Quantitative Analysis of Newly Evolving Patterns of International Trade

Fragmentation, Offshoring of Activities, and Vertical Intra-Industry Trade

World Scientific Studies in International Economics

(ISSN: 1793-3641)

---

*Published**

Vol. 12 The Japanese Economy in Retrospect, Volume I and Volume II
Selected Papers by Gary R. Saxonhouse
by Robert M Stern (University of Michigan, USA), Gavin Wright (Stanford University, USA) & Hugh Patrick (Columbia University, USA)

Vol. 13 Light the Lamp
Papers on World Trade and Investment in Memory of Bijit Bora
edited by Christopher Findlay (University of Adelaide, Australia), David Parsons (KADIN Indonesia) & Mari Pangestu (Trade Minister of Indonesia)

Vol. 14 The International Financial Crisis: Have the Rules of Finance Changed?
edited by Asli Demirgüç-Kunt (The World Bank, USA), Douglas D Evanoff (Federal Reserve Bank of Chicago, USA) & George G Kaufman (Loyola University of Chicago, USA)

Vol. 15 Systemic Implications of Transatlantic Regulatory Cooperation and Competition
edited by Simon J Evenett (University of St Gallen, Switzerland) & Robert M Stern (University of Michigan, USA)

Vol. 16 Comparative Advantage, Growth, and the Gains from Trade and Globalization
A Festschrift in Honor of Alan V Deardorff
edited by Robert M Stern (University of Michigan, USA)

Vol. 17 Macroprudential Regulatory Policies: The New Road to Financial Stability?
edited by Stijn Claessens (International Monetary Fund, USA), Douglas D Evanoff (Federal Reserve Bank of Chicago, USA), George G Kaufman (Loyola University Chicago, USA) & Laura Kodres (International Monetry Fund, USA)

Vol. 18 Quantitative Analysis of Newly Evolving Patterns of International Trade: Fragmentation, Offshoring of Activities, and Vertical Intra-Industry Trade
edited by Robert M Stern (University of Michigan and University of California-Berkeley, USA)

*The complete list of the published volumes in the series can be found at http://www.worldscibooks.com/series/wssie_series.shtml.

18 World Scientific Studies in International Economics

QUANTITATIVE ANALYSIS OF NEWLY EVOLVING PATTERNS OF INTERNATIONAL TRADE

Fragmentation, Offshoring of Activities, and Vertical Intra-Industry Trade

Editor

Robert M Stern

University of Michigan and
University of California-Berkeley, USA

World Scientific

NEW JERSEY • LONDON • SINGAPORE • BEIJING • SHANGHAI • HONG KONG • TAIPEI • CHENNAI

Published by

World Scientific Publishing Co. Pte. Ltd.

5 Toh Tuck Link, Singapore 596224

USA office: 27 Warren Street, Suite 401-402, Hackensack, NJ 07601

UK office: 57 Shelton Street, Covent Garden, London WC2H 9HE

Library of Congress Cataloging-in-Publication Data

Quantitative analysis of newly evolving patterns of international trade : fragmentation, offshoring of activities, and vertical intra-industry trade / edited by Robert M Stern.

p. cm. -- (World Scientific studies in international economics, ISSN 1793-3641 ; vol. 18)

Includes bibliographical references.

ISBN 978-9814383479

1. International trade--Statistical methods. I. Stern, Robert M. (Robert Mitchell), 1927–

HF1379.Q363 2012

382.01'5195--dc23

2012003413

British Library Cataloguing-in-Publication Data

A catalogue record for this book is available from the British Library.

Typeset by Stallion Press

Email: enquiries@stallionpress.com

Printed in Singapore by B & Jo Enterprise Pte Ltd

Contents

Acknowledgments

Zana Kwaiser, the Program Administrator/Project Coordinator in the Ford School's International Policy Center, and Judith Jackson are to be thanked for their efforts in administering the research program and for arranging the logistics for and overseeing the October 2009 conference. Judith Jackson is also to be especially thanked for handling the manuscripts and for the preparation of this conference volume. Chris Myers prepared the website for the research program and conference. Melanie Standish, Associate Program Officer in the Center for Global Partnership, provided helpful oversight of the grant process and administration on behalf of The Japan Foundation. Sandhya Ventakesh and the editorial and production staff of World Scientific are to be thanked for their able assistance in bringing this volume to conclusion.

Robert M. Stern
Ann Arbor, Michigan
12 April 2010

Introduction and Overview

Robert M. Stern

This volume contains the papers that were prepared in connection with a project funded by The Japan Foundation, Center for Global Partnership (CGP), entitled *Quantitative Analysis of Newly Evolving Patterns of International Trade: Fragmentation; Offshoring of Activities; and Vertical Intra-Industry Trade.*

Robert M. Stern was the project director, and Kyoji Fukao and Kozo Kiyota were co-directors. Twelve papers were commissioned and presented and critiqued at a conference held at the University of Michigan on October 16 and 17, 2009. The papers were subsequently revised based on the comments made by appointed discussants and other participants in the October 2009 conference. The papers and discussant comments that comprise the substantive chapters that follow have been edited by Professor Stern.

I. OBJECTIVES OF THE PROGRAM OF RESEARCH

In recent decades, international trade and foreign direct investment (FDI) have grown especially rapidly. In this "globalization" process, we can observe rapid expansion in the U.S., Japan, and other major trading countries of new modes of the international division of labor. Thus, U.S., Japanese, and other countries' multinational enterprises (MNEs) have been fragmenting their production activities into several processes and relocating labor-intensive processes, such as assembling, to developing countries. MNEs have also started to outsource or offshore labor-intensive service activities, such as call centers and some types of accounting activities. Furthermore, intra-industry trade with vertical division of labor has been increasing markedly. For example, the U.S. exports expensive semiconductors based on frontier technologies to China and imports more standardized inexpensive semiconductors from China.

According to standard international trade theory, the impact of trade in goods and services on factor markets can be evaluated by regarding trade as international transactions of production factors that are embodied in the traded goods and services. For example, an industrialized country like the U.S. or Japan can mitigate their scarcity of unskilled labor by importing unskilled-labor–intensive products. For the standard analysis, it is imperative to determine the factor contents of traded goods and services, that is, how much each unit of traded goods and services embodies production factors, such as unskilled and skilled labor, capital, land, and technology.

It is widely believed among international economists that the three new modes of the international division of labor must have significant impacts on factor markets in the trading countries. However, quantitative studies of these impacts have been limited, inasmuch as methods and data to measure factor contents within these new modes of trade are still underdeveloped. For example, we do not know the extent to which expensive semiconductors with frontier technologies are more intensive in skilled labor and technology than standardized, inexpensive semiconductors. Data on factor inputs in production processes, such as assembling and production of key components, are also very limited.

In our project, the objective was to develop new methods and data to measure the factor contents of emerging new modes of international trade. Such methods and data are crucially important for evaluating impacts of the new modes on factor markets in the U.S., Japan, and other major trading countries, and also for forecasting the future development of world trade and FDI, evaluating welfare gains from trade, estimating impacts of free trade agreements, and designing effective trade and FDI policies. There are a number of issues that arise accordingly, as follows:

(1) **Fragmentation.** How do factor contents (including the stock of research and development (R&D)) differ among different production processes? And based on this information, what are the main factors that are due to fragmentation? To what extent can we evaluate welfare gains from this type of division of labor? Are trade data based on ordinary commodity classifications, input–output (IO) tables, and factor-input statistics at the disaggregated industry level good enough to measure the magnitude of division of labor due to fragmentation? What evidence do we have about the effects of fragmentation on factor markets?

(2) **Offshoring of activities, including services.** How much and what types of offshoring are being conducted? How do factor contents differ among different production tasks? And based on this information, what are the main factors involved in the task trade? Can we evaluate welfare gains from this type of division of labor? Are existing commodity trade and services statistics, IO tables, and factor-input statistics at the disaggregated industry levels different enough to measure the magnitude of division of labor though task trade?

(3) **Task trade.** What evidence do we have about the effects of task trade on factor markets in developed and developing economies?

(4) **Vertical intra-industry trade.** Are there any relationships between unit values of commodities and factor contents? Based on this information, what factors are actually traded in the context of vertical intra-industry trade? Can we evaluate the welfare gains from this type of division of labor? What evidence do we have about the effects of vertical intra-industry trade on factor markets?

(5) **Product varieties.** What production factors are needed in order to increase the variety of commodities that a country can produce?

(6) **Division of labor.** How does the division of labor involving the new types of trade patterns compare to the classical inter-industry trade of the U.S., Japan, and the European Union? How does the division of labor involving the new types of trade patterns compare to the classical inter-industry trade of the developing economies?

(7) **MNE intra-firm trade.** What percentages of the new modes of trade are conducted as intra-firm trade by MNEs?

(8) **Foreign direct investment.** To what extent does FDI, which is conducted in parallel with the new modes of trade, bring about new technology and improvement in total factor productivity (TFP)?

(9) **Policy implications.** Do we need to change trade and labor-market policies and the conduct of trade negotiations to deal with the new modes of trade?

II. RESEARCH AGENDA

International Trade and Factor Markets

The relationship between international trade and factor markets has been of central importance for many decades in the study of international economics. In view of the increases in income inequality between skilled and unskilled labor in the U.S. and other major trading countries, there has been a debate about whether or not the increases in imports from low-wage countries have been a key determinant of wage inequality. In this connection, Katz and Autor (1999) concluded in their study that the key determinant of wage inequality was not imports but skill-biased technology growth. However, Feenstra and Hanson (2003) later pointed out that imports really mattered once offshoring was taken into account.

With recent improvements in transportation and communication technology, it is becoming easier for MNEs to divide finely their production and services activities and locate them to different countries. This offshoring is a relatively new phenomenon in international economics, but it is closely related to traditional issues such as wage inequality, intra-industry trade, and the international division of labor. It also brings to life the new theoretical concept known as task trade.

Wage Inequality

As noted earlier, how offshoring affects factor markets is an issue that has attracted great interest. Accordingly, a number of studies have addressed this issue. Feenstra and Hanson (1999) focused on U.S. manufacturing industries for 1979–1990 and estimated the effects of trade through offshoring and technology on wage inequality. Trade through offshoring was measured by intermediate input trade while technology was measured by expenditures on high-technology capital such as computers. Their results indicated that there were significantly positive correlations between total factor productivity (TFP) and adjusted value-added prices, the computer share of capital stock, and the computer share of investment. Their results suggested that not only technology but also trade was an important factor in explaining wage inequality. Their results thus differ from other studies such as Katz and Autor (1999).

It is noteworthy that these studies were not extended beyond 1990, and that they were confined to U.S. experience. In view of the rapid growth of offshoring in the past two decades, it is important to address the effects of offshoring on wage inequality in more detail. Some of the questions for new research include the following:

- Has offshoring accelerated the wage inequality between skilled and unskilled workers in the U.S., Japan, and other major economies since 1990?
- In explaining U.S. and Japanese wage inequality, how important have skill-biased technology growth or offshoring been in each nation?
- How does offshoring by U.S. and Japanese firms to China and India affect wage inequality?
- How does the offshoring of services activities such as R&D affect wage inequality?

Vertical Intra-industry Trade

Vertical intra-industry trade is also by no means a new phenomenon. There have been a number of studies that have examined the relationship between FDI and vertical intra-industry trade (e.g., Fukao, Ishido, and Ito, 2003). However, as concerns the relationship between offshoring and vertical intra-industry trade, most of the existing studies (e.g., Ando, 2006) have been limited to fact finding. Indeed, there have been only a few attempts to link theory with empirical analysis. Kimura, Takahashi, and Hayakawa (2007) examined the validity of fragmentation theory, using a gravity-model approach. They found that the key elements of fragmentation such as differences in service-link costs have significant effects on the magnitude of intra-industry trade.

Because of the comparative lack of empirical studies, several important questions remain unresolved. These include:

- How does offshoring affect vertical intra-industry trade?
- Is the relationship between offshoring and vertical intra-industry trade different from the relationship between FDI and vertical intra-industry trade? If so, how?
- Is the relationship between offshoring and vertical intra-industry trade in Japan different from the U.S.? If so, how?
- Are there any relationships between the unit values of commodities and factor content in Japanese and U.S. trade?

Vertical Specialization and Intra-firm Trade

There have been two types of studies analyzing vertical specialization and intra-firm trade. Hummels, Ishii, and Yi (2001) used IO tables for OECD countries and four emerging market economies and calculated the degree of vertical specialization (imported-input content or foreign value-added embodied in exports). They found that vertical specialization accounted for 20% of exports in 1990.

Other studies have used firm-level data. Hanson, Mataloni, and Slaughter (2006) examined the determinants of vertical linkage, as measured by trade in intermediate inputs between U.S. parent firms and their affiliates. They found that the trade in intermediate inputs increases with lower trade costs, lower wages for unskilled labor in host countries, and lower corporate income taxes in host countries.

These studies can be extended to the following questions:

- Are trade data based on ordinary commodity classifications, IO tables, and factor-input statistics at a disaggregated industry level good enough to measure the magnitude of division of labor through offshoring?
- Do Japanese firms have similar intra-firm patterns as compared to U.S. firms?
- Which production processes locate in which countries?

International Division of Labor

While there have been several theoretical studies, such as Leamer (1999), that have examined the relationship between international trade and the international division of labor, there are few studies that have examined the relationship between offshoring and the international division of labor. Marin (2006) examined the patterns of international division of labor in Europe, but her analysis in fact analyzed the determinants of intra-firm trade, offshoring, and outsourcing, and did not examine directly the magnitude of the international division of labor. It appears, therefore, that there are several important questions that remain unresolved:

- How do we measure the international division of labor? That is, in other words, how do labor inputs differ among different production processes?

- In this connection, how do factor contents (including R&D stock) differ among different production processes?
- How and how much does the international division of labor affect domestic factor markets?
- To what extent are factors actually traded through offshoring?
- Does the international division of labor enhance welfare gains?

Productivity

Since Bernard and Jensen (1999) found a systematic relationship between exports and productivity at the firm level, a number of studies have focused on the firm-level nexus between exports and productivity. Some studies have been extended not only to exports but also to FDI (e.g., Helpman, Melitz, and Yeaple, 2004; Kimura and Kiyota, 2006). More recently, Tomiura (2007) has extended the analysis to offshoring. Using firm-level, cross-section data for Japan, he found that exporting or offshoring firms were less productive than firms that engage in FDI but more productive than domestic firms.

Tomiura's study can be extended in a dynamic framework as Bernard and Jensen (1999) and Kimura and Kiyota (2006) have done. Possible questions for further research are as follows:

- Are there any sequential relationships between exports, FDI, and offshoring in Japan and the U.S.?
- Which activities may make Japanese and U.S. firms more productive: exports, FDI, or offshoring?
- Are offshoring firms in Japan and the U.S. less productive than firms that engage in FDI? Can we identify the differences of sunk costs between exports, FDI, and offshoring?

Task Trade

Task trade is a new concept developed by Grossman and Rossi-Hansberg (2006) to describe recent increases in offshoring production and services activities by MNEs. Some of the questions for further study include the following:

- Can we measure the magnitude of task trade for Japan and the U.S.? If so, how?

- How much and what types of task trade are being conducted by Japanese and U.S. MNEs?
- How do factor contents differ among different tasks? Based on this information, what factors are being incorporated into task trade?

In developing the topics that comprised our research agenda, we carried out a literature survey of the pertinent academic publications that highlight the salient features of the new modes of international trade that have been described. As a next step, we circulated the preceding descriptions of the pertinent questions for research to a number of specialists in Japan, the U.S., and Western Europe to solicit their possible interest in participating in our proposed program. The individuals solicited were drawn from academia, government agencies, and research institutes, based upon our knowledge of their published and ongoing research.

III. SUMMARIES OF PAPERS

While there are many topics in the research agenda noted, only selected ones were addressed in the papers, as will be noted in the chapters mentioned below. To aid the reader in focusing on the papers of interest, summaries of the papers and conference discussant comments are provided in what follows.

Chapter 1, by Toshiyuki Matsuura, Kiyoyasu Tanaka and Shujiro Urata, "The Determinants of Offshore Production by Multinational Corporations: A Comparison of Japanese and U.S. Multinational Corporations," notes that the rise of offshore production by multinational corporations (MNCs) has been a central force in the recent economic globalization. Their study employs confidential *affiliate-level* panel data to improve measures of foreign affiliate activities of Japanese firms in manufacturing sectors. Combining existing data on U.S. MNCs with the Japanese data, they illustrate the pattern and determinants of their foreign affiliate sales by destination market across countries and industries for the period 1989–2005. The results indicate that Japanese and U.S. MNCs are similar in the substantial growth of their foreign affiliate sales, the importance of sales to local markets, and a systematic variation of sales by destination market across regions. However, Japanese MNCs are distinctive from U.S. MNCs in that their foreign affiliates increased worldwide employment massively and various sales largely in host countries with lower average years of schooling. In particular, Japanese affiliate sales in Asia were prominently higher in host markets with lower educational attainment. They interpret these results as evidence that comparative advantage motives play a larger role in explaining offshore production by Japanese MNCs than U.S. MNCs.

In her comment, **Linda Tesar** has a number of concerns: (1) the industry designation may be too coarse. It may happen that at an aggregate level an industry appears to use skilled labor, but the segment of production that is conducted offshore may be the segment of production that is low-skilled-labor intensive; (2) because the data are averaged over the period 1989–2005, the average may not capture the state of offshoring at the end of the period of rapidly increasing offshore activity; (3) reporting the results for broad groupings of countries may be misleading because MNC activity may be distinctive between individual countries; (4) by reporting a wide range of results, it is difficult to discern a "bottom line" of what the authors consider to be the overall message from the data; and (5) it might be useful to include variables in the analyses that capture the differences in the determinants of the location of production between countries/regions.

Chapter 2, by Keiko Ito and Kiyoyasu Tanaka, "Does Material and Service Offshoring Improve Domestic Productivity? Evidence from Japanese Manufacturing Industries," notes that there is an increasing number of stages of production processes being shifted offshore. Their study investigates the effects of offshoring on productivity in Japanese manufacturing industries for the period 1988–2004. Material offshoring, as measured by the import share of intermediate material inputs, has steadily increased during the period, with a pronounced increase in offshoring to Asian countries. In a wide range of specifications, they find significantly positive correlations between material offshoring and productivity at the industry level. The estimates are particularly robust for offshoring to Asia. These results suggest that Japanese manufacturing firms extensively developed international division of labor in East Asia, which possibly generated a strong productivity-enhancing effect. In contrast, they find that service offshoring, as measured by the import ratio of service inputs, is not associated with industry-level productivity. They find a positive correlation between offshoring and productivity only for information services, suggesting that in this segment, offshoring offers potential benefits.

In his comment, **Isao Kamata** notes that the study by Ito and Tanaka is the first that investigates the impacts of offshoring on domestic productivity for Japanese manufacturing industries, highlighting the difference between the offshoring of intermediate material inputs and that of service inputs. The study also takes advantage of the precision of Japanese data (the IO tables of the JIP Database 2009) and employs a direct measure of imported inputs from each industry to each industry, which is in contrast to the preceding studies that use a proxy measure of offshored inputs. Further, the study separately examines the productivity impacts of material offshoring to different regions, reflecting on potential differences in the motivation behind offshoring to different countries (i.e., comparative advantage versus variety in intermediate inputs). Finally, the study examines different types of offshored services — information services and business services — for the impacts of the offshoring of these services on domestic productivity, considering the difference of the degree to which the services are standardized and offshorable. Kamata has some concerns with the study: (1) it may be difficult to draw a firm conclusion about offshoring because of the stagnation of the Japanese economy during the period studied and the comparatively small amount of offshoring observed; (2) the annualization procedure used for the data raises the possibility of losing information on the original direct measure (or variation in the original data), especially since the annualized offshoring intensity is later linearly detrended to use for estimation purposes; (3) there may be a problem of endogeneity in the relation between output growth and the change in offshoring; (4) the detailed empirical results suggest that the findings about the impacts of offshoring may not be robust; (5) the choice of control variables in estimating the effects of offshoring on labor productivity and the effects of skill upgrading is not altogether clear; and (6) the estimation of the effects of offshoring broken down by region and type may be biased because of omitted variables.

Chapter 3, by Banri Ito, Eiichi Tomiura, and Ryuhei Wakasugi, "Does Firm Boundary Matter? The Effect of Offshoring on Productivity of Japanese Firms," notes that there has been great interest in the examination of the impact of offshore sourcing that has increased rapidly and expanded over various tasks. Theoretical studies have shown that offshore sourcing contributes to higher productivity. This chapter aims to provide evidence of the effect of offshore sourcing on productivity, on the basis of original survey data of offshore sourcing of Japanese firms. The estimation results show that offshore insourcing within multinationals has a positive impact on productivity, but there is a time lag in the appearance of the impact. On the other hand, it is found that offshore outsourcing through arms-length contracting out did not appear to affect productivity, despite the expectation that the reallocation of resources to more advanced production processes contributes to productivity.

In his comment, **Wilhelm Kohler** notes that the contribution of the paper is twofold. On the methodological side, it tries to address the issue of *causality.* And on the data side, it incorporates the distinction between *intra-firm* and *arms-length* offshoring and, to some extent, the distinction between offshoring of *components* and offshoring of *service inputs* (by manufacturing firms). Both are welcome innovations, but the issue of causality surely is of particular interest. He suggests that the paper would be strengthened by an explicit consideration of the theoretical background designed to sort out causality in models of offshoring that stress a productivity effect of offshoring, as well as models that suggest a reverse channel of causality. Kohler notes that the authors do not explain why some firms do offshoring of one type or another, while others do not. Nor is it specified why offshoring should improve a firm's productivity. Hence, the empirical analysis is not attempting to *test any specific model prediction.* While leaving theoretical details in the background is legitimate, given that there are several models that stress productivity effects of offshoring, as well as models that explain firms' sourcing strategy, Kohler argues that our understanding of the exercise and the results obtained may be enhanced by *adding a theoretical perspective,* which he provides in his comment.

Chapter 4, by Wilhelm Kohler and Marcel Smolka, "Global Sourcing: Evidence from Spanish Firm-Level Data," investigates the link between productivity of firms and their sourcing behavior. They distinguish between domestic and foreign sourcing, as well as between outsourcing and vertical integration. A firm's choice is driven by a "hold-up" problem caused by lack of enforceable contracts. They use Spanish firm-level data to examine the productivity premia associated with the different sourcing strategies. They find strong empirical support for the predictions of the model.

In his comment, **Jagadeesh Sivadasan** notes that Kohler and Smolka examine the link between productivity and firm choices related to their sourcing decisions. In particular, they investigate how productivity relates to two binary choices — foreign versus domestic sourcing, and outsourcing versus vertical integration. This yields four (potentially non-exclusive) strategic choices: (1) Domestic Outsourcing; (2) Domestic Integration, (3) Foreign Outsourcing, and (4) Foreign Integration. A number of interesting aspects are pointed out: (1) the authors have information in their dataset that is fairly unique insofar as there are few plant-level datasets that have the detailed information on input sourcing required for empirical analyses; (2) the key driver of the theoretical prediction appears to be the assumption regarding the fixed costs of each of the aforementioned strategies. What is noteworthy is that the theory could accommodate different rank orderings of the fixed costs and hence support alternative rank orderings of productivity; (3) an important simplification in the theoretical framework is that it models one "headquarter" firm deciding about one critical input — whether to outsource (domestically or abroad) or integrate into manufacturing (domestically or abroad). In practice, all firms have multiple inputs that they wish to procure. Key parameters of the model (particularly "headquarters intensity") could vary across inputs, so that the firm may make different strategic choices in relation to different inputs. As the authors note, this is very much evident in the data. A large majority of the firms pursue multiple strategies; and (4) the theoretical framework as well as the empirical work looks at vertical "backward" integration. The focus is on how productivity relates to purchasing of inputs. But firms could also vertically integrate in the "forward" direction, especially to foreign markets by undertaking foreign FDI or become MNCs.

Chapter 5, by Anna M. Falzoni and Lucia Tajoli, "The Effects of Offshoring on the Composition of Employment in Italy," assesses the extent of offshoring in the Italian manufacturing industries and studies how this phenomenon is affecting the skill composition of employment. Measuring offshoring using the import-use matrices of IO tables, they first estimate the impact of offshoring on the general level of employment, and do not find any significant relationship. Then, they examine the relationship between offshoring and employment composition by skills. The results show that the use of offshoring is not restricted to the search for cheaper unskilled labor, and its impact on the composition of employment seems to vary for different industry groups.

In his comment, **Kei-Mu Yi** has concerns about the measurement of offshoring and the empirical methodology used in the study. He notes that the offshoring measure used is either total imported intermediates (broad) or own-industry imported intermediates (narrow) as a share of total intermediates used by an industry. But there have been other measures used in empirical research, such as imported intermediate inputs as a share of gross output, which may yield significant results. For example, an alternative measure is imported intermediate inputs as a share of gross output. Another issue is that, by their very nature, IO tables capture the repeated sequences of inputs being made into output, much of which is used as inputs to make other outputs, etc. In terms of imported intermediates, some of them become embodied in domestic intermediates that are later used to produce another industry's goods that are eventually used for final demand. It is suggested accordingly that efforts could be made to calculate the "true" domestic value-added and imported input content of exports. Furthermore, it is noted that account should be taken of the offshoring of goods that do not return to Italy. The more general point is that offshoring is considerably more complex than what can be captured by measures that focus on imported intermediate goods. Finally, it will be interesting to consider the next version of Italy's IO tables because it will capture some of the major inroads that China has made on Italian markets.

Yi also notes that the econometric specification used for the skill intensity of production is probably most justified when offshoring is driven by lower costs of fragmentation. But other forces could plausibly affect the skill intensity of production in addition to affecting offshoring. It would be useful then to discuss this issue and to consider pursuing steps to isolate and focus on that part of offshoring that is driven by lower costs of fragmentation only. He notes finally that more discussion of the determinants of the skill premium would be useful.

Chapter 6, by Mitsuyo Ando and Fukunari Kimura, "International Production/Distribution Networks in East Asia and Domestic Operations: Evidence from Japanese Firms," investigates the pattern of globalizing corporate activities of Japanese firms and their domestic operations and international trade, using firm-level data for 1998–2004. The journalistic literature often claims that the globalization of corporate activities in less developed countries reduces operations and employment domestically. However, the analysis compares firms expanding operations in East Asia with those not expanding operations and finds that Japanese manufacturing firms expanding operations in the region, particularly in machinery sectors, are more likely to maintain or increase domestic employment. In addition, machinery firms expanding operations in the region do not necessarily reduce the number of domestic establishments/affiliates. Furthermore, manufacturing firms with expanding operations, particularly in machinery sectors, tend to intensify export/import activities with the region, suggesting a complementary relationship between international trade and FDI. At least at the individual firm level, the fragmentation of production by Japanese manufacturing firms, particularly in the machinery sectors, seems to generate additional jobs and operations at home by effectively utilizing the mechanics of the production process *vis-â-vis* the division of labor in East Asia.

In his comment, **Vitor Trindade** notes the main findings of the Ando–Kimura study, which are: (1) expansion of Japanese firms into East Asia seems to be associated with higher growth of employment and with higher probability of no decrease in the employment of the expanding firms; (2) expansion of Japanese firms into East Asia seems to be associated with more intense trade (both imports and exports) by those firms; and (3) expansions of Japanese firms seem to be in some cases associated with the closing of some of the firms' domestic establishments or affiliates. Based on the aggregate results (1) above, one can infer then that the evidence is not suggestive of the broad decreases in domestic employment that so worry many observers of the international economic scene. Furthermore, result (3) may simply indicate firms' rationalization of their domestic activities, once due account is taken of result (1). The evidence of a correlation between globalizing activities and no decrease of domestic employment uncovered is both plausible and important. Trindade shares the authors' reluctance in drawing causal inferences about globalizing firms, particularly if there are omitted variables. It may simply be that some firms are more successful than others, for reasons that go beyond the controls that the authors include. Successful firms are more likely than unsuccessful ones to expand *both* domestically *and* abroad, by reason of their very success. Trindade also cautions about any inferences regarding "networks," in the absence of evidence that Japanese firms are forming or are part of any networks.

Trindade offers some suggestions for further research: (1) it would be interesting to distinguish between firms that invest abroad within their own industries (with "industry" as narrowly defined as possible, not just "machinery," for example), versus those firms that invest in different sectors, and to examine different patterns of international diversification; and (2) it would be useful to investigate the role of actual outsourcing in firms' domestic employment and domestic affiliates, perhaps by linking these firm-level data with Japanese international trade data, and, if there is a possibility of linking these data with more detailed data on employment of skilled versus non-skilled labor.

Chapter 7, by Kozo Kiyota, "Japan's Exports and Employment," considers how much employment is created by rising Japanese exports and how the export dependence of employment has changed over time. Using newly developed Japanese IO table data from 1975 to 2006, this chapter estimates the effect of exports on industry employment (i.e., direct effect) and the effect on other industries' employment (i.e., indirect effect). Estimation results indicate that the export dependence of Japan's employment gradually increased for the last three decades. In 2006, approximately 30% of manufacturing employment was created by exports, which is twice as much as it was in 1975. The magnitude of the indirect effect is almost the same as that of the direct effect. Less export-oriented industries sometimes have heavy export dependence of employment due to the intra-industry linkages with export-oriented industries.

In her comment, **Katherine Terrell** notes that Kiyota addresses four important questions:(1) how much employment is created by Japanese exports; (2) the relative size of direct (own industry) and indirect (intra-industry linkages) effects of trade on employment; (3) whether the dependence on exports has changed over time and if so, is it concentrated in a few industries; and (4) which countries' demand for exports affects Japanese employment the most. Terrell raises some questions on the data and methodology, in particular whether the input–output coefficients are changing over time, in which industries are the indirect effects especially large, and how the indirect effect of exports on employment is calculated. She also suggests clarification of the differences in indirect effects between the manufacturing and non-manufacturing industries, and the possible extension of the analysis to provide more detail for the industries especially involved in exports to East Asia and the U.S. and the importance of skilled and unskilled labor.

In **Chapter 8, Peter Debaere and Shalah Mostashari**, in **"What Determines the Extensive Margin of International Trade? An Investigation of the Cross-Section of U.S. Imports,"** investigate the sector and country determinants of the range of goods, the extensive margin, within a sector that countries export to the U.S. They relate the traditional determinants of comparative advantage, sectors' factor intensities interacted with countries' factor abundance, to the extensive margin in a sector, as well as the interactions between sector-level measures of intermediate-use intensity and the quality of countries' institutions. In addition, they study the impact of trade frictions such as U.S. import tariffs and distance from the U.S., which are thought to be a greater hindrance to intermediate intensive sectors. They consider two measures of sectors' intermediate intensity or fragmentation: a sector's intermediate cost share and 1 minus the Herfindahl index of industry concentration, which increases with the number of intermediates used. Consistent with hypotheses about fragmentation of production, they find that closer countries and countries with lower tariffs imposed on them export a wider range of goods in sectors that have large intermediate-cost shares. The impact of trade frictions is, however, far less pronounced for the more skilled-labor–intensive sectors that are characterized by use of a greater range of intermediates and a large degree of intra-industry trade.

In his comment, **Andrei Levchenko** notes that the authors demonstrate that countries with better institutions tend to export more product categories in sectors that have: (1) lower intermediate-use intensity and (2) higher product complexity. Levchenko focuses first on disentangling the role of institutions for the extensive margin versus the overall trade volumes. Second, he argues that in spite of the large amount of empirical and theoretical work in this area, we do not yet have a good grasp of whether, and how, the extensive margin of trade has an appreciable impact on economic welfare. Levchenko suggests that the authors' estimates could simply be driven by a mechanical correlation between the overall trade volumes and the number of product categories as recorded in the trade data. The impact of institutions on the extensive margin as distinct from its impact on the total trade volumes must then be sorted out. Finally, Levchenko provides a model designed to evaluate the welfare impact of the extensive margin of trade.

In **Chapter 9, K.C. Fung, Hitomi Iizaka, and Alan Siu**, in "**Modes of East Asian Trade and Foreign Direct Investment: U.S. and Japan,**" analyze the growing importance of trade in parts and components and other modes of trade in East Asia. The empirical analysis shows that FDI plays a particularly important role in facilitating trade of parts and components and trade in capital goods in East Asia. This is true for aggregate FDI as well as FDI from two important source countries: the U.S. and Japan. Furthermore, it is shown that compared with U.S. FDI, FDI from Japan has a stronger influence on both trade in parts and components as well as trade in capital goods. One policy implication is that to integrate further into the East-Asian production network, economies need to adopt policies that are friendly not only to trade, but also FDI.

In her comment, **Theresa Greaney** notes that the use of a gravity model to analyze the authors' research questions needs further development. She observes that there are some changes from the traditional usage of a gravity model by: (1) omitting the multilateral resistance term; (2) restricting the sample of trading countries to only nine East Asian countries; and (3) changing the dependent variable to parts of bilateral trade (i.e., parts and components, and capital goods) rather than total bilateral trade. She suggests that the authors include benchmark results for total bilateral trade involving many countries in addition to East Asian countries, and include a dummy variable when both trade partners are located in East Asia. She also recommends including more trade partners throughout the authors' use of the gravity model and including benchmark results for total bilateral trade versus results for just parts and components trade or just capital goods trade to see if the results differ when trade is broken down into sub-groupings. Further, in assessing the impact of FDI on trade and avoiding the inherent endogeneity problem, the authors use instrumental variables to estimate FDI and then use these estimated values as independent variables in the gravity model. She notes that, while the approach seems reasonable, the description of their methodology could be improved.

In **Chapter 10, Deborah Swenson,** in **"The Influence of Multinational Exposure on Private Chinese Trade,"** examines Chinese trade data at the sector-city level to study how exposure to multinational firms affected export volumes and export participation by private Chinese exporters between 1998 and 2005. Using panel regressions that control for city-sector fixed effects, the data show that private Chinese export outcomes improved when local firms were surrounded by a growing presence of multinational firms. This effect is apparent whether private export outcomes are measured by export volumes or the number of export transactions. In addition, the results suggest that an important channel generating positive spillovers to local firms is transmitted via input or capital goods imports by multinational firms.

In her comment, **Lucia Tajoli** notes that what is most interesting with the Swenson study is her examination of a specific effect whether the export capacity of Chinese domestic firms is enhanced or reduced by the presence of MNCs. The answer is *a priori* uncertain because there exists the possibility that foreign firms displace domestic firms through some form of crowding out, by increasing the competitive pressure or raising the price of factors of production. This concern is especially relevant for smaller economies (the Irish case is a relevant example), but it seems less pertinent for very large and fast growing economies such as China. The evidence provided suggests that there are indeed positive spillover effects from foreign MNCs to domestic private firms. Tajoli suggests a number of issues deserving of further analysis: (1) the peculiarity of Chinese exporting firms, which for a large fraction are state-owned, and whether the increase of private exports is due to "new" exports or instead to a privatization process, which has turned SOEs' exports into private exports; (2) the very rapid increase of overall Chinese exports to the world coupled with the effects of the many important structural, institutional, and policy changes that have occurred in the Chinese economy; (3) problems arising from introducing MNCs' imports into the regression analysis and the role especially of imports of capital goods; (4) the role of the processing trade; and (5) the need for some robustness checks that could be done on the estimation techniques.

In **Chapter 11, Theresa Greaney and Yao Li**, in **"The Effects of Foreign Direct Investment on China's Labor Market,"** examine how FDI has affected the labor market in China. In particular, they analyze industrial and regional data from the National Bureau of Statistics of China to assess how FDI has impacted wages and employment. Since most of the data from China distinguishes between FDI from overseas Chinese investors (i.e., those located in Hong Kong, Macao, and Taiwan) and FDI from foreign investors, they examine possible differences in investment patterns and effects across these different FDI sources. They first present a descriptive analysis of China's industrial sector in 2004, focusing on industry-level and regional differences in the shares of capital coming from the state; from Hong Kong, Macao, and Taiwan; from foreigners; and from others. They use the descriptive analysis to guide a regression analysis in looking for the effects of FDI on earnings and employment in China's manufacturing industries, while controlling for other determinants of earnings and employment. The regression analysis seeks to explain variations in earnings and employment across industries using capital ownership as an explanatory variable. They attempt to identify FDI effects separately from privatization effects by considering the effects of capital contributions sourced from the state, from collectives, and from private domestic investors, as opposed to those sourced from FDI. They also conduct separate analyses of two particularly large employment industries — textiles and communication equipment, computers and electronics — seeking to explain earnings and employment variations across regions. The advantages of the study are the use of an extensive and relatively new data source, *China's Economic Census Yearbook 2004*, the method of allowing ownership to be defined as a continuous variable based on capital contributions from different sources, the ability to examine the effects of investment from overseas Chinese separately from investment from foreigners, and the in-depth inquiries into two specific industries as case studies of a labor-intensive sector and a capital-intensive sector.

In his comment, **Francesc Ortega** notes that it would be useful to provide more background information on the goals of FDI in China, in particular whether FDI is mainly aimed at serving the Chinese domestic market or to re-export and if there are variations by industry. Also, the regression analysis could be used, with industry-fixed effects, to produce sets of stylized facts on the average firm characteristics by ownership structure and to focus on the following set of outcomes: wages, output per worker, relative size (in employment or output), export share of output, and capital intensity. Ortega raises a number of questions on the specification of the regression analysis, and he suggests a new instrumental approach designed to determine whether foreign ownership in an industry leads to higher productivity or whether it is attracted by high productivity. Finally, he notes that a main limitation of the data being used is that there are no firm-level observations, and that it would be interesting to focus on presenting a set of stylized facts on average firm characteristics by ownership, controlling for industry that could become an important benchmark for future studies on FDI in China.

In **Chapter 12, Eric Y. Cho and Hideki Yamawaki**, in **"Clusters, Productivity, and Exports in Taiwanese Manufacturing Industries,"** note that the Taiwanese government has been devoting its effort towards building industrial and science parks since the 1980s. Although the rationale that underlies this policy is to capitalize on the economies of agglomeration, there exists no evidence in the existing literature that examines empirically if clusters promote productivity and exports in Taiwan. In this study, they construct indices to measure the extent of cluster in industry and municipals for Taiwan. They then apply the indices to examine the effect of clustering on labor productivity, growth, and export propensity. The statistical results provide some evidence that supports the hypothesis that clustering enhances the growth rate of labor productivity and promotes exports in Taiwanese manufacturing industries.

In his comment, **Kozo Kiyota** notes that, while the authors ask whether the clusters promote the growth of labor productivity and exports, there is, however, no discussion about the effects of Taiwanese industrial policy on the clusters. If the clusters are formed by factors other than industrial policy, it is difficult to justify Taiwanese industrial policy. It may thus be important to examine the effects of the Taiwanese industrial policy on the clusters to obtain some policy implications from the analysis. He also questions why the focus is on labor productivity rather than total factor productivity (TFP). Another concern is the desirability of checking the robustness of the results and controlling for unobservable industry heterogeneity (i.e., fixed/random effects), and employing panel data estimation methods. Finally, Kiyota suggests that labor productivity should be treated as an endogenous variable because it also depends upon the clusters.

Having summarized the main themes and results of the chapters and the discussant comments, the reader may now turn to the substantive chapters and comments in the chapters that follow.

REFERENCES

Ando, Mitsuyo (2006). "Framentation and Vertical Intra-Industry Trade in East Asia," *North American Journal of Economics and Finance*, 17(3): pp. 257–281.

Bernard, Andrew B. and J. Bradford Jensen (1999). "Exceptional Exporter Performance: Cause, Effect, or Both?" *Journal of International Economics*, 47(1): pp. 1–26.

Feenstra, Robert C. and Gordon H. Hanson (2003). "Global Production Sharing and Rising Inequality: A Survey of Trade and Wages," in E. Kwan Choi and James Harrigan, eds., *Handbook of International Trade*, Oxford, UK: Blackwell Publishing, pp. 146–185.

Fukao, Kyoji, Hikari Ishido and Keiko Ito (2003). "Vertical Intra-Industry Trade and Foreign Direct Investment in East Asia," *Journal of the Japanese and International Economics*, 17(4): pp. 468–506.

Grossman, Gene M. and Esteban Rossi-Hansberg (2006). "Trading Tasks: A Simple Theory of Offshoring," NBER Working Paper No. 12721.

Hanson, Gordon H., Raymond J. Mataloni and Matthew J. Slaughter (2006). "Vertical Production Networks in Multinational Firms," *Review of Economics and Statistics*, 87(4): pp. 664–678.

Helpman, Elhanan, Marc J. Melitz and Stephen R. Yeaple (2004). "Export versus FDI with Heterogeneous Firms," *American Economic Review*, 94(1): pp. 300–316.

Hummels, David, Jun Ishii and Kei-Mu Yi (2001). "The Nature and Growth of Vertical Specialization in World Trade," *Journal of International Economics*, 54(1): pp. 75–96.

Katz, Lawrence F. and David Autor (1999). "Changes in the Wage Structure and Earnings Inequality," in Orely Ashenfelter and David Card, eds., *Handbook of Labor Economics*, Volume 3A, pp. 1463–1555, Amsterdam: Elsevier Science.

Kimura, Fukunari, Yuya Takahashi and Kazunobu Hayakawa (2007). "Fragmentation and Parts and Components Trade: Comparison between East Asia and Europe," *North American Journal of Economics and Finance*, 18(1): pp. 23–40.

Leamer, Edward E. (1999). "Effort, Wages, and the International Division of Labor," *Journal of Political Economy*, 107(6): pp. 1127–1162.

Marin, Dalia (2006). "A New International Division of Labor in Europe," *Journal of European Economic Association*, 4(2–3): pp. 612–622.

Tomiura, Eiichi (2007). "Foreign Outsourcing, Exporting, and FDI: A Productivity Comparison at the Firm Level," *Journal of International Economics*, 72(1): pp. 113–127.

PART I

FRAGMENTATION AND OUTSOURCING

CHAPTER 1

The Determinants of Offshore Production by Multinational Corporations: A Comparison of Japanese and U.S. Multinational Corporations

Toshiyuki Matsuura,[*,§] Kiyoyasu Tanaka,[†,¶] and Shujiro Urata[‡,||]

[*] Institute for Economic and Industrial Studies (Keio Economic Observatory)
Tokyo, Japan
[†] Interdisciplinary Studies Center
Institute of Developing Economics, Chiba, Japan
[‡] Graduate School of Asia Pacific Studies
Shinjuku, Tokyo, Japan
[§] Matsuura@sanken.keio.ac.jp
[¶] Tanakak@ier.hit-u.ac.jp
[||] Surata@waseda.jp

I. INTRODUCTION

Economic integration across borders has been rapidly developing as policy and technical barriers to foreign direct investment (FDI) and international trade have declined in recent decades. According to UNCTAD (2008), the volume of global GDP and exports of goods and non-factor services in current prices increased 4.5 and 7.1 times from 1982 to 2007, respectively. World FDI inflows, however, increased even more rapidly, 31.6 times for the period. In 2007, the presence of multinational corporations (MNCs) in the world economy, measured by the value-added of all foreign affiliates, accounted for an estimated 11% of global GDP. Furthermore, global trading chains by MNCs represent a substantial portion of world trade flows. Indeed, U.S. MNCs accounted for close to 80% of U.S. exports and imports in 2000 (Bernard *et al.*, 2005). MNCs have been a driving force in the process of economic globalization.

In order to understand the role of MNCs in the conduct of international commerce and production, it is crucial to understand the nature of offshore production by MNCs. It has long been documented that manufacturing firms are widely engaged in global production networks by geographically fragmenting particular stages of the production process (Feenstra, 1998). For instance, MNCs maintain headquarter services and production of intermediate goods at home, and their foreign subsidiaries assemble intermediates that are imported from the home country so as to produce final goods. The fragmentation of production by MNCs is motivated by the desire to shift production activities to countries in which factor costs are relatively low (Helpman, 1984; Markusen, 2002). As many markets are geographically segmented by borders, MNCs face a rich array of production organization to serve final consumers around the globe. An optimal form of global supply chains that stretches over various countries concerns the degree of vertical specialization within multinational production networks in order to save international transportation costs (Yeaple, 2003a; Grossman, Helpman, and Szeidl, 2006).

A large number of empirical studies have investigated a fundamental force in MNC decisions as to the location of offshore production. From a policy perspective, this issue is at the center of the debate over the extent to which the recent waves of trade and investment liberalization induce MNCs to relocate domestic production abroad. As briefly described, MNCs may systematically shift production facilities to countries with lower wages and factor costs. As such, multinational behavior raises great concern that a reduction of trade barriers for freer trade could accelerate the pace of hollowing-out of domestic manufacturing sectors if MNCs organize offshore production primarily for factor-cost considerations.

Although the concern is critically dependent on the question of what factors determine FDI activity, the prevalence of evidence indicates that MNCs primarily pursue horizontal FDI that is motivated by access to foreign markets in the face of trade barriers (Brainard, 1997; Carr, Markusen, and Maskus, 2001). On the other hand, there is mixed evidence of vertical FDI that is motivated by international differences in factor costs, as predicted by the factor-proportions theory of trade (Blonigen, 2005). These findings suggest that the factor-cost motivation may not be prevalent in accounting for the general location of multinational production. Instead, only a few particular manufacturing industries such as machinery and electronics are conducive to offshoring of production in the host countries that have comparative advantage (Yeaple, 2003b). From a theoretical point of view, the existing evidence does not appear to bear out the significance of production fragmentation by MNCs. Thus, the empirical literature remains largely inconclusive as to whether a hollowing-out scenario afflicts the global economy in a quantitatively important way.

However, one of the key issues in prior research concerns the prevalence of evidence based on offshore production by U.S. MNCs. There is considerable evidence that U.S. MNCs have extensively engaged in vertical production networks in Canada and Mexico — the members of the North American Free Trade Agreement (NAFTA) — by exporting intermediate inputs to their affiliates for further processing (Feinberg and Keane, 2001; Hanson, Mataloni, and Slaughter, 2001, 2005). Apparently, these countries enjoy low trade costs for shipments, and wage-cost advantages in the case of Mexico. Their geographic location could present a strong incentive for U.S. firms to consolidate vertical production chains in the NAFTA. As such, FTAs may generate a strong force against the shift of production to non-FTA member countries with lower factor costs, which would make it difficult to take the prediction of factor-proportions theory to U.S. MNCs data. An open question is whether U.S. MNCs–based results can be generalized to apply to the nature of offshore production by MNCs originating from other parent countries. Furthermore, the issue is aggravated by the limited existing data on multinational activity. A number of data problems on the measurement of multinational production, including the definition of foreign affiliates, sectoral classification, and survey methods, undermine comparability of the measures of multinational production. Thus, currently available data pose a challenge for an empirical analysis of multinational activities of MNCs of different nationality on a uniform basis as well as for the exploration of the peculiarity of the structure of U.S. multinational production.

To fill these gaps in the current literature, we exploit confidential *affiliate-level* panel data from the Ministry of Economy, Trade, and Industry, Japan, in order to construct improved measures of foreign affiliate sales by Japanese MNCs (Matsuura, 2004). In particular, we assemble the official surveys to estimate missing sales of a large number of foreign affiliates during 1989–2005. The estimated data on affiliate sales that vary by destination market are aggregated over industry and country solely for majority-owned foreign subsidiaries to match the Japanese data with U.S. data.[1] This new dataset enables us to make a rigorous comparison on the nature of offshore production between Japanese and U.S. MNCs. Then, we combine the Japanese and U.S. data to explore the following questions. What are the characteristics of offshore production by Japanese and U.S. firms? What are the determinants of their foreign production? To what extent is the pattern of Japanese and U.S. multinational production consistent with factor-cost and market-access motives of FDI? These questions should shed new light on the distinctiveness of U.S. multinational production as compared to Japanese MNCs. Furthermore, a comparative analysis helps us to evaluate the influence of the U.S. data on the empirical evidence that factor-seeking motivation is not prevalent in the general pattern of FDI activity.

The descriptive analysis illustrates several features of Japanese and U.S. multinational activities. In the past decades, foreign affiliate sales by Japanese and U.S. MNCs substantially increased alike. But the employment growth of Japanese affiliates was much more rapid than that of U.S. affiliates. For both Japanese and U.S. MNCs, local sales explain the majority of affiliate total sales across country and industry categories, indicating the importance of local markets for attracting offshore production by multinationals. Second, the similarity between Japanese and U.S. affiliates figures prominently in the composition of affiliate sales across three regions: Asia, Europe, and South America. Regional-market characteristics, rather than sectoral characteristics, are influential in explaining the target market for offshore production by Japanese and U.S. MNCs. In contrast, there also exist some differences between Japanese and U.S. MNCs. In particular, Japanese affiliates are distinctive in that the composition of affiliate exports for a home country becomes progressively larger across sectors as the income level of host country declines; it also becomes progressively greater across country-income levels as the sectoral skill intensity decreases.

In the regression analysis, we use a comprehensive panel data on foreign affiliate sales disaggregated by country, industry, and destination market

[1] More details of the dataset are presented in Section IV.

to explore what factors motivate multinational sales. Our interest lies in examining comparative advantage (vertical) and market access (horizontal) motives of offshore production by Japanese and U.S. MNCs. In this respect, we find several interesting patterns. First, foreign affiliate sales by Japanese MNCs tend to be larger in unskilled-labor–abundant countries, with the more pronounced impact of unskilled labor on Japanese affiliates in Asia. Since this pattern is consistent with the model of vertical FDI, Japanese MNCs appear to engage substantially in vertical production chains across borders to take advantage of international differentials in factor costs. In contrast, the evidence suggests that foreign affiliate sales by U.S. MNCs are only marginally sensitive to variation in host country's unskilled-labor abundance. This is not to say that U.S. MNCs do not pursue vertical FDI strategies. Rather, we find that the comparative advantage motive of offshore production by U.S. manufacturing affiliates seems to be, *on average*, weaker than that by Japanese affiliates. The results for the determinants of export versus local sales also bear out these assertions.

The rest of this chapter is organized as follows. Section II briefly reviews the literature on the determinants of FDI. Section III explains the econometric framework for the analysis of offshore production by multinationals. Section IV describes our primary data sources of Japanese and U.S. MNCs and other data sources. In Section V, we illustrate the overall picture of Japanese and U.S. affiliate activities by focusing on the composition of affiliate sales by destination markets across sectoral skill intensity and host-country characteristics. Section VI presents the regression results of the determinants of affiliate sales. Section VII concludes.

II. LITERATURE REVIEW

We begin by describing theoretical studies of FDI in order to motivate the empirical work on the determinants of multinational production. Then, we discuss the recent empirical works that attempt to identify the role of comparative advantages in FDI activity. Lastly, we review prior research using U.S. and/or Japanese MNCs data to clarify the contribution of our study.[2]

[2] For a more comprehensive review, see Blonigen (2005) and Helpman (2006).

The literature has previously made a clear distinction between factor-seeking (vertical) and market-seeking (horizontal) motives of FDI activity. First, Helpman (1984) and Helpman and Krugman (1985) have examined the role of factor-proportions differences in accounting for multinational production. Some firms fragment the production process into various stages that differ by factor proportions; for instance, skilled labor is used more intensively in headquarters services than in final assembly. Differences in relative skilled-labor endowments across countries generate international differentials in skilled-labor costs, which may not be equalized by international trade. In this case, these firms locate headquarters activity in the country where skilled labor is relatively cheap, but move production activity to the country where unskilled labor is relatively cheap. Comparative advantage creates an incentive for vertical MNCs that are headquartered in one country but produce in another country. Then, the model predicts that offshore production by vertical MNCs should occur primarily between countries that are sufficiently different in relative skill abundance. From the standpoint of firms in skilled-labor–abundant countries, the supply of unskilled labor in a foreign country is a crucial factor in undertaking vertical investment.

Second, Markusen (1984) and Brainard (1997) have analyzed a firm's decision between exporting and local production. In contrast to the vertical models, firms have identical factor intensities across stages of the production process, which rule out vertical fragmentation of production. Instead, these firms are motivated by trade barriers between countries to shift production facilities offshore. If gains from the savings of trade costs exceed additional fixed costs of building a foreign plant, these firms become horizontal MNCs that are headquartered in one country but produce in multiple countries. In the absence of comparative advantage motives, the horizontal model predicts that horizontal FDI should occur between countries of similar factor proportions.

The recent literature maintains factor-cost and market-access motives as a primary explanation of multinational production, but goes beyond the traditional distinction between vertical and horizontal FDI by extending the analysis at least in two ways. First, Yeaple (2003a) and Ekholm *et al.* (2007) analyze a three-country (region) framework in which multinational firms with production facilities in a low-cost market can serve their home market and/or a third market by exports from their offshore production. These studies highlight cross-country dependence as an important determinant of FDI; MNCs take into account regional market characteristics in determining a host country for their offshore production. Second, Helpman *et al.* (2004) introduce firm-level heterogeneity in the firm's decision between exporting and horizontal direct investment. As only the most productive firms are shown to engage in FDI, they shed light on the role of within-sector firm-productivity differences in accounting for the cross-sectoral pattern of multinational sales.

The early empirical analysis, including Brainard (1997); Carr, Markusen, and Maskus (2001); and Blonigen, Davies, and Head (2003), is motivated to estimate the prediction of the general equilibrium models of horizontal and vertical FDI. These studies find that affiliate/FDI activities are prevalent between similar countries and respond positively to trade barriers as measured by tariffs and transportation costs. These results are taken as evidence of market-seeking FDI. In contrast, the data do not strongly support the hypothesis of vertical FDI models that larger differences in relative factor abundance should increase MNCs activity from skilled-labor–abundant to unskilled-labor–abundant countries. In addition, Markusen and Maskus (2001) find that skilled-labor abundance in a host country increases export sales by foreign affiliates of U.S. MNCs that are aggregated over manufacturing industry at the country-level for the period 1986–1994. This suggests that U.S. multinationals, *on average*, tend to consolidate offshore production for export in more skilled-labor–abundant countries.

To resolve the mixed evidence of vertical FDI, recent studies have taken a closer look at U.S. MNCs activity. Hanson, Mataloni, and Slaughter (2001) document a detailed pattern of outward U.S. FDI across industries and countries in the 1980s and 1990s. Their analysis points to the concentration of U.S. multinational activities in high-income countries in the 1980s, but a subsequent shift towards low-income countries in the 1990s. Hanson, Mataloni, and Slaughter (2005) use U.S. firm-level data to study trade in intermediate inputs between foreign affiliates and parent firms. Their results indicate that lower trade costs and wages for unskilled labor encourage affiliate demand for imported inputs. In addition, Yeaple (2003b) finds that host-country relative skill endowments tend to increase (decrease) affiliate activity by U.S. MNCs in less (more) skilled-labor–intensive sectors, thereby supporting a chain of comparative advantage across industries and countries. All of these studies provide evidence that U.S. MNCs engage in vertical activity for certain sectors and countries. However, the evidence does not support the claim that vertical motivations of offshore production are prevalent in the general pattern of U.S. FDI. The vertical model of FDI does not receive strong support from the data on U.S. MNCs in which skilled-labor–abundant countries account for the dominant share of their offshore production. These issues provide a motivation for comparing the role of comparative advantage in the structure of Japanese and U.S. multinational activities.

There is limited empirical work that analyzes factor-cost motivations of offshore production for multinationals of different nationality. Braconier, Norback, and Urban (2005a) define vertical FDI as FDI driven by factor-cost differentials across countries. Their study finds that wage costs for low-skilled workers decrease foreign affiliate sales of U.S. and Swedish MNCs from the late 1980s through 1990s, suggesting that these MNCs invest more in a low-wage country for less-skilled labor. However, their results show that affiliate sales increase in high-skilled labor costs. It is not clear why both U.S. and Swedish MNCs tend to seek *higher* wages for skilled labor. These results are inconsistent with vertical FDI as defined earlier. Furthermore, Braconier, Norback, and Urban (2005b) estimate the knowledge-capital model of multinational enterprises, as described in Markusen (2002), to study whether FDI activity is driven by differences in relative skill endowments. Using a dataset on affiliate sales collected from a wide range of country sources, they find support for a vertical component of the model. But the study does not address comparability in affiliate data sources.

Prior research on a comparative analysis of Japanese and U.S. MNCs includes that of Eaton and Tamura (1994), who studied bilateral FDI stocks in Japan and the U.S. during the period 1985–1990. They find that host-country educational level was likely to significantly increase U.S. FDI activities, but have little influence on Japanese FDI. Lipsey (2000) also examines Japanese and U.S. affiliate production for export in East Asia since the mid-1970s. His findings indicate that the pattern of affiliate export by Japanese firms was more consistent with host-country comparative advantages than U.S. firms, but the pattern of Japanese and U.S. affiliates became alike over time.

All of these studies suggest that comparative advantage motives play a certain role in explaining a cross-country pattern of overall offshore production by MNCs. However, no attempt was made to harmonize the measurement of foreign affiliate activities across data sources. Measurement discrepancies are likely to arise for a variety of reasons, including the definition of foreign affiliate, the survey quality, and industry classification. Pooling MNC data may invalidate the consistency of estimated effects of factor-cost differentials as measured by wage levels or relative skill endowments. In general, prior work has paid little attention to the issue of whether data inconsistency may distort the estimate of determinants of multinational activity.

To construct a dataset on affiliate activity that is comparable across data sources, we exploit confidential *affiliate-level* panel data for foreign affiliates owned by Japanese firms. Estimating missing sales by foreign affiliates in the original survey, the dataset improves publicly available data on Japanese affiliate sales. We aggregate estimated affiliate sales by country and industry to construct panel data on the majority-owned foreign affiliates by Japanese firms, which improve comparability with U.S. MNCs data. Combining the improved Japanese data with existing U.S. data, we explore the patterns and determinants of offshore production by Japanese and U.S. MNCs in a consistent fashion. This approach is close to the study of Tanaka (2009), which showed that offshore production by Japanese MNCs was attracted to unskilled-labor–abundant countries more strongly than U.S. MNCs in the 1990s. Our study is distinctive in that our dataset is constructed solely from majority-owned foreign affiliates in which their sales are disaggregated by both country and industry.

III. EMPIRICAL MODEL

This section presents our empirical framework that is designed to examine underlying motivations of offshore production by multinationals. In order to make our results comparable to prior research on FDI, we adopt a reduced-form estimation that links country and industry characteristics with a measure of multinational activity. In general, FDI theory does not offer a theoretically derived standard specification for determinants of FDI, but a commonly used specification is based on the knowledge-capital model as specified in Carr, Markusen, and Maskus (2001). Roughly speaking, their estimating equation captures the simulated distribution of affiliate production that varies by cross-country differences in country size, relative skill endowments, and transportation costs. We modify the estimating equation to meet the nature of our dataset by introducing a sectoral variation in the affiliate data. In particular, we mainly exploit a variation in host-country skilled-labor abundance to examine comparative advantage motives of FDI, which are allowed to differ by Japanese and U.S. MNCs.

We estimate the following empirical model:

$$\begin{aligned}\text{ASALE}_{ijkt} = {} & \beta_0 + \beta_1\text{SKILL}_{jt} + \beta_2\text{SKINT}_{ikt} + \beta_3\text{GDP}_{jt} + \beta_4\text{DIST}_{ijt} \\ & + \beta_5\text{SPATIAL}_{ijt} + \eta X'_{jt} + (\beta_6\text{SKILL}_{jt} + \beta_7\text{SKINT}_{ikt} \\ & + \beta_8\text{GDP}_{jt} + \beta_9\text{DIST}_{ijt} + \beta_{10}\text{SPATIAL}_{ijt} + \eta X'_{jt}) \\ & \times\text{U.S.} + \varepsilon_{ijkt} \qquad (1)\end{aligned}$$

where the subscripts indicate home country i, host country j, industry k, and time t. ASALE is a type of foreign affiliate sales as a proxy for affiliate production for local and export markets. SKILL is a measure of supply of skilled labor in a host country. SKINT is a sectoral intensity of skilled labor in a parent country. GDP is a measure of host-market size. DIST represents the geographic distance between parent and host countries. SPATIAL measures a spatial dispersion of third-countries' affiliate activity originating from the same parent nation. X includes region and year dummies. U.S. indicates a dummy variable which takes on unity if a home country is the U.S. and zero if the home country is Japan.

We estimate the model (1) to explore the main hypothesis that comparative advantage motives play a driving force in explaining the pattern of offshore production by multinationals. The factor-proportions theory suggests that a cross-country difference in skilled-labor abundance generates an incentive for firms to locate unskilled-labor–intensive production in the country where the unskilled-labor wage is relatively low. In the specification, the strength of comparative advantage motives is captured primarily by the SKILL variable; from a standpoint of firms headquartered in skilled-labor–abundant countries such as Japan and the U.S., factor-seeking offshore production should be located in less skilled-labor–abundant countries. Vertical MNCs are encouraged not only to invest more in unskilled-labor–abundant countries but also to expand the scale of production operation in such countries. If the data are consistent with the prediction of factor-seeking FDI, then we expect $\beta_1 < 0$. Note that there is only a host-country variation in SKILL so that we estimate the *average* response of MNCs to host-country skill abundance at the industry level.

The interaction term between SKILL and U.S. in the model allows us to test the second main hypothesis that the strength of comparative advantage motives may systematically differ by Japanese and U.S. MNCs. Under the null hypothesis, there is no difference in the intensity of comparative advantage motives, suggesting that the coefficient of the interaction is not statistically different from zero. However, we argue that a regional concentration of vertical production networks could systematically differentiate the cross-country distribution of offshore production by Japanese MNCs from that by U.S. MNCs. Vertical production chains within multinational firms are driven not only by low wages for unskilled labor, but by low trading costs for moving intermediate inputs and/or final products across borders. So, vertical FDI activity takes into account factor-cost considerations and the savings of transportation costs in an inherently intricate manner. As a host country is more distant from a home market, a reduction in production cost of taking advantage of low wages could be offset by greater transport costs that increase for shipping goods multiple times. Mutually reinforcing influences of factor and trade costs could generate an agglomeration force to the pattern of vertical FDI in the proximate region.

The preponderance of evidence points to the important role of East Asia and North America for vertical production networks by Japanese and U.S. firms, respectively. Japanese firms are widely engaged in vertical trading chains across East Asia, which serves as a hub for offshore production networks (Kimura and Ando, 2005). U.S. MNCs extensively create vertical production networks by locating input processing in their foreign affiliates in Canada and Mexico (Feinberg and Keane, 2001; Hanson, Mataloni, and Slaughter, 2001, 2005). The distinctive feature of Japanese vertical production networks relative to the U.S. is the diversity of the region; East Asia consists of many countries of different factor proportions, whereas North America comprises only Canada and Mexico. A possible hypothesis is that the geographic proximity of East Asia to Japan may disproportionately highlight the comparative advantage motives, as measured by cross-country variations in skill endowments, in explaining the pattern of Japanese multinational sales. If this is the case, host country's skilled-labor abundance is likely to have a greater negative impact on Japanese MNCs relative to U.S. MNCs. Thus, we predict $\beta_6 > 0$.

The comparative advantage explanation may have different implications for different types of multinational sales because some component of affiliate activity is encouraged by other investment motivations such as market access, fiscal incentives, and tax evasion. The strength of the comparative advantage motives should be weaker in affiliate sales to local markets as MNCs build offshore production for local sales in order to gain access to foreign markets. The impact of skill endowments in a host country can be different across affiliate sales for local and export markets. Hence, we estimate the model separately for each type of affiliate sales to allow for different coefficients of SKILL across sales destinations.

We include industry- and country-specific variables that are important determinants of FDI. SKINT enters the model to control for sectoral intensity of knowledge capital as a source of multinational expansion. Firms in relatively high-skilled-labor–intensive industries may invest more in a foreign market, whereas firms in relatively low-skilled-labor–intensive industries may invest less abroad. The host-market size as measured by GDP increases the entry of multinational firms as well as the scale of affiliate production. As horizontal MNCs are encouraged by trade frictions between countries, DIST as a proxy for international transport costs is expected to encourage foreign affiliate sales. Further, recent theory of FDI suggests that multinationals take into account the spatial location of FDI activity originating from the same parent country (Coughlin and Segev, 2000; Baltagi, Egger, and Pfaffermayr, 2007; Blonigen *et al.*, 2007). As export-platform FDI may cluster in a specific region to exploit gains from agglomeration, SPATIAL can have a positive impact on foreign affiliate sales. Thus, we expect $\beta_2 > 0, \beta_3 > 0, \beta_4 > 0, \beta_5 > 0$. Additionally, we allow these independent variables to have different coefficients between Japanese and U.S. MNCs by interacting them with the U.S. dummy.

Finally, X is a vector of other control variables. We introduce a dummy variable for time to control for aggregate time effects that influence multinational sales around the globe. The model includes a dummy variable for three regions (Asia, Europe, and South America) to address the effects of regional characteristics on affiliate sales. By including an interaction term with these dummy variables, the year and regional effects are also allowed to vary by Japanese and U.S. MNCs.

IV. DATA DESCRIPTION

Data on Foreign Affiliates of Japanese and U.S. Firms

In this section, we first describe data sources on foreign affiliates of Japanese and U.S. MNCs. Japanese data come from *the basic survey of overseas business activities* (BSOBA) by Japanese firms. The survey is annually conducted by the Ministry of Economy, Trade, and Industry (METI). Since responding to the METI survey is not mandatory for parent firms, the official data on Japanese MNCs are known to suffer from low response rates of around 60%, varying samples of parent firms over time, and widely fluctuating sales at the affiliate level. Using affiliate samples in the survey, METI reports aggregate information on foreign affiliate activity of Japanese firms. However, the officially available data on foreign affiliates are likely to suffer seriously from the varying quality of surveys across years. Variation in foreign affiliate sales in the survey may not be sufficiently correlated with variation in real economic activity of foreign affiliates even at the aggregate level such as industry and country. As these data problems are not well understood, it is even unknown to what extent the survey quality affects the aggregate information on foreign affiliate activity. Thus, the existing government data on Japanese MNCs are not appropriate for rigorous empirical analysis on multinational activity.

Many unresolved data problems motivate us to devote much effort on improving the Japanese survey data. One key issue lies in the fact that there are many foreign affiliates that enter and exit a host market in an apparently inconsistent way, possibly reflecting serious reporting errors. As a complete list of foreign affiliates in operation is crucial for the consistent measurement of multinational sales at the aggregate level, we construct *affiliate-level* panel data by linking parent firms and foreign affiliates from the *confidential* data of BSOBA questionnaire. The affiliate-level panel data are used to pin down affiliate samples with missing information on their activity, which are likely to arise from reporting errors. Then, missing sales of foreign affiliates are estimated by linear interpolation at the affiliate level during the years 1989–2005. To permit public access to the dataset, the improved dataset aggregates affiliate sales, purchases, and employment over country, industry, and year.[3]

The previous dataset on Japanese FDI activity, however, remains to have several issues for a comparative analysis of multinational activity. One issue of comparability between Japanese and U.S. MNCs data is that the concept of foreign affiliate ownership differs between Japanese and U.S. data. Building on our previous work, this paper addresses the deviation of the ownership concept to improve comparability with existing data on U.S. MNCs. Specifically, we compile the improved data on foreign affiliates for which more than 50% of their equity stakes are owned by Japanese parent firms. For the following analysis, we employ the resulting dataset on foreign affiliates by Japanese firms.

The data on foreign affiliate activities of U.S. parent firms in non-bank manufacturing come from the survey of *U.S. Direct Investment Abroad*, published by the U.S. Bureau of Economic Analysis (BEA). To match with the definition of affiliate ownership in the Research Institute for Economy, Trade and Industry (RIETI) data, we use the data on the majority-owned foreign affiliates in the BEA source. There are five items that are commonly available variables in the data sources and used for the analysis: affiliate total sales, local sales, exports to the home market, exports to the third market, and the number of employees. The BEA switched from the Standard Industry Classification (SIC) system to the North American Industry Classification System (NAICS) for the industry category of foreign affiliates in 1999. Because the industry-by-country analysis using all samples is likely to suffer from a discontinuity in the industry classification, we separately examine the pre- and post-1999 samples in the regression analysis.

Both the improved dataset on Japanese MNCs and existing U.S. MNCs data are used in Tanaka (2009), which reports that the measurement of the volume of affiliate sales across the RIETI and BEA datasets is fairly consistent. However, when comparing aggregate sales by Japanese manufacturing affiliates in the U.S. from the RIETI source with those from

[3]Available at http://www.rieti.go.jp/jp/database/FDI2009/index.html. Accessed 30 December 2009. See Matsuura (2004) for details.

the *Foreign Direct Investment in the U.S.* published by the BEA, the former data exceeds the latter to large extent. While the discrepancy may not necessarily be extended to affiliate activities in other countries, we suspect that the industry classification method is a primary reason for an observed deviation between data sources. Specifically, an industry to which certain foreign affiliates belong is determined by sectoral sales of the affiliates at the four-digit-level in the BEA survey, but by the subjective judgment of a person who files a report in the METI survey. Some foreign affiliates of Japanese firms that are assigned to manufacturing could be classified as wholesale affiliates. The comparability issue on industry classification between Japanese and U.S. sources is not addressed in our study.

There are at least two other issues for a comparison on the real volume of foreign affiliate sales. First, affiliate sales in the RIETI are reported in millions of Yen, but those in the BEA are in millions of U.S. dollars. While it is possible to measure the RIETI's affiliate sales in the U.S. dollars using Yen-dollar exchange rates, the dollar-denominated affiliate sales are highly sensitive to an exchange-rate movement across years. Second, affiliate sales in both datasets are measured in nominal terms so that price deflators by country and industry are necessary for measuring a real volume of sales. While the price deflators such as wholesale and consumer price index are readily available at the country-by-year level, a deflated volume of affiliate sales can be extremely large in countries that experienced high inflation in the 1980s and 1990s.

All of these problems suggest that the nature of affiliate data does not allow for a straightforward comparison of the volume of offshore affiliate sales by Japanese and U.S. MNCs. To proceed in a meaningful way, we assume that foreign affiliates in the METI and BEA surveys report the composition of their sales by destination in a consistent way over time. Instead of the volume of sales, we focus on the share and growth of affiliate sales by destination in the descriptive analysis. In the regression analysis for a pooled sample, we attempt to control for some component of systematic deviations between these data sources by including dummy variables for U.S. MNCs, year, and an interaction term between U.S. MNCs and year. This approach helps us to mitigate an influence of systematic measurement errors on the investigation of comparative advantage motives of FDI.

Other Data Sources

We use other data sources on country and industry characteristics. Data on skilled-labor abundance are taken from Barro and Lee (2001). Educational attainment is measured by the average years of schooling of the population older than 25 years, which serves as a proxy for supply of skilled labor in a country. Data on real GDP measured in billions of year 2000 U.S. dollars come from the *World Development Indicators.*[4] For geographic distance, we employ the dataset on geographic variables compiled by the CEPII, the research center in international economics in France.[5] To construct a measure of spatial dispersions of FDI activity, we define a spatial-lag variable as:

$$\text{SPATIAL}_{ijt} = \sum_{s} \frac{\sum_k \text{ASALES}_{iskt}}{\text{Distance}_{js}} \tag{2}$$

where the subscript s indicates a third country. Data on ASALES come from the RIETI and BEA survey used for our dependent variable, respectively. The CEPII's distance data are used to measure a geographic distance between host and third countries.

Data on industry characteristics used in the analysis include the composition of skilled labor in employment. For the Japanese sample, we use the ancillary dataset on sectoral employees by occupation in the Japan Industrial Productivity Database 2009.[6] Data on skilled-labor intensity in the U.S. manufacturing sector come from the NBER manufacturing productivity database constructed by Bartelsman and Gray (1996). In these datasets, skilled labor is measured by the share of non-production workers in total employment. Thus, unskilled labor is approximated by the composition of production labor in the labor force in an industrial sector. These datasets on industry skill intensity are aggregated over industries to match the industry classification of foreign affiliates by Japanese and U.S. firms, respectively.

[4]Taiwan GDP data are obtained from the Department of Commerce, Taiwan.

[5]Available at http://www.cepii.fr/anglaisgraph/bdd/distances.htm. Accessed 30 December 2009.

[6]See the data at http://www.rieti.go.jp/en/database/JIP2009/index.html. Accessed 30 December 2009.

V. THE PATTERN OF FOREIGN AFFILIATE ACTIVITY BY JAPANESE AND U.S. MNCs

Before proceeding with the formal econometric analysis, this section provides a descriptive analysis of offshore production of Japanese and U.S. MNCs. The main purpose of this section is to present the stylized facts on the pattern and trend of foreign affiliate activities in a consistent way in order to make a comparison of Japanese and U.S. MNCs. As briefly explained in the data description, we illustrate the composition of affiliate sales by destination and affiliate employment to characterize the nature of foreign production.

Worldwide Pattern of Foreign Affiliate Activity

We start by describing the overall growth of Japanese and U.S. and multinational activity. Figure 1 illustrates the worldwide pattern of their affiliate activities for the years 1985–2005. The left-hand panel shows the rapid growth of foreign affiliate sales for both Japanese and U.S. MNCs. During the period, U.S. affiliate sales increased more than fivefold from 250 to over

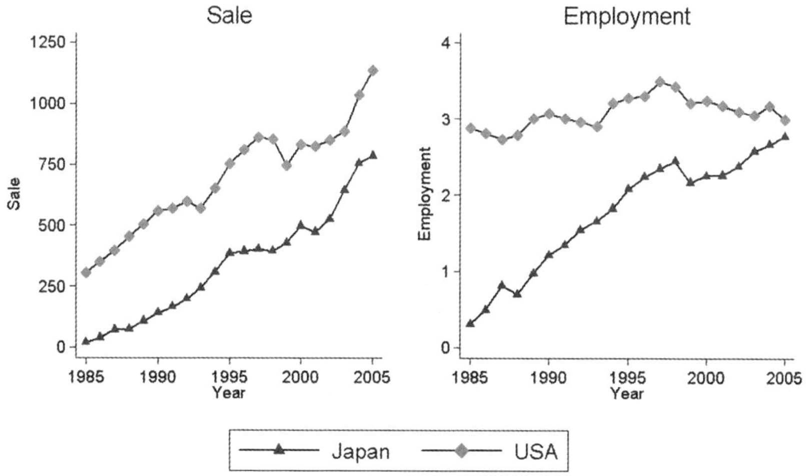

Note: Affiliate sales are in billions of U.S. dollars; employment is in millions of employees.

Source: RIETI and U.S. BEA.

Fig. 1. Worldwide pattern of Japanese and U.S. multinational activities affiliate sales and employment for year 1985–2005.

1,100 billion U.S. dollars in nominal terms. More impressively, Japanese affiliate sales increased from less than 10 billion to over 750 billion dollars during the period 1985–2005. These figures represent the massive expansion of offshore production by Japanese and U.S. companies for the past decades. Furthermore, the right-hand panel illustrates that Japanese and U.S. multinationals employed around 3 million workers around the globe in 2005, respectively. While foreign employment by U.S. MNCs remained virtually constant in the past decades, Japanese affiliate employment increased at a remarkably rapid pace. In summary, U.S. affiliate sales increased rapidly without much expansion of foreign employment. But the rapid growth of Japanese affiliate sales occurred together with increased employment.

Foreign Affiliate Sales by Country Income and Sectoral Skill Intensity

To organize the descriptive analysis, we place the comparative-advantage motive of FDI at the center of the analysis as discussed in Yeaple (2003b). Specifically, we sort Japanese and U.S. affiliate industries by the intensity of skilled labor according to the industry information. Using the median value of skilled-labor intensity in year 1985 as a cutoff point, we classify the above- and below-median industries as high- and low-skill–intensive sectors, respectively.[7] As to the characteristics of the host countries, we use World Bank's country classification, i.e., high, upper middle, lower middle, and lower income countries, according to gross national income per capita. To avoid the change of income category for the countries, we adopt the classification in the year 1987. Additionally, we introduce the regional dimension to explore the characteristics of Japanese and U.S. MNCs in Asia, Europe, and South America.

Figure 2 illustrates the composition of foreign affiliate sales by destination across country income and industry-skill intensity. Because of data availability, we take the average shares for the period 1989–2005 of

[7] High-skill sectors in the U.S. sample include chemicals and allied products, industrial machinery and equipment, and electronic and other electric equipment. The other sectors are defined to be low skill intensive. In the case of Japan, transportation equipment is also classified as high-skill–intensive according to the cutoff point of skill intensity. The conclusions are not affected in a significant way by classifying the transportation equipment as a low-skill sector.

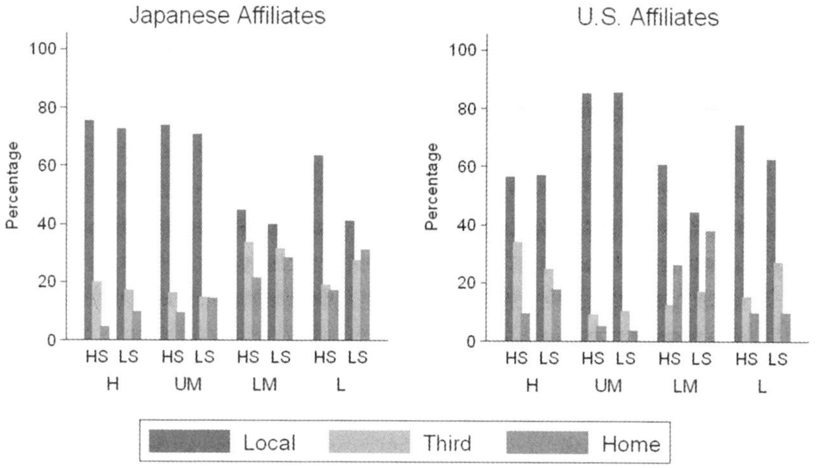

Note: HS and LS indicate high- and low-skilled-labor–intensive sectors; H, UM, LM, and L mean high, upper middle, lower middle, and low income countries; U.S. industry category changed in 1999 from SIC to NAICS.

Source: RIETI and U.S. BEA.

Fig. 2. Japanese and U.S. affiliate sales by destination market average share by industry and income group for 1989–2005.

the U.S. and Japanese samples. First, local sales of U.S. affiliates account for the majority of total sales across country and industry groups. The same feature is also observed for Japanese affiliates. These findings imply that offshore production by multinationals serves primarily local markets. However, the importance of local markets varies more significantly across countries than industries. The portion of local sales is relatively larger in upper-middle and low-income countries for both the Japanese and U.S. samples. Second, U.S. affiliate exports to a third market are relatively higher in high-income countries, but a cross-industry difference appears to be small. In contrast, Japanese affiliate exports to a third country are relatively larger in high and lower-middle income countries. Roughly speaking, a distinctive pattern of third-market exports is not clearly observed.

Lastly, U.S. and Japanese affiliate sales to the home country account for a small share of total sales across countries and sectors. In contrast with the U.S. sample, the Japanese sample is distinctive in that the share of affiliate exports for the home market becomes progressively larger in both low- and high-skill–intensive sectors as the level of host country income declines. Also, the home-export share appears to be larger in low-skill–intensive industries as the country income declines progressively. These patterns seem to be consistent with a comparative advantage motive of FDI in which the degree of offshore production motivated by factor price differentials varies with country and industry characteristics.

Foreign Affiliate Sales by Region and Sectoral Skill Intensity

In Figure 3, we disaggregate the sectoral composition of various affiliate sales by region: Asia, Europe, and South America. Consistent with the previous figures, affiliate sales to a local market explain the dominant share of total sales across the regions for both the U.S. and Japanese samples. The fraction of local sales is relatively larger in South America, possibly suggesting that multinational production in the region is driven strongly by market access.

In Europe, U.S. affiliate sales to a third market account for the prominent portion of total sales. A similar pattern can be also observed for the Japanese sample. These findings imply that Europe plays a large role in

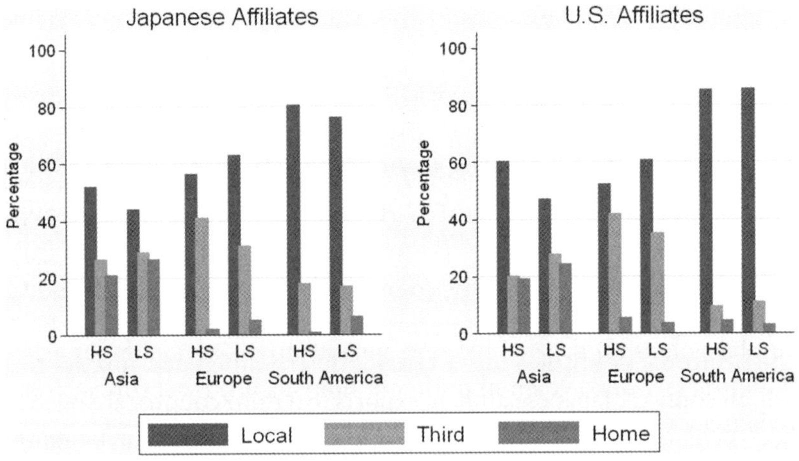

Note: HS and LS indicate high- and low-skilled intensive sectors; the U.S. industry classification changed in 1999 from SIC to NAICS.

Source: RIETI and U.S. BEA

Fig. 3. Japanese and U.S. affiliate sales by destination market and region average share by industry for 1989–2005.

explaining the somewhat higher share of affiliate exports to a third country that were previously observed in high-income countries. Lastly, affiliate sales to a home market represent the small part of total sales in Europe and South America. In contrast, home-market exports appear to be a relatively important portion of affiliate sales in Asia. These patterns can be seen in both U.S. and Japanese samples. When illustrating the composition of offshore production by Japanese and U.S. MNCs across the regions, we can observe similar patterns on the relative importance of affiliate sales by destination. This suggests that both U.S. and Japanese MNCs respond to the regional characteristics in a similar fashion by choosing the main market for local production.

Growth of Foreign Affiliate Sales by Country Income in High- and Low-Skill Industry

Figure 4 shows the three-year average growth rate of Japanese and U.S. affiliate sales by destination market in high skill-intensive sector for the period 1990–2004. The left- and right-hand panels show the Japanese and U.S. samples, respectively. Over the early and middle 1990s, every type of Japanese affiliate sales across country groups had recorded high growth. In particular, affiliate exports in low-income countries exhibited a remarkably high increase. Each type of U.S. affiliate sales had on average moderate growth rates in the 1990s. From the late 1990s to the early 2000s, we observe a decline in the growth rates of affiliate sales by destination. Thereafter, affiliate sales started to grow at a positive rate. As observed in the U.S. sample, the Japanese affiliate activities declined at the end of the 1990s. Subsequently, the growth rates of affiliate production by Japanese MNCs remained moderate during the early 2000s.

In Figure 5, we display the average growth rates of Japanese and U.S. affiliate sales in low-skill–intensive industry. The left-hand panel displays the growth rate of Japanese affiliate sales. The affiliate activities exhibit a high growth rate over the 1990s. Foreign affiliate sales by Japanese firms in low-income countries appear to grow at a relatively fast pace. However, each type of affiliate sales declined to a low growth rate in the early 2000s. In the right-hand panel, U.S. affiliate sales appear to exhibit a

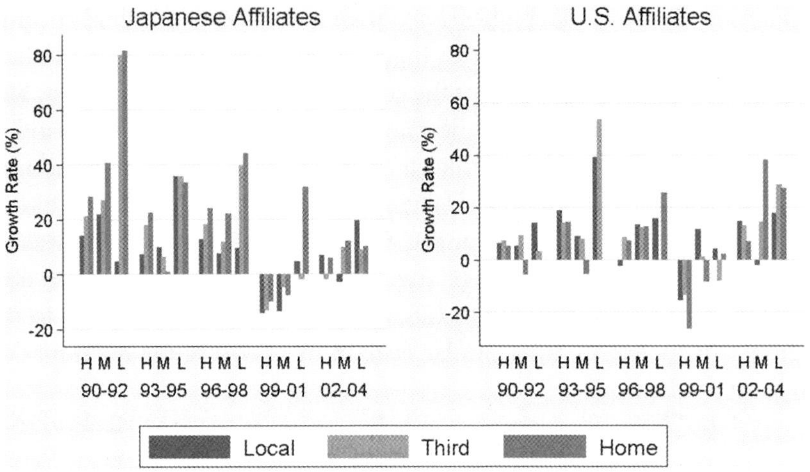

Note: H, M, and L mean high-, middle-, and low-income countries; the U.S. industry classification changed in 1999 from SIC to NAICS.

Source: RIETI and U.S. BEA.

Fig. 4. Growth of Japanese and U.S. affiliate sales in high-skill industry three-year average growth rate by destination market and country income for 1990–2004.

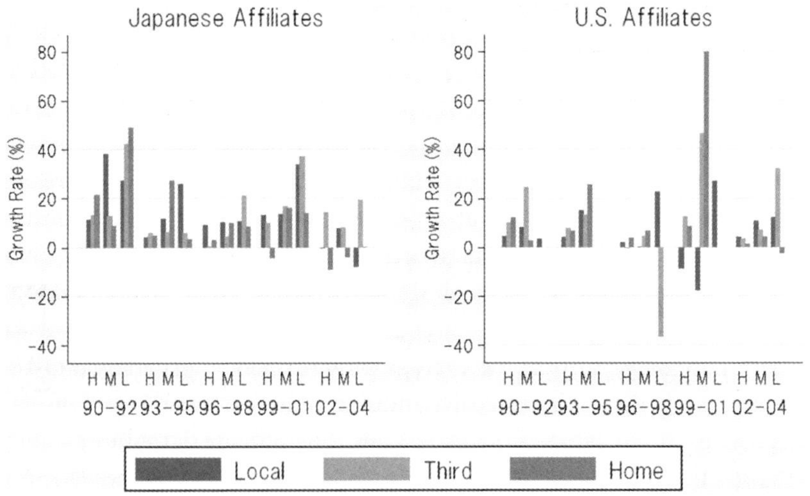

Note: H, M, and L mean high-, middle-, and low-income countries; the U.S. industry classification changed in 1999 from SIC to NAICS.

Source: RIETI and U.S. BEA.

Fig. 5. Growth of Japanese and U.S. affiliate sales in low-skill industry three-year average growth rate by destination market and country income for 1990–2004.

moderate growth rate in the 1990s.[8] In contrast to the high-skill industry, we can observe a surge in the growth rate of affiliate sales to third and home markets in middle-income countries for the end of the 1990s. As expected, the growth rate of affiliate sales in high-income countries remained low over time. Overall, we do not observe a clear trend in the growth of U.S. affiliate sales by destination.

In summary, these figures demonstrate the substantially high growth rates for Japanese affiliate sales in both high- and low-skill industries over the periods. Particularly, low-income countries played an important role in the expansion of Japanese affiliate activities. In contrast, no clear pattern on the growth of U.S. affiliate sales in the 1990s and early 2000s can be observed.

Growth of Foreign Affiliate Employment

Finally, we describe the growth of foreign affiliate employment by Japanese and U.S. multinationals during the period 1990–2004 in Figure 6. The growth of employment by U.S. MNCs in low-income countries was relatively high over time across high- and low-skill industries. The employment in high- and middle-income countries exhibited no prominent growth during the period. In contrast, the employment growth in Japanese affiliates was remarkably high across countries of different income levels in the 1990s. At the beginning of the 2000s, however, the increase in affiliate employment slowed down. From a comparative point of view, affiliate employment seems to grow more rapidly in the 1990s for Japanese MNCs than U.S. MNCs. During the 2000s, however, both Japanese and U.S. affiliates appear to exhibit a slowdown or decline in the employment expansion.

---

[8]A 1996–1998 dip in U.S. third-market export for low-income country was caused by primary and fabricated metal industry in India. A 1999–2001 jump in U.S. home-market export for middle-income country resulted primarily from computers in Malaysia and the Philippines. These observations imply that the suppression of some observations for confidentiality in the U.S. survey could lead to less imprecise estimates of the growth rate at the country and industry level.

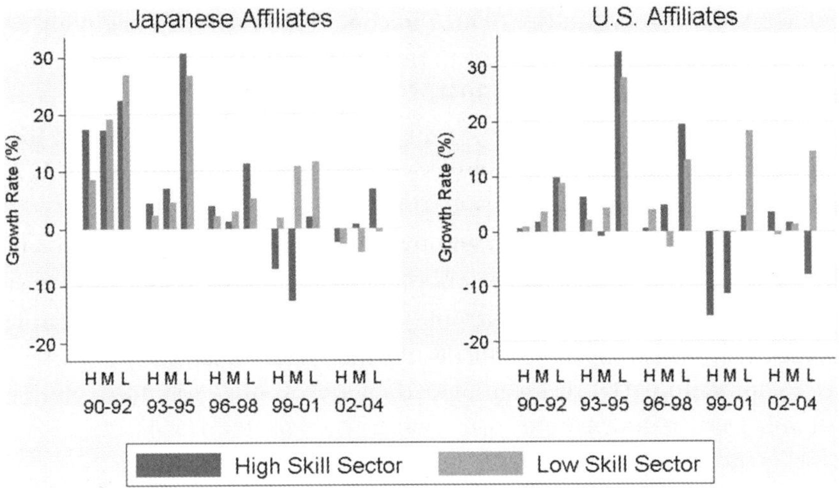

Note: H, M, and L mean high-, middle- and low-income countries; the U.S. industry classification changed in 1999 from SIC to NAICS.

Source: RIETI and U.S. BEA

Fig. 6. Growth of Japanese and U.S. affiliate employment three-year average growth rate by country income and sectoral skill intensity for 1990–2004.

Summary

The descriptive analysis produces several characterizations of the pattern of foreign affiliate activities in the case of Japanese and U.S. MNCs. The growth of Japanese and U.S. affiliate sales was remarkably rapid in the past decades. The rise of affiliate sales coincided with the massive expansion of employment for Japanese MNCs. The composition of Japanese affiliate sales to a home country varies by country income and industry skill intensity in a consistent way with comparative advantage motives. The composition of U.S. and Japanese affiliate sales shows significantly similar patterns across regions. Finally, Japanese affiliate activities exhibited a remarkably high growth in the 1990s as compared to the U.S. affiliates.

VI. ESTIMATION RESULTS ON DETERMINANTS OF AFFILIATE SALES BY JAPANESE AND U.S. MNCs

In this section, we investigate the factors that motivate Japanese and U.S. MNCs to engage in offshore production. To organize the regression analysis, we first explore the determinants of the level of foreign affiliate sales for the whole sample. Then, we divide the sample by the location of their affiliates — Asia and Europe — to study whether Japanese and U.S. firms respond differently to regional characteristics. Next, we examine the determinants of the composition of affiliate sales by destination markets to identify the determinants of the destination market of foreign affiliate sales. Basic Statistics for variables used in the regression analysis is presented in the Appendix.

Throughout this section, we are interested in estimating the coefficient of SKILL as measured by the average years of schooling of the population in a host country. As we intend to exploit a new dataset on Japanese multinational activity to conduct a comparative analysis on Japanese and U.S. MNCs, we will not address causal effects of country/industry characteristics on affiliate activity. Thus, we mainly contrast the difference in estimated coefficients between Japanese and U.S. samples, which are less subject to omitted variables bias.

Benchmark Results

Table 1 presents the results of Equation (1) estimated by ordinary least squares (OLS) with standard errors clustered at the industry level. To address a discontinuity in the U.S. industry classification, the sample covers the period 1989–1998 in columns (1)–(4) and the years 1999–2005 in columns (5)–(8). The dependent variable is a natural logarithm of foreign affiliate sales that vary by target market across specifications.

Column (1) shows the result for total affiliate sales. The coefficient of SKILL is significantly negative, suggesting that a 1% increase in the average years of schooling in a host country is expected to reduce Japanese affiliate sales by 3.6%. The interaction term between host-country skilled-labor–abundance and the U.S. dummy has a significantly positive coefficient. Taking into account the coefficient of skill endowments, a change in host-country skill endowment has little influence on U.S. affiliate sales. In columns (2)–(4), the results show that skilled-labor abundance in a host country is also negatively correlated with Japanese affiliate sales to local, home, and third markets. A negative impact of SKILL appears to be pronounced for local sales and third-country export sales. On the other hand, the negative link between skill endowment and affiliate sales becomes

Table 1. **Regression results of determinants of Japanese and U.S. affiliate sales**

Period	1989–1998				1999–2005			
Variable / Sale	Total (1)	Local (2)	Home (3)	Third (4)	Total (5)	Local (6)	Home (7)	Third (8)
SKILL	−3.55[a]	−6.45[a]	−2.44[a]	−5.62[a]	−3.07[a]	−0.85[b]	1.32	−0.92
	[−7.76]	[−7.20]	[−3.47]	[−7.94]	[−5.54]	[−2.05]	[1.41]	[−1.03]
SKILL × U.S.	3.25[a]	6.39[a]	1.89[a]	5.56[a]	2.36[a]	−0.15	−2.95[a]	−0.65
	[7.20]	[7.82]	[4.71]	[6.70]	[3.70]	[−0.23]	[−3.43]	[−0.55]
SKINT	0.88	1.66	0.36	1.43	0.48	0.46	1.07	1.31
	[0.64]	[0.94]	[0.26]	[0.76]	[0.34]	[0.33]	[0.99]	[0.61]
SKINT × U.S.	0.88	0.83	2.17	1.48	1.33	1.37	2.98[a]	2.45
	[0.80]	[0.47]	[1.63]	[1.02]	[0.87]	[0.82]	[4.92]	[1.19]
GDP	0.69[a]	1.88[a]	1.21[a]	1.04[a]	0.42[b]	0.35[b]	0.48	−0.06
	[3.25]	[9.89]	[4.77]	[3.91]	[2.40]	[2.23]	[1.17]	[−0.22]
GDP × U.S.	−0.11	−0.82[a]	−0.79[b]	−0.54	0.23	0.71[a]	0.27	0.85[a]
	[−0.51]	[−4.74]	[−2.31]	[−1.56]	[1.30]	[3.49]	[0.50]	[3.07]
DIST	−1.67[a]	−2.49[a]	−1.89[a]	−2.27[a]	−0.95[a]	−0.46[b]	0.27	0.19
	[−4.94]	[−4.77]	[−3.92]	[−2.66]	[−3.65]	[−2.11]	[0.29]	[0.50]
DIST × U.S.	1.10[b]	2.12[a]	0.83[b]	1.77[c]	0.49	0.04	−1.40	−0.97
	[2.55]	[3.45]	[2.30]	[1.74]	[1.38]	[0.16]	[−1.25]	[−1.12]
SPATIAL	1.50[a]	2.61[a]	1.83[a]	2.63[a]	0.85[a]	0.37	0.33	0.57[b]
	[9.55]	[10.7]	[12.3]	[15.9]	[4.32]	[1.39]	[1.64]	[2.57]
SPATIAL × U.S.	−0.83[a]	−1.91[a]	−0.37	−1.17[a]	−0.33[c]	0.24	0.92[a]	0.73[a]
	[−4.52]	[−5.52]	[−1.52]	[−4.59]	[−1.94]	[0.95]	[3.24]	[3.11]
R-squared	0.52	0.47	0.47	0.45	0.72	0.77	0.58	0.62
Observations	3,167	3,038	2,799	2,893	2,138	1,932	1,833	1,814

[a] Significant at 1%
[b] Significant at 5%
[c] Significant at 10%
Note: Dependent variable: log of foreign affiliate sales. Total, Local, Home, and Third indicate affiliate total sales, local sales, export to a home market, and export to a third market, respectively; constant and dummy variables for year, region, U.S., U.S. × region, and U.S. × year are included, but not reported; t-statistics computed from standard errors clustered at the industry level are in parentheses.

weak in the case of U.S. MNCs, after accounting for the coefficient of the interaction.

A plausible interpretation of these findings is that Japanese MNCs tend to locate offshore production in less-skilled-labor–abundant countries, whereas U.S. MNCs place little emphasis on host-country skill endowment for the location of offshore production. As the coefficient of SKILL represents an average effect of foreign skilled labor across sectors, this pattern holds, on average, for multinational sales at the manufacturing industry level. From a theoretical point of view, the comparative advantage story appears to be an important force in driving affiliate production more strongly for Japanese MNCs than U.S. MNCs. Using the country-level data, similar evidence has been provided in Eaton and Tamura (1994) and Tanaka (2009). Furthermore, we find little correlation between industry skill intensity and affiliate sales across the specifications. In the work of Hanson, Mataloni, and Slaughter (2001), a sectoral intensity of skilled labor is positively correlated with U.S. affiliate sales in 12 manufacturing and non-manufacturing industries. As our regression covers only manufacturing in the sample, the smaller variation across industries is likely to produce an estimate with large standard errors.

The economic size of a host market as measured by real GDP has a significantly positive coefficient across various affiliate sales. The significant negative coefficient of the interaction between GDP and the U.S. dummy implies that the positive effect of host-country GDP is weaker for U.S. affiliates than Japanese affiliates. Japanese MNCs are more sensitive to the size of the host market for their affiliate activity. On the other hand, the coefficient of the distance variable is significantly negative. The coefficient of the distance interaction with the U.S. dummy is significant but smaller in size than the distance coefficient. This suggests that proximity to a home country encourages offshore production by both Japanese and U.S. firms, with the negative impact more pronounced for Japanese MNCs. With respect to the estimated effects of host-country characteristics for U.S. affiliates, these findings are in line with the evidence in prior research such as Brainard (1997); Carr, Markusen, and Maskus (2001); and Hanson, Mataloni, and Slaughter (2001).

Lastly, the spatial lag variable denoted by SPATIAL is positively associated with various types of affiliate sales, with the magnitude of the effect being smaller for U.S. affiliates. Blonigen *et al.* (2007) and Baltagi, Egger, and Pfaffermayr (2007) find a positive influence of the spatial lag for U.S. outward FDI. We add further evidence that Japanese MNCs tend to locate offshore production in the market with greater spatial distribution of FDI from Japan. Furthermore, Japanese MNCs exhibit a stronger responsiveness to the spatially distributed FDI from the same parent country than do U.S. MNCs. A possible interpretation is that Japanese MNCs are widely engaged in production chains around the globe, with a strong network with other Japanese firms through transactions in intermediate and final goods. As a result, direct investment by Japanese firms in a third country could improve an environment for Japanese firms to promote offshore production in a host country. A sequential improvement of investment climate specific to Japanese firms through production networks could reflect the larger positive coefficient of SPATIAL for Japanese MNCs.

Columns (5)–(8) of Table 1 display the results for the period 1999–2005. Roughly speaking, the pattern of coefficient signs and statistical significance across variables and specifications is similar to the results before the year 1999. However, there are some differences in the magnitude of the coefficients. Host-country skilled-labor abundance has a smaller negative impact on various affiliate sales in the recent period, with the unsystematic difference between Japanese and U.S. MNCs. The implication is that foreign investment motivated by factor-cost differentials in the 1990s could have declined in the early 2000s. Perhaps, a rapid development of offshore production in unskilled-labor–abundant countries in the past decades might lead to an increase in labor costs, which weaken the comparative advantage motive of offshore production. This interpretation is in line with a decline in the growth rate of affiliate sales in low income countries since the late 1990s. Furthermore, the results indicate that the SPATIAL variable has smaller coefficients in the post-1999 sample. This suggests that Japanese affiliate sales became less sensitive to the spatially distributed FDI of the same parent country in the 2000s. Consistent with the estimated coefficients of SKILL, we interpret that offshore production of Japanese MNCs for a factor-cost motivation was extensively established in the 1990s, so that cross-country dependency of FDI activity originating from Japan might have declined over time.

Determinants of Foreign Affiliate Sales in Asia versus Europe Samples

In the descriptive analysis, we illustrate that the composition of affiliate sales by destination varies by the host-country region for both Japanese and U.S. MNCs. However, the benchmark results have assumed that the determinants of foreign affiliate sales are identical across the regions. As Blonigen and Wang (2005) empirically demonstrate a systematic difference

Table 2. Regression results of determinants of Japanese and U.S. affiliate sales in Asia

Variable	Period Sale	1989–1998 Total (1)	Local (2)	Home (3)	Third (4)	1999–2005 Total (5)	Local (6)	Home (7)	Third (8)
SKILL		-3.67^a	-4.83^a	-8.94^a	-4.95^a	-2.11^a	-1.31^a	-6.35^a	-3.47^a
		[−4.64]	[−3.61]	[−5.80]	[−3.82]	[−3.56]	[−3.45]	[−3.73]	[−2.79]
SKILL × U.S.		5.11^a	7.10^a	10.84^a	7.06^a	2.01^a	0.66	4.69^a	1.69
		[5.50]	[4.94]	[8.30]	[5.10]	[3.28]	[1.32]	[2.73]	[1.11]
SKINT		0.08	0.10	0.06	0.15	1.17	0.63	2.36	2.38
		[0.13]	[0.11]	[0.04]	[0.13]	[0.92]	[0.63]	[0.90]	[1.04]
SKINT × U.S.		2.42^a	4.33^a	2.73	3.66^a	2.12	2.84^b	3.54^c	4.13^c
		[3.81]	[3.11]	[1.25]	[4.38]	[1.50]	[2.00]	[1.84]	[1.90]
GDP		-1.29^a	-1.54^a	-3.31^a	-2.11^a	−0.18	0.24^a	-1.28^b	−0.65
		[−4.60]	[−3.73]	[−8.25]	[−4.55]	[−0.78]	[2.89]	[−2.24]	[−1.52]
GDP × U.S.		1.75^a	2.63^a	3.41^a	2.45^a	0.45^b	0.39^b	1.21^b	0.66
		[5.87]	[7.29]	[8.12]	[3.93]	[1.97]	[2.01]	[2.01]	[1.20]
DIST		-3.21^a	-4.34^a	-7.99^a	-4.34^a	-1.10^b	-0.69^b	-3.70^a	−1.15
		[−4.91]	[−3.77]	[−10.7]	[−3.50]	[−2.34]	[−2.09]	[−2.81]	[−1.04]
DIST × U.S.		6.28^a	9.74^a	10.11^a	7.98^a	−0.60	-2.48^c	−2.97	-6.06^a
		[4.41]	[5.24]	[6.41]	[2.83]	[−0.71]	[−1.74]	[−1.15]	[−2.75]
SPATIAL		0.74^a	1.08^a	1.13^a	1.35^a	0.37	0.36	0.83^a	0.76^a
		[3.24]	[2.81]	[12.0]	[6.88]	[1.47]	[1.27]	[3.85]	[2.93]
SPATIAL × U.S.		−0.45	−0.81	−0.04	−0.29	−0.02	0.19	0.33	0.51
		[−1.49]	[−1.55]	[−0.12]	[−0.84]	[−0.07]	[0.67]	[1.00]	[1.87]
R-squared		0.75	0.62	0.62	0.61	0.85	0.84	0.72	0.72
Observations		1,277	1,221	1,141	1,187	956	880	843	818

[a] Significant at 1%
[b] Significant at 5%
[c] Significant at 10%
Note: Dependent variable: log of foreign affiliate sales. Total, Local, Home, and Third indicate affiliate total sales, local sales, export to a home market, and export to a third market, respectively; constant and dummy variables for year, U.S., and U.S. × year are included, but not reported; t-statistics computed from standard errors clustered at the industry level are in parentheses.

between developed and developing countries in the empirical model of FDI, we relax this assumption by estimating Equation (1) separately for the Asia and Europe samples.

Table 2 displays the regression results for Japanese and U.S. affiliate sales in Asia. In columns (1)–(4), we find that SKILL has a significantly negative coefficient for various affiliate sales by Japanese firms during the period 1989–1998. In particular, affiliate export to a home market exhibits the largest coefficient in absolute value; a 1% increase in the average years of schooling in Asian countries was associated with a 9% decline in Japanese affiliate exports to a home country. Hence, it is suggested that Japanese MNCs significantly increased their offshore production in relatively unskilled-labor–abundant countries of Asia in order to export products back to the Japanese market. In contrast, SKILL has a positive impact on U.S. affiliate sales after accounting for the interaction term; U.S. MNCs tend to have larger affiliate sales in more skilled-labor–abundant countries of Asia. While the prior analysis of Tanaka (2009) shows that host-country educational attainment significantly reduces Japanese affiliate sales at the country level, our findings further imply that a comparative advantage motive appears to be pronounced for foreign subsidiaries by Japanese companies in Asia. In sum, we could interpret our results as suggesting that Japanese MNCs were seeking unskilled labor in Asia, but U.S. MNCs were attracted to skilled labor.

Industry skill intensity is mostly insignificant across specifications for the Japanese sample, but the coefficient of the interaction term of U.S. and SKINT points to a positive impact of skill intensity on U.S. affiliate sales. Taken together with the results of SKILL, U.S. multinational activity in Asia is larger for the relatively skill-intensive sector and skilled-labor–abundant countries. The results can be interpreted as suggesting that U.S. firms in skill-intensive sectors were seeking skilled labor for their offshore production in Asia. Next, the impact of host-market size on affiliate sales significantly differs for Japanese and U.S. MNCs in Asia. Host country's GDP in Asia is negatively associated with Japanese affiliate sales. As the negative effect of GDP is largest for affiliate exports to a home country, Japanese firms tend to undertake local production for export in a smaller market. In contrast, U.S. affiliate sales of any type are positively correlated with the economic size of the host nation. As many prior studies find a positive effect of host-market size, this finding is taken as evidence of a market-access motive of FDI (Brainard, 1997; Braconier, Nornack, and Urban, 2005a). In contrast, our results are consistent with the hypothesis that Japanese MNCs motivated by factor-cost differences in Asia consolidate offshore production in the small market.

Geographic distance is significantly and negatively associated with Japanese affiliate sales in Asia, suggesting that the distance effect would capture in part transport costs for intermediate input trade in vertical offshore production. On the other hand, U.S. affiliate sales in Asia are positively correlated with distance, consistent with a market-access story. The spatial lag variable has a positive impact on both Japanese and U.S. affiliate sales, but there is little difference. In addition, columns (5)–(8) present the results for the period 1999–2005. The overall pattern of coefficient signs and statistical significance is generally consistent with the previous discussion. Nevertheless, the distinction between Japanese and U.S. MNCs becomes statistically weak as to the determinants of host-country characteristics. Possibly, these results imply that the nature of offshore production by Japanese and U.S. MNCs became alike in the 2000s.

Table 3 presents the results for Japanese and U.S. affiliates in Europe. Because many European countries are classified as high-income countries, our hypothesis is that market access rather than comparative advantage would play a large role in explaining the variation of affiliate sales in the region. Using the sample for 1989–1998, columns (1)–(4) show that various Japanese affiliate sales in European countries are negatively correlated with skilled labor abundance, with weak statistical significance. As the interaction variable with the U.S. dummy has insignificant coefficients, host country's skill endowment has little influence on U.S. affiliate sales in Europe. Furthermore, the regression results for 1999–2005 in columns (5)–(8) indicate little association between affiliate sales and skill abundance. As there is no clear pattern between sectoral skill intensity and affiliate sales, it is reasonable to conclude that skilled labor abundance in European countries exerts little systematic influence on foreign affiliate activities by Japanese and U.S. MNCs.

Market size has significantly positive coefficients across various affiliate sales in the sample period. Taking into account the U.S. interaction term, both Japanese and U.S. affiliate sales in Europe increased with respect to the economic size of the host market. These results imply that Japanese and U.S. firms in Europe concentrate offshore production plants in the larger market. However, the distance variable as a proxy for international transportation costs is insignificant. While the saving of shipping cost

Table 3. Regression results of determinants of Japanese and U.S. affiliate sales in Europe

		1989–1998				1999–2005			
Variable	Period Sale	Total (1)	Local (2)	Home (3)	Third (4)	Total (5)	Local (6)	Home (7)	Third (8)
SKILL		−3.58	−9.76[b]	−1.42	−8.84[c]	−7.30[c]	4.13	8.19	5.90
		[−1.54]	[−1.99]	[−0.57]	[−1.95]	[−1.88]	[0.95]	[1.19]	[0.93]
SKILL × U.S.		1.46	6.78	0.19	5.76	6.32[c]	−5.45	−7.79	−7.27
		[0.57]	[1.27]	[0.09]	[1.30]	[1.75]	[−1.22]	[−1.06]	[−1.20]
SKINT		3.50	4.46	3.84[b]	4.48	2.73	1.97	3.70[b]	2.51
		[1.39]	[1.25]	[2.02]	[1.32]	[1.21]	[0.82]	[1.98]	[0.79]
SKINT × U.S.		−1.88	−3.07	−0.49	−1.80	−1.66	−1.10	0.01	−0.90
		[−0.85]	[−0.91]	[−0.36]	[−0.58]	[−0.68]	[−0.42]	[0.01]	[−0.30]
GDP		1.58[a]	3.06[a]	2.34[a]	2.33[a]	1.15[a]	0.17	1.55	−0.07
		[4.95]	[9.97]	[5.53]	[6.27]	[6.30]	[0.36]	[1.55]	[−0.09]
GDP × U.S.		−0.50	−1.65[a]	−1.19[b]	−1.47[a]	−0.13	1.02[b]	−0.27	0.90
		[−1.50]	[−4.12]	[−2.34]	[−3.37]	[−1.04]	[2.11]	[−0.25]	[1.14]
DIST		17.8[c]	33.5[b]	23.7	29.7[c]	6.32	−2.95	20.4	2.01
		[1.90]	[2.09]	[1.38]	[1.75]	[0.85]	[−0.32]	[1.23]	[0.17]
DIST × U.S.		−21.5[b]	−38.5[b]	−27.4	−34.0[c]	−9.27	−1.10	−21.0	−4.15
		[−2.12]	[−2.28]	[−1.53]	[−1.81]	[−1.06]	[−0.11]	[−1.23]	[−0.34]
SPATIAL		4.13[a]	7.83[a]	4.99[a]	7.94[c]	3.30[a]	−0.26	2.18	−0.25
		[5.20]	[14.37]	[4.49]	[8.81]	[2.71]	[−0.17]	[0.88]	[−0.15]
SPATIAL × U.S.		−3.15[a]	−6.98[a]	−3.86[a]	−6.24[a]	−2.80[b]	0.64	−1.21	1.31
		[−3.20]	[−12.00]	[−3.04]	[−5.68]	[−2.11]	[0.40]	[−0.50]	[0.84]
R-squared		0.45	0.51	0.47	0.43	0.68	0.70	0.44	0.47
Observations		1,094	1,046	972	1,003	694	642	612	627

[a]Significant at 1%
[b]Significant at 5%
[c]Significant at 10%
Note: Dependent variable: log of foreign affiliate sales. Total, Local, Home, and Third indicate affiliate total sales, local sales, export to a home market, and export to a third market, respectively; constant and dummy variables for year, U.S., and U.S. × year are included, but not reported; t-statistics computed from standard errors clustered at the industry level are in parentheses.

can be important for market-seeking FDI by Japanese and U.S. firms, distance may pick up the negative effect of monitoring cost of foreign affiliates.

Lastly, the spatial lag variable has a significantly positive coefficient across the type of affiliate sales. The interaction term with the U.S. dummy shows a significantly negative coefficient, but the size of the coefficient is small. These results imply that Japanese and U.S. MNCs tend to clustered with other investors from the same country in European markets during the 1990s. The tendency of clustering in Europe is stronger for Japanese affiliates than U.S. affiliates. However, it appears possible to interpret that the importance of clustering declined for the location of Japanese and U.S. MNCs in Europe over time since the late 1990s.

Determinants of Affiliate Sales for Export versus Local Market

The previous regressions have focused on the level of various affiliate sales, but paid little attention to the factors that determine the target market of affiliate sales. To examine this issue, we specify the dependent variable as a share of affiliate export sales in affiliate total sales. Then, we estimate model (1) with the share variable to study the determinants of the relative importance of the destination market of affiliate sales, conditional on the total size of affiliate total sales. This specification allows us to explore factors that motivate foreign affiliates to shift from production for local markets toward export markets.

Table 4 presents the results of the new specification estimated by OLS for the period 1989–1998 and 1999–2005. We also divide the sample by region to take into account regional attributes of the data; a dummy variable for region is excluded from these regressions. In column (1) using the world sample, the estimated coefficient of SKILL is insignificant. Columns (2) and (3) present the regressions for the Asia and Europe samples in order to check the influence of regional characteristics on the imprecisely estimated coefficient of SKILL. For the Asia sample, the SKILL variable has a significantly negative coefficient, with its U.S. interaction having a significantly positive coefficient. The OLS estimate suggests that a 10% increase in the host country's average years of schooling is associated with a four point *decrease* in the ratio of export sales to total sales for Japanese affiliates in Asia. On the other hand, the corresponding change would lead to a two point *increase* for U.S. affiliates in Asia. Hence, Japanese MNCs increase the share of production for export in *less* skilled-labor–abundant countries, whereas U.S. MNCs increase the ratio of export production in *more* skilled-labor–abundant countries.

Table 4. Determinants of local versus export sales for Japanese and U.S. affiliates

		1989–1998			1999–2005		
Variable	Period sample	World (1)	Asia (2)	Europe (3)	World (5)	Asia (6)	Europe (7)
SKILL		−9.42	−39.2[a]	12.3	−0.51	−42.2[c]	37.7
		[−0.99]	[−3.32]	[0.48]	[−0.05]	[−1.94]	[0.37]
SKILL × U.S.		15.2[c]	55.5[a]	−24.0	−1.61	39.9	−35.0
		[1.88]	[3.66]	[−0.97]	[−0.15]	[1.52]	[−0.39]
SKINT		−1.93	−1.67	22.2	2.99	25.9	−9.96
		[−0.15]	[−0.08]	[1.23]	[0.27]	[0.74]	[−0.71]
SKINT × U.S.		11.42	−0.80	5.39	12.8[b]	3.38	28.8
		[0.62]	[−0.07]	[0.19]	[2.24]	[0.13]	[1.64]
GDP		−10.3[a]	−21.9[a]	−4.48	−7.48[a]	−16.9[a]	−4.88
		[−3.12]	[−4.53]	[−0.67]	[−3.17]	[−3.22]	[−0.50]
GDP × U.S.		3.36	13.6[a]	−5.80	2.69	6.90	−1.40
		[0.83]	[3.46]	[−0.92]	[0.90]	[1.45]	[−0.15]
DIST		−15.2[a]	−36.4[a]	28.6	3.44	−18.4	44.8
		[−2.73]	[−6.08]	[0.25]	[0.67]	[−1.33]	[0.30]
DIST × U.S.		15.4[a]	33.4	6.53	−3.37	−26.1	−8.24
		[2.60]	[1.60]	[0.06]	[−0.51]	[−1.57]	[−0.05]
SPATIAL		3.95[c]	3.12	13.0	0.71	4.28[c]	−3.28
		[1.70]	[0.96]	[0.88]	[0.34]	[1.86]	[−0.13]
SPATIAL × U.S.		10.7[a]	10.6[a]	7.37	9.70[a]	6.55[b]	12.6
		[3.31]	[2.70]	[0.38]	[7.75]	[2.29]	[0.57]
R-squared		0.23	0.29	0.21	0.22	0.31	0.13
Observations		2,980	1,172	1,041	1,910	865	638

[a] Significant at 1%
[b] Significant at 5%
[c] Significant at 10%
Note: Dependent variable: Affiliate export sales to total sales. Constant and dummy variables for year, U.S., U.S. × year are included in each specification; region and U.S. × region dummies are included in the world sample; t-statistics computed from standard errors clustered at the industry are in parentheses.

These results for Japanese affiliates are carried over to the sample period for 1999–2005 although the statistical evidence for U.S. affiliates becomes weak. In addition, skilled-labor abundance has little effect on the relative importance of affiliate sales for export, as is consistent with the hypothesis that FDI activity in Europe is primarily driven by market-access motives. Taken together, we interpret the evidence as suggesting that comparative advantage motives of FDI played a larger role in offshore production by Japanese MNCs in Asia than that of U.S. MNCs.

Industry skill intensity has insignificant coefficients across specifications for different periods, suggesting that sectoral characteristics had little impact on the composition of affiliate sales by target market. The coefficients of the GDP variable are significantly negative across the models; Japanese and U.S. affiliates tend to increase the share of local sales in the larger host market. The distance variable indicates the significantly negative coefficients in columns (1) and (2), with the negative coefficient being larger in Asia. But the coefficients are insignificant for the Europe sample. Consistent with the prediction of factor-seeking FDI models, Japanese affiliates in Asia tend to engage in production for the local market when their host country is distant from Japan. On the other hand, Japanese affiliates are likely to concentrate on export sales when their host country is closer to Japan. These patterns lend support to the idea that multinationals have an incentive to reduce transportation costs of delivering final goods that are assembled at their offshore production site. Lastly, the spatial lag variables have only weakly significant coefficients across specifications. Thus, clustering plays little role in the target market of their foreign production.

VII. CONCLUSION

The rise of multinational firms in the world economy is a distinguishing feature of the economic globalization. As multinationals play an increasingly important role in the conduct of international commerce and production, it is of great interest to understand the nature of offshore production by multinationals. Consequently, there is a growing number of empirical studies on multinational behavior. In particular, the location of multinational production has been a central question from a policy perspective because many countries attempt to attract foreign investment in order to internalize spillover effects of the presence of multinational firms. However, widely available data on multinational activity such as FDI stock and foreign subsidiary sales are subject to a variety of measurement issues, including international comparability, country coverage, and quality of surveys. Thus, previously available measures of multinational activity pose a challenge for exploring the nature of multinational behavior using various data sources in a consistent way. In practice, researchers have chosen either to focus on multinational behavior from a single parent country such as the U.S., or analyze multinational data from various country sources that are not sufficiently harmonized.

In this chapter, we have attempted to fill these gaps by improving the measurement of various activities of foreign affiliates by Japanese parent firms in a comparable way with widely used data on U.S. multinationals. In particular, we employ confidential affiliate-level panel data from the Ministry of Economy, Trade, and Industry, Japan, to construct a consistent dataset on manufacturing foreign subsidiaries of Japanese and U.S. firms at the country- and industry-level during the period 1989–2005. Furthermore, we improve comparability of affiliate sales by destination market across two data sources by including solely majority-owned foreign affiliates.

The descriptive analysis illustrates that Japanese and U.S. affiliate sales around the globe increased substantially in past decades, but Japanese multinationals increased their foreign employment much more rapidly than U.S. multinationals. As to the destination market, affiliate sales to a host market accounts for the majority of their total sales across various country and industry categories. On the other hand, the pattern of Japanese affiliate sales is distinctive from that of U.S. affiliates in that the proportion of affiliate exports to a home market increases progressively as host-country income levels and sectoral skill intensity decline. Moreover, the regression analysis shows that sales of Japanese affiliates are higher in host countries with lower educational attainment, but U.S. affiliate sales are larger in host nations with higher educational levels. These patterns figure prominently in Asian countries. Taken together, we interpret these results as evidence for comparative-advantage motives of offshore production in the case of Japanese multinationals. In contrast, our analysis is consistent with the previous findings that factor-cost motives play a limited role in offshore production of U.S. multinationals in specific industries and countries.

While we have illustrated the distinctive characteristics of foreign affiliate activities by Japanese and U.S. multinationals in a fairly comparable way, we have not explicitly addressed the question of what factors would lead to different patterns of foreign activities by multinationals from different nationalities. It is beyond the scope of this chapter to discuss a wide range of reasons behind these different patterns. Having noted this, we interpret the results on Japanese multinationals as indicating that they establish offshore production plants in unskilled-labor–abundant countries to conduct unskilled-labor–intensive stages of production. Under these schemes, Japanese parent firms supply intermediate inputs to their foreign affiliates, which perform the final assembly, and subsequently export the final products back to the home market or to the third markets. As such, international fragmentation of the production process necessarily involves a multitude of transportation of intermediate inputs and final goods across borders. Multinationals are likely to face a trade-off between wage and trade costs in moving their plants abroad. In this respect, the geographic proximity of labor-abundant Asian countries to Japan can provide a distinctive advantage for Japanese companies to expand production networks internationally.

As a final note, we emphasize some of the issues that are not explored in this chapter but merit further research using the new dataset on Japanese affiliates. As argued by Yeaple (2003b), multinational firms in skilled-labor–intensive industries may prefer to locate their production plants in relatively skilled-labor–abundant countries. On the other hand, firms in unskilled-labor–intensive industries are likely to build their plants in relatively unskilled-labor–abundant countries. The factor intensity of production processes and factor abundance in foreign countries could interact in a systematic way to determine the pattern of multinational sales across countries and sectors. As such, it would be interesting to extend our study to the sectoral analysis of multinational activity, which may shed further light on the comparative features of multinationals. However, it is also likely to involve comparability issues in the measurement of industry characteristics across countries.

APPENDIX

Table A1. Summary statistics

	Mean		S.D.		Min		Max	
Variable	JP	U.S.	JP	U.S.	JP	U.S.	JP	U.S.
Total sale, ¥/$ million (JP/U.S.)	11.4	7.23	2.43	1.91	−0.04	−0.17	16.5	11.3
Local sale, ¥/$ million (JP/U.S.)	11.2	6.74	1.71	1.94	5.68	−0.17	16.4	10.4
Home export, ¥/$ million (JP/U.S.)	8.13	4.28	3.30	2.59	−0.26	−0.17	13.7	10.8
Third export, ¥/$ million (JP/U.S.)	9.81	5.63	2.45	2.68	−0.26	−0.17	14.4	10.3
Export share	38.1	36.4	25.1	25.4	0.00	0.00	97.0	99.3
Home export share	12.5	10.6	16.1	15.0	0.00	0.03	77.9	100
Third export share	25.7	27.6	21.5	21.7	0.00	0.27	92.3	100
SKILL, years of schooling	2.10	2.10	0.27	0.27	1.43	1.43	2.51	2.51
SKINT, non-prod. workers /total workers	−1.08	−1.13	0.20	0.28	−1.31	−1.46	−0.71	−0.61
GDP, $ billion	6.15	6.15	1.23	1.23	3.94	3.94	9.31	9.31
DIST, km	8.81	9.04	0.67	0.66	7.05	6.60	9.82	9.70
SPATIAL	10.1	5.83	0.98	1.08	8.45	4.04	12.7	8.67

Note: All variables except for export ratios are defined in log.

Table A2. Correlation coefficients

Sample		[1]	[2]	[3]	[4]	[5]	[6]	[7]	[8]	[9]	[10]	[11]
Japanese												
[1]	TSALE	1.00										
[2]	LSALE	0.95	1.00									
[3]	HEXPORT	0.64	0.53	1.00								
[4]	THEXPORT	0.78	0.63	0.56	1.00							
[5]	EXSHR	0.08	−0.22	0.34	0.47	1.00						
[6]	SKILL	0.12	0.14	0.07	0.07	−0.05	1.00					
[7]	SKILL × SKINT	0.05	0.04	0.02	0.11	0.03	−0.01	1.00				
[8]	SKINT	−0.08	−0.10	−0.03	0.02	0.10	−0.80	0.57	1.00			
[9]	GDP	0.20	0.31	−0.08	0.05	−0.35	0.29	0.02	−0.28	1.00		
[10]	DIST	−0.08	−0.05	−0.40	0.02	−0.11	−0.03	0.04	0.01	0.36	1.00	
[11]	SPATIAL	0.12	0.07	0.16	0.23	0.20	0.45	−0.01	−0.32	−0.22	−0.14	1.00
U.S.												
[1]	TSALE	1.00										
[2]	LSALE	0.95	1.00									
[3]	HEXPORT	0.82	0.70	1.00								
[4]	THEXPORT	0.90	0.78	0.78	1.00							
[5]	EXSHR	0.40	0.13	0.59	0.64	1.00						
[6]	SKILL	0.15	0.14	0.18	0.17	0.14	1.00					
[7]	SKILL × SKINT	0.32	0.25	0.40	0.35	0.25	0.01	1.00				
[8]	SKINT	0.15	0.09	0.18	0.18	0.13	−0.65	0.73	1.00			
[9]	GDP	0.56	0.65	0.37	0.43	−0.09	0.05	−0.04	−0.05	1.00		
[10]	DIST	−0.47	−0.49	−0.50	−0.32	−0.11	−0.32	0.08	0.29	−0.37	1.00	
[11]	SPATIAL	0.34	0.25	0.27	0.50	0.50	0.32	−0.02	−0.18	0.13	−0.12	1.00

Note: All variables except for export ratios are defined in log.

Table A3. List of countries and industries

Country			
Argentina	Germany	Mexico	Switzerland
Australia	Hong Kong	Netherlands	Taiwan
Belgium	India	New Zealand	Thailand
Brazil	Indonesia	Philippines	United Kingdom
Canada	Italy	Singapore	
China	Japan	South Korea	
France	Malaysia	Spain	

Industry	
SIC for years 1989–1998	NAICS for years 1999–2005
Food and kindred products	Food
Primary and fabricated metals	Chemicals
Chemicals and allied products	Primary and fabricated metals
Electronic and other electric equipment	Machinery
Industrial machinery and equipment	Computers and electronic products
Transportation equipment	Electrical equipment, appliances, and components
Other manufacturing	Transportation equipment

REFERENCES

Baltagi, Badi H., Peter Egger, and Michael Pfaffermayr (2007). "Estimating Models of Complex FDI: Are There Third-Country Effects?" *Journal of Econometrics*, 140(1): pp. 260–281.

Barro, Robert J. and Jong-Wha Lee (2001). "International Data on Educational Attainment: Updates and Implications." *Oxford Economic Papers*, 53(3): pp. 541–563.

Bartelsman, Eric J. and Wayne Gray (1996). "The NBER Manufacturing Productivity Database." National Bureau of Economic Research, Inc, NBER Technical Working Paper: 205.

Bernard, Andrew B., J. Bradford Jensen and Peter K. Schott (2005). "Importers, Exporters, and Multinationals: A Potrait of Firms in the U.S. That Trade Goods." National Bureau of Economic Research, Inc. Working Paper 11404.

Blonigen, Bruce A. (2005). "A Review of the Empirical Literature on FDI Determinants," *Atlantic Economic Journal*, 33(4): pp. 383–403.

Blonigen, Bruce A. and Miao Grace Wang (2005). "Inappropriate Pooling of Wealthy and Poor Countries in Empirical FDI Studies," in Does Foreign Direct Investment Promote Development? Theodore H. Moran, Edward

M. Graham, and Magnus Blomstrom, eds., Washington, D.C.: Institute for International Economics; Washington, D.C.: Center for Global Development, pp. 221–244.

Blonigen, Bruce A., Ronald B. Davies, Glen R. Waddell, and Helen T. Naughton (2007). "FDI in Space: Spatial Autoregressive Relationships in Foreign Direct Investment," *European Economic Review*, 51(5): pp. 1303–1325.

Blonigen, Bruce A., Ronald B. Davies, and Head, Keith (2003). "Estimating the Knowledge-Capital Model of the Multinational Enterprise". [Comment] *American Economic Review*, 93(3): pp. 980–994.

Braconier, Henrik, Pehr-Johan Norback, and Dieter Urban (2005a). "Multinational Enterprises and Wage Costs: Vertical FDI Revisited." *Journal of International Economics*, 67(2): pp. 446–470.

Braconier, Henrik, Pehr-Johan Norback, and Dieter Urban (2005b). "Reconciling the Evidence on the Knowledge-Capital Model." *Review of International Economics*, 13(4): pp. 770–786.

Brainard, S. Lael (1997). "An Empirical Assessment of the Proximity-Concentration Trade-off between Multinational Sales and Trade." *American Economic Review*, 87(4): pp. 520–544.

Carr, David L., James R. Markusen, and Keith E. Maskus (2001). "Estimating the Knowledge-Capital Model of the Multinational Enterprise." *American Economic Review*, 91(3): pp. 693–708.

Coughlin, Cletus C. and Eran Segev (2000). "Foreign Direct Investment in China: A Spatial Econometric Study." *World Economy*, 23(1): pp. 1–23.

Eaton, Jonathan and Akiko Tamura (1994). "Bilateralism and Regionalism in Japanese and U.S. Trade and Direct Foreign Investment Patterns." *Journal of the Japanese and International Economies*, 8(4): pp. 478–510.

Ekholm, Karolina, Rikard Forslid, and James R. Markusen (2007). "Export-Platform Foreign Direct Investment." *Journal of the European Economic Association*, 5(4): pp. 776–795.

Feenstra, Robert C. (1988). "Integration of Trade and Disintegration of Production in the Global Economy," *Journal of Economic Perspectives*, 12(4): pp. 31–50.

Feinberg, Susan E. and Keane, Michael P (2001). " U.S.-Canada Trade Liberalization and MNC Production Location." *Review of Economics and Statistics*, 83(1): pp. 118–132.

Grossman, Gene M., Elhanan Helpman, and Adam Szeidl (2006). "Optimal Integration Strategies for the Multinational Firm." *Journal of International Economics*, 70(1): pp. 216–238.

Hanson, Gordon H., Raymond J. Mataloni, Jr., and Matthew J. Slaughter (2001). "Expansion Strategies of U.S. Multinational Firms." National Bureau of Economic Research, Inc, NBER Working Papers: 8433.

Hanson, Gordon H., Raymond J. Mataloni, Jr., and Matthew J. Slaughter (2005). "Vertical Production Networks in Multinational Firms." *Review of Economics and Statistics*, 87(4): pp. 664–678.

Helpman, Elhanan (1984). "A Simple Theory of International Trade with Multinational Corporations." *Journal of Political Economy*, 92(3): pp. 451–471.

Helpman, Elhanan (2006). "Trade, FDI, and the Organization of Firms." *Journal of Economic Literature*, 44(3): pp. 589.

Helpman, Elhanan, Marc J. Melitz, and Stephen R. Yeaple. (2004). "Export versus FDI with Heterogeneous Firms," *American Economic Review*, 94(1): 300–316.

Helpman, Elhanan and Paul R. Krugman (1985). *Market Structure and Foreign Trade: Increasing Returns, Imperfect Competition, and the International Economy*. Cambridge, MA: MIT Press.

Kimura, Fukunari and Mitsuyo Ando (2005). "Two-Dimensional Fragmentation in East Asia: Conceptual Framework and Empirics." *International Review of Economics and Finance*, 14(3): pp. 317–348.

Lipsey, Robert E. (2000). "Affiliates of U.S. and Japanese Multinationals in East Asian Production and Trade," in *The Role of Foreign Direct Investment in East Asian Economic Development*. Takatoshi Ito and Anne O. Krueger eds. NBER-East Asia Seminar on Economics, Vol. 9. Chicago and London: University of Chicago Press: pp. 147–185.

Markusen, James R (1984). "Multinationals, Multi-plant Economies, and the Gains from Trade." *Journal of International Economics*, 16(3–4): pp. 205–226.

Markusen, James R (2002). *Multinational Firms and the Theory of International Trade*, Cambridge and London: MIT Press.

Markusen, James R. and Keith E. Maskus (2001). "Multinational Firms: Reconciling Theory and Evidence," in *Topics in Empirical International Economics: A Festscrift in Honor of Robert E. Lipsey* Magnus Blomström and Linda S. Goldeberg eds. Chicago: University of Chicago Press: pp. 71–95.

Matsuura, Toshiyuki (2004). "Estimating Economic Activity, Sales, and Procurements of the Overseas Affiliates of Japanese Multinational Firms (in Japanese)." *Keizai Toukei Kenkyu*, 32(4): pp. 1–16.

Tanaka, Kiyoyasu (2009). "Vertical Foreign Direct Investment: Evidence from Japanese and U.S. Multinational Enterprises." *Global COE Hi-Stat Discussion Paper No. 46.*

United Nations Conference on Trade and Development (UNCTAD) (2008). *World Investment Report 2008: Transnational Corporations, and the Infrastructure Challenge.* New York and Geneva: United Nations Publications.

Yeaple, Stephen Ross (2003a). "The Complex Integration Strategies of Multinationals and Cross Country Dependencies in the Structure of Foreign Direct Investment." *Journal of International Economics*, 60(2): pp. 293–314.

Yeaple, Stephen Ross (2003b). "The Role of Skill Endowments in the Structure of U.S. Outward Foreign Direct Investment." *Review of Economics and Statistics*, 85(3): pp. 726–734.

Comment

Linda Tesar

I am glad to be given the opportunity to discuss this paper on the determinants of offshore production by U.S. and Japanese multinational corporations.

The purpose of this paper, as stated by the authors, is to illustrate the commonalities and the differences in the pattern of Japanese and U.S. affiliate production. The goal is to identify the characteristics of offshore production by Japanese and U.S. firms and then determine the extent to which offshore production is consistent with market access and comparative advantage.

To address this question, the authors compare data from two difference sources. On the Japanese side, the authors make use of data from METI, which provides a survey of overseas business activities. The data cover affiliate sales by destination (local, home and third market), affiliate employment, production by country, industry and year. Some data are estimated to fill in missing sales. On the U.S. side, similar data are gathered from the BEA, which reports survey data of nonbank manufacturing firms with foreign affiliates.

There are several key differences in the databases that could be important for interpreting the results, especially if the ultimate focus of the analysis is going to be the differences between U.S. and Japanese multinational operations. The authors should be commended for their care with the data, as exemplified in their comparison of U.S. and Japanese bilateral flows. The fact that these flows differ across the two datasets (e.g. what Japan reports as an inflow from the U.S. does not match what the U.S. reports as an outflow to Japan) is not fully explained in the paper, but the authors should be credited for bringing this type of discrepancy to light. The authors also highlight the fact that the data are reported in nominal local currency and note that they must use exchange rates and local deflators to make the series comparable. Again, the authors should be credited with their care in treating the data, but in this reviewer's opinion, they make too much out of this issue — any analysis of international data invariably leads one to rely country-specific databases that require exchange rates and deflators to make the data comparable. There's no need to be so apologetic on this score and I think the authors do a good job of noting the possible weaknesses of the data sources.

I do, however, have some other concerns about the results that I think require further analysis for robustness.

1. In order to study differences across the two countries, industries are sorted by their use of skilled labor. The question is whether the location of offshore affiliates and the volume of sales by affiliates are related to local skill abundance. One concern I have is that the industry designation may be too coarse. It may happen that at an aggregate level an industry appears to use skilled-labor, but the segment of production that is conducted offshore may be the segment of production that is low-skilled-labor intensive. I don't know exactly what to recommend here but to obtain more disaggregated data, or to note in which industries the discrepancy lies between onshore and offshore labor intensities could be particularly important.
2. Another issue is that the data are averaged over the period 1989–2005. This is a period of rapidly increasing offshore activity. I am concerned that the average does not capture the state of offshoring in 2005. Trying different dates would be a good robustness check.
3. The descriptive plots and tables sort countries by income and report the results for broad groupings of countries. This may cluster countries in ways that could be misleading and may lead to counter-intuitive conclusions. For example, U.S. multinational activity in Canada and Mexico — much of which reflects production-sharing arrangements to produce goods for the *U.S.* market — is quite different from U.S. multinational production in Europe — much of which is intended to serve the *European* market. Lumping that activity together could hide some interesting results.
4. The descriptive analysis and the regressions produce a wide range of results, but it is hard to discern a clear "bottom line." Rather than report all of the results, it would be helpful if the paper were to focus on what the authors take to be the overall message from the data.

5. When all is said and done, it is hard to know how to interpret the results. For example, if the data suggest that comparative advantage matters more for one country than another, what do we conclude from this result? Usually, we are looking for determinants of trade that hold across countries. If the determinants hold in one location, but fail to hold in another, what is the explanation? If we are missing some factor (such as an institutional or legal difference across the two countries), shouldn't that be incorporated in the regression from the beginning? In other words, do the authors anticipate finding a difference between the two countries, and if they do, can they propose some variables to capture that difference?

CHAPTER 2

Does Material and Service Offshoring Improve Domestic Productivity? Evidence from Japanese Manufacturing Industries*

Keiko Ito[†,§] and Kiyoyasu Tanaka[‡,¶]

[†] *Faculty of Economics, Senshu University*
Kanagawa, Japan
[‡] *Interdisciplinary Studies Center*
Institute of Developing Economics, Chiba, Japan
[§] *keiko-i@isc.senshu-u.ac.jp*
[¶] *kiyoyasu_tanaka@ide.go.jp*

I. INTRODUCTION

Relocating business activities abroad, or "offshoring," has become one of the most important issues in international economics in recent years.[1] Advances in technology have reduced transportation costs significantly, which has contributed to the international fragmentation of the value-added chain. The production of individual commodities within an industry is divided into ever smaller production processes, some of which are then

*This research was conducted as part of a project entitled "Research on Productivity Growth in Service Industries" at the Research Institute of Economy, Trade and Industry (RIETI).

[1] Following Olsen (2006), we use the term "offshoring" to refer to the relocation of jobs and processes to a foreign country without distinguishing whether the provider is external or affiliated with the firm. Strictly speaking, the relocation of business activities to unaffiliated foreign firms is typically referred to as "international outsourcing," while that to affiliated foreign firms is called "international insourcing." But there is a growing number of studies that simply use the term "offshoring" to refer to both international outsourcing and international insourcing.

relocated to low-wage foreign countries so as to minimize total production costs. Such international fragmentation has brought about a substantial increase in offshoring of intermediate inputs in many regions around the world. Moreover, the development of information technology (IT) means that many services that were traditionally non-tradable have become tradable. Particularly, in the U.S. and other English-speaking developed countries, offshoring of services has become increasingly important.

Triggered by the rise in offshoring, there has been growing interest in many developed countries regarding its impact on factor demand and productivity at home. In the case of offshoring of intermediate material inputs (hereafter, "material offshoring"), production processes requiring low-skilled human capital tend to be relocated to low-wage foreign countries, which potentially affects the wages and employment levels of low-skilled workers at home. On the other hand, in the case of service offshoring, a growing range of activities is relocated abroad, including even tasks requiring high-skilled human capital. The potential negative impact of offshoring on wages and employment in jobs that are more likely to be offshored is probably the main reason why much of the research on offshoring has focused on labor-market issues.[2]

However, offshoring may have long-term economic benefits for domestic industries through factor-cost reductions and productivity gains. If offshoring enables firms to lower costs by relocating abroad production processes in which they are relatively inefficient, this allows them to specialize in processes where they have a comparative advantage, or to engage in new business activities. Moreover, the productivity-enhancing effect of offshoring may not be limited to incumbent firms. Offshoring may increase productivity at a more aggregate level if it leads to the exit of inefficient firms and the creation of new firms (Antràs, Garicano,

[2]There is a substantial body of empirical research that has explored the impact of offshoring on labor demand at home. Most of the research confirms that offshoring has a skill-upgrading effect: the relative demand for unskilled labor decreases and the relative demand for skilled labor increases when unskilled-labor–intensive tasks are outsourced to unskilled-labor–abundant countries. Such studies exist for the U.S. (Feenstra and Hanson, 1999), the United Kingdom (Hijzen, Görg, and Hine, 2005), France (Strauss-Kahn, 2004), Sweden (Ekholm and Hakkala, 2006), Japan (Head and Ries, 2002; Ito and Fukao, 2005; and Ahn, Fukao, and Ito, 2008), and other countries.

and Rossi-Hansberg, 2006). While these issues are critical in understanding the impact of offshoring activities, it is an empirical question of whether the offshoring activity can generate productivity gains for domestic industries.

Although there is a growing number of studies empirically examining the productivity effects of offshoring either at the firm or industry level, the statistical evidence so far that offshoring indeed enhances productivity is still weak.[3] This is especially the case for service offshoring. Amiti and Wei (2009), estimating the effects of both service offshoring and material offshoring on productivity using industry-level data for the U.S. manufacturing sector, find that offshoring has a significant positive effect on productivity, and that the magnitude is much larger for service offshoring than for material offshoring. In contrast, other empirical studies applying the Amiti and Wei–type industry-level analysis for Italy and Korea do not find any productivity-enhancing effects of service offshoring (Daveri and Jona-Lasinio, 2008; Lin and Ma, 2011). Moreover, there have been few firm- or plant-level studies finding evidence of a productivity-enhancing effect of service offshoring, with a notable exception being the study by Görg, Hanley, and Strobl (2008) for the case of Irish manufacturing.[4]

In this chapter, we investigate a relationship between offshoring and domestic productivity, employing industry-level panel data for Japanese manufacturing for the period 1988–2004. The Japanese manufacturing sector is an interesting case because Japanese firms have been playing an important role in the fragmentation of production in East Asia since the 1980s. The rapid expansion of international division of labor is expected to have some impact on domestic productivity. Furthermore, studying the case of Japan should help us understand the nature of service offshoring and its impact on productivity. It is sometimes claimed that business practices in Japanese firms are different from those in U.S. firms. Therefore, the

[3]See Olsen (2006) for a survey on the productivity impact of offshoring. Section II of this chapter also provides an updated survey on this issue.

[4]Ito, Wakasugi, and Tomiura (2008) also find that offshoring of tasks for production of intermediate goods and final assembly, as well as the offshoring of tasks for R&D and information services, positively affects firm-level productivity growth. However, their analysis is based on information on whether or not the firm carries out offshoring, and the information on the amount of offshoring is not available.

productivity-enhancing effect of service offshoring confirmed by Amiti and Wei (2009) for U.S. manufacturing may not be found in the case of Japan because of the different business practices. In this respect, the case of Japanese manufacturing possibly provides an interesting implication for factors that play a role in determining the productivity effects of offshoring.

This chapter also examines whether the effects of offshoring on productivity depend on the region to which activities are outsourced and whether the effects depend on the type of service tasks offshored. By doing so, we try to provide clues to understanding determinants of the productivity effects of offshoring, which have not yet been sufficiently investigated in previous studies.

In order to make our analysis comparable to previous studies, we follow the empirical methodology of Amiti and Wei (2009). We find that Japan's material offshoring to Asia has been increasing drastically, which is consistent with the widely described fact that there has been a significant increase in the fragmentation of production between Japan and East Asian countries in the last two decades or so. On the other hand, we find no clearly increasing trend in service offshoring in the Japanese manufacturing sector. These findings imply that Japanese firms have shifted a substantial part of the production processes for intermediate inputs to foreign countries, while they have been slow in relocating service tasks offshore.

Our statistical investigation finds that material offshoring tends to be positively associated with domestic productivity. In particular, material offshoring to Asia has a robust productivity-enhancing effect. On the other hand, there is little correlation between service offshoring and productivity, which is at odds with the result for U.S. manufacturing in Amiti and Wei (2009). While material offshoring mainly aims at cost savings through the relocation of relatively inefficient parts of the production process to another country, service offshoring is more likely to promote restructuring or improving the way activities are performed. The contrasting result between Japan and the U.S. may imply that Japanese firms are lagging behind in restructuring the way activities are performed, or that peculiar business practices in Japanese firms prevent them from streamlining their service activities across borders.

However, we find that service offshoring tends to be positively associated with productivity at home when we focus on offshoring of information services only. Information services such as data processing and computer programming are conducive to standardization of tasks, in the sense that the performance of these tasks involves less judgment skill compared with commercial services such as business, legal, and engineering consultancy activities. Our findings imply that in this segment, offshoring offers potential benefits.

The remainder of the chapter is organized as follows. Section II presents a review of the literature on the relationship between offshoring and productivity at both the industry and the firm level and, moreover, provides a more thorough discussion of the potential productivity-enhancing effects of offshoring. Next, Section III explains our methodology for measuring offshoring, considers offshoring trends in Japanese manufacturing, and outlines our empirical framework. Section IV then presents our results with a discussion on the nature of offshoring in Japan. Section V concludes.

II. LITERATURE REVIEW

Empirical work to date has failed to produce clear evidence that offshoring helps to lift productivity. A likely explanation is that the productivity-enhancing effects of offshoring depend on a variety of country and/or firm characteristics as well as market or institutional factors. The purpose of this literature review is to summarize possible reasons why offshoring is expected to raise domestic productivity and to present previous empirical results on this issue. We also discuss factors that may prevent firms or industries from enjoying an improvement in domestic productivity through offshoring.

Although there is still little theoretical work on the relationship between offshoring and domestic productivity, it seems reasonable to assume that offshoring contributes to productivity increases in domestic manufacturing operations. The reason is that, first, by relocating inefficient tasks to low-cost countries, the unit cost of the firm's product falls, which can be interpreted as an improvement in productivity.[5] Second, offshoring allows

[5]Grossman and Rossi-Hansberg (2008) show that a decline in the cost of trade in a particular task directly boosts the productivity of the factor whose tasks become easier to move offshore. However, they also show that whether both low-skilled and high-skilled workers can share in the gains from improved opportunities for offshoring depends on

firms to move abroad less productive stages of the production process and shift corporate resources to high-productivity activities, such as product development and process innovation. The remaining workers may become more efficient if offshoring enables firms to restructure in a way that shifts the production possibility frontier outward (Amiti and Wei, 2009). Third, the use of new varieties of imported material or service inputs may enable firms to lower costs of intermediate inputs or streamline production processes, which possibly increases domestic productivity. Taken together, there are reasonable channels through which offshoring improves domestic productivity.

Meanwhile, advances in IT have brought about a drastic reduction in the cost of offshoring. Technological innovations in information and communication processes, such as the Internet, have dramatically reduced communication costs across borders and barriers to trade in service tasks (Freund and Weinhold, 2002). In general, the provision of service inputs requires physical contact between suppliers and manufacturers, which in the past made the offshoring of service tasks impossible. However, the introduction of new information technologies in manufacturing production at home has enabled firms to coordinate production processes with foreign suppliers of service tasks at a low cost, resulting in an increase in service offshoring in developed countries. Technology has also played a key role in the global expansion of material offshoring, for example, through the way that it has revolutionized logistic-management techniques. These technological advances, combined with low labor costs abroad as well as the erosion of trade barriers, have created opportunities for manufacturers to reduce production costs by integrating foreign suppliers into their global supply chains.

The rapid increase in offshoring, boosted by such technological innovation, has attracted considerable attention in many countries around the world. In recent years, a growing number of empirical studies have analyzed the productivity effects of offshoring. Industry-level studies include Egger and Egger (2006), who, using industry-level data for the European Union (EU) manufacturing sector, find that offshoring has a positive impact

the changes in the relative price between low-skilled and high-skilled workers and on the changes in labor supply for each type of worker.

on real-value-added per low-skilled worker in the long run. Specifically, they find that the change in offshoring intensity accounts for about 6% of the increase in value added per low-skilled worker during the period 1992–1997. Amiti and Wei (2009) analyze the impact of offshoring on productivity, distinguishing between the effects of service and material offshoring for the U.S. manufacturing sector for the period 1992–2000. Their findings indicate that service offshoring has a significant positive effect on productivity, accounting for around 10% of productivity growth in U.S. manufacturing. Although material offshoring also has a positive effect on productivity, the magnitude is much smaller.

The findings by Amiti and Wei (2009) are consistent with results reported in Mann (2004) and McKinsey Global Institute (2003, 2005), which show that service offshoring has a positive effect on the U.S. economy. However, similar studies applying an Amiti and Wei-type framework to Italy and Korea do not find any positive effect of service offshoring. Daveri and Jona-Lasinio (2008) find that in the case of the Italian manufacturing sector, there is a positive relationship between productivity growth and material offshoring, but not service offshoring, while Lin and Ma (2011) find that service offshoring leads to a decline in productivity in the case of the Korean manufacturing sector. In addition, McKinsey Global Institute (2005) reports that in contrast with the positive impact of service offshoring on the U.S. economy, the impact on the French and German economies is negative, although it should be noted that the analytical framework is very different from that employed by Amiti and Wei (2009).[6] These empirical studies indicate that while material offshoring generally tends to improve productivity at home, this is not necessarily the case for service offshoring, as not every country has benefited from service offshoring.

[6]The McKinsey Global Institute (2003, 2005) reports estimate the potential economic value created from offshoring by assessing the cost savings for customers and investors, the direct benefits arising from any increase in export to the offshore location and repatriated profits from affiliated offshore providers, and the value of labor re-employed. According to McKinsey Global Institute (2005), every dollar of corporate spending on back-office and IT services offshored to India generates more than $1.14 of new wealth for the U.S. economy. However, Germany earns back only €0.74 for every euro of spending on corporate-service jobs that are moved offshore. France falls between the two (€0.86).

Turning to micro-level analyses, Görg and Hanley (2005) explore the impact of offshore outsourcing of materials and services on electronics firms in the Republic of Ireland over the period 1990–1995. They find a significantly positive effect on Total Factor Productivity (TFP) when looking at offshore outsourcing of materials and services combined. When distinguishing between offshoring of services and materials, however, the productivity impact of service offshoring is found to be insignificant while that of material offshoring is still significantly positive. Moreover, the positive productivity effect of material offshoring holds only for plants with low export intensities. Their interpretation of this result is that offshoring generates productivity increases for plants with low export intensity because offshoring enables these plants to benefit from greater flexibility in production techniques and to learn from international best practice. On the other hand, using Irish data again, but this time for the manufacturing sector overall, Görg, Hanley, and Strobl (2008) obtain robust evidence for a positive effect of service offshoring only for exporters. They argue that in the case of service offshoring, the search for partners to which to outsource activities involves costs, makes exporting firms with sufficient knowledge and experiences in foreign markets advantageous in conducting such a search efficiently.

Meanwhile, using Japanese firm-level data for the period 1994–2000, Hijzen, Inui, and Todo (2010) find that offshoring generally has a positive effect on productivity growth. Although they do not distinguish between service and material offshoring, they separately examine the effects of subcontracting at arm's length internationally (international outsourcing) and domestically (domestic outsourcing).[7] They find that the impact on TFP growth in the case of international outsourcing is four times greater than that in the case of domestic outsourcing. They also find that the size of the effect of offshoring does not vary between firms in high- and low-technology industries, between multinationals and domestic firms, or between exporting and non-exporting firms. Finally, for the case of Spanish manufacturing, Fariñas and Martín-Marcos (2010), using firm-level data

[7]They also examine the effects of purchases of intermediate inputs from a firm's foreign affiliates (international insourcing).

for the period 1990–2002, find a positive relationship between the intensity of offshoring and productivity.

The industry-level and firm- or plant-level studies cited here, focusing on a variety of countries, generally support the hypothesis that material offshoring has a positive impact on domestic productivity. In contrast, the results on the effects of service offshoring are less clear. There are several potential explanations for the zero or negative correlation between service offshoring and productivity. Daveri and Jona-Lasinio (2008) argue that it may take time for the compositional or structural gains from service offshoring to offset the transitional adjustment costs. As pointed out by McKinsey Global Institute (2005), such adjustment costs may arise from low re-employment rates among workers losing their jobs to offshoring because of low labor market flexibility and job creation. Daveri and Jona-Lasinio (2008) also point out that, depending on a country's factor endowments, it may be the most productive service activities that are offshored in order to escape existing inefficiencies at home resulting from insufficient liberalization in the market for such services. On the other hand, Lin and Ma (2011), focusing on the case of Korea, conjecture that language barriers as well as cultural differences may be main reasons why service offshoring has a negative effect on productivity. In addition, McKinsey Global Institute (2005) points out that the size of cost savings varies across countries to which business activities are offshored, depending on the wage levels of destination countries. It also points out that the size of other direct costs or benefits from offshoring differs depending on the size and productivity of industries in the home country and the ownership structure of offshore providers, i.e., whether or not the offshore providers are affiliates of the home country firms. Such factors affect the magnitude of exports from the home country to the offshore location as well as the repatriated profits of affiliated offshore providers and hence the balance of the impact overall.

Turning to trends in Japan's manufacturing sector, there has been a substantial increase in the role of material offshoring, as indicated by the considerable growth in intra-regional outsourcing of intermediate inputs within East Asia (Ahn, Fukao, and Ito, 2008; Wakasugi, Ito, and Tomiura, 2008). Since there are large factor price differences within the region, the division of labor through material offshoring may have contributed to cost savings of domestic operations, which potentially produces a significant impact on productivity in Japan. Although the firm-level study by Ito, Wakasugi, and Tomiura (2008) finds that firms conducting offshoring show higher productivity growth than firms not conducting offshoring, such evidence is still scarce. Moreover, their study does not take account of the impact of changes in magnitude of offshoring.

Thus, previous studies find mixed results for the relationship between offshoring and domestic productivity. Particularly, empirical evidence for the productivity-enhancing effect of service offshoring is scarce. Against such a background, it is important to accumulate empirical evidence from various countries with differing characteristics in terms of factor costs, technological level, business practice, institutional and market characteristics, etc., in order to evaluate the economic benefits of offshoring. Japan's case should be particularly interesting because Japanese firms play an important role in the fragmentation of production in East Asia and also because business practices in Japanese firms are pointed out to be very different from those in Western developed countries, which may result in different impacts of offshoring on domestic productivity. This study employs a similar analytical framework to the one in Amiti and Wei (2009) in order to evaluate our findings in comparison to their results for the U.S. However, by investigating different impacts of offshoring by destination and by type of activities, we try to provide a clue to understanding the mechanism whereby offshoring enhances domestic productivity.

In the next section, we present the analytical framework for our examination of the impact of material and service offshoring on productivity in Japanese manufacturing.

III. ANALYTICAL FRAMEWORK

Measurement of Offshoring

A number of recent studies, using a variety of data sources, have tried to analyze trends in the trade in intermediate inputs. One of the empirical issues in these studies has been the measurement of the importance of trade in intermediate inputs or offshoring. There are two widely used methodologies to measure offshoring. One of these is the methodology by Feenstra and Hanson (1999), in which offshoring is only indirectly measured utilizing the import propensity for each good. They estimate offshoring in industry *i*, for example, by assuming that the share of imported input purchases of good *j* in total input purchases of good *j* for industry *i* equals the import propensity for good *j for the entire economy* (i.e., the share of imports of good *j* in total domestic demand for good *j*).[8] The other methodology is to use direct information on the value of imported intermediate inputs for each industry from and within each sector. In the case of Japan, data on imported intermediate inputs can be obtained directly from the input–output tables, and we therefore employ the second methodology.[9] Hence, our measure of offshoring is:

$$z_i = \frac{\sum_{j=1}^{N} m_{ij}}{Y_i} \qquad (1)$$

where m_{ij} is industry *i*'s use of imported intermediate inputs from industry *j* and Y_i stands for the total non-energy intermediate inputs used by industry *i*. For the purposes of our analysis, we construct separate offshoring measures for material offshoring and service offshoring. Therefore, in the case of the material offshoring measure ($z = MO$), industry *j* denotes all manufacturing industries, while in the case of the service offshoring measure ($z = SO$), industry *j* denotes offshorable service industries. Following Amiti and Wei (2009), when considering imported service inputs in manufacturing, inputs from the following five sectors are considered: telecommunications, insurance, finance, business services, and information services.[10]

[8]Amiti and Wei (2009) and Lin and Ma (2011), for example, employ this methodology.

[9]Examples of studies employing this methodology include Hijzen, Görg, and Hine (2005); Ekholm and Hakkala (2006); and Daveri and Jona-Lasinio (2008).

[10]These services correspond to 11 JIP industries, as shown in Table A1. While Daveri and Jona-Lasinio (2008) include transportation services in their service offshoring measure, we exclude transportation sectors. The reason is that the amount of imported transportation services greatly depends on the volume of goods trade and does not purely consist of supporting services for manufacturing activities similar to back-office or IT services.

Comprehensive and detailed input–output tables are available in Japan for every five years. Utilizing the input–output tables for 1990, 1995, and 2000 as benchmark data, we construct a time series for our offshoring measures as follows:

Equation (1) can be rewritten as:

$$z_i = \sum_{j=1}^{N} \frac{m_{ij}}{IM_j} \frac{IM_j}{Y_i} \tag{2}$$

where IM_j denotes imports in industry j. We observe industry i's use of imported intermediate inputs from industry j as a share of total imports in industry j, m_{ij}/IM_j, for 1990, 1995, and 2000. We also have information on the ratio of imports in industry j to total non-energy intermediate inputs used in industry $i(IM_j/Y_i)$ every year. We use a linear interpolation of 1990, 1995, and 2000 values of m_{ij}/IM_j for the years 1991–1994 and 1996–1999. For 1988 and 1989, we use m_{ij}/M_j for the year 1990, and for 2001–2004, we use m_{ij}/IM_j for the year 2000. Thus, we assume that an industry's use of imported inputs from the same and other industries as a share of its total imports (m_{ij}/IM_j) changes at a certain growth rate for the estimated values. However, total imports in industry $j(IM_j)$ and total non-energy intermediate inputs used in industry $i(Y_i)$ are directly taken from the JIP (Japan Industry Productivity) Database 2009 for each year.[11]

Material and Service Offshoring by the Japanese Manufacturing Sector

Table 1 presents the trends in the intensity of material and service offshoring for the Japanese manufacturing sector during the period 1990–2004.[12] The table shows that the share of imported material inputs in

[11]The JIP Database 2009 is available at <http://www.rieti.go.jp/en/database/JIP2009/index.html>. Refer to Fukao and Miyagawa (2008) for details of the data construction and methodology. The primary objective of the JIP Database 2009 is to provide a consistent database for the industry-level analysis of structural change and economic growth in Japan from a long-term perspective. To this end, the JIP Database 2009 includes a wide variety of indicators on industry characteristics for 108 sectors from 1970 to 2006: capital service input indices and capital costs, labor service input indices and labor costs, nominal and real values of inputs and outputs, and TFP. Additional datasets on trade, FDI, and market reforms are also provided.

[12]We also construct offshoring measures by region, assuming that the country distribution of imports in industry i is the same for intermediate inputs as for final products. Our regional classification is as follows: North America denotes Canada and the U.S.,

Table 1. **Material and service offshoring in Japanese manufacturing**

	1990 (%)	1995 (%)	2000 (%)	2004 (%)	Change 1990–2004 (% points)	(%)
Imported inputs as a percentage share of total inputs						
Materials	**5.95**	**6.29**	**7.69**	**8.89**	**2.95**	**49.57**
of which:						
from North America	2.16	2.08	2.29	1.96	−0.21	−9.63
from EU	1.21	1.14	1.32	1.56	0.35	28.81
from Asia	1.60	2.24	3.23	4.40	2.80	175.56
from China	0.29	0.60	0.98	1.73	1.44	505.10
from ASEAN4	0.48	0.61	0.96	1.16	0.68	140.19
from NIEs4	0.76	0.96	1.20	1.39	0.63	82.70
Services	**0.21**	**0.21**	**0.23**	**0.19**	**−0.02**	**−11.50**
of which:						
from North America	0.09	0.09	0.1	0.08	−0.003	−3.72
from EU	0.06	0.04	0.05	0.06	−0.008	−11.72
from Asia	0.04	0.05	0.05	0.04	−0.008	−18.78
from China	0.01	0.01	0.01	0.01	0.003	47.09
from ASEAN4	0.01	0.01	0.01	0.01	−0.002	−20.16
from NIEs4	0.03	0.03	0.03	0.02	−0.008	−30.65

Note: The shares for 1990 and 1995 are calculated using the regional distribution in 1996 as weights. Data on the regional distribution of services trade are only available from 1996 onward.
Source: Authors' calculation.

2004 was 8.9%, while the share of imported service inputs was only 0.2%. It also clearly shows that the share of material inputs has been increasing and that particularly, material offshoring to Asia has grown rapidly during this period.[13] Remarkably, material offshoring to China increased by nearly

not including Mexico; EU includes both Western and Eastern European countries; and Asia denotes East, Southeast, and South Asian countries, not including Middle Eastern countries.

[13]It should be noted that, as pointed out by Ekholm and Hakkala (2006), this outsourcing measure may underestimate the magnitude of the shift of intermediate goods production to low-income countries in Asia because outsourcing is measured based on the value of imports, which is affected by price changes and exchange rates. If lower production costs in low-income Asian countries lead to a shift of intermediate goods production to these countries, similar goods can be imported at lower prices from Asia than from higher-income countries. Therefore, the increase in outsourcing to Asia may be more pronounced on a volume basis.

sixfold. On the other hand, service offshoring has been very small and remained essentially unchanged during this period.[14] In fact, the degree of offshoring in 2004 was smaller than that in 1990. The regional distribution of service offshoring has also seen little change, although the share of North America, which accounted for the largest slice, has decreased slightly. On the other hand, China's share has increased somewhat (see the percentage increase during the period 1990–2004), although the overall amount is still very small and the change in terms of China's share is therefore not discernable in the table.

Comparing Table 1 with corresponding figures for other countries that have been the subject of previous empirical studies, certain characteristics of Japanese offshoring patterns stand out. In Amiti and Wei (2009), the intensity of material offshoring for the U.S. manufacturing sector is around 15% for the period 1992–2000, while the corresponding figures for Italy and Korea, calculated by Daveri and Jona-Lasinio (2008) and Lin and Ma (2011), respectively, are around 24%. The corresponding figure for Japan in Table 1 suggests that the extent of material offshoring in Japan is much smaller than that in the U.S., Italy, and Korea, though our figures cannot be directly compared with corresponding figures in other studies because of definitional or methodological differences. Moreover, the low degree of material offshoring for Japan that we find (6%–9%) likely reflects the large size of the domestic manufacturing sector and the high technological capability and efficiency of intermediate input producers in Japan.

On the other hand, as for the degree of service offshoring, our figure for Japan is comparable to that for the U.S. in Amiti and Wei (2009), although the corresponding figures for Italy and Korea in Daveri and Jona-Lasinio (2008) and Lin and Ma (2011), respectively, are much larger.[15] Again, the size of the domestic sector, in this case services, may be responsible, with the

[14]For imported services, we use the information from the regional balance of payment statistics provided by the Bank of Japan. Because the regional balance of payment statistics are available only for 1996 onward, we assume that the regional distribution of imports in service industry i for the years before 1996 is the same as the regional distribution in 1996.

[15]In Amiti and Wei (2009), the measure of service offshoring is estimated in the range of 0.18%–0.29% for the U.S., while corresponding figures for Italy in Daveri and Jona-Lasinio (2008) and for Korea in Lin and Ma (2011) are estimated to be more than 1%.

domestic service sectors in Japan and the U.S. being much larger than those in Italy and Korea. However, there is an important difference between Japan and the U.S. in that the intensity of service offshoring has grown rapidly in the latter, while it has stagnated in the former. In the U.S., the intensity of service offshoring increased from 0.18% in 1992 to 0.29% in 2000 (Amiti and Wei, 2009; Table 1). In contrast, in the case of Japan, the corresponding intensity was steady around 0.2% for the period 1990–2004.

Table 2 presents a breakdown of the material and service offshoring intensity for each industry.[16] This shows that while the levels of material and service offshoring intensity vary substantially across industries, many industries — in line with the manufacturing sector overall — have seen an increase in the intensity of material offshoring. This is particularly the case for machinery industries. On the other hand, when it comes to service offshoring, none of the industries shows any clear trend, mirroring the finding for the manufacturing sector as a whole.

In fact, balance-of-payment statistics show that the growth rate of Japan's service trade in the last decade has been much smaller than that of other developed countries, suggesting that service offshoring by Japanese firms has not increased at a similarly rapid pace as that by firms in the U.S. and other developed countries.[17] Moreover, several pieces of anecdotal evidence lend further support to the conclusion that service offshoring in Japan did not increase during the period 1990–2004. First, from around 2000, international service outsourcing to developing countries such as India and its impact on domestic white-collar jobs received much attention both from the media and from political circles in the U.S., the United Kingdom, and Australia (Amiti and Wei, 2005, Mankiw and Swagel, 2006). In contrast, in Japan, service offshoring has never been a major issue of public discussion or the cause for fear of job losses, although some supporting services, such as software development, customer services, and professional services, have been moved to China and other Asian countries. The likely

[16]Although we calculated the offshoring intensity for each JIP industry (52 manufacturing industries), we present the intensities at a more aggregated industry level in Table 2. For a list of the JIP industries, see Table A1.

[17]According to the OECD statistics, for example, the average annual growth rate of Japan's imports of services (in terms of nominal U.S. dollar) was 3.3% for the period 2000–2005, while the corresponding rates for the U.S. and for the EU15 were 8.1% and 13.3%, respectively.

Table 2. **Material and service offshoring by industry**

	1990	1995	2000	2004
(a) Imported material inputs as a percentage of total inputs (%)				
Food & beverages	10.73	10.06	11.01	11.40
Textiles	10.47	9.13	10.65	15.07
Wood products	24.89	20.11	19.81	21.05
Pulp & paper	8.49	8.98	8.93	9.42
Printing	2.19	2.77	1.82	2.26
Leather	24.11	19.55	21.68	26.43
Rubber & Plastics	4.47	4.89	6.45	8.07
Chemicals	6.71	7.08	7.35	8.47
Non-metallic minerals	1.36	1.03	1.93	2.59
Basic metals	3.47	3.41	2.38	3.12
Fabricated metal products	11.64	9.63	10.68	13.99
Machinery & equipment	2.43	3.19	5.84	6.30
Electrical machinery	5.07	8.30	12.13	16.55
Transport equipment	2.01	1.67	3.16	3.70
Precision machinery	4.89	9.10	12.10	14.63
Mfg.n.e.c.	5.77	6.45	6.99	8.59
(b) Imported service inputs as a percentage of total inputs (%)				
Food & beverages	0.21	0.22	0.26	0.23
Textiles	0.19	0.21	0.19	0.19
Wood products	0.10	0.04	0.07	0.06
Pulp & paper	0.14	0.16	0.16	0.14
Printing	0.23	0.29	0.33	0.26
Leather	0.16	0.14	0.17	0.18
Rubber & Plastics	0.15	0.16	0.17	0.13
Chemicals	0.44	0.40	0.43	0.37
Non-metallic minerals	0.19	0.16	0.20	0.17
Basic metals	0.09	0.07	0.07	0.04
Fabricated metal products	0.15	0.16	0.17	0.13
Machinery & equipment	0.24	0.19	0.21	0.16
Electrical machinery	0.30	0.24	0.27	0.24
Transport equipment	0.16	0.14	0.19	0.14
Precision machinery	0.30	0.25	0.26	0.22
Mfg.n.e.c.	0.21	0.22	0.29	0.29

Source: Authors' calculation.

reason is that the scale of the relocation of such supporting services abroad was not very large. Second, it can be pointed out that service offshoring is not easy for Japanese firms because of language problems and different business practices. For instance, Japanese firms tend to maintain long-term relationships with supporting service providers and to purchase various custom-made services from these providers. As a result, large manufacturing firms tend to possess service affiliates. Even in the case of outsourcing, they are likely to require frequent face-to-face consultations for the development of custom-made services.

Thus, service offshoring by Japanese firms so far has not expanded dramatically. However, the Information-Technology Promotion Agency survey (IPA, 2009) indicates that IT service offshoring, particularly to China, India, and Vietnam, is projected to steadily increase in the future. Moreover, it has often been argued that an increase in the degree of international openness may improve the productivity of the Japanese service sector that has stagnated in recent years (Jones and Yoon, 2008). Against this background, and despite the fact that the degree of service offshoring in Japan is still at a low level, whether or not the offshoring of services has some impact on productivity in the manufacturing sector is becoming an important issue that deserves to be scrutinized.

Estimation Model

This section describes our empirical specification for the analysis of the link between offshoring activities and manufacturing productivity in Japan. In order to render our empirical results comparable to previous findings for other countries, we adopt the standard production-function approach as employed by Amiti and Wei (2009). The production function for industry i at time t is defined as follows:

$$Q_{i,t} = T(SO_{i,t}, MO_{i,t})F(S_{i,t}, M_{i,t}, L_{i,t}, K_{i,t}) \qquad (3)$$

where Q is the level of output in industry i as a function of service inputs, S, material inputs, M, labor, L, and capital, K. The technological level of the production function is expressed as T, which depends on our key variables of sectoral offshoring activities: service offshoring, SO, and material offshoring, MO. In Equation (3), it is assumed that the offshoring of service and material input purchases contributes to Hicks-neutral technological change in the production function for industry i. In this approach, global sourcing activities change the technology level without affecting the balance between factor inputs such as labor and capital. Therefore, we assume that offshoring leads to a shift of the industry's production function because domestic production processes are reorganized to take advantage of sourcing material and service inputs from foreign providers.

For the regression analysis, we assume a general Cobb–Douglas production function for Equation (3).[18] Taking the natural logarithm of the Cobb–Douglas function, the equation can be expressed as follows:

$$LnQ_{i,t} = \alpha_0 + \alpha_1 SO_{i,t} + \alpha_2 MO_{i,t} + \beta_1 LnS_{i,t} + \beta_2 LnM_{i,t} + \beta_3 LnL_{i,t} + \beta_4 LnK_{i,t} + \gamma_i + \gamma_t + e_{i,t} \quad (4)$$

where γ_i *and* γ_t are industry- and time-specific effects, respectively, and $e_{i,t}$ is the error term. By estimating the coefficients of *SO* and *MO*, α_1 and α_2, we examine whether an increase in the offshoring intensity (*SO* or *MO*) leads to higher output, holding all factors of production constant (total service input, total manufacturing input, labor input, and capital stock). That is, the coefficients α_1 and α_2 denote the effect of offshoring on TFP. To control for the unobserved industry-specific fixed effects (γ_i), we take the first difference of Equation (4). Denoting the first-differenced variables by Δ, our central regression equation is as follows[19]:

$$\Delta LnQ_{i,t} = \alpha_0 + \alpha_1 \Delta SO_{i,t} + \alpha_2 \Delta MO_{i,t} + \beta_1 \Delta LnS_{i,t} + \beta_2 \Delta LnM_{i,t} + \beta_3 \Delta LnL_{i,t} + \beta_4 \Delta LnK_{i,t} + \pi_i \delta'_i + \pi_t \delta'_t + \varepsilon_{i,t} \quad (5)$$

[18] Egger and Egger (2006) estimate a Constant Elasticity of Substitution (CES) production function to study the effect of foreign outsourcing on labor productivity of low-skilled workers in 12 EU countries during the period 1992–1997.

[19] Some may argue that changes in the material and service offshoring measures include both changes in imported intermediate input and in composition of material inputs and service inputs. That is, in our offshoring measures expressed in Equation (1), the denominator is the total non-energy intermediate inputs used by each manufacturing industry. Therefore, the material and service offshoring would likely be affected by changes in the composition of material intermediate inputs and service intermediate inputs, not only by changes in import ratio of material or service inputs. In our central regression Equation (5), we include material inputs (M) and service inputs (S) separately as input factors of the production function. By doing so, we control for the changes in composition of material and service intermediate inputs. Moreover, we also checked trends of material offshoring and service offshoring by calculating the measures using only material intermediate inputs as the denominator for the former and only service intermediate inputs as the denominator for the latter. The trends of the alternative material and service offshoring measures were consistent with the trends of our original offshoring measures, suggesting that the impact of changes in the composition of material and service inputs would not be crucial.

Although the time-constant, industry-specific fixed effects on the productivity level are removed by taking the first difference of Equation (4), we still include industry dummies (δ'_i) in Equation (5) in order to take account of the possibility that the growth rate of industry productivity can be influenced by time-constant industry characteristics. For instance, some industries may exhibit substantially higher productivity growth rates than other industries due to technological innovation during our period of interest. On the other hand, some industries may show considerably lower productivity growth rates, perhaps because their products have reached a mature stage in the product cycle, and production efficiency is already high, leaving little room for productivity improvements. Thus, it is possible that low-growth industries are more likely to exploit global sourcing strategies for efficiency reasons than high-growth industries. Alternatively, high-growth industries may be more likely to take advantage of foreign sourcing because of the global production networks that have been established. Such tendencies could give rise to a spurious relationship between offshoring activities and productivity growth, and it is for this reason that we include industry dummies in the time-differenced equation. The year dummies (δ'_t) in Equation (5) address the concern that aggregate time effects on industry productivity growth can vary across years. For the regression analysis, we also include one-period lags of the offshoring variables to take account of the possibility that productivity effects may not be instantaneous.

Econometric Issues

The main hypothesis in this study is that manufacturing firms that engage in offshoring of service and material inputs are likely to experience a higher growth rate of manufacturing productivity through the adoption of more efficient technology such as a more efficient supply chain system. A standard regression framework allows us to disentangle the effects of offshoring from those of other important determinants of productivity growth in an industry. However, we are faced with a potential problem of endogeneity between offshoring and productivity growth, which would yield biased coefficients on the offshoring variables in the production function estimation.

Specifically, the question is whether firms' decisions whether to purchase intermediate inputs domestically or from abroad can plausibly be isolated from cross-industry patterns of productivity growth. For example, Tomiura

(2005) finds that in 1998, less than 3% of firms in Japan engaged in foreign outsourcing, and that in particular, high-productivity firms that produce labor-intensive products are more likely to rely on foreign outsourcing. His findings raise the reasonable concern that the offshoring variables could be positively correlated with productivity at the industry level, if more productive firms are concentrated in high-growth industries.

Because of this concern, we remove the industry-specific fixed effects by taking the first difference of Equation (4) to control for industry heterogeneity such as the distribution of firm productivity. This ensures that any positive correlation between offshoring and productivity growth would not merely be due to the concentration of offshoring firms in high-growth industries. Moreover, the inclusion of industry dummies in our regression Equation (5) alleviates the potential endogeneity problem that high-growth industries over time may tend to exhibit an increase of offshoring activities.[20]

Another concern is that firms simultaneously determine the composition of material and service inputs from domestic and foreign suppliers for production, which can give rise to biases in a standard linear regression. To address the endogeneity of input choices, we also estimate the effect of offshoring activities on labor productivity, measured as value added per worker, at the industry level.

Description of Industry-level Data

The data used for our empirical analysis are taken mainly from the JIP Database 2009. The dependent variable, Q, is the real volume of aggregate output at constant prices in industry i. For service and material inputs, we use the real value of intermediate inputs taken from the input–output tables of the JIP Database 2009. Material and service inputs, M and S, are defined as intermediate inputs purchased from JIP industries 1–59 and

[20]The inclusion of industry fixed effects in the first-difference Equation (5) allows us to estimate the short-run effect of offshoring on productivity, which illustrates the *ex post* productivity gain of industries that engage in offshoring activities. However, the fixed-effects specification can produce a downward bias in the estimates in the presence of measurement errors. Since the measurement of offshore sourcing is obviously a difficult task, it is possible that the short-run effect of offshoring on productivity is underestimated in our analysis.

60–107, respectively. Labor input, L, is the total number of employees in an industry. Data on the share of workers by occupation are taken from the supplementary tables of the JIP Database 2009. Data on capital stocks are created by aggregating IT and non-IT capital stocks, which are also taken from the JIP Database 2009. In the JIP Database, the IT capital stock is estimated by the perpetual inventory method using the aggregate value of software and hardware investment for each industry. These data are also used to calculate the share of IT capital stock in total capital stock for each industry. Data on the degree of import penetration are constructed by dividing the value of imports by domestic demand, i.e., imports/(domestic production + imports – exports). The offshoring variables, SO and MO, are constructed following the methodology explained in above.

IV. ESTIMATION RESULTS

In this section, we present the estimation results of our central regression model (Equation (5)) for a panel dataset covering the Japanese manufacturing sector for the period 1988–2004. Regression results are reported with standard errors corrected for cluster correlation within industries. All independent variables except for the offshoring variables are the first difference of the natural logarithm of the variables. We begin with our main results of the effects of offshoring on productivity and then explore the relationship between industries' productivity and offshoring disaggregated by region and type.

Total Factor Productivity and Labor Productivity

Table 3 shows the Ordinary Least Square (OLS) estimation results for the production function (Equation (5)). Columns (1) to (4) show the results for the first-differenced specification with year fixed effects only, while columns (5) to (8) include industry dummies. To begin with, we estimate the coefficients of the contemporaneous variables for service and material offshoring, presented in column (1). The coefficient for current service offshoring is negative, but not statistically significant, while that for material offshoring is positive and significant. Next, since offshoring activities may affect domestic operations in subsequent periods, in column (2) we used offshoring variables lagged by one period. The estimated coefficients

Table 3. OLS estimates of the effect of offshoring on TFP

Dependent variable: Δ ln (Real Output)

	(1)	(2)	(3)	(4)	(5)	(6)	(7)	(8)	(9)
Δ Service Offshoring	−0.58		−0.588	−0.588	−0.613		−0.635	−0.658	−5.028
	(1.627)		(1.511)	(1.497)	(1.716)		(1.603)	(1.604)	(2.554)
Δ Service Offshoring$_{t-1}$		0.374	0.374	0.31		0.249	0.136	0.095	
		(1.048)	(0.706)	(0.753)		(1.044)	(0.674)	(0.691)	
Δ Material Offshoring	0.408**		0.445**	0.380**	0.151		0.19	0.175	0.822
	(0.198)		(0.183)	(0.152)	(0.132)		(0.130)	(0.129)	(0.423)
Δ Material Offshoring$_{t-1}$		0.229	0.258	0.207		0.062	0.101	0.092	
		(0.257)	(0.230)	(0.191)		(0.179)	(0.171)	(0.163)	
Δ ln(Material Input)	0.542***	0.533***	0.544***	0.542***	0.479***	0.478***	0.484***	0.486***	0.754***
	(0.048)	(0.047)	(0.050)	(0.050)	(0.049)	(0.048)	(0.052)	(0.052)	(0.106)
Δ ln(Service Input)	0.07*	0.071**	0.071**	0.075**	0.062*	0.062*	0.062*	0.063*	0.167*
	(0.036)	(0.032)	(0.035)	(0.035)	(0.032)	(0.031)	(0.033)	(0.033)	(0.063)
Δ ln (Number of Workers)	0.084	0.062	0.074		0.104*	0.088	0.09		0.286**
	(0.057)	(0.066)	(0.065)		(0.057)	(0.069)	(0.068)		(0.094)

(Continued)

Table 3. (*Continued*)

Dependent variable: Δln (Real Output)

	(1)	(2)	(3)	(4)	(5)	(6)	(7)	(8)	(9)
Δ ln(Number of Non-production Workers)				0.159				0.103	
				(0.130)				(0.136)	
Δ ln(Number of Production Workers)				−0.079				−0.012	
				(0.131)				(0.133)	
Δ ln(Capital Stock)	0.262**	0.280**	0.267**	0.267**	0.124***	0.155***	0.152***	0.149**	0.114
	(0.105)	(0.109)	(0.109)	(0.109)	(0.055)	(0.057)	(0.056)	(0.057)	(0.090)
Year Dummies	yes	yes	yes	yes	yes	yes	yes	yes	yes
Industry Dummies	no	no	no	no	yes	yes	yes	yes	no
Observations	800	750	750	750	800	750	750	750	100
R-squared	0.641	0.629	0.635	0.637	0.700	0.692	0.693	0.693	0.803

Note: Clustered standard errors at the industry level are shown in parentheses, with ***, **, and * indicating significance at the 1%, 5%, and 10% levels, respectively. The constant term is not reported.
Source: Authors' estimation.

for the offshoring variables, however, are not statistically significant. In column (3), we then estimate a specification that includes both the contemporaneous and lagged values of the offshoring variables. We find that only the current variable for material offshoring has a significant positive coefficient. All of these results imply that TFP growth in Japan's manufacturing sector was positively related with contemporaneous increases in material offshoring, but not service offshoring.

It is often argued that international sourcing of intermediate inputs can play a role in the skill upgrading of domestic workers. The positive impact of material offshoring on manufacturing TFP may therefore reflect a change in the skill composition of workers at domestic plants across industries rather than a shift in the production function. To examine this issue in more detail, we disaggregate for each industry the number of workers employed into production and non-production workers. Column (4) indicates that the contemporaneous variable for material offshoring is still positive and significant, meaning that the result in column (3) is robust to a change in the skill composition of workers. However, the coefficient for contemporaneous material offshoring in column (4) is smaller than in column (3), suggesting that the effect of material offshoring on production may in part reflect the positive effect of the resulting skill upgrading on production.

Next, we estimate time-differenced specifications with industry dummies to address the concern that certain high-growth industries may be more likely to rely on offshoring than other industries. The results are shown in columns (5) through (8). In contrast with the results in columns (1) to (4), however, the coefficients for both service and material offshoring are not statistically significant in all specifications. The coefficient on the contemporaneous material offshoring variable is still positive, but much smaller. As the estimations in columns (5) to (8) contain industry dummies controlling for cross-industry variations in TFP growth and offshoring intensity, these results are driven primarily by the time-series variation in offshoring and TFP. The implication is that the TFP growth rate is higher in industries with greater reliance on global sourcing, but industries that increase their offshoring intensity do not necessarily experience *ex post* a higher growth rate of TFP in subsequent periods.

Column (9) shows the results using observations only for years 1990, 1995, and 2000. As explained in the previous section, the measures of offshoring are constructed partly by linear interpolation. Although there is no better way to construct the annual measures under data constraints, this methodology may induce some spurious time-series correlations between the offshoring measures and productivity. In order to check the sensitivity of the results, we drop the years for which the offshoring measures are estimated. The estimated coefficient of the material offshoring variable in column (9) is not statistically significant. This result suggests that the significantly positive impact of material offshoring in columns (1) to (4) may be partly due to the estimation method of offshoring variables.

A possible problem with the foregoing results is that input choices with regard to material and service inputs are endogenously determined by firms' output choices, which may produce a bias in the OLS estimates for the offshoring variables. A conventional solution to such an endogeneity problem is to employ an instrumental variable for offshoring that is significantly correlated with a change in offshoring intensity but sufficiently uncorrelated with unobserved determinants of industry output. As such an instrument is not readily available, we take an alternative approach and estimate the effect of offshoring on labor productivity, where labor productivity is measured as the total output minus material and service inputs, divided by the number of workers.

Table 4 presents the estimation results of the labor-productivity specification. All models are first differenced, with specifications (1) to (5) including year dummies only, while (6) to (10) also include industry dummies. As in Table 3, column (11) shows the result using observations only for years 1990, 1995, and 2000 as a robustness check. We find that in specifications (1) to (3), the coefficient for service offshoring is not significant, but that for material offshoring is positive and significant. In order to check whether these results are driven by omitted variables, we include the IT capital share and the import penetration ratio as additional control variables. If an increase in the IT capital share and/or the import penetration ratio improved productivity, and this was associated with an increase in offshoring, then omitting these variables may cause the coefficients on the offshoring variables to be inflated. The estimation results including these additional variables are shown in columns (4) and (5). We find that the coefficient for material offshoring remains positive and significant. These results lead us to conclude that material offshoring has a significant

Table 4. OLS estimates of the effect of offshoring on labor productivity

Dependent variable: Δ ln (Real value added per worker)

	(1)	(2)	(3)	(4)	(5)	(6)	(7)	(8)	(9)	(10)	(11)
Δ Service Offshoring	0.858		0.534	1.430	0.818	1.215		1.217	2.210	1.478	−43.350
	(5.404)		(5.399)	(4.976)	(5.575)	(5.237)		(5.188)	(4.821)	(5.181)	(24.520)
Δ Service Offshoring$_{t-1}$		0.855	1.790	2.048	1.776		0.921	1.841	2.245	2.091	
		(3.417)	(2.152)	(2.273)	(2.137)		(3.554)	(2.386)	(2.722)	(2.429)	
Δ Material Offshoring	2.101**		1.970***	2.200***	2.384**	0.430		1.373***	1.406***	2.124***	3.548
	(0.936)		(0.717)	(0.693)	(0.904)	(0.715)		(0.370)	(0.384)	(0.486)	(2.407)
Δ Material Offshoring$_{t-1}$		1.769*	1.888**	2.089*	1.715**		1.084	1.359	1.367	1.533	
		(0.997)	(0.905)	(1.082)	(0.785)		(1.098)	(0.088)	(1.087)	(1.269)	
ln(Capital Stock)	0.854	0.933	0.920	0.952	0.950	0.397	0.533	0.532	0.638	0.545	1.645
	(0.691)	(0.725)	(0.731)	(0.725)	(0.755)	(0.503)	(0.525)	(0.524)	(0.588)	(0.494)	(0.050)
Δ IT Capital Stock Share				−0.731					−0.654		
				(1.818)					(1.149)		
Δ IT Capital Stock Share$_{t-1}$				−3.547					−2.974		
				(3.140)					(2.138)		

(Continued)

Table 4. (*Continued*)

Dependent variable: Δ ln (Real value added per worker)

	(1)	(2)	(3)	(4)	(5)	(6)	(7)	(8)	(9)	(10)	(11)
Δ Import Share					−1.254					−2.484***	
					(0.776)					(0.630)	
Δ Import Share$_{t-1}$					0.422					−0.858	
					(0.363)					(0.678)	
Year Dummies	yes	yes	yes	yes	yes	yes	yes	yes	yes	yes	yes
Sector Dummies	no	no	no	no	no	yes	yes	yes	yes	yes	no
Observations	795	747	747	747	747	795	747	747	747	747	99
R-squared	0.049	0.049	0.059	0.070	0.069	0.184	0.171	0.175	0.181	0.205	0.093

Note: Clustered standard errors at the industry level are shown in parentheses, with ***, **, and * indicating significance at the 1%, 5%, and 10% levels respectively. The constant term is not reported.
Source: Authors' estimation.

positive impact on the growth rate of labor productivity, consistent with the results from Table 3.[21]

Next, we look at the results for the specification including the industry dummies (columns (6) to (10)). While the estimated coefficients for the offshoring variables are not statistically significant in columns (6) and (7), the coefficient for material offshoring is significantly positive in columns (8) to (10). The results in columns (8) to (10) suggest that the growth rate of labor productivity significantly increased in those industries where the share of material offshoring expanded, while the estimation results of the TFP specification in Table 3 suggest that the TFP growth rate did not necessarily increase in industries where the share of material offshoring expanded. However, the insignificant coefficient for the material offshoring variable in column (11) indicates that our estimation results may not be robust enough to conclude that global sourcing of material inputs enhances the domestic productivity.

Material Offshoring by Region

The regression models up to this point have assumed that TFP and labor productivity are related to aggregate international sourcing of service and material inputs. However, it is possible that the effects of offshoring on manufacturing productivity depend on the region to which activities are outsourced. As mentioned earlier, our analysis is based on the notion that firms engage in offshoring in the search for cheaper inputs to lower costs, and that lower costs can be interpreted as a shift in the production function. Yet, the extent to which offshoring indeed lowers costs is likely to vary by partner country or region to which activities are offshored. For instance, unskilled-labor–intensive intermediate inputs can be imported from unskilled-labor–abundant developing countries at low cost, which would have a strong cost-saving effect on domestic production. If unskilled-labor–intensive inputs are more easily offshored than skilled-labor–intensive inputs, we would expect that offshoring to developing countries has a larger positive

[21]The results are qualitatively similar when we estimate the model by robust regression estimation using an iterative process that gives less weight to outlier observations. Moreover, simply excluding outlier observations from the estimation also produces similar results.

impact on manufacturing productivity at home than offshoring to developed countries.

To examine whether there are any regional differences in the effect of offshoring on productivity growth, we disaggregate material offshoring by region: offshoring to Asia, Europe, and North America. As is well known, Asian countries play a prominent role in the international production networks of Japanese firms. The estimation results for material offshoring to Asia are shown in Table 5.[22] Column (1) shows that a change in material offshoring to Asia has a significant positive impact on TFP, while column (2) shows a positive correlation between TFP and the lagged variable for material offshoring. Including both the contemporaneous and the lagged variables (column (3)) yields significant positive coefficients for both variables.

Moreover, as shown in column (4), the coefficients for the material offshoring variables are still significant even controlling for the skill composition of workers, indicating that our results are not driven by a change in the skill composition. In columns (5) to (8), we include industry dummies to rule out that our results reflect industry-specific dynamics, such as an increase in offshoring by only a few fast-growing industries. Columns (9) and (10) show the Generalized Method of Moments (GMM) estimation results and column (11) shows the results using observations only for years 1990, 1995, and 2000 as robustness checks. These results show that the coefficient for material offshoring to Asia is significantly positive. Our results in Table 5 thus demonstrate that material offshoring to Asia brings a significant productivity gain in domestic manufacturing operations while the results in Tables 3 and 4 suggest that the productivity-enhancing effect of material offshoring as a whole is less robust.

In contrast to offshoring to Asia, the coefficients for material offshoring to Europe and North America are not significant.[23] The implication is that whether offshoring activities improve domestic TFP depends on the foreign country from which domestic firms import material inputs. The likely reason for our result is that factor-price differences between Japan and Asia

[22]To refine our analysis, we further distinguish offshoring to China, the ASEAN4, and the NIEs4 countries. The estimation results for these three regions are available upon request to the authors.
[23]These results are available upon request to the authors.

Table 5. Estimate of the effect of material offshoring to Asia on TFP

Dependent variable: Δ ln (Real Output)

	(1) OLS	(2) OLS	(3) OLS	(4) OLS	(5) OLS	(6) OLS	(7) OLS	(8) OLS	(9) GMM	(10) GMM	(11) OLS
Δ Service Offshoring	−0.638		−0.481	−0.489	−0.637		−0.565	−0.575	−5.852	−5.562	−3.718
	(1.649)		(1.528)	(1.523)	(1.720)		(1.613)	(1.615)	(6.171)	(5.029)	(2.926)
Δ Service Offshoring$_{t-1}$		0.304	0.034	0.031		0.232	−0.027	−0.037	−1.443	−0.329	
		(1.033)	(0.674)	(0.691)		(1.048)	(0.652)	(0.652)	(6.016)	(5.134)	
Δ Material Offshoring to Asia	1.037***		1.015***	0.966***	0.466**		0.622**	0.606**	2.460	2.112*	2.027**
	(0.303)		(0.220)	(0.288)	(0.225)		(0.234)	(0.287)	(1.473)	(1.106)	(0.802)
Δ Material Offshoring to Asia$_{t-1}$		1.242**	0.963***	0.915***		0.728*	0.690**	0.675**	0.834**	0.964**	
		(0.547)	(0.356)	(0.310)		(0.425)	(0.337)	(0.320)	(0.401)	(0.417)	
Δ ln(Material Input)	0.536***	0.509***	0.530***	0.530***	0.480***	0.465***	0.484***	0.484***	0.550***	0.445***	0.714***
	(0.045)	(0.044)	(0.046)	(0.046)	(0.047)	(0.045)	(0.049)	(0.048)	(0.132)	(0.106)	(0.112)
Δ ln(Service Input)	0.071**	0.074***	0.077**	0.078**	0.063*	0.064**	0.066**	0.067**	0.062	0.046	0.179***
	(0.035)	(0.027)	(0.032)	(0.032)	(0.032)	(0.028)	(0.031)	(0.031)	(0.064)	(0.068)	(0.064)
Δ ln(Number of Workers)	0.091	0.091*	0.094		0.105*	0.116**	0.098				0.327***
	(0.061)	(0.051)	(0.067)		(0.060)	(0.053)	(0.069)				(0.091)

(Continued)

Table 5. (*Continued*)

Dependent variable: Δ ln (Real Output)

	(1) OLS	(2) OLS	(3) OLS	(4) OLS	(5) OLS	(6) OLS	(7) OLS	(8) OLS	(9) GMM	(10) GMM	(11) OLS
Δ ln(Number of Non-production Workers)				0.083				0.067	0.104		
				(0.120)				(0.130)	(0.272)		
Δ ln(Number of Production Workers)				0.012				0.031	0.222		
				(0.124)				(0.130)	(0.265)		
Δ ln(Number of Technical and Managerial Workers)										0.077	
										(0.130)	
Δ ln(Number of Non-technical and Managerial Workers)										0.326	
										(0.304)	
Δ ln(Capital Stock)	0.258**	0.268**	0.260**	0.261**	0.127**	0.141***	0.156***	0.154***	0.056	0.024	0.094
	(0.104)	(0.102)	(0.105)	(0.105)	(0.055)	(0.049)	(0.056)	(0.055)	(0.077)	(0.077)	(0.095)

(*Continued*)

Table 5. (*Continued*)

Dependent variable: Δ ln (Real Output)

	(1) OLS	(2) OLS	(3) OLS	(4) OLS	(5) OLS	(6) OLS	(7) OLS	(8) OLS	(9) GMM	(10) GMM	(11) OLS
Δ ln(Real Output)$_{t-1}$									0.206 (0.140)	0.232** (0.115)	
Year Dummies	yes	yes	yes	yes	yes	yes	yes	yes	yes	yes	yes
Industry Dummies	no	no	no	no	yes	yes	yes	yes	no	no	no
Observations	800	800	750	750	800	800	750	750	750	750	100
R-squared	0.646	0.631	0.646	0.646	0.701	0.691	0.697	0.697			0.809
p-value of Hansen Statistic									0.178	0.208	
p-value of AR Test Statistic									0.056	0.033	
Number of Included Industries									50	50	

Note: Clustered standard errors at the industry level are shown in parentheses, with ***, **, and * indicating significance at the 1%, 5%, and 10% levels, respectively. The constant term is not reported. For the GMM estimations (models 9 and 10), we use as instruments the first, second, and third lags of each variable except for year dummies.

Source: Authors' estimation.

are greater on average than those with Europe and North America. The geographic proximity of Asia to Japan also results in lower transportation costs. In addition, by distinguishing material offshoring to China, ASEAN4, and NIEs4, we find that material offshoring to ASEAN4 tends to be positively associated with productivity with a time lag while the contemporaneous material offshoring variable tends to be positively associated with productivity in the case of offshoring to NIEs4.[24] In the case of offshoring to China, neither contemporaneous nor lagged offshoring variables has a significant coefficient, suggesting that material offshoring to China is not associated with domestic productivity. Although material offshoring from a low-cost country appears to matter for domestic productivity, the quality or technology level of the offshored material should be crucial to have a productivity-enhancing effect.

Previous studies such as Amiti and Wei (2009) and Görg and Hanley (2005) have estimated the impact of aggregate offshoring activities on productivity without breaking these down into regions. In contrast, we empirically demonstrate that the effects of offshoring of material inputs on domestic productivity depend on the region from which domestic firms import materials. Our results suggest that material offshoring to a low-cost region is likely to bring greater productivity gains for domestic manufacturing sectors.

Service Offshoring by Type

One of the topics widely discussed in the literature, with the aim of trying to understand the impact of offshoring on domestic service employment, is what type of service jobs are likely to be transferred offshore (see, e.g., Jensen and Kletzer 2006). Service activities such as R&D and corporate management require close contact between service workers to facilitate the flow of tacit knowledge, so outsourcing these activities offshore involves large fixed costs. On the other hand, activities such as data input, computer programming, and customer services are relatively standardized in the sense that the performance of these tasks involves less judgment skill. Consequently, the costs of offshoring such information-related tasks are relatively small.

[24]These results are available upon request to the authors.

Despite the fact that there has been great interest in the matter, there has been little empirical work on the issue that the existence and magnitude of productivity-enhancing effects of service offshoring are likely to depend on the nature of offshored service tasks. Thus, we also investigate the impact of offshoring for different types of service tasks. To do so, we construct separate offshoring measures for information services and business services. Specifically, information services include the use of computers, information processing, and the provision of information, while business services comprise business, legal, and engineering consultancy activities.

For the estimation, service offshoring disaggregated by type of activity is entered in the first-differenced specification. The results for information services offshoring are shown in Table 6. The estimations shown in columns (1) to (4) include year dummies, while those in columns (5) to (8) include both year and industry dummies. Column (9) shows the result using observations only for years 1990, 1995, and 2000 as a robustness check. While the contemporaneous variable for information services offshoring is not significant in any of the specifications where it is included except column (3), the lagged variable is positive and significant in all specifications where it is included. A possible explanation is that productivity gains from information service offshoring do not show up instantaneously, but would take time to materialize.

In contrast to offshoring of information services, the estimated coefficient of business service offshoring is not statistically significant in most cases, suggesting that business services offshoring does not play a significant role in improving domestic productivity in manufacturing.[25] In the case of offshoring of business services, there still seem to be various tasks that are difficult to define in a standardized manner, such as business and legal consultancy. These business services involve a substantial amount of judgment and communication between clients and professionals engaged in the production of such services. Moreover, congruence of language and business culture is likely to play a large role in whether domestic firms can exploit and benefit from business services offshoring. In the case of Japan, peculiarities of the Japanese language and culture seem to be a barrier to international transactions in such business service tasks. Therefore,

[25] The results are available upon request to the authors.

Table 6. **OLS estimates of the effect of information services offshoring on TFP**

Dependent variable: Δ ln (Real Output)

	(1)	(2)	(3)	(4)	(5)	(6)	(7)	(8)	(9)
Δ Information Services Offshoring	10.753		48.847*	43.996	−0.341		65.724	65.404	−8.684
	(21.485)		(27.719)	(32.420)	(24.464)		(43.043)	(47.453)	(83.960)
Δ Information Services Offshoring$_{t-1}$		82.621***	116.420***	108.504***		84.851***	146.501***	145.918**	
		(24.364)	(33.407)	(37.795)		(25.024)	(49.006)	(55.442)	
Δ Material Offshoring	0.409**		0.377**	0.343**	0.152		0.130	0.129	0.821*
	(0.197)		(0.164)	(0.144)	(0.132)		(0.124)	(0.126)	(0.435)
Δ Material Offshoring$_{t-1}$		0.347	0.204	0.178		0.148	0.056	0.055	
		(0.285)	(0.213)	(0.184)		(0.186)	(0.160)	(0.155)	
Δ ln(Material Input)	0.542***	0.517***	0.542***	0.541***	0.480***	0.465***	0.482***	0.482***	0.756***
	(0.049)	(0.044)	(0.050)	(0.050)	(0.049)	(0.045)	(0.052)	(0.052)	(0.106)
Δ ln(Service Input)	0.071*	0.068**	0.074**	0.076**	0.063*	0.061**	0.066*	0.066*	0.169**
	(0.036)	(0.030)	(0.036)	(0.036)	(0.032)	(0.030)	(0.034)	(0.034)	(0.064)
Δ ln(Number of Workers)	0.084	0.070	0.071		0.105*	0.105*	0.082		0.288***
	(0.057)	(0.057)	(0.068)		(0.057)	(0.057)	(0.072)		(0.096)
Δ ln(Number of Non-production Workers)				0.105				0.042	
				(0.144)				(0.141)	

(Continued)

Table 6. (*Continued*)

Dependent variable: Δ ln (Real Output)

	(1)	(2)	(3)	(4)	(5)	(6)	(7)	(8)	(9)
Δ ln(Number of Production Workers)				−0.031				0.040	
				(0.145)				(0.137)	
Δ ln(Capital Stock)	0.261**	0.272**	0.258**	0.259**	0.124**	0.130**	0.135**	0.135**	0.105
	(0.105)	(0.107)	(0.112)	(0.111)	(0.055)	(0.052)	(0.062)	(0.061)	(0.088)
Year Dummies	yes	yes	yes	yes	yes	yes	yes	yes	yes
Industry Dummies	no	no	no	no	yes	yes	yes	yes	no
Observations	800	800	750	750	800	800	750	750	100
R-squared	0.641	0.626	0.643	0.643	0.700	0.693	0.703	0.703	0.803

Note: Clustered standard errors at the industry level are shown in parentheses, with ***, **, and * indicating significance at the 1%, 5%, and 10% levels, respectively. The constant term is not reported.
Source: Authors' estimation.

it would still be costly to offshore these tasks, and Japanese manufacturing firms seem not yet to be able to take advantage of doing so.

On the other hand, in the case of information-service offshoring, recent innovations in information and communication technology have dramatically improved the ability to transmit information across borders at low cost. Our finding that information-service offshoring is positively associated with domestic productivity indicates that Japanese manufacturing firms benefit from innovations in information and communication technology. However, we should note that we do not see a clear and rapid increase in information-service offshoring in the case of Japanese manufacturing. Although it is beyond the scope of our study to explore a barrier to service offshoring, it is important to pin down possible reasons why Japanese firms have not been able to fully take advantage of overseas IT suppliers.

According to a survey conducted by IPA of Japan in 2008, the biggest concern about IT service offshoring is language and communication problems, followed by difficulties concerning quality control and differences in cultural and business practices (IPA, 2009). In fact, Japanese firms tend to use custom-made IT systems and software rather than ready-made IT systems or packaged software, which makes it difficult for them to outsource such IT services to foreign companies. Even in Japan, large firms tend to have affiliated firms, from which they insource such services, rather than outsourcing them to independent firms. This reflects part of a general pattern in Japan, where outsourcing to completely unrelated firms is not very common. Moreover, because of firms' reliance on custom-made IT systems and software, outsourcing in many cases would be unlikely to reduce the costs of IT services, particularly when the development of such systems and software requires long-term and frequent face-to-face communication.

Furthermore, a survey conducted by the Research Institute of Economy, Trade and Industry (RIETI) in 2007 shows that the Chief Information Officers (CIOs) in Japanese firms tend to be in charge of duties other than IT systems while the CIOs in U.S. firms tend to be full-time CIOs being in charge of IT systems exclusively (RIETI, 2007). Analyzing the survey results, Motohashi (2007) argues that U.S. firms place greater importance on using IT as a tool to accomplish corporate strategy than Japanese firms. In addition, U.S. firms maintain a relationship with outsourcing firms as partners for consulting on technology trends, whereas a large number of Japanese firms perceive them as a means of cost reduction.

The results of these surveys and analyses suggest that peculiarities of the Japanese language and business culture as well as a lack of strategic IT management prevent Japanese firms from increasing service offshoring and from enjoying productivity gains from doing so.

V. CONCLUSION

This study has analyzed the effect of offshoring of services and material inputs on domestic productivity using industry-level data for Japanese manufacturing. We found that material offshoring tends to be positively associated with domestic productivity, while service offshoring does not appear to have any significant relationship. Therefore, our results suggest that service offshoring does not contribute to productivity in the manufacturing sector, which is in line with findings for Italy and Korea obtained by Daveri and Jona-Lasinio (2008) and Lin and Ma (2011). However, our results for service offshoring are at odds with results by Amiti and Wei (2009) for the U.S. manufacturing sector, where service offshoring has a large positive effect on productivity.

One notable finding is that material offshoring to Asia has a significant positive effect on productivity growth, while material offshoring to Europe and North America does not have any significant effects. This implies that whether offshoring activities improve domestic productivity depends on the foreign country, from which domestic firms import material inputs. In the case of Japan, the large differences between factor prices at home and in Asian countries, coupled with geographic proximity, appear to have yielded a significant productivity-enhancing effect of material offshoring. In fact, material offshoring to Asia has increased dramatically in the 1990s through the early 2000s. As a result, offshoring to Asia could contribute to productivity growth in Japanese manufacturing.

In the case of service offshoring, we find that offshoring is positively associated with productivity in the subsequent period when we focus on offshoring of information services, though the statistical robustness is somewhat weak. The statistical weakness may be partly due to the stagnancy of service offshoring in Japan. However, our results suggest that even though the level of offshoring is still low, offshoring of services, at least in the segment of information services, is likely to produce productivity gains with a time lag. What, then, hinders Japanese firms from increasing offshoring of such services? It has often been indicated that the corporate organization of Japanese firms is not well suited to IT systems, which are designed to use standardized software. In addition, it has also been pointed out that the decision-making processes in Japanese firms, requiring substantial interdivisional communication, are obstacles to the effective use of state-of-the-art IT systems (see, e.g., Motohashi, 2008). These factors would make it difficult for Japanese firms to utilize foreign service providers. As the U.S. evidence implies potentially large productivity gains from exploiting service offshoring, it is worth further scrutinizing the determinants of service offshoring in Japanese manufacturing industries. In this respect, our findings shed light on the importance of IT management in determining whether firms import IT services and realize productivity gains from offshoring of information services.

As a final note, we discuss some of the issues that are not sufficiently addressed in this study. First, we found no significant effect of offshoring of business services on productivity. We conjecture that the nature of business services, which involve a substantial amount of communication between clients and professionals as well as peculiarities of the Japanese language and culture, hinder Japanese firms from effectively using offshored business services. However, if it is the peculiarities of the Japanese language and culture that are the biggest obstacles to the international outsourcing of business services, outsourcing of such services to domestic suppliers may nevertheless have a positive productivity effect. Thus, it would be interesting to examine whether domestic service outsourcing has a productivity-enhancing effect, and also which has the stronger productivity effect, international or domestic outsourcing.

Second, this study does not address the effects of offshoring on each type of worker, i.e., low-skilled workers and high-skilled workers. From a theoretical perspective, task-level analysis has attracted much attention in the literature (e.g., Grossman and Rossi-Hansberg, 2008). Particularly in the context of service offshoring, high-skilled tasks have been increasingly moved overseas due to advances in IT. Investigating the productivity effect of offshoring separately on low-skilled workers (or tasks) and on high-skilled workers (or tasks) is another possible item for a future research agenda.

Finally, we did not explore the productivity effect of service offshoring by region in this study because sufficient data on the regional distribution of service offshoring were not available. So far, the magnitude of service offshoring in Japanese manufacturing has remained low and has not shown as conspicuous an increasing trend as in the case of material offshoring. However, it will become important to analyze the effect of service offshoring by region if the volume of service offshoring increases in the future. If services offshored to developed countries embody greater knowledge or know-how while services offshored to developing countries are less knowledge-intensive but cheaper, the productivity-enhancing effect of service offshoring may differ by region/country to which activities are outsourced. Regional differences in the effect of service offshoring on productivity are another issue that it would be useful to further scrutinize in the future. Exploring these issues will help to shed light on the mechanism whereby offshoring can increase productivity.

ACKNOWLEDGMENTS

The authors would like to thank Isao Kamata, Theresa Greaney, and participants in the CGP conference for their helpful comments. The authors are also grateful for helpful comments and suggestions by seminar participants at RIETI.

APPENDIX

Table A1. List of industries

Sector	Industry	JIP industry classification
Primary	—	1 Rice, wheat production
Primary	—	2 Miscellaneous crop farming
Primary	—	3 Livestock and sericulture farming
Primary	—	4 Agricultural services
Primary	—	5 Forestry
Primary	—	6 Fisheries
Energy-related	—	7 Mining
Manufacturing	Food & beverages	8 Livestock products

(Continued)

Table A1. (*Continued*)

Sector	Industry	JIP industry classification
Manufacturing	Food & beverages	9 Seafood products
Manufacturing	Food & beverages	10 Flour and grain mill products
Manufacturing	Food & beverages	11 Miscellaneous foods and related products
Manufacturing	Food & beverages	12 Prepared animal foods and organic fertilizers
Manufacturing	Food & beverages	13 Beverages
Manufacturing	Food & beverages	14 Tobacco
Manufacturing	Textiles	15 Textile products
Manufacturing	Wood products	16 Lumber and wood products
Manufacturing	Mfg. n.e.c.	17 Furniture and fixtures
Manufacturing	Pulp & paper	18 Pulp, paper, and coated and glazed paper
Manufacturing	Pulp & paper	19 Paper products
Manufacturing	Printing	20 Printing, plate making for printing and bookbinding
Manufacturing	Leather	21 Leather and leather products
Manufacturing	Rubber & Plastics	22 Rubber products
Manufacturing	Chemicals	23 Chemical fertilizers
Manufacturing	Chemicals	24 Basic inorganic chemicals
Manufacturing	Chemicals	25 Basic organic chemicals
Manufacturing	Chemicals	26 Organic chemicals
Manufacturing	Chemicals	27 Chemical fibers
Manufacturing	Chemicals	28 Miscellaneous chemical products
Manufacturing	Chemicals	29 Pharmaceutical products
Energy-related	—	30 Petroleum products
Energy-related	—	31 Coal products
Manufacturing	Non-metallic minerals	32 Glass and its products
Manufacturing	Non-metallic minerals	33 Cement and its products
Manufacturing	Non-metallic minerals	34 Pottery
Manufacturing	Non-metallic minerals	35 Miscellaneous ceramic, stone and clay products
Manufacturing	Basic metals	36 Pig iron and crude steel
Manufacturing	Basic metals	37 Miscellaneous iron and steel
Manufacturing	Basic metals	38 Smelting and refining of non-ferrous metals
Manufacturing	Fabricated metal products	39 Non-ferrous metal products
Manufacturing	Fabricated metal products	40 Fabricated constructional and architectural metal products
Manufacturing	Fabricated metal products	41 Miscellaneous fabricated metal products

(*Continued*)

Table A1. (*Continued*)

Sector	Industry	JIP industry classification
Manufacturing	Machinery & equipment	42 General industry machinery
Manufacturing	Machinery & equipment	43 Special industry machinery
Manufacturing	Machinery & equipment	44 Miscellaneous machinery
Manufacturing	Machinery & equipment	45 Office and service industry machines
Manufacturing	Electrical machinery	46 Electrical generating, transmission, distribution and industrial apparatus
Manufacturing	Electrical machinery	47 Household electric appliances
Manufacturing	Electrical machinery	48 Electronic data processing machines, digital and analog computer equipment and accessories
Manufacturing	Electrical machinery	49 Communication equipment
Manufacturing	Electrical machinery	50 Electronic equipment and electric measuring instruments
Manufacturing	Electrical machinery	51 Semiconductor devices and integrated circuits
Manufacturing	Electrical machinery	52 Electronic parts
Manufacturing	Electrical machinery	53 Miscellaneous electrical machinery equipment
Manufacturing	Transport equipment	54 Motor vehicles
Manufacturing	Transport equipment	55 Motor vehicle parts and accessories
Manufacturing	Transport equipment	56 Other transportation equipment
Manufacturing	Precision machinery	57 Precision machinery & equipment
Manufacturing	Rubber & Plastics	58 Plastic products
Manufacturing	Mfg. n.e.c.	59 Miscellaneous manufacturing industries
—	—	60 Construction
—	—	61 Civil engineering
Energy-related	—	62 Electricity
Energy-related	—	63 Gas, heat supply
Energy-related	—	64 Waterworks
Energy-related	—	65 Water supply for industrial use
Services	—	66 Waste disposal
Services	—	67 Wholesale
Services	—	68 Retail
Services	Finance	69 Finance
Services	Insurance	70 Insurance
Services	—	71 Real estate
Services	—	72 Housing

(*Continued*)

Table A1. (*Continued*)

Sector	Industry	JIP industry classification
Services	Transportation	73 Railway
Services	Transportation	74 Road transportation
Services	Transportation	75 Water transportation
Services	Transportation	76 Air transportation
Services	Transportation	77 Other transportation and packing
Services	Telecommunication	78 Telegraph and telephone
Services	—	79 Mail
Services	—	80 Education (private and non-profit)
Services	—	81 Research (private)
Services	—	82 Medical (private)
Services	—	83 Hygiene (private and non-profit)
Services	—	84 Other public services
Services	Business Services	85 Advertising
Services	Business Services	86 Rental of office equipment and goods
Services	Business Services	87 Automobile maintenance services
Services	Business Services	88 Other services for businesses
Services	—	89 Entertainment
Services	Information Services	90 Broadcasting
Services	Information Services	91 Information services and internet-based services
Services	Information Services	92 Publishing
Services	Information Services	93 Video picture, sound information, character information production and distribution
Services	—	94 Eating and drinking places
Services	—	95 Accommodation
Services	—	96 Laundry, beauty and bath services
Services	—	97 Other services for individuals
Services	—	98 Education (public)
Services	—	99 Research (public)
Services	—	100 Medical (public)
Services	—	101 Hygiene (public)
Services	—	102 Social insurance and social welfare (public)
Services	—	103 Public administration
Services	—	104 Medical (non-profit)
Services	—	105 Social insurance and social welfare (non-profit)
Services	—	106 Research (non-profit)
Services	—	107 Other (non-profit)
—	—	108 Activities not elsewhere classified

REFERENCES

Ahn, Sanghoon, Kyoji Fukao, and Keiko Ito (2008). "Outsourcing in East Asia and Its Impact on the Japanese and Korean Labour Markets." OECD Trade Policy Working Paper 65, January, Organisation for Economic Co-operation and Development.

Amiti, Mary and Shang-Jin Wei (2005). "Fear of Service Outsourcing: Is it Justified?" *Economic Policy*, 20(42): pp. 308–347.

Amiti, Mary and Shang-Jin Wei (2009). "Service Offshoring and Productivity: Evidence from the U.S." *World Economy*, 32(2): pp. 203–220.

Antràs, Pol, Luis Garicano, and Esteban Rossi-Hansberg (2006) "Offshoring in a Knowledge Economy." *Quarterly Journal of Economics*, 121(1): pp. 31–77.

Daveri, Francesco, and Cecilia Jona-Lasinio (2008). "Off-Shoring and Productivity Growth in the Italian Manufacturing Industries." *CESifo Economic Studies*, 54(3): pp. 414–450.

Egger, Hartmut, and Peter Egger (2006). "International Outsourcing and the Productivity of Low-Skilled Labor in the EU." *Economic Inquiry*, 44(1): pp. 98–108.

Ekholm, Karolina, and Katariina Hakkala (2006). "The Effect of Offshoring on Labor Demand: Evidence from Sweden." Working Paper 654, May, Research Institute of Industrial Economics, Stockholm.

Fariñas, José C. and Ana Martín-Marcos (2008). "Foreign Sourcing and Productivity: Evidence at the Firm Level." *World Economy*, 33(3): pp. 482–506.

Feenstra, Robert C. and Gordon H. Hanson (1999). "The Impact of Outsourcing and High-Technology Capital on Wages: Estimates for the U.S., 1979–1990." *The Quarterly Journal of Economics*, 114(3): pp. 907–940.

Freund, Caroline, and Diana Weinhold (2002). "The Internet and International Trade in Services." *American Economic Review*, 92(2): pp. 236–240.

Fukao, Kyoji, and Tsutomu Miyagawa (2008). *Productivity and Economic Growth in Japan: Firm- and Industry-level Empirical Analysis Based on JIP Database* (in Japanese), Tokyo: University of Tokyo Press.

Görg, Holger, and Aoife Hanley (2005). "International Outsourcing and Productivity: Evidence from the Irish Electronics Industry." *North American Journal of Economics and Finance*, 16(2): pp. 255–269.

Görg, Holger, Aoife Hanley, and Eric Strobl (2008). "Productivity Effects of International Outsourcing: Evidence from Plant-Level Data." *Canadian Journal of Economics*, 41(2): pp. 670–688.

Grossman, Gene M. and Esteban Rossi-Hansberg (2008). "Trading Tasks: A Simple Theory of Offshoring." *American Economic Review*, 98(5): pp. 1978–1997.

Head, Keith and John Ries (2002). "Offshore Production and Skill Upgrading by Japanese Manufacturing Firms." *Journal of International Economics*, 58(1): pp. 81–105.

Hijzen, Alexander, Holger Görg and Robert C. Hine (2005). "International Outsourcing and the Skill Structure of Labour Demand in the United Kingdom." *Economic Journal*, 115(506): pp. 860–878.

Hijzen, Alexander, Tomohiko Inui and Yasuyuki Todo (2010). "Does Offshoring Pay? Firm-level Evidence from Japan." *Economic Inquiry*, 48(4): pp. 880–895.

Ito, Banri, Ryuhei Wakasugi and Eiichi Tomiura (2008). "Offshoring and Productivity: Evidence from Japanese Firm-Level Data." RIETI Discussion Paper Series 08-E-028, Research Institute of Economy, Trade and Industry.

Ito, Keiko and Kyoji Fukao (2005). "Physical and Human Capital Deepening and New Trade Patterns in Japan." in Takatoshi Ito and Andrew K. Rose, eds., *International Trade in East Asia*, NBER-East Asia Seminar on Economics, Volume 14, Chapter 1, pp. 7–49, Chicago and London: University of Chicago Press.

IPA (2009). *IT Jinzai Shijo Doko Chosa* (Survey on Trends of IT Job Markets), Information-Technology Policy Agency, Japan.

Jensen, J. Bradford and Lori G. Kletzer (2006). "Tradable Services: Understanding the Scope and Impact of Services Offshoring." in Lael Brainard and Suan M. Collins, eds., *Brookings Trade Forum: 2005 — Offshoring White-Collar Work*, Brookings Institution Press, pp. 75–116.

Jones, Randall S. and Taesik Yoon (2008). "Enhancing the Productivity of the Service Sector in Japan." Economics Working Papers No. 651, December, Organisation for Economic Co-operation and Development.

Lin, Songhua and Alyson C. Ma (2011). "Outsourcing and Productivity: Evidence from Korean Data." Forthcoming in *Journal of Asian Economics*.

Mankiw, Gregory N. and Phillip Swagel (2006). "The Politics and Economics of Offshore Outsourcing." *Journal of Monetary Economics*, 53(5): pp. 1027–1056.

Mann, Catherine L. (2004). Globalization of IT Services and White Collar Jobs: The Next Wave of Productivity Growth, *International Economics Policy Briefs*, pp. 3–11, Institute of International Economics.

McKinsey Global Institute (2003). *Offshoring: Is It a Win-Win Game?*, McKinsey and Company. Available at: www.mckinsey.com/mgi/publications/win_win_game.asp. Accessed 10 June 2009.

McKinsey Global Institute (2005). *How Offshoring of Services Could Benefit France*, McKinsey and Company. Available at: www.mckinsey.com/mgi/ publications/offshoringbenefits.asp. Accessed 10 June 2009.

Motohashi, Kazuyuki (2007). "A Comparative Analysis of Japanese, U.S., and Korean Firms on IT and Management." RIETI Discussion Paper Series 07-E-047, Tokyo: Research Institute of Economy, Trade and Industry.

Motohashi, Kazuyuki (2008). "Comparative Analysis of IT Management and Productivity Between Japanese and U.S. Firms" (sic), RIETI Discussion

Paper Series 08-E-007, Tokyo: Research Institute of Economy, Trade and Industry.

Olsen, Karsten B. (2006). "Productivity Impacts of Offshoring and Outsourcing: A Review." STI Working Paper 2006/a, OECD Directorate for Science, Technology and Industry (STI), Organisation for Economic Co-operation and Development.

RIETI (2007). *IT Senryaku to Kigyo Pafomansu ni kansuru Nichi-Bei-Kan no Kokusai Hikaku: Anketo Chosa Shukei Kekka Gaiyo* (International Comparison on IT Strategies and Corporate Performance for Japanese, U.S., and Korean Firms: A Summary Result of the Questionnaire Survey), Research Institute of Economy, Trade and Industry, Tokyo.

Strauss-Kahn, Vanessa (2004). "The Role of Globalization in the Within-Industry Shift Away from Unskilled Workers in France." in Robert E. Baldwin and L. Alan Winters, eds., *Challenges to Globalization: Analyzing the Economics*, Chapter 6, pp. 209–231, Chicago and London: University of Chicago Press.

Tomiura, Eiichi (2005). "Foreign Outsourcing and Firm-Level Characteristics: Evidence from Japanese Manufacturers." *Journal of the Japanese and International Economies*, 19(2): pp. 255–271.

Wakasugi, Ryuhei, Banri Ito and Eiichi Tomiura (2008). "Offshoring and Trade in East Asia: A Statistical Analysis." *Asian Economic Papers*, 7(3): pp. 105–128.

Comment*

Isao Kamata

Foreign outsourcing or offshoring is common today not only for intermediate material inputs but also for service inputs, and the impacts of offshoring on the productivity of domestic industries are of growing research interest. Although the offshoring of intermediate material inputs and service inputs might be motivated by different reasons, research that separately examines the impacts of the two modes of offshoring is not yet very abundant. Moreover, previous studies have not agreed on the significance of service offshoring in terms of its impact on domestic productivity for different countries. In this study, Ito and Tanaka empirically investigate differences between the impacts of material offshoring and service offshoring on domestic productivity, using industry-level data for Japanese manufacturing for the years 1988 through 2004. They also examine whether and how material offshoring to different regions has different impacts on domestic productivity, and whether and how the productivity impacts of service offshoring is different across the types of offshored services. Their key findings are: (1) in Japanese manufacturing industries, material offshoring has a positive impact on domestic productivity, while service offshoring does not have a significant impact; (2) the positive productivity impact is significant for material offshoring to Asian countries but not for Europe and North America; and (3) although offshoring of business services does not have a significant impact on domestic productivity in Japanese manufacturing industries, offshoring of information services has a significant positive impact.

While it follows preceding studies such as Amiti and Wei (2009) for its methodology, the authors' study contributes to the literature in the following ways. First, to the best of my knowledge, it is the first study that investigates the impacts of offshoring on domestic productivity for Japanese manufacturing industries, highlighting the difference between the offshoring of intermediate material inputs and service inputs. Second, the study takes advantage of the precision of Japanese data (the input–output tables of the JIP Database 2009) and employs a direct measure of imported inputs from each industry to each industry, in contrast to earlier studies that use a proxy measure of offshored inputs. Third, the study separately examines the productivity impacts of material offshoring to different regions, reflecting potential differences in the motivation behind offshoring to different countries (i.e., comparative advantage *versus* variety in intermediate inputs). The study also examine different types of offshored services — information services and business services — for the impacts of these services on domestic productivity, considering the difference of the degree to which the services are standardized and offshorable.

My major comments are the following.

Period of the Study

While the study investigates Japanese manufacturing industries for the years 1988 through 2004, Ito and Tanaka mention that the Japanese economy stagnated during the most of this period, and thus output growth in manufacturing observed in the data should be very small. In addition, as presented in Table 1, change in service offshoring (as the share in the total input) in Japanese manufacturing was also very small during this period. It may therefore be difficult to draw a firm conclusion about the relationship between offshoring — especially that of service inputs — and the productivity of Japanese manufacturing industry from an empirical study using data for this period.

Measure of Offshoring Intensity

One of the major advantages of this study is that, unlike preceding studies, Ito and Tanaka directly measure the values of imported intermediate inputs of both materials and services, for each manufacturing industry (i.e., m_{ij} in Equation (1)). However, there is a drawback: the data for this direct measure of imported inputs are available only for every five years. Ito and Tanaka thus "annualize" their measure of offshoring intensity, m_{ij}/Y_i (see Equation (1)), by decomposing it into the product of two terms, $(m_{ij}/IM_j) \cdot (IM_j/Y_i)$ (see Equation (2)) and applying a linear interpolation to the first term to compute its values for the years for which the data on m_{ij} are not available. This annualization, however, might raise concern about the possibility of losing the information in the original direct measure (or variation in the original data), especially given that the annualized offshoring intensity is later linearly detrended for use in estimation.[26] An alternative approach that I would consider is to use the original data only for the years 1990, 1995, and 2000 for estimation. Although this would significantly reduce the number of observations, it could maintain the information contained in the original data. This approach could also address the above-mentioned issue of the small variation in the variables of output growth and service offshoring by measuring changes of those variables over five years.

Endogeneity

Ito and Tanaka point out a major potential issue in their benchmark regression — the estimation of a production function — that there should be potential endogeneity between output growth (the regressand) and change in material and service offshoring (regressors). Because of lack of appropriate instruments, however, they do not address this issue directly in their benchmark specification. Instead, they add an alternative specification in which they regress value added per worker on the offshoring measures. However, for their benchmark estimation, at least they could try the Arellano–Bond GMM estimator that has been suggested and used by Amiti and Wei (2009) to address the endogeneity issue.[27]

Interpretation of the Result of the Benchmark Estimation

From the estimation results for their benchmark specification, Ito and Tanaka conclude that, in Japanese manufacturing industries, material

[26] I also see difficulty in finding a meaningful economic interpretation of this decomposition, especially for the second term IM_j/Yi_i. The study by Amiti and Wei (2009) has also applied decomposition to the measure of offshoring but in a different way. They have applied such decomposition primarily to construct a proxy measure of offshoring with lack of a direct measure of imported inputs, unlike the current study that has the advantage of a direct measure of imported intermediate inputs in each output industry.

[27] Using separately measured TFP instead of estimating a production function could also be an alternative approach. While they do not mention it in the text, the authors should also have discussed this alternative TFP specification in the main body of the paper.

offshoring positively impacts domestic TFP but service offshoring does not. However, the results in Table 3 seem to be too weak in support of this conclusion. The table indicates that the positive correlation between the increase in material offshoring and output growth is significant only at the 10% level, and it is indeed insignificant when the industry dummies are included in the regression. In addition, with regard to the point estimate of the coefficient for the contemporaneous variable of service offshoring, although the estimate is not statistically significant, it has a relatively large negative value. This negative coefficient might indicate that service offshoring in Japanese manufacturing industries has indeed negatively impacted the domestic productivity, or that, in Japan, productivity-declining industries have tended to offshore service inputs (i.e., reverse causality).

Alternative Specification for the Labor-Productivity Effects

Ito and Tanaka also estimate the effects of offshoring on labor productivity, measured as the value added per worker. In some versions of this specification, they include the IT capital share and the import penetration ratio as additional control variables to check for omitted-variable bias in estimation. However, it is not obvious why these two variables should be chosen for additional control. Ito and Tanaka are not clear, either, about why they control for each of these two variables separately but not for both together.

Controlling for the Effects of Skill Upgrading

Ito and Tanaka discuss the possibility of skill upgrading of domestic workers through offshoring and its impacts on productivity. To see the direct productivity effects of offshoring, they try to control for the domestic skill-upgrading effect in estimation for the benchmark specification but not for the alternative labor-productivity specification. However, the effects of a change in the skill composition of workers should be more significant in the labor-productivity specification. That is, the average labor productivity (or value-added per worker) is expected to increase as the average skill level of labor rises. I therefore think that, to address this issue consistently, they should control for the skill composition of workers in both specifications.

Material Offshoring by Region and Service Offshoring by Type

Ito and Tanaka also examine whether the productivity impacts of material offshoring differ depending on the region from which materials are sourced. This is done by replacing the variable for the aggregate material offshoring with that for offshoring to a particular region (Asia, Europe, or North America) and running separate regression for their benchmark specification with each regional offshoring variable. However, this might cause the estimated impact of the regional offshoring in each regression to be biased due to the omission of the variables for offshoring to other regions. For instance, material offshoring to both Asia and non-Asian regions could have increased together, and the material offshoring could have positively impacted domestic productivity regardless of the destination. In such a case, the estimated productivity impact of offshoring to Asia under the current specification might be biased upward. To address this issue and compare the productivity impacts of material offshoring to different regions, Ito and Tanaka might want to include the variables for offshoring to different regions (Asia, Europe, North America, and other regions) in one regression for simultaneous estimation. By the same token, for the estimation of productivity impacts of offshoring of different types of services, they might want to include the variables for information service offshoring and other service offshoring together for estimation.

To conclude, I should mention that Ito and Tanaka address various issues on foreign outsourcing and its productivity impacts, each of which can be an interesting topic for further research.

REFERENCE

Amiti, Mary and Shang-Jin Wei (2009). "Service Offshoring and Productivity: Evidence from the U.S." *The World Economy*, 32(2): pp. 203–220.

CHAPTER 3

Does Firm Boundary Matter? The Effect of Offshoring on Productivity of Japanese Firms

Banri Ito*, Eiichi Tomiura†, and Ryuhei Wakasugi‡

*Senshu University, Kawasaki-shi Kanagawa, Japan
†Yokohama National University, Yokohama, Japan
‡Kyoto University, Kyoto, Japan
§ito-banri@isc.senshu-u.ac.jp
¶tomiura@ynu.ac.jp
‖wakasugi@kier.kyoto.u.ac.jp

I. INTRODUCTION

Recently, there has been great interest in the examination of the impact of offshore sourcing to foreign countries that has increased rapidly and expanded over various tasks. It is remarkable that the offshore sourcing of not only production parts, intermediate goods, and final assemblies but also financial, legal, and customer support services have increased. There have been several theoretical studies of offshore sourcing. Grossman and Rossi-Hansberg (2009) and Baldwin and Robert-Nicoud (2007) have shown that offshore sourcing contributes to higher production efficiency. Antràs (2003) and Antràs and Helpman (2004) have indicated that on the basis of productivity and sectoral characteristics, firms decide whether to produce intermediate inputs or outsource them. A number of empirical studies have focused on the effect of offshore sourcing on the labor market in source countries (e.g., Ekholm and Hakkala (2006); Egger and Egger (2006); Feenstra and Hanson (1996, 1999); Geishecker and Görg (2005); Head and Ries (2002); Helg and Tajoli (2005); and Hijzen, Görg, and Hine (2005)). But there are few studies at the firm level that have examined the economic impact of offshore sourcing. This chapter aims to provide empirical evidence of the causal effect of offshore sourcing on the growth of firm productivity using unique microdata for Japanese manufacturing firms.

Previous empirical studies that have explored this issue using industry-level data suggest that offshore sourcing positively affects productivity (e.g., Amiti and Wei (2006); Egger and Egger (2006); and Ito and Tanaka (2009)). The first attempt using firm-level data, Görg and Hanley (2005) examined the effect of offshore outsourcing on labor productivity using Irish firm-level data in the electronics industry over the period, 1990–1995. They found a positive impact of offshore outsourcing on total factor productivity (TFP) when estimating the effect of outsourcing of materials and services combined. However, they observed the effect of outsourcing of services not to have a significant impact when distinguishing between two tasks.[1] Their advantage is no doubt that the data on offshore outsourcing can be distinguished according to materials and services inputs. However, the measurement of "offshore outsourcing" used in their study includes not only outsourcing but also insourcing, for it is defined as the ratio of total imported inputs to total inputs. Taking into account the firm's boundaries, offshore outsourcing to local firms through arm's-length transactions should be distinguished from total offshore sourcing. Hijzen, Inui, and Todo (2006) also estimated the impact of offshore sourcing on firm productivity, using Japanese firm-level data for the period 1994–2000. They found that offshore sourcing defined as the ratio of the expenditure on subcontracting to foreign suppliers has a positive and significant effect on TFP, even after controlling offshore insourcing, which is defined as all intermediate purchases from the firm's own foreign subsidiaries. Although they suggested the positive impact of offshore sourcing regardless of the firm's boundaries, the definition of their data does not explicitly identify both offshore insourcing and outsourcing. Furthermore, their definition of offshore sourcing is restricted to the manufacturing of goods and materials, while firms' offshoring activities were extended to a wide range of tasks,

[1] Görg, Hanley, and Stroble (2008), which extended data coverage to 1990–1998 and all manufacturing industries and took into account the status of trade activity and ownership, report similar results on labor productivity.

including not only production parts, intermediate goods, and final assemblies but also financial, legal, and customer support services. Thus, there is a possibility of underestimating offshore sourcing due to the restriction of micro-data.

In this chapter, we examine the impacts of both offshore outsourcing and insourcing on the productivity by using firm-level data that directly identify outsourcing firms and insourcing firms. The data cover the firms that conduct offshore sourcing, not only production outsourcing, but also outsourcing of service-related tasks such as R&D, information services, customer support, and professional services through contracting out. To identify the causal effect on firm productivity, we implement a propensity score matching (PSM) technique with a difference-in-differences (DID) technique. The results indicate that offshore outsourcing has no impact on firm productivity, though offshore insourcing has a positive impact with a time lag of several years.

This chapter is organized as follows. Section II describes the construction of the data set and general features of offshoring firms. In Section III, we present an analytical framework to examine the effect of offshoring on firm productivity and empirical strategy. Section IV presents the empirical results of the effect of offshoring on productivity and discusses the results, and Section V, the conclusions.

II. DATA AND STATISTICAL DESCRIPTIONS

Data

To obtain basic information on firm characteristics and performance, we used the *Basic Survey of Japanese Business Structure and Activities* (*Kigyo Katsudo Kihon Chosa*, in Japanese) for the period 1997–2005, conducted by Japan's Ministry of Economy, Trade and Industry (henceforth METI survey). This annual national survey is mandatory for all firms with 50 or more employees and whose paid-up capital or investment fund is over 30 million yen in mining, manufacturing, wholesale, retail, and food and beverage industries. The firm-level data allow us to construct a panel-data set. As for the data on offshore sourcing activity, we used the *Survey of Corporate*

Offshore Activities (*Kigyo Kaigai Katsudo Chosa*, in Japanese),[2] which is an academic survey conducted by the Research Institute of Economy, Trade and Industry (henceforth RIETI survey) on 14,062 manufacturing firms listed in the METI survey. The RIETI survey collected responses from 5,528 firms. Considering that other previously available firm-level data sets on offshoring include only a limited number of firms and are not designed to cover the entire manufacturing industry, this survey has a clear advantage in terms of its coverage. It has direct information on a binary choice of foreign outsourcing with contracting out, explicitly distinguished from domestic outsourcing and from arm's-length purchases in foreign markets. The survey covers not only outsourcing of production-related tasks, including final assembly, production of intermediates, and production of jigs/dies, but also outsourcing of service-related tasks, such as R&D, information services, customer support, and professional services. Although it is a one-shot survey, the data include the status of offshore sourcing of five years earlier, as a retrospective question. Hence, we matched the METI and RIETI data for 2000 and 2005. As a result, we could draw on more than 3,000 observations for each 2000 and 2005 sample with accurate information on the variables of interest.

With regard to the outsourcing partners, the survey distinguishes three types of firms: (a) own offshore subsidiaries, which are defined by majority ownership, (b) subsidiaries owned by other Japanese multinationals, and (c) foreign-owned firms, including either local firms or subsidiaries of multinationals from third countries.[3] As for the respondent firms, because two or more answers are permitted, the overlapping answer across three choices is potentially included in the data. In order to estimate the impact of offshoring, respectively, for offshore insourcing and offshore outsourcing separately, we constructed two dummy variables. One is the offshore insourcing dummy variable that takes a value of 1 if the firm engages in contracts with its own offshore subsidiaries and 0 for non-offshoring firms. The other dummy is for offshore outsourcing, which takes a value of 1 if

[2]Firm-level data of this survey cannot be publicly disclosed. The authors are allowed to access this firm-level data set as a part of a RIETI research project. For details and aggregate statistics of the survey, Ito *et al.* (2007) provided a comprehensive description of this survey.

[3]Since the category (a) concentrates on the majority-owned subsidiaries, the categories (b) and (c) could include minority-owned affiliates of the outsourcing firm.

the firm engages in exclusively arm's-length contracts with local firms and 0 for non-offshoring firms. Thus, the former dummy potentially includes the firms positively responding to the choice of both or either (b) or (c). The latter dummy covers the firms exclusively engaging in both or either (b) or (c), while the firms engaging in offshore insourcing are excluded from the sample.

To measure firm performance, we first calculated the value added as the total sales minus the sum of cost of goods sold and general and administrative costs minus wages, rental, depreciation, and tax costs. The total sales and part of the intermediate input are deflated by the output and input deflators, respectively. The deflators have been taken from the Japan Industrial Productivity (JIP) database for 2008, which has comprehensive Japanese industry-level data. The real capital stock is calculated by the perpetual inventory method, using the book value of fixed tangible assets and investment data from the METI surveys. The deflator of investment goods and the depreciation rate have also been sourced from the JIP database for 2008. The labor input indicates the number of total employees reported in the METI surveys. We estimate the TFP level for each firm using the above data for sampled firms for the period 1997–2005. The direct calculation of TFP using the estimated coefficients of capital stock and labor in the Cobb-Douglas function form has an endogeneity problem. As the benchmark of TFP, the estimated labor share and capital share are 0.76 and 0.23, respectively, when estimating the production function according to the Levinsohn and Petrin (2003) procedure.[4]

Differences of Productivity between Offshoring and Non-offshoring

Before analyzing the causal effect of offshoring, we examine the difference in the TFP distribution between offshoring firms and non-offshoring firms by pooling the data for 2000 and 2005. Figures 1 and 2 present the kernel density estimate of productivity for the firms engaging in offshore insourcing

[4]In this procedure, the purchase of inputs is used as a proxy variable for a productivity shock. We also applied an alternative method by using investment as the proxy, as proposed by Olley and Pakes (1996). However, the results were almost the same. In consideration of omitted firms with zero investment, we relied on the estimator by the Levinsohn–Petrin procedure.

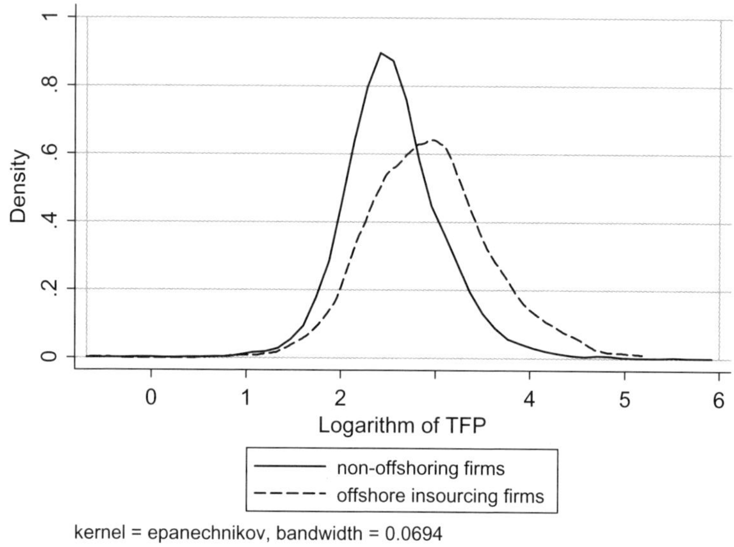

Note: Kernel density estimate is applied to the pooled data of 2000 and 2005.

Fig. 1. Differences in TFP: Offshore insourcing versus non-offshoring.

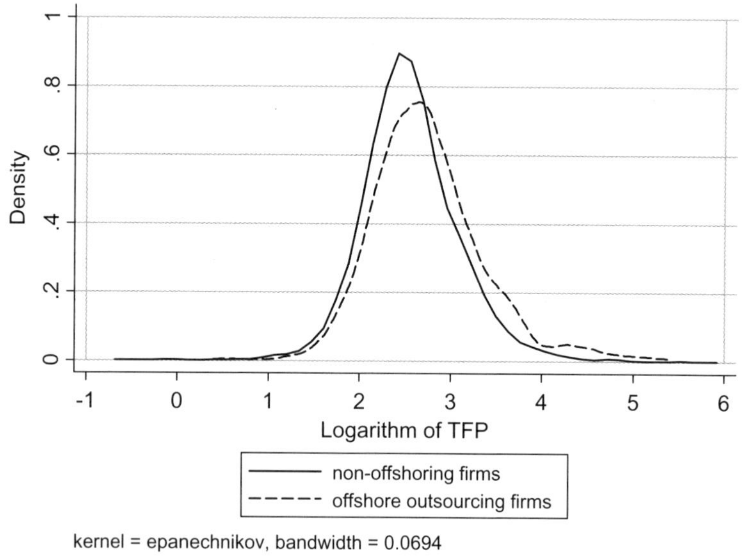

Note: Kernel density estimate is applied to the pooled data of 2000 and 2005.

Fig. 2. Differences in TFP: Offshore outsourcing versus non-offshoring.

and outsourcing compared to non-offshoring firms. Both results indicate that offshoring firms are likely to be more productive than non-offshoring firms. Further, we examined the difference in the TFP distribution by applying t-tests for equality of differences in the means of the distributions and two-sample Kolmogorov–Smirnov tests for equality of distribution functions. The differences with offshoring firms were statistically significant in the two tests. These results suggest that the productivity distribution of offshoring firms dominates that of non-offshoring firms.

Next, we graphically compare the changes in the productivity level of both offshoring and non-offshoring firms over time by using the panel data. The basic information at the firm-level is taken from the METI survey as the source for Japanese manufacturing firms, while the data on outsourcing are from the RIETI survey. Using the offshore insourcing and outsourcing dummies mentioned above and the panel data for the periods 1997–2005, we distinguished firms according to non-offshoring firms, offshore insourcing firms, and offshore outsourcing firms in 2000 and repeated this for later years. Non-offshoring firms are restricted to firms that did not engage in offshoring in either 2000 or 2005. Figure 3

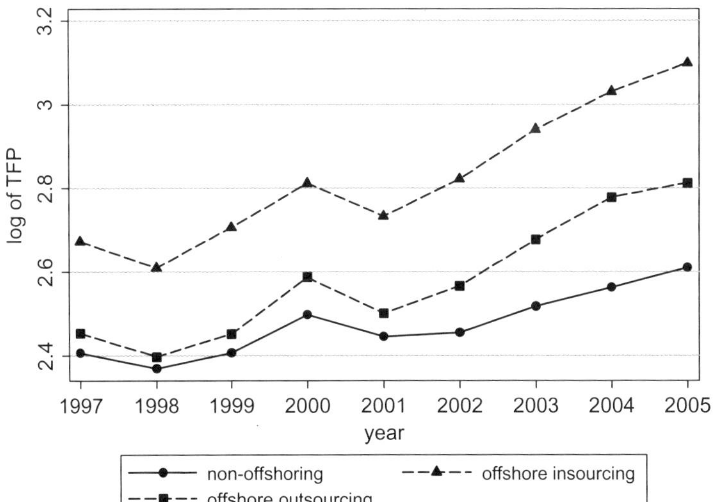

Note: Each mean value over time is calculated in terms of the firms that engage in offshore insourcing, outsourcing, and non-offshoring firms in 2000.

Fig. 3. Differences in TFP over time.

depicts the difference in the average of the logarithm of the TFP level over time between the three types as of 2000. The trends in the productivity level of offshoring firms provide important information to show the dynamic change attributed to offshoring. The figure shows that even before 2000, the TFP of offshore insourcing firms and offshore outsourcing firms was already higher than that of non-offshoring firms. Further, the difference in TFP between offshoring firms and non-offshoring firms has apparently expanded from year to year since around 2002. Although the difference in trend between the two would imply that offshoring activity yields high productivity, it cannot be identified as an influence by offshoring, and a further examination by econometric analysis would be required. More precisely, to compare the difference between offshoring firms and non-offshoring firms is not appropriate because the characteristics of both firms are potentially different, and it may be due to other factors. In the next section, we present a procedure to estimate the causal effect of offshoring on productivity.

III. THE EFFECT OF OFFSHORING ON PRODUCTIVITY GROWTH

Analytical Framework

The production of goods is a multistage process. Each stage of production activity can be considered to be a bundled task in the process of transformation from an intermediate product to a final product. At every stage, capital, labor, and intermediate goods are inputs. Outsourcing of a task is defined as unbundling the task from the production process and replacing it with intermediate goods produced outside of the firm.[5] If (1) the production activity of each stage is competitive, (2) prices of intermediate products are market dependent, and (3) primary factors such as capital and labor are available at a given price in the factor market, similar to the availability of labor at fixed wages in a labor market, a firm may be deficient in some stages of production because of the gap between the value of the marginal product of labor and the wage rate. In such a case, the firm will choose to: (1) unbundle a task from the production process and offshore it to a foreign

[5]See Feenstra and Hanson (1999), Antràs (2003), Grossman and Rossi-Hansburg (2008), and others.

country where the wage rate is lower than the value of marginal product of labor, (2) re-import processed intermediate products, and (3) include them in the production process of the final product. In this manner, outsourcing enables a firm to work around the deficits in its own production process.

Such a shift in resources to more efficient stages of a production process raises productivity growth. Previous studies have included offshoring by productivity growth in the aggregate production function. Our research investigates how a one-shot change in the production process affects the TFP as does the previous research by Görg and Hanley (2005) and Hijzen, Inui, and Todo (2006).

Empirical Strategy

On the basis of the framework of offshoring and productivity growth, we expect that offshoring positively affects a firm's TFP growth. The statistical analysis presented in the former section identifies only the average difference in the productivity between offshoring firms and non-offshoring firms but it cannot clarify the causality. In order to capture the causal effect of offshoring on firm productivity, we implement the PSM technique developed by Rosenbaum and Rubin (1983) with the DID technique. First, we estimate the binary response model on the choice of offshoring and gain the propensity score for each firm. In the second step, we match the similar non-offshoring firms with offshoring firms in terms of various firm characteristics using the propensity score by matching algorithms. Finally, we examine the difference in productivity growth between treated and matched control observations.

The data on offshoring used in this analysis are dichotomous, and we constructed the dummy variable, O_{it} that takes a value of 1 if the firm i enters into contracts with foreign suppliers in year t and 0 for non-offshoring firms. The productivity of firm i in year $t + s$ ($s \geq 0$) and the firm characteristics in year $t - 1$ are $Y_{i,t+s}$ and $X_{i,t-1}$, respectively. We define the causal effect of offshoring on productivity as the difference in the performance between the offshoring and non-offshoring firms by introducing the conditional independence assumption. This means that the decision on offshore sourcing and the potential productivity are stochastically independent for the firms having the same exogenous characteristics, $x_{i,t-1}$. The average causal effect is written as;

$$\begin{aligned}\delta' = {} & E(Y^1_{i,t+s}|O_{it} = 1, X_{i,t-1} = x_{i,t-1}) \\ & - E(Y^0_{i,t+s}|O_{it} = 0, X_{i,t-1} = x_{i,t-1})\end{aligned} \tag{1}$$

where $Y^1_{i,t+s}$ and $Y^0_{i,t+s}$ are potential outcomes according to the status of offshoring, and δ' is the average effect of treatment on the treated (ATT). The counterfactual group is created by using a selected group of non-offshoring firms that have similar firm characteristics, $x_{i,t-1}$. Thus, we need to extract non-offshoring firms with similar firm characteristics from the sample. Rosenbaum and Rubin (1983) propose using the propensity score to find the counterfactual group from the control group. The concrete procedure of this method is, first, to estimate predicted probabilities on entry of offshoring $\Pr(O_{it} = 1|X_{i,t-1} = x_{i,t-1})$ for each firm by probit or logit, and secondly, to select non-offshoring firms for which the probability is close to the probability of offshoring firms as the counterfactual group and, finally, to estimate the difference of its productivity among both. The ATT estimates under the PSM procedure are shown by the following form.

$$\delta^{PSM} = \frac{1}{N}\sum_{i\in T}\left(Y^1_{i,t+s} - \sum_{j\in C} W(\Pr(X_{i,t-1}), \Pr(X_{j,t-1}))Y^0_{j,t+s}\right) \tag{2}$$

where N is the number of offshoring firm and T refers to the treatment group. C refers to the control group. $W(\Pr(X_{i,t-1}), \Pr(X_{j,t-1}))$ and is a matching weight ($0 < W \leq 1$) which depends on the probabilities of both offshoring and non-offshoring firms.

The panel data enable us to control for the unobserved time-invariant firm individual effects by taking difference and to obtain more robust estimates. The PSM technique can be enhanced to the DID estimate for which time invariable, individual effects can be removed by taking the difference. The ATT estimates in this case can be written as follows.

$$\delta^{PSM-DID} = \frac{1}{N}\sum_{i\in T}\left(\Delta Y^1_{i,t+s} - \sum_{j\in C} W(\Pr(X_{i,t-1}), \Pr(X_{j,t-1}))\Delta Y^0_{j,t+s}\right) \tag{3}$$

We use two matching techniques, nearest-neighbor matching and kernel matching, to match offshoring firms with non-offshoring firms. Nearest-neighbor matching is to search out similar firms to which the difference of the participation probability is minimized as shown in the next expression from the control group (non-offshoring firms).

$$|p_i - p_j| = \min_{k \in \{D=0\}} \{|p_i - p_k|\} \tag{4}$$

In the case of nearest-neighbor matching, three different matching methods are tested. One is one-to-one matching, which matches each observation in the treatment group to only one control observation that has the closest propensity score. The second is k-nearest-neighbor matching, which allows matching more than one observation in the control group. The third is caliper matching, which each observation in the treatment group is matched with a observation in the control group that has the closest propensity score within the caliper that is set at 0.01 in this analysis.

Kernel matching is to apply the following matching weight in the Equations (2) and (3).

$$W = \frac{K(\Pr(X_{j,t-1}) - \Pr(X_{i,t-1}))/b}{\sum_{k \in \{R=0\}} K(\Pr(X_{k,t-1}) - \Pr(X_{i,t-1}))/b} \tag{5}$$

where K is a kernel function and b is bandwidth.[6]

IV. EMPIRICAL RESULTS

Propensity Score and Balancing Test

It is necessary to estimate the participation probability of whether to outsource to a foreign supplier with a contract as a procedure of the PSM technique. Following the empirical studies on determinants of offshoring (e.g., Girma and Görg, 2004; Kimura, 2002; Tomiura, 2005), we select the firm attributes expected to have an influence on the offshoring decision as explanatory variables, and obtain the predicted probabilities by estimating

[6] The Epanechnikov kernel function is applied, and bandwidth is set to be 0.06 in this analysis.

the following logit model

$$\ln\left(\frac{p_i}{1-p_i}\right) = \beta_0 + \beta_1(R/Q)_{it-1} + \beta_2 \ln L_{it-1} + \beta_3(K/L)_{it-1} + \beta_4 W_{it-1} + \beta_5(R\&D/Q)_{it-1} + \beta_6(S/L)_{it-1} + \beta_7 AGE_{it-1} \quad (6)$$

where subscript *it* denotes the index of the firm in the period t. The dependent variable is the log-odds ratio in terms of the probability on the participation in offshoring. We use lagged explanatory variables to avoid the simultaneity problem. The profit-to-total sales R/Q is included as a measure of business performance to control for possible self-selection.[7] The labor cost-saving strategies would be a major motivation to start offshoring in order to focus on core competencies. On the other hand, firms may need high technological capacity and skills to absorb output through offshoring activities. We add the capital–labor ratio K/L, wage per employees W, R&D expenditures over total sales *R&D*/Q and skill intensity defined as the number of employees in headquarters over total employees S/L. As other firm attributes, we employ the logarithm of the number of employees as a proxy for firm size ln$L$ and the firm age *AGE* to control for the firm's vintage effect. The variation among industries is controlled by two-digit industry dummy variables. Table 1 describes the summary statistics for each variable on the basis of the status of offshore insourcing and outsourcing.

Since we have the METI data with basic information at the firm-level for the period 1997–2005 and the RIETI data on offshore sourcing activity in 2000 and 2005, the logit model is estimated by cross-sectional data for 2000. Offshoring firms in 2000 are matched with non-offshoring firms that have similar characteristics,[8] and ATT-DID is estimated after 2000. Therefore, the explanatory variables in year 1999 are included in the model. The estimation results are displayed in Table 2. In both cases of offshore insourcing and outsourcing, the coefficient of the lagged profit rate is not statistically

---

[7]As suggested by Antràs and Helpman (2004), the productivity level would affect the decision of offshoring. We also confirmed that the results of ATT-DID is not substantially changed even if the lagged productivity level is added or adopted instead of the profit rate in the logit model. However, we rely on the model excluding the lagged productivity level in order to avoid a possible violation of the conditional independence assumption.

[8]The control group is defined as non-offshoring firms that did not perform offshore sourcing in both years of 2000 and 2005.

Table 1. **Descriptive statistics**

	Non-offshoring firms (2,840 obs.)		Offshore insourcing firms (273 obs.)		Total	
Variable	Mean	S.D	Mean	S.D	Mean	S.D
R/Q	0.027	0.056	0.032	0.054	0.027	0.056
lnL	5.041	0.845	6.167	1.398	5.138	0.959
K/L	13.395	19.844	15.096	14.127	13.541	19.423
W	4.764	1.52	5.418	1.615	4.82	1.539
R&D/Q	0.008	0.019	0.022	0.028	0.01	0.021
S/L	0.15	0.117	0.18	0.124	0.152	0.118
AGE	37.977	15.383	44.748	16.771	38.558	15.62
	Non-offshoring firms (2,840 obs.)		Offshore outsourcing firms (265 obs.)		Total	
Variable	Mean	S.D	Mean	S.D	Mean	S.D
R/Q	0.027	0.056	0.026	0.052	0.027	0.056
lnL	5.041	0.845	5.342	0.954	5.066	0.858
K/L	13.395	19.844	11.879	13.869	13.266	19.412
W	4.764	1.52	4.955	1.585	4.78	1.526
R&D/Q	0.008	0.019	0.015	0.025	0.009	0.02
S/L	0.15	0.117	0.18	0.124	0.152	0.118
AGE	37.977	15.383	39.799	15.753	38.131	15.421

significant, although it was forecast that the firms with good performance would be selected. The results show that firm size and skill intensity have a positive impact on the probability of participation in offshoring. The coefficient of the number of employees is significantly positive in both estimations. As the firm-level analyses on the determinants of internationalization have shown, the larger the firm size is, the more active offshoring is. The skill intensity measured by the ratio of employees in headquarters has a positive sign, suggesting that offshoring activities require firms to strengthen skill capabilities. As for the capital–labor ratio, a negative coefficient is expected if labor cost saving as a motivation of offshoring is supported. The coefficient of capital–labor ratio is not statistically significant in the case of insourcing, and is negative and significant in the case of outsourcing. Both coefficients of wage per employee and R&D intensity are not significant, while firm age is positively correlated with offshore

Table 2. Estimation results of logit

	Insourcing	Outsourcing
R/Q	1.771	0.436
	[1.332]	[1.194]
lnL	0.934	0.379
	[0.075]**	[0.078]**
K/L	−0.01	−0.012
	[0.005]	[0.006]*
W	−0.042	0.023
	[0.059]	[0.054]
R&D/Q	3.374	2.2
	[3.057]	[3.039]
S/L	2.143	1.907
	[0.611]**	[0.564]**
AGE	0.012	0.005
	[0.005]*	[0.005]
Industry dummies	Yes	Yes
Constant	−7.733	−4.504
	[0.448]**	[0.456]**
Observations	3,113	3,105
Log likelihood	−725.63	−833.31
Pseudo R2	0.216	0.08

Note: Standard errors in parenthesis; *, ** indicate significance at the 5% and 1% levels, respectively.

insourcing. The older firms are more inclined to engage in offshoring than the younger firms.[9]

It is necessary to match similar non-offshoring firms in terms of firm attributes with offshoring firms to obtain the ATT estimate by the PSM technique with high accuracy. The sample is restricted by imposing the common support condition, which means that non-offshoring firms whose probability is higher than offshoring firms with the maximum probability and offshoring firms whose probability is lower than non-offshoring firms

[9]As for the ATT estimated value using the PSM technique, the result was influenced by selecting the explanatory variable used for estimating participation probability (Heckman *et al.* (1998)). However, a substantial change was not evident in the following ATT estimate, even though the combination of explanatory variables changed as the variables were added or dropped, one by one, and the ATT estimate was tested. We also omit the variables that have no explanatory power and estimate ATT, but the change in the results was negligible.

with the minimum probability are excluded from the sample.[10] After the match, we carry out the balancing test to judge whether the difference of the mean value in terms of firm attributes used in the estimation for the participation probability between both groups is statistically different from 0. It can be judged that non-offshoring firms with firm attributes similar to offshoring firms are correctly matched if a significant difference is not statistically found for each variable between the two. As in all matching techniques, the null hypothesis that the difference of the means of the variable between offshoring firms and matched non-offshoring firms is zero is not rejected for all variables after the match, although the hypothesis is rejected in many cases before the match. This result indicates that the matched non-offshoring firms resemble the offshoring firms in terms of the firm attributes. The results of balancing tests for each variable used in the logit estimation are displayed in Tables A1 and A2.

Estimate of Offshoring Effect on Productivity

Using the propensity score on participation in offshoring gained from the logit estimation, we estimate the ATT with DID in terms of the logarithm of TFP in the matched sample. The effects of offshore insourcing and outsourcing on productivity may be different in magnitude. We estimate the effects of offshoring on TFP with respect to both offshore insourcing and outsourcing, distinguishing offshoring firms into firms engaging in both insourcing to a firm's foreign subsidiaries and outsourcing to local firms through arm's-length transactions and firms engaging in exclusively offshore outsourcing. In both cases, the control group is non-offshoring firms.

Table 3 presents the results of ATT with the DID estimate in the case of offshore insourcing. Since the effects of offshoring might have a time lag, the ATT estimate is calculated from the time of t to five years later, namely from 2000 to 2005 for which data are available. The difference in lnTFP is defined as lnTFP in each year minus that in year 2000. Hence, the estimates indicate the TFP growth rate due to offshoring. The first and second columns present the mean value of each status of offshoring, the third column displays ATT with DID estimates, and the results for testing the null of equivalence between groups are indicated in the right

[10]The loss of the number of observations by common support condition was limited.

Table 3. ATT with DID results on offshore insourcing

	One-to-one matching					k-nearest-neighbor matching				
	Offshoring		ATT with	t-test for mean equivalence		Offshoring		ATT with	t-test for mean equivalence	
Variable	Yes	No	DID	t-value	$p > \|t\|$	Yes	No	DID	t-value	$p > \|t\|$
ΔlnTFP2001	−0.062	−0.046	−0.016	−0.710	0.481	−0.062	−0.057	−0.005	−0.220	0.829
ΔlnTFP2002	−0.003	−0.007	0.003	0.120	0.907	−0.003	0.008	−0.012	−0.410	0.683
ΔlnTFP2003	0.133	0.087	0.045	1.310	0.190	0.133	0.092	0.040	1.150	0.252
ΔlnTFP2004	0.218	0.132	0.086	2.130	0.033	0.218	0.112	0.106	2.540	0.011
ΔlnTFP2005	0.284	0.187	0.097	2.120	0.034	0.284	0.168	0.116	2.600	0.010
	Caliper matching					Kernel matching				
	Offshoring		ATT with	t-test for mean equivalence		Offshoring		ATT with	t-test for mean equivalence	
Variable	Yes	No	DID	t-value	$p > \|t\|$	Yes	No	DID	t-value	$p > \|t\|$
ΔlnTFP2001	−0.061	−0.058	−0.003	−0.130	0.896	−0.062	−0.062	0.000	0.000	0.999
ΔlnTFP2002	−0.002	−0.003	0.001	0.030	0.977	−0.003	−0.005	0.001	0.040	0.965
ΔlnTFP2003	0.134	0.083	0.051	1.430	0.153	0.133	0.080	0.053	1.470	0.142
ΔlnTFP2004	0.224	0.121	0.103	2.500	0.013	0.218	0.121	0.097	2.320	0.021
ΔlnTFP2005	0.288	0.176	0.112	2.460	0.014	0.284	0.176	0.108	2.370	0.018

side of each panel. The difference after four or five years is positive and statistically significant at the significance level of 5% while those before 2003 are not significant. The results indicate that offshoring through intra-firm insourcing has a positive impact on productivity growth after controlling unobserved firm individual effects, but the effects appear with a time lag of four or five years. The estimated ATT with DID of Table 3, for instance, implies that offshore insourcing leads to a 9%–11% increase in TFP four or five years after offshoring.

We also examine the effect of offshore outsourcing to local firms in foreign countries on TFP growth. The ATT with DID estimates of offshore outsourcing are presented in Table 4. The estimates show the positive sign in most cases, but they are not statistically significant in any of the matching techniques. This result indicates that there is no difference in average productivity growth between non-offshoring firms matched to the treated and the firms conducting offshore outsourcing, and it is suggested that offshore outsourcing to local suppliers does not contribute to productivity growth.[11]

Discussion

The estimated results show that offshore insourcing increases productivity growth with a time lag of several years. On the other hand, the results of estimation for offshore outsourcing indicate that outsourcing through arm's-length contracts has no impact on productivity growth. It would be an interesting issue to discuss why the effect of offshore insourcing has a time-lag and why the results are different according to firm boundaries.

One possible explanation for our finding of a time lag is that the relocation of resources to other production processes within the firm takes a time to affect productivity. Offshoring activities enable firms to specialize in production processes with core competencies. However, resources shifted to other production processes, which are supposed to be more skill intensive than the processes that can be outsourced, would improve productivity through learning by doing. Therefore, it is expected that time is required until the reallocation of the resources can indeed contribute to productivity growth. The time lag until the appearance of the effect of offshore insourcing in our result may reflect this interpretation.

[11]We obtained the comparable result of the ATT estimate without the DID. See Tables A3 and A4.

Table 4. ATT with DID results on offshore outsourcing

	One-to-one matching					k-nearest-neighbor matching				
	Offshoring		ATT with	t-test for mean equivalence		Offshoring		ATT with	t-test for mean equivalence	
Variable	Yes	No	DID	t-value	$p > \|t\|$	Yes	No	DID	t-value	$p > \|t\|$
ΔlnTFP2001	−0.072	−0.073	0.0	0.020	0.986	−0.072	−0.079	0.007	0.280	0.782
ΔlnTFP2002	−0.024	−0.045	0.021	0.570	0.571	−0.024	−0.059	0.035	1.010	0.314
ΔlnTFP2003	0.087	0.098	−0.011	−0.270	0.784	0.087	0.054	0.033	0.820	0.415
ΔlnTFP2004	0.181	0.162	0.019	0.430	0.669	0.181	0.118	0.063	1.530	0.128
ΔlnTFP2005	0.218	0.209	0.009	0.170	0.865	0.218	0.165	0.052	1.070	0.286
	Caliper matching					Kernel matching				
	Offshoring		ATT with	t-test for mean equivalence		Offshoring		ATT with	t-test for mean equivalence	
Variable	Yes	No	DID	t-value	$p > \|t\|$	Yes	No	DID	t-value	$p > \|t\|$
ΔlnTFP2001	−0.072	−0.080	0.008	0.290	0.772	−0.072	−0.068	−0.004	−0.170	0.865
ΔlnTFP2002	−0.024	−0.060	0.036	1.030	0.306	−0.024	−0.044	0.019	0.610	0.543
ΔlnTFP2003	0.087	0.053	0.033	0.840	0.402	0.087	0.047	0.040	0.990	0.321
ΔlnTFP2004	0.181	0.117	0.064	1.550	0.121	0.181	0.107	0.074	1.770	0.077
ΔlnTFP2005	0.218	0.164	0.053	1.090	0.276	0.218	0.151	0.067	1.390	0.166

Regarding the second question, the result might reflect that the outsourced task is different according to firm boundaries. The survey on offshoring used in this study also contains disaggregated information on the types of tasks outsourced offshore at the firm level. The survey distinguishes three production-related tasks (production of intermediates, final assembly, and production of jigs/dies), four service-related tasks (R&D, information services, customer support, professional (legal, accounting, or financial) services, and the other tasks. We found that two tasks (the production of intermediates and final assembly) are most frequently offshore sourced and their share to total offshore sourcing is 35%. Moreover, the data show that final assembly tends to be relatively often insourced to firms' own foreign subsidiaries, while the production of intermediates concentrates on the case of outsourcing through arm's-length contracting.[12] Therefore, our results might be associated with the difference of tasks between insourcing and outsourcing. Firms engaging in insourcing the more labor-intensive production processes, such as final assembly, might possibly be able to concentrate on more advanced production processes compared with firms that choose to outsource the production of intermediates. The gain from specializing in more advanced production processes is expected to be larger than in other production processes that can be outsourced beyond the firm's boundaries. As a result, the rise of productivity is observed by the insourcing firm that has succeeded in subcontracting the final assembly stage in which productivity is expected to be low to outside the firm.[13]

Of course, it is expected that there are various factors affecting the different results besides the difference in tasks outsourced. First, our finding that the offshore insourcing has a positive impact on productivity while offshore outsourcing has no impact may be due to the difference in the level of offshoring.[14] More precisely, the productivity effects can be distinguished according to the extensive margin and the intensive margin depending on

[12]According to our survey as reported in Ito, Wakasugi, Tomiura (2007), Table 6, in around half of the cases, the final assembly and the production of intermediates are insourced within the boundary of multinationals and outsourced to foreign unrelated suppliers, respectively.

[13]Although it could be examined whether this interpretation is correct by further disaggregating data according to the task, we have not tested this because the number of observations decreased sharply.

[14]Grossman and Rossi-Hansberg (2008) suggest theoretically that the magnitude of the productivity effect depends on the range of offshored tasks.

the intensity of offshoring activities. However, we do not examine this issue because the data on the amount of offshore sourcing are not available. The magnitude of productivity effects would surely be different if the firms increase offshore sourcing. Also, one would expect that transfer pricing may affect the behavior of insourcing firms and cause the different result through the difference in offshoring costs across arm's-length and owned subsidiary. If multinational firms prefer to shift profits from abroad to the home country to avoid taxation abroad, the firms may have an incentive to engage in insourcing their tasks to foreign subsidiaries at a lower than arm's length price. As a result, it can be observed that the productivity gains concentrate on insourcing firms. However, an opposite influence is foreseen in the case of Japanese firms because the effective corporate tax rate in Japan is approximately 41% as of 2009, which is the highest in the world. It seems that the enterprise has moved the profit to foreign countries through transfer pricing. Therefore, transfer pricing is not expected to have a positive effect of insourcing at least while such a tax incentive should be controlled. Further examination of these issues would be required for a comprehensive understanding of the productivity effect of offshoring.

V. CONCLUSIONS

In recent years, there has been great interest in the examination of the impact of offshore sourcing that has increased rapidly and expanded over various tasks. This chapter has examined the causal effect of offshore sourcing on TFP growth by shedding light on the organizational form in terms of the ownership of suppliers and on the time lag in appearance of the effects, using Japanese firm-level data in manufacturing industries over the period, 2000–2005. The advantage of our study, over previous studies, is a distinctive investigation of offshore sourcing between offshore insourcing and outsourcing based on firm-level data. The effect of offshore sourcing has been examined separately with respect to offshore insourcing and outsourcing by distinguishing offshore sourcing firms into firms engaging in both insourcing to firm's foreign subsidiaries and outsourcing to local firms through arm's-length transactions and firms engaging in exclusively offshore outsourcing.

The results are summarized as follows. First, the impact of offshore insourcing within multinationals on productivity measured as TFP is found to be positive. One interesting finding is that there was a time-lag in the appearance of the impacts. This result implies that the effect is dynamic through learning by doing in more skill-intensive processes. Second, it is found that offshore outsourcing through arm's-length contracting out did not affect productivity. These contrasting results between offshore insourcing and outsourcing may indicate that the productivity gain is associated with the difference in offshoring tasks between the two types of sourcing.

ACKNOWLEDGMENTS

The authors deeply appreciate insightful comments from Wilhelm Kohler and other participants. The authors also thank the statistics offices of the Ministry of Economy, Trade and Industry and the Research Institute of Economy, Trade and Industry for granting permission to access firm-level data.

APPENDIX

Table A1. Balancing tests on offshore insourcing

(a) One-to-one matching

Variable	Sample	Offshoring Yes	Offshoring No	% bias (Yes−No)/No × 100	% reduction of |bias|	t-test for mean equivalence: t-value	t-test for mean equivalence: $p > \|t\|$
R/Q_{t-1}	Unmatched	0.035	0.028	12.5		1.90	0.057
	Matched	0.034	0.028	10.9	12.9	1.35	0.178
lnL_{t-1}	Unmatched	6.261	5.083	102.0		20.53	0.000
	Matched	6.103	6.040	5.5	94.6	0.59	0.555
K/L_{t-1}	Unmatched	15.250	13.559	9.9		1.35	0.177
	Matched	15.011	12.873	12.6	−26.4	1.85	0.064
W_{t-1}	Unmatched	5.463	4.795	43.5		7.00	0.000
	Matched	5.369	5.268	6.6	85.0	0.72	0.469
RD/Q_{t-1}	Unmatched	0.024	0.009	59.7		11.08	0.000
	Matched	0.022	0.020	8.8	85.3	0.86	0.389
S/L_{t-1}	Unmatched	0.180	0.150	25.9		4.17	0.000
	Matched	0.180	0.179	1.2	95.2	0.13	0.893
AGE_{t-1}	Unmatched	45.828	38.417	47.3		7.55	0.000
	Matched	45.115	44.096	6.5	86.2	0.70	0.483

(Continued)

Table A1. (*Continued*)

(b) k-nearest-neighbor matching

Variable	Sample	Offshoring Yes	Offshoring No	% bias (Yes−No)/No × 100	% reduction of [bias]	t-test for mean equivalence t-value	$p > \|t\|$
R/Q_{t-1}	Unmatched	0.035	0.028	12.5		1.90	0.057
	Matched	0.034	0.033	1.5	87.6	0.19	0.852
$\ln L_{t-1}$	Unmatched	6.261	5.083	102.0		20.53	0.000
	Matched	6.103	6.094	0.8	99.2	0.08	0.934
K/L_{t-1}	Unmatched	15.250	13.559	9.9		1.35	0.177
	Matched	15.011	14.617	2.3	76.7	0.28	0.776
W_{t-1}	Unmatched	5.463	4.795	43.5		7.00	0.000
	Matched	5.369	5.387	−1.2	97.3	−0.13	0.897
RD/Q_{t-1}	Unmatched	0.024	0.009	59.7		11.08	0.000
	Matched	0.022	0.023	−2.2	96.4	−0.21	0.834
S/Lt−1	Unmatched	0.180	0.150	25.9		4.17	0.000
	Matched	0.180	0.181	−0.8	97.0	−0.09	0.932
AGE_{t-1}	Unmatched	45.828	38.417	47.3		7.55	0.000
	Matched	45.115	45.032	0.5	98.9	0.06	0.954

(c) Caliper matching

Variable	Sample	Offshoring Yes	Offshoring No	% bias (Yes−No)/No × 100	% reduction of [bias]	t-test for mean equivalence t-value	$p > \|t\|$
R/Q_{t-1}	Unmatched	0.035	0.028	12.5		1.90	0.057
	Matched	0.033	0.033	0.7	94.7	0.08	0.938
$\ln L_{t-1}$	Unmatched	6.261	5.083	102.0		20.53	0.000
	Matched	6.017	6.007	0.8	99.2	0.09	0.928
K/L_{t-1}	Unmatched	15.250	13.559	9.9		1.35	0.177
	Matched	14.614	14.280	2.0	80.2	0.24	0.812
W_{t-1}	Unmatched	5.463	4.795	43.5		7.00	0.000
	Matched	5.333	5.354	−1.4	96.8	−0.15	0.880
RD/Q_{t-1}	Unmatched	0.024	0.009	59.7		11.08	0.000
	Matched	0.021	0.022	−1.6	97.4	−0.15	0.880
S/L_{t-1}	Unmatched	0.180	0.150	25.9		4.17	0.000
	Matched	0.182	0.181	1.2	95.3	0.13	0.899
AGE_{t-1}	Unmatched	45.828	38.417	47.3		7.55	0.000
	Matched	44.749	45.341	−3.8	92.0	−0.40	0.690

(*Continued*)

Table A1. (*Continued*)

(d) Kernel matching

Variable	Sample	Offshoring Yes	Offshoring No	% bias (Yes−No)/No × 100	% reduction of [bias]	t-test for mean equivalence t-value	t-test for mean equivalence $p > \|t\|$
R/Q_{t-1}	Unmatched	0.035	0.028	12.5		1.90	0.057
	Matched	0.034	0.033	1.7	86.4	0.20	0.841
lnL_{t-1}	Unmatched	6.261	5.083	102.0		20.53	0.000
	Matched	6.103	6.052	4.4	95.7	0.46	0.644
K/L_{t-1}	Unmatched	15.250	13.559	9.9		1.35	0.177
	Matched	15.011	14.508	3.0	70.3	0.38	0.704
W_{t-1}	Unmatched	5.463	4.795	43.5		7.00	0.000
	Matched	5.369	5.299	4.6	89.5	0.51	0.607
RD/Q_{t-1}	Unmatched	0.024	0.009	59.7		11.08	0.000
	Matched	0.022	0.022	0.9	98.6	0.08	0.934
S/L_{t-1}	Unmatched	0.180	0.150	25.9		4.17	0.000
	Matched	0.180	0.176	3.7	85.6	0.40	0.689
AGE_{t-1}	Unmatched	45.828	38.417	47.3		7.55	0.000
	Matched	45.115	44.156	6.1	87.1	0.66	0.508

Table A2. Balancing tests on offshore outsourcing

(a) One-to-one matching

Variable	Sample	Offshoring Yes	Offshoring No	% bias (Yes−No)/No × 100	% reduction of [bias]	t-test for mean equivalence t-value	t-test for mean equivalence $p > \|t\|$
R/Q_{t-1}	Unmatched	0.028	0.028	−0.4		−0.05	0.958
	Matched	0.028	0.030	−3.9	−1026.0	−0.46	0.643
lnL_{t-1}	Unmatched	5.360	5.083	31.6		5.09	0.000
	Matched	5.356	5.263	10.6	66.6	1.14	0.255
K/L_{t-1}	Unmatched	11.197	13.559	−14.1		−1.86	0.062
	Matched	11.231	9.672	9.3	34.0	1.62	0.105
W_{t-1}	Unmatched	4.956	4.795	10.5		1.66	0.096
	Matched	4.965	4.806	10.3	1.7	1.22	0.223
RD/Q_{t-1}	Unmatched	0.014	0.009	23.9		4.08	0.000
	Matched	0.014	0.016	−7.4	69.1	−0.70	0.486
S/L_{t-1}	Unmatched	0.176	0.150	22.4		3.58	0.000
	Matched	0.177	0.176	0.5	97.8	0.05	0.958
AGE_{t-1}	Unmatched	39.796	38.417	9.0		1.39	0.164
	Matched	39.663	39.682	−0.1	98.6	−0.01	0.988

(*Continued*)

Table A2. (*Continued*)

(b) k-nearest-neighbor matching

Variable	Sample	Offshoring Yes	Offshoring No	% bias (Yes−No)/ No × 100	% reduction of [bias]	t-test for mean equivalence t-value	t-test for mean equivalence $p > \|t\|$
R/Q_{t-1}	Unmatched	0.028	0.028	−0.4		−0.05	0.958
	Matched	0.028	0.027	2.1	−512.0	0.24	0.808
lnL_{t-1}	Unmatched	5.360	5.083	31.6		5.09	0.000
	Matched	5.356	5.320	4.0	87.2	0.43	0.666
K/L_{t-1}	Unmatched	11.197	13.559	−14.1		−1.86	0.062
	Matched	11.231	10.824	2.4	82.8	0.39	0.695
W_{t-1}	Unmatched	4.956	4.795	10.5		1.66	0.096
	Matched	4.965	4.954	0.7	93.2	0.08	0.933
RD/Q_{t-1}	Unmatched	0.014	0.009	23.9		4.08	0.000
	Matched	0.014	0.015	−4.3	82.1	−0.42	0.673
S/L_{t-1}	Unmatched	0.176	0.150	22.4		3.58	0.000
	Matched	0.177	0.180	−2.6	88.4	−0.28	0.780
AGE_{t-1}	Unmatched	39.796	38.417	9.0		1.39	0.164
	Matched	39.663	40.401	−4.8	46.5	−0.56	0.574

(c) Caliper matching

Variable	Sample	Offshoring Yes	Offshoring No	% bias (Yes−No)/ No × 100	% reduction of [bias]	t-test for mean equivalence t-value	t-test for mean equivalence $p > \|t\|$
R/Q_{t-1}	Unmatched	0.028	0.028	−0.4		−0.05	0.958
	Matched	0.028	0.027	2.1	−487.1	0.23	0.815
lnL_{t-1}	Unmatched	5.360	5.083	31.6		5.09	0.000
	Matched	5.356	5.317	4.4	85.9	0.48	0.632
K/L_{t-1}	Unmatched	11.197	13.559	−14.1		−1.86	0.062
	Matched	11.231	10.811	2.5	82.2	0.40	0.686
W_{t-1}	Unmatched	4.956	4.795	10.5		1.66	0.096
	Matched	4.965	4.950	0.9	91.2	0.11	0.914
RD/Q_{t-1}	Unmatched	0.014	0.009	23.9		4.08	0.000
	Matched	0.014	0.015	−3.8	84.3	−0.37	0.711
S/L_{t-1}	Unmatched	0.176	0.150	22.4		3.58	0.000
	Matched	0.177	0.179	−2.3	89.7	−0.25	0.804
AGE_{t-1}	Unmatched	39.796	38.417	9.0		1.39	0.164
	Matched	39.663	40.448	−5.1	43.1	−0.60	0.550

(*Continued*)

Table A2. (*Continued*)

(d) Kernel matching

Variable	Sample	Offshoring Yes	Offshoring No	% bias (Yes−No)/No × 100	% reduction of |bias|	*t*-test for mean equivalence *t*-value	*t*-test for mean equivalence $p > \|t\|$
R/Q_{t-1}	Unmatched	0.028	0.028	−0.4		−0.05	0.958
	Matched	0.028	0.028	−0.1	68.6	−0.01	0.990
lnL_{t-1}	Unmatched	5.360	5.083	31.6		5.09	0.000
	Matched	5.356	5.305	5.8	81.7	0.62	0.537
K/L_{t-1}	Unmatched	11.197	13.559	−14.1		−1.86	0.062
	Matched	11.231	11.592	−2.2	84.7	−0.31	0.758
W_{t-1}	Unmatched	4.956	4.795	10.5		1.66	0.096
	Matched	4.965	4.931	2.2	79.2	0.25	0.802
RD/Q_{t-1}	Unmatched	0.014	0.009	23.9		4.08	0.000
	Matched	0.014	0.014	3.5	85.3	0.36	0.719
S/L_{t-1}	Unmatched	0.176	0.150	22.4		3.58	0.000
	Matched	0.177	0.172	3.6	83.7	0.39	0.698
AGE_{t-1}	Unmatched	39.796	38.417	9.0		1.39	0.164
	Matched	39.663	39.599	0.4	95.4	0.05	0.962

Table A3. ATT estimates on offshore insourcing

	One-to-one matching					k-nearest neighbor matching				
	Offshoring			t-test for mean equivalence		Offshoring			t-test for mean equivalence	
Variable	Yes	No	ATT	t-value	$p > \|t\|$	Yes	No	ATT	t-value	$p > \|t\|$
lnTFP2000	2.786	2.741	0.044	0.980	0.330	2.786	2.777	0.009	0.190	0.848
lnTFP2001	2.721	2.692	0.029	0.600	0.547	2.721	2.719	0.002	0.030	0.973
lnTFP2002	2.791	2.741	0.051	0.980	0.328	2.791	2.796	−0.004	−0.080	0.935
lnTFP2003	2.924	2.836	0.088	1.600	0.110	2.924	2.874	0.050	0.910	0.364
lnTFP2004	3.005	2.865	0.140	2.450	0.015	3.005	2.888	0.117	2.070	0.039
lnTFP2005	3.070	2.929	0.141	2.380	0.018	3.070	2.945	0.125	2.160	0.031
	Caliper matching					Kernel matching				
	Offshoring			t-test for mean equivalence		Offshoring			t-test for mean equivalence	
Variable	Yes	No	ATT	t-value	$p > \|t\|$	Yes	No	ATT	t-value	$p > \|t\|$
lnTFP2000	2.757	2.758	−0.001	−0.010	0.990	2.786	2.762	0.024	0.540	0.589
lnTFP2001	2.695	2.702	−0.006	−0.130	0.895	2.721	2.700	0.022	0.450	0.651
lnTFP2002	2.766	2.764	0.001	0.020	0.982	2.791	2.763	0.028	0.530	0.597
lnTFP2003	2.895	2.844	0.051	0.920	0.356	2.924	2.847	0.077	1.390	0.165
lnTFP2004	2.981	2.875	0.106	1.870	0.062	3.005	2.882	0.123	2.150	0.032
lnTFP2005	3.045	2.934	0.111	1.900	0.058	3.070	2.937	0.133	2.250	0.025

Table A4. ATT estimates on offshore outsourcing

	One-to-one matching					k-nearest neighbor matching				
	Offshoring			t-test for mean equivalence		Offshoring			t-test for mean equivalence	
Variable	Yes	No	ATT	t-value	$p > \|t\|$	Yes	No	ATT	t-value	$p > \|t\|$
lnTFP2000	2.575	2.577	−0.002	−0.060	0.951	2.575	2.590	−0.015	−0.390	0.698
lnTFP2001	2.499	2.511	−0.012	−0.300	0.767	2.499	2.513	−0.014	−0.330	0.741
lnTFP2002	2.552	2.532	0.020	0.430	0.666	2.552	2.533	0.018	0.390	0.699
lnTFP2003	2.675	2.673	0.002	0.040	0.968	2.675	2.643	0.032	0.610	0.542
lnTFP2004	2.759	2.740	0.018	0.340	0.733	2.759	2.707	0.052	0.960	0.337
lnTFP2005	2.793	2.786	0.006	0.110	0.915	2.793	2.756	0.037	0.620	0.535
	Caliper matching					Kernel matching				
	Offshoring			t-test for mean equivalence		Offshoring			t-test for mean equivalence	
Variable	Yes	No	ATT	t-value	$p > \|t\|$	Yes	No	ATT	t-value	$p > \|t\|$
lnTFP2000	2.575	2.589	−0.014	−0.360	0.722	2.575	2.568	0.007	0.170	0.862
lnTFP2001	2.499	2.511	−0.012	−0.290	0.770	2.499	2.502	−0.003	−0.070	0.943
lnTFP2002	2.552	2.532	0.020	0.430	0.669	2.552	2.528	0.024	0.520	0.601
lnTFP2003	2.675	2.641	0.034	0.650	0.513	2.675	2.616	0.060	1.130	0.258
lnTFP2004	2.759	2.704	0.054	1.010	0.315	2.759	2.674	0.084	1.540	0.124
lnTFP2005	2.793	2.753	0.039	0.660	0.509	2.793	2.719	0.074	1.250	0.213

REFERENCES

Amiti, M. and S. Wei (2006). "Services Offshoring and Productivity: Evidence from the U.S." NBER Working Paper, No. 11926.

Antràs, P. (2003). "Firms, Contracts, and Trade Structure." *Quarterly Journal of Economics*, 118(4): pp. 1375–1418.

Antràs, P. and E. Helpman (2004). "Global Sourcing." *Journal of Political Economy*, 112(3): pp. 552–580.

Baldwin, R. and F. Robert-Nicoud (2007). "Offshoring: General Equilibrium Effects on Wages, Production and Trade." NBER Working Papers 12991, National Bureau of Economic Research, Inc.

Egger, P. and H. Egger (2006). "International Outsourcing and the Productivity of Low-skilled Labor in the EU." *Economic Inquiry*, 44(1): pp. 98–108.

Ekholm, K. and K. Hakkala (2006). "The Effect of Offshoring on Labor Demand: Evidence from Sweden." CEPR Working Paper No. 5648.

Feenstra, R. C. and G. H. Hanson (1996). "Globalization, Outsourcing, and Wage Inequality." *American Economic Review*, 86(2): pp. 240–245.

Feenstra, R. C. and G. H. Hanson (1999). "The Impact of Outsourcing and High-Technology Capital on Wages: Estimates for the U.S., 1979–1990." *Quarterly Journal of Economics*, 114(3): pp. 907–941.

Geishecker, I. and H. Görg (2005). "Do Unskilled Workers Always Lose From Fragmentation?" *The North American Journal of Economics and Finance*, 16(1): pp. 81–92.

Girma, S. and H. Görg (2004). "Outsourcing, Foreign Ownership, and Productivity: Evidence from UK Establishment-level Data." *Review of International Economics*, 12: pp. 817–832.

Görg, H. and A. Hanley (2005). "International Outsourcing and Productivity: Evidence from the Irish Electronics Industry." *The North American Journal of Economics and Finance*, 16(2): pp. 255–269.

Görg, H., A. Hanley and E. Strobl (2008). "Productivity Effects of International Outsourcing: Evidence from Plant Level Data." *Canadian Journal of Economics*, 41(2): pp. 670–688.

Grossman, G. M. and E. Rossi-Hansberg (2008). "Trading Tasks: A Simple Theory of Offshoring." *American Economic Review*, 98(5): pp. 1978–1997.

Head, K. and J. Ries (2002). "Offshore Production and Skill Upgrading by Japanese Manufacturing Firms." *Journal of International Economics*, 58(1): pp. 81–105.

Heckman, J., H. Ichimura, J. Smith and P. Todd (1998). "Characterizing Selection Bias Using Experimental Data." *Econometrica*, 66(5): pp. 1017–1098.

Helg, R. and L. Tajoli (2005). "Patterns of International Fragmentation of Production and Implications for the Labour Markets." *North American Journal of Economics and Finance*, 16(2): pp. 233–254.

Hijzen, A., H. Görg and R. C. Hine (2005). "International Outsourcing and the Skill Structure of Labour Demand in the United Kingdom." *Economic Journal*, 115(506): pp. 860–878.

Hijzen, A., T. Inui and Y. Todo (2006). "Does Offshoring Pay? Firm-Level Evidence from Japan." RIETI Discussion Paper Series 07-E-005.

Ito, B., E. Tomiura and R. Wakasugi (2007). "Dissecting Offshore Outsourcing and R&D: A Survey of Japanese Manufacturing Firms." RIETI Discussion Paper Series 07-E-060.

Ito, K. and K. Tanaka (2009). "Does Offshoring Improve Domestic Productivity? Evidence from Japanese Manufacturing Industries." (mimeo).

Kimura, F. (2002). "Subcontracting and the Performance of Small and Medium Firms in Japan." *Small Business Economics*, 18(1–3): pp. 163–175.

Levinsohn, J. and A. Petrin (2003). "Estimating Production Functions Using Inputs to Control for Unobservables." *Review of Economic Studies*, 70(2): pp. 317–341.

Olley, S. G. and A. Pakes (1996). "The Dynamics of Productivity in the Telecommunications Equipment Industry." *Econometrica*, 64(6): pp. 1263–1297.

Rosenbaum, P. and D. Rubin (1983). "The Central Role of the Propensity Score in Observational Studies for Causal Effects." *Biometrika*, 70: pp. 41–55.

Tomiura, E. (2005). "Foreign Outsourcing and Firm-level Characteristics: Evidence from Japanese Manufacturers." *Journal of the Japanese and International Economies*, 19: pp. 255–271.

Comment

Wilhelm K. Kohler

I. INTRODUCTION

The public discussion and anxiety about offshoring are mainly focused on wage inequality and job losses. This is mirrored by a corresponding focus also of the academic literature, both theoretical and empirical. Ito, Tomiura, and Wakasugi (henceforth ITW) look at the productivity effect of offshoring, which has repeatedly been pointed out in theoretical models of offshoring, but which has taken somewhat of a back seat in empirical research. The paper is entirely empirical, and its contribution is twofold: On the methodological side, it tries to address the issue of *causality*. And on the data side, it incorporates the distinction between *intra-firm* and *arms-length* offshoring and, to some extent, the distinction between offshoring of *components* and offshoring of *service inputs* (by manufacturing firms). Both are welcome innovations, but the issue of causality surely is of particular interest.

The problem of causality is relatively obvious. But perhaps the paper could still gain from a somewhat clearer picture of the theoretical background, which could reinforce the case for trying to sort out causality. There are models of offshoring that stress a productivity effect of offshoring, as well as models that suggest a reverse channel of causality. Among the former, we can distinguish three different types of channels. One is the variety effect stressed by Ethier (1982) without reference to offshoring, but clearly relevant in the present context. It would suggest that firms may enhance the variety of inputs available through offshoring. If inputs are imperfect substitutes in a Dixit–Stiglitz fashion, then offshoring should increase a firm's productivity. But even if inputs are perfect substitutes, as in Grossman and Rossi-Hansberg (2008) where inputs are dubbed tasks, there is a potential productivity effect from a higher degree of "north-south" task trade, provided that this trade is driven by a reduction in real trade cost. In Grossman and Rossi-Hansberg (2011) it is shown that even "north–north" trade may increase firms' productivity, due to economies of scale. However, the effect is not unambiguous, since it is driven by external economies of scale, with the usual multiplicity of equilibria that comes along with such externalities.

So much for the first type of causality that is at the center of this study. At the same time, however, there are models stressing that firms pursue different sourcing strategies, *because* they are differently productive. The most relevant case in point has been stressed in Antràs and Helpman (2004, 2008), where firms select themselves into different modes of domestic and foreign sourcing, including intra-firm as well as arms-length offshore sourcing, based on different productivity levels. If this plays a role in the data, then inferring a productivity effect of offshoring from cross-section firm-level evidence on offshoring and productivity is bound to be fraught with methodological problems.

Given this two-sided causality stressed in the literature, the case for the ITW study seems quite obvious. Causality certainly has not been adequately addressed in existing literature, hence this is a welcome contribution. To sort out causality, ITW propose to apply propensity score matching (PSM) techniques to a panel data set, in order to avoid these problems in testing for causality running *from offshoring to productivity*. Such techniques enjoy huge popularity in other areas of applied economic research, particularly in labor economics, but have so far not been applied to test for a productivity effect of offshoring.

Entirely empirical in nature, the study's focus lies squarely with how to design an appropriate framework to exploit the information contained in two firm-level data sets, one (METI-survey) giving detailed firm characteristics from 1997 through 2005, the other (RIETI-survey) revealing the offshoring status of firms in 2000 and 2005. The authors are able to match these data sets, and they try to exploit the information through a *treatment analysis* based on *propensity-score-matching* of firms.

Treatment is defined as the status of a firm engaging in intrafirm or arm's-length offshoring, respectively, in 2000. The outcome of interest is a firm's productivity level in each of the years from 2001 to 2005. The treatment effect is defined as the *difference in difference*. Specifically, ITW first compute the difference between a firm's productivity level in each of these years and its level in 2000, i.e., its productivity growth, and then compare productivity-growth rates across offshoring and non-offshoring firms. This comparison, of course, must control for relevant firm heterogeneity. Ideally, one would compare "twin firms" where one receives treatment (offshoring) and the other does not. The study tries to achieve this by means of propensity-score-matching, based on firm-level characteristics of 1999 and using three alternative matching criteria.

As noted, the analysis is entirely empirical, with a methodological emphasis on alternative propensity score matching criteria. It is not explained why some firms do offshoring of one type or another, while others do not. Nor is it specified why offshoring should improve a firm's productivity. Hence, the empirical analysis is not attempting to *test any specific model prediction.* I think that leaving theoretical details in the background is legitimate, given that we have several models that stress productivity effects of offshoring, as well as models that explain firms' sourcing strategy. But I would argue that our understanding of the exercise and the results obtained may be enhanced by *adding a theoretical perspective.* This is the main purpose of my comment.

II. A THEORETICAL PERSPECTIVE ON THE APPROACH

What is the type of scenario through which ITW hope to identify a causal effect of offshoring on a firm's productivity growth? Suppose we observe a universe of firms in year $t-1$, which may be heterogeneous in several ways. Some of this heterogeneity is observed through a host of firm characteristics $X_{i,t-1}$. In particular, some of them are involved in offshoring, while others are not. Some do so by arm's-length transactions (outsourcing), some do it in an intrafirm mode. Suppose that the difference in year t sourcing strategies is based on firms' contemporaneous productivity levels, as in Antràs and Helpman (2004). Each of these firms has its own trajectory of productivity growth, with productivity levels $Y_{i,t+s}$, $s = 1 \ldots 5$. Potentially, these growth trajectories may also reflect a firm's year-t-sourcing strategy.

In a *deterministic* world without any exogenous shocks, we would not expect to find any "twin firms" (with the same characteristics $X_{i,t-1}$) with two different sourcing strategies in period t. In a *stochastic* world, we might stipulate that firm characteristics X explain the *probability* that firm i is engaged in a specific mode of offshoring, but due to noise the data would have "twin firms" with different sourcing modes, both in period $t-1$ and in period t. If offshoring does have a productivity effect, and if there is some persistence in the dynamics (of both the offshoring status and the productivity effect), the subsequent productivity trajectories of firms with the same characteristics $X_{i,t-1}$ would differ, depending on whether or not they do offshoring in $t-1$. Then, we would expect to detect the productivity effect of offshoring through

$$[\Delta_{2000+1,2000} Y_i | O_{i,2000} = 1, X_{i,1999}] \\ - [\Delta_{2000+1,2000} Y_j | O_{j,2000} = 0, X_{j,1999} = X_{i,1999}]$$

where Δ is the difference operator and $O_{i,2000} = 1$ indicates offshoring in year 2000, and $O_{i,2000} = 0$ otherwise. The magnitude of this productivity effect is likely to be industry specific. In the empirical analysis, this could be accommodated through industry-dummies. In the empirical analysis, the condition $X_{j,1999} = X_{i,1999}$ is approximated by close propensity scores of firms i and j, based on a Logit-estimation of an offshoring regression.

The probabilistic interpretation of offshoring would seem to offer some "theoretical" justification for ITW using the propensity-score techniques. But the specification of the Logit model of offshoring estimated for subsequent score matching seems a bit *ad hoc* to me. The specification views offshoring as driven by scale and skill intensity. It is not obvious why this should be the case. Of special relevance to the present purpose: Why does the specification not allow for the productivity level to play a role, as suggested by Antràs and Helpman (2004)? As regards the factor intensity, I think one should make a distinction, conceptually at least, between average and marginal factor intensities, as I have suggested in Kohler (2004). But presumably the data available here do not allow the authors to empirically capture this distinction.

There is an additional question that worries me. Might there be unobserved heterogeneity across firms pertaining to the time span 2001–2005, unrelated to their offshoring behavior in 2000, and not captured by their propensity score? If so, this might affect the legitimacy of the treatment analysis. It seems to me that, in general, such heterogeneity should be expected. Put somewhat differently, there might be idiosyncratic firm-specific shocks that arrive in the years 2001 up to 2005, which may lead firms j who had $O_{j,2000} = 0$ to start up offshoring some time in between 2000 and 2005, with an ensuing positive productivity effect during that same time span. If so, then this would seem to compromise the analysis. It might, therefore, be desirable to define non-offshoring "twins" as firms that exhibit both, $O_{j,2000} = 0$ and $O_{j,2005} = 0$.

Related to the previous point: What if a firm identified as $O_{i,t-1} = O_{i,t} = 1$ has in fact started offshoring already 10 years ago? From the data, we cannot tell whether or not this is the case. This firm is now compared to a "twin firm" with $O_{j,t-1} = O_{j,t} = 0$. If there is a productivity *level effect*, then — other things equal — t should still have a higher productivity *level* than j in periods $t + s$ for which we do the treatment analysis. But since, for good reason, we do it in a diff-in-diff manner, and if — plausibly — the entire productivity level effect has been reached by t, then both firms will exhibit the same stationary level of TFP, assuming for the sake of the argument that TFP-changes are driven *only* by offshoring.

Finally, let me venture a more speculative thought. Think about some initial equilibrium with purely domestic sourcing, and offshoring arising as a new technological option, in the sense of a discrete "regime switch". The work by Antràs and Helpman (2004, 2008) suggests a certain relative frequency distribution of different types of offshoring, which reflects an underlying productivity distribution across firms. If the noise in the offshoring status that I have alluded to just before is uncorrelated to productivity (and if the model is correct), then this relationship between the two types of distributions should also be present in the data. Now, if offshoring exerts a positive influence on a firm's productivity growth, this should have an effect on its subsequent sourcing decisions, in line with Antràs and Helpman (2004). In other words, offshoring generates a repeated adjustment of firms' sourcing decisions, in response to the productivity effects of *earlier* offshoring decisions.

Pressing this into a one-period framework, we should obtain something like a mapping of the productivity distribution into a distribution of productivity *changes*. In its most general form, then, the research question of ITW is whether there is an *ergodic distribution of productivity* that emerges under offshoring, and whether or not this dominates the distribution without offshoring. Answering this question is surely beyond this study, but it would still be interesting to see if the productivity growth effect in 2001–2005 of offshoring in 2000 has a systematic effect on offshoring behavior in 2005, which *is* observed in the RIETI data set.

III. THE NATURE OF THE PRODUCTIVITY EFFECT

Why should a firm's productivity be affected by its sourcing of inputs? The notion of a positive productivity effect of offshoring was first brought into focus by Feenstra and Hanson (1999), but has recently been formulated in a particularly illuminating and sharp way by Grossman and Rossi-Hansberg (2008). In a very general sense, by the logic of revealed preference, the possibility of offshoring, compared to a case where all inputs must be procured domestically, *is* a productivity increase, at least for the firms that make use of this option. Looked at in this way, the positive productivity effect is trivial.

However, on closer inspection, and including variations in the *degree* of offshoring, in addition to the question of *whether* or not firms are offshoring, the productivity effect of offshoring becomes far less trivial. In general, offshoring and productivity changes are both endogenous phenomena and the direction of their co-movement in the data depends on the type of exogenous shock that drives both things. If it is a *reduction of offshoring cost*, as in Grossman and Rossi-Hansberg (2008), then it seems fairly obvious that TFP, if measured correctly, should rise. Indeed, the kind of task-trade alluded to by the authors may be modeled in such a way that the reduction in offshoring cost and the associated increase in the extensive margin of offshoring (types of tasks imported instead of performed domestically) ultimately shows up in an *equivalent sector-biased TFP-change*; see Kohler (2009). This effect might be difficult to measure, given available data, but the principal presence and nature of a positive productivity effect is clear.

However, things are different, if such an extension of the extensive margin of offshoring happens as an integral part of a firm's structural adjustment, say to a terms of trade shock, as in Kohler (2004). If offshoring more tasks is a way to absorb an unfavorable change in the final goods price, relative to domestic input prices, then a TFP measure derived from the value of sales relative to the value of inputs need not improve as the firm raises its level of offshoring.

The analysis of Grossman and Rossi-Hansberg (2008) and Antràs and Helpman (2004) also suggests a distinction between the *extensive task-margin* of offshoring (separating, for each firm, domestic from delocalized tasks), and the *extensive firm margin*, which separates firms with qualitatively different sourcing behavior (domestic versus foreign, intra-firm versus arms-length). In this connection, it seems important that the Grossman and Rossi-Hansberg productivity effect does not arise for firms at the extensive margin, at least not for small amounts of offshoring, because it works only through *infra-marginal* tasks.

Against this backdrop, it seems to me that a matching technique based exclusively on a Logit estimation of the *extensive firm margin* is a crude instrument, perhaps too crude. Remember that in Grossman and Rossi-Hansberg (2008) the magnitude of the productivity effect, given the size of the cost-shock, depends on the level of offshoring that a firm has already achieved, *prior* to the shock. One might, therefore, also think about a matching procedure that relies, not on a Logit estimation of the extensive firm margin alone, but on a *Tobit model* which includes the *intensive firm margin* (level of offshoring achieved by a firm). This may sound a bit strange at first flush, since it departs from question of treatment, but in my view there is nothing fundamental that would negate such an approach.

IV. MEASURING THE PRODUCTIVITY EFFECT

One would expect that measuring the productivity effect is difficult. I had problems finding out exactly how ITW go about it, but I somehow get the impression that their measure comes closer to a measure of *profit* than TFP.

At any rate, there is a further principal problem that arises here. In a perfect competition general equilibrium, any TFP increase is passed on to domestic input prices, particularly domestic primary input prices. Hence, any TFP-measure using output and input values is liable to underestimate a positive TFP effect, if present. ITW deflate output and input prices by corresponding price indices, but this is a partial remedy at best. Think of a case where all inputs are entirely sector specific. Then the Grossman and Rossi-Hansberg type productivity effect will be passed on, in its entirety, to sector-specific factors, separately and independently for each sector. Now, if some sectors experience an offshoring-driven TFP-increase and others do not, then an index-based deflation of input prices is not enough to achieve a correct measure of TFP-increase.

V. WHAT IS SPECIAL ABOUT INTRA-FIRM OFFSHORING?

A key message that ITW convey is that the expected positive TFP effect arises only if offshoring takes the intra-firm form, and that it takes a four- to five-year lag. The lag seems a bit long to me, but I would accept the explanation offered by ITW. The *mode restriction* is more interesting and, perhaps, puzzling. The authors suggest that it may have to do with the fact that different types of tasks are involved if firms offshore within their boundaries from when they do it via arms-length. This may be true, but we would like to see evidence. Moreover, why is there a larger productivity effect for offshoring *final assembly* than for arms-length offshoring of *service related inputs*? Also, ITW give the impression that the data sets of METI and RIETI should allow for this distinction in the entire analysis, so one could do the analysis separately for the two types of inputs.

What are the likely candidates of explanation? In my view, one is the *level* of offshoring achieved, as opposed to the simpler question of *whether* a firm is in offshoring. This is motivated by the Grossman and Rossi-Hansberg (2008) analysis, as I have emphasized above. And it could be addressed with a Tobit model.

Another explanation is a hold-up problem of the kind stipulated in Antràs and Helpman (2004). In their analysis, intra-firm offshoring (offshore insourcing in the ITW terminology) arises in cases where the need to *incentivize the input supplier* is less important. In the negotiation about the surplus, this shows up in a lower *ex post* revenue share that accrues to the input supplier. If this effect is present in the data, then it depends on accounting practices in integrated firms, as well as on the precise definition of the TFP measure, whether or not this eventually shows up in larger TFP-gains for intra-firm outsourcing.

However, a separate channel is involved that runs in the opposite direction. The incentive problem on the input is less severe whenever the headquarter input, which — by assumption and definition — is a domestic input, has a large share in the value-added chain. If this is true, then any increase in the level of offshoring will have relatively little leverage on the firm's TFP level.

There is a further explanatory candidate that is perhaps the most relevant: Integrated firms may have a tax incentive to shift profits from abroad to the domestic tax jurisdiction, or vice versa. If the former is the case, then they would tend to import their foreign tasks at low *transfer prices.* It is conceivable, and in my view quite likely, that something like this is behind the finding of ITW that the productivity enhancement of offshoring comes through only for intrafirm offshoring.

REFERENCES

Antràs, P. and E. Helpman (2004). "Global Sourcing." *Journal of Political Economy*, 112(3): pp. 552–580.

Antràs, P. and E. Helpman (2008). "Contractual Frictions and Global Sourcing." In *The Organization of Firms in a Global Economy*, Helpman, E., Marin, D., and Verdier, T., eds., Harvard University Press: Cambridge, MA.

Ethier, W. (1982). "National and International Returns to Scale in the Modern Theory of International Trade." *The American Economic Review*, 72(3): pp. 389–405.

Feenstra, Robert C. and G. H. Hanson (1999). "The Impact of Outsourcing and High-Technology Capital on Wages: Estimates for the U.S., 1979–1990." *Quarterly Journal of Economics*, 114(3): pp. 907–940.

Grossman, G. M. and E. Rossi-Hansberg (2011). "Trading Tasks: A Simple Theory of Offshoring." *American Economic Review*, 98(5): pp. 1978–1997.

Grossman, G. M. and E. Rossi-Hansberg (2009). *Task Trade between Similar Countries.* Forthcoming *Econometrica.*

Kohler, W. (2004). "International Outsourcing and Factor Prices with Multistage Production." *Economic Journal*, 114(1): pp. 166–185.

Kohler, W. (2009). "Offhsoring: Why Do Stories Differ?" In *The EU and Emerging Markets*, Tondl, G., ed., Springer-Verlag: Vienna, pp. 17–49.

CHAPTER 4

Global Sourcing: Evidence from Spanish Firm-Level Data*

Wilhelm K. Kohler† and Marcel Smolka‡

University of Tübingen, Nauklerstraße 47, 72074 Tübingen, Germany
† *wilhelm.kohler@uni-tuebingen.de*
‡ *marcel.smolka@uni-tuebingen.de*

We investigate the link between productivity of firms and their sourcing behavior. Following Antràs and Helpman (2004) we distinguish between domestic and foreign sourcing, as well as between outsourcing and vertical integration. A firm's choice is driven by a hold-up problem caused by lack of enforceable contracts. We use Spanish firm-level data to examine the productivity premia associated with the different sourcing strategies. We find strong empirical support for the predictions of the model.

I. INTRODUCTION

During the past decade, trade theory has turned *micro*: The individual firm has entered the stage of analysis. Of course, this is of interest only to the extent that firms are not entirely symmetric. We have ample evidence indicating that firms exhibit substantial heterogeneity in the degree as well as the organizational form of internationalization. Importantly, this heterogeneity is not random, but features a characteristic pattern. The general picture is one of so-called "exporter-premia," whereby exporting firms show higher performance in several dimensions than non-exporting firms, most notably in the level of productivity; see Bernard *et al.* (2007) for a convenient survey. A similar pattern is also observed for horizontal foreign direct investment

*An earlier version of this chapter was presented at the conference "*Fragmentation, Offshoring of Activities, and Vertical Intra-Industry Trade*," held at The University of Michigan, Gerald R. Ford School of Public Policy, 16–17 October 2009.

†Corresponding author.

(FDI); see Helpman, Melitz, and Yeaple (2004) and Helpman (2006). The dominant theoretical explanation of such heterogeneity in exports and FDI invokes the celebrated model of firm heterogeneity in a monopolistic competition framework developed in Melitz (2003). This explanation features self-selection of firms based on productivity. In other words, the causation runs from productivity to exports or FDI. However, such causality is more difficult to establish empirically than the pattern of heterogeneity as such; see Bernard and Jensen (1999). Although the bulk of the literature focuses on exports and horizontal FDI, Bernard *et al.* (2007) find a picture of premia also on the import side. In other words, more-productive firms tend to do both, more exporting and more importing than less-productive firms. Any theoretical explanation for an "importer premium" must address firms' sourcing behavior. Production requires intermediate inputs, and in many cases these inputs may be obtained either domestically or through imports. Moreover, provision of intermediates may take different organizational forms, such as arms-length market transactions or vertical integration within a firm's own boundary. In other words, a firm's sourcing decision for intermediates involves a *location* dimension (domestic or offshore) and an *organizational* dimension (markets or in-house). Do we find a characteristic pattern of performance premia across these sourcing modes? What does this pattern look like? How can it be explained?

Drawing on Antràs (2003) as well as Melitz (2003), Antràs and Helpman (2004) develop a model of global sourcing that addresses both the location of sourcing and its organizational mode. The model emphasizes a hold-up problem that arises if the inputs in question are relationship-specific and cannot be contracted. As a result, the firm and the input-supplier face the need to negotiate on dividing the surplus from the relationship. Institutional environments in developed economies typically offer several organizational forms that firms may rely on for their sourcing strategies. Drawing on Grossman and Hart (1986), Antràs and Helpman (2004) assume that firms may choose between two forms, one relying on arms-length transactions, the other relying on so-called vertical integration. The two forms differ in the outside options of the two negotiating parties, whereby vertical integration gives the firm a property right in the input. This enhances the firm's outside option when negotiating with the supplier about sharing the fruits of the relationship, but it also reduces the incentive for the input-supplier to invest in that relationship. This is the key trade-off modeled in Antràs and Helpman (2004). The model generates relatively sharp predictions where a firm's sourcing strategy is determined by its productivity as well as certain structural characteristics of the underlying production relationship. Antràs and Helpman (2004) assume complete lack of contractibility, which may risk overdoing the point. In Antràs and Helpman (2008), the model is extended to allow for a varying degree of contractibility over a continuum of tasks required for each of the two inputs in question. The extended model generates additional predictions, but the spirit of the original model survives without a stain.

Empirical evidence on firm heterogeneity in importing and sourcing is less abundant than evidence on exports and horizontal FDI. The reason has to do with data limitations. Offshoring is notoriously difficult to measure. This is aggravated by the need to observe the prevalence of organizational forms, if we aim at a comprehensive empirical investigation that covers both dimensions of sourcing. As a result, empirical analysis seems inherently more challenging in this line of research than for the export side, as suggested by Greenaway and Kneller (2007, p. F156). No wonder, then, that the literature on firm heterogeneity in trade has mainly focused on exports and FDI, and less on imports and sourcing. Existing empirical work has mostly focused on the organizational form of offshoring, thus ignoring domestic sourcing strategies; see Defever and Toubal (2007) and Nunn and Trefler (2008). However, a consistent investigation of "importer-premia," or a full test of the Antràs–Helpman model, requires a comprehensive approach that includes observing both, domestic sourcing as well as import sourcing.

In Kohler and Smolka (2011), we have derived general conditions that result in an unambiguous mapping of a firm's productivity level into the organizational form and location of its input sourcing; see also Mřazová and Neary (2011). Against this backdrop, we have conducted an "open search" for premia sourcing modes, using a Spanish firm-level data set. In this chapter, we draw on the same data set, but we now interpret the pattern of sourcing strategies in light of the Antrás–Helpman model.

A crucial feature of our data is that they allow us to consistently investigate both sourcing dimensions (location and organizational form) in a unified setting. Tomiura (2007) mainly provides evidence on both dimensions from a Japanese data set, without investigating performance premia associated with different sourcing modes, and without observing the organizational dimension for domestic sourcing. A recent study by Federico (2009), relying on Italian firm-level data, does observe all possible dimensions, and it looks at the relationship between firm productivity and sourcing behavior. However, this relationship is inherently more complex in this setup than in the standard case because of the hold-up problem mentioned earlier. For this reason, we first present a theoretical model of the hold-up problem that highlights how firm productivity interacts with structural characteristics of the underlying production relationship in determining a firm's sourcing strategy.

Given this interaction, can we expect a clear pattern looking at "productivity-premia" alone? Our theoretical section tells us we can do so only up to a point. In other words, we need to bring in certain controls. It also tells us that we need to be very cautious about whether the units of observation are indeed firms as defined in the model. Theory defines the firm as a true headquarter that decides about the organizational form of sourcing. We must therefore avoid our data being "contaminated" by firms who are in fact positioned at the opposite side of the hold-up problem, i.e., purchasing an input from foreign or domestic headquarters. Our data set is unique in that it allows us to clearly separate firms that correspond to the theoretical notion of a headquarter from those which are themselves subsidiaries of foreign or domestic parental companies.

The chapter is structured as follows. Section II presents the essentials of the hold-up model of global sourcing, aiming at a rigorous derivation of the "sourcing-premia" implied by this model. In Section III, we then describe our data set and present a few descriptive statistics. Section IV is divided into two parts. First, we compare the true productivity distributions of subsets of firms that differ in their sourcing strategies. More specifically, we compare firms engaged in domestic outsourcing versus domestic vertical integration, as well as firms engaged in foreign outsourcing versus foreign vertical integration. A final comparison is between firms with offshore sourcing (whether at arms-length or with vertical integration) versus domestic sourcing. Secondly, we estimate "sourcing-premia" by regressing firm productivity on dominant sourcing strategies, as well as a host of controls. Section V concludes with a brief summary and outlook on open questions and further research.

II. THEORY OF SOURCING WITHOUT CONTRACTIBILITY

Stripped down to its bare bones, what are the essentials of the "hold-up model" of global sourcing? A key tenet of all models in the spirit of Antràs (2003) is that production requires essential inputs that the firm cannot generate within its firm (or command) hierarchy, but must be obtained from a supplier. Importantly, the line separating "firm-inputs" and "supplier-inputs" is exogenous to the model. What is endogenous is the organizational mode and location of the "supplier-input." Alternative modes of organization differ in their implications for the incentive structure for the firm and the input-supplier. Thus, by choosing a specific organizational mode the firm may alleviate the problem of distorted input levels. More specifically, vertical integration lowers the incentive for the input-supplier which may, therefore, not be an optimal strategy if the input looms large in the production relationship. In Antràs and Helpman (2004, 2008), this mechanism is extended to include firm heterogeneity. It turns out that firms select into different sourcing strategies, based on their productivity in interaction with the importance of "firm-inputs" relative to "supplier-inputs" in the production relationship.

The Framework

There are two types of agents, firms and input-suppliers. Firms have access to some market where they raise revenue from selling final goods which are produced from two essential inputs that are provided, respectively, by the firms themselves (the so-called "headquarter service") and by the input-suppliers. Input-suppliers may either be located in the domestic economy or in the foreign economy, but all firms are assumed to be located in the domestic economy. Firms are unable to produce non-headquarter inputs which we shall henceforth call supplier-inputs. Therefore, they must always resort to input-suppliers in order to generate revenue at all. In turn, production of both, the headquarter- and the supplier-input, requires primary factors which must be purchased in the factor market of the country where the input provider is located.

Final goods feature product differentiation along the lines of Dixit and Stiglitz (1977). Importantly, each firm produces its own distinct brand which affords market power. However, it also implies that inputs must be provided in a unique specification for each brand. We assume extreme specificity, so that any input, once provided, has economic value only from production and sale of the corresponding final good. This is called relationship-specificity. Moreover, we assume that the quality and/or quantity of input provision cannot be verified by a third party, so that firms and input-suppliers cannot write enforceable contracts for input provision. Therefore, firms and input-suppliers must ensure corresponding specifications, and when deciding about the amounts of labor to invest into generating their respective inputs, they expect to be pitted against each other in a negotiation about how to share the revenue from selling the output generated by their specific inputs. Negotiation is assumed to take the form of Nash-bargaining, with a bargaining power equal to β for the firm, and $1 - \beta$ for the input-supplier. In addition to the variable cost of input provision, raising revenue from the production relationship requires an organizational effort which causes a fixed cost. As we shall detail below, the magnitude of this cost is assumed to differ across organizational forms as well as between locations of input provision.

For simplicity, we assume that, in both countries, input-suppliers are in infinitely elastic supply, with zero outside options. Thus, any input-supplier is willing to engage in a production relationship with a firm, if and only if it may expect to obtain a share of the revenue that is at least equal to the cost of input provision. We assume perfect competition among input-suppliers, so that in equilibrium the expected profit from participating in production as an input-supplier must be zero. A firm may thus attract a suitable input-supplier by charging a participation fee which is equal to the surplus of the supplier's expected revenue-share over the cost for input provision. Note that this surplus need not be positive. If it is negative, then the firm must pay a participation price to the input-supplier.

The cost of input provision for the input-supplier is determined by domestic factor prices or foreign factor prices, depending on whether a firm chooses a domestic or foreign supplier. This is the location dimension mentioned in the introduction. We assume a foreign location advantage for the supplier-input, which means that the foreign unit-cost of production is lower than the unit-cost under domestic factor prices. In the domestic economy, there is an infinitely elastic supply of potential firms that may enter the market, with an uncertain total productivity of the relationship between the two inputs. Firm entry evolves as in Melitz (2003), meaning that entry is governed by a sunk entry cost and zero expected profits from a potential relationship with an input-supplier.

A fundamental premise of this type of models is that there is a key asymmetry between firms and input-suppliers. In the very first stage of decision making, firms may "purchase" an outside option for the *ex-post* Nash-bargaining, which takes the form of property rights in the supplier-input. Following Antràs and Helpman (2004), we call this *vertical integration*, but it is important to bear in mind that it does not mean the firm has command over the entire input provision. The meaning is as follows. If bargaining breaks down, the firm may invoke a property right on the supplier-input and still sell the output. However, securing this outside option involves two types of cost. First, there is an iceberg-type cost of invoking property rights in that the revenue accruing to the firm is only a fraction δ of market revenue.[1] And second, the organizational fixed cost to the firm is higher with vertical integration than without. We call an organizational form of input provision that does not involve any acquisition of property rights *outsourcing*.

The organizational cost is likely to be larger if the firm relies on a foreign input-supplier, whatever the organizational form of sourcing. Antràs and Helpman (2004) make further assumptions that ultimately lead to the following ranking of the fixed organizational cost: $F^{FI} > F^{FO} > F^{DI} > F^{DO}$, whereby the superscripts I and O indicate vertical integration and outsourcing, respectively, while F and D indicate a foreign or domestic input-supplier. All organizational costs are expressed in units of the (domestic) headquarter-input. One may also assume that δ is larger for an input provided domestically: $\delta^D > \delta^F$. Notice that this share is always zero if the firm chooses outsourcing.

With this legal environment of property rights, the firm may influence the expected pay-off from *ex-post* Nash-bargaining through an *ex ante* choice of its organizational form of sourcing. More specifically, with vertical integration the share of revenue that accrues to the firm is equal to

[1]Antràs and Helpman (2004) assume that the iceberg-cost parameter applies to the quantity of the final good produced. But this translates into an iceberg-cost parameter for revenue in a straightforward way, depending on the details of the revenue function that are not important for our purpose.

$\beta^{\ell I} := \delta^\ell + \beta(1 - \delta^\ell)$, and with outsourcing it is equal to $\beta^{FO} = \beta^{DO} = \beta < \beta^{\ell\kappa}$ $(I = F, D; K = I, O)$. Notice that $1 - \delta^\ell$ times the revenue to be generated from the market represents the "gains from trade," with trade meaning completion of the production relationship through successful Nash-bargaining.

Decision Making

Decision making takes place in a multi-stage manner. In a *first step*, firms enter the market in order to find out about their productivity level θ (TFP). In *stage 2*, conditional upon θ being large enough to avoid losses from the subsequent stages,[2] each firm decides about its optimal sourcing strategy, which means the simultaneous choice of a location $\ell = F$ or $\ell = D$ and an organizational form $\kappa = I$ or $\kappa = O$. In the *third stage*, the two input providers (i.e., the firm and the supplier) choose levels of their inputs that maximize the difference between their expected shares of revenue, to be generated from the relationship, and their respective cost of input provision. Expected shares depend on the anticipated Nash-bargaining power and the outside options of the two parties. Importantly, the revenue depends on the levels of each input chosen. *Stage 4* then involves production of the final good, with the revenue shared among the two input providers according to the Nash-bargaining solution. When contemplating entry, a potential firm anticipates its optimal choice of an organizational form in stage 2, which in turn will anticipate the optimal input levels emerging in stage 3. Thus, the sourcing strategy chosen is an integral part of a subgame-perfect equilibrium. In the following, we focus on stages 2–4 of decision making, employing the usual backward induction.[3]

Revenue (stage 4): Under the above assumptions, revenue R is concave in x, the quantity of the final good produced:

$$R(x) = A^{1-\alpha}x^\alpha \quad \text{with } x = \theta y(h, m) \tag{1}$$

The first expression follows from Dixit-Stiglitz-type product differentiation, with an elasticity of substitution equal to $1/(1 - \alpha)$, whereby

[2]Details of this first stage are as in Melitz (2003) and will not be looked at in detail here.

[3]For the first stage of firm entry and a "general equilibrium" embedment of this sector, with a second numéraire sector, see Antràs and Helpman (2004).

$0 < \alpha < 1$. In the second expression, $y(h, m)$ is a linearly homogeneous production function for the final good, with input levels h and m for the headquarter service and the supplier-input, respectively, and θ as the firm-specific TFP-level. In the sequel, we denote the elasticity of x with respect to h by η. Given linear homogeneity, the elasticity with respect to m is equal to $1 - \eta$.

Input levels (stage 3): Input-providers simultaneously, but independently, choose input levels h and m that maximize $\gamma R(x) - c^h(w^D)h$ and $(1 - \gamma) R(x) - c^m(w^\ell)m$, respectively, where ℓ denotes the location of the input-supplier, and the terms $c^h(\cdot)$ and $c^m(\cdot)$ denote minimum unit-cost for the headquarter- and supplier-input, respectively, as functions of factor prices w^ℓ. The parameter γ denotes the revenue share accruing to the firm in *ex-post* Nash-bargaining. This depends on the organizational choice $\kappa \in \{I, O\}$. However, for the time being we ignore this dependency, in order to better grasp the strategic role of this share. It can be shown that the optimal input levels (indicated by an asterisk) satisfy

$$h^* = \gamma\alpha R^*\eta / c^h(w^D) \quad \text{and} \quad m^* = (1 - \gamma)\alpha R^*(1 - \eta)/c^m(w^\ell) \tag{2}$$

In this equation, R^* denotes the relationship-specific total revenue deriving from input levels h^* and m^*, determined simultaneously in this stage of decision making. The lack of contractibility introduces a distortion, relative to the environment with *ex ante* enforceable contracts. Both inputs are provided in less than optimal amounts, whereby the share parameter γ determines the distortion (under-provision) of the headquarter input, relative to the supplier-input.

Organizational form (stage 2): In addition to the input levels h^* and m^*, the firm's entire profit from the relationship depends on the participation fee that it may charge (or has to pay) the input-supplier, as well as on the fixed organizational cost it has to bear. The participation fee is equal to $(1-\gamma)R^* - c^m(w^\ell)m^*$, which may be zero, positive, or negative. Equilibrium firm profits now emerge as

$$\begin{aligned}\Pi^* &= R^* - c^h(w^D)h^* - c^m(w^\ell)m^* - c^h(w^D)F^{\ell\kappa} \\ &= R^*[1 - \gamma\alpha\eta - (1 - \gamma)\alpha(1 - \eta)] - c^h(w^D)F^{\ell\kappa}\end{aligned} \tag{3}$$

where $F^{\ell\kappa}$ denotes the corresponding organizational fixed cost in units of domestic labor. The second line uses the above first-order conditions on the two input levels. It is now crucial to recognize that R^* depends on the organizational choice through the above mentioned property rights that may be acquired through vertical integration. Using c_y to denote the unit-cost function dual to $y(h, m)$, we may write

$$R^* = A\left[\frac{1}{\alpha\theta}c_y\left(\frac{c^h(w^D)}{\gamma}, \frac{c^m(w^\ell)}{1-\gamma}\right)\right]^{-(\alpha/1-\alpha)} \tag{4}$$

Notice that the elasticity of c_y with respect to $c^h(w^D)$ is equal to η, and analogously for the other input cost. Notice also that the lack of complete contracts affects maximum revenue that can be generated from the final goods market in a way which is equivalent to a tax on the two inputs. If $\gamma \neq 1/2$, then the "equivalent tax" also distorts the input mix. Equilibrium firm profits now emerge as

$$\Pi^* = Z^{\ell\kappa}\theta^{\alpha/(1-\alpha)} - c^h(w^D)F^{\ell\kappa} \tag{5}$$

where

$$Z^{\ell\kappa} := \frac{A[1-\alpha\gamma\eta - \alpha(1-\gamma)(1-\eta)]}{\left[c_y\left(\frac{c^h(w^D)}{\gamma}, \frac{c^m(w^\ell)}{1-\gamma}\right)/\alpha\right]^{\frac{\alpha}{1-\alpha}}} \tag{6}$$

In stage 2 of the game, the firm chooses a sourcing strategy $\ell \in \{D, F\}$ and $\kappa \in \{I, O\}$ that maximizes profits Π^*.

Organizational Modes of Sourcing

Equation (5) depicts a firm's profits from a production relationship as a linear function of $\Theta := \theta^{\alpha/(1-\alpha)}$. Remember that $0 < \alpha < 1$, hence Θ is unambiguously increasing in the productivity level θ. The negative intercept in (5) represents the fixed organizational cost $F^{\ell\kappa}$ and the domestic unit-cost of the headquarter input. In turn, Equation (6) reveals the slope of this line as a relatively complex function of the expected revenue share parameter γ and the two countries' unit-cost for the inputs. Together, Equations (5) and (6) reveal how firm productivity interacts with other characteristics of the production relationship in determining maximum firm profits. Setting demand characteristics (A, α) aside, these are the revenue share γ, reflecting the bargaining situation that stems from lack of enforceable contracts, the share of the firm's own input (η), and the factor intensities of the two inputs, reflected in $c^h(w^D)$ and $c^m(w^\ell)$.

Up to this point we have not considered the choice of organizational form for the production relationship and the location of the input-supplier. How does firm productivity impact on these choices? We first discuss the organizational mode for a given location of supply. For any given sourcing market and for given characteristics of the production relationship (γ, η), the slope term $Z^{\ell\kappa}$ tells us how differences in firm productivity Θ translate into differences in maximum operating profits. If there are fixed costs, these need to surpass a certain threshold for the firm to remain in the market. But this is not what we want to focus on now. We want to consider the role that γ and η play for the slope of the profit function. Antràs and Helpman (2004) suggest that the organizational dimension of the sourcing strategy is best understood by first considering the effect of an unrestricted variation of the share parameter γ on a firm's profit from the relationship with an input-supplier. Unrestricted simply means that the firm can pick γ at will. It is obvious that a firm should not expect positive profits if its bargaining power approaches zero, $\gamma \to 0$. Remembering that the lack of enforceable contracts is equivalent to a tax on the two inputs, this case is recognized as an infinite "equivalent tax" on the headquarter-input, which wipes out all firm profits. Perhaps less obviously, a firm could not expect positive profits also if $\gamma \to 1$. Intuitively, in this case it would simply lack an essential input, since the input-supplier lacks any incentive to invest in the relationship at all. Formally, in either of the two cases $\gamma \to 0$ and $\gamma \to 1$ we have $c_\gamma(\cdot) \to \infty$, provided that $0 < \eta < 1$, and from (5) and (6) a firm's maximum profit function would be flat at $-c^h(w^D)F^{\ell\kappa}$. Independent of its productivity level, a firm would make negative maximum profits.

All of this suggests that there should be a level of γ which maximizes the slope of our profit-line. We now call this the optimal value of γ, always bearing in mind that, ultimately, the choice of γ will be subject to institutional restrictions. We shall turn to the equilibrium value of γ below. Intuitively, the incentive problem of a high γ is the more severe, the more important the supplier-input for the relationship, as measured by the elasticity $1 - \eta$. Put differently, for a given sourcing location, the optimal firm-share

γ should be increasing in η, the elasticity of the output x with respect to the headquarter service. Antràs and Helpman (2004) derive such a monotonic relationship for the optimal level of γ as a function of η. Let us denote this relationship by $\gamma(\eta)$, with $\gamma > 0$. It is interesting to note that the optimal value of γ is independent of the unit-cost functions for the two inputs. Moreover, both $\gamma(\eta)$ and $Z^{\ell\kappa}$ are independent of the firm's productivity level θ. Importantly, however, the level of the slope $Z^{\ell\kappa}$ that is reached at the optimal value of γ does depend on the unit-cost $c_y(\cdot)$ and, thus, on the extent of the foreign cost advantage. For this reason, an increase in the firm's revenue share γ also implies a variation in the slope $Z^{\ell\kappa}$ which comes about through the "equivalent tax" on the supplier-input in $c^m(w^\ell)/(1-\gamma)$. It is also worth noting that, given a certain pattern of factor price differences between the two countries, the extent of the foreign cost advantage depends on the factor intensity of the supplier-input.

Next, we must recognize that the bargaining and institutional environment typically requires a discrete choice among a limited set of options, rather than unconstrained optimization on γ. In our case, a firm has but two options. Vertical integration gives a revenue share equal to $\beta^{\ell I} := \delta^\ell + \beta(1-\delta^\ell)$, depending on the sourcing location. Outsourcing ties this share down to $\beta < \beta^{\ell I}$, independent of the sourcing location.

We proceed by first conditioning the firm's organizational choice on a given sourcing location $\ell \in \{D, F\}$. There is a critical value of $\tilde{\eta}$, implicitly defined through $\gamma(\tilde{\eta}) = \beta < \beta^{\ell I}$, such that, for any $\eta < \tilde{\eta}$, firms will never choose vertical integration, whatever their productivity, and independently of the fixed organizational cost. The supplier-input is simply too important in the production relationship. Ideally, the firm would even want to enhance the input-supplier's incentive through a revenue share larger than $1-\beta$, but by assumption β is as low as the firm's share can get.[4]

There is a further critical value $\bar{\eta}^\ell$ which is implicitly defined by $\gamma(\bar{\eta}^\ell) = \delta^\ell + \beta(1-\delta^\ell)$. It might be tempting to argue that for any elasticity value, $\eta > \bar{\eta}^\ell$, the firm should choose vertical integration. However, this is not true. While it is true that in such industries the profit line has a larger slope for vertical integration than for outsourcing, i.e., $Z^{\ell I} > Z^{\ell O}$, this does

[4]This may seem like a paradox. Why, after all, should a firm not be able to *reduce* its bargaining power? The underlying assumption here is that for some reason the firm cannot credibly commit to a lower bargaining power than β.

not unambiguously dictate a vertical integration strategy, if integration involves a higher fixed cost of organization. Therefore, firm productivity must surpass some threshold level for this strategy to be worthwhile. Notice that $\Theta^{\ell O}$ depends on the level of η, conditional on $\eta > \bar{\eta}^{\ell}$.

For intermediate elasticity values that satisfy $\tilde{\eta} < \eta < \bar{\eta}^{\ell}$ the comparison of $Z^{\ell I}$ and $Z^{\ell O}$ is ambiguous. By monotonicity of $\gamma(\eta)$, for values in the upper range of this interval, we have $Z^{\ell I} > Z^{\ell O}$, so that the logic of the preceding paragraph applies, meaning that firms below some threshold productivity choose outsourcing instead of vertical integration, and *vice versa.* Thus, the true threshold level of η that separates outsourcing firms from integrated ones is implicitly determined by $Z^{\ell I} = Z^{\ell O}$. We denote this level by $\eta^{\ell *}$, whereby $\tilde{\eta} < \eta^{\ell *} < \bar{\eta}^{\ell}$.

Summarizing what we have found so far, we may state that, whatever the input-supplier's location, we should expect to see more productive firms organizing their sourcing through vertical integration, and less productive firms to choose outsourcing. But there are two important caveats. First the threshold productivity level $\Theta^{\ell O}$ separating the two types of firms generally depends on the headquarter-elasticity η. Secondly, if this elasticity falls below a threshold value, then firm productivity simply does not matter, and all firms choose an outsourcing strategy. These caveats are important for estimation of "sourcing-premia" using the methodology of Bernard and Jensen (1999), as we do in the empirical part below. Suppose, for instance, that we compare productivity levels across sourcing strategies of firms in different industries with differing headquarter-elasticities. Suppose, moreover, that we have an industry with a headquarter-elasticity below $\eta^{\ell *}$ alongside others with elasticity values well above $\eta^{\ell *}$. If the former industry has a large mass of firms with a high productivity, then we should not expect to observe a clear productivity ranking across sourcing modes.[5]

[5]There is a further caveat that we should like to add here. Suppose that we reverse the fixed cost assumption, such that $F^{\ell I} < F^{\ell O}$, which does not seem all that implausible. Then we would observe firms with a headquarter-elasticity below $\eta^{\ell *}$ potentially pursuing both strategies. If so, it would indeed be the less productive firms that do vertical integration. It becomes obvious that the predictions of the model heavily depend on the fixed cost ranking assumption. As we shall see below, the case assumed in the text is supported by our data.

Adding the Offshoring-Dimension

So far we have looked at organizational choice assuming that the input-supplier's location is given. We now look at the choice of location explicitly. Remember our assumption relating to the fixed organizational cost: $F^{FI} > F^{FO} > F^{DI} > F^{DO}$. With this ranking, it is obvious that foreign sourcing will never be attractive, unless the foreign economy has an absolute cost advantage in the supplier-input. In terms of Equation (6), this requires $c_y(\frac{w^D}{\gamma}, \frac{w^F}{1-\gamma}) < c_y(\frac{w^D}{\gamma}, \frac{w^D}{1-\gamma})$. We therefore assume that this inequality holds, which implies that $Z^{F\kappa} > Z^{D\kappa}$. We may then say that a firm's productivity level Θ is a leverage for the cost-advantage of foreign sourcing. Moreover, we assume that the extent of the foreign cost advantage is specific to the industry, not the firm. With both dimensions explicitly in the picture, we have a more complex choice problem. Figure 1 depicts a case where all possible sourcing strategies will emerge in equilibrium, whereby the headquarter-elasticity is assumed to satisfy $\eta > \eta^{F*} > \eta^{D*}$. Hence, the profit-lines for vertical integration are steeper than those for outsourcing in either location. At the same time, by the assumption of a foreign cost

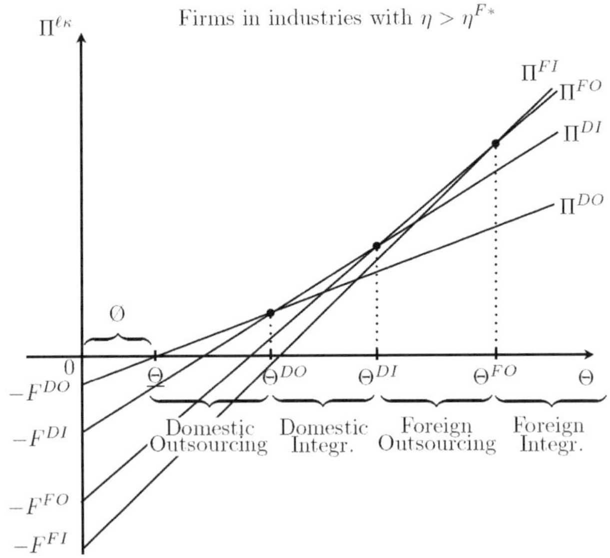

Fig. 1. Productivity ranking for an equilibrium with all sourcing modes.

advantage, they are steeper for offshoring than for domestic sourcing for either of the two organizational modes. However, these assumptions do not guarantee that all four sourcing strategies will appear in equilibrium. We must distinguish between two types of "degenerate" equilibria.

First, we may have a case where the fixed cost-disadvantage of the integration strategy over the outsourcing strategy is small enough and/or the variable cost advantage large enough for integration to be the dominant strategy for all firms, irrespective of their productivity.[6] This may happen for the foreign or the domestic location, or indeed for both. However, even in this latter case, we would still observe foreign integration only for more productive firms.

Second, the fixed cost of offshoring relative to domestic sourcing may be small enough, compared to the locational advantage in variable cost, so that the equilibrium features only offshoring firms. This may happen independently for either of the two organizational modes. But again, we would still expect to see the more productive firms pursuing an integration strategy.

Both of these degenerate equilibria still entail a clear productivity ranking, provided that one can control for variations in the headquarter-elasticity and variations in the degree of foreign cost advantage. As an extreme case, by adding the two lines of reasoning behind these degenerate equilibria, we might even envisage a complete dominance of foreign integration. While not being in contradiction with the model, an industry of this type would simply not contribute any variation that could be used to empirically establish any "sourcing-premia."

Finally, we may allow for a modification in the fixed cost ranking, such that $F^{FI} > F^{DI} > F^{FO} > F^{DO}$. Notice that this still preserves the fundamental idea of an extra fixed cost deriving from executing property rights, as well as the idea of a fixed cost of offshoring within a given organizational mode. It might be tempting to argue, by looking at Figure 1, that this just removes the domestic integration strategy. But this is not the case, since there is no fundamental reason within our model that forces us to assume, as we do in Figure 1, that the profit line for domestic integration is flatter

[6]All of this is, of course, conditional on positive expected profits, i.e., on remaining in the market in the first place.

than the profit line for foreign outsourcing. We should thus not expect from the fundamental premises of the model to observe the productivity ranking depicted in Figure 1. Observing domestic integration to be chosen by more productive firms than foreign outsourcing is perfectly consistent with the model. This is an important qualification for the empirical analysis of "sourcing-premia" below.

This completes our theoretical view of the hold-up problem in a firm's global sourcing decision, based on the seminal contribution of Antràs and Helpman (2004). Section III turns to an empirical analysis based on Spanish firm-level data. Our analysis will focus entirely on the productivity-sourcing-nexus. We eschew the problem of finding a valid empirical measure of the headquarter intensity. The literature often uses the capital-intensity or skill-intensity of production as a proxy.[7] But it clearly transpires from the above analysis that factor intensities may capture an entirely different channel, viz. the extent of the foreign cost advantage. We therefore chose to follow a procedure that avoids this problem altogether.

III. DATA

Our empirical analysis is based on the Spanish "Survey on Business Strategies" (ESEE)[8] from the Fundación SEPI.[9] The Fundación SEPI surveys approximately 2,000 firms with 10 or more employees from all over Spain on a yearly basis since 1990 and addresses strategic business issues, as well as revenue and balance sheet statistics. The sample covers approximately 70% of all Spanish manufacturing firms with more than 200 employees, plus 5% of all firms with a number of employees between 10 and 200.[10] The coverage of firms is representative for each of the two firm-size categories, and special care has been taken to control for the time dynamics in the panel which result from firms exiting and entering markets.[11]

[7] See Antràs (2003), Yeaple (2006), and Nunn and Trefler (2008).

[8] "Encuesta sobre Estrategias Empresariales."

[9] "Sociedad Estatal de Participaciones Industriales."

[10] Small-sized firms have been selected by a stratified sampling procedure.

[11] For a comprehensive data description, see http://www.funep.es/esee/en/einfo_que_es.asp. Accessed 30 July 2008.

There are three primary advantages associated with the use of these data compared to prior empirical research. First, we know for each firm whether it acquires intermediate inputs through each of the four sourcing strategies (foreign integration, foreign outsourcing, domestic integration, and domestic outsourcing). In the survey, intermediate inputs are defined as goods that have been acquired from a *different legal entity* (either related or unrelated to the firm) and "*incorporated and transformed in the production process.*" This perfectly fits into the Antràs and Helpman (2004) modeling setup.[12] Clearly, the simultaneous and coherent coverage of all four sourcing modes generates a much more comprehensive picture of global sourcing decisions than was the case with earlier studies.[13] Second, the data allow us to compute several common measures of firm productivity. We can thus evaluate the robustness of our findings in a convincing manner. This is an important point, since previous research has shown that empirical results are often sensitive to the specific way in which productivity is defined and/or estimated. Third, all firms in the sample are categorized by the degree of participation of other companies in a firm's joint capital. We use this information to construct a subsample of firms that satisfy the crucial assumption that the input-supplier never has a controlling stake in the headquarters' capital.[14] In other words, our firms do have complete discretion over the organizational mode of sourcing.

Table 1 presents the absolute numbers and the percentages of firms with different sourcing strategics in the year 2007. We distinguish between foreign integration (*FI*), foreign outsourcing (*FO*), domestic integration (*DI*), and domestic outsourcing (*DO*), as well as all possible combinations thereof. This distinction implies that sourcing categories are *mutually exclusive* in the sense that each firm is assigned to exactly one specific

[12]We again emphasize that the modeling framework does not envisage a situation in which there is a command hierarchy in the strict sense of the word between firm and input producer.

[13]In principle, our data set covers the years 2000–2007 but we can distinguish the four strategic options for intermediate input sourcing only for the two most recent years. Nonetheless, we take the whole panel into account where its use provides us with additional insights or more accurate estimates (for example, we rely on the whole panel data set when it comes to total factor productivity estimation).

[14]Note also that all data refer to a specific legal entity and not to a corporate group comprising a number of economically interdependent entities.

Table 1. Firms' sourcing strategies in 2007

DO	*DI*	*FO*	*FI*	*DODI*	*DOFO*	*DOFI*	*DODIFO*	*DODIFI*	*DOFOFI*	*DIFO*	*DIFI*	*DIFOFI*	*FOFI*	*DODIFOFI*
Large firms (>200 employees)														
97	8	14	3	45	144	12	68	8	73	2	0	5	4	50
17.7	1.5	2.6	0.5	8.2	26.3	2.2	12.4	1.5	13.3	0.4	0.0	0.9	0.7	9.1
Small firms (<201 employees)														
809	9	19	1	50	389	9	46	2	23	0	0	0	1	11
56.3	0.6	1.3	0.1	3.7	28.4	0.7	3.4	0.1	1.7	0.0	0.0	0.0	0.1	0.8
Sample firms														
906	17	33	4	95	533	21	114	10	96	2	0	5	5	61
45.7	0.9	1.7	0.2	4.8	26.9	1.1	5.7	0.5	4.8	0.1	0.0	0.3	0.3	3.1

Note: In each subtable, the first and second rows give the numbers and the percentages of firms in the various sourcing categories, respectively. All percentages are of the total number of firms in the respective size category in the 2007 sample ($N = 548$ for large firms, $N = 1,436$ for small firms, and $N = 1,984$ for the whole 2007 sample). We represent foreign integration (FI), foreign outsourcing (FO), domestic integration (DI), and domestic outsourcing (DO), as well as all combinations thereof.

(though potentially mixed) sourcing strategy. Close to 50% of the firms in our sample engage in two or more sourcing modes simultaneously. Looking at large firms only, we find an even more telling picture: almost 80% of all firms with more than 200 employees make use of such complex sourcing strategies. Strictly speaking, a combinatory use of sourcing channels is ruled out in Antràs (2003) and Antràs and Helpman (2004), where each firm is assumed to buy a single specific manufacturing component, for which there is a unique optimal sourcing strategy.[15] In our sample, however, only 2.7% of firms pursue pure sourcing strategies other than domestic outsourcing. To give an example, the overwhelming majority (more than 98%) of all foreign-integration-firms take advantage of at least one additional type of sourcing channel. Therefore, and with an eye on the subsequent econometric analysis, the notion of complex strategies is highly relevant. We also find that nearly half of the firms are active in foreign sourcing in the sense that they do engage in either vertical FDI or offshore outsourcing, or both. By way of comparison, the equivalent percentage number for Japan's manufacturing firms is 5%; see Tomiura (2007). The high share of international firms in Spain seems to reflect the high degree of economic integration in Europe.[16] Indeed, more than 70% of the total value of imported goods have a member country of the European Union as origin, but only 5% come from Latin America.[17]

In Table 2 we assign firms to groups *DO*, *DI*, *FO*, and *FI* in a *mutually inclusive* way such that a single firm may appear in more than one category. Integration as opposed to outsourcing of intermediate input-suppliers is reserved for only a minority of firms. A total of 304 firms (15%) procure intermediate inputs from related parties in Spain, 202 firms (10%) acquire them from related parties abroad. By contrast, nearly all firms outsource part of their production to independent suppliers in the domestic economy, and more than 40% do so in the foreign economy. Another important observation is that in 2007 (2006) there is a small fraction of around 4%(6%) of firms that do not report purchasing any intermediate inputs at

[15]Schwarz and Sudekum (2011) extend the model to allow for multiple sourcing strategies.
[16]Admittedly, the number is somewhat overstated since large firms are overrepresented in the sample. Still, the difference is impressive even when looking at small firms only.
[17]These numbers correspond to imports in 2006. In Kohler and Smolka (2011) we provide a more extensive description of stylized facts that transpire from this data set.

Table 2. **Firms in mutually inclusive sourcing categories in 2007**

	Large firms (>200 employees)		Small firms (<201 employees)		Sample firms	
	Number	in %	Number	in %	Number	in %
Domestic outsourcing	497	90.7	1,339	93.2	1,836	92.5
Domestic integration	186	33.9	118	8.2	304	15.3
Foreign outsourcing	360	65.7	489	34.1	849	42.8
Foreign integration	155	28.3	47	3.3	202	10.2
Non-sourcing	15	2.7	67	4.7	82	4.1

Note: With mutually inclusive strategies, a single firm may show up in more than one sourcing category. All percentages are of the total number of firms in the respective size category in the 2007 sample ($N = 548$ for large firms, $N = 1{,}436$ for small firms, and $N = 1{,}984$ for the whole 2007 sample).

all. These firms appear to manufacture and combine all inputs necessary for final goods production within their own legal entity's command structure. In terms of our model, such firms are able to avoid any "hold-up" problem of the type considered above, and to achieve efficient investment levels in all inputs. On the other hand, they also forego the option to arbitrage on factor price differences across countries. We shall address this issue further, when discussing our empirical results in the next section.

The disaggregation into large and small firms in Table 2 reveals at least two interesting regularities. On one hand, sourcing inputs from a vertically integrated supplier is a much more common strategy for large firms than for small firms. In fact, one-third of firms with more than 200 employees are domestic-integration-firms, and close to 30% are foreign-integration-firms. The corresponding numbers for small firms are 8% and 3%, respectively. On the other hand, large firms are on average much more present in international sourcing markets than small firms, which is very much in line with earlier evidence on export markets. Both observations taken together provide us with a clear hint with regard to the fixed cost ranking of global sourcing strategies. Since high fixed costs constitute an especially high hurdle for smaller firms, the Spanish data point towards a ranking that satisfies $F^{FI} > F^{FO}$ and $F^{DI} > F^{DO}$ as well as $F^{D\kappa} > F^{D\kappa}$, as assumed in Antràs and Helpman (2004).

IV. EMPIRICAL ANALYSIS

As we have detailed in the theoretical section, the Antràs and Helpman (2004) model suggests that firms facing a hold-up problem in sourcing select themselves into different sourcing strategies, depending on their productivity level and certain structural characteristics of the underlying production relationship. In this section, we want to examine whether our data lend empirical support to the hypothesized productivity ranking. We proceed in two steps. First, we apply a non-parametric test based on the principle of first-order stochastic dominance, in order to compare cumulative productivity distributions for certain groups of firms that differ in their sourcing behavior. To be more precise, we test for stochastic dominance among the two groups of firms that choose different organizational forms, viz. outsourcing and vertical integration. We do so separately for the domestic sourcing and for offshoring. We also test for stochastic dominance among the two groups that differ in sourcing domestically or offshore, whatever the organizational form. In the second step, we adopt the Bernard and Jensen (1999) methodology, which has seen extensive use in estimation productivity- and size-premia of exporting relative to non-exporting firms. We modify this approach so that it allows us to estimate productivity-premia for firms engaging in different sourcing modes (relative to a baseline category) in a unified econometric framework.

Throughout our analysis, we use four different measures of firm productivity θ, in order to evaluate the sensitivity of our results with respect to different specifications of productivity. The specifications chosen are labor productivity ($PROD_L$) computed as valued added per hour worked and three different measures of total factor productivity computed from estimations of sectoral production functions. The first uses standard ordinary least squares (OLS) regressions, the second uses a fixed-effects model, and the third employs the Olley and Pakes (1996) framework. We denote these measures as $PROD_{OLS}$, $PROD_{FE}$, and $PROD_{OP}$, respectively.[18] We treat $PROD_{OP}$ as the preferred measure, since the Olley and Pakes (1996) method controls for endogeneity problems that may arise from unobserved productivity shocks and/or firms' market exit decisions. Our results are

[18]See Appendix for details.

assuringly robust to the use of different productivity measures. We report results only for $PROD_{OP}$.[19]

The entire empirical analysis is conducted relying on two types of samples. The first is restricted to true headquarter firms, meaning that we exclude a firm if some other company owns more than 50% of the firm's capital and/or if the firm is subject to foreign ownership.[20] As we have already pointed out in Section II, restricting the sample along this dimension is important, in order to ensure that we only observe firms with full discretion over their sourcing strategies. The second is the unrestricted sample, which has the advantage of a larger number of observations, but risks including firms whose sourcing strategy is dictated by their parental company. If we obtain differing results, this is an indication that controlling for true headquarter-status, which to the best of our knowledge is a unique feature of our analysis relative to existing literature, is empirically important.[21]

Evidence from a Non-parametric Test

In this subsection, we employ a non-parametric approach to evaluate the productivity ranking hypothesized in Section II. For this purpose, we plot empirical cumulative distribution functions for estimates of total factor productivity for firms belonging to different sourcing groups. Suppose we compare two cumulative distribution functions $F(z)$ and $G(z)$, each of which represents the productivity distribution of one sourcing mode. We say that $F(z)$ stochastically dominates $G(z)$ at first order, if $F(z) - G(z) \leq 0 \, \forall z \in \mathbb{R}$ and $\exists \, z \in \mathbb{R}$ with $F(z) - G(z) < 0$. Computing the distribution-free Kolmogorov–Smirnov test statistic (K-S test), we can then conclude (a) whether or not the two groups share the same underlying productivity distribution (two-sided test) and (b) whether or not the distribution of one

[19] All other results are available from the authors upon request.

[20] The threshold value of control is not decisive. For example, in 2007 we exclude roughly 30% of the total number of firms ($N = 1{,}984$). Reducing the threshold value to 25% would eliminate only a slightly larger number of firms but leave all of our results unchanged.

[21] It should be noted that restricting the sample along the ownership dimension significantly decreases the share of large firms in the sample.

group dominates the other (one-sided test). Formally, we test the following hypotheses:

(i) The two-sided test we are interested in is whether

$$H_0\colon F(z) - G(z) = 0 \quad \forall z \in \mathbb{R} \text{ against}$$
$$H_1\colon \exists\, z \in \mathbb{R} \quad \text{with} \quad F(z) - G(z) \neq 0$$

can be rejected.

(ii) The one-sided test is to see if it is true that

$$H_0\colon F(z) - G(z) \leq 0\, \forall z \in \mathbb{R} \text{ against}$$
$$H_1\colon \exists\, z \in \mathbb{R} \quad \text{with} \quad F(z) - G(z) > 0$$

cannot be rejected.

The K-S test uses the maximum vertical distance between the curves of two cumulated distribution functions as the statistic D, which makes it a particularly robust and useful test whenever the true distributions are unknown.

In Figure 2 we display the cumulative distribution functions for 2006 and 2007 separately since the K-S testing procedure assumes independence across observations.[22] Each panel depicts two functions, representing a distinct sourcing strategy, as indicated in the legend. For a firm to be assigned to a specific sourcing category, we require that it obtains some intermediate inputs through the respective sourcing mode.[23] Any firm that uses both of the two strategies considered is assigned to the group for which our maintained hypothesis implies a higher fixed cost; see Section II above. The samples do not exclude firms that are additionally active in any other sourcing mode.[24] The graphs suggest a first order stochastic dominance of the productivity distribution for integration over that of outsourcing and for offshoring over domestic sourcing of inputs. This is as expected from theory.

[22]We only show distribution functions from the unrestricted sample since there are no qualitative differences when using the restricted sample instead. Also, results from the K-S testing procedure are qualitatively identical.

[23]Thus, we ignore non-sourcing firms in this subsection.

[24]We redo the whole exercise excluding all firms that are additionally sourcing through other modes, but the results remain basically unchanged.

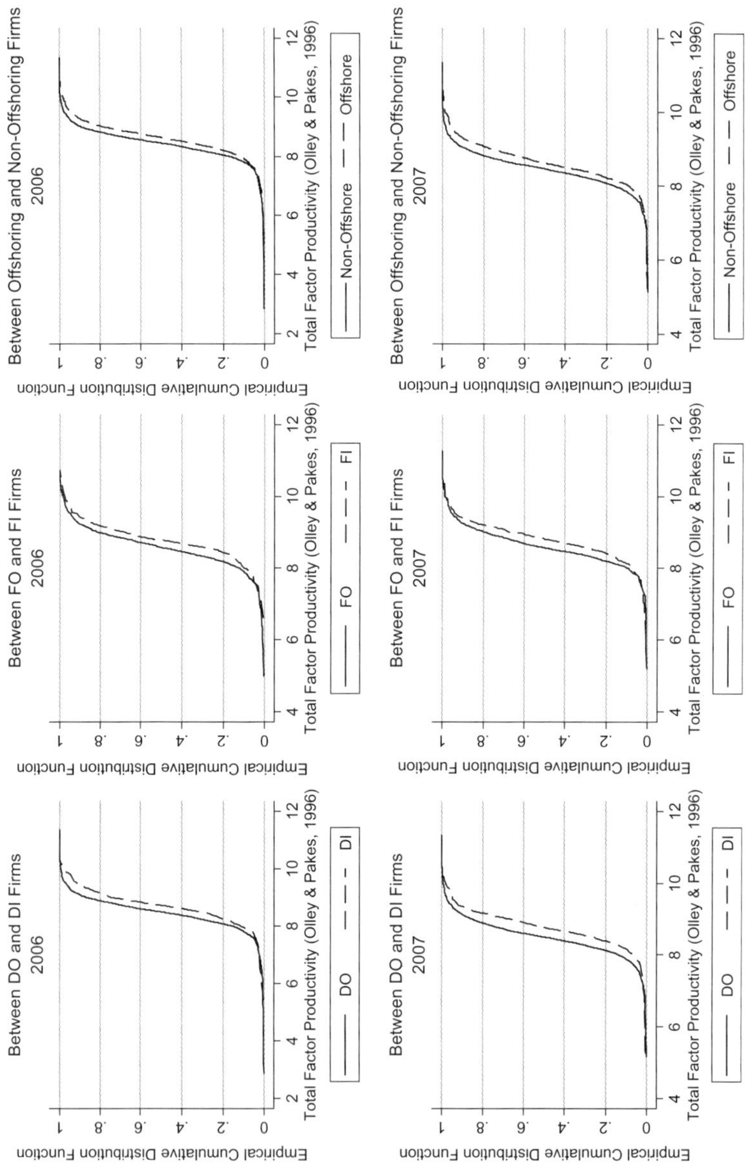

Fig. 2. Empirical cumulative distribution functions for $PROD_{OP}$.

Table 3. Kolmogorov–Smirnov testing procedure with total factor productivity

	2006		2007	
	Maximum Vertical Distance	P-value	Maximum Vertical Distance	P-value
$PROD_{OP}^{DO} > PROD_{OP}^{DI}$	0.2161	0.000	0.2629	0.000
$PROD_{OP}^{DO} < PROD_{OP}^{DI}$	−0.0094	0.957	−0.0053	0.986
Two-Sided Test	0.2161	0.000	0.2629	0.000
$PROD_{OP}^{FO} > PROD_{OP}^{FI}$	0.2196	0.000	0.2252	0.000
$PROD_{OP}^{FO} < PROD_{OP}^{FI}$	−0.0011	1.000	−0.0110	0.963
Two-Sided Test	0.2196	0.000	0.2252	0.000
$PROD_{OP}^{D} > PROD_{OP}^{F}$	0.1795	0.000	0.1708	0.000
$PROD_{OP}^{D} < PROD_{OP}^{F}$	−0.0009	0.999	−0.0039	0.985
Two-Sided Test	0.1795	0.000	0.1708	0.000

Note: Column one gives the null hypotheses to be tested. Two-Sided Test stands for the null hypothesis that the two considered samples come from the same distribution. Columns two and four provide the maximum vertical distance between the two cumulative distribution functions. Vertical arrangement of test results congruent with horizontal arrangement of subfigures in Figure 2.

The formal test for stochastic dominance using the K-S procedure confirms what the figures suggest. The null hypothesis of the two-sided test under which the samples are drawn from the same distribution has to be rejected in all cases; see Table 3. Furthermore, we can never reject the null hypothesis of the one-sided test where we evaluate whether integration dominates outsourcing and offshoring dominates domestic sourcing. By way of contrast, we always have to reject the null hypothesis when performing the one-sided test with sourcing group categories reversed.[25]

[25]Since the sampling properties of our data vary depending on whether or not firms have more than 200 employees, we are worried about the possibility that the results might not generalize to the Spanish manufacturing industry as a whole. Therefore, we repeat the entire procedure for the two size categories separately. We find that our results are strongly confirmed for small-size firms, while there are some ambiguities as regards very large firms. The true productivity distribution of Spanish manufacturing firms could then be obtained by weighting the two distributions according to their appearance in the Spanish universe of manufacturing firms. Since the small-size firms are underrepresented in our sample, we argue that our findings may be generalized without any further concerns.

What do we learn from this first stage of our empirical analysis? We draw two main conclusions. First, there are significant productivity differentials between firms that choose a strategy of vertical integration and those that go for outsourcing. The productivity distribution for the first group of firms features clear stochastic dominance over the second. Notably, this statement holds true for both, the domestic and the foreign sourcing markets, as suggested by theory. Second, as regards the locational choice of intermediate input production, we find clear-cut evidence in favor of the idea that offshoring requires a higher productivity than domestic sourcing. Again, this result is in line with our theoretical model.

Estimating Sourcing Premia

In this subsection, we estimate productivity premia for firms in different sourcing groups using a regression framework borrowed from Bernard and Jensen (1999). We regress a firm's productivity level on binary variables that indicate a firm's specific sourcing strategy. In the theoretical model of Section II, firms face a quaternary choice of intermediate input production, where the unique profit-maximizing strategy is *either* foreign integration (*FI*), *or* foreign outsourcing (*FO*), *or* domestic integration (*DI*), *or* domestic outsourcing (*DO*). In the subsequent regression analysis, we capture this idea by computing "sourcing dummies" in a *hierarchical* and *mutually exclusive* way. If a firm is active in two or more sourcing modes, we assign it to the category which, according to our maintained hypothesis, is associated with the highest fixed cost. In an alternative specification, we depart from this approach and construct the sourcing indicators in a *mutually inclusive* way. For example, the dummies for *FI* and *FO* both take on a value of one, and the dummies for *DI* and *DO* a value of zero, if a firm engages in both vertical FDI and offshore outsourcing, but not in domestic sourcing. We thus allow for more flexibility in the estimation procedure, in order to detect differences to the former, more restrictive coding structure that satisfies mutual exclusion.

Formally, we estimate the following panel model:

$$y_{it} = \mathbf{x}_{it}\lambda + u_{it}, \quad i = 1, \ldots, N, \quad t = 1, \ldots, T, \tag{7}$$

where $u_{it} = c_i + \varepsilon_{it}$.

In this expression, y_{it} is the dependent variable for firm i at time t, $\mathbf{x}_{it} = (1, x_{it2}, \ldots, x_{itk})$ is a vector of explanatory variables, $\lambda = (\lambda_1, \lambda_2, \ldots, \lambda_k)'$ is a vector of parameters to estimate (including an intercept), and u_{it} is a composite error term including an unobserved firm-effect c_i and an idiosyncratic error ε_{it}.

We implement three estimation methods. The first simply pools the data and applies OLS. This estimator yields consistent estimates, as long as there is no systematic contemporaneous correlation between the composite error term and the explanatory variables. To take into account serial correlation within panel units arising from the unobserved firm-level effect c_i, we always report robust standard errors clustered by firm. Second, we average all variables across the two time periods and apply OLS, whereby we again disregard the time-variation in the data.[26] This estimator is called the "between-estimator" in the literature. The model reads as

$$\bar{y} = \bar{\mathbf{x}}_i\lambda + \bar{u}_i, \quad i = 1, \ldots, N, \qquad (8)$$
$$\text{where } \bar{u}_i = c_i + \varepsilon_i,$$

Bars indicate mean values over time. For this model to deliver consistent estimates, the variables in $\mathbf{x}_{it}$ need to be strictly exogenous, conditional on c_i, and $\mathbf{x}_{it}$ has to be independent from c_i. The third estimation method explicitly treats the data as a panel and controls for unobserved heterogeneity across firms by estimating a random-effects model. Under the same assumptions as before, this is an efficient estimator.

Our theoretical analysis in Section II highlights the interplay between firm-specific productivity θ and industry-specific headquarter-elasticity η in shaping firms' global sourcing decisions. Obviously, this interaction implies that the productivity premia may differ across industries, provided that industries feature different η-values. Although we do include industry dummies, we emphasize that this does not amount to controlling for this "headquarter-elasticity-effect".[27] From previous research we must expect that there is a productivity premium also on exporting; see Bernard *et al.*

[26] Note again that we observe the sourcing strategies for the years 2006 and 2007 only.

[27] As we have shown in Section II, the productivity ranking also depends on a certain fixed cost ranking.

(2007). To control for this, we additionally incorporate a firm's export status (*EXPORT*) in our set of regressors. Otherwise, we would be liable to observe spurious positive correlation between foreign sourcing modes and productivity. This could happen, for instance, if firms obtain access to new information through exporting, and if that information reduces the fixed cost of offshoring. Furthermore, we follow the empirical literature on productivity premia by including a firm's age (*AGE*) and size in terms of employees (*SIZE*) as control variables. From established theory, we expect a positive sign on the size coefficient. Where relevant, we always include a year dummy in our regressions, in order to isolate our estimates from any year-specific effects.

As already mentioned, our sample includes observations where firms report not to source any inputs outside their own hierarchical control. For both of our coding rules, these firms should be assigned zero values for all indicator variables for sourcing. Strictly speaking, the global sourcing model of Section II is silent on why such firms should exist. It assumes at the outset that generating revenue requires *two different agents* to be involved in the production relationship. We tackle this problem in two ways. First, we exclude all "non-sourcing firms" from the sample and estimate all productivity premia relative to the baseline category of domestic outsourcing. Our model suggests a productivity-dependent sorting pattern such that only the most productive firms source through vertical integration of a foreign input-supplier, and only the least productive firms outsource intermediate input production in the domestic economy. Moreover, firms that outsource the input to a foreign supplier are expected to feature a higher productivity level than firms pursuing vertical integration of a domestic supplier. Under the fixed cost ordering hypothesized in Section II, we thus expect the following coefficient ranking for our three indicator variables: $FI > FO > DI$. The second strategy is to include indicator variables for all four sourcing modes in the regression and treat the "non-sourcing firm" as the baseline category, where we have no *ex ante* view on the productivity level of non-sourcing firms relative to the other modes. In this case, the coefficient ranking is expected to satisfy $FI > FO > DI > DO$.

Tables 4 and 5 present the first set of results for total factor productivity premia, based on the restricted sample of true headquarter firms. We summarize the most relevant results as follows. First, we find the

Table 4. Total factor productivity premia (mutually exclusive sourcing dummies, non-sourcing firms excluded)

	Pooled OLS			Between estimator			Random effects		
Variables	(1)	(2)	(3)	(4)	(5)	(6)	(7)	(8)	(9)
FI	0.447***	0.403***	0.236**	0.532***	0.484***	0.295**	0.371***	0.324***	0.192**
	(0.107)	(0.109)	(0.105)	(0.131)	(0.133)	(0.134)	(0.089)	(0.091)	(0.085)
FO	0.192***	0.163***	0.118***	0.224***	0.192***	0.142***	0.145***	0.117***	0.081***
	(0.027)	(0.030)	(0.029)	(0.032)	(0.035)	(0.035)	(0.027)	(0.029)	(0.029)
DI	0.177**	0.171**	0.076	0.177**	0.170**	0.059	0.118*	0.110*	0.040
	(0.073)	(0.074)	(0.076)	(0.081)	(0.081)	(0.082)	(0.065)	(0.065)	(0.067)
Age		−0.000	−0.002**		−0.000	−0.001*		−0.000	−0.001*
		(0.001)	(0.001)		(0.001)	(0.001)		(0.001)	(0.001)
Export		0.088***	0.030		0.0812**	0.019		0.101***	0.048
		(0.029)	(0.031)		(0.032)	(0.033)		(0.028)	(0.030)
Size			0.085***			0.086***			0.085***
			(0.014)			(0.014)			(0.014)

(*Continued*)

Table 4. (*Continued*)

	Pooled OLS			Between estimator			Random effects		
Variables	(1)	(2)	(3)	(4)	(5)	(6)	(7)	(8)	(9)
Constant	8.318***	8.286***	8.009***	8.280***	8.248***	7.973***	8.320***	8.274***	7.994***
	(0.069)	(0.071)	(0.080)	(0.080)	(0.082)	(0.092)	(0.068)	(0.070)	(0.080)
Industry-fixed effects	Yes	Yes	Yes	Yes	Yes	Yes	Yes	Yes	Yes
Year-fixed effects	Yes	Yes	Yes	No	No	No	Yes	Yes	Yes
$H0$: $FI = FO$	0.02	0.03	0.26	0.02	0.03	0.25	0.01	0.02	0.19
$H0$: $FI = DI$	0.04	0.07	0.20	0.02	0.04	0.12	0.02	0.05	0.14
$H0$: $FO = DI$	0.84	0.92	0.58	0.57	0.79	0.32	0.67	0.92	0.53
Observations	2,474	2,474	2,474	2,474	2,474	2,474	2,474	2,474	2,474
R^2	0.14	0.14	0.17	0.16	0.17	0.19	0.16	0.16	0.19

The table gives estimation results obtained with the Bernard and Jensen (1999) methodology. Each column represents a separate regression where the dependent variable $PROD_{OP}$ is a function of dummy variables for foreign integration (*FI*), foreign outsourcing (*FO*), domestic integration (*DI*), and a firm's size in terms of employees (*SIZE*), age (*AGE*), and export status (*EXPORT*). The sourcing dummies are mutually exclusive. If a firm is active in two or more sourcing modes simultaneously, it is assigned to the category which is supposed to be associated with the highest fixed costs. The sample excludes firms with domestic or foreign parent companies as well as non-sourcing firms. The lower part of the table gives p-values of tests for equality of coefficients. Robust standard errors are clustered by firm (except for the between estimator) and given in parentheses. The size variable is in natural logs. *, **, *** indicate significance at the 10%, 5%, 1% levels, respectively.

Table 5. Total factor productivity premia (mutually exclusive sourcing dummies, non-sourcing firms included)

	Pooled OLS			Between estimator			Random effects		
Variables	(1)	(2)	(3)	(4)	(5)	(6)	(7)	(8)	(9)
FI	0.428***	0.380***	0.205*	0.509***	0.461***	0.266*	0.346***	0.299***	0.162*
	(0.112)	(0.113)	(0.109)	(0.141)	(0.142)	(0.143)	(0.093)	(0.093)	(0.088)
FO	0.169***	0.140***	0.088**	0.198***	0.171**	0.112*	0.117***	0.092**	0.053
	(0.045)	(0.045)	(0.044)	(0.066)	(0.067)	(0.066)	(0.038)	(0.039)	(0.038)
DI	0.153*	0.150*	0.048	0.149	0.149	0.030	0.089	0.086	0.012
	(0.081)	(0.081)	(0.084)	(0.099)	(0.099)	(0.099)	(0.070)	(0.070)	(0.071)
DO	−0.022	−0.017	−0.024	−0.027	−0.018	−0.026	−0.024	−0.019	−0.023
	(0.043)	(0.042)	(0.041)	(0.064)	(0.064)	(0.063)	(0.035)	(0.035)	(0.034)
Age		−0.000	−0.002**		−0.000	−0.001		0.000	−0.001*
		(0.001)	(0.001)		(0.001)	(0.001)		(0.001)	(0.001)
Export		0.100***	0.041		0.091***	0.029		0.108***	0.054*
		(0.028)	(0.030)		(0.031)	(0.032)		(0.027)	(0.029)
Size			0.086***			0.086***			0.087***
			(0.013)			(0.013)			(0.013)

(*Continued*)

Table 5. (*Continued*)

	Pooled OLS			Between estimator			Random effects		
Variables	(1)	(2)	(3)	(4)	(5)	(6)	(7)	(8)	(9)
Constant	8.347***	8.303***	8.030***	8.324***	8.275***	8.007***	8.357***	8.298***	8.016***
	(0.077)	(0.079)	(0.085)	(0.0968)	(0.0989)	(0.106)	(0.074)	(0.076)	(0.083)
Industry-fixed effects	Yes	Yes	Yes	Yes	Yes	Yes	Yes	Yes	Yes
Year-fixed effects	Yes	Yes	Yes	No	No	No	Yes	Yes	Yes
H0: FI = FO	0.02	0.02	0.25	0.02	0.03	0.02	0.01	0.02	0.18
H0: FI = DI	0.03	0.07	0.20	0.02	0.04	0.11	0.02	0.05	0.14
H0: FO = DI	0.83	0.89	0.60	0.55	0.80	0.32	0.66	0.92	0.53
H0: FI = DO	0.00	0.00	0.03	0.00	0.00	0.03	0.00	0.00	0.03
H0: FO = DO	0.00	0.00	0.00	0.00	0.00	0.00	0.00	0.00	0.01
H0: DI = DO	0.02	0.02	0.35	0.03	0.04	0.49	0.08	0.10	0.60
Observations	2,632	2,632	2,632	2,632	2,632	2,632	2,632	2,632	2,632
R^2	0.14	0.14	0.17	0.16	0.17	0.19	0.16	0.16	0.19

The table gives estimation results obtained with the Bernard and Jensen (1999) methodology. Each column represents a separate regression where the dependent variable $PROD_{OP}$ is a function of dummy variables for foreign integration (*FI*), foreign outsourcing (*FO*), domestic integration (*DI*), domestic outsourcing (*DO*), and a firm's size in terms of employees (*SIZE*), age (*AGE*), and export status (*EXPORT*). The sourcing dummies are mutually exclusive. If a firm is active in two or more sourcing modes simultaneously, it is assigned to the category which is supposed to be associated with the highest fixed costs. The sample excludes firms with domestic or foreign parent companies but includes non-sourcing firms. The lower part of the table gives p-values of tests for equality of coefficients. Robust standard errors are clustered by firm (except for the between estimator) and given in parentheses. The size variable is in natural logs. *, **, *** indicate significance at the 10%, 5%, 1% levels, respectively.

hypothesized ranking of coefficients in the overwhelming majority of cases. Notice that the ranking is preserved when firm size is controlled for. Among the indicator variables, foreign integration consistently exhibits the largest of all coefficients, and it is always significantly different from zero. The results indicate that firms sourcing through vertical integration of a foreign supplier are roughly 50% more productive than firms which source through an independent domestic supplier, assuming that firm size does not play a role.[28] Second, firms engaged in domestic outsourcing are consistently revealed as the least productive of all. In Table 4, all coefficients of all other sourcing-dummies are positive and mostly significant, while in Table 5 the dummy for domestic outsourcing is the only sourcing indicator with a negative coefficient. Translating our regression coefficients into magnitudes of premia, we recognize that firms engaged in foreign outsourcing are somewhat above 20% more productive than those which do so in the home economy. For domestic integration the premium is somewhat below 20%.[29] Third, we do not find a statistically significant difference between firms which choose a strategy of foreign outsourcing and those which source through domestic vertical integration, although the point estimates of the coefficients for *FO* and *DI* suggest that the former are more productive than the latter. Generally speaking, our regressions elucidate important structural differences in the productivity levels of firms depending on their sourcing channels, and these differences are consistent with the model of global sourcing introduced by Antràs and Helpman (2004).

How do things change if we code our indicator variables for the sourcing strategies in a *mutually inclusive* way? Tables 6 and 7 reveal that the picture changes dramatically. First, the results no longer suggest a robust ranking of sourcing coefficients. Although we can still be confident that firms engaged in domestic outsourcing belong to the least productive firms in the sample (together with "non-sourcing firms"), we do not find a significant difference between any two of the remaining sourcing coefficients. How does this fit with our earlier results obtained with mutually exclusive sourcing dummies? Strictly speaking, our regressions suggest that *any* sourcing category

[28]The premia are calculated from the coefficients as follows: $\text{PREMIUM}^{\ell\kappa} = 100 \times [\exp(\lambda^{\ell\kappa}) - 1]$.

[29]Again, we are looking at Table 3 at the columns where we do not control for size.

Table 6. **Total factor productivity premia (mutually inclusive sourcing dummies, non-sourcing firms included)**

	Pooled OLS			Between estimator			Random effects		
Variables	(1)	(2)	(3)	(4)	(5)	(6)	(7)	(8)	(9)
FI	0.194*	0.182	0.096	0.258*	0.242*	0.144	0.197**	0.179*	0.102
	(0.116)	(0.115)	(0.108)	(0.133)	(0.134)	(0.133)	(0.096)	(0.095)	(0.087)
FO	0.173***	0.146***	0.111***	0.204***	0.174***	0.133***	0.131***	0.104***	0.076***
	(0.026)	(0.029)	(0.028)	(0.032)	(0.034)	(0.034)	(0.027)	(0.029)	(0.028)
DI	0.196***	0.193***	0.097	0.174***	0.170***	0.064	0.164***	0.159***	0.078
	(0.055)	(0.056)	(0.060)	(0.058)	(0.058)	(0.060)	(0.053)	(0.053)	(0.056)
Age		−0.001	−0.002**		−0.000	−0.001*		−0.000	−0.001*
		(0.001)	(0.001)		(0.001)	(0.001)		(0.001)	(0.001)
Export		0.087***	0.033		0.083***	0.022		0.101***	0.050*
		(0.029)	(0.031)		(0.032)	(0.033)		(0.028)	(0.030)
Size			0.081***			0.084***			0.082***
			(0.014)			(0.014)			(0.014)

(*Continued*)

Table 6. (*Continued*)

Variables	Pooled OLS (1)	Pooled OLS (2)	Pooled OLS (3)	Between estimator (4)	Between estimator (5)	Between estimator (6)	Random effects (7)	Random effects (8)	Random effects (9)
Constant	8.298***	8.269***	8.013***	8.265***	8.235***	7.974***	8.301***	8.259***	7.997***
	(0.069)	(0.070)	(0.080)	(0.080)	(0.082)	(0.092)	(0.068)	(0.070)	(0.080)
Industry-fixed effects	Yes	Yes	Yes	Yes	Yes	Yes	Yes	Yes	Yes
Year-fixed effects	Yes	Yes	Yes	No	No	No	Yes	Yes	Yes
$H0$: $FI = FO$	0.86	0.77	0.89	0.71	0.63	0.94	0.52	0.46	0.79
$H0$: $FI = DI$	0.99	0.93	0.99	0.59	0.64	0.60	0.78	0.86	0.82
$H0$: $FO = DI$	0.71	0.45	0.83	0.65	0.96	0.31	0.57	0.36	0.98
Observations	2,474	2,474	2,474	2,474	2,474	2,474	2,474	2,474	2,474
R^2	0.14	0.15	0.17	0.17	0.17	0.19	0.16	0.17	0.19

The table gives estimation results obtained with the Bernard and Jensen (1999) methodology. Each column represents a separate regression where the dependent variable $PROD_{OP}$ is a function of dummy variables for foreign integration (*FI*), foreign outsourcing (*FO*), domestic integration (*DI*), and a firm's size in terms of employees (*SIZE*), age (*AGE*), and export status (*EXPORT*). The sourcing dummies are mutually inclusive. The sample excludes firms with domestic or foreign parent companies as well as non-sourcing firms. The lower part of the table gives p-values of tests for equality of coefficients. Robust standard errors are clustered by firm (except for the between estimator) and given in parentheses. The size variable is in natural logs. *, **, *** indicate significance at the 10%, 5%, 1% levels, respectively.

Table 7. **Total factor productivity premia (mutually exclusive sourcing dummies, non-sourcing firms excluded)**

	Pooled OLS			Between estimator			Random effects		
Variables	(1)	(2)	(3)	(4)	(5)	(6)	(7)	(8)	(9)
FI	0.198*	0.182	0.095	0.262**	0.242*	0.145	0.200**	0.180*	0.101
	(0.115)	(0.114)	(0.106)	(0.132)	(0.132)	(0.131)	(0.095)	(0.094)	(0.085)
FO	0.170***	0.137***	0.103***	0.204***	0.168***	0.128***	0.124***	0.096***	0.069**
	(0.026)	(0.028)	(0.027)	(0.032)	(0.034)	(0.034)	(0.026)	(0.028)	(0.027)
DI	0.193***	0.190***	0.091	0.170***	0.165***	0.059	0.161***	0.155***	0.073
	(0.055)	(0.055)	(0.059)	(0.057)	(0.057)	(0.059)	(0.052)	(0.052)	(0.055)
DO	0.011	0.017	0.009	−0.013	−0.003	−0.011	0.006	0.010	0.004
	(0.037)	(0.037)	(0.036)	(0.054)	(0.054)	(0.054)	(0.032)	(0.031)	(0.031)
Age		−0.000	−0.002**		−0.000	−0.001*		−0.000	−0.001*
		(0.001)	(0.001)		(0.001)	(0.001)		(0.001)	(0.001)
Export		0.100***	0.044		0.093***	0.032		0.109***	0.057**
		(0.028)	(0.030)		(0.031)	(0.032)		(0.027)	(0.029)
Size			0.083***			0.084***			0.083***
			(0.014)			(0.013)			(0.014)

(Continued)

Table 7. (*Continued*)

	Pooled OLS			Between estimator			Random effects		
Variables	(1)	(2)	(3)	(4)	(5)	(6)	(7)	(8)	(9)
Constant	8.299***	8.256***	8.004***	8.297***	8.249***	7.994***	8.312***	8.257***	7.996***
	(0.075)	(0.077)	(0.083)	(0.091)	(0.094)	(0.101)	(0.073)	(0.074)	(0.082)
Industry-fixed effects	Yes	Yes	Yes	Yes	Yes	Yes	Yes	Yes	Yes
Year-fixed effects	Yes	Yes	Yes	No	No	No	Yes	Yes	Yes
$H0$: $FI = FO$	0.81	0.71	0.95	0.68	0.60	0.90	0.46	0.41	0.73
$H0$: $FI = DI$	0.97	0.95	0.98	0.55	0.62	0.57	0.73	0.82	0.79
$H0$: $FO = DI$	0.70	0.41	0.86	0.61	0.97	0.31	0.54	0.33	0.96
$H0$: $FI = DO$	0.12	0.17	0.44	0.06	0.09	0.28	0.05	0.09	0.28
$H0$: $FO = DO$	0.00	0.01	0.05	0.00	0.01	0.04	0.01	0.06	0.14
$H0$: $DI = DO$	0.01	0.01	0.23	0.02	0.03	0.37	0.01	0.01	0.26
Observations	2,632	2,632	2,632	2,632	2,632	2,632	2,632	2,632	2,632
R^2	0.14	0.15	0.17	0.16	0.17	0.19	0.16	0.17	0.19

The table gives estimation results obtained with the Bernard and Jensen (1999) methodology. Each column represents a separate regression where the dependent variable $PROD_{OP}$ is a function of dummy variables for foreign integration (*FI*), foreign outsourcing (*FO*), domestic integration (*DI*), domestic outsourcing (*DO*), and a firm's size in terms of employees (*SIZE*), age (*AGE*), and export status (*EXPORT*). The sourcing dummies are mutually inclusive. The sample excludes firms with domestic or foreign parent companies but includes non-sourcing firms. The lower part of the table gives p-values of tests for equality of coefficients. Robust standard errors are clustered by firm (except for the between estimator) and given in parentheses. The size variable is in natural logs. *, **, *** indicate significance at the 10%, 5%, 1% levels, respectively.

contributes equally to a firm's productivity premium, relative to the pure domestic outsourcing (or "non-sourcing") case. For each additional sourcing mode, the productivity premium rises by roughly 20 percentage points when size is not controlled for. Thus, the interpretation seems straightforward: foreign integration *per se* does not imply that a firm is among the most productive ones. Rather, high productivity premia seem related to the fact that firms simultaneously combine *various* sourcing channels. This is remarkable in that it points to the need for further refinements to theory, so that it may explain such complex strategies.

It is worth noting that the inclusion of firm size affects the coefficients for outsourcing and integration dummies differently. While it picks up all productivity differences of the two integration modes with respect to the baseline categories, the coefficient for *FO* continues to be highly significant. Apparently, firm size plays a superior role in explaining productivity premia of vertically integrating firms.

In the text, we only report the results for the restricted sample, but we find at least two interesting differences between the estimates with the unrestricted and the restricted samples.[30] First, the coefficient ranking obtained with mutually exclusive coding of the indicator variables changes slightly once we include "non-headquarter" firms in the sample. Indeed, what we observe is a reversal in the ranking of the coefficients for foreign outsourcing and domestic integration, and this reversal is at least marginally significant in several specifications. This finding is consistent with empirical evidence reported by Federico (2010), who cannot identify true headquarters in his sample of Italian manufacturing firms.[31] Second, all point estimates of the sourcing coefficients are smaller with the unrestricted sample than with the restricted sample, with one exception: The *DI*-dummy features a larger coefficient with the unrestricted sample when "non-sourcing firms" are excluded. Generally, this observation suggests that true headquarter firms have to overcome higher productivity hurdles relative to the domestic outsourcing category than "non-headquarter" firms whose sourcing strategy

[30] See the appendix for estimation results with the unrestricted sample.

[31] It should be noted, however, that this sort of ambiguity in the data cannot be interpreted as evidence against the model. In fact, a potential reversal in the productivity ranking of *DI* and *FO* firms can easily be rationalized within the model by assuming sufficiently high fixed costs for domestic integration compared to foreign outsourcing.

might not always reflect their own decision, but that of a domestic or foreign parental company.

V. FINAL REMARKS

Recent theoretical developments have helped us understand why firm heterogeneity in productivity might be a long-run equilibrium phenomenon. Such theoretical models imply that firms with different productivity levels behave differently, even when facing the same market environment. This seems corroborated by a wealth of empirical literature which shows that more productive firms are more likely to actively pursue strategies of internationalization both in generating revenue and sourcing inputs. We now have an impressive body of theory that explains such "globalization premia" through a self-selection of firms into different strategies of internationalization, based on exogenous differences in their productivity.

In this chapter, we have presented empirical evidence on such premia, based on a very prominent model of this type developed by Antràs and Helpman (2004). In this model, firm heterogeneity is determined as in Melitz (2003), and firms face the problem of sourcing their inputs in an environment that is characterized by a hold-up problem due to lack of enforceable contracts. They react to this environment by choosing between two organizational forms of sourcing, viz. outsourcing *via* arms-length transactions and acquiring property rights in the desired inputs, respectively. In addition, firms face the more familiar choice between domestic and foreign sourcing. Thus, there are four possible strategies, and the model suggests that firms with different productivity levels adopt different strategies. In this chapter, we have first examined the interplay between a firm's productivity and other characteristics of production that should determine its sourcing strategy. We have then examined the empirical relevance of the "global sourcing premia" implied by the model, relying on Spanish firm-level data that are uniquely geared towards such an empirical exercise. In doing so, we have used both, non-parametric methods as well as an estimation approach.

We find a productivity ranking across different sourcing strategies, which is impressively consistent with the model. Firms that choose vertical integration tend to be more productive than those who rely on arms-length transactions, and firms who source offshore are generally more productive than those who source their inputs domestically. This is in line with the theoretical model, provided that foreign sourcing unambiguously requires larger fixed costs than domestic sources, and that exercising property rights always entails a larger fixed cost than arms-length transactions, as hypothesized by Antràs and Helpman (2004). We do not offer any independent empirical support for this ranking, but the ranking seems very plausible.

We see the following agenda for future research on this issue. First, as regards theoretical modeling, we feel that the model should be generalized so as to generate outcomes where a firm adopts foreign and domestic sourcing strategies as well as different organizational modes at the same time, because this is what we find in the data. A step in this direction has been achieved in Antràs and Helpman (2008) where the assumption of complete lack of enforceable contracts has been relaxed. In our view, a more general and flexible modeling framework relating to the notion of offshoring and/or vertical integration would constitute further progress.

As regards empirical analysis, a more comprehensive examination of how a firm's sourcing strategy relates to further characteristics of the underlying production relationship would seem important. In particular, the notion of a "headquarter-elasticity" which is a key variable in the model should also be brought into the realm of empirical observations. Our analysis suggests that doing so through empirical measures of capital intensity or skill intensity as a proxy risks confounding strategic issues pertaining to the hold-up problem with cost advantages from offshoring. These two aspects need to be clearly separated, both in the theoretical framework and the empirical analysis.

ACKNOWLEDGMENTS

We thank seminar participants at the University of Tübingen, the 5th Danish International Economics Workshop, Aarhus School of Business, the International Workshop on Firm and Product Heterogeneity, H.U. Brussels, the ETSG 2009, University of Rome, the Japanese and U.S. International

Trade Conference, University of Michigan, the 9th FIW Workshop, Vienna, and *THE* Christmas Workshop 2009, University of Hohenheim, for useful comments. We are especially grateful to Jörn Kleinert, Jagadeesh Sivadasan, and Dieter Urban for their very helpful suggestions. Thanks are also due to Inga Heiland and Ina Charlotte Jäkel for editorial assistance.

APPENDIX

This appendix gives information on how we compute the different measures of productivity at the level of the firm. Where necessary, we calculate real values in terms of 2007 prices using sectoral price indexes provided by the National Statistics Institute (INE) in Spain.

Labor productivity. $PROD_L$. Computed as value added divided by the approximation of hours effectively worked. The units of the hourly productivity may be interpreted as Euros per hour. This variable is calculated only for companies with non-negative value added. Value added is defined as the sum of sales, changes in the stock of inventory, and other operating income minus the sum of purchases and the costs of external services.

Total factor productivity. $PROD_{OLS}$. Computed as the residual of sectoral production function estimates according to the following regression equation (estimated by standard OLS).

$$y_t = \lambda_1 k_t + \lambda_2 l_t + \lambda_3 a_t + u_t, \qquad \text{(A1)}$$

where y_t is log-value added in year $t = 2000, \ldots, 2007$, k_t is the log value of the capital stock net of amortization and depreciation, l_t is the log value of the average number of employees per year, a_t is the age of the firm (in years), and u_t is the error term. The capital stock excludes all immaterial and financial assets. The average number of employees over the year is the sum of full-time regular employees, 1/2 of part-time regular employees (both items as of December 31st), and the average number of eventual workers.

Total factor productivity. $PROD_{FE}$. Computed as the residual of sectoral estimates of Equation (A1) with a fixed-effects model in order to account for unobserved time-invariant firm heterogeneity. The basic idea is as follows.

Table A1. TFP premia (unrestricted sample, mutually exclusive sourcing dummies, non-sourcing firms excluded)

	Pooled OLS			Between estimator			Random effects		
Variables	(1)	(2)	(3)	(4)	(5)	(6)	(7)	(8)	(9)
FI	0.331***	0.287***	0.142***	0.363***	0.319***	0.160***	0.278***	0.236***	0.118***
	(0.041)	(0.043)	(0.046)	(0.045)	(0.047)	(0.050)	(0.037)	(0.039)	(0.041)
FO	0.179***	0.147***	0.095***	0.205***	0.172***	0.115***	0.138***	0.110***	0.070***
	(0.025)	(0.026)	(0.026)	(0.028)	(0.030)	(0.030)	(0.023)	(0.024)	(0.024)
DI	0.234***	0.219***	0.123***	0.253***	0.239***	0.133**	0.185***	0.172***	0.094**
	(0.045)	(0.045)	(0.046)	(0.052)	(0.053)	(0.053)	(0.040)	(0.040)	(0.040)
Age		−0.000	−0.001**		−0.000	−0.001**		0.000	−0.001*
		(0.001)	(0.001)		(0.001)	(0.001)		(0.001)	(0.001)
Export		0.096***	0.020		0.090***	0.011		0.108***	0.035
		(0.025)	(0.027)		(0.028)	(0.029)		(0.024)	(0.026)
Size			0.090***			0.090***			0.090***
			(0.010)			(0.010)			(0.010)

(*Continued*)

Table A1. (*Continued*)

	Pooled OLS			Between estimator			Random effects		
Variables	(1)	(2)	(3)	(4)	(5)	(6)	(7)	(8)	(9)
Constant	8.352***	8.309***	8.019***	8.332***	8.293***	8.005***	8.372***	8.317***	8.021***
	(0.065)	(0.067)	(0.075)	(0.067)	(0.069)	(0.075)	(0.067)	(0.069)	(0.077)
Industry-fixed effects	Yes	Yes	Yes	Yes	Yes	Yes	Yes	Yes	Yes
Year-fixed effects	Yes	Yes	Yes	No	No	No	Yes	Yes	Yes
$H0$: $FI = FO$	0.00	0.00	0.28	0.00	0.00	0.34	0.00	0.00	0.22
$H0$: $FI = DI$	0.08	0.22	0.72	0.09	0.22	0.67	0.05	0.19	0.62
$H0$: $FO = DI$	0.22	0.12	0.54	0.37	0.22	0.75	0.24	0.13	0.54
Observations	3717	3717	3717	3717	3717	3717	3717	3717	3717
R^2	0.15	0.15	0.18	0.17	0.18	0.21	0.17	0.18	0.21

The table gives estimation results obtained with the Bernard and Jensen (1999) methodology. Each column represents a separate regression where the dependent variable $PROD_{OP}$ is a function of dummy variables for foreign integration (*FI*), foreign outsourcing (*FO*), domestic integration (*DI*), and a firm's size in terms of employees (*SIZE*), age (*AGE*), and export status (*EXPORT*). The sourcing dummies are mutually exclusive. If a firm is active in two or more sourcing modes simultaneously, it is assigned to the category which is supposed to be associated with the highest fixed costs. The sample includes firms with domestic or foreign parent companies but excludes non-sourcing firms. The lower part of the table gives p-values of tests for equality of coefficients. Robust standard errors are clustered by firm (except for the between estimator) and given in parentheses. The size variable is in natural logs. *, **, *** indicate significance at the 10%, 5%, 1% levels, respectively.

Table A2. TFP premia (unrestricted sample, mutually exclusive sourcing dummies, non-sourcing firms included)

	Pooled OLS			Between estimator			Random effects		
Variables	(1)	(2)	(3)	(4)	(5)	(6)	(7)	(8)	(9)
FI	0.292***	0.246***	0.104*	0.307***	0.264***	0.111	0.243***	0.204***	0.089*
	(0.052)	(0.052)	(0.053)	(0.069)	(0.070)	(0.071)	(0.045)	(0.045)	(0.046)
FO	0.140***	0.109***	0.058	0.149**	0.119**	0.067	0.103***	0.078**	0.039
	(0.041)	(0.040)	(0.039)	(0.060)	(0.060)	(0.059)	(0.034)	(0.034)	(0.033)
DI	0.195***	0.183***	0.088	0.198***	0.189**	0.086	0.147***	0.138***	0.0634
	(0.055)	(0.054)	(0.054)	(0.075)	(0.075)	(0.074)	(0.046)	(0.046)	(0.046)
DO	−0.037	−0.032	−0.032	−0.055	−0.047	−0.042	−0.031	−0.026	−0.026
	(0.039)	(0.038)	(0.037)	(0.059)	(0.059)	(0.058)	(0.032)	(0.031)	(0.030)
Age		−0.000	−0.001**		−0.000	−0.001**		0.000	−0.001**
		(0.001)	(0.001)		(0.001)	(0.001)		(0.001)	(0.001)
Export		0.110***	0.032		0.103***	0.023		0.117***	0.044*
		(0.024)	(0.026)		(0.028)	(0.028)		(0.023)	(0.025)
Size			0.090***			0.091***			0.090***
			(0.010)			(0.010)			(0.010)

(*Continued*)

Table A2. (*Continued*)

	Pooled OLS			Between estimator			Random effects		
Variables	(1)	(2)	(3)	(4)	(5)	(6)	(7)	(8)	(9)
Constant	8.393***	8.336***	8.047***	8.396***	8.339***	8.046***	8.411***	8.343***	8.045***
	(0.072)	(0.074)	(0.080)	(0.085)	(0.087)	(0.091)	(0.071)	(0.073)	(0.079)
Industry-fixed effects	Yes	Yes	Yes	Yes	Yes	Yes	Yes	Yes	Yes
Year-fixed effects	Yes	Yes	Yes	No	No	No	Yes	Yes	Yes
$H0: FI = FO$	0.00	0.00	0.29	0.00	0.00	0.33	0.00	0.00	0.21
$H0: FI = DI$	0.08	0.26	0.77	0.09	0.25	0.69	0.04	0.18	0.59
$H0: FO = DI$	0.22	0.11	0.51	0.37	0.20	0.72	0.26	0.13	0.54
$H0: FI = DO$	0.00	0.00	0.00	0.00	0.00	0.00	0.00	0.00	0.00
$H0: FO = DO$	0.00	0.00	0.00	0.00	0.00	0.00	0.00	0.00	0.01
$H0: DI = DO$	0.00	0.00	0.01	0.00	0.00	0.02	0.00	0.00	0.02
Observations	3915	3915	3915	3915	3915	3915	3915	3915	3915
R^2	0.15	0.15	0.18	0.17	0.18	0.21	0.17	0.18	0.21

The table gives estimation results obtained with the Bernard and Jensen (1999) methodology. Each column represents a separate regression where the dependent variable $PROD_{OP}$ is a function of dummy variables for foreign integration (*FI*), foreign outsourcing (*FO*), domestic integration (*DI*), domestic outsourcing (*DO*), and a firm's size in terms of employees (*SIZE*), age (*AGE*), and export status (*EXPORT*). The sourcing dummies are mutually exclusive. If a firm is active in two or more sourcing modes simultaneously, it is assigned to the category which is supposed to be associated with the highest fixed costs. The sample includes firms with domestic or foreign parent companies as well as non-sourcing firms. The lower part of the table gives p-values of tests for equality of coefficients. Robust standard errors are clustered by firm (except for the between estimator) and given in parentheses. The size variable is in natural logs. *, **, *** indicate significance at the 10%, 5%, 1% levels, respectively.

Table A3. TFP premia (unrestricted sample, mutually inclusive sourcing dummies, non-sourcing firms excluded)

	Pooled OLS			Between estimator			Random effects		
Variables	(1)	(2)	(3)	(4)	(5)	(6)	(7)	(8)	(9)
FI	0.159***	0.139***	0.053	0.169***	0.149***	0.054	0.142***	0.123***	0.052
	(0.042)	(0.042)	(0.043)	(0.045)	(0.045)	(0.045)	(0.038)	(0.038)	(0.039)
FO	0.114***	0.083***	0.048**	0.139***	0.106***	0.068**	0.085***	0.058***	0.033
	(0.023)	(0.025)	(0.024)	(0.027)	(0.028)	(0.028)	(0.021)	(0.022)	(0.022)
DI	0.148***	0.140***	0.058	0.155***	0.147***	0.061*	0.125***	0.117***	0.048
	(0.034)	(0.035)	(0.036)	(0.035)	(0.035)	(0.035)	(0.031)	(0.031)	(0.033)
Age		0.000	−0.001**		0.000	−0.001**		0.000	−0.001*
		(0.001)	(0.001)		(0.001)	(0.001)		(0.001)	(0.001)
Export		0.108***	0.029		0.102***	0.020		0.117***	0.042
		(0.025)	(0.027)		(0.028)	(0.029)		(0.024)	(0.026)
Size			0.092***			0.093***			0.091***
			(0.011)			(0.011)			(0.011)

(*Continued*)

Table A3. (*Continued*)

	Pooled OLS			Between estimator			Random effects		
Variables	(1)	(2)	(3)	(4)	(5)	(6)	(7)	(8)	(9)
Constant	8.362***	8.310***	8.019***	8.343***	8.294***	8.004***	8.378***	8.316***	8.021***
	(0.063)	(0.066)	(0.074)	(0.067)	(0.069)	(0.075)	(0.065)	(0.068)	(0.077)
Industry-fixed effects	Yes	Yes	Yes	Yes	Yes	Yes	Yes	Yes	Yes
Year-fixed effects	Yes	Yes	Yes	No	No	No	Yes	Yes	Yes
$H0$: $FI = FO$	0.40	0.29	0.93	0.59	0.44	0.79	0.24	0.18	0.69
$H0$: $FI = DI$	0.85	0.99	0.94	0.82	0.97	0.90	0.73	0.91	0.92
$H0$: $FO = DI$	0.40	0.17	0.83	0.73	0.37	0.88	0.28	0.12	0.70
Observations	3717	3717	3717	3717	3717	3717	3717	3717	3717
R^2	0.14	0.15	0.17	0.17	0.17	0.20	0.17	0.17	0.21

The table gives estimation results obtained with the Bernard and Jensen (1999) methodology. Each column represents a separate regression where the dependent variable $PROD_{OP}$ is a function of dummy variables for foreign integration (FI), foreign outsourcing (FO), domestic integration (DI), and a firm's size in terms of employees ($SIZE$), age (AGE), and export status ($EXPORT$). The sourcing dummies are mutually inclusive. The sample includes firms with domestic or foreign parent companies but excludes non-sourcing firms. The lower part of the table gives p-values of tests for equality of coefficients. Robust standard errors are clustered by firm (except for the between estimator) and given in parentheses. The size variable is in natural logs. *, **, *** indicate significance at the 10%, 5%, 1% levels, respectively.

Table A4. TFP premia (unrestricted sample, mutually inclusive sourcing dummies, non-sourcing firms included)

	Pooled OLS			Between estimator			Random effects		
Variables	(1)	(2)	(3)	(4)	(5)	(6)	(7)	(8)	(9)
FI	0.158***	0.136***	0.052	0.167***	0.145***	0.053	0.143***	0.123***	0.054
	(0.042)	(0.042)	(0.043)	(0.044)	(0.045)	(0.045)	(0.038)	(0.038)	(0.038)
FO	0.111***	0.077***	0.042*	0.135***	0.098***	0.060**	0.081***	0.054**	0.028
	(0.023)	(0.024)	(0.024)	(0.026)	(0.028)	(0.028)	(0.021)	(0.022)	(0.021)
DI	0.146***	0.137***	0.056	0.152***	0.143***	0.058	0.121***	0.113***	0.045
	(0.034)	(0.034)	(0.036)	(0.034)	(0.034)	(0.035)	(0.031)	(0.031)	(0.032)
DO	−0.002	0.002	0.012	−0.019	−0.013	0.003	−0.004	−0.001	0.005
	(0.032)	(0.032)	(0.031)	(0.044)	(0.044)	(0.044)	(0.028)	(0.027)	(0.027)
Age		0.000	−0.001**		0.000	−0.001**		0.000	−0.001*
		(0.001)	(0.001)		(0.001)	(0.001)		(0.001)	(0.001)
Export		0.121***	0.041		0.115***	0.032		0.124***	0.050**
		(0.024)	(0.026)		(0.027)	(0.028)		(0.023)	(0.025)
Size			0.092***			0.093***			0.092***
			(0.010)			(0.010)			(0.010)

(*Continued*)

Table A4. (*Continued*)

	Pooled OLS			Between estimator			Random effects		
Variables	(1)	(2)	(3)	(4)	(5)	(6)	(7)	(8)	(9)
Constant	8.370***	8.305***	8.006***	8.372***	8.308***	8.003***	8.391***	8.318***	8.016***
	(0.068)	(0.070)	(0.077)	(0.076)	(0.078)	(0.084)	(0.068)	(0.070)	(0.079)
Industry-fixed effects	Yes	Yes	Yes	Yes	Yes	Yes	Yes	Yes	Yes
Year-fixed effects	Yes	Yes	Yes	No	No	No	Yes	Yes	Yes
$H0$: $FI = FO$	0.38	0.27	0.86	0.57	0.40	0.90	0.20	0.16	0.60
$H0$: $FI = DI$	0.83	0.99	0.94	0.79	0.97	0.93	0.67	0.86	0.86
$H0$: $FO = DI$	0.40	0.15	0.75	0.72	0.32	0.96	0.28	0.12	0.66
$H0$: $FI = DO$	0.00	0.01	0.46	0.00	0.01	0.43	0.00	0.01	0.31
$H0$: $FO = DO$	0.01	0.08	0.47	0.00	0.04	0.30	0.02	0.13	0.52
$H0$: $DI = DO$	0.00	0.00	0.35	0.00	0.01	0.33	0.00	0.00	0.33
Observations	3915	3915	3915	3915	3915	3915	3915	3915	3915
R^2	0.14	0.15	0.18	0.17	0.17	0.21	0.17	0.17	0.21

The table gives estimation results obtained with the Bernard and Jensen (1999) methodology. Each column represents a separate regression where the dependent variable $PROD_{OP}$ is a function of dummy variables for foreign integration (FI), foreign outsourcing (FO), domestic integration (DI), domestic outsourcing (DO), and a firm's size in terms of employees ($SIZE$), age (AGE), and export status ($EXPORT$). The sourcing dummies are mutually inclusive. The sample includes firms with domestic or foreign parent companies as well as non-sourcing firms. The lower part of the table gives p-values of tests for equality of coefficients. Robust standard errors are clustered by firm (except for the between estimator) and given in parentheses. The size variable is in natural logs. *, **, *** indicate significance at the 10%, 5%, 1% levels, respectively.

If $u_t = \Omega + \varepsilon_t$, where ε_t is an error term with usual properties and Ω is a time-invariant productivity differential that is being observed by the firm (but not the econometrician), then there may be systematic correlation between u_t and k_t and l_t because the firm will incorporate this additional information in the decision of how many inputs to use (*simultaneity bias*). Thus, the OLS estimates are biased. With the fixed-effects specification we eliminate Ω and get consistent estimates.

Total factor productivity. $PROD_{OP}$. Computed as the residual of estimates of Equation (A1) with the Olley and Pakes (1996) methodology. Suppose Ω changes over time such that $u_t = \Omega_t + \varepsilon_t$. Then, the fixed-effects model yields biased estimates. We account for this endogeneity issue by applying a consistent three-step estimation procedure proposed by Olley and Pakes (1996) where capital investment I_t is meant to proxy for the unobserved productivity shock Ω_t. In doing so, we automatically address the *selection bias* problem that results from inefficient firms exiting the market and constitutes another potential source of inconsistency. For details regarding the estimation algorithm, see Olley and Pakes (1996).

REFERENCES

Antràs, Pol (2003). "Firms, Contracts, and Trade Structure," *The Quarterly Journal of Economics*, 118(4): pp. 1375–1418.

Antràs, Pol and Elhanan Helpman (2004). "Global Sourcing," *Journal of Political Economy*, 112(3): pp. 552–580.

Antràs, Pol and Elhanan Helpman (2008). "Contractual Frictions and Global Sourcing," In *The Organization of Firms in a Global Economy*, E. Helpman, D. Marin, and T. Verdier, eds., Harvard University Press: Cambridge, MA.

Bernard, Andrew B. and J. Bradford Jensen (1999). "Exceptional Exporter Performance: Cause, Effect or Both?" *Journal of International Economics*, 47(1): pp. 1–25.

Bernard, Andrew B., J. Bradford Jensen, Stephen J. Redding and Peter K. Schott (2007). "Firms in International Trade," *Journal of Economic Perspectives*, 21(3): pp. 105–130.

Defever, Fabrice and Farid Toubal (2011). "Productivity, Relationship-specific Input and the Sourcing Modes of Multinationals," CEPR Discussion Paper No. 8656.

Dixit, Avinash K. and Joseph E. Stiglitz (1977). "Monopolistic Competition and Optimum Product Diversity," *American Economic Review*, 67(3): pp. 297–308.

Federico, Stefano (2010). "Outsourcing versus Integration at Home or Abroad and Firm Heterogeneity," *Empirica* 37(1): pp. 47–63.

Greenaway, David and Richard Kneller (2007). "Firm Heterogeneity, Exporting and Foreign Direct Investment," *Economic Journal*, 117(517): pp. F134–F161.

Grossman, Sanford J. and Oliver D. Hart (1986). "The Costs and Benefits of Ownership: A Theory of Vertical and Lateral Integration," *Journal of Political Economy*, 94(4): pp. 691–719.

Helpman, Elhanan (2006). "Trade, FDI, and the Organization of Firms," *Journal of Economics Literature*, 44(3): pp. 589–630.

Helpman, Elhanan, Marc J. Melitz and Stephen R. Yeaple (2004). "Exports versus FDI with Heterogeneous Firms," *American Economic Review*, 94(1): pp. 300–316.

Kohler, Wilhem and Marcel Smolka (2011). "Sourcing Premia with Incomplete Contracts: Theory and Evidence," *The B. E. Journal of Economic Analysis & Policy*, 11(1), Contributions.

Melitz, Marc J. (2003). "The Impact of Trade on Intra-Industry Reallocations and Aggregate Industry Productivity," *Econometrica*, 71(6): pp. 1695–1725.

Mrázová, Monika and J. Peter Neary (2011). "Selection Effects with Heterogenous Firms," mimeo, Oxford.

Nunn, Nathan and Daniel Trefler (2008). "The Boundaries of the Multinational Firm: An Empirical Analysis," In *The Organization of Firms in a Global Economy*, E. Helpman, D. Marin, and T. Verdier, eds., Harvard University Press: Cambridge, MA.

Olley, S. and A. Pakes (1996). "The Dynamics of Productivity in the Telecommunications Equipment Industry," *Econometrica*, 64(6): pp. 1263–1298.

Schwarz, Christian and Jens Südekum (2011). "Global Sourcing of Complex Production Process," CESifo Working Paper No. 3559, Munich.

Tomiura, Eiichi (2007). "Foreign Outsourcing, Exporting, and FDI: A Productivity Comparison at the Firm Level," *Journal of International Economics*, 72(1): pp. 113–127.

Yeaple, Stephen R. (2006). "Offshoring, Foreign Direct Investment, and the Structure of U.S. Trade," *Journal of the European Economic Association*, 4(2–3): pp. 602–611.

Comment

Jagadeesh Sivadasan

In Chapter 4, Wilhelm Kohler and Marcel Smolka examine the link between productivity and firm choices related to their sourcing decisions. In particular, they investigate how productivity relates to two binary choices — foreign versus domestic sourcing, and outsourcing versus vertical integration. This yields four (potentially non-exclusive) strategic choices: (i) Domestic Outsourcing (*DO*), (ii) Domestic Integration (*DI*), (iii) Foreign Outsourcing (*FO*), and (iv) Foreign Integration (*FI*).

To frame their empirical investigation, the authors present a rich theoretical framework, based on Antras and Helpman (2004). This model yields the prediction that firms within certain productivity (TFP) bands make particular strategic choices. The productivity bands yield the following rank ordering of productivity levels for the four choices: $\text{TFP}^{DO} < \text{TFP}^{DI} < \text{TFP}^{FO} < \text{TFP}^{FI}$.

The authors use a rich and interesting Spanish firm-level dataset to test this key prediction and find evidence consistent with the theoretical predictions. In particular, the data clearly show that domestic outsourcing is predominant for the least productive firms, and only the more productive firms undertake integration, and/or foreign sourcing.

This is a well-executed chapter, with a very apt theoretical framework and good data, and carefully done empirical work. The non-parametric explorations very nicely document the key patterns in the data, and these are confirmed by the more rigorous regression results. I shall highlight below for readers some of the interesting aspects of the Chapter, acknowledging that the authors have carefully thought and discussed many of the issues noted.

1. *Fairly unique data and hence relatively unique empirical findings*: The authors have information in their dataset that is fairly unique. Few plant-level datasets have the detailed information on input sourcing required

to test the Antras-Helpman model carefully. For example, the widely used U.S. Annual Survey of Manufactures or the Census of Manufactures (Bernard and Jensen, 1999), or Chilean and Colombian (Roberts and Tybout, 1996) plant level datasets, do not have information on whether inputs are sourced from a related party or whether they are outsourced. Thus, the question they address has not been as widely investigated in the literature, in contrast to the very large number of studies that have looked at the productivity premium for exporters.

Two other studies, mentioned by the authors, which find broadly similar results as this chapter, are Tomiura (2007) and Federico (2010). Both studies find that foreign integration/FDI is undertaken by the most productive firms, and that the firms that use pure domestic outsourcing are the least productive. Contrary to this paper, Federico concludes that $\text{TFP}^{DI} > \text{TFP}^{FO}$ (see discussion in point 2 below).

Another related paper of interest is Kugler and Verhoogen (2009), who document that firms that import inputs (though they do not distinguish between foreign integration and outsourcing) are clearly superior performers than firms that obtain inputs only domestically.

2. *Key driver of theoretical results, and the most robust empirical findings*: As the authors carefully discuss, the key driver of the theoretical prediction appear to be the assumption regarding the fixed costs of each of the strategies. Assuming $F^{DO} < F^{DI} < F^{FO} < F^{FI}$ yields the rank ordering that the authors find most support for. However, the theory could accommodate different rank orderings of the fixed costs and hence support alternative rank orderings of productivity.

   The most robust results obtained that seem to be consistent with integration being costlier than outsourcing (and more weakly foreign integration being the costliest). The result relating to whether $\text{TFP}^{DI} > \text{TFP}^{FO}$ is sometimes contradicted (see particularly specifications in the appendix tables). As discussed above and as the authors note, this does not necessarily contradict theory, but instead informs us about the relative magnitude of the fixed costs of these individual strategies. Taken together with the results in Federico (2009), it seems that in some cases domestic integration may in fact be costlier than foreign outsourcing. As barriers to trade continue to decline, this finding may get stronger over time.

3. *Theory versus empirics*: An important simplification in the theoretical framework is that it models one "headquarter" firm deciding about one critical input — whether to outsource (domestically or abroad) or integrate into manufacturing (domestically or abroad). In practice, all firms have multiple inputs that it wishes to procure. Key parameters of the model (particularly "headquarters intensity") could vary across inputs, so that the firm may make different strategic choices in relation to different inputs. As the authors note, this is very much evident in the data. A large majority of the firms pursue multiple strategies. It is also plausible that in practice fixed costs may be heterogeneous across inputs and firms; if this is the case, then a strict ordering of productivity may not hold, potentially biasing against finding strict ordering of productivity across strategies in the data (though the theory may be valid for single inputs). This could explain the non-significant coefficients for some specifications.
4. *Relation to FDI and export literature*: The theoretical framework here as well as the empirical work looks at vertical "backward" integration. The focus is on how productivity relates to purchasing of inputs. An extensive literature has looked at exporters and domestic firms, and found that exporters are more productive. Firms could also vertically integrate in the "forward" direction, especially to foreign markets by undertaking foreign FDI or become MNCs. Helpman, Melitz, and Yeaple (2008) propose a model where MNC firms are more productive, and find evidence for this. If a lot of the foreign FDI is related to forward integrating into the foreign markets in distribution/marketing, then this is closely related vertical "forward" integration. Just as the authors here break down sourcing into four choices, there are potentially four choices on the sales side too: domestic manufacturing only, domestic forward integration into marketing/distribution, exports only, and forward integration into foreign markets (FDI). It would be interesting to investigate the rank ordering on this dimension of vertical integration and trade.

REFERENCES

Antràs, Pol and Elhanan Helpman (2004). "Global Sourcing." *Journal of Political Economy*, 112(3): pp. 552–580.

Bernard, A.B. and Jensen J.B. (1999). "Exceptional Exporter Performance: Cause, Effect, or Both?" *Journal of International Economics*, 47(1): pp. 1–25.

Federico, Stefano (2010). "Outsourcing versus Integration at Home or Abroad and Firm Heterogeneity." *Empirica* [Online], 10 December 2009.

Helpman, Elhanan, Marc J. Melitz and Stephen R. Yeaple (2004). "Exports versus FDI with Heterogeneous Firms." *American Economic Review*, 94(1): pp. 300–316.

Kugler, M. and E. Verhoogen (2008). "The Quality-Complementarity Hypothesis: Theory and Evidence from Colombia." NBER working paper #14418, Oct. 2008.

Roberts, Mark J. and James R. Tybout (1996). *Industrial Evolution in Developing Countries: Micro Patterns of Turnover, Productivity, and Market Structure*, Oxford: Oxford University Press.

Tomiura, Eiichi (2007). "Foreign Outsourcing, Exporting, and FDI: A Productivity Comparison at the Firm level." *Journal of International Economics*, 72(1): pp. 113–127.

CHAPTER 5

The Effects of Offshoring on the Composition of Employment in Italy

Anna M. Falzoni*,‡ and Lucia Tajoli†,§

*Department of Economic Studies
Universitã di Bergamo, Bergamo, Italy
†Department of Management, Economics and Industrial Engineering
Politecnico di Milano, Milano, Italy
‡anna-maria.falzoni@unibg.it
§lucia.tajoli@polimi.it

I. INTRODUCTION

The debate on the effects of the offshoring practices of firms on the labor market has been revived by the recent theoretical approaches that extend the possibilities of offshoring to a much larger number of sectors and tasks.[1] The earlier models of offshoring and the related empirical evidence show that the delocalization of phases of production was a phenomenon well established only in a small number of sectors and involving a selection of firms. Not surprisingly, therefore, the effects of offshoring on the labor markets produced by the existing empirical studies are, in many

[1]The definition of offshoring (and consequently its measures) is not clear-cut in the economic literature or in the public debate. Here we adopt the definition given by OECD (2007): offshoring is used to designate outsourcing (i.e. use of goods and services produced outside the firm) abroad. The term covers the situation where production of goods or services is effected or (partially) transferred abroad within the same company, say to a foreign affiliate, as well as transfer of production abroad to a non-affiliated enterprise. Offshoring to non-affiliates implies subcontracting of a permanent and regular character, even if this particular characteristic is very difficult to measure. See, among others, Hijzen (2005) and OECD (2007) for an extensive discussion of the definition and measurement issues.

cases, quite limited. But the new approaches suggest that offshoring might increase rapidly, both in its extension (the number of sectors involved, including services) and depth (the number of production phases or tasks that can be delocalized) (see, among others, Grossman and Rossi-Hansberg, 2006, 2008). The reported empirical evidence indicates that this is indeed occurring.[2]

In this chapter, we assess the evidence of such an increase in offshoring for Italy, and how this is affecting the Italian labor market. As the theoretical models of international fragmentation of production and offshoring illustrate, the effect on factors of production depends crucially on which sectors are involved and on the factor intensity of the imported inputs (see, for example, Deardorff, 2001, 2005; Kohler, 2008). Furthermore, the recent literature indicates that firms' recourse to offshoring depends not only on factor price differences and technological feasibility but also on goods' and countries' "institutional characteristics" (Antràs and Helpman, 2008). Different patterns of offshoring can then be observed across countries and industries, with different implications for the domestic labor markets.

In this respect, the Italian case is interesting, as Italy's comparative advantages and model of international specialization is quite peculiar when compared to other industrialized countries, and this leads to a somewhat peculiar pattern of offshoring too.[3] Previous works on Italian international fragmentation of production measured through outward processing data (see, for example, Helg and Tajoli, 2005) suggest that this practice was concentrated in a few traditional sectors, and it was almost negligible in many industries. But much of the previous work had severe data limitations. Offshoring is a much broader phenomenon than what is usually recorded in the statistics of outward processing trade or international production sharing. But it is more narrowly defined than overall imports of components and parts, and it is therefore difficult to measure when only trade data

[2]See, for example, Havik and Mc Morrow (2006) on the growth of the phenomenon in the EU, IMF (2007), and OECD (2007). For a general survey, see among others, Feenstra and Hanson (2003) and Crinò (2009).

[3]Italy displays a strong revealed comparative advantage in traditional manufacturing industries such as apparel, footwear, and furniture, which is in contrast to the revealed comparative advantages of most other countries with similar income levels (see, for example, De Benedictis, 2005).

are available.[4] Here we measure offshoring in the Italian manufacturing sectors using the import-use matrices of input–output tables, and computing both a broad and a narrow indicator of the phenomenon. The use of input–output tables allows combining trade data with information on the underlying structure of the economy.

In this chapter, based on an industry/year panel covering the Italian manufacturing sectors over the period 1992–2003, we first estimate the impact of offshoring on the general level of employment and do not find any significant relationship. Then, we examine the relationship between offshoring and the employment composition to determine if this process is associated with a significant shift in the composition by skills of the labor force employed domestically.[5]

As mentioned, the recent theory of offshoring suggests that the sign of these relations is *a priori* quite uncertain. On one hand, the extension of offshoring to a larger number of tasks and countries will not necessarily affect unskilled workers only. On the other hand, if the new division of labor increases the average productivity, it might benefit different workers' groups (see, among others, Dluhosch, 2006). In fact, our results show that the use of offshoring is not restricted to the search for cheaper unskilled labor, and its impact on the composition of employment seems to be quite different in different industry groups.

The chapter is organized as follows. Section II describes the recent developments of the Italian labor market, particularly the composition of labor demand between skilled and unskilled workers. In Section III, we discuss the trends of various measures of offshoring based on the import-use matrices

[4]The use of data on outward processing trade (OPT) to measure the extent of international fragmentation of production has the advantage of capturing a precise organizational choice of the firms. But unfortunately, not all international fragmentation decisions give rise to processing trade flows that are officially recorded. Therefore, OPT measures systematically underestimate the phenomenon. On the other hand, analyses based on statistics on trade in intermediate goods are difficult, given the different level of aggregation for different industries.

[5]Recently, other studies have investigated the relationship between offshoring and labor-market outcomes in Italy, following different lines of research. Broccolini *et al.* (2008) analyze the impact of international outsourcing and technological change on wages. Using firm-level data, Costa and Ferri (2007) study the employment effects of offshoring. Bertoli (2008) investigates the relevance of intersectoral effects of offshoring on employment.

of input–output tables. The empirical model and the estimation results are presented in Section IV. Section V offers some conclusions.

II. EMPLOYMENT LEVELS AND COMPOSITION IN THE ITALIAN MANUFACTURING SECTOR

We start our analysis by observing the changes in employment in the manufacturing sector. We are especially interested in the relative employment of skilled and unskilled workers in Italy, using the available definitions and sources.[6] From ISTAT, we have data on the employment of managers and employees (white collar), and laborers, apprentices and, home workers (blue collar) at the two-digit industry level in Italy. These data series allow us to examine how employment changes over time. Using this classification to define skilled and unskilled workers, we follow most of the literature distinguishing between production and non-production workers or white- and blue-collar workers. Unfortunately, the ratio of white- and blue-collar workers is at best an incomplete representation of changes in the actual skill intensity of production, especially when the skills used are not codified. To better assess the characteristics of our skill measure, we compare it with other measures of skill intensity.

An alternative possible indicator of the skills of the employed workers comes from a recent study by Bruno *et al.* (2008), based on an INPS matched employer–employee data set. Their measure of skill is the individual worker's effect obtained as a latent variable from a wage equation. Each individual worker effect is fixed over time, and it captures unchanging personal attributes, such as the unobservable worker's innate ability. Skill intensity indices of Italian manufacturing industries are then obtained as averages of the individual skill estimates, but unfortunately they are available for a short time span (years 2000–2002). Using these estimates of the skill intensity of each sector, we obtain a ranking of sectors which is quite

[6]Our main source for disaggregated data on employment by industry is the ISTAT (Italian National Statistical Institute) publication "*Conti Economici delle Imprese*," covering 23 manufacturing sectors at the level of disaggregation corresponding to two-digit ATECO 91-NACE Rev.1. We have homogenous data that allow distinguishing between white and blue collar workers for the period, 1992–2003, for all Italian manufacturing firms in ATECO sectors 17–36 with more than 20 employees. For the period, 1998–2003, data for the employment composition of all manufacturing firms in ATECO sectors 15–37 are available.

close to the one obtained using the white-/blue-collar ratio computed from ISTAT; the correlation between the two skill measures is equal to 0.67.

Another possibility is to consider workers' educational attainments rather than their ability. This type of classification is more closely related to the supply side of the labor market. But the composition of employment in terms of educational categories might provide some information complementary to that provided by the employment categories. For this reason, we also look at another variable to examine the skill composition of the Italian labor force, measuring the share of hours worked in each sector by workers with a tertiary education.[7] Also, this measure gives rise to a comparable ranking of sectors, and over our observation period the correlation between the education-based measure of skill intensity and the white-/blue-collar ratio is 0.80.

Overall, the sectors that appear to use relatively more skilled workers do so with reference to all the available measures. In our view, the comparison between skill indicators means that, in spite of its limits, the white-/blue-collar ratio is a good proxy of the skill intensity of the Italian manufacturing industries, and this is why we use it in our analysis.

Looking at changes in employment in our sample of manufacturing firms with more than 20 employees in ATECO sectors 17–36, we observe that the number of employees in 2003 had decreased by 7.4% since 1992.[8] During the same period, the number of white-collar workers increased by 1.3%, while the number of blue-collar workers declined by 11%, giving rise to an overall increase in the ratio between white-collar and blue-collar workers, from 0.40 to 0.46 (see Figures 1 and 2).

For the period 1998–2003, we can compute the white-/blue-collar ratio in ATECO manufacturing sectors 15–37, including also the very small firms. In this case, the skill/unskill ratio is lower, indicating that in Italy smaller firms use relatively less skill labor, or at least employ fewer white-collar workers. Skill upgrading occurs also for this larger sample, but, when also including the smaller firms, it turns out to be more modest: the number of white-collar workers increased by 2.4% in six years and number

[7]This measure of workers' education by sector is provided in the EUKLEMS database supported by the European Commission (www.euklems.net).

[8]The official employment statistics by ISTAT for the entire manufacturing sector indicate a 7% reduction of employment over the same period.

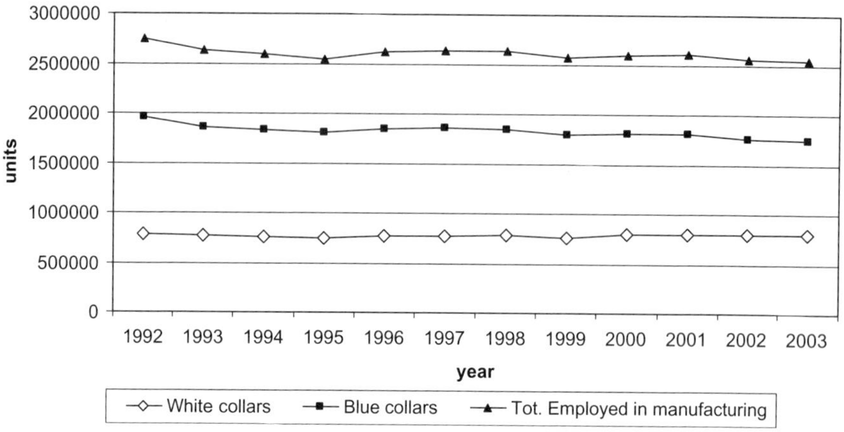

Source: Our elaboration on ISTAT, Conti Economici delle Imprese, various years.
Fig. 1. Employment levels in Italy (manufacturing firms with more than 20 employees in ATECO sectors 17–36).

of blue-collar workers declined by 2.8%, increasing the white-/blue-collar ratio from 0.34 in 1998 to 0.36 in 2003 (see Figure 2).

The process of skill upgrading is in line with the expectations, especially for an advanced country. A number of studies have shown that in many countries, there has been a shift over time in labor demand toward skilled workers.[9] In most countries, such an increase occurred not only because of the increasing weight of technology-intensive sectors in manufacturing and of advanced services in the tertiary sector, but especially because, within a number of industries, production became more skill-intensive (Berman, Bound, and Griliches, 1994; Strauss-Kahn, 2004).

Also in Italy, the relative increase in skilled labor employment is common to most sectors, both skill-intensive and unskill-intensive, with a few

[9]According to OECD (2007) data, using International Standard Classification of Occupations, categories 1, 2, and 3 to define skilled workers (a narrower definition than ours, as it leaves out clerks), in Italy the share of skilled workers in total manufacturing employment increased from 12% in 1997 to 23% in 2004, moving closer, but still lower than the analogous share in Germany and France, which was around 30% in 2004. For an early assessment of the changes in the use of skilled and unskilled labor in Italian manufacturing in relation to internationalization of production, see Brenton and Pinna (2001), and for a recent analysis of the increase in the skill intensity of many manufacturing sectors, see Giovannetti and Quintieri (2007).

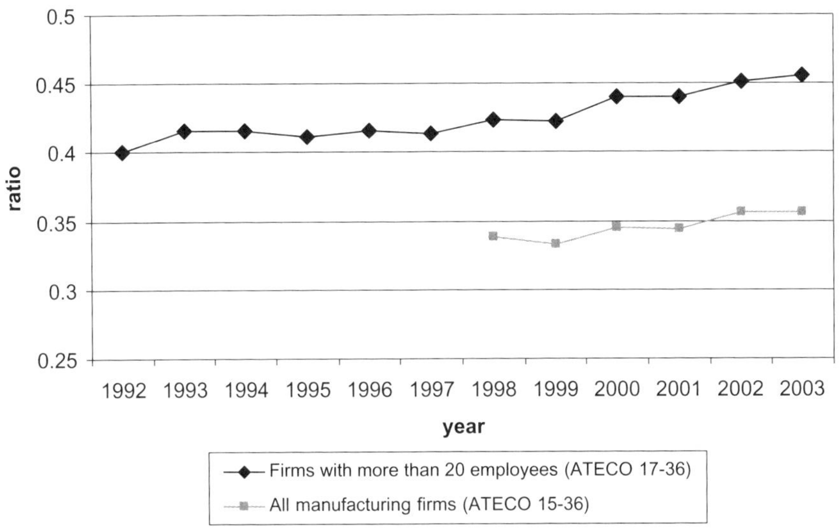

Source: Our elaboration on ISTAT, Conti Economici delle Imprese, various years.

Fig. 2. Skill upgrading in the Italian manufacturing industry (white-/blue-collar ratio).

exceptions. In 2003, only the office machinery sector displayed a lower white-/blue-collar ratio than in 1992, while most other industries display an increase in the ratio between 1992 and 2003 (Table 1), with the strongest skill upgrading observed in communication equipment (a skill-intensive sector), followed by chemicals and then by apparel, which was a highly unskill-intensive sector at the beginning of the observation period.

To assess the relative importance of changes within individual industries and changes in the composition of the manufacturing sector, it is possible to decompose the change in employment in a *within* and *between* effect, following Berman, Bound, and Griliches (1994). The overall change in the proportion of skilled workers in manufacturing can be written as

$$\Delta W = \Sigma_i \, \Delta E_i \, \omega_i + \Sigma_i \, \Delta W_i \, \xi_i \tag{1}$$

where W and W_i represent the ratio of white collars over total employment in the entire manufacturing sector and in industry i respectively, E_i is the share of employment in industry i, Δ represents change over time (from 1992 to 2003 in our case), ω_i is the mean of W_i over time, and ξ_i is the mean of E_i over time. The first term on the right-hand-side of expression (1)

Table 1. Skill intensity by sector

Skill-intensive sectors (white-/blue-collar ratio higher than average)			Unskill-intensive sectors (white-/blue-collar ratio lower than average)		
	White-/Blue-collar ratio			White-/Blue-collar ratio	
ATECO Sector	1992	2003	ATECO Sector	1992	2003
22. Publishing and printing	0.84	0.96	15. Food and beverages		0.40
23. Fuels	1.04	1.35	16. Tobacco		0.45
24. Chemical products	1.14	1.51	17. Textiles	0.23	0.31
29. Mechanical equipment	0.51	0.53	18. Wearing apparel	0.18	0.37
30. Office machinery	2.70	1.53	19. Leather and footwear	0.14	0.19
31. Electrical machinery	0.53	0.53	20. Wood, cork and straw products	0.20	0.22
32. Communication equipment	0.90	1.48	21. Paper products	0.28	0.32
33. Precision instruments	0.80	0.89	25. Rubber and plastic products	0.30	0.30
35. Transportation equipment other than auto vehicles	0.47	0.59	26. Non-metallic mineral products	0.28	0.36
			27. Basic metals	0.29	0.30
			28. Fabricated metal products	0.27	0.27
			34. Motor vehicles	0.31	0.32
			36. Furniture and other manufactures	0.28	0.30
			37. Recycling		0.23

Note: See the Appendix for the exact definition of industries.
Source: Our elaboration from ISTAT, Conti Economici delle Imprese, firms with more than 20 employees.

reports the change in the proportion of white-collar workers attributable to shifts in employment *between* industries, and the second term reports the change attributable to changes in the proportion of white-collar workers *within* each industry.

Applying this decomposition to the Italian manufacturing firms with more than 20 employees in sectors 17–36, we obtain some interesting results. The share of white-collar workers in manufacturing goes from 0.29 in 1992 to 0.31 in 2003, increasing by 0.027 (ΔW). This change is the result of an increase in the within component of 0.03, and a decrease of the between component of 0.003. As suggested by the observation of the data, the skill upgrading in Italian manufacturing is entirely due to changes within individual industries. In Italy, the negative change between component shows that there has not been a shift in the composition of employment in favor of more skill-intensive sectors, contrary to the scenario in other countries.[10] Overall, the composition effect in terms of sectors of the total skilled/unskilled ratio appears quite modest, in line with all the studies showing the persistence over time of the Italian model of specialization (see, for example, De Benedictis, 2005).

The variations in the level of employment of managers and clerks and production workers behind the trend in the ratio are differentiated among industries (Figure 3). In some of the most advanced sectors, there is an increase in the number of white-collar workers. In contrast, the upward trend in the skilled/unskilled labor ratio in the textiles and apparel industries is essentially due to the fall of employment of blue-collar workers *vis-à-vis* a stable number of white-collar workers. Some sectors, such as wood, furniture, and metal products, show an increase in skill intensity in spite of the increase in the number of blue-collar workers. Even in the presence of a generalized trend of skill upgrading, the different movements in the level of employment of the different groups might imply different types of re-organization of production. One of these is the recourse to offshoring that we discuss in the following section.

III. HAS ITALY EXPERIENCED AN INCREASE IN OFFSHORING?

The empirical literature has used various proxies to measure the extent of international fragmentation of production: data on outward processing

[10] This result is in line with the result of a similar decomposition performed at the firm-level for the Italian mechanical industry by Manasse, Stance, and Turrini (2004).

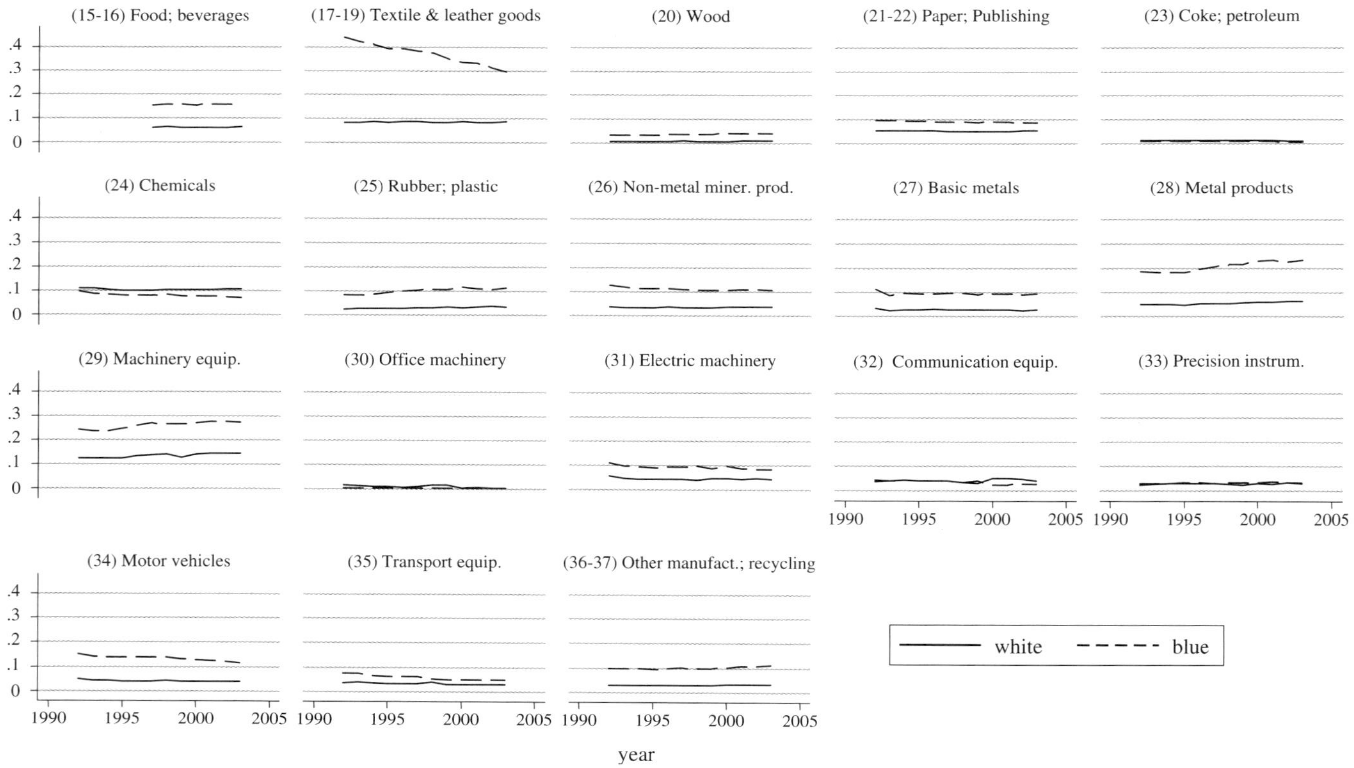

Source: ISTAT, Conti Economici delle Imprese.

Fig. 3. White-and blue-collars employment levels in Italian manufacturing industries (firms with more than 20 employees).

trade, statistics on trade in intermediate goods, and input–output tables. Each proxy has pros and cons. However, aiming to analyze whether Italy shows an increase in offshoring and if this has an impact on the domestic labor market, data from input–output tables (specifically "import-use" matrices) have been preferred as they allow analyzing developments across industries and over time, while keeping track of the vertical and horizontal linkages between industries.

The proxy for offshoring intensity (OFF) is constructed as:

$$OFF_{it} = \frac{\left(\sum_{k=1}^{K} M_{\text{ikt}}\right)}{II_{\text{it}}} \qquad (2)$$

where M_{ikt} are imports of intermediate input (service) k by industry i at time t, whereas II_{it} is total usage of intermediate inputs in the same industry. Many indices of offshoring are used in the literature. For example, the amount of imported intermediate inputs can alternatively be normalized by industry output or value added. In a recent paper, Horgos (2009) discusses the properties of different offshoring measures and their performance in explaining the labor market effects of offshoring. He shows that for Germany, there is a high correlation between an index normalized using gross industry output and an index normalized using total use of inputs. But the latter seems particularly appropriate when measuring offshoring disaggregating by industries. We chose this normalization because it emphasizes the choice of obtaining intermediate inputs from abroad rather than domestically.

We use recently released input–output matrices for Italy up to 2003 to retrieve the main components of OFF_{it}. M_{ikt} comes from the "Import" matrices, giving the amount of intermediate inputs and services acquired by each industry from abroad. II_{it} comes instead from the "Use" matrices, giving the total amount (domestic plus foreign) of intermediate inputs and services used by each industry. Compared to Feenstra and Hanson (1999), who employ "combined-use" matrices, in combination with trade data, using import-use matrices has the advantage that offshoring is measured directly and is no longer driven by increased import penetration of all goods.[11]

[11]For Italy, the advantages of using import-use matrices have been illustrated in Daveri and Jona-Lasinio (2008), who study the link between offshoring and productivity growth.

We construct two similar measures for material offshoring and service offshoring. For material offshoring, we use imports of all products classified in ATECO categories 15–37 (broad offshoring). We also compute a narrow proxy, using only imports from the same industry (the diagonal elements of the import matrix). For service offshoring, we use imports of the following services: financial and insurance services (ATECO: 64 to 67), rental services (ATECO 71), computer services (ATECO 72), research and developments services (ATECO 73), professional services (ATECO 74), other private services (ATECO 93).

As for material offshoring, the narrow measure is usually preferred as it best captures the idea of the fragmentation of production within the same industry, and of delocalization abroad of production phases (Feenstra and Hanson, 1999; Hijzen, 2005). In addition, it seems particularly convenient here because we have to rely on the relatively high aggregation level of two-digit industries.

As shown in Table 2, when considering the whole manufacturing industry, the broad measure of offshoring of materials shows an increasing trend. The narrow proxy of offshoring, instead, remains fairly constant over the period, from 10.98% in 1992, to a maximum of 12.05% in 1994, with a moderate decline in the last years of our analysis to around 11%. In line with the evidence emerging from other countries (Hijzen, 2005; Amiti and Wei, 2005), offshoring of services is growing substantially, but its importance is far from the one of offshoring of goods.[12]

Figures 4 and 5 show the different trends in two-digit ATECO industries of our measures of offshoring. A clear upward trend in the narrow offshoring indicator appears in chemical products and motor vehicles, while other industries show smaller changes in this respect. The picture emerging is one in which the importance of offshoring differs widely across industries. Focusing on the measures of material offshoring, on average in the period 1992–2003, the three most important offshoring industries were "Office and computing machinery" (ATECO 30), "Chemicals" (ATECO 24),

[12]There are computational and normalization differences between our offshoring measures and the ones presented in other studies using similar datasets, such as Daveri and Jona-Lasinio (2008). One difference is the inclusion of energy inputs in our indices, which we decided not to drop, energy being a relevant element of overall costs, even if the value of these inputs can be subject to larger fluctuations.

Table 2. Offshoring indices for Italy (percentages, unweighted averages)

	1992	2003
All Industries		
Broad offshoring	18.34	24.62
Narrow offshoring	10.98	10.83
Service offshoring	0.52	2.06
Industries by Skill-Intensity (based on ISTAT, see Table 1)		
Skill-Intensive Industries		
Broad offshoring	23.60	32.17
Narrow offshoring	15.08	13.99
Service offshoring	0.61	3.61
Unskill-Intensive Industries		
Broad offshoring	14.73	19.87
Narrow offshoring	7.72	8.72
Service offshoring	0.49	0.81
Industries by Skill-Intensity (based on INPS) (*)		
Skill-Intensive Industries		
Broad offshoring	22.64	31.63
Narrow offshoring	14.83	15.22
Service offshoring	0.57	3.02
Unskill-Intensive Industries		
Broad offshoring	13.56	17.12
Narrow offshoring	5.98	5.45
Service offshoring	0.51	0.86

Note: (*) Skill-intensive industries: ATECO 21–22, 24, 27, 29, 30, 31, 32, 33, 34, 35. Unskill-intensive industries or industries with ambiguous skill-intensity: ATECO 15–16, 17–19, 20, 25, 26, 28, 36–37. The ATECO 23 sector (Fuels) is excluded. For details, see Bruno *et al.* (2008).
Source: Elaborations from ISTAT, Tavole Input–Output, various years.

and "Communication equipment" (ATECO 32) in terms of the broad index (respectively with average intensity 54.5, 38.5, and 38.3). "Chemicals," "Basic metals" (ATECO 27), and "Communication equipment" were at the top of the ranking in terms of the narrow definition of offshoring (respectively with average intensity 30.5, 24.9, and 22.4).

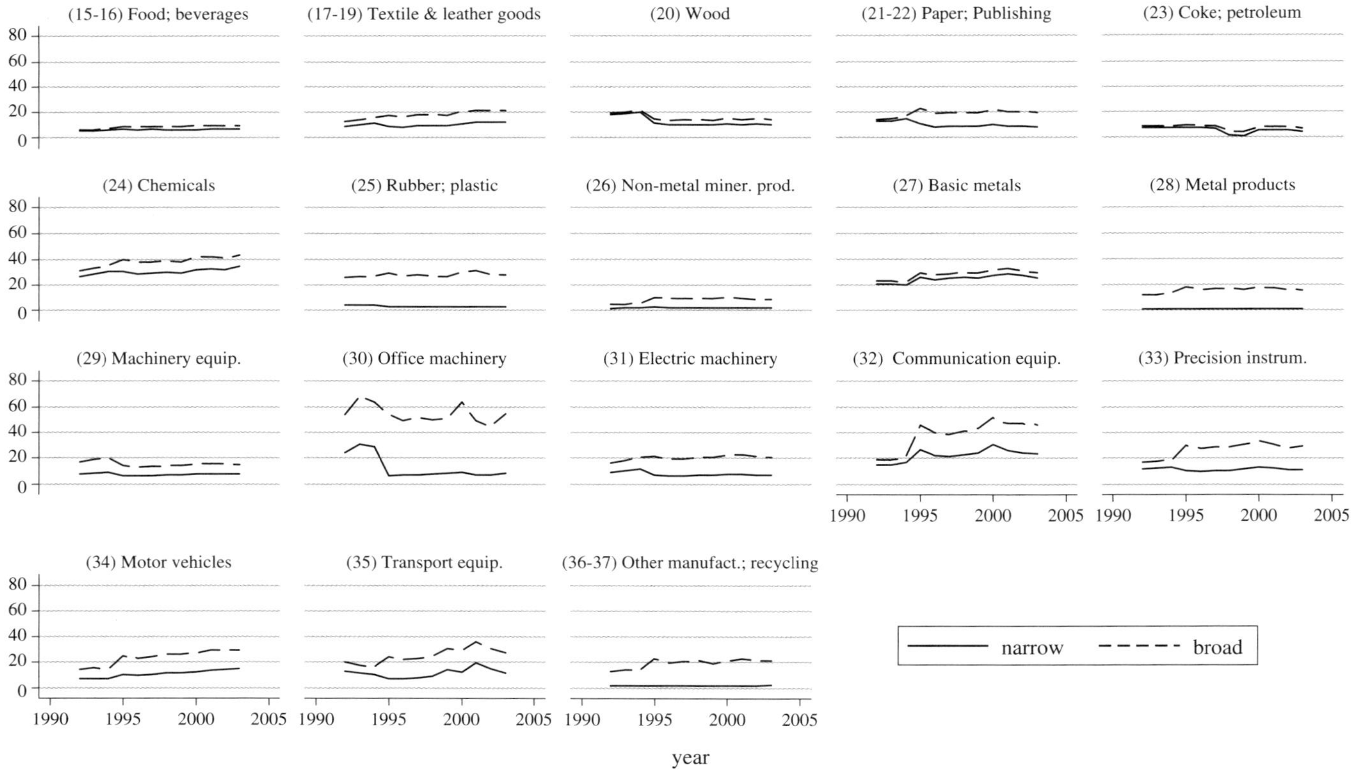

Source: Elaborations from ISTAT, Tavole Input–Output.

Fig. 4. Narrow and broad material offshoring indices in Italian manufacturing industries (%).

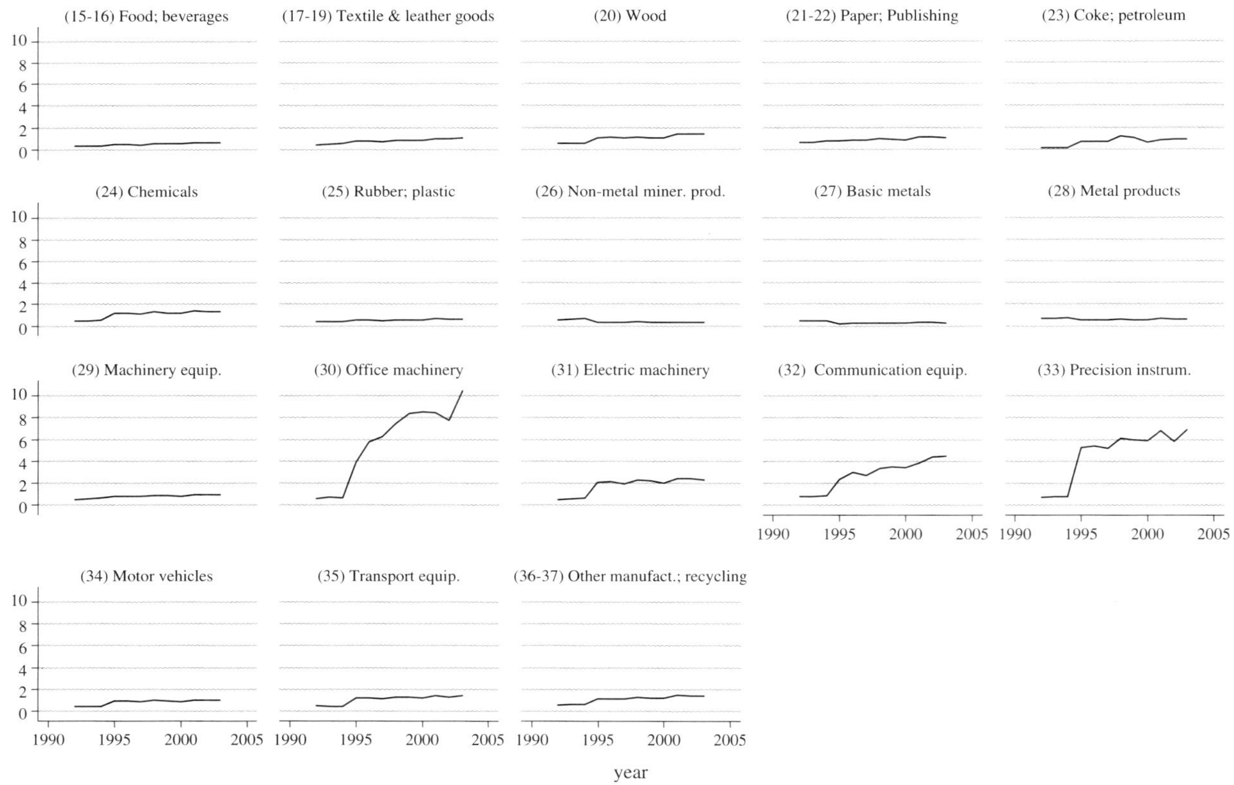

Source: Elaborations from ISTAT, Tavole Input–Output.

Fig. 5. Service offshoring index in Italian manufacturing industries (%).

Even with strong differences in the development of offshoring, the industries' ranking does not change much during the period under study. Contrary to anecdotal evidence, but in line with the developments reported for the advanced economies in IMF (2007) and De Backer and Yamano (2007),[13] in Italy international fragmentation of production measured through input–output tables seems to characterize mostly high-tech and/or scale intensive industries rather than traditional unskill-intensive productions, typical of the Italian pattern of specialization.

To shed some light on this point, we continue our analysis looking at the existing relationship between offshoring and industries' skill intensity. Interestingly, Table 2 shows that, whichever classification we use to distinguish industries according to their skill intensity, high-skill intensive industries show intensity of offshoring greater than low-skill intensive ones.

There may be various reasons for this evidence. The intensity of material offshoring may represent not only (or not specifically) the search for low labor cost through international fragmentation of the production process but also the extent of the Italian comparative disadvantage in high-tech and scale-intensive industries and the need to rely on import of sophisticated or complex components.[14]

Furthermore, one might suspect that the intensity of offshoring in some industries could be related to the large presence of foreign-owned firms in Italian high-tech and scale-intensive industries. In this case, the proxies of offshoring could capture production transfer within multinational enterprises (MNEs). To verify to what extent offshoring in Italy is related to the activities of MNEs, we check the correlation between inward and outward FDI intensity and our offshoring indices. We also consider whether our

[13]According to IMF (2007) calculations, the rise in offshoring in advanced economies has been driven mostly by imports of skilled rather than unskilled inputs. In spite of this increase, the extent of offshoring is still quite limited in advanced economies, and in 2003 the offshoring of non-energy manufacturing and services inputs averaged roughly 10% of total intermediate inputs in these countries.

[14]This explanation diverges from that suggested in IMF (2007), where the fact that the rise in offshoring is driven mostly by imports of skilled rather than unskilled inputs is related to advanced economies' comparative advantages. In IMF (2007, Chapter 5), it is suggested that, in line with developed economies' specialization in skill-intensive productions, goods produced in unskilled sectors are more likely to be imported as final goods rather than intermediates.

Table 3. **Correlation between internationalization indicators for Italy, 1992–2003 (17 sectors, excluding fuels, 189 yearly observations)**

	Narrow off-shoring index	Broad off-shoring index	Service off-shoring index	Imports/ Production	Exports/ Production	Inward FDI intensity	Outward FDI intensity
Narrow offshoring index	1.0000						
Broad offshoring index	0.5934	1.0000					
Service offshoring index	0.0346	0.5539	1.0000				
Imports/ Production	0.3395	0.7831	0.7397	1.0000			
Exports/ Production	0.0923	0.6167	0.5101	0.7008	1.0000		
Inward FDI intensity	0.4918	0.7755	0.4096	0.6803	0.5333	1.0000	
Outward FDI intensity	0.1941	0.1867	0.0219	0.3179	0.1912	0.3684	1.0000

Source: See the Appendix for variables' definitions and sources.

measure of offshoring might represent a general propensity to import in a given industry, by checking the correlation between import over production and offshoring indices.

The correlation matrix is reported in Table 3. The correlation between narrow offshoring and inward FDI is fairly high, and even higher is the correlation with the broad offshoring index, confirming that foreign MNEs in Italy, being connected to an international production network, are responsible for part of the offshoring observed. More surprising is the low correlation between outward FDI intensity and offshoring. It seems that most foreign investments by Italian firms are not undertaken to serve the domestic market from abroad to exploit lower production costs. The correlation between the narrow offshoring index and import over production is only 0.34, suggesting that the two measures are not capturing the same phenomenon, and that the narrow index is a better approximation for the offshoring choices of industries than the broad one, much more highly correlated with imports.

IV. THE RELATIONSHIP BETWEEN OFFSHORING AND EMPLOYMENT

We now examine the relationship between labor demand in Italy and the use of offshoring, described in the Section III. As mentioned, changes in employment levels and composition can result from a number of factors, and they might be affected by different forms of internationalization in addition to offshoring. Therefore, in assessing the relationship between offshoring and employment, it is important to control for the various changes in the organization of production that can affect labor demand. In particular, to isolate the role of offshoring, we want to control for other channels of influence by introducing different proxies for the propensity of the industry to interact with international markets. The use of offshoring as an explanatory variable in a labor demand equation rests on the hypothesis that offshoring decisions are exogenous in this context. This is not always necessarily the case: if technology or the factor endowment changes, this could simultaneously affect labor demand and offshoring. We maintain the hypothesis that offshoring is exogenous, and it is pushed by factors not directly affecting labor demand (such as lower trade barriers between countries) because of the relatively short time span of our observations, which makes unlikely a significant change in technology or endowment.

The first issue we examine is whether offshoring has an impact on the overall level of employment. The empirical framework adopted is the one most often used in the literature, derived from a conditional labor demand model (Hamermesh, 1993) and it is represented by the following log-linear expression:

$$\ln L_{it} = \beta_0 + \mu_i + \tau_t + \beta_1 OFF_{it} + \beta_2 \ln W_{it} + \beta_3 \ln Y_{it} + \beta_4 \ln (K_{it}/Y_{it}) + \beta_5 \ln X_{it} + \varepsilon_{it} \qquad (3)$$

where L is total labor employed in industry i at time t, W is the wage rate of industry i, Y is gross output, K/Y is the capital-output ratio (gross fixed capital formation relative to gross production), OFF is our offshoring index (broad, narrow or referring to services), X is a vector of additional control variables at industry level, and μ_i and τ_t are group-specific (industry) and time-specific fixed effects. The proxies for offshoring and the vector of variables X are introduced as demand shifters, inducing parallel movements in the labor demand function. Two main types of demand shifters have been included. First, demand shifters that account for the factor bias of technological change. Variables that have been typically used are based on computer use or R&D intensity. We have chosen to use ICT intensity, representing the gross fixed capital formation in software, office, and communication equipments over production. This proxy seems more adapt to capture the organizational changes that can be related both to the recourse to offshoring and to shifts in employment (see, among others, Benfratello, Razzolini, and Sembenelli 2009). Second, a set of control variables is added to capture shifts in labor demand related to modalities of presence on international markets other than offshoring, such as export propensity (exports relative to gross production) and outward FDI and different forms of sourcing from abroad, such as import penetration (imports relative to gross production) or links to foreign firms (inward FDI).

We estimate Equation (3) in levels across industries and time, and adopt a dynamic specification via the introduction of the lagged dependent variable. The characteristics of the Italian labor market suggest that indeed employment in many sectors is sticky, and it takes time to absorb the effects of changes in the production function. This specification allows us to preserve the information contained in the levels of variables, while taking into account labor adjustment costs.[15]

Turning to the estimation methods, we have adopted a two-way fixed-effects specification, but we face some relevant econometric issues. First, the standard LSDV (least squares dummy variables) estimator applied to a first-order autoregressive model is consistent only for large T (number of years), which is not the case for most panels, ours included. The usual solution in this case is to adopt the generalized method of moments estimator approach suggested by Arellano and Bond (A–B), widely used in most recent dynamic panel data applications, which takes the model

[15]A specification in first differences was also estimated, giving the same results reported in Table 4 in terms of sign and significance of the coefficients. These results are not reported to save on space, but are available from the authors upon request.

in first differences and exploits all available linear orthogonality conditions.[16] Our empirical set-up, however, is one in which both N (number of sectors) and T (number of years) are small, and in this case the A–B estimator finite sample performance is not better than the inconsistent LSDV estimator. A useful solution to this problem has been proposed by Bruno (2005a, b), developing a small sample alternative based on bias-corrected LSDV estimator (the LSDVC estimator), derived from the Kiviet estimator for dynamic panels. Based on these considerations, in estimating our empirical models, we have applied and showed three different estimation approaches (LSDV, A–B, and LSDVC).

Table 4 presents the results for Equation (3). The results of the regressions show the expected signs for the control variables and a stable and reasonable fit of the equation. In all regressions, with all types of offshoring indicators, offshoring is not significantly affecting the overall employment level.[17] This result is preserved even in regressions of the unconditional labor-demand function (dropping the production variable) and without any control for all other forms of internationalization. These findings seem to confirm that the general level of employment in the manufacturing industries is not significantly affected by delocalization choices. Rather, a small negative effect on employment seems to exist due to the competition of imports.

Most of the impact of offshoring is expected to be not on the overall level of employment, but on the composition of employment used in manufacturing, and this is the main issue we want to address. To test the effect of international trade and offshoring on relative wages and the composition of labor demand, the recent literature uses a quasi-fixed translog cost function with two variable factors, skilled and unskilled labor, and capital as a quasi-fixed factor. Fixing the short-run levels of capital and output, imposing cost minimization and some parameter restrictions to make the function linearly homogeneous in factor prices, generates the equations that are usually estimated.[18] In the literature, there are estimates both for

[16]The A–B estimator has attractive asymptotic properties compared, for example, to the LSDV (inconsistent) and the Anderson and Hsiao (AH) (inefficient) estimators (see Bruno, 2005b).

[17]This result is in line with the results of Hijzen and Swaim (2007), that offshoring has no effect on sectoral employment in a group of OECD countries that includes Italy.

Table 4. Regression results for employment levels

Dependent variable: *ln* (total number of employees)

	Eq 4.1 LSDV	Eq 4.2 A–B	Eq 4.3 LSDVC	Eq 4.4 LSDV	Eq 4.5 A–B	Eq 4.6 LSDVC	Eq 4.7 LSDV	Eq 4.8 A–B	Eq 4.9 LSDVC
OFF narrow	0.001	0.001	0.001						
	(0.001)	(0.001)	(0.001)						
OFF broad				0.000	0.001	0.000			
				(0.001)	(0.001)*	(0.001)			
OFF services							−0.001	−0.003	−0.001
							(0.004)	(0.003)	(0.004)
ln(K/Y)	0.07	0.02	0.07	0.07	0.02	0.07	0.07	0.02	0.07
	(0.02)***	(0.02)	(0.02)***	(0.02)***	(0.02)	(0.03)***	(0.2)***	(0.02)	(0.03)***
lnY	0.21	0.18	0.21	0.21	0.16	0.21	0.21	0.18	0.21
	(0.04)***	(0.03)***	(0.04)***	(0.04)***	(0.03)***	(0.04)***	(0.04)***	(0.03)***	(0.04)***
lnW	−0.81	−0.91	−0.80	−0.82	−0.92	−0.80	−0.81	−0.91	−0.80
	(0.04)***	(0.03)***	(0.04)***	(0.04)***	(0.03)***	(0.04)***	(0.04)***	(0.03)***	(0.04)***
ln(Imp/Y)	−0.09	−0.08	−0.08	−0.09	−0.08	−0.08	−0.08	−0.07	−0.08
	(0.03)***	(0.02)***	(0.03)***	(0.03)***	(0.02)***	(0.03)**	(0.03)***	(0.02)***	(0.03)**
ln(Exp/Y)	−0.02	−0.07	−0.02	−0.02	−0.09	−0.02	−0.02	−0.08	−0.01
	(0.03)	(0.03)***	(0.03)	(0.03)	(0.03)***	(0.03)	(0.03)	(0.03)***	(0.03)
lnFDIin	−0.01	−0.01	−0.01	−0.004	−0.01	−0.004	−0.004	−0.01	−0.004
	(0.01)	(0.01)	(0.01)	(0.008)	(0.01)	(0.01)	(0.01)	(0.01)	(0.01)

(Continued)

Table 4. (*Continued*)

	Eq 4.1 LSDV	Eq 4.2 A–B	Eq 4.3 LSDVC	Eq 4.4 LSDV	Eq 4.5 A–B	Eq 4.6 LSDVC	Eq 4.7 LSDV	Eq 4.8 A–B	Eq 4.9 LSDVC
lnFDIout	−0.01	−0.01	−0.01	−0.01	−0.01	−0.01	−0.01	−0.01	−0.01
	(0.01)	(0.01)	(0.01)	(0.01)	(0.01)	(0.01)	(0.01)	(0.01)	(0.01)
ln(ICT/Y)	−0.01	−0.01	−0.01	−0.01	−0.01	−0.01	−0.01	0.01	−0.01
	(0.02)	(0.01)	(0.02)	(0.02)	(0.02)	(0.02)	(0.02)	(0.01)	(0.02)
lnEmp(-1)	0.24	0.08	0.26	0.24	0.07	0.27	0.25	0.08	0.27
	(0.04)***	(0.03)***	(0.04)***	(0.04)***	(0.03)**	(0.04)***	(0.04)***	(0.03)**	(0.04)***
Time dummies	yes	yes	yes	yes	yes	yes	yes	yes	yes
No. of obs.	179	161	179	179	161	179	179	161	179
No. of sectors	18	18	18	18	18	18	18	18	18
R-squared	0.81			0.81			0.81		
ABII (p-value)		0.0321			0.0436			0.0200	

Note: Coefficients with ***, **, * are significant at the 99%, 95%, and 90% level, respectively. LSDV indicates least squares dummy variables estimation method, A–B indicates estimates obtained with the Arellano–Bond method for dynamic panels, and LSDVC indicates corrected least squares dummy variables estimation. ABII: Arellano–Bond test for H_0: no second-order correlation in the residuals.

these cost-share equations as well as estimates of the employment-share equations.

In order to highlight the labor market outcome in the presence of labor market rigidities and lacking reliable data on wages for different groups of workers, we adopt the latter approach estimating the following employment ratio equation:

$$S_{it} = \beta_0 + \mu_i + \tau_t + \beta_1 OFF_{it} + \beta_2 \ln Y_{it} + \beta_3 \ln(K_{it}/Y_{it}) + \beta_4 \ln X_{it} + \varepsilon_{it} \tag{4}$$

where S is the ratio of skilled (S_{sk}) and unskilled workers (S_{unsk}) employed in industry i at time t, K/Y is the capital–output ratio in industry i, Y is gross output of industry i, OFF is our offshoring index (broad, narrow or referring to services), X is the vector of additional control variables, and μ_i and τ_t are group-specific (industry) and time-specific fixed effects.[19] As in Equation (3), logarithmic transformation has been applied to all variables, except than to the offshoring indices. We estimate Equation (4) in levels across industries and time.[20]

In Table 5, we present the baseline regressions of our model. Both the coefficient of the capital–output ratio and the coefficient of the output variable are positive and significant in all specifications. The positive sign indicates complementarity between capital and skills, and that an increase in skill-intensity is associated with higher output, as usually expected. Our main variable of interest is of course the index of offshoring, but in all the panel regressions, this variable appears to be non-significant. Without any control on specific industry characteristics, offshoring does not seem to affect the composition of employment.

In Table 6, we introduce additional control variables, to check possible complementarities or substitution effects between offshoring and other

[18]See for example Feenstra (2004), Chapter 4, for the derivation of these equations.

[19]Time effects are introduced as a proxy of the change over time of the relative wage of skilled and unskilled workers. As mentioned, we lack reliable data on wages for different groups of workers, and time effects is a proxy often used in the literature (see again Feenstra (2004), Chapter 4). See also the Appendix for the exact definition of variables.

[20]As a robustness check, we also estimated Equation (4) in differences, like we did for Equation (3). Results for the sign and the significance of the coefficients are the same, but we prefer the specification in levels, as this allows preserving absolute differences between industries.

Table 5. **Baseline regression results for skilled/unskilled employment ratio**

Dependent variable: *ln*(*S*)

	Eq. 5.1 LSDV	Eq. 5.2 A–B	Eq. 5.3 LSDVC	Eq. 5.4 LSDV	Eq. 5.5 A–B	Eq. 5.6 LSDVC	Eq. 5.7 LSDV	Eq. 5.8 A–B	Eq. 5.9 LSDVC
OFF narrow	0.005	0.006	0.004						
	(0.003)	(0.004)	(0.003)						
OFF broad				−0.001	−0.006	−0.001			
				(0.002)	(0.003)	(0.003)			
OFF services							−0.005	−0.01	−0.003
							(0.01)	(0.01)	(0.01)
ln(K/Y)	0.29	0.37	0.29	0.28	0.35	0.28	0.28	0.36	0.28
	(0.05)***	(0.05)***	(0.05)***	(0.05)***	(0.05)***	(0.05)***	(0.05)***	(0.05)***	(0.05)***
lnY	0.25	0.35	0.26	0.28	0.42	0.28	0.26	0.36	0.27
	(0.12)**	(0.12)***	(0.12)*	(0.12)**	(0.13)***	(0.12)**	(0.12)**	(0.12)***	(0.12)**
lnS(−1)	0.41	0.35	0.51	0.42	0.36	0.52	0.42	0.35	0.52
	(0.08)***	(0.08)***	(0.08)***	(0.08)***	(0.08)***	(0.08)***	(0.08)***	(0.08)***	(0.08)***
Time dummies	yes	yes	yes	yes	yes	yes	yes	yes	yes
No. of observations	179	161	179	179	161	179	179	161	179
No. of sectors	18	18	18	18	18	18	18	18	18
R-squared	0.57			0.49			0.53		
AB II (*p*-value)		0.3351			0.3203			0.3589	

Note: See Table 4.

Table 6. Regression results for skilled/unskilled employment ratio using additional controls

Dependent variable: ln(*S*)

	Eq. 6.1 LSDV	Eq. 6.2 A–B	Eq. 6.3 LSDVC	Eq. 6.4 LSDV	Eq. 6.5 A–B	Eq. 6.6 LSDVC
OFF narrow	0.008	0.01	0.007	0.007	0.008	0.007
	(0.003)**	(0.004)**	(0.003)**	(0.003)**	(0.004)*	(0.004)*
ln(K/Y)	0.10	0.26	0.11	0.11	0.25	0.11
	(0.07)	(0.09)***	(0.08)	(0.08)	(0.09)***	(0.09)
lnY	0.09	0.30	0.09	0.08	0.28	0.09
	(0.12)	(0.13)**	(0.13)	(0.12)	(0.14)**	(0.13)
ln(Imp/Y)	−0.06	−0.17	−0.02	−0.07	−0.20	−0.03
	(0.09)	(0.12)	(0.11)	(0.10)	(0.13)	(0.11)
ln(Exp/Y)	−0.15	−0.28	−0.16	−0.16	−0.28	−0.16
	(0.10)	(0.12)**	(0.11)	(0.10)	(0.12)**	(0.12)
lnFDIin				0.01	0.03	0.01
				(0.03)	(0.03)	(0.03)
lnFDIout				0.01	0.001	0.01
				(0.03)	(0.04)	(0.03)
ln(ICT/Y)	0.09	−0.004	0.08	0.09	−0.002	0.08
	(0.07)	(0.07)	(0.08)	(0.07)	(0.07)	(0.08)
Δlntotdip	0.66	0.51	0.69	0.65	0.52	0.69
	(0.13)***	(0.13)***	(0.14)***	(0.13)***	(0.14)***	(0.14)***
lnS(−1)	0.50	0.42	0.60	0.51	0.42	0.61
	(0.07)***	(0.08)***	(0.07)***	(0.08)***	(0.08)***	(0.07)***
Time dummies	yes	yes	yes	yes	yes	yes
No. of observations	179	161	179	179	161	179
No. of sectors	18	18	18	18	18	18
R-squared	0.94			0.93		
AB II (*p*-value)		0.9529			0.8765	

Note: See Table 4.

phenomena bringing about shifts in relative labor demand. We focus on the narrow index, which should better capture the phenomenon of offshoring. The index of narrow offshoring is significant and positive when additional control variables are included in the regression, even if small.[21] In Equations (6.1) through (6.6), we control for the various channels of internationalization of production, but these variables do not seem to impact

[21]Given our specification, results in Table 6 indicate that a one-point increase of the offshoring index implies on average an increase of 0.7% of the skilled/unskilled workers ratio.

on the composition of employment across manufacturing industries or on the significance of the offshoring index. In all the specifications, we added a variable measuring the change in the total sectoral employment level, to control for the presence of major restructuring processes in some manufacturing sectors. This variable is always highly significant with a positive sign, showing that expansion or contraction of total employment induces changes in the same direction in the skill intensity of the related industry.[22]

The results of the previous set of estimates suggested pursuing more checks. While these panel estimates across all industries and over time are very common in the literature, they require making very strong assumptions, such as that the cost function is the same across industries. Instead, our estimates show a great deal of heterogeneity between industries.[23] For these reasons, we also ran our regressions splitting the sample in two different industry groups, to take into account the fact that offshoring can have contradictory effects across industries, if it affects different parts of the production process. Following the theoretical suggestion that offshoring, like international trade in goods, should be consistent with the factor content of production, we split our sample according to the skill intensity of each industry, using the two different indicators presented in section II: one based on the white/blue collar ratio computed from ISTAT data, and the other based on estimates from INPS data.[24]

The results for the two groups of industries are quite different both from the ones obtained for the entire sample and between groups. Looking at the sign and the value of the coefficients in Table 7, we can confirm that there are remarkable differences in the organization of production of the different

[22] As a robustness check, we also estimated Equation (4) in differences, like we did for Equation (3). Results on the sign and the significance of the coefficients are the same, but we prefer the specification in levels, as this allows preserving absolute differences between industries. In addition, we estimated Equation (4) without the variable measuring the change in total sectoral employment level. The coefficient of the capital-output ratio variable becomes always significant and the other results do not change.

[23] The heterogeneity between sectors seems confirmed by the large difference displayed in the regressions in the values of the within and between R-squared, not reported in the tables. Egger and Egger (2005) also raise some doubts on the assumptions made in most empirical studies on the labor effects of offshoring across industries.

[24] A similar split of manufacturing industries in two groups with different skill intensities is presented in Geishecker and Gorg (2005), with different results for the two groups.

Table 7. **Regression results for skilled/unskilled employment ratio in different industry groups**

Dependent variable: *ln*(*S*)

	Unskill-intensive industries (a) (white-/blue-collar ratio below average)			Skill-intensive industries (b) (white-/blue-collar ratio above average)			Skill-intensive industries (based on INPS) (c)		
	Eq 7.1 LSDV	Eq 7.2 A–B	Eq. 7.3 LSDVC	Eq 7.4 LSDV	Eq 7.5 A–B	Eq. 7.6 LSDVC	Eq. 7.7 LSDV	Eq 7.8 A–B	Eq. 7.9 LSDVC
OFF narrow	−0.01	−0.01	−0.01	0.01	0.01	0.01	0.01	0.01	0.01
	(0.004)*	(0.004)**	(0.004)*	(0.005)**	(0.005)***	(0.006)**	(0.004)*	(0.005)*	(0.005)
ln(*K/Y*)	−0.13	−0.07	−0.13	0.03	0.17	0.05	0.14	0.33	0.16
	(0.05)**	(0.07)	(0.05)**	(0.15)	(0.17)	(0.16)	(0.13)	(0.15)**	(0.14)
lnY	−0.18	−0.18	−0.17	0.50	0.73	0.49	0.31	0.42	0.33
	(0.08)**	(0.09)**	(0.08)**	(0.25)**	(0.27)***	(0.27)*	(0.19)*	(0.21)**	(0.20)
ln(*Imp/Y*)	0.13	0.10	0.12	−0.13	−0.40	−0.06	−0.04	−0.33	0.06
	(0.09)	(0.11)	(0.10)	(0.21)	(0.23)*	(0.22)	(0.18)	(0.21)	(0.20)
ln(*Exp/Y*)	−0.23	−0.16	−0.22	−0.28	−0.23	0.35	−0.11	−0.13	−0.16
	(0.12)**	(0.14)	(0.12)*	(0.20)	(0.21)	(0.22)	(0.17)	(0.19)	(0.19)
lnFDIin	0.02	0.02	0.02	−0.01	−0.04	0.01	−0.04	−0.05	−0.03
	(0.02)	(0.02)	(0.02)	(0.07)	(0.08)	(0.09)	(0.06)	(0.07)	(0.07)
lnFDIout	0.03	0.03	0.02	−0.001	−0.02	0.01	0.01	−0.01	0.02
	(0.02)	(0.03)	0.03	(0.05)	(0.06)	(0.06)	(0.05)	(0.05)	(0.05)
ln(*ICT/Y*)	0.07	0.05	0.07	0.07	−0.11	0.07	0.01	−0.17	−0.01
	(0.05)	(0.05)	(0.05)	(0.15)	(0.17)	(0.16)	(0.13)	(0.14)	(0.14)

(*Continued*)

Table 7. (*Continued*)

	Unskill-intensive industries (a) (white-/blue-collar ratio below average)			Skill-intensive industries (b) (white-/blue-collar ratio above average)			Skill-intensive industries (based on INPS) (c)		
	Eq 7.1 LSDV	Eq 7.2 A–B	Eq. 7.3 LSDVC	Eq 7.4 LSDV	Eq 7.5 A–B	Eq. 7.6 LSDVC	Eq. 7.7 LSDV	Eq 7.8 A–B	Eq. 7.9 LSDVC
Δ*lntotdip*	−0.01	−0.01	−0.01	1.26	1.30	1.29	1.04	0.99	1.08
	(0.14)	(0.15)	(0.15)	(0.24)***	(0.25)***	(0.25)***	(0.20)***	(0.21)***	(0.22)***
lnS(-1)	0.44	0.36	0.56	0.64	0.61	0.75	0.58	0.55	0.69
	(0.11)***	(0.13)***	(0.11)***	(0.11)***	(0.11)***	(0.10)***	(0.10)***	(0.10)***	(0.09)***
Time dummies	yes	yes	yes	yes	yes	yes	yes	yes	yes
No. of observations	90	81	90	78	70	78	98	88	98
No. of sectors	9	9	9	8	8	8	10	10	10
R-squared	0.1003			0.0026			0.3260		
ABII (*p*-value)		0.9411			0.6115			0.4929	

Note: See Table 4.

(a) It includes ATECO sectors 15–16, 17–19, 20, 25, 26, 27, 28, 34, 36–37.

(b) It includes ATECO sectors 21–22, 24, 29, 30, 31, 32, 33, 35. The fuel sector (ATECO 23) has been dropped from these regressions.

(c) In this regression we included ATECO sectors 21–22, 24, 27, 29, 30, 31, 32, 33, 34 and 35. According to this classification, only four industries are unambiguously unskill-intensive, leaving too few observations to perform regressions over the unskill industries subset (see for details Bruno *et al.*, 2008).

industries. The output variable has a negative coefficient in the unskilled industries, and a positive one in the skill-intensive ones. This result has quite reasonable implications: an increase of production increases unevenly the employment of unskilled workers in the unskilled industries, while in the skill-intensive industries, the skilled labor force expands more than proportionally with output. The K/Y variable is mostly non-significant, but it presents a similar switch of sign between industry groups. Export over production is significant, with a negative sign only for the unskilled industries. It seems that for this group of industries, if an increase in exports increases labor demand, it does so especially with respect to the workers qualified as blue collar, or unskilled, thereby decreasing the skill/unskilled ratio. The variable measuring the overall change in employment is not significant for the unskilled industries, but it is positive and highly significant for the skill-intensive ones: in these industries, an increase in employment seems to expand especially the number of skilled workers. The estimates for the two subsets of skill-intensive industries present similar results for all the control variables.

Moving to our main variable of interest, we see that for the group of skill-intensive industries, the offshoring indicator has a small positive sign, and it is almost always significant, while for the unskill-intensive group, the sign of the coefficient is negative. This last result appears puzzling, but a possible explanation of this difference in signs lies in the structure of Italian comparative advantage and specialization, giving rise to different types of offshoring. Offshoring should be undertaken by firms to offset comparative disadvantage in some phases of production. As mentioned, offshoring in Italy is generally stronger, first of all, in some skill-intensive industries, where on average we observe a revealed comparative disadvantage for Italy, and where the productivity gap with respect to other industrialized countries is higher.[25] In these sectors, offshoring of relatively high-tech components could be complemented by an increase of skilled personnel. Second, the index of offshoring is high in some traditional industries such as apparel and footwear, displaying an overall comparative advantage. It is normally assumed that in these sectors the production phases intensive in unskilled

[25] For Italy, there is a negative simultaneous correlation between our offshoring indices and all available measures of productivity at the industry level.

labor — relatively expensive in Italy — are delocalized abroad. But if this organization of production allows the output to expand, the net effect on employment composition might be ambiguous. Unfortunately, the data so far do not allow us to check which production phases are offshored in the different industries. But the disadvantage leading to fragmentation production internationally could come from factor price differences as well as from productivity gaps. If the pattern of offshoring does not have the same factor intensity across production phases and industries (e.g., not all production phases which are located abroad are intensive in unskilled labor), offshoring might very well affect factors differently in different industries.

V. CONCLUSIONS

Considering the evidence of the last few years, Italy shows, like most other countries, a general increase in skill-intensity in manufacturing industries, as well as an increase in the use of offshoring in many manufacturing sectors. The relationship between the two phenomena is not straightforward. The increase in offshoring is occurring especially in some of the more advanced industries.

Given these "stylized facts," it is not surprising that in Italy the relationship between offshoring and changes in the labor market appears weak in our regressions. It seems in fact that offshoring is pushed only to a limited extent by the search for low-cost blue-collar workers. Offshoring is more related to the integration of industries in the international production networks for some advanced goods, where Italy does not have a comparative advantage, and it needs to obtain many components from abroad. Our analysis underlines the importance of taking into account industry heterogeneity and the possibility of offshoring production phases with different factor intensities.

Overall, this change in the organization of production does not seem to have dramatically affected the Italian labor market. While the general increase in employment of skilled labor is expected to continue and it can be enhanced in some sectors by the internationalization choices of firms, as some of our results show, in Italy offshoring is not the main reason behind the slow changes we observe in the labor market.

ACKNOWLEDGMENTS

This chapter was prepared within the research project "Intensità di capitale umano nella specializzazione internazionale dell'Italia, outsourcing internazionale di merci e servizi e riflessi sull'occupazione." Financial support from UniCredit Group for this project is gratefully acknowledged. Thanks are due to Gianluca Orefice for his valuable research assistance and to Rosario Crinò for kindly providing us with the proxies of offshoring. The authors are especially grateful to Kei-Mu Yi for discussing the chapter and giving us useful insights, and to participants of the SIE 2008 Annual Conference, the 2009 Workshop of the project "International Fragmentation of Italian Firms," the CGP 2009 Conference at the University of Michigan for comments to an earlier version of the paper. Anna M. Falzoni acknowledges additional financial support from Università degli Studi di Bergamo "Fondi di Ateneo" (60FALZ07). All remaining errors are our own.

APPENDIX

Data and Sources

The empirical analysis in this chapter was undertaken on 23 manufacturing sectors classified according to the classification ATECO 91 — NACE rev.1

The industry codes and definitions are the following:

15 Manufacture of food and beverages
16 Manufacture of tobacco
17 Manufacture of textiles
18 Manufacture of wearing apparel; dressing and dyeing of fur
19 Tanning and dressing of leather; manufacture of luggage, handbags, saddlery, harness and footwear
20 Manufacture of wood and of products of wood and cork, except furniture; manufacture of articles of straw and plaiting materials
21 Manufacture of paper and paper products
22 Publishing, printing and reproduction of recorded media
23 Manufacture of coke, refined petroleum products and nuclear fuel
24 Manufacture of chemicals and chemical products
25 Manufacture of rubber and plastic products

26 Manufacture of other non-metallic mineral products
27 Manufacture of basic metals
28 Manufacture of fabricated metal products, except machinery and equipment
29 Manufacture of machinery and equipment, nec (not elsewhere classified)
30 Manufacture of office, accounting and computing machinery
31 Manufacture of electrical machinery and apparatus, nec
32 Manufacture of radio, television and communication equipment and apparatus
33 Manufacture of medical, precision and optical instruments, watches and clocks
34 Manufacture of motor vehicles, trailers and semi-trailers
35 Manufacture of other transport equipment
36 Manufacture of furniture; manufacturing, n.e.c.
37 Treatment and preparation for recycling

In the econometric analysis, to combine industry data to the offshoring indices computed from input–output tables, some sectors have been aggregated. Our industry/year panel then covers 18 industries, due to the following aggregations: ATECO 15–16, 17–19, 21–22, and 36–37.

VARIABLE DEFINITION AND SOURCES

Offshoring index (OFF): $OFF_{it} = (\sum_{k=1}^{K} M_{ikt})/II_{it}$
where M_{ikt} are imports of intermediate input (service) k by industry i at time t, whereas II_{it} is total usage of intermediate inputs. More specifically, for the numerator of the narrow offshoring index we have the value of the imported inputs i by industry i at current prices, where i is a two-digit NACE sector; for the broad offshoring index we have the sum of the value of imported inputs in NACE sectors 15 through 37 by industry i; and for the service offshoring index we used the sum of values of imported inputs in NACE sectors 71–74 and 93 by industry i. The imported input values are taken from ISTAT, Tavola delle Importazioni. At the denominator of all indices instead we have the value at current prices of all used input by industry i from ISTAT, Tavola degli impieghi (use) a prezzi base. *Source:*

ISTAT, Conti nazionali: il nuovo sistema input–output, 1995–2003, released on October 2006.

Skill intensity (S): computed as the ratio of the number of managers and employees (skilled workers) over the number of workers, apprentices and home workers (unskilled workers) for each manufacturing sector. *Source*: ISTAT, Conti Economici delle Imprese, various years.

Capital (K): gross fixed capital formation by sector at current prices. *Source*: OECD, STAN Database for Industrial Analysis.

Employment (L): total employment by sector. *Source*: ISTAT, Conti Economici delle Imprese, various years.

Wage rate (W): total wages over total employment by sector. *Source*: ISTAT, Conti Economici delle Imprese, various years.

Production (Y): production (gross output) by sector at current prices. *Source*: OECD, STAN Database for Industrial Analysis.

ICT: gross fixed capital formation in software, office and communication equipments. *Source*: ISTAT, Conti Economici Nazionali, various years.

Imports (Imp): imports of goods by sector at current prices. *Source*: OECD, STAN Database for Industrial Analysis.

Exports (Exp): exports of goods by sector at current prices. *Source*: OECD, STAN Database for Industrial Analysis.

FDI intensity (FDIin and FDIout): the share of employment in domestic affiliates of foreign MNEs (inward FDI) on total employment, and the share of employment in foreign affiliates of domestic MNEs (outward FDI) on total employment, in a given sector. *Source*: Reprint database, Politecnico di Milano and ICE.

Δtotdip: change in total sectoral employment level. *Source*: ISTAT, Conti Economici delle Imprese, various years.

REFERENCES

Amiti, M. and S. Wei (2005). "Fear of Outsourcing: Is it Justified?" *Economic Policy*, 20: pp. 308–348.

Antràs, P. and E. Helpman (2008). "Contractual frictions and Global Sourcing," in E. Helpman, D. Marin, and T. Verdier (Eds.), *The Organization of Firms in a Global Economy*, Cambridge, MA: Harvard University Press, pp. 9–54.

Benfratello, L., T. Razzolini and A. Sembenelli (2009). "Does ICT Investment Spur or Hamper Offshoring? Empirical Evidence From Microdata," (mimeo).

Berman, E., J. Bound and Z. Griliches (1994). "Changes in the Demand For Skilled Labor within U.S. Manufacturing: Evidence from the Annual Survey of Manufacturers." *Quarterly Journal of Economics*, 109(2): pp. 367–397.

Bertoli, S. (2008). "The Impact of Material Offshoring on Employment in the Italian Manufacturing Industries: The Relevance of Intersectoral Effects," Centro Studi Luca d'Agliano, Development Studies Working Paper, No. 244.

Brenton, P. and A. M. Pinna (2001). "The Declining Use of Unskilled Labor in Italian Manufacturing: Is Trade to Blame?" CEPS Working Document, No. 178.

Broccolini, C., A. Lo Turco, A. Presbitero and S. Staffolani (2008). "Individual Earnings, International Outsourcing and Technological Change. Evidence from Italy," Centro Studi Luca d'Agliano, Development Studies Working Paper, No. 242.

Bruno, G. S. F. (2005a). "Approximating the Bias of the LSDV Estimator for Dynamic Unbalanced Panel Data Models." *Economic Letters*, 87: pp. 361–366.

Bruno, G. S. F. (2005b). "Estimation and Inference in Dynamic Unbalanced Panel-Data Models with a Small Number of Individuals." *The Stata Journal*, 5(4): pp. 473–500.

Bruno, G., O. Dessy, A. Falzoni and R. Helg (2008). "Estimating Skills in the Italian Manufacturing Sector Using the INPS Archives: An Application to the Italian Pattern of Trade," (mimeo).

Costa, S. and G. Ferri (2007). "The Determinants and Employment Effects of International Outsourcing: The Case of Italy," SERIES Working Paper, No. 16.

Crinò, R. (2009). "Offshoring, Multinationals and Labor Market: A Review of the Empirical Literature." *Journal of Economic Survey*, 23(2): pp. 197–249.

Daveri, F. and C. Iona-Lasinio (2008). "Off-shoring and Productivity Growth in the Italian Manufacturing Industries." *CESifo Economic Studies*, 54(3): pp. 414–450.

Deardorff, A. V. (2001). "Fragmentation across cones," in S. W. Arndt and H. Kierzkowski (Eds.), *Fragmentation. New Production Patterns in the World Economy*, pp. 35–51, Oxford: Oxford University Press.

Deardorff, A. V. (2005). "A Trade Theorist's Take on Skilled Labor Outsourcing." *International Review of Economics and Finance*, 14: pp. 259–271.

De Benedictis, L. (2005). "Three Decades of Italian Comparative Advantages." *The World Economy*, 28(11): pp. 1679–1709.

De Backer, K. and N. Yamano (2007). "The Measurement of Globalisation using International Input-Output Tables," OECD, STI Working Paper, No. 2007/8.

Dluhosch, B. (2006). "Intraindustry Trade and the Gains from Fragmentation." *North American Journal of Economics and Finance*, 17: pp. 49–64.

Egger, H. and P. Egger (2005). "Labor Market Effects of Outsourcing under Industrial Interdependence." *International Review of Economics and Finance*, 14: pp. 349–363.

Feenstra, R. C. (2004). *Advanced International Trade. Theory and Evidence*, Princeton: Princeton University Press.

Feenstra, R. C. and G. H. Hanson (1999). "The Impact of Outsourcing and High-Technology Capital on Wages: Estimates for the United States, 1979–1990," *The Quarterly Journal of Economics*, 114(3): pp. 907–940.

Feenstra, R. C. and G. H. Hanson (2003). "Global Production Sharing and Rising Inequality: A Survey on Trade and Wages," in K. Choi and J. Harrigan (Eds.), *Handbook of International Trade*, pp. 146–185, Oxford; Malden, MA; Carlton, Vicotria: Basil Blackwell.

Geishecker, I. and H. Gorg (2005). "Do Unskilled Workers Always Lose From Fragmentation?" *North American Journal of Economics and Finance*, 16: 81–92.

Giovannetti, G. and B. Quintieri (2007). "Globalizzazione, specializzazione produttiva e mercato del lavoro," Working Paper Fondazione Masi (in Italian).

Grossman, G. M. and E. Rossi-Hansberg (2006). "The Rise of Offshoring: It's Not Wine for Cloth Anymore," *Proceedings of the Federal Reserve Bank of Kansas City*, pp. 59–102.

Grossman, G. M. and E. Rossi-Hansberg (2008). "Trading Tasks: A Simple Theory of Offshoring." *American Economic Review*, 98(5): pp. 1978–1997.

Hamermesh, D. (1993). *Labor Demand*, Princeton New Jersey: Princeton University Press.

Havik, K. and K. McMorrow (2006). "Global Trade Integration and Outsourcing: How Well is the EU Coping with the New Challenges?," European Economy, *Economic paper*, No. 259, European Commission, DG for Economic and Financial Affairs.

Helg, R. and L. Tajoli (2005). "Patterns of International Fragmentation of Production and the Relative Demand for Labor." *North American Journal of Economics and Finance*, 16: pp. 233–254.

Hijzen, A. (2005). "A Bird's Eye View of International Outsourcing: Data, Measurement and Labor Demand Effects," *Economie Internationale*, CEPII Research Center, 4Q, pp. 45–63.

Hijzen, A. and P. Swaim (2007). "Does Offshoring Reduce Industry Employment?" *National Institute Economic Review*, 201: pp. 86–96.

Horgos, D. (2009). "Labor Market Effects of International Outsourcing: How Measurement Matters." *International Review of Economics & Finance*, 18(4): pp. 611–623.

IMF (2007). *World Economic Outlook*, Washington D.C., April.

Kohler, W. (2008). "Offshoring: Why Do Stories Differ?," CESifo Working Paper, No. 2231.

Manasse, P., L. Stanca and A. Turrini (2004). "Wage Premia and Skill Upgrading in Italy: Why Didn't the Hound Bark?" *Labor Economics*, 11(1): pp. 59–83.

OECD (2007). *Offshoring and Employment. Trends and Impacts*, Paris: OECD.

Strauss-Kahn, V. (2004). "The role of globalization in the within-industry shift away from unskilled workers in France," in R. E. Baldwin and L. A. Winters (Eds.), *Challenges to Globalization*, pp. 209–233, London: NBER and University of Chicago Press.

Comment

Kei-Mu Yi

I. INTRODUCTION AND OVERVIEW

One of the most important topics in international trade over the past decade is the research on offshoring. This phenomenon has captured such a high level of interest that it has more than one name! It has also been called by terms such as fragmentation, vertical specialization, production sharing, and outsourcing. But, what all these terms aim to capture or characterize is the increased specialization over the past several decades — by firms, industries, and countries — in particular stages of a good's production chain. Understanding the causes and consequences of this phenomenon has motivated a great deal of empirical and theoretical research. The research has been complementary; the empirical research has informed the development of theories and models and vice versa.

The paper by Falzoni and Tajoli (hereafter, FT) is a good contribution to the empirical research and stimulates thinking on this topic. FT study the effect of offshoring on overall employment and skill composition across Italian manufacturing industries between 1992 and 2003. Italy is an interesting country to study for three reasons. First, it has been one of the primary countries to offshore production to central Europe. Second, like the rest of Europe, its manufacturing markets have been affected by the emergence of China. Finally, Italy is unique among the G7 nations in that it still has an innovative and relatively vibrant textile and apparel industry.

FT first construct measures of changes in the skill composition and in offshoring. They find that over time, the skill intensity of production has increased broadly across two-digit manufacturing sectors. Among the unskilled-intensive industries, textiles and wearing apparel had the largest increases. FT construct two measures of offshoring. Each measure captures imported intermediate inputs as a share of total intermediates used by an industry. The broad measure includes all industries as sources, while the narrow measure includes only the same industry as a source. FT find that the broad measure increased by about 25% between 1992 and 2003, while the narrow measure changed little.

FT then turn to their main analysis, an econometric analysis of the effect of offshoring on overall employment and on the skill composition of employment. Specifically, they conduct a panel estimation of a labor-demand equation that includes time and industry fixed effects, several control variables, and offshoring.[26] They find that offshoring has had little effect on overall employment, but that it has had some effect on the skill composition of employment. If the change in total industry employment is controlled for, offshoring has a statistically significant positive effect on the skill composition of employment. Also, the effect of offshoring differs according to the skill intensity of the industry. Offshoring reduces the skill composition of the unskilled-intensive industries, but increases the skill composition of the skill-intensive industries.

Taken together, these findings lead to the conclusion that the effects of offshoring are not as sweeping and broad as is sometimes claimed, but, in fact are more nuanced and subtle, and also consistent with standard international trade theory. My comments below focus on the measurement of offshoring and on the empirical methodology.

II. MEASUREMENT OF OFFSHORING

I have several comments on the measurement of offshoring. The offshoring measure used in this paper is either total imported intermediates (broad) or own-industry imported intermediates (narrow) as a share of total intermediates used by an industry. There are other measures used in empirical research. For example, an alternative measure is imported intermediate inputs as a share of gross output. Consider the following situation: intermediate use in gross output increases, but the share of imported intermediates in total intermediates is unchanged. The measure in this paper will be unchanged, but the alternative measure will have increased. It may be

[26]One of their control variables is a lagged dependent variable; FT employ several estimators that make the appropriate econometric adjustment for the endogeneity caused by that variable.

useful therefore to consider a wider range of measures, simply to see if the broad findings are robust to them.

By their very nature, input–output tables capture the repeated sequences of inputs being made into output, much of which is used as inputs to make other outputs, etc. In terms of imported intermediates, some of them become embodied in domestic intermediates that are later used to produce another industry's goods that are eventually used for final demand. The expression below captures the value of all imported intermediates that are embodied in final demand:

$$[uA_{\text{im}}(I - A_{\text{ID}})^{-1}]'FD_I$$

where u is a $1 \times K$ vector of 1s, K is the number of industries, A_{im} is the Italian imported input coefficient matrix, A_{ID} is the Italian domestic input coefficient matrix, and FD_I is the $K \times 1$ vector of final demand. This yields a $K \times 1$ vector of imported intermediate values, where row K gives the value of imported intermediates used to produce industry K output used for final demand.[27]

Some imported intermediates actually embody domestic content. Johnson and Noguera (2009) and Wang, Powers, and Wei, (2009), among others, have shown how to appropriately calculate the "true" domestic value-added and imported input content of exports. I would conjecture that the appropriate expression for the true value of imported intermediates into Italy is given by:

$$[u(A_{\text{im}} - A_{\text{WM}}(I - A_{\text{WD}})^{-1}A_{\text{IM}})]'GO_I$$

where A_{WM} is the world imported input coefficient matrix from Italy, and A_{WD} is the world domestic input coefficient matrix. (Note that if $A_{\text{WM}} = 0$, then the measure above is identical to that employed by FT.) The above measure can be constructed from a database like GTAP. Johnson and Noguera (2009) apply their methodology to a number of countries and find that it can significantly change estimates of sectoral domestic value-added input (and, consequently, estimates of sectoral imported input content).

A related measurement issue is: how do we measure the offshoring of goods that do not return to Italy? I would guess that much of the Italian

[27] *Note*: this measure would not be appropriate to use to study the effects of offshoring on labor demand.

apparel manufacturing that has been offshored to Central Europe involves production of final or intermediate goods that are then exported to countries other than Italy. My more general point is that offshoring is considerably more complex than what can be captured by measures that focus on imported intermediate goods. One advantage of the Johnson and Noguera framework is that it can begin to address these more complex notions of offshoring, although I believe the ultimate answers will arise from a combination of models and data.

Finally, studying the next version of Italy's input–output tables will be very interesting, because it will capture some of the major inroads that China has made on Italian markets. The table below shows that China's importance as a source for Italy's industrial supplies and parts and components increased by more than a factor of four between 2003 and 2008, more than twice the pace of the increase in overall imports.

ITALY IMPORTS

Variable	1995 $ billion	2003 $ billion	2008 $billion
Imports from world	204.0	297.0	554.0
Imports of industrial. supplies from world, excluding China	78.6	88.0	160.0
Imports of industrial supplies from China	1.14	2.6	11.0
Imports of parts and components from world, excluding China	25.1	33.1	52.1
Imports of parts and components from China	0.24	1.1	4.6

Source: U.N. Comtrade Database

Two Estimation Issues

Offshoring can arise from many forces: lower costs of trade (tariffs, transport costs, etc.), lower costs of fragmentation (e.g., cheaper and improved communication networks), changes in factor endowments, and changes in the technology of sectoral production. The econometric specification for the skill intensity of production is probably most justified when offshoring is driven by lower costs of fragmentation. The other forces could plausibly affect the skill intensity of production in addition to affecting offshoring.

It would be useful therefore to discuss this issue; also FT should consider pursuing steps to isolate and focus on that part of offshoring that is driven by lower costs of fragmentation only.

In the standard approach to estimating labor–demand equations, the wage share of skilled (or unskilled) labor is the dependent variable. FT's rationale for using the employment share instead of the wage share is that time-fixed effects pick up variation in the skill premium. More discussion of this would be useful. Perhaps FT could give an example to illustrate when time fixed effects work and when they do not.

An alternative is to consider the following. A simple CES production framework implies:

$$S_u = \left(\frac{a_i}{1 - a_i}\right)\left(\frac{w_{\mathrm{ut}}}{w_{\mathrm{st}}}\right)\rho$$

In log terms, S_{it} should be captured by industry-fixed-effects and by time-fixed effects. Hence, why not run regression of S_{it} on industry-fixed effects, time-fixed effects, and the offshoring term alone?

Two Other Comments

It would be useful to provide more economic interpretations to the coefficient estimates. For example, it would be good to know the answer to the following question: If offshoring in unskilled-intensive industries overall rose to the apparel's level of offshoring, what would happen to S_i?[28]

Finally, I would like to mention a potentially useful theoretical framework by Burstein and Vogel (2009), which studies the increase in the skill premium with a model that includes both Heckscher–Ohlin (factor abundance and intensity) and Ricardian (productivity) reasons for offshoring. The model also includes for the skill bias of technology. Offshoring costs are characterized as the costs of transferring technology abroad (per unit cost). Overall, this is a useful and rich framework that can support the empirical research.

[28] Also, I have one question for clarification: A coefficient of 0.01 from Table 6.2 means that an increase in narrow offshoring by 1 percentage point raises the skilled–unskilled unemployment ratio by 1% or by 0.01%?

REFERENCES

Burstein, Ariel and Jonathan Vogel (2009). "Globalization, Technology, and the Skill Premium," (manuscript), UCLA and Columbia University.

Johnson, Robert and Guillermo Noguera (2009). "Accounting for Intermediates: Production Sharing and Trade in Value Added," (manuscript), Dartmouth College and U.C. Berkeley.

Wang, Zhi, William Powers and Shang-Jin Wei (2009). "Value Chains in East Asian Production Networks: An International Input-Output Model Based Analysis," U.S. International Trade Commission Working Paper 2009-10-C.

PART II

EFFECTS OF TRADE AND FOREIGN DIRECT INVESTMENT

CHAPTER 6

International Production/Distribution Networks in East Asia and Domestic Operations: Evidence from Japanese Firms*

Mitsuyo Ando[†,¶] and Fukunari Kimura[‡,§]

[†] *Faculty of Business and Commerce*
Keio University, Japan
[‡] *Faculty of Economics, Keio University, Japan*
[§] *ERIA*
[¶] *ando@fbc.keio.ac.jp*

I. INTRODUCTION

In East Asia, international production/distribution networks began to be formulated in the 1990s and have further developed in recent years. These networks have been accompanied by large increases in vertical back-and-forth transactions of parts and components.[1] Japanese firms have been major players in the networks. Since the late 1990s in particular, Japanese investment in East Asia has accelerated; as shown in Figure 1, with an upward trend that is observed for the direct investment position of Japan in East Asia, based on the balance of payments statistics. A predominant

*The METI (Ministry of Economy, Trade, and Industry) database was analyzed under the auspices of the RIETI (Research Institute of Economy, Trade, and Industry) project, "Productivity of Companies and Industries, and Japan's Economic Growth." This is a revised version of the paper that appeared as *RIETI DP* 07-E-063.

[1] See Kimura and Ando (2005), Ando and Kimura (2006), Ando (2006), and Kimura (2006) for empirical analyses and established facts on production/distribution networks in East Asia. For a theoretical framework for production sharing, based on fragmentation theory, see Jones and Kierzkowski (1990) and Arndt and Kierzkowski (2001).

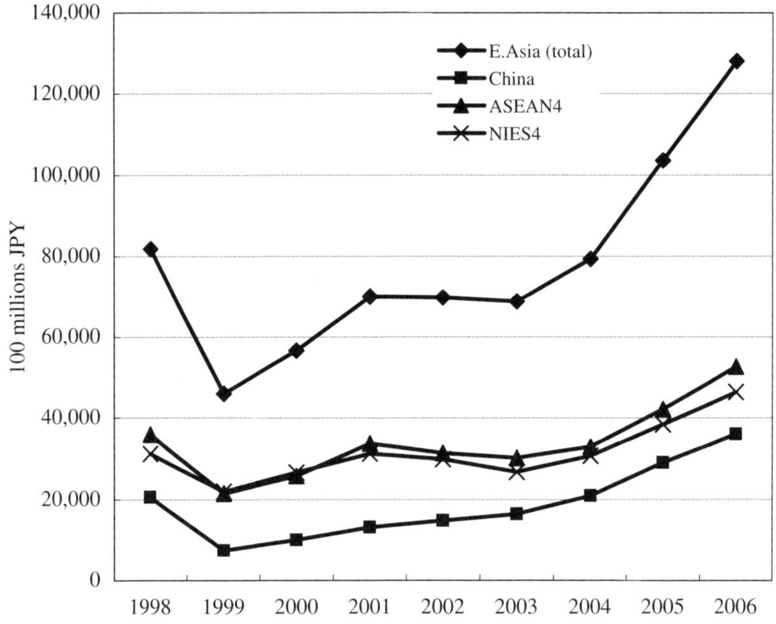

Source: Authors' calculation, based on balance of payments statistics available from the website of the Bank of Japan.

Fig. 1. Direct investment position of Japan in East Asia.

portion of the investment is in the manufacturing sectors — the manufacturing share of the Japanese direct investment position for 2006 is 72% for East Asia as a whole, 78% for China, 82% for the Association of Southeast Asian Nations (ASEAN), including the Philippines (86%), Indonesia (77%), Thailand (79%), and Malaysia (89%), and 57% for the Newly Industrializing Economies (NIEs), including Taiwan (73%), Korea (59%), Singapore (64%), and Hong Kong (30%).

Outsourcing and offshoring in lower-income countries by multinational enterprises (MNEs) raise concerns about activities in high-income countries. A popular argument claims that domestic employment and operations may shrink due to the relocation of economic activities by taking advantage of a large wage gap between developed and developing countries. In particular, the fear of losing jobs, in both the manufacturing and services sectors, and other possible disruptive effects in wealthier societies seem to be emphasized in journalistic as well as intellectual literature in Europe and North America.[2] However, even in the case when foreign direct investment (FDI) is pursuing inexpensive labor in developing countries, the effect of FDI on domestic operations is not necessarily negative; it depends on the extent to which the cost reduction through FDI allows the firm to strengthen its competitiveness and whether the firm maintains activities at home that are complementary to operations abroad. There is sometimes further shifting of activities to the procurement of specialized parts and components, headquarters functions, and the development of new products. Figure 2 illustrates an example of complementary operations. When a firm realizes cost reduction by fragmentation with FDI in lower income countries, it may be able to sell more products at cheaper prices than before. Larger sales require an increase in the production of both final goods and intermediate inputs, including specialized parts and components (P&C), as well as larger research and development (R&D) activities for new products and more extensive headquarter (HQ) services. If the firm shifts home activities to those that are complementary to activities abroad, it would rather expand domestic employment overall even if it might reduce employment in assembly lines.

As Becker *et al.* (2005) note, the effect of FDI on the labor market at home is inherently an empirical issue. Their analysis of German MNEs for 2000 and Swedish MNEs for 1998 finds that affiliate employment abroad tends to substitute for parent employment. Blomstrom, Fors, and Lipsey (1997) demonstrate that affiliate production in developing countries had a stronger negative effect on parent employment in the U.S. in 1989, while Swedish parents employed more labor at home in 1970–1994.[3] Rather than

[2]See, for example, Samuelson (2004) and Blinder (2006).

[3]See Brown and Spletzer (2005) for the relationship between offshoring and mass layoffs in the U.S. The recent study by Ebenstein *et al.* (2009) links industry-level data on offshoring activities of U.S. MNEs, import penetration, and export shares with individual level worker data and measures the impact on the wages of domestic workers. They find that offshoring to high wage countries is positively correlated with U.S. manufacturing employment while offshoring to low wage countries is negatively associated.

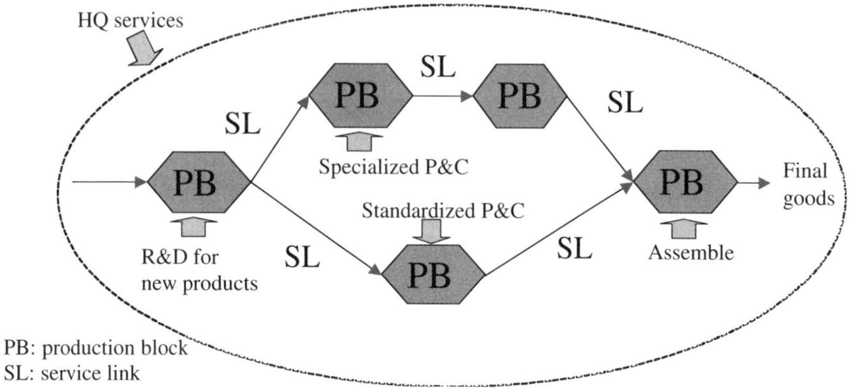

Fig. 2. Complementary operations with fragmentation: an illustration.

focusing on MNEs only as in the previous literature including the above-mentioned studies, Federico and Minerva (2008) assess the impact of Italy's outward FDI in the period between 1996 and 2001, comparing employment performance across local provinces. They find that FDI is associated with faster employment growth at home, relative to the national industry average.

Japan has for long been a typical country with "hollowing-out (*Kūdōka*)" concerns since the mid-1980s, reflecting the rapid development of the international division of labor in East Asia. In particular, Japan is located in the neighborhood of China and has recently been expanding manufacturing operations there. Fukao and Amano (2004) provide an extensive literature survey on the effect of outward FDI by Japanese firms on the skill composition in labor demand at home at the macro level, industry level,[4] and firm level, suggesting possible job creation or at least job retainment on the side of skilled labor with globalizing corporate

[4]Also, see Ito and Fukao (2005) for analysis at the detailed industry level. They use the share of vertical intra-industry trade as a broad outsourcing measure and find that vertical intra-industry trade, particularly with Asia, raises the skill intensity calculated as the share of professional and technical or managerial and administrative workers in the period, 1988–2000. This may reflect the fact that vertical FDI in Asia consists of the transfer of low-skilled production work to the region while high-skilled employees remain at home. They note that Japanese manufacturing industries realized skill upgrading as a result of the international division of labor with Asian economies.

activities.[5] At the same time, they emphasize the importance of further comprehensive research at the firm level.

In what follows, we investigate the globalizing activities of Japanese firms, with a particular emphasis on East Asia, and their domestic operations, using comprehensive firm-level panel data, including both firms with and without operations abroad. This is in contrast with most of the previous studies using data only for MNEs. More specifically, we compare the domestic operations of firms expanding foreign operations with those of firms not expanding foreign operations. That is, how do firms expanding foreign operations differ, compared with other firms, in reorganizing domestic operations in terms of employment, establishments and affiliates at home, and export/import activities? In doing so, we also examine both cases that include firms that expand foreign operations with their first FDI during the sample period and those firms that do not, in order to see whether any difference exists among globalizing firms.[6] By analyzing these patterns, we wish to determine whether the hollowing-out of industries exists directly due to globalizing activities, whether domestic operations and foreign operations are substitutes or complements, and whether trade and FDI are substitutes or complements at the firm level. In particular, we are interested in the implications of production fragmentation, typically in machinery industries, for retaining domestic operations through assigning different activities at home and abroad.

The chapter proceeds as follows. Section II provides a description of the micro data employed and examines patterns of the globalizing activities of

[5] Head and Ries (2002) have investigated the influence of offshore production by Japanese multinationals on domestic skill intensity at the firm level, using Toyo Keizai's survey on Japanese Overseas Investment 1992–1993 (1,070 firms). They find that additional foreign affiliate employment in low-income countries raises skill intensity, expressed as the non-production share of the wage bill at home. For other studies on the effect of offshoring on the skill composition of domestic labor demand at the firm level, see Ekholm and Hakkala (2006) with evidence from Sweden and Hijzen, Gorg, and Hine (2005) with evidence from the United Kingdom.

[6] Hijzen, Inui, and Todo (2007) investigate the causal effect of becoming a multinational or establishing their first foreign affiliate during the sample period between 1995 and 2002, on home performance. They use propensity matching techniques in combination with a difference-in-difference estimator. They find that Japanese outward FDI tends to strengthen the economic activities in terms of output and employment, but not productivity.

Japanese firms and their domestic operations. Then, Section III quantitatively investigates those patterns, employing logit and ordinary least squares (OLS) regression analyses. Section IV concludes.

II. JAPANESE INVESTMENT IN EAST ASIA AT THE FIRM LEVEL: OVERVIEW

Data

The analysis in this and the following sections is based on firm-level statistics in *The Basic Survey of Business Structure and Activity*, available from the Ministry of Economy, Trade, and Industry (METI), Government of Japan (the former name was the Ministry of International Trade and Industry (MITI)). This database provides detailed information on (parent) firms located in Japan as well as the number, industry, and regional location of their foreign affiliates with no less than 20% Japanese ownership. Note that the location of foreign affiliates is not identified on a country basis; the questionnaires from *the 1997F/Y Basic Survey* include only East Asia, North America, and Europe as regional categories.[7]

The samples in the survey cover firms with more than 50 workers, capital of more than 30 million yen, and establishments in mining, manufacturing, wholesale/retail trade, and restaurants. Our industry classification is presented in Table A1. We use this survey for the latest available seven years containing the data from 1998 to 2004.

Characteristics of Japanese Firms Investing in East Asia

This subsection investigates the globalizing patterns of Japanese firms, with a particular emphasis on firms investing in East Asia. To shed light on the features for East Asia, we compare them with firms investing in North America and Europe. Table 1 presents the number of all sized firms and small and medium enterprises (SMEs) with affiliates in East Asia/North America/Europe and the number of affiliates in East Asia/North America/Europe by the industry of parent firms and by the industry of affiliates.[8] In 2004, 4,590 out of 28,340 firms located in Japan (in the data set)

[7] East Asia includes all Asian countries east of Pakistan. Note that Japanese FDI in South Asia is small in this period.

[8] SMEs are here defined as firms with regular workers of less than 300.

Table 1. Sectoral patterns of Japanese parent firms and their affiliates in East Asia, North America, and Europe for 2004

Industry of parent firm	Number of parent firms: all sized	(%)	Number of affiliates by the industry of parent firms	(%)	Share by the industry of affiliates: Manufacturing (machinery)		Non-manufacturing (wholesales)		Number of parent firms: SMEs	(%)	Number of affiliates by the industry of parent firms	(%)	Share by the industry of affiliates: Manufacturing (machinery)		Non-manufacturing (wholesales)	
			(a-1) East Asia								(a-2) East Asia					
Manufacturing	2,610	68	10,070	70	73	(38%)	27	(18%)	1,280	66	1,962	62	84	(39%)	16	(12%)
-Machinery	1,200	31	5,387	37	69	(65%)	31	(20%)	534	27	916	29	82	(76%)	18	(14%)
Non-manufacturing	1,237	32	4,412	30	33	(8%)	67	(42%)	668	34	1,202	38	35	(9%)	65	(55%)
-Wholesales	812	21	3,645	25	36	(9%)	64	(50%)	528	27	1,094	35	36	(9%)	64	(60%)
Total	3,847	100	14,482	100	61	(29%)	39	(25%)	1,948	100	3,164	100	65	(28%)	35	(28%)
			(b-1) North America								(b-2) North America					
Manufacturing	1,250	68	3,123	69	49	(29%)	51	(24%)	367	60	386	61	55	(29%)	45	(33%)
-Machinery	660	36	1,955	43	44	(41%)	56	(25%)	195	32	222	35	50	(47%)	50	(40%)
Non-manufacturing	592	32	1,392	31	16	(4%)	84	(40%)	249	40	246	39	11	(6%)	89	(66%)
-Wholesales	353	19	1,034	23	20	(4%)	80	(51%)	176	29	197	31	13	(7%)	87	(78%)
Total	1,842	100	4,515	100	39	(21%)	61	(29%)	616	100	632	100	38	(20%)	62	(46%)
			(c-1) Europe								(c-2) Europe					
Manufacturing	717	70	3,003	73	42	(24%)	58	(37%)	128	56	158	56	48	(17%)	52	(43%)
-Machinery	389	38	2,008	49	34	(33%)	66	(42%)	64	28	88	31	34	(31%)	66	(56%)
Non-manufacturing	306	30	1,137	27	13	(4%)	87	(43%)	101	44	125	44	18	(14%)	82	(63%)
-Wholesales	193	19	945	23	15	(5%)	85	(50%)	81	35	114	40	20	(16%)	80	(68%)
Total	1,023	100	4,140	100	34	(19%)	66	(39%)	229	100	283	100	35	(16%)	65	(52%)

Note: The figures for (a-1, b-1, c-1) are those of all sized parent firms and figures for (a-2, b-2, c-2) are of parent SMEs. The figures for "share" manufacturing, machinery, non-manufacturing, and wholesales expresses the shares of manufacturing affiliates, machinery affiliates, non-manufacturing affiliates, and wholesales affiliates in total number of affiliates of all sized/SMEs firms in each sectoral category.

Source: Authors' calculation, based on METI database.

have affiliates abroad. Among them, 3,847 firms have affiliates in East Asia. That is, over 80% of the Japanese firms going abroad have at least one affiliate in East Asia.

Japanese manufacturing parent firms, particularly machinery parent firms, are active investors in East Asia. Almost 70% of the Japanese firms with affiliates in East Asia are in the manufacturing sector and close to half are in machinery industries. Moreover, Japanese manufacturing affiliates, regardless of the industries of their parent firms, account for 61% of the total Japanese affiliates in the region, compared to 39% for North America and 34% for Europe.

A parent firm often conducts various types of operations at the same time and establishes foreign affiliates in order to conduct a subset of those activities.[9] Japanese manufacturing parent firms have 73% of their total affiliates in East Asia in the manufacturing sector. The corresponding portion is even higher for manufacturing SMEs; 84% of their affiliates in East Asia are in manufacturing. Such investment patterns by SMEs reflect a typical strategy for firms involved in manufacturing activities, aiming at supplying intermediate goods for other firms and/or for their own affiliates and forming a critical mass of industrial clusters in the manufacturing sector. Japanese manufacturing parent firms also have non-manufacturing affiliates in East Asia (27% of total affiliates of manufacturing firms), particularly in the wholesales sector (18%), to establish distribution networks by internalizing wholesale trade activities.

In contrast with East Asia, the share of manufacturing affiliates of manufacturing parent firms is relatively low, and the share of their non-manufacturing affiliates is as high as 51% for North America and 58% for Europe. This indicates that Japanese manufacturing investment in North America or Europe aims at selling their products or producing goods to be sold there, rather than being involved in dense vertical production chains as is the case in East Asia.

Table 2 presents globalizing patterns of Japanese firms in the two-period balanced panel data for 1998–2004. Although the expansion of globalizing activities at the firm level may be measured in various ways, we regard an

---

[9] The industrial classification is based on the largest activities in terms of the value of sales. See Table A2 for the sector matching between industries of parent firms and affiliates in terms of the number of affiliates.

Table 2. Globalizing patterns from 1998 to 2004: share by the type of firms

The type of firms	Foreign (incl. East Asia)	East Asia	North America	Europe	Foreign (incl. East Asia)	East Asia	North America	Europe
	(a) All firms				(b) Manufacturing firms			
No entry in	79%	82%	86%	92%	74%	78%	84%	91%
Expansion (i + ii)	12%	11%	7%	4%	15%	14%	9%	6%
— (i) already had FDI	6%	5%	0%	0%	8%	7%	1%	0%
— (ii) with 1st FDI	5%	5%	6%	4%	7%	7%	8%	5%
Steady in	5%	4%	1%	0%	7%	6%	1%	0%
Shrinkage	2%	1%	0%	0%	3%	1%	1%	0%
Shrinkage (withdrawal)	2%	2%	6%	3%	2%	2%	6%	3%
Total	100%	100%	100%	100%	100%	100%	100%	100%
	(c) SMEs				(d) Manufacturing SMEs			
No entry in	86%	89%	92%	96%	84%	87%	91%	96%
Expansion (i + ii)	7%	7%	3%	1%	9%	8%	3%	1%
— (i) Already had FDI	2%	2%	0%	0%	3%	2%	0%	0%
— (ii) with 1st FDI	5%	5%	3%	1%	6%	6%	3%	1%
Steady in	4%	3%	0%	0%	5%	4%	0%	0%
Shrinkage in	1%	0%	0%	0%	1%	0%	0%	0%
Shrinkage (withdrawal)	2%	1%	5%	3%	2%	1%	5%	3%
Total	100%	100%	100%	100%	100%	100%	100%	100%

Note: The type of firms, expansion (i), is used for firms that already had atleast 1st FDI in the region before 1998 and increased, expansion (ii) is for firms that have the 1st (and more) FDI in the region during the sample period, shrinkage (withdrawal) is for firms that withdrew from the region during the sample period.
Source: Table A3 in the Appendix

increase in the number of foreign affiliates or affiliates in a specific region as the indication of globalizing activities.[10] During the six years, 12% of firms in all industries and 15% of manufacturing firms in the sample enlarged their activities abroad. Very close to these proportions, 11% of firms in all industries and 14% of manufacturing firms in the sample expanded their operations in East Asia.[11] It suggests that most of the Japanese

[10]Matsuura and Nagata (2005) investigate patterns of domestic job creation and destruction by Japanese firms by decomposing them into three types of firms, that is, those without foreign operations, those expanding operations abroad, and those reducing operations abroad. They employ unbalanced panel data for 1991–2002 and use the number of workers in manufacturing affiliates abroad to distinguish those expanding from those reducing operations abroad.

[11]These ratios are lower for North America and Europe: 7% and 4% of the firms in all industries and 9% and 6% of manufacturing firms, respectively. In addition, most of these firms started operations in these regions during the sample period, unlike the case of East Asia. The ratios for those expanding operations, excluding those with first FDI in North America and Europe, are less than 0.5%. Furthermore, almost all of them enlarged their

globalizing firms in the sample period enlarged their activities in East Asia, contributing to further development of production/distribution networks in East Asia, particularly in the manufacturing sector. We therefore focus on their expanding activities, mainly in manufacturing, in East Asia.

Interestingly, many firms that established their affiliates for the first time in East Asia during the sample period are SMEs. The share of SMEs in terms of their numbers is 63% for all sectors and 62% for the manufacturing sector. Their active FDI certainly contributes to the development of vertical production chains in the region.

While some firms globalize their activities, how do Japanese firms reorganize their domestic operations? In the period 1998–2004, 60% of the firms in the balanced panel dataset reduced domestic employment, and aggregate employment in the domestic market dropped, mainly in the manufacturing sector (Table 3). The shrinkage of employment shows a gradual but steady trend in the manufacturing sector. Even in the manufacturing sector, however, the share of firms reducing domestic employment is relatively low for firms expanding operations in East Asia (61%), particularly those starting operations in East Asia (by establishing their first affiliate in the region during the sample period) (55%), compared with those reducing operations or remaining intact in East Asia (by withdrawing (some of) their affiliates or simply maintaining their affiliates in the region) (69%–75%) and those without entry in the region (63%). The average growth rate of domestic employment at the firm level is not low for manufacturing firms expanding operations in East Asia compared to those not expanding. The average growth rate at the firm level during the six years is 0.0% for those with expansion in East Asia as a whole (5.7% for firms conducting the first FDI in the region and −5.7% for the rest), while it is −2.1% for those without entry in East Asia, −8.5% and −16.3% (exit) for those with reduction, and −7.6% for those intact.[12]

activities in East Asia at the same time. See Table A3 for the matrix of globalizing patterns in East Asia and other regions.

[12]In the following regression analysis of the effect of expanding operations in East Asia on domestic operations, we conservatively use the other firms, including firms both with and without having affiliates in East Asia, as a control group. MNEs not expanding operations in East Asia (i.e., excluding non-MNEs) could also be a control group, although the results are likely to be even stronger in such a case.

Table 3. Changes in domestic operations from 1998 to 2004 by the type of firms

The type of firms	Domestic employment: Share of firms with reduction	Domestic employment: Average growth rates at the firm level	Domestic employment: Aggregate change	Domestic establishments: Share of firms with reduction	Domestic establishments: Aggregate change	Domestic affiliates: Share of firms with reduction	Domestic affiliates: Aggregate change
(a) All firms							
No entry in East Asia	59%	0.049	215,001	30%	21,788	18%	−1,003
Expansion in East Asia (i + ii)	59%	0.0030	−146,750	42%	2,303	31%	817
(i) already had FDI	64%	−0.041	−182,215	51%	−674	40%	189
(ii) with 1st FDI	54%	0.096	35,465	34%	2,977	23%	628
Steady	70%	−0.054	−60,318	38%	1,760	34%	−577
Shrinkage	71%	−0.080	−9,819	52%	−587	57%	−2,458
Shrinkage (withdrawal)	69%	−0.073	−1,623	41%	358	48%	−747
Total	60%	0.038	−3,509	32%	25,622	21%	−3,968
(b) Manufacturing firms							
No entry	63%	−0.021	−111,204	26%	1,860	15%	−571
Expansion (i + ii)	61%	0.000	−181,593	40%	−627	31%	437
(i) already had FDI	66%	−0.057	−171,659	50%	−775	41%	−143
(ii) with 1st FDI	55%	0.057	−9,934	31%	148	22%	580
Steady	69%	−0.076	−46,325	37%	119	34%	−442
Shrinkage	74%	−0.085	−64,814	51%	−330	56%	−974
Shrinkage (withdrawal)	75%	−0.163	−28,045	41%	−97	47%	−343
Total	63%	−0.025	−431,981	29%	925	20%	−1,893

(Continued)

Table 3. (*Continued*)

The type of firms	Domestic employment			Domestic establishment		Domestic affiliates	
	Share of firms with reduction	Average growth rates at the firm level	Aggregate change	Share of firms with reduction	Aggregate change	Share of firms with reduction	Aggregate change
(c) SMEs							
No entry	58%	0.051	59,710	27%	7,390	15%	−586
Expansion (i + ii)	50%	0.096	10,771	30%	219	21%	94
(i) already had FDI	50%	0.048	1,457	35%	−10	23%	−11
(ii) with 1st FDI	50%	0.115	9,314	28%	229	20%	105
Steady	65%	−0.039	−3,805	30%	−40	24%	−81
Shrinkage	63%	0.039	181	31%	22	26%	−8
Shrinkage (withdrawal)	64%	−0.073	−2,496	31%	24	36%	−55
Total	58%	0.049	64,361	27%	7,615	16%	−636
(d) Manufacturing SMEs							
No entry	61%	−0.007	−23,291	23%	527	14%	−394
Expansion (i + ii)	51%	0.087	6,906	26%	129	20%	65
(i) already had FDI	56%	−0.031	696	34%	−26	23%	−14
(ii) with 1st FDI	49%	0.108	6,210	23%	155	18%	79
Steady	62%	−0.037	−2,588	29%	−45	24%	−53
Shrinkage	67%	0.070	199	33%	8	30%	−6
Shrinkage (withdrawal)	69%	−0.103	−1,813	35%	−17	34%	−39
Total	60%	−0.002	−20,587	24%	602	15%	−427

Note: The two-period balanced panel data is used. Industry classification and firm size are based on data for 1998. The type of firms, expansion (i), is used for firms that already had atleast 1st FDI in the region before 1998 and increased, expansion (ii) is for firms that have the 1st (and more) FDI in the region during the sample period, shrinkage (withdrawal) is for firms that withdrew from the region during the same period.
Source: Authors' calculation, based on METI database.

Moreover, the share of firms reducing domestic employment is much lower for SMEs expanding operations in East Asia than for those not expanding activities in East Asia. For manufacturing SMEs, the ratios are 51% for SMEs expanding operations in East Asia (56% for those expanding further and 49% for those with the first FDI in the region) while 61% for those with no entry, 67% for those reducing, 69% for those with exit, and 62% for those remaining. Furthermore, SMEs expanding operations in East Asia, including those in the manufacturing sector, have much higher average growth rates of domestic employment and indeed contribute to net domestic job creation at the aggregate level.[13]

Firms establishing their first affiliates in East Asia during the sample period, regardless of whether they are in manufacturing and are SMEs, show an increase in the number of domestic establishments and domestic affiliates as well, rather than diminishing domestic operations. All of the above-mentioned features indicate that intensified globalizing activities of Japanese firms through FDI particularly in East Asia might be complements of domestic operations, rather than substitutes, and reduce direct negative impacts on employment, establishments, and affiliates at home. We now turn to formal econometric analysis with a control of firm size and other variables to confirm these features.

III. GLOBALIZING CORPORATE ACTIVITIES AND DOMESTIC OPERATIONS AT THE FIRM LEVEL

This section analyzes patterns of globalizing activities of Japanese firms, focusing on their domestic operations and transactions with foreign markets. Given the fact that most Japanese firms expanding operations abroad activate their operations in East Asia, as discussed in the previous section, this section investigates how these firms with expanding activities in East Asia reorganize domestic operations and export/import activities compared with other firms, employing logit/OLS regression analyses.

[13] Large firms may reduce domestic operations by themselves and outsource some processes of productions to other firms, particularly SMEs. In this case, it would be more likely for SMEs to increase new employment at home, resulting in the increase in domestic employment for SMEs.

Empirical Method And Data

The equation for our logit/OLS estimation analyses is as follows:

$$Y_{t_0}^{t} = \beta_0 + \beta_1 X_{t_0}^{t} + \beta_2 S_{t_0} + \beta_3 KL_{t_0} + \beta_4 EX_{t_0} + \beta_5 RD_{t_0} \\ + \beta_6 AD_{t_0} + \beta_7 FC_{t_0} + \varepsilon,$$

where $Y_{t_0}^{t}$ expresses a change in domestic operations or a change in export/import activities with East Asia from base year t_0 to the targeted year t. As for domestic operations, 0/1 binary variables are used for a change in domestic employment, the number of domestic establishments, and the number of domestic affiliates; $Y_{t_0}^{t}$ is one if a firm does not reduce domestic employment/the number of domestic establishments/the number of affiliates, and is zero otherwise. Another variable for a change in domestic employment, $Y_{t_0}^{t}$, a growth rate of domestic employment, is also used. As for export/import activities with East Asia, a change in the ratio of exports to/imports from East Asia in total sales/purchases is applied; $Y_{t_0}^{t}$ is a difference obtained by subtracting the ratio for the base year from the ratio for the targeted year.

$X_{t_0}^{t}$ is a binary variable for expanding corporate activities in East Asia; $X_{t_0}^{t}$ is one if a firm increases the number of affiliates in East Asia from the base year to the targeted year and is zero otherwise.[14] Regarding domestic operations, if a firm increases (does not decrease) domestic employment/the number of domestic establishments/the number of domestic affiliates with their globalizing activities, or their activities in East Asia are complements of domestic operations, the coefficient for $X_{t_0}^{t}$ is expected to be positive. In the case of transactions with East Asia, if a firm expanding operations in East Asia intensifies transactions with that region, the coefficient for $X_{t_0}^{t}$ is expected to be positive. In particular, if FDI and exports are complements rather than substitutes, the coefficient is expected to be positive. Although firms expanding operations in East Asia basically include those that start operations during the sample period in the region (wider definition), the case of firms expanding operations in East Asia, excluding

[14]Although the marginal impact of an increase in one (or more) affiliate(s) abroad may be different between large firms and SMEs, such a difference, if any, would be partially controlled in regression analyses with the size of firms as one of the control variables.

those firms (narrower definition), is also examined to check whether or not the results would significantly change.

Other independent variables are included as conventional control variables for the base year: the size of firm in terms of the number of regular workers in Japan (natural log) (S_{t0}), the capital–labor ratio in terms of tangible assets per regular workers (natural log) (KL_{t0}), the foreign sales ratio (in total sales) (EX_{t0}), an in-house R&D expenditure ratio (in total sales) (RD_{t0}), the advertisement expenditure ratio (in total sales) (AD_{t0}), and the foreign capital ratio (FC_{t0}). These are all for domestic (parent) firms.[15] Note that to control industry characteristics, industry dummies according to the industry classification shown in Table A1 are also included in all regression equations.

As discussed in Section II, the reorganization of domestic operations may differ according to the size of the firm. The variable of firm size is included to control such differences, if at all. The capital–labor ratio, foreign sales, R&D expenditure, and advertisement expenditure are variables representing firm-specific intangible assets. As a firm expanding operations abroad would have superior technology (or more capital-intensive technology), the coefficient for tangible assets per worker is expected to be positive. A firm's relatively large foreign sales would indicate that the firm is exposed to the global market and is internationally competitive, and may be significantly involved in production sharing activities. Therefore, the coefficient for the variable of foreign sales is expected to be positive, particularly for relatively strengthened export/import activities with East Asia. The expenditure on R&D and advertisement activities would reflect a firm's intangible assets and technological competitiveness, and therefore, the coefficient for these variables is expected to be positive. A variable for foreign capital is included to examine whether any significant difference exists between purely domestic firms and firms with (higher) foreign capital in Japan.

For each of the dependent variables mentioned above, logit estimation analysis is conducted when they are binary variables measuring changes in domestic operations, while OLS estimation analysis is conducted when

[15]The foreign capital ratio of a firm is denoted from zero to 1000: 10 times percentage of the ratio of foreign capital to total capital of a firm.

they are growth rates of domestic employment or a change in exports to/imports from East Asia as a share of total sales/purchases. In addition, the sample set is divided into manufacturing firms and non-manufacturing firms, considering that their FDI strategies would be different.

Our main analysis focuses on the period from 1998 (base year) to 2004 (targeted year), using a balanced panel dataset.[16] We set a change between 1998 and 2004 as a benchmark. A firm's decision on FDI and domestic reshuffling takes a long time. In order to plan FDI, it typically takes at least two to three years from a planning stage to the actual initiation of investment. After starting investment, another two to three years are needed to reach full operation. The accompanied adjustment in domestic operations is also likely to proceed gradually during these four to six years. Our exercise with six-year changes should thus primarily be interpreted as a sort of contemporaneous, one-shot regression focusing on the association of changes in domestic operations with the expansion of East Asian operations. It might be useful to investigate the time lag structure of adjustments in foreign and domestic operations in more detail. Accordingly, regressions with balanced-panel datasets with different base years and targeted years are also demonstrated.

Empirical Results

Tables 4–6 report results of logit regression analyses and OLS regression analyses for: (a) manufacturing firms, (b) machinery firms, and (c) non-manufacturing firms. As Table 3 suggests, control of the size of firm is crucial for our analysis. For manufacturing firms, the coefficient for the size of firm is negative and statistically significant in all equations for domestic operations. It indicates that Japanese manufacturing firms with larger employment size at home are more likely to reduce domestic operations in terms of domestic employment, domestic establishments, and domestic affiliates.

[16]See Table A4 for summary statistics and Table A5 for correlation matrix of independent variables for two-period balanced data for 1998-2004. Notice that the portion of entry-exit firms is relatively small in Japan. If we could include the information on exit firms, however, our results on the globalizing activities would be even larger than the results presented in this paper since those firms should be included in the category of firms not expanding operations abroad.

Table 4. Production networking in East Asia and domestic operations in 1998–2004: manufacturing firms

	Dependent variable					
	(1)	(2)	(3)	(4)	(5)	(6)
Independent variables	d. employment [logit]	d. employment [OLS]	d. establishments [logit]	d. affiliates [logit]	Exports to E.Asia [OLS]	Imports from E.Asia [OLS]
a) Wider definition for expanding operations						
Constant	1.351***	0.315***	3.369***	4.709***	0.003	0.017**
	(0.196)	(0.035)	(0.198)	(0.228)	(0.005)	(0.008)
Expansion in East Asia (including new entry)	0.415***	0.084***	−0.088	−0.090	0.028***	0.032***
	(0.067)	(0.012)	(0.069)	(0.075)	(0.002)	(0.003)
Firm size	−0.421***	−0.069***	−0.497***	−0.543***	0.000	−0.002*
	(0.026)	(0.004)	(0.026)	(0.028)	(0.001)	(0.001)
Capital–labor ratio	0.085***	0.015***	−0.053**	−0.213***	−0.0001	0.000
	(0.023)	(0.004)	(0.024)	(0.030)	(0.001)	(0.001)
Foreign sales ratio	0.246	−0.063	−0.503**	−0.635**	0.027***	0.041***
	(0.242)	(0.044)	(0.245)	(0.006)	(0.006)	(0.011)
In-house R&D ratio	3.341***	0.546***	−0.867	−0.863	0.095***	0.011
	(1.093)	(0.189)	(1.149)	(1.297)	(0.028)	(0.049)
Advertisement ratio	−1.101	0.352	−4.147***	−4.690***	−0.040	−0.049
	(1.430)	(0.252)	(1.379)	(1.471)	(0.035)	(0.059)
Foreign capital ratio	0.00041*	0.00007*	0.00011	0.00153***	0.0001	0.00356
	(0.000)	(0.000)	(0.000)	(0.000)	(0.000)	(0.062)
Industry dummies	Yes	Yes	Yes	Yes	Yes	Yes
Log likelihood	−6495		−5832	−4700		
AdjR2		0.034			0.056	0.027
Number of obs.	10,218	10,218	10,218	10,218	10,218	10,036

(Continued)

Table 4. (*Continued*)

	Dependent variable					
	(1)	(2)	(3)	(4)	(5)	(6)
Independent variables	d. employment [logit]	d. employment [OLS]	d. establishments [logit]	d. affiliates [logit]	Exports to E.Asia [OLS]	Imports from E.Asia [OLS]
b) Narrower definition for expanding operations						
Constant	1.278***	0.296***	3.312***	4.658***	0.002***	0.016*
	(0.197)	(0.035)	(0.200)	(0.231)	(0.005)	(0.009)
Expansion in East Asia	0.273***	0.043**	−0.221**	−0.196**	0.027***	0.029***
	(0.096)	(0.017)	(0.093)	(0.098)	(0.002)	(0.004)
Firm size	−0.401***	−0.064***	−0.487***	−0.535***	0.001	−0.001
	(0.026)	(0.004)	(0.026)	(0.029)	(0.001)	(0.001)
Capital–labor ratio	0.091***	0.016***	−0.052**	−0.212***	0.000	0.001
	(0.023)	(0.004)	(0.024)	(0.030)	(0.001)	(0.001)
Foreign sales ratio	0.302	−0.046	−0.440*	−0.582**	0.027***	0.042***
	(0.243)	(0.044)	(0.248)	(0.267)	(0.006)	(0.011)
In-house R&D ratio	3.554***	0.678***	−0.779	−0.782	0.103***	0.021
	(1.091)	(0.201)	(1.152)	(1.301)	(0.028)	(0.049)
Advertisement ratio	−1.158	0.334*	−4.195***	−4.730***	−0.041	0.002
	(1.426)	(0.253)	(1.378)	(1.471)	(0.036)	(0.062)
Foreign capital ratio	0.00038	0.00007	0.00010	0.00153***	0.00000	0.00001
	(0.000)	(0.000)	(0.000)	(0.000)	(0.000)	(0.000)
Industry dummies	Yes	Yes	Yes	Yes	Yes	Yes
Log likelihood	−6510		−5830	−4698		
Adj R2		0.030			0.044	0.020
Number of obs.	10,218	10,218	10,218	10,218	10,218	10,036

Note: Figures in parenthesis are standard deviation. *** indicates that the results are statistically significant at the 1% level, ** at the 5% level, and * at the 10% level. Regressions are as follows:

(1) dependent variable: 1 if a firm does not reduce the number of domestic employments and 0 otherwise
(2) dependent variable: growth rate of the number of domestic employment
(3) dependent variable: 1 if a firm does not reduce the number of domestic establishments and 0 otherwise
(4) dependent variable: 1 if a firm does not reduce the number of domestic affiliates and 0 otherwise
(5) dependent variable: a change in the ratio of expoprts to East Asia in total sales
(6) dependent variable: a change in the ratio of imports from East Asia in total purchases.

Table 5. Production networking in East Asia and domestic operations in 1998–2004: machinery firms.

	Dependent variable					
	(1)	(2)	(3)	(4)	(5)	(6)
Independent variables	d. employment [logit]	d. employment [OLS]	d. establishments [logit]	d. affiliates [logit]	Exports to E. Asia [OLS]	Imports from E. Asia [OLS]
a) Wider definition for expanding operations						
Constant	1.744***	0.327***	3.325***	4.994***	0.004	0.020*
	(0.234)	(0.041)	(0.244)	(0.287)	(0.008)	(0.012)
Expansion in East Asia	0.409***	0.069***	−0.094	−0.007	0.033***	0.030***
(including new entry)	(0.094)	(0.017)	(0.097)	(0.110)	(0.003)	(0.005)
Firm size	−0.419***	−0.065***	−0.372***	−0.551***	0.002	0.001
	(0.040)	(0.007)	(0.039)	(0.002)	(0.001)	(0.002)
Capital–labor ratio	0.091**	0.013*	−0.052	−0.136***	0.0009	0.002
	(0.038)	(0.007)	(0.042)	(0.052)	(0.001)	(0.002)
Foreign sales ratio	0.183	−0.087*	−0.595**	−0.739**	0.030***	0.057***
	(0.288)	(0.053)	(0.287)	(0.313)	(0.010)	(0.015)
In-house R&D ratio	2.583*	0.632**	−2.334	−1.571	0.086*	−0.102
	(1.418)	(0.264)	(1.451)	(1.684)	(0.050)	(0.076)
Advertisement ratio	−0.945	−0.432	−14.694**	−19.346***	−0.091	0.250
	(6.108)	(1.135)	(6.231)	(6.784)	(0.214)	(0.327)
Foreign capital ratio	0.00048	0.00007	0.00019	0.00129**	0.00001	0.00002
	(0.000)	(0.000)	(0.000)	(0.001)	(0.000)	(0.000)
Industry dummies	Yes	Yes	Yes	Yes	Yes	Yes
Log likelihood	−2487		−2228	−1745		
Adj R2		0.035			0.048	0.024
Number of obs.	3,903	3,903	3,903	3,903	3,903	3,846

(*Continued*)

Table 5. (*Continued*)

	Dependent variable					
	(1)	(2)	(3)	(4)	(5)	(6)
Independent variables	d. employment [logit]	d. employment [OLS]	d. establishments [logit]	d. affiliates [logit]	Exports to E. Asia [OLS]	Imports from E. Asia [OLS]
b) Narrower definition for expanding operations						
Constant	1.702***	0.315***	3.247***	4.902***	0.002	0.021*
	(0.237)	(0.042)	(0.248)	(0.291)	(0.008)	(0.012)
Expansion in East Asia	0.344***	0.045*	−0.250*	−0.176	0.029***	0.032***
	(0.131)	(0.024)	(0.128)	(0.139)	(0.005)	(0.007)
Firm size	−0.407***	−0.062***	−0.357***	−0.532***	0.003**	0.001
	(0.041)	(0.007)	(0.040)	(0.046)	(0.001)	(0.002)
Capital–labor ratio	0.098***	0.014*	−0.051	−0.133**	0.001	0.002
	(0.038)	(0.007)	(0.041)	(0.052)	(0.001)	(0.002)
Foreign sales ratio	0.190	−0.080	−0.524*	−0.666**	0.030***	0.054***
	(0.290)	(0.053)	(0.290)	(0.317)	(0.010)	(0.015)
In-house R&D ratio	2.683*	0.654**	−2.272	−1.469	0.093*	−0.098
	(1.417)	(0.264)	(1.453)	(1.690)	(0.050)	(0.076)
Advertisement ratio	0.068	−0.257	−14.941**	−19.391***	−0.008	0.326
	(6.063)	(1.136)	(6.234)	(6.782)	(0.216)	(0.327)
Foreign capital ratio	0.00046	0.00007	0.00018	0.00127**	0.00001	0.00002
	(0.000)	(0.000)	(0.000)	(0.001)	(0.000)	(0.000)
Industry dummies	Yes	Yes	Yes	Yes	Yes	Yes
Log likelihood	−2493		−2227	−1744		
Adj R2		0.032			0.034	0.021
Number of obs.	3,903	3,903	3,903	3,903	3,903	3,846

Note: Figures in parenthesis are standard deviation. *** indicates that the results are statistically significant at the 1% level, ** at the 5% level, and * at the 10% level. Regressions are as follows:

(1) dependent variable: 1 if a firm does not reduce the number of domestic employments and 0 otherwise
(2) dependent variable: growth rate of the number of domestic employment
(3) dependent variable: 1 if a firm does not reduce the number of domestic establishments and 0 otherwise
(4) dependent variable: 1 if a firm does not reduce the number of domestic affiliates and 0 otherwise
(5) dependent variable: a change in the ratio of expoprts to East Asia in total sales
(6) dependent variable: a change in the ratio of imports from East Asia in total purchases.

Source: Authors' calculation, based on METI database.

Table 6. Production networking in East Asia and domestic operations in 1998–2004: non-manufacturing firms

Independent variables	Dependent variable					
	(1) d. employment [logit]	(2) d. employment [OLS]	(3) d. establishments [logit]	(4) d. affiliates [logit]	(5) Exports to E. Asia [OLS]	(6) Imports from E. Asia [OLS]
a) Wider definition for expanding operations						
Constant	0.540***	0.353***	2.246***	4.411***	0.000	0.002
	(0.148)	(0.063)	(0.153)	(0.184)	(0.002)	(0.005)
Expansion in East Asia	0.324***	0.073*	−0.245**	−0.058	0.025***	0.026***
(including new entry)	(0.096)	(0.042)	(0.097)	(0.109)	(0.001)	(0.003)
Firm size	−0.139***	−0.030	−0.300***	−0.467***	−0.0002**	0.0003
	(0.025)	(0.011)	(0.025)	(0.029)	(0.000)	(0.001)
Capital–labor ratio	−0.080***	−0.022***	−0.043**	−0.240***	−0.0002	−0.0005
	(0.017)	(0.007)	(0.018)	(0.024)	(0.000)	(0.001)
Foreign sales ratio	−0.059	−0.326*	0.233	−0.298	0.016***	−0.0041
	(0.403)	(0.173)	(0.421)	(0.464)	(0.005)	(0.014)
In-house R&D ratio	0.604	−0.177	0.798	−2.107	0.011	0.060
	(1.153)	(0.465)	(1.479)	(1.291)	(0.014)	(0.037)
Advertisement ratio	9.368***	3.739***	2.873*	2.399	−0.019	0.028
	(1.691)	(0.592)	(1.571)	(1.971)	(0.018)	(0.046)
Foreign capital ratio	0.00036*	0.00004	−0.00014	0.00071*	0.00000	−0.00002***
	(0.000)	(0.000)	(0.000)	(0.000)	(0.000)	(0.000)
Industry dummies	Yes	Yes	Yes	Yes	Yes	Yes
Log likelihood	−5412		−5105	−3991		
Adj R2		0.014			0.060	0.011
Number of obs.	7,994	7,994	7,994	7,994	7,994	7,955

(Continued)

Table 6. (*Continued*)

	Dependent variable					
	(1)	(2)	(3)	(4)	(5)	(6)
Independent variables	d. employment [logit]	d. employment [OLS]	d. establishments [logit]	d. affiliates [logit]	Exports to E. Asia [OLS]	Imports from E. Asia [OLS]
b) Narrower definition for expanding operations						
Constant	0.514***	0.333***	2.229***	4.411***	0.001	0.001
	(0.148)	(0.064)	(0.154)	(0.185)	(0.002)	(0.005)
Expansion in East Asia	0.247*	−0.016	−0.375***	−0.063	0.034***	0.021***
	(0.142)	(0.061)	(0.142)	(0.152)	(0.002)	(0.005)
Firm size	−0.133***	−0.026**	−0.298***	−0.467***	−0.0003	0.0008
	(0.025)	(0.011)	(0.025)	(0.029)	(0.000)	(0.001)
Capital–labor ratio	−0.080***	−0.021***	−0.043**	−0.239***	−0.0002	−0.0005
	(0.017)	(0.007)	(0.018)	(0.024)	(0.000)	(0.001)
Foreign sales ratio	0.059	−0.249	0.286	−0.303	0.014***	0.005
	(0.405)	(0.175)	(0.427)	(0.468)	(0.005)	(0.014)
In-house R&D ratio	0.617	−0.155	0.869	−2.103	0.007	0.061*
	(1.158)	(0.465)	(1.520)	(1.290)	(0.014)	(0.037)
Advertisement ratio	9.368***	3.753***	2.909*	2.400	−0.021	0.028
	(1.691)	(0.592)	(1.572)	(1.971)	(0.018)	(0.046)
Foreign capital ratio	0.00035*	0.00003	−0.00014	0.00071*	0.00000*	−0.00002***
	(0.000)	(0.000)	(0.000)	(0.000)	(0.000)	(0.000)
Industry dummies	Yes	Yes	Yes	Yes	Yes	Yes
Log likelihood	−5416		−5104	−3992		
Adj R2		0.014			0.056	0.006
Number of obs.	7,994	7,994	7,994	7,994	7,994	7,955

Note: Figures in parenthesis are standard deviation. *** indicates that the results are statistically significant at the 1% level, ** at the 5% level, and * at the 10% level. Regressions are as follows:

(1) dependent variable: 1 if a firm does not reduce the number of domestic employments and 0 otherwise
(2) dependent variable: growth rate of the number of domestic employment
(3) dependent variable: 1 if a firm does not reduce the number of domestic establishments and 0 otherwise
(4) dependent variable: 1 if a firm does not reduce the number of domestic affiliates and 0 otherwise
(5) dependent variable: a change in the ratio of expoprts to East Asia in total sales
(6) dependent variable: a change in the ratio of imports from East Asia in total purchases.

Source: Authors' calculation, based on METI database.

The coefficient for the capital–labor ratio is statistically significant with a positive value in the analysis of domestic employment for manufacturing firms, including machinery firms.[17] On the other hand, the corresponding coefficient is negative only in the analysis of domestic affiliates for machinery firms, although it is negative in both analyses of domestic establishments and affiliates for manufacturing firms as a whole. These results suggest that Japanese manufacturing firms, in particular non-machinery manufacturing firms, with capital-intensive technology tend to keep or expand domestic employment and strengthen transactions with East Asia, while they tend to reshuffle domestic corporate organizations in terms of both domestic establishments and affiliates. What is interesting here is that machinery firms with capital-intensive technology tend to keep or expand domestic employment and do not necessarily reshuffle domestic operations in terms of domestic establishments. Machinery firms are active investors in East Asia as well as important players in developing international production/distribution networks in the region.

Furthermore, for manufacturing firms, including machinery firms, the coefficient for in-house R&D ratio is positive with statistical significance for domestic employment, regardless of whether we use the binary variable or the growth rate, and export activities with East Asia.[18] This implies that R&D intensive manufacturing firms are more likely to expand domestic operations in terms of employment at home and relatively intensify export activities with East Asia, probably because they succeed in reorganizing competitive activities and strengthening their competitiveness.

Given the size of firm and other controls, our results provide several interesting insights. First, the expansion of operations in East Asia is positively associated with no decline in domestic employment and their growth rates with statistical significance for manufacturing firms, once the size of firm is controlled. Interestingly, the coefficient is even larger for

[17]On the contrary, the coefficient for the capital–labor ratio is negative with statistical significance for non-manufacturing firms, indicating that capital-intensive non-manufacturing firms tend to reduce domestic employment.

[18]In the case of non-manufacturing firms for the analysis of domestic employment, the coefficient is positive and statistically insignificant for R&D expenditure ratio, while positive and significant for advertisement expenditure ratio, in contract with those for manufacturing firms. It suggests that advertisement-intensive non-manufacturing firms tend to keep or increase domestic employment.

only machinery firms than for manufacturing firms in general, when firms that conduct the first FDI in the region are excluded from the category of firms expanding foreign operations.[19] On the other hand, the coefficient is smaller and is not always statistically significant for non-manufacturing firms. This suggests that manufacturing firms expanding operations in East Asia, particularly in the machinery sectors, are unlikely to reduce their domestic employment, compared with those that do not. Moreover, their growth rates of domestic employment are likely to be higher than those for other manufacturing firms by as much as 7%–8% during the six years (Tables 4(2) and 5(2)).

Since we regress six-year changes in domestic operations on the expansion of activities in East Asia in six years, some may have concern about a timing issue in the econometric analysis. We thus conduct casual robustness checks by employing each year's data. Table 7 reports the results of regression analysis of domestic employment for manufacturing firms, using various time-lag versions with one-year or two-year balanced-panel data. The table presents only the results of the variable for the expansion in East Asia. As the table clearly shows, the positive association of domestic employment with the expansion of operations in East Asia is robust, although the lag structure may differ across firms as well as sample periods.

Although total domestic employment in manufacturing sectors declines at the aggregate level, globalizing corporate manufacturing activities, particularly by machinery firms, tend to partially offset job destruction and sometimes even contribute to net job creation in the domestic market at the firm level. As discussed earlier, a rise in domestic employment by Japanese manufacturing firms, in particular machinery firms, expanding operations in East Asia would partially reflect a need to expand domestic production of key parts and components to be exported to East Asia, strengthen R&D activities for new products, or intensify specialization in headquarter services at home, as a result of active and effective fragmentation of production and specialization. The fragmentation with successful cost reduction would allow firms to expand employment engaged in production or services of these PBs, although it may indeed decrease employment at home in other

[19]The results do not change even when a variable for the expansion of manufacturing operations abroad is used.

Table 7. Robustness check for time lag structure: domestic employment for manufacturing firms

		Expansion in East Asia (including new entry)					
1 year		2003–2004	2002–2003	2001–2002	2000–2001	1999–2000	1998–1999
D. employment: binary variable	2003–2004	0.438***	0.178**				
		(0.103)	(0.089)				
	2002–2003		0.210**	0.209**			
			(0.087)	(0.100)			
	2001–2002			0.044	−0.033		
				(0.098)	(0.110)		
	2000–2001				0.093	−0.001	
					(0.111)	(0.115)	
	1999–2000					0.106	0.004
						(0.104)	(0.124)
	1998–1999						0.085
							(0.121)

		Expansion in East Asia (including new entry)				
2 years		2002–2004	2001–2003	2000–2002	1999–2001	1998–2000
D. employment: binary variable	2002–2004	0.419***	0.275***	0.211**		
		(0.074)	(0.081)	(0.088)		
	2001–2003		0.250***	0.014	−0.072	
			(0.079)	(0.090)	(0.090)	
	2000–2002			−0.034	−0.137	0.031
				(0.091)	(0.097)	(0.104)
	1999–2001				0.196**	0.013
					(0.087)	(0.102)
	1998–2000					0.196**
						(0.094)

		Expansion in East Asia (including new entry)					
1 year		2003–2004	2002–2003	2001–2002	2000–2001	1999–2000	1998–1999
D. employment: growth	2003–2004	0.019	0.007				
		(0.014)	(0.006)				
	2002–2003		0.037***	−0.003			
			(0.008)	(0.009)			
	2001–2002			0.003	−0.006		
				(0.008)	(0.008)		
	2000–2001				0.024***	0.005	
					(0.007)	(0.008)	

(*Continued*)

Table 7. (*Continued*)

1 year	Expansion in East Asia (including new entry)					
	2003–2004	2002–2003	2001–2002	2000–2001	1999–2000	1998–1999
1999–2000					0.013	0.001
					(0.009)	(0.010)
1998–1999						0.020*
						(0.012)

2 years	Expansion in East Asia (including new entry)				
	2002–2004	2001–2003	2000–2002	1999–2001	1998–2000
D. employment: growth					
2002–2004	0.039***	0.023**	0.010		
	(0.009)	(0.009)	(0.009)		
2001–2003		0.022**	0.002	−0.005	
		(0.009)	(0.009)	(0.010)	
2000–2002			0.020**	−0.001	0.001
			(0.008)	(0.009)	(0.010)
1999–2001				0.030***	0.003
				(0.009)	(0.011)
1998–2000					0.027**
					(0.010)

Note: Although the table presents only the results of a variable for expansion in East Asia, all the regressions above include other control variables and are conducted by using corresponding balanced panel dataset.

Source: Authors' calculation, based on METI database.

PBs, which results in an expansion of employment at home in total. Another possible explanation for a relative rise in domestic employment by globalizing manufacturing (machinery) firms would be that they succeed in differentiating products to be produced in the domestic market from those to be produced in East Asia.

Second, for manufacturing firms, there is a negative, though statistically insignificant, relationship between the expansion of manufacturing operations in East Asia and no decline in the number of domestic establishments as well as domestic affiliates when a wider definition for expanding operations in East Asia is applied (Table 4(3a) and 4(4a)). The coefficients, however, become negative and statistically significant when a narrower definition is applied (Table 4(3b) and 4(4b)). On the other hand, when only machinery firms are focused on, the negative relationship with statistical significance cannot be observed, except for the case of domestic establishment with a narrower definition for expanding operations (Table 5(3a), 5(4a), 5(3b), and 5(4b)). These results suggest that the expansion of operations in East Asia is effectively utilized as an opportunity to reshuffle the domestic corporate structure, particularly by non-machinery manufacturing firms expanding operations in East Asia (excluding those with the first FDI in the region during the sample period). They also suggest that machinery firms expanding operations in East Asia, in particular, do not necessarily reduce domestic corporate operations and rather maintain or even expand domestic employment when they expand operations in the region.

Third, export/import activities with East Asia are relatively intensified by globalizing firms in East Asia, and such a tendency is stronger for machinery firms (Tables 4(5), 4(6), 5(5), and 5(6)). The relationship between the expansion of manufacturing operations in East Asia and the relative intensification of transactions with East Asia is positively associated with statistical significance, with a larger coefficient for machinery firms in most cases than for manufacturing firms in general. It suggests that firms expanding operations in East Asia intensify their transactions with East Asia compared to other manufacturing firms, which is particularly true in the case of machinery firms. This is other supporting evidence for expanding fragmentation of production by Japanese firms mainly in machinery industries and their involvement in further development of production/distribution networks in East Asia where trade and FDI are in a sense complementary.

IV. CONCLUSION

Japanese firms have recently accelerated their investment in East Asia, mainly in manufacturing sectors, and have contributed to the development of international production/distribution networks in machinery sectors as the major players. Our study has attempted to investigate patterns of globalizing activities of Japanese firms, with a particular emphasis on firms investing in East Asia, and their domestic impacts by using comprehensive firm-level data including both firms with and without foreign operations. In addition to changes in domestic operations, such as domestic (parent) employment, domestic establishments, and domestic affiliates, changes in transactions with East Asia are also examined.

Our descriptive analysis shows that most of the Japanese firms developing their foreign operations for the period 1998–2004 have expanded their activities in East Asia, particularly in the manufacturing sector. Moreover, our logit/OLS estimation analyses with a distinction among manufacturing, machinery, and non-manufacturing firms demonstrate that, given the size of firm and other controls, globalizing manufacturing firms are unlikely to reduce their domestic employment and rather have tended to increase in by 7%–8% during the six years, compared with other manufacturing firms. Such a tendency is salient for machinery firms that are one of active players in international production/distribution networks mainly in machinery sectors in East Asia. Furthermore, globalizing manufacturing firms, particularly globalizing machinery firms, in East Asia have intensified export/import activities with East Asia while sometimes restructuring domestic activities in terms of the number of domestic establishments and domestic affiliates, compared with other firms. Their expanding manufacturing operations in East Asia, particularly by machinery firms, seem to be complements, rather than substitutes, for domestic operations, and contribute to the further development of production/distribution networks in the region where trade and FDI are in a sense complementary.

Unfortunately, our dataset does not allow us to directly analyze changes in the skill structure of employed labor. However, we can observe that Japanese firms intensifying operations in East Asia tend to retain domestic operations more successfully than other firms. Particularly in the case of SMEs globalizing their activities, domestic operations are even expanded. Further investigation of the Japanese case would thus provide a crucial argument against unwarranted anti-globalism sentiment.

ACKNOWLEDGMENTS

We thank Beata Javorcik, Kyoji Fukao, Sven Arndt, Hyun-Hoon Lee, Vitor Trindade, Kei-Mu Yi, and other participants in various workshops for helpful comments. Mitsuyo Ando acknowledges financial support from Seimeikai.

APPENDIX

Table A1. Industry classification

Manufacturing sector		Non-manufacturing sector	
090	Food processing	490	Wholesale trade
100	Beverages, tobacco, and animal feed	550	Retail trade
110	Textiles	Other	Mining, services, and other
120	Apparel		
130	Wood and wood products		
140	Furniture and fixtures		
150	Pulp, paper, and paper products		
160	Publishing and printing		
170	Chemicals		
180	Petroleum and coal products		
190	Plastic products		
200	Rubber products		
210	Leather and leather products		
220	Ceramics, clay, and stone products		
230	Iron and steel		
240	Nonferrous metal		
250	Metal products		
260	General machinery		
270	Electric machinery		
280	Telecommunications machinery		
290	Electronic parts and device		
300	Transport equipment		
310	Precision machinery		
320	Other manufacturing		
260–310	Machinery		

Table A2. Sector switching and non-sector switching Japanese affiliates abroad for 2004

(a-1) The number of affiliates in East Asia with all sized parent firms

Industry of affiliates (columns); Industry of parent firms (rows)

Industry of parent firms	090	100	110	120	130	140	150	160	170	180	190	200	210	220	230	240	250	260	270	280	290	300	310	320	490	550	Other
090	233	5		1			2	1	10		1			1				3							35	2	44
100	7	42							2									1						2	19	3	22
110			82	15			1		2		4						1		1		1	8			29		4
120			4	70			2				3		1					1			3				12		4
130					21																				1		1
140						18											2	1			1				5	3	
150			5				68	2	2		1	4			1		1	1			1			2	7		5
160			1					106			2			1						9	5		18				7
170	8	4	29	13				3	777	2	41	4		7		12	11	12	1		20	2	5	7	247	10	82
180										5															8	3	22
190			11	1		1	1		20		291			1	2		14	5	3	1	15	3	2	10	71		9
200			1			1			4	1	4	143	1				4	2			2	3	2	7	42	6	7
210													10												1		
220	1		2						22		3	1		206			7	4	2	13	40		4	3	38	9	27
230									2						63	3	20	6	1	2	4	2		2	4	1	20
240									2		2	10		5		239	24	2	4	12	47	46	1	1	59		33
250					1			1			3	1		4	2	1	236	9	4	5	10	11	5	4	39	2	12
260	2	1			2			1		1	2	1		1	8	1	17	580	19	36	4	41	4	16	338	10	112
270			1		1	1			9					8	1	27	7	14	485	4	44	7	17	6	218	28	66
280								1			4						6	26	68	246	72	12	5	1	171	3	143
290	2			2				1	11					1		3	5	13	12	8	466	4	8	2	160	2	38
300			1	1					3		25	13		1	13	4	11	34	25	2	16	991	11	2	105	45	98
310						1			4		4	3		3			1	10	10		24	3	160	3	93	10	20
320				1			2	1			8		1				9	2		2	2	3	8	186	64	4	18
490	99	3	74	171	9	19	14	6	170	5	108	29	4	35	60	35	62	60	48	20	125	44	28	101	1824	68	424
550	3	1	4	9		2					2	1			1	1	2			5			5	16	23	107	29
Other	6			3	2		1	3			1			3			4	16	9	2		4	4	7	25	11	455

(b-1) The number of affiliates in North America with all sized parent firms

Industry of affiliates (columns); Industry of parent firms (rows)

Industry of parent firms	090	100	110	120	130	140	150	160	170	180	190	200	210	220	230	240	250	260	270	280	290	300	310	320	490	550	Other
090	46								2																14	1	14
100	1	7																						2	18	2	11
110			4	1																		2			5		3
120											1										1				1		4
130					4																						1
140						2																			1	1	1
150			1				10		1																4		1
160								20						1						3	7		6			2	7
170	1	3	2						151		2			2		1	2	2			6	3	2	2	107	2	74
180																									2		5
190	1								4		40							1	1		1	4		4	16	1	10
200											2	24					2	1						3	13	6	22
210																											
220									3		1			33				1		9	14				14		10
230															9	1	1	1							5		7
240									1			5		2		41	10			3		20			13	1	24
250																	56	1		1	1	6	1		19	1	4
260						1			1		1				1		1	130	6	4		13	2	3	171	6	76
270									4							15	1	2	58		9	4		1	68	18	23
280																		6	8	80	4	1	1		71		289
290									3		1			1		1		1	2	2	49		1	2	60	1	21
300											2	4			3		4	12	2		1	380	3	2	72	18	117
310									1		2			2				1	3		2	2	22		46	6	24
320			2								5				1	1	1	1			1			35	36	2	26
490	25	2	4	8	5		4		31	1	16	8		2	12	7	10	12	4	2	8	12	7	28	531	26	269
550	1											1												3	16	23	20
Other	1				2				1					1			1	1	1	2					16	35	233

(c-1) The number of affiliates in Europe with all sized parent firms

Industry of affiliates (columns); Industry of parent firms (rows)

Industry of parent firms	090	100	110	120	130	140	150	160	170	180	190	200	210	220	230	240	250	260	270	280	290	300	310	320	490	550	Other
090	13								6															1	17		12
100		3																						11	7	2	9
110			1															1							2		1
120											1														4		
130					1																						
140						1																			1		
150			1		1		4																		7		1
160								16												1			13	1			5
170			3					1	130	1	5					3		1			2	2	5	3	116	2	43
180																									2		4
190									2		34						1							5	18	1	2
200						1					1	20					2								25	25	3
210																											
220									4		1			107			1		6	16	10				10	1	4
230															3		2								2		2
240									1			2				16	5					19			8	1	6
250																	53				1				7		
260		1													1		2	102	7	3		15			326	5	54
270								1	2					2		7		1	81	1	9	4			162	36	26
280																		26	9	105	3	3			133		178
290									3					3					2	10	40				49		5
300											2	1		1				14			1	189	1	4	89	59	79
310														1				2	2		2	1	20		88	7	28
320											2													39	52	2	5
490	6	1	1	9	3	1			27	1	8				7	1		7	2		13	16	5	36	475	31	295
550											1	1													8	30	6
Other				1											1			2	1					1	7	2	131

(Continued)

Table A2. (*Continued*)

(a-2) The number of affiliates in East Asia with SMEs

Industry of affiliates (columns); Industry of parent firms (rows)

	090	100	110	120	130	140	150	160	170	180	190	200	210	220	230	240	250	260	270	280	290	300	310	320	490	550	Other
090	52			1					3					1				1							2		6
100		2																1							1		
110			40	5					1													4			9		
120			2	36			2						1												7		2
130					14																				1		1
140						10											1	1			1				4		
150							21	1				4			1		1							2	2		
160			1					14						1									1				2
170	2							1	139		6	1		1		2	6	4						2	22		10
180										5															4		1
190									7		114				2		10	4	3				2	4	12		2
200			1			1			4		1	34													4		
210													10												1		
220			1											29				1						3	12	9	1
230															22		2	4	1							1	2
240																48	2		2	2	4	1			6		
250					1			1			1				1		112	3	3		9	6	1	2	11		4
260		1						1			1			1			8	193	6		3	8	1	10	37	1	9
270			1											1			2	3	110		3	1	1	5	37	1	11
280											3						5	5		33	2		1		13	1	2
290	1							1									4		6	2	119	4		1	31		3
300			1	1					2			1			1		3	4	7	1	6	114	5		3	1	2
310														1					9		3		47	2	5	1	3
320				1			1				1		1					1			2	1	7	31	6		1
490	40	1	17	55	3	8	5	5	27		42	12	1	17	3	14	25	20	14	8	26	12	15	28	656	18	22
550	1		1	1							1					1	1								5	4	5
Other				1													1	4	2			4		1	5	3	67

(b-2) The number of affiliates in North America with SMEs

Industry of affiliates (columns); Industry of parent firms (rows)

	090	100	110	120	130	140	150	160	170	180	190	200	210	220	230	240	250	260	270	280	290	300	310	320	490	550	Other
090	4																										
100		1																							2		2
110			1																						1		
120																											1
130					3																						
140																											
150							2																		2		
160								4																		2	2
170									25		1							1						1	12		9
180																									1		
190									2		13													2	2	1	
200												2													1	2	
210																											
220														3				1							2		1
230															2										1		1
240																6									1		1
250																	16					2	1		7	1	1
260						1					1						1	29	1	1		1			30	2	7
270																			9		1	1		1	19	2	3
280																		1		3	1				8		1
290											1										11				15		
300																	2	3	1			34	2		7		2
310																							6		10		4
320			2												1						1			4	6		1
490	3	1	2		1		1		2		1					1		4				5	4	1	154	3	14
550																									3	3	1
Other																				1					5	3	33

(c-2) The number of affiliates in Europe with SMEs

Industry of affiliates (columns); Industry of parent firms (rows)

	090	100	110	120	130	140	150	160	170	180	190	200	210	220	230	240	250	260	270	280	290	300	310	320	490	550	Other
090																											
100																											1
110																											
120																									1		
130					1																						
140																											
150																											
160								2																1			
170								1	10															1	5		3
180																									1		
190											6						1							4	2		
200											1																
210																											
220														2											2	1	
230															1												
240																2											
250																	12								3		
260		1													1		1	7	2						20	3	1
270																					1				12	3	
280																		7		1					6		
290																					2				5		
300																						3	1		2		1
310																							3		4		1
320																								1	5		
490					1				2									5	1		2	6	4	2	78	5	8
550																									1	2	
Other																											8

Data source: Authors' calculation, based on METI database.

Table A3. Globalizing patterns from 1998 to 2004 in East Asia and other regions: the number of firms

			Matrix between patterns of operations in East Asia and those in other regions																	
			In foreign countries (incl. E.Asia)						In North America						In Europe					
	Number of firms	Share in total	No entry	Expansion	Expansion (1st FDI)	Steady	Shrinkage	Shrinkage (with drawal)	No entry	Expansion	Expansion (1st FDI)	Steady	Shrinkage	Shrinkage (with drawal)	No entry	Expansion	Expansion (1st FDI)	Steady	Shrinkage	Shrinkage (with drawal)
(a) All firms																				
No entry in E.A.	14,986	82%	14, 381	54	175	198	37	141	13, 896	4	276	32	24	754	14, 461	0	97	7	3	418
Expansion in E.A.	933	5%	—	847	—	37	49	0	314	49	453	36	29	52	471	24	371	9	16	42
Expansion in E.A. (entry)	983	5%	—	130	808	37	8	0	659	7	161	16	10	130	809	2	86	6	5	75
Steady in E.A.	816	4%	—	89	—	642	85	0	511	5	174	21	14	91	640	3	99	3	7	64
Shrinkage in E.A.	215	1%	—	15	—	12	188	0	86	6	90	9	3	21	126	1	69	0	3	16
Shrinkage in E.A. (exit)	304	2%	—	12	—	15	34	243	236	0	26	4	0	38	271	0	9	0	1	23
Total	18,237	100%	14, 381	1, 147	983	941	401	384	15, 702	71	1180	118	80	1086	16, 778	30	731	25	35	638
Share in total	*100%*		*79%*	*6%*	5%	5%	2%	2%	*86%*	*0%*	6%	*1%*	*0%*	6%	*92%*	*0%*	*4%*	*0%*	*0%*	3%
(b) Manufacturing firms																				
No entry in E.A.	7,939	78%	7, 547	34	123	143	23	69	7, 344	3	183	27	18	364	7, 655	0	64	6	3	211
Expansion in E.A.	691	7%	—	632	—	28	31	0	223	38	351	23	21	35	337	20	288	5	11	30
Expansion in E.A. (entry)	697	7%	—	95	572	27	3	0	457	7	124	11	6	92	576	2	62	4	2	51
Steady in E.A.	597	6%	—	61	—	474	62	0	372	3	126	15	11	70	469	2	75	2	6	43
Shrinkage in E.A.	134	1%	—	10	—	8	116	0	54	4	55	6	2	13	76	1	46	0	1	10
Shrinkage in E.A. (exit)	176	2%	—	8	—	6	25	137	135	0	20	1	0	20	159	0	6	0	1	10
Total	10,234	100%	7, 547	840	695	686	260	206	8, 585	55	859	83	58	594	9, 272	25	541	17	24	355
Share in total	*100%*		*74%*	*8%*	7%	7%	3%	2%	*84%*	*1%*	*8%*	*1%*	*1%*	6%	*91%*	*0%*	*5%*	*0%*	*0%*	3%

(*Continued*)

Table A3. (*Continued*)

	Number of firms	Share in total	In foreign countries (incl. E.Asia): No entry	Expansion	Expansion (1st FDI)	Steady	Shrinkage	Shrinkage (with drawal)	In North America: No entry	Expansion	Expansion (1st FDI)	Steady	Shrinkage	Shrinkage (with drawal)	In Europe: No entry	Expansion	Expansion (1st FDI)	Steady	Shrinkage	Shrinkage (with drawal)
			Matrix between patterns of operations in East Asia and those in other regions																	
(c) SMEs																				
No entry in E.A.	11,749	89%	11,416	23	103	115	11	81	11,065	3	158	13	13	497	11,423	0	44	3	1	278
Expansion in E.A.	243	2%	—	229	—	11	3	0	155	2	55	7	4	20	192	1	31	1	4	14
Expansion in E.A. (entry)	618	5%	—	41	556	18	3	0	454	0	71	2	3	88	538	0	31	1	1	47
Steady in E.A.	430	3%	—	24	—	379	27	0	321	2	43	10	2	52	362	0	25	2	2	39
Shrinkage in E.A.	54	0%	—	2	—	3	49	0	33	0	11	4	1	5	44	0	4	0	0	6
Shrinkage in E.A. (exit)	143	1%	—	3	—	10	10	120	119	0	7	1	0	16	130	0	3	0	0	10
Total	13,237	100%	11,416	322	659	536	103	201	12,147	7	345	37	23	678	12,689	1	138	7	8	394
Share in total			*86%*	*2%*	5%	4%	1%	2%	*92%*	*0%*	*3%*	*0%*	*0%*	*5%*	*96%*	*0%*	*1%*	*0%*	*0%*	3%
(d) Manufacturing SMEs																				
No entry in E.A.	6,454	87%	6,232	15	74	82	6	45	6,075	3	105	11	11	249	6,280	0	30	2	1	141
Expansion in E.A.	161	2%	—	153	—	7	1	0	107	1	34	2	3	14	129	1	18	1	3	9
Expansion in E.A. (entry)	429	6%	—	25	388	15	1	0	315	0	48	1	1	64	381	0	16	0	0	32
Steady in E.A.	301	4%	—	14	—	270	17	0	233	1	26	5	2	34	259	0	17	1	1	23
Shrinkage in E.A.	30	0%	—	0	—	2	28	0	19	0	6	2	1	2	26	0	1	0	0	3
Shrinkage in E.A. (exit)	80	1%	—	1	—	4	7	68	69	0	5	0	0	6	74	0	2	0	0	4
Total	7,445	100%	6,232	208	462	380	60	113	6,818	5	224	21	18	369	7,149	1	84	4	5	212
Share in total	*100%*		*80%*	*6%*	5%	5%	4%	0%	*91%*	*1%*	*2%*	*4%*	*1%*	*1%*	*95%*	*1%*	*1%*	*2%*	*1%*	*1%*

Note: Figures are based on the two-period balanced panel dataset. "Entry" means and "exit" mean the 1st FDI in the region and withdrawal from the region, respectively.

Source: Authors' calculation, based on METI database.

Table A4. Summary statistics for firms in 1998 in the two-period panel dataset, 1998–2004

	Mean	SD	Min	Max
(a) All firms (obs. = 18,212)				
Expansion in East Asia	0.105	0.307	0	1
Firm size	457	1,866	50	71,237
Capital–labor ratio (mill. JPY)	10	16	0.001	905
Foreign sales ratio	0.022	0.082	0	1
In-house R&D ratio	0.006	0.022	0	1.646
Advertisement ratio	0.006	0.017	0	0.363
Foreign capital ratio	16	103	0	1,000
(b) Manufacturing firms				
Expansion in East Asia (obs. = 10,218)	0.136	0.343	0	1
Firm size	469	1,944	50	67,900
Capital–labor ratio (mill. JPY)	11	15	0.004	870
Foreign sales ratio	0.030	0.096	0	1
In-house R&D ratio	0.010	0.022	0	0.355
Advertisement ratio	0.005	0.016	0	0.287
Foreign capital ratio	15	92	0	1,000
(c) Non-manufacturing firms				
Expansion in East Asia (obs. = 7,994)	0.066	0.248	0	1
Firm size	443	1,761	50	71,237
Capital–labor ratio (mill. JPY)	9	17	0.001	905
Foreign sales ratio	0.011	0.059	0	0.967
In-house R&D ratio	0.002	0.021	0	1.646
Advertisement ratio	0.008	0.017	0	0.363
Foreign capital ratio	17	115	0	1,000

Table A5. Correlation matrix for the two-period panel dataset, 1998–2004

	Expansion in East Asia	Firm size (log)	Capital–labor ratio (log)	Foreign sales ratio	In-house R&D ratio	Advertisement ratio	Foreign capital ratio
(a) All firms (obs. = 18212)							
Expansion in East Asia	1						
Firm size (log)	0.263	1					
Capital-labor ratio (log)	0.100	0.092	1				
Foreign sales ratio	0.241	0.169	0.075	1			
In-house R&D ratio	0.162	0.180	0.085	0.209	1		
Advertisement ratio	−0.011	0.132	−0.003	−0.0110	0.034	1	
Foreign capital ratio	0.027	0.092	0.006	0.123	0.104	0.103	1
(b) Manufacturing firms (obs. = 10218)							
Expansion in East Asia	1						
Firm size (log)	0.338	1					
Capital-labor ratio (log)	0.121	0.150	1				
Foreign sales ratio	0.228	0.245	0.083	1			
In-house R&D ratio	0.202	0.303	0.094	0.257	1		
Advertisement ratio	0.009	0.121	0.046	0.017	0.083	1	
Foreign capital ratio	0.040	0.129	0.059	0.142	0.113	0.076	1
(c) Non-manufacturing firms (obs. = 7994)							
Expansion in East Asia	1						
Firm size (log)	0.141	1					
Capital-labor ratio (log)	0.045	0.039	1				
Foreign sales ratio	0.242	0.027	0.029	1			
In-house R&D ratio	0.042	0.025	0.021	0.066	1		
Advertisement ratio	−0.019	0.147	−0.012	−0.036	0.010	1	
Foreign capital ratio	0.015	0.055	−0.033	0.116	0.105	0.127	1

REFERENCES

Ando, Mitsuyo (2006). "Fragmentation and Vertical Intra-industry Trade in East Asia." *North American Journal of Economics and Finance*, 17(3): pp. 257–281.

Ando, Mitsuyo and Fukunari Kimura (2006). "Fragmentation in East Asia: Further Evidence," *KUMQRP Discussion Paper* No. 2006-23.

Arndt, W. Sven and Henryk Kierzkowski (2001). *Fragmentation: New Production Patterns in the World Economy*, Oxford: Oxford University Press.

Becker, Sascha, Karoline Ekholm, Robert Jäckle and Marc-Andreas Muendler (2005). "Location Choice and Employment Decisions: A Comparison of German and Swedish Multinationals." *Weltwirtschaftliches Archiv*, 141(4): pp. 693–731.

Blinder, Alan S. (2006). "Offshoring: The Next Industrial Revolution?" *Foreign Affairs*, 85(2): pp. 113–128.

Blomstrom, Magnus, Gunnar Fors and Robert E. Lipsey (1997). "Foreign Direct Investment and Employment: Home Country Experience in the U.S. and Sweden." *Economic Journal*, 107(445): pp. 1787–1797.

Brown, Sharon and James Spletzer (2005). "Labor Market Dynamics Associated with Movement of Works Overseas," Presented at the November 2005 OECD Conference on The Globalization of Production, Impacts of Employment, Productivity, and Economic Growth, Paris.

Ebenstein, Avraham, Ann Harrison, Margaret McMillan and Shannon Phillips (2009). "Estimating the Impact of Trade and Offshoring on American Workers using the Current Population Surveys," NBER Working Paper Series No. 15107.

Ekholm, Karolina and Katariina Hakkala (2006). "The Effect of Offshoring on Labor Demand: Evidence from Sweden," CEPR Working Paper No. 5648.

Federico, Stefano and Gaetano Alfredo Minerva (2008). "Outward FDI and Local Employment Growth in Italy." *Review of World Economics*, 144(2): pp. 295–324.

Fukao, Kyoji and Tomofumi Amano (2004). *Inward Direct Investment in Japan and the Japanese Economy (Tainichi Chokusetsu Toshi to Nihon Keizai)*. Nihon Keizai Shinbunsha. (In Japanese).

Head, Keith and John Ries (2002). "Offshore Production and Skill Upgrading by Japanese Manufacturing Firms." *Journal of International Economics*, 58(1): pp. 81–105.

Hijzen, Alexander, Holger Gorg and Robert C. Hine (2005). "International Outsourcing and the Skill Structure of Labor Demand in the United Kingdom." *Economic Journal*, 115(506): pp. 860–878.

Hijzen, Alexander, Tomohiko Inui and Yasuyuki Todo (2007). "The Effects of Multinational Production on Domestic Performance: Evidence from Japanese Firms" RIETI Discussion Paper Series No. 07-E-0006.

Ito, Keiko and Kyoji Fukao (2005). "Physical and Human Capital Deepening and New Trade Patters in Japan," In Takatoshi Ito and Andrew Rose (Eds.), *International Trade (NBER-East Asia Seminar on Economics)*, Vol. 14, Chicago: The University of Chicago Press.

Jones, W. Ronald and Henryk Kierzkowski (1990). "The Role of Services in Production and International Trade: A Theoretical Framework." In Ronald W. Jones and Anne O. Krueger, (Eds.), *The Political Economy of International Trade: Essays in Honor of Robert E. Baldwin*, pp. 31–48, Oxford: Basil Blackwell.

Kimura, Fukunari (2006). "International Production and Distribution Networks in East Asia: Eighteen Facts, Mechanics, and Policy Implications." *Asian Economic Policy Review*, 1(2): pp. 326–344.

Kimura, Fukunari and Mitsuyo Ando (2005). "Two-Dimensional Fragmentation in East Asia: Conceptual Framework and Empirics." *International Review of Economics and Finance*, 14(4): pp. 317–348.

Matsuura, Toshiyuki and Yosuke Nagata (2005). "Activities of Japanese Affiliates Abroad and their Effects on Domestic Employment" — Analysis Based on the Constructed FDI Database. *Keizai Toukei Kenkyu*, 33(4), 39–57. (In Japanese)

Samuelson, Paul (2004). "Where Richard and Mill Rebut and Confirm Arguments of Mainstream Economists Supporting Globalization." *Journal of Economic Perspectives*, 18(3): pp. 135–146.

Comment

Vitor Trindade

Among all of the concerns that both policy-making elite and the public have about globalization, arguably none surpasses the impact that the globalizing activities of domestic firms have on domestic employment. Are these firms more likely to reduce domestic employment when they diversify their activities internationally? This seems to be the question, and the general public seems to have made up its mind that the answer is an unalloyed yes.[1]

This makes it ever more urgent that economists investigate the same and related questions, which have to do with firms' decisions to diversify their activities abroad, and the impact of those decisions in their countries of origin. The Ando–Kimura study is one nice effort in that direction. In particular, it finds that alarmism about globalization is hardly justified. Specifically, the authors accomplish that by asking the following questions:

1. When Japanese firms expand abroad (especially in East Asia), do they tend to increase or decrease domestic employment?
2. Do they tend to increase or decrease exports and imports?
3. And finally, do they tend to open or close new domestic affiliates and establishments?

From a theoretical perspective, a firm's expansion abroad can as plausibly lead to an increase in domestic employment as it could lead to a

[1]Two phrases from recent presidential elections in the U.S. serve as illustrations of economic concerns about globalization, as they were expressed in the public arena. The first is Ross Perot's "great sucking sound" of 1992, a sound, one supposes, to be caused by the massive loss of employment that would ensue after the creation of NAFTA. The second is John Kerry's 2004 use of "outsourcing" as a campaign motif. Many other examples in other contexts of course are readily available.

decrease. As an example of the former, consider a firm whose expansion is mostly into the commercial sector associated with its manufactures (a car maker expanding abroad into car dealerships, for example). This activity, if successful, would lead to domestic expansion accompanying the expansion abroad. An example could be a tariff-jumping firm, whose foreign-made output is a perfect substitute for its domestic-made one. Many other stories are possible, of course, and the authors correctly argue from this that the question then becomes essentially an empirical one.

To study this, they have gathered firm-level data for Japan, for the years 1998–2004. These data contain information on: domestic employment; the international trade of each firm; their domestic affiliates and their foreign affiliates (with a special focus on East Asia, a focus that seems warranted because East Asia received the lion's share of Japanese foreign investment in those years; and information needed for controls such as size of the firms, R&D expenditures, and so on. The main findings are:

1. Expansion of Japanese firms into East Asia seems to be associated with higher growth of employment and with higher probability of no decrease in the employment of the expanding firms.
2. Expansion of Japanese firms into East Asia seems to be associated with more intense trade (both imports and exports) by those firms.
3. However, expansions of Japanese firms seem to be in some cases associated with the closing of some of the firms' domestic establishments or affiliates.

Based on the aggregate results 1 above, one infers then that the evidence is not suggestive of the broad decreases in domestic employment that so worry many observers of the international economic scene. Furthermore, one may argue, along with the authors, that result 3 may simply indicate firms' rationalization of their domestic activities, once due account is taken of result 1.

I find that the evidence of a correlation between globalizing activities and no decrease of domestic employment uncovered here is both plausible and important. Furthermore, I share the authors' reluctance in drawing causal inferences about globalizing firms from it. This may be especially problematic if there are omitted variables. It may simply be that some firms are more successful than others, for reasons that go beyond the controls that the authors include.[2] Successful firms are more likely than unsuccessful ones to expand *both* domestically *and* abroad, by reason of their very success. This would of course produce the kind of correlation that is seen here, between a firm's increase in foreign affiliates (the main right-hand side variable of interest) and, say, an increase in domestic employment (the left-hand side variable in one of the results).

In the same vein, I would also caution about any inferences regarding "networks." It does seem that what we know is: Japanese firms that have increased their affiliates abroad in the years of the sample do not seem, on average, to be decreasing their domestic employment. As I already pointed out, this is a useful result, but is there any evidence that these firms are forming or are part of any networks? For example, do firms that belong to keiretsu behave in any different ways than those that do not?

These points notwithstanding, this paper gives us a picture that is at odds with the layperson's over-simplistic view of globalization. This and further papers along the same lines should prove to be a strong corrective against anti-globalizing pessimism.

Finally, what follows are some suggestions for further research. First, it would be interesting to distinguish between firms that invest abroad within their own industries (with "industry" as narrowly defined as possible, not just "machinery," for example), versus those firms that invest in different sectors. One would guess that the former are more likely to be reducing employment domestically, unlike the latter type, whose foreign activities are more likely to complement their domestic activities. In my view, this would also better support the use of the word "fragmentation." Indeed, it seems that we do not really know whether there is any "fragmentation" happening in the strict sense, given the information contained in the authors' dataset. By the way, there is evidence (see Table 1) which indicates that, for example in machinery, about two-thirds of East Asian affiliates of Japanese firms remain in the same sector (machinery), while the same is true for only one-third of affiliates in North America and Europe. To me, this suggests

[2]These include some reasonable variables, such as R&D expenditures, expenditures on advertisements, and others. But of course, one could argue as well that these are variables whose variations across firms in the same industry stand in need of explanation themselves. At any rate, they may be simply insufficient to explain the relative success of individual firms.

very different patterns of international diversification, which may prove worthwhile of further investigation.

It would also be a useful exercise to investigate the role of actual outsourcing in firms' domestic employment and domestic affiliates, perhaps by linking these firm-level data with Japanese international trade data. Furthermore, if there is a possibility of linking these data with more detailed data on employment of skilled versus non-skilled labor, it would also be useful to check whether the impact on the two kinds of labor is any different. This is likely to provide further insights about international investment and skill upgrading.

In summary, this is a useful addition to the literature on foreign investment and domestic labor markets, and in particular gives cause for cautious optimism on the impact of globalization on domestic employment.

CHAPTER 7

Japan's Exports and Employment

Kozo Kiyota

Faculty of Business Administration, Yokohama National University, Japan
Research Institute of Economy, Trade and Industry (RIETI), Japan

I. INTRODUCTION

The effect of international trade on employment is one of the central concerns of business circles and policy makers in many countries, including Japan.[1] While the financial effect of turbulence in 2008 was initially expected to be relatively small, it hit the Japanese economy severely. It is said that the effect mostly came through the trade channel, originating from "the collapse in demand for consumer durable goods and capital goods in (non-Asian) advanced economies" (IMF, 2009, p. 71).[2]

The effect of trade on the Japanese labor market has been widely discussed in the literature. Tachibanaki, Morikawa, and Nishimura (1998) have examined the effect of manufacturing imports from Asian countries on employment and wages in Japan. Matching the Japanese trade statistics with the *Census of Manufactures* at the two-digit industry level, they found a negative effect of imports on employment, although the effect was not large. Tomiura (2003) has used more detailed data to extend the analysis of Tachibanaki, Morikawa, and Nishimura (1998). Using the data for 380 manufacturing industries for 1988–1995, he found a significant effect of the changes in import prices on Japan's employment.[3] Sakurai

[1] See, for example, Sachs *et al.* (1994) for a discussion of the effects of trade on U.S. manufacturing employment.

[2] Similarly, OECD (2009) pointed out that "[t]he global crisis has taken a heavy toll on Japan's trade-dependent economy" (p. 73).

[3] A recent study by Sasaki (2007) has further extended Tomiura (2003), using more recent data covering the period 1994–2003. He also found that the fall in import prices had significant negative impact on employment in import-competing industries.

(2004) has examined the effect of import penetration on manufacturing employment, using Japanese input–output (IO) data in 1980 and 1990. He found increased imports had a small effect on Japanese employment.

While these studies have made significant contributions to the understanding of the effect of imports on employment in Japan, there are at least two dimensions to be extended. First, previous studies on trade and Japanese labor markets focused on the effect of imports rather than exports. For countries with large trade deficits, such as the U.S., the effect of import competition from low-wage countries can be a major concern. However, for countries with large trade surpluses, such as Japan and China, the effect of exports on employment is also an important factor because the contribution of foreign demand to domestic employment could be large.[4] A study on the effect of exports on employment can thus contribute to a deeper understanding of the current Japanese economy and the discussion on its future prospects.

Second, previous studies focused only on the effect on the industry's own employment.[5] To examine the effect of trade on employment, previous studies regressed sectoral employment on sectoral trade on the basis of the import–penetration ratio.[6] Note that the demand for labor can be affected not only by the industry's own trade (i.e., direct effect) but also by the trade of other industries through intra-industry linkages (i.e., indirect effect). If the indirect effect is not small, the previous studies overestimated the effect on the industry's own employment while underestimating the effect on other industries' employment.

This chapter examines the following questions: How much employment is created by rising Japanese exports? How has the export dependence of employment changed over the time? Are the changes in the export–dependence ratio attributable to the changes in productivity? Is the indirect effect from exports small? Do the increases in the export dependence

[4]Several studies have examined the effects of exports on employment. See, for example, Feenstra and Hong (2007) which examined the effect of China's exports on employment.

[5]An exception is a study by Sakurai (2004) that has utilized the IO table to capture the indirect effects. However, his interest is the effect of imports, not the effect of exports.

[6]Some studies such as Tomiura (2003) and Sasaki (2007) have utilized sectoral import prices to examine the effects of international trade. Similarly, Dekle (1998) has examined the effects of exchange-rate fluctuations on Japanese manufacturing employment for the period 1975–1994.

concentrate in a few industries? If the demand from the U.S. declines, which industries are strongly affected?

To estimate both the direct and indirect demand for labor from exports, I use Japanese IO table data from 1975 to 2006, which have been newly developed as a part of a research project of the Research Institute of Economy, Trade and Industry (RIETI), and Hitotsubashi University. The IO table consists of 52 manufacturing and 56 non-manufacturing industries, available on an annual basis for 1975–2006. This enables us to capture the detailed intra-industry linkages. Following Feenstra and Hong (2007), I identify employment created through the direct and indirect effects as "implied employment."

The analysis of the indirect effect of exports on employment also contributes to the literature on the linkages of multinational firms. Several studies such as Hanson, Matoloni, and Slaughter (2005) and Kiyota *et al.* (2008) have examined the determinants of the linkages of multinational firms. However, little attention has been paid on how the effect of foreign demand is transmitted to home country employment through the linkages.[7] Based on the fact that multinational firms dominate more than 90% of Japanese exports (Kiyota and Urata, 2008, Table 1) and that intra-firm trade accounted for more than 40% of Japanese exports (Kiyota *et al.*, 2008, Table 1), the analysis of the effect of exports on employment contributes to the deeper understanding of the effects through the linkages of multinational firms.

In what follows, the Section II presents the methodology and data. Estimation results are presented in Section III. A summary of the findings and policy implications are presented in Section IV.

II. METHODOLOGY AND DATA

Methodology

A logical starting point to estimate the implied employment effect of exports is to look at the calculation from IO tables for Japan, with both the

[7] An exception is a study by Yamashita and Fukao (2008) that examined the effect of overseas operation by multinational firms on employment in Japan, although their study did not take into account the indirect effect.

Table 1. Japan's employment and GDP

	Employment (Thousands of persons)			GDP (Billions of Yen, 2000 constant prices)				
	Total	Manufacturing	Non-manufacturing	Total	Domestic final demand	Exports	Imports	Trade balance
1975	55,797	14,158	41,639	237,867	234,182	13,708	10,022	3,686
1980	58,571	14,165	44,406	299,448	289,912	22,181	12,645	9,536
1985	60,945	15,297	45,649	353,167	346,105	22,004	14,941	7,062
1990	64,187	15,307	48,880	442,988	436,370	29,303	22,685	6,618
1995	66,632	14,106	52,526	474,485	469,441	45,536	40,492	5,044
2000	65,252	12,649	52,603	499,683	489,615	57,694	47,625	10,068
2006	64,199	11,344	52,855	549,601	530,633	82,515	63,547	18,968
Share								
	(Total employment = 100%)			(GDP = 100%)				
1975	100	25.4	74.6	100	98.5	5.8	4.2	1.5
1980	100	24.2	75.8	100	96.8	7.4	4.2	3.2
1985	100	25.1	74.9	100	98.0	6.2	4.2	2.0
1990	100	23.8	76.2	100	98.5	6.6	5.1	1.5
1995	100	21.2	78.8	100	98.9	9.6	8.5	1.1
2000	100	19.4	80.6	100	98.0	11.5	9.5	2.0
2006	100	17.7	82.3	100	96.5	15.0	11.6	3.5

(*Continued*)

Table 1. (*Continued*)

	Employment (Thousands of persons)			GDP (Billions of Yen, 2000 constant prices)				
	Total	Manufacturing	Non-manufacturing	Total	Domestic final demand	Exports	Imports	Trade balance
Growth Rate (percent per year, compound)								
1975–1980	1.0	0.0	1.3	4.6	4.3	9.6	4.6	19.0
1980–1985	0.8	1.5	0.6	3.3	3.5	−0.2	3.3	−6.0
1985–1990	1.0	0.0	1.4	4.5	4.6	5.7	8.4	−1.3
1990–1995	0.7	−1.6	1.4	1.4	1.5	8.8	11.6	−5.4
1995–2000	−0.4	−2.2	0.0	1.0	0.8	4.7	3.2	13.8
2000–2006	−0.3	−1.8	0.1	1.6	1.3	6.0	4.8	10.6
1975–2006	0.5	−0.7	0.8	2.7	2.6	5.8	6.0	5.3

Note: Domestic final demand is defined as the sum of consumption, investment, and government expenditure.
Source: JIP 2009 Database.

direct and indirect demand for labor from exports. The growth of implied employment is then decomposed into the contribution of domestic final demand and exports.[8]

Let i ($i = 1, \ldots, n$) be an index of an industry in the economy. Denote $n \times 1$ vectors of domestic final demand, exports, and imports as **D**, **E**, and **M**, respectively, whose elements are D_i, M_i, and E_i. Let **Q** and **F** be $n \times 1$ vectors of gross output and final demand, respectively. Final demand consists of domestic final demand and net external demand (i.e., exports minus imports): $\mathbf{F} \equiv \mathbf{D} + \mathbf{E} - \mathbf{M}$.[9] Denote an $n \times n$ intermediate input matrix as **q**, whose element is q_{ij}. Let **A** be an $n \times n$ input coefficient matrix, whose element is $a_{ij} = q_{ij}/Q_i$ where Q_i is the gross output of industry i. Output thus is written as:

$$\mathbf{Q} \equiv \mathbf{AQ} + \mathbf{F} \tag{1}$$

Because final demand consists of domestic final demand and external demand, we have:

$$\mathbf{Q} = \mathbf{AQ} + \mathbf{D} + \mathbf{E} - \mathbf{M} \tag{2}$$

Note that imports are "endogenously" determined in the sense that imports depend upon domestic demand. To take account of this "endogeneity," following Sakurai (2004), assume that imports are proportional to sectoral domestic demand at $\bar{m}_i$, where $\bar{m}_i = M_i/(\sum_j q_{ij} + D_i)$. Denote an $n \times n$ diagonal matrix as $\bar{M}$, whose diagonal element is $\bar{m}_i$. Equation (2) is rewritten as:

$$\mathbf{Q} = \mathbf{AQ} + \mathbf{D} + \mathbf{E} - \bar{\mathbf{M}}(\mathbf{AQ} + \mathbf{D}) \tag{3}$$

Solving Equation (3) for the output vector **Q**, we have:

$$\mathbf{Q} = \{\mathbf{I} - (\mathbf{I} - \bar{\mathbf{M}})\mathbf{A}\}^{-1}\{(\mathbf{I} - \bar{\mathbf{M}})\mathbf{D} + \mathbf{E}\} \tag{4}$$

where **I** is an $n \times n$ identity matrix. Let $\mathbf{Q}^{\mathrm{D}}$ and $\mathbf{Q}^{\mathrm{E}}$ be the implied gross outputs from domestic final demand and exports, respectively. Therefore,

---

[8]A similar growth decomposition framework has been employed by Feenstra and Hong (2007).

[9]Domestic final demand is defined as the sum of consumption, investment, and government expenditure.

the effects of domestic final demand and exports on the gross output are written as:

$$Q^D = \left\{I - \left(I - \bar{M}\right) A\right\}^{-1} \left(I - \bar{M}\right) D \tag{5}$$

and

$$Q^E = \{I - \left(I - \bar{M}\right) A\}^{-1} E \tag{6}$$

respectively.

Let l_i be the industry i's labor-input coefficients: $l_i = L_i/Q_i$, where L_i is industry i's employment. Let **L** be the $n \times 1$ employment vector, whose element is L_i. Let $\bar{L}$ be the $n \times n$ diagonal matrix, whose diagonal element is l_i. Denote the implied employment from domestic final demand and exports as L^D and L^E. The effects of domestic final demand and exports on employment thus are written as:

$$L^D = \bar{L}Q^D = \bar{L}\{I - (I - \bar{M})A\}^{-1}(I - \bar{M})D \tag{7}$$

and

$$L^E = \bar{L}Q^E = \bar{L}\{I - (I - \bar{M})A\}^{-1}E \tag{8}$$

respectively.[10]

Let L_{it}^D and L_{it}^E be the implied employment from domestic final demand and exports in industry i at year t, respectively. Let L_t^D and L_t^E be the total implied employment from domestic final demand and exports at year t, respectively. Total employment is decomposed into the implied employment from domestic final demand and exports:

$$L_t = \sum_i L_{it}^D + \sum_i L_{it}^E = L_t^D + L_t^E \tag{9}$$

The export–dependence ratio of employment is defined as: L_t^E/L_t. Taking the difference of (9) between years t and $t - 1$, we obtain:

$$\Delta L_t = \Delta L_t^D + \Delta L_t^E \tag{10}$$

Therefore, the employment growth is written as:

$$\Delta L_t/L_t = \Delta L_t^D/L_t + \Delta L_t^E/L_t \tag{11}$$

[10]Note that the equation will be the standard formula of factor contents if imports do not depend on domestic demand.

Equation (11) is used to capture the effect of exports on employment growth.

Data

As mentioned earlier, the data cover 108 industries in Japan between 1975 and 2006. The major source of the data is the Japan Industrial Productivity database 2009 (JIP 2009 database), which is compiled as a part of a research project of the RIETI and Hitotsubashi University. The database runs annually from 1970 to 2006, covering 52 manufacturing and 56 non-manufacturing industries.[11] The major sources of the database are government statistics and, therefore, the industrial classification of the JIP 2009 database is based on the Japan Standard Industry Classification (JSIC) that complies with the International Standard Industry Classification (ISIC) developed by the United Nations and JSIC.

The database compiles detailed information on sectoral output and inputs, including information on the number of workers.[12] From the JIP 2009 database, the IO table and sectoral employment (i.e., the number of workers) for 1975–2006 are obtained. Exports and imports include trade in services. All IO tables are valued at 2000 constant prices.

Descriptive Analysis

Table 1 indicates Japan's employment and GDP. Major findings are summarized as follows. First, total employment showed negative growth after 1995. The annual average growth rate of total employment was greater than 0.5% before 1995 but fell to −0.4% for 1995–2000 and −0.3% for 2000–2006. Second, for manufacturing, there was negative growth from 1990. The annual average growth rate of manufacturing employment was positive before 1990 but fell to −1.6% for 1990–1995 and continued to be negative afterwards. As a result, the share of manufacturing employment relative to total employment decreased from 25.4% in 1975 to 17.7% in 2006. Third, the growth rate of real GDP was small after 1990. The annual

[11] IO tables for 1971–1972 are not available in the JIP 2009 database. Table A1 presents the list of 108 industries. Industries codes 8–59 are classified as manufacturing while the others are classified as non-manufacturing.

[12] For more details about the JIP database, see Fukao *et al.* (2007).

average growth rate of real GDP was less than 2% for 1990–2006. Fourth, on the other hand, the exports showed large positive growth throughout the period, except for 1980–1985. The annual average growth rate of exports for 1975–2006 was 5.8%. Finally, although exports showed remarkable growth after 1985, imports also expanded rapidly throughout the period. The annual average growth rate of imports for 1975–2006 was 6.0%, which is greater than that for exports. Therefore, in spite of the rapid growth of exports, the share of domestic final demand relative to GDP continued to be high for the past three decades. The share of domestic final demand was 96.5%–98.9% over the period. In this connection, it should be noted that the trade imbalance declined from 3.2% in 1980 to 1.1% in 1995.

III. RESULTS

How Much Employment Is Created by Rising Japanese Exports?

Table 2 presents the implied employment from domestic final demand and exports in Japan. Implied employment is estimated, based on Equation (10). The major findings are threefold. First, the contribution of exports to employment is rather small in Japan. The share of implied employment from domestic final demand is greater than 90% throughout the period. This implies that the employment created by Japan's exports was less than 10%. Second, however, the contribution of exports to total employment is gradually increasing after 1990. The share of implied employment increased from 6.4% in 1990 to 9.9% in 2006. Third, exports showed a significant contribution to manufacturing employment. Also, the contribution of exports to manufacturing employment increased over the period. The share of implied employment from exports to total implied employment increased from 15.1% in 1975 to 28.7% in 2006. This result means that approximately 30% of manufacturing employment was created by exports in 2006.

How Did the Export Dependence of Employment Change Over Time?

Table 3 indicates the growth of implied employment from domestic final demand and exports. The growth of implied employment is calculated, based on Equation (12). Three messages stand out from this table. First,

Table 2. **Implied Japanese employment from domestic final demand and exports**

	All industries			Manufacturing			Non-manufacturing		
	Total	Domestic final demand	Exports	Total	Domestic final demand	Exports	Total	Domestic final demand	Exports
Number of workers (thousands of persons)									
1975	55,797	52,147	3,650	14,158	12,017	2,142	41,639	40,130	1,509
1980	58,571	54,091	4,480	14,165	11,637	2,529	44,406	42,455	1,951
1985	60,945	57,040	3,905	15,297	13,075	2,221	45,649	43,965	1,684
1990	64,187	60,088	4,099	15,307	13,027	2,280	48,880	47,062	1,819
1995	66,632	61,294	5,338	14,106	11,078	3,028	52,526	50,216	2,310
2000	65,252	59,392	5,860	12,649	9,572	3,077	52,603	49,820	2,782
2006	64,199	57,817	6,382	11,344	8,085	3,259	52,855	49,732	3,123
Share (total = 100%)									
1975	100	93.5	6.5	100	84.9	15.1	100	96.4	3.6
1980	100	92.4	7.6	100	82.1	17.9	100	95.6	4.4
1985	100	93.6	6.4	100	85.5	14.5	100	96.3	3.7
1990	100	93.6	6.4	100	85.1	14.9	100	96.3	3.7
1995	100	92.0	8.0	100	78.5	21.5	100	95.6	4.4
2000	100	91.0	9.0	100	75.7	24.3	100	94.7	5.3
2006	100	90.1	9.9	100	71.3	28.7	100	94.1	5.9

Note: Domestic final demand is defined as the sum of intermediate input demand, consumption, investment, and government expenditure.
Source: JIP 2009 Database.

Japan's employment has begun to decline since the late 1990s. Total employment showed positive growth before the period, 1990–1995, but was negative after 1995–2000. This negative growth was largely attributable to the negative contribution of domestic final demand. The growth of domestic final demand was also negative after the period 1995–2000. Second, on the other hand, the implied employment from exports was positive throughout the period, except for 1980–1985, when exports had negative growth (Table 1). This result implies that exports offset the drops in domestic final demand for 1995–2006. In other words, there is a potential risk that negative shocks on exports fall from the employment growth.

Finally, in manufacturing, negative growth had already started in the early 1990s. The growth of manufacturing employment was negative

Table 3. Implied growth in Japanese employment from domestic final demand and exports

	All industries			Manufacturing			Non-manufacturing		
	Total	Domestic final demand	Exports	Total	Domestic final demand	Exports	Total	Domestic final demand	Exports
(Growth rate: percent per year for total/all industries and percentage point for others, compound)									
1975–1980	0.97	0.68	0.29	0.00	−0.13	0.14	0.97	0.81	0.15
1980–1985	0.79	0.99	−0.19	0.38	0.48	−0.10	0.42	0.51	−0.09
1985–1990	1.04	0.97	0.06	0.00	−0.02	0.02	1.03	0.99	0.04
1990–1995	0.75	0.37	0.38	−0.37	−0.60	0.23	1.11	0.96	0.15
1995–2000	−0.42	−0.58	0.16	−0.44	−0.46	0.01	0.02	−0.12	0.14
2000–2006	−0.27	−0.41	0.13	−0.34	−0.38	0.05	0.06	−0.02	0.09
1975–2006	0.45	0.30	0.15	−0.15	−0.21	0.06	0.60	0.52	0.09

Note: The sum of percentage points is not necessarily equal to the total because of rounding. For the definition of domestic final demand, see the note in Table 2.
Source: JIP 2009 Database.

during 1990–1995 and continued to be negative afterward. Also, the negative growth of implied employment from domestic final demand was observed throughout the period, except for 1980–1985. As a result, the contribution of domestic final demand to the growth of manufacturing employment was a −0.21% point for 1975–2006.

Note that manufacturing employment declined after 1990 and total employment declined after 1995 (Table 1). Note also that the trade imbalance declined from 3.2% in 1980 to 1.1% in 1995 (Table 1). These findings imply that the increases in export dependence are not necessarily attributable to the increases in total employment or the increases in trade balance.

Are the Changes in the Export–Dependence Ratio Attributable to the Changes in Productivity?

One may be concerned that the increases in the export dependence of employment are largely attributable to the growth of productivity rather than exports. This is because export dependence can be decomposed into the growth of productivity and exports:

$$\frac{L_t^E}{L_t} = \frac{L_t^E}{E_t} \times \frac{E_t}{Q_t} \times \frac{Q_t}{L_t} = \frac{E_t}{Q_t} \times \left(\frac{Q_t/L_t}{E_t/L_t^E} \right) \tag{12}$$

where E/Q is the export–output ratio; Q/L is the macroeconomic labor productivity; and E/L^E is the export labor productivity.

In terms of growth, Equation (13) can be written as:

$$\frac{\Delta(L_t^E/L_t)}{L_t^E/L_t} = \frac{\Delta(E_t/Q_t)}{E_t/Q_t} + \left\{ \frac{\Delta(Q_t/L_t)}{Q_t/L_t} - \frac{\Delta(E_t/L_t^E)}{E_t/L_t^E} \right\} \tag{13}$$

The first term captures the contribution of exports while the second term captures the contributions of productivity growth. Note that the productivity term consists of two opposite effects. Increases in the export–dependence ratio are caused by increases in the growth of macroeconomic labor productivity and/or decreases in the growth of export labor productivity.

Table 4 presents the decomposition of the export–dependence ratio of employment. Major findings are threefold. First, the growth of the export–output ratio is positive from 1975 to 2006, except for 1980 to 1985. This implies that the expansion of exports contributes to the increase in the export dependence of employment. Second, on the other hand, the productivity term is negative throughout the period. The negative effect of the export labor productivity exceeds the positive effect of the macroeconomic labor productivity, which results in a negative contribution to the export dependence. Finally, the negative effect of productivity is not large enough to offset the positive effect of exports. Therefore, the increases in export dependence are largely attributable to the increases in exports.

The results suggest that the high export dependence of the Japanese employment comes from the rapid growth of exports. The heavy export dependence has to be considered as a vulnerability in the Japanese economy. Note, however, that the export dependence of employment can be mitigated if the export labor productivity improves even when the Japanese economy increases exports. The growth of export labor productivity might be a possible solution to mitigate the external shocks from abroad.

Table 4. Decomposition of the export–dependence ratio: level and growth

	All industries					Manufacturing				
	Export dependence	Exports	Productivity			Export dependence	Exports	Productivity		
Level	L^E/L	E/Y	$(Y/L)/(E/L^E)$	Y/L	E/L^E	L^E/L	E/Y	$(Y/L)/(E/L^E)$	Y/L	E/L^E
Decomposition of level										
1975	0.065	0.031	2.135	8.019	3.755	0.151	0.068	2.238	10.852	4.849
1980	0.076	0.039	1.938	9.595	4.952	0.179	0.086	2.073	13.653	6.586
1985	0.064	0.033	1.924	10.838	5.634	0.145	0.074	1.970	15.271	7.752
1990	0.064	0.035	1.825	13.045	7.149	0.149	0.078	1.899	19.255	10.141
1995	0.080	0.051	1.578	13.458	8.530	0.215	0.126	1.703	20.782	12.204
2000	0.090	0.062	1.457	14.350	9.846	0.243	0.155	1.568	23.624	15.070
2006	0.099	0.082	1.205	15.582	12.929	0.287	0.200	1.436	28.846	20.093

(*Continued*)

Table 4. (*Continued*)

	All industries					Manufacturing				
	Export dependence	Exports	Productivity			Export dependence	Exports	Productivity		
Growth rate	$\Delta L^E/L$	$\Delta E/Y$	$\Delta Y/L - \Delta E/L^E$	$\Delta Y/L$	$\Delta E/L^E$	$\Delta L^E/L$	$\Delta E/Y$	$\Delta Y/L - \Delta E/L^E$	$\Delta Y/L$	$\Delta E/L^E$
Decomposition of growth (annual average)										
1975–1980	0.031	0.051	−0.019	0.036	0.055	0.033	0.048	−0.015	0.046	0.061
1980–1985	−0.035	−0.034	−0.001	0.024	0.026	−0.041	−0.031	−0.010	0.022	0.033
1985–1990	−0.001	0.010	−0.011	0.037	0.048	0.005	0.012	−0.007	0.046	0.054
1990–1995	0.045	0.074	−0.029	0.006	0.035	0.073	0.095	−0.022	0.015	0.037
1995–2000	0.023	0.039	−0.016	0.013	0.029	0.025	0.042	−0.017	0.026	0.042
2000–2006	0.017	0.049	−0.032	0.014	0.045	0.028	0.042	−0.015	0.033	0.048

Note: Δ means growth rate in this table. For the definition of variables, see main text.
Source: JIP 2009 Database.

Is the Indirect Effect from Exports Small?

The effect of exports on employment is further decomposed into the direct effect (i.e., employment created by the industry's own exports) and indirect effect (i.e., employment created by other industries' exports). If the indirect effect is large, a study of the relationship between trade and employment focusing on the direct effect will overestimate the effect on the industry's employment while underestimating the effect on other industries' employment. How much employment then is created through the indirect effect?

Table 5 presents the decomposition results of implied employment from exports and indicates that the indirect effect is surprisingly large. The magnitude of the indirect effect is almost the same as the direct effect

Table 5. Implied Japanese employment from exports: direct versus indirect effects

	All industries			Manufacturing			Non-manufacturing		
	Total	Direct effect	Indirect effect	Total	Direct effect	Indirect effect	Total	Direct effect	Indirect effect
Number of workers (thousands of persons)									
1975	3,650	1,710	1,940	2,142	1,358	783	1,509	352	1,157
1980	4,480	1,992	2,487	2,529	1,564	964	1,951	428	1,523
1985	3,905	1,778	2,127	2,221	1,368	854	1,684	410	1,274
1990	4,099	1,768	2,331	2,280	1,327	953	1,819	441	1,378
1995	5,338	2,381	2,957	3,028	1,895	1,133	2,310	486	1,824
2000	5,860	2,713	3,147	3,077	1,937	1,140	2,782	776	2,006
2006	6,382	3,237	3,145	3,259	2,146	1,113	3,123	1,091	2,032
Share (total = 100%)									
1975	100	46.8	53.2	100	63.4	36.6	100	23.3	76.7
1980	100	44.5	55.5	100	61.9	38.1	100	21.9	78.1
1985	100	45.5	54.5	100	61.6	38.4	100	24.4	75.6
1990	100	43.1	56.9	100	58.2	41.8	100	24.2	75.8
1995	100	44.6	55.4	100	62.6	37.4	100	21.0	79.0
2000	100	46.3	53.7	100	62.9	37.1	100	27.9	72.1
2006	100	50.7	49.3	100	65.8	34.2	100	34.9	65.1

Note: Direct effect is defined as the effect of the industry's own exports on its employment. Indirect effect is defined as the effect of other industries' exports on the industry's employment.

Source: JIP 2009 Database.

between 1975 and 2006. This implies that about half of the effects of exports appeared through intra-industry linkages. The results suggest that it is important to take into account the indirect effect in analyzing the effect of exports on employment. Note that the effect is different between the manufacturing and non-manufacturing sectors. Table 5 indicates that the indirect effect is smaller in manufacturing than non-manufacturing because many non-manufacturing industries produce non-tradable services. In manufacturing, however, the indirect effect still accounts for more than one-third of the total effect. This result suggests that the indirect effect is not small even in manufacturing.

Do the Increases in the Export Dependence Concentrate in a Few Industries?

The difference between manufacturing and non-manufacturing suggests that the export dependence of employment may be different across industries. It is often pointed out that Japan's major export-oriented industries are electrical machinery, motor vehicles, and general machinery (e.g., METI, 2009, p. 220). However, it is not clear whether the increases in the export dependency of employment are limited to these industries because of the indirect effect.

Do the increases in the export dependence concentrate in a few industries? Figure 1 plots the export–dependence ratio in 1975 and 2006 for all industries and manufacturing. Numbers correspond to the industry code presented in Table A1. The industries located above the 45-degree line are the industries that increased their export dependence between 1975 and 2006.

The results are striking. The majority of industries locate above the 45-degree line. This implies that the increases in the export dependence of employment occurred in the majority of industries, although the magnitude is different across industries. Japan's major export-oriented industries are electrical machinery, motor vehicles, and general machinery. However, the increases in the export dependency of employment are not limited to these industries. Another concern may be that the increases in export dependence are simply due to the increases in the volume of the industry's exports. Figure 2 plots the relationship between the changes in the export–output ratio and export–dependence ratio for manufacturing

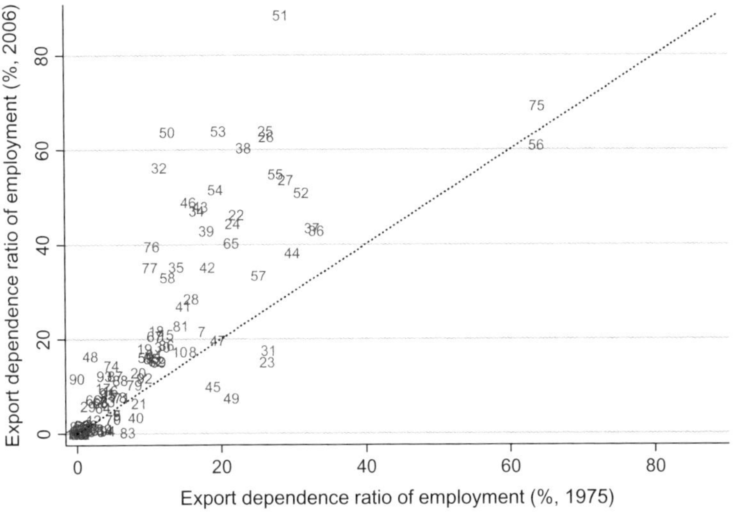

(a) All industries

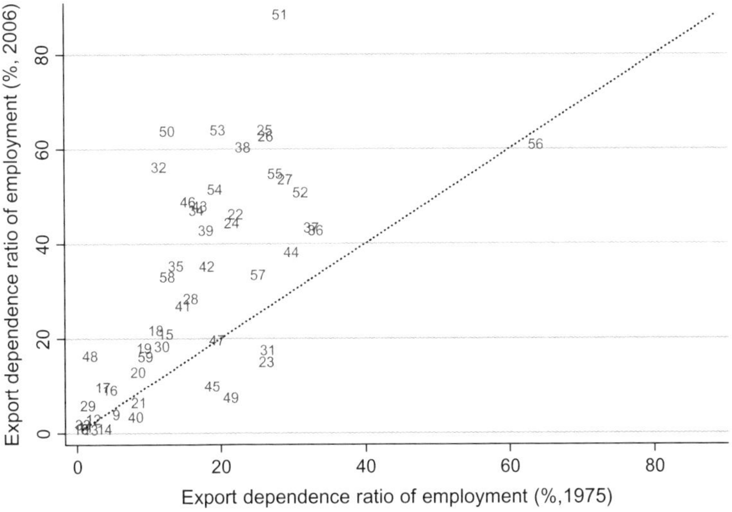

(b) Manufacturing

Note: The export dependence ratio of employment is defined as the implied employment from exports devided by the sum of the implied employment from the domestic demand and exports. Numbers correspond to the industry code in Table A1.

Source: JIP 2009 Database.

Fig. 1. Distribution of export dependence ratio of employment across industries, 1975–2006.

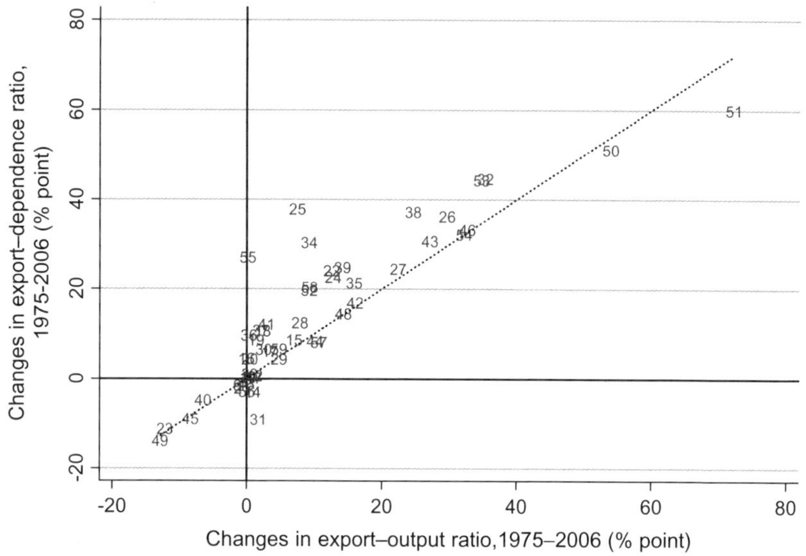

Note: The export–dependence ratio of employment is defined as the implied employment from exports divided by the sum of implied employment from domestic final demand and exports. The export–output ratio is defined as exports divided by the gross output. Numbers correspond to the industry code in Table A1.
Source: JIP 2009 Database.

Fig. 2. Relationship between export–output ratio and export–dependence ratio for manufacturing industries, 1975–2006.

industries between 1975 and 2006 (percentage point).[13] Numbers correspond to the industry code presented in Table A1. The industries located above the 45-degree line are the industries that increased the export dependence of employment at a faster pace than the industry's exports (relative to outputs).

Figure 2 shows that a number of industries located above the 45-degree line. This result implies that the export dependence of employment grew faster than the industry's exports in many industries. Note that some industries such as motor vehicle parts and accessories (Code 55) showed increases in the export dependence of employment while holding the export–output ratio constant. The increases in the export dependence are not necessarily attributable to the increases in the volume of the industry's exports.

[13]The export–output ratio is defined as exports divided by gross output.

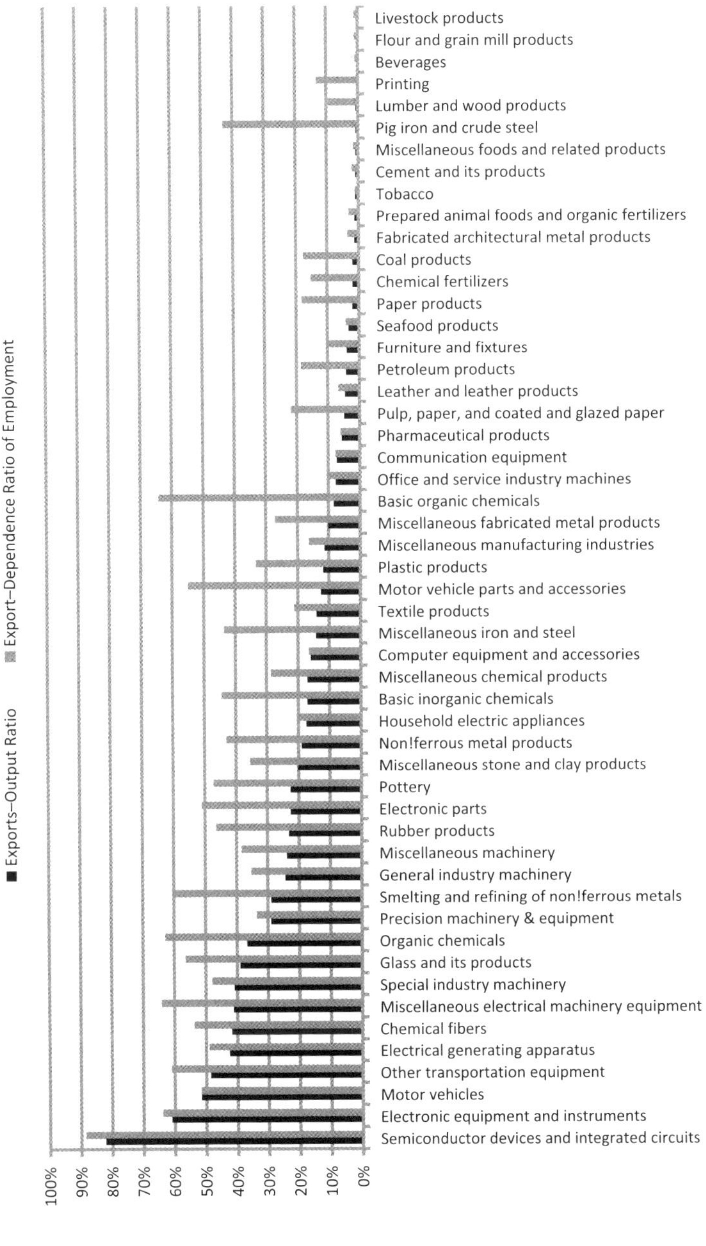

Note: The export–dependence ratio of employment is defined as implied employment from exports divided by the sum of implied employment from domestic final demand and exports. The export–output ratio is defined as exports divided by the gross output.

Source: JIP 2009 Database.

Fig. 3. Export–input ratio and export–dependence ratio of employment in 2006, by manufacturing industry.

Figure 3 presents the export–output ratio and export–dependence ratio of employment in 2006, by manufacturing industry. An important inference from this figure is that the industries with a low export–output ratio do not necessarily have a low export dependence of employment. The gap between the export–output ratio and the export–dependence ratio is notably high in such industries as metal industries (e.g., non-ferrous metals, steels), parts industries (e.g., electronic parts and motor vehicle parts), and chemical industries (e.g., organic chemicals and basic inorganic chemicals).

These results together imply that a less export-oriented industry does not necessarily mean that the industry is free from negative shocks on exports. The industry's export dependence will be large if downstream producers have high export dependence. Producers need to be aware not only of the export dependence of their industry but also of the export dependence of their upstream producers and downstream customers in different industries. Non-exporters can be significantly affected by negative external shocks through intra-industry linkages.

If the Demands from East Asia and the U.S. Decline, Which Industries Are Strongly Affected?

The effects of exports on employment can be different across export destination countries due to the difference in the volume and structure of trade.[14] How much employment is created by the exports to East Asia? If the demands from the U.S. decline, which industries are strongly affected?

To answer these questions, I decompose the export destinations, focusing on five major export partners, including China, NIES, ASEAN4, EU15, and the U.S.[15] In 2006, these destinations accounted for 84.1% of Japan's manufacturing exports. In the JIP 2009 database, a country breakdown is available from 1980 to 2004, and services trade data are not available.[16] This

---

[14]Using the Japanese IO table, Kiyota (2005) showed that the R&D contents of Japanese machinery exports (i.e., R&D spillovers through Japanese machinery exports) toward East and Southeast Asia are different from those toward U.S.

[15]NIES includes Hong Kong, Korea, Singapore, and Taiwan. ASEAN4 includes Indonesia, Malaysia, the Philippines, and Thailand. EU15 includes Austria, Belgium, Denmark, Finland, France, Germany, Greece, Ireland, Italy, Luxembourg, the Netherlands, Portugal, Spain, Sweden, and the United Kingdom.

Table 6. Implied Japanese employment from manufacturing exports, by major partners

	Total	China	NIES	ASEAN4	EU15	U.S.
Number of workers (thousands of persons)						
1980	3,546	132	544	248	536	784
1985	3,161	201	428	134	433	1,126
1990	3,334	65	645	244	684	1,061
1995	4,454	226	1,073	527	719	1,215
2000	4,623	304	1,080	432	753	1,365
2004	4,675	621	1,144	427	669	1,034
Share (total = 100%)						
1980	100	3.7	15.3	7.0	15.1	22.1
1985	100	6.4	13.5	4.3	13.7	35.6
1990	100	1.9	19.4	7.3	20.5	31.8
1995	100	5.1	24.1	11.8	16.1	27.3
2000	100	6.6	23.4	9.3	16.3	29.5
2004	100	13.3	24.5	9.1	14.3	22.1

Note: NIES includes Hong Kong, Korea, Singapore, and Taiwan. ASEAN4 includes Indonesia, Malaysia, the Philippines, and Thailand. EU15 includes Austria, Belgium, Denmark, Finland, France, Germany, Greece, Ireland, Italy, Luxembourg, the Netherlands, Portugal, Spain, Sweden, and the United Kingdom.
Source: JIP 2009 Database.

section thus focuses on Japan's manufacturing exports between 1980 and 2004.

Table 6 presents the implied employment from manufacturing exports, by major export destinations.[17] There are three notable findings in this table. First, Japan's implied employment from exports highly depends on exports to the five major regions. These regions combined accounted for

[16]Precisely, the nominal exports and imports are available at the country-industry level but the real exports and imports are available only at the industry-level in the JIP 2009 database. To obtain the real exports at the country-industry level, this paper first calculated the share of each country of exports from the nominal exports at the industry level and then multiplied the real sectoral exports by the share.

[17]Note that the implied employment in Table 6 is different from the implied employment in Table 2. This is because Table 6 focuses on the implied employment from manufacturing exports while Table 2 focuses on the implied manufacturing employment from total exports.

83.3% of Japan's implied employment from exports in 2004. Besides, the share of China, NIES, and ASEAN4 combined was 46.9% in 2004. These results imply that exports toward East and Southeast Asian countries contribute significantly to Japan's employment.

Second, the relative share of the U.S. to Japan's total implied employment gradually declined after 1985. The share of the U.S. decreased from 35.6% in 1985 to 22.1% in 2004. From 1980 to 2000, the U.S. was the major export destination. In 2004, the share of the U.S. was exceeded by the share of NIES. Finally, the relative share of China shows remarkable growth after 1990. The share of China in Japan's implied employment from exports grew from 1.9% in 1990 to 13.3% in 2004. Although the share of China was still significantly smaller than that of NIES and the U.S., it exceeded that of ASEAN4 and EU15.

Which industries depend on exports to these destinations? Table 7 reports the top 10 industries of implied employment in 2004, by export

Table 7. Implied Japanese employment from manufacturing exports, by major partners and by manufacturing industries in 2004: top 10 industries

	Number of workers (1,000)	Share (%)		Number of workers (1,000)	Share (%)
All countries	4,675	100.0	ASEAN4	427	100.0
1 Motor vehicle parts and accessories	373	8.0	1 Motor vehicle parts and accessories	27	8.0
2 Special industry machinery	265	5.7	2 Semiconductor devices and integrated circuits	23	5.7
3 Electronic parts	221	4.7	3 Special industry machinery	22	4.7
4 Semiconductor devices and integrated circuits	156	3.3	4 Electronic parts	22	3.3
5 Miscellaneous electrical machinery equipment	150	3.2	5 Miscellaneous electrical machinery equipment	20	3.2

(Continued)

Table 7. (*Continued*)

	Number of workers (1,000)	Share (%)		Number of workers (1,000)	Share (%)
6 Plastic products	147	3.2	6 Miscellaneous fabricated metal products	16	3.2
7 General industry machinery	145	3.1	7 General industry machinery	14	3.1
8 Miscellaneous fabricated metal products	140	3.0	8 Plastic products	14	3.0
9 Textile products	132	2.8	9 Miscellaneous iron and steel	12	2.8
10 Motor vehicles	126	2.7	10 Miscellaneous machinery	12	2.7
China	621	100.0	EU15	669	100.0
1 Textile products	52	8.4	1 Motor vehicle parts and accessories	64	8.4
2 Special industry machinery	49	7.9	2 Electronic parts	36	7.9
3 Electronic parts	36	5.7	3 General industry machinery	27	5.7
4 Semiconductor devices and integrated circuits	26	4.2	4 Special industry machinery	26	4.2
5 Miscellaneous electrical machinery equipment	20	3.3	5 Motor vehicles	25	3.3
6 Plastic products	19	3.1	6 Plastic products	19	3.1
7 Motor vehicle parts and accessories	19	3.1	7 Miscellaneous electrical machinery equipment	19	3.1
8 Electrical generating apparatus	18	2.9	8 Miscellaneous fabricated metal products	19	2.9
9 General industry machinery	18	2.9	9 Semiconductor devices and integrated circuits	15	2.9

(*Continued*)

Table 7. (*Continued*)

	Number of workers (1,000)	Share (%)		Number of workers (1,000)	Share (%)
10 Miscellaneous fabricated metal products	17	2.8	10 Household electric appliances	15	2.8
NIES	1,144	100.0	U.S.	1,034	100.0
1 Special industry machinery	91	7.9	1 Motor vehicle parts and accessories	140	7.9
2 Semiconductor devices and integrated circuits	73	6.4	2 Motor vehicles	49	6.4
3 Electronic parts	68	6.0	3 Special industry machinery	48	6.0
4 Miscellaneous electrical machinery equipment	45	3.9	4 Electronic parts	41	3.9
5 Plastic products	44	3.8	5 Miscellaneous fabricated metal products	33	3.8
6 Precision machinery & equipment	33	2.9	6 General industry machinery	32	2.9
7 Miscellaneous fabricated metal products	32	2.8	7 Plastic products	31	2.8
8 Textile products	31	2.7	8 Miscellaneous electrical machinery equipment	29	2.7
9 General industry machinery	30	2.6	9 Miscellaneous machinery	22	2.6
10 Electrical generating apparatus	29	2.5	10 Rubber products	21	2.5

Note: For the regional classification, see Table 6.
Source: JIP 2009 Database.

destinations. Table 7 clearly shows that exports to different destinations have different effects across industries. Exports to the U.S. have significant effects in motor vehicles. Motor vehicle parts and accessories and motor vehicles account for 13.3% of the implied employment from exports to the

U.S. On the other hand, exports to East and Southeast Asia mainly include electronics parts and the textile products industry. Semiconductor devices and electronics parts are within the top four industries in China, NIES, and ASEAN4, whereas semiconductor devices are not ranked within the top ten industries in the U.S. Similarly, the textile products industry is the top industry in China but is not ranked within the top ten industries in the U.S.

These results also show the reason why the motor vehicles industries in Japan were hit severely by the financial turbulence in 2008. The implied employment of motor vehicle parts and accessories and motor vehicles from manufacturing exports is 499,00 workers, 55.6% of which is attributable to the exports to EU15 and the U.S. Because of the high export dependence on EU15 and the U.S., the negative demand shocks on these countries had a strong impact on these industries.

IV. CONCLUDING REMARKS

In light of the growing linkages between exports and employment in Japan, this chapter examined how much employment is created by rising Japanese exports and how the export dependence of employment has changed over the time. Using newly developed Japanese IO table data from 1975 to 2006, both the direct and indirect demand for labor from exports has been estimated.

The results indicate that Japan's employment gradually increased its export dependence over the past three decades. In 2006, approximately 30% of manufacturing employment was created by exports, which is twice as much as it was in 1975. On the other hand, domestic final demand had a negative contribution to the growth of employment in the late 1990s. Moreover, in manufacturing, the negative contribution of domestic final demand had already started in the early 1990s. The high export dependence of employment comes from the increases in exports rather than productivity growth.

The magnitude of the indirect effect is almost the same as that of the direct effect. This means that if an industry's exports create 1,000 jobs in the industry, they also create an additional 1,000 jobs in other industries. Less export-oriented industries sometimes have heavy export dependence of employment through intra-industry linkages with export-oriented industries. These results suggest the importance of intra-industry linkages.

The foregoing results have interesting implications to trade theory and economic policy. It has been shown that not only the direct effect but also the indirect effect is important in understanding how negative external shocks are transmitted to domestic industries. Models without intermediate input sectors do not seem to capture such mechanisms. Theoretical studies need therefore to introduce intra-industry linkages to capture the indirect as well as the direct effects of trade on factor demand.

In identifying the potential risks of negative external shocks, it is important for policy makers to know how much employment is indirectly as well as directly involved in exports. Given that Japan's employment has increased its export dependence since 1985, any policy measures to limit exports will have negative effects on employment. The heavy export dependence has to be considered to be an important vulnerability in the Japanese economy. Sensible risk management would seem to call for some efforts to mitigate negative external shocks. In this connection, the construction of the detailed data is imperative in performing reliable policy studies. Policy makers should recognize the importance of the construction of detailed data.

ACKNOWLEDGMENTS

I wish to thank Katherine Terrell and conference participants at the University of Michigan, Ann Arbor, for their helpful comments on an earlier draft. Financial support from the Center for Global Partnership (CGP), Japan Foundation, and Research Institute of Economy, Trade and Industry (RIETI) is gratefully acknowledged. The usual disclaimer applies.

APPENDIX

Table A1. List of industries in JIP 2009 Database

No.	Industry
1	Rice, wheat production
2	Miscellaneous crop farming
3	Livestock and sericulture farming
4	Agricultural services
5	Forestry
6	Fisheries

(*Continued*)

Table A1. (*Continued*)

No.	Industry
7	Mining
8	Livestock products
9	Seafood products
10	Flour and grain mill products
11	Miscellaneous foods and related products
12	Prepared animal foods and organic fertilizers
13	Beverages
14	Tobacco
15	Textile products
16	Lumber and wood products
17	Furniture and fixtures
18	Pulp, paper, and coated and glazed paper
19	Paper products
20	Printing
21	Leather and leather products
22	Rubber products
23	Chemical fertilizers
24	Basic inorganic chemicals
25	Basic organic chemicals
26	Organic chemicals
27	Chemical fibers
28	Miscellaneous chemical products
29	Pharmaceutical products
30	Petroleum products
31	Coal products
32	Glass and its products
33	Cement and its products
34	Pottery
35	Miscellaneous stone and clay products
36	Pig iron and crude steel
37	Miscellaneous iron and steel
38	Smelting and refining of non-ferrous metals
39	Non-ferrous metal products
40	Fabricated architectural metal products
41	Miscellaneous fabricated metal products
42	General industry machinery
43	Special industry machinery
44	Miscellaneous machinery
45	Office and service industry machines
46	Electrical generating apparatus
47	Household electric appliances

(*Continued*)

Table A1. (*Continued*)

No.	Industry
48	Computer equipment and accessories
49	Communication equipment
50	Electronic equipment and instruments
51	Semiconductor devices and integrated circuits
52	Electronic parts
53	Miscellaneous electrical machinery equipment
54	Motor vehicles
55	Motor vehicle parts and accessories
56	Other transportation equipment
57	Precision machinery & equipment
58	Plastic products
59	Miscellaneous manufacturing industries
60	Construction
61	Civil engineering
62	Electricity
63	Gas, heat supply
64	Waterworks
65	Water supply for industrial use
66	Waste disposal
67	Wholesale
68	Retail
69	Finance
70	Insurance
71	Real estate
72	Housing
73	Railway
74	Road transportation
75	Water transportation
76	Air transportation
77	Other transportation and packing
78	Telegraph and telephone
79	Mail
80	Education (private and non-profit)
81	Research (private)
82	Medical (private)
83	Hygiene (private and non-profit)
84	Other public services
85	Advertising
86	Rental of office equipment and goods
87	Automobile maintenance services
88	Other services for businesses

(*Continued*)

Table A1. (*Continued*)

No.	Industry
89	Entertainment
90	Broadcasting
91	Information services
92	Publishing
93	Video picture and sound information
94	Eating and drinking places
95	Accommodation
96	Laundry, beauty and bath services
97	Other services for individuals
98	Education (public)
99	Research (public)
100	Medical (public)
101	Hygiene (public)
102	Social insurance and social welfare (public)
103	Public administration
104	Medical (non-profit)
105	Social insurance and social welfare (non-profit)
106	Research (non-profit)
107	Other (non-profit)
108	Activities not elsewhere classified

Note: Industries codes 8–59 are classified as manufacturing while the others are classified as non-manufacturing.

REFERENCES

Dekle, Robert (1998). "The Yen and Japanese Manufacturing Employment," *Journal of International Money and Finance*, 17(5): 785–801.

Feenstra, Robert C. and Chang Hong (2007). "China's Exports and Employment," NBER Working Paper No. 13552.

Fukao, Kyoji, Sumio Hamagata, Tomohiko Inui, Keiko Ito, Hyeog Ug Kwon, Tatsuji Makino, Tsutomu Miyagawa, Yasuo Nakanishi, and Joji Tokui (2007). "Estimation Procedures and TFP Analysis of the JIP Database 2006," RIETI Discussion Paper Series 07-E-003.

Hanson, Gordon H., Raymond J. Mataloni, Jr., and Matthew J. Slaughter (2005). "Vertical Production Networks in Multinational Firms." *Review of Economics and Statistics*, 87(4): pp. 664–678.

Kiyota, Kozo (2005). "Services Content of Japanese Trade." *Japan and the World Economy*, 17(3): pp. 261–292.

Kiyota, Kozo, Toshiyuki Matsuura, Shujiro Urata, and Yuhong Wei (2008). "Reconsidering the Backward Vertical Linkage of Foreign Affiliates: Evidence from Japanese Multinationals." *World Development*, 36(8): pp. 1398–1414.

Kiyota, Kozo and Shujiro Urata (2008). "The Role of Multinational Firms in International Trade: The Case of Japan." *Japan and the World Economy*, 20(3): pp. 338–352.

International Monetary Fund (IMF) (2009). *World Economic Outlook: Crisis and Recovery*, April 2009, Washington, D.C.: IMF.

Ministry of Economy, Trade and Industry (METI) (2009). *White Paper on International Economy and Trade 2009*, Tokyo: METI, (In Japanese).

Organisation for Economic Co-operation and Development (OECD) (2009). *OECD Economic Outlook*, 85, June 2009, Paris: OECD.

Sachs, Jeffrey D., Howard J. Shatz, Alan V. Deardorff, and Robert E. Hall (1994). "Trade and Jobs in U.S. Manufacturing." *Brooking Papers on Economic Activity*, 1: pp. 1–84.

Sakurai, Kojiro (2004). "How Does Trade Affect the Labor Market? Evidence from Japanese Manufacturing." *Japan and the World Economy*, 16(2): pp. 139–161.

Sasaki, Hitoshi (2007). "Import Competition and Manufacturing Employment in Japan," Bank of Japan Working Paper Series, No. 07-E-25, Bank of Japan.

Tachibanaki, Toshiaki, Masayuki Morikawa, and Taro Nishimura (1998). "Economic Development in Asian Countries, and the Effect of Trade in Asia on Employment and Wages in Japan." *Asian Economic Journal*, 12(2): pp. 123–151.

Tomiura, Eiichi (2003). "The Impact of Import Competition on Japanese Manufacturing Employment." *Journal of the Japanese and International Economies*, 17(2): pp. 118–133.

Yamashita, Nobuaki and Kyoji Fukao (2008). "The Effects of Overseas Operations on Home Employment of Japanese Multinational Enterprises," Hi-Stat Discussion Paper, No. 251, Hitotsubashi University.

Comment*

Katherine Terrell

In his chapter, Kiyota addresses four important questions: (1) how much employment is created by Japanese exports; (2) the relative size of direct (own industry) and indirect (intra-industry linkages) effects of trade on employment; (3) whether the dependence on exports has changed over time and if so, how is it concentrated in a few industries; and (4) which countries' demand for exports affects Japanese employment the most. Kiyota reaches a number of interesting findings:

- Employment creation through exports grew from 1975 to 2006 (from 6.5% of all employment creation to 9.9%), with the greatest effect is in manufacturing, from 15% to 30%, and not much effect in non-manufacturing, from 4% to 6%. From 1995 to 2006, exports were driving employment growth in both manufacturing and non-manufacturing sectors, when declining demand was causing overall employment to fall.
- The direct versus indirect effects accounted for similar (indirect, slightly higher) shares of employment creation from exports for all industries. But direct demand was driving employment growth in manufactures (58%–66%), whereas indirect demand was more important in non-manufacturing (65%–79%).
- Employment from exports was not increasingly concentrated in a few industries over time. Rather, a large share of industries was increasing their "export dependence."
- With respect to Japan's trading partners and sectors, since 2004 East Asia was the most important, contributing 47% of implied employment from exports in manufacturing, mainly in electronics and textiles.

---

* Editor's Note. Katherine Terrell, Professor of Business Economics and Public Policy at the University of Michigan, died from respiratory complications on December 29, 2009, in the Dominican Republic. She was 59. This comment was prepared by the editor based on the PowerPoint slides that she had prepared for her conference presentation.

U.S. importance declined, contributing 22% of employment (down from 36% in 1985), mainly in the auto industry.

There are some issues involving Kiyota' data and methodology that deserve attention:

- It should be clarified how many IO tables have been used and the extent to which the input coefficients were changing over time.
- Some characteristics of the 56 non-manufacturing industries could be mentioned, especially those in which the indirect employment effects have been especially large. An equation for calculating the indirect effect of exports on employment is also needed.

The section in which increases in export dependence are concentrated in a few industries is not entirely clear. The motivating paragraph asks why findings on the indirect effects are so different between manufactures and non-manufactures. But then, the rest of section deviates from this and asks whether the increase in "export dependence" is growing over time in only a few industries. There is no mention of direct versus indirect effects.

More clarification is needed in addressing what is meant by "export dependence," and why it is an important question? Export dependence $= L^E/(L^E + L^D) = L^E/L$. The analysis could be more to the point:

— Figure 1 plots cumulative (?) distribution of L^E/L.
— Why not simply plot L^E/L for each industry in 1985 on 2006 and draw a 45-degree line to see if they fall above or below?

Further, why should we be concerned that export dependence is correlated with increases in the volume of exports? It is not clear why plotting the export–output ratio and the export–dependency ratio (Figures 2 and 3) is important. The conclusion that follows from the motivating paragraph is interesting:

> "The industry's export dependence will be large if downstream producers have high export dependence. . . . Non-exporters can be significantly affected by negative external shocks through intra-industry linkages."

However, none of the analysis in between seems to address this point. Thus, why not show in which manufacturing and especially non-manufacturing sectors the indirect effect of trade is most important? It would be interesting to know if they are the inputs and services to the electronics and auto industries, or if they are completely different. Finally, there are some possible extensions worth considering:

- With respect to the demand from East Asia and the U.S., it would be interesting to look at the industries with high L^E/L ratios and see to which countries they are exporting — would show which are most vulnerable. Could this analysis be done in terms of the indirect export effect?
- It would also be interesting to carry out the analysis (at least for Tables 2 and 3) for skilled versus unskilled labor. This would be important in relation to questions of income distribution as well as trade theory.

CHAPTER 8

What Determines the Extensive Margin of International Trade? An Investigation of the Cross-Section of U.S. Imports

Peter Debaere[*,†,§] and Shalah Mostashari[‡,¶]

*Darden School of Business University of Virginia, VA, USA
†CEPR, London, UK
‡Tippie College of Business, University of Iowa, IA, USA
§DebaereP@darden.virginia.edu
¶Shalah-mostashari@uiowa.edu; shalah.mostashari@gmail.com

I. INTRODUCTION

This chapter addresses an important dimension of international trade that only recently has been the subject of intense study: the extensive margin of international trade, or the range of goods that different countries export or import to one another. Specifically to be investigated is what determines the cross-sectional variation of the range of goods that the U.S. imports from different countries in different industries, noting which sector characteristics are prone to give way to an expanding extensive margin within a sector, and how these interact with the country characteristics of the exporting country. At this point, these determinants are not very well understood, even though the changing range of goods is quite important. More available varieties through international trade tend to increase consumer welfare. Changing extensive margins may reflect the ever-changing and increasing international division of labor that is often linked to the international fragmentation of the production process. Finally, extensive-margin growth is a non-trivial source of real trade growth.

The extensive margin is a new frontier of international trade research that fits well within the framework of recent trade models developed to address firm and product heterogeneity. Not so long ago, the smallest unit of analysis in international trade was a sector or industry. With ever new and more detailed datasets becoming available, the individual firm and the individual varieties of goods that are traded have attracted more attention.[1] The focus on heterogeneity at the industry and firm level and the changing ranges of goods that countries export have given way to a new set of theoretical questions that the traditional comparative advantage theories and imperfect competition models are hard-pressed to answer. That is, what are the dynamics within a sector? What explains intra-firm trade, and how do we explain the different ways in which firms organize their international production? In return, firm and product heterogeneity have enriched the traditional theories and have made them more general and realistic. Melitz (2003) introduced firm heterogeneity in Krugman's (1980) canonical "new" trade analysis. Complementing this approach, Bernard, Redding, and Schott (2007) have enhanced the traditional Heckscher–Ohlin model with firm heterogeneity; Eaton and Kortum (2002) and Bernard *et al.* (2003) have incorporated heterogeneity into Dornbusch–Fisher–Samuelson's (1977) Ricardian model and, in doing so, have taken the model beyond its two-country framework.

As has been well documented by, among others, Hummels and Klenow (2005), Evenett and Venables (2002), Besedes and Prusa (2003), Kang (2004), and Feenstra and Kee (2004), the range of goods that countries trade varies significantly across sectors, across destination countries, across countries of origin, as well as across time.[2] As Feenstra (1994) and later Broda and Weinstein (2006) have pointed out, this variation poses new challenges for measuring prices, constructing price indices, as well as for accurately assessing welfare gains or losses. The changing extensive margin also matters in the assessment of the impact of trade frictions on trade flows, and the policy prescriptions can be different in case the adjustment is mainly along the intensive or the extensive margin. In addition, a changing extensive margin can introduce a selection bias in estimates of the impact of trade frictions on the volume of trade, which is why Helpman, Melitz, and Rubinstein (2004) introduced a two-step Heckman procedure with a

[1] For a good survey on this issue, see Helpman (2004).

[2] Recent firm-level studies are investigating the changing product mix within and across firms, as in Bernard, Redding, and Schott (2009).

selection equation that explains the extensive margin in their gravity model of countries' bilateral trade.[3]

The variation of the extensive margin also offers an opportunity to begin addressing phenomena that are not well understood, such as the growth of world trade. As Yi (2003) has pointed out, the rapid growth in post-WWII trade coinciding with only moderate tariff reductions presents a quantitative challenge. The elasticities of trade to tariffs that are needed to explain the growth of international transactions are too high relative to what traditional models suggest.[4] In order to address this puzzle, Yi put forward the hypothesis that a changing extensive margin due to international fragmentation of production or vertical specialization, could help reconcile the moderate tariff reductions on the one hand, and the rapid trade expansion on the other. Minor trade liberalizations can have a strong impact on international trade flows when production becomes internationally fragmented as new goods may begin being traded and parts of goods may start to cross borders multiple times.

In previous work, inspired by Yi (2003)'s question, Debaere and Mostashari (2009) used very detailed international trade and tariff data to study the extensive margin of international trade. In particular, in a probit analysis, they investigated the importance of tariffs in explaining whether or not countries exported a good to the U.S.[5] They found that

[3]Felbemayr and Kohler (2006) employ a Tobit model.

[4]For example, Yi (2003) argues a demand elasticity of 10 or more is needed to rationalize world-trade growth in recent decades; Anderson, Balistreri, Fox, and Hillberry (2005) argue that only an elasticity of 17 can match world-bilateral-trade patterns, and Feinberg and Keane (2009) need an elasticity in the range of 25 to 30 to explain the increase of intra-firm trade as a fraction of total sales for Canadian Multinationals between 1983 and 1996. As for the actual elasticity estimates, Broda and Weinstein's (2006) median estimate of the elasticity of substitution is in the order of 3.1; Romalis' (2007) demand elasticities range between 6.2 and 10.9. For further discussion on this issue, see Ruhl (2005).

[5]Work by Ruhl (2005), Kehoe and Ruhl (2002), and Hilberry and McDaniel (2002) documented how the extensive margin of trade tends to increase significantly in the wake of trade liberalizations such as NAFTA. However, these analyses did not include countries that are not directly affected by trade liberalization. Our detailed cross-country analysis revealed that many countries, including those not benefiting from significant trade liberalization by the U.S., experienced significant increases in their extensive margin of trade between 1989 and 1999. This observation already suggested what our econometric results confirmed, which was that tariff reductions are not the alpha and omega of a changing extensive margin. In another study finding similar results, Klenow and Rodriguez-Clare (1997) focus on Costa Rica.

tariffs did matter for the extensive margin. However, from a quantitative perspective, tariffs were only of moderate importance. At best, declining tariffs could explain only about 12% of the increase in the extensive margin of U.S. imports between 1989 and 1999. The analysis suggested that much of the actual change seen in the extensive margin was left to country- and good-specific effects. In this chapter, we want to begin to understand what other factors affect the extensive margin of trade.[6]

In order to investigate the role that sector and country characteristics play in determining the range of goods exported within a sector, we merge U.S. import and production data. We are particularly interested in industry characteristics that suggest a greater inclination toward international fragmentation. Therefore, we employ various measures of an industry's use of intermediate goods and investigate what country characteristics give way to a comparative advantage in intermediate-intensive industries. At the same time, we investigate how these sector-level intermediate-intensity measures interact with measures of institutional quality and trade frictions such as distance and tariffs in determining the extensive margin. Our hypothesis is that goods from sectors that are intermediate intensive will be more sensitive to trade frictions to the extent that some of these inputs are part of an international production process. In other words, if it is the case that some of these intermediate inputs are coming from abroad because they cannot be produced at home, or if it is the case that an intermediate in a sector crosses international borders multiple times before it gets assembled into a final product, then we would expect that the extensive margin in such a sector would be quite sensitive to trade frictions.

To investigate our hypothesis, we use two different measures of intermediate intensity and investigate whether or not these industry characteristics amplify or dampen the effects of trade frictions. The first measure is the share of costs spent on intermediates in total expenditures on labor and intermediates. This measure indicates the relative importance of intermediates relative to labor. The second measure of intermediate intensity that we

[6]From Hummels and Klenow (2005), we know that the size of a country and also its per capita GDP play an important role in determining the range of goods that a country exports or imports. Evenett and Venables (2002) also find that distance matters. Feenstra and Rose (2000) and Xiang (2008) investigate patterns of the extensive margin over time and whether these are consistent with product cycles. These papers, however, do not address what underlying factors drive these patterns.

use is calculated as one minus the Herfindahl index of input concentration, which increases with the number of inputs used in an industry. We find that these two measures capture very different aspects of fragmented industries. The intermediate cost share term addresses the transactions-costs aspects of internationally fragmented production processes since the larger the value of intermediates traded, the greater the potential transportation costs from acquiring intermediates from many foreign countries. The Herfindahl measure, which is related to what we consider the degree of complexity, is potentially more dependent on institutional quality since the need to assemble many different intermediate goods from possibly many different suppliers, poses a greater dependence on contract enforcement. We also include other measures that capture additional costs associated with industries that use many intermediate inputs, such as Nunn's (2007) measure of relationship-specific investment requirements, which are similarly more dependent on high-quality judicial institutions.

Our empirical analysis focuses on the interactions between the sector and country characteristics, and how these affect the extensive margin. Our methodology is similar to that employed by Rajan and Zingales (1998) and Romalis (2004), who were the first to exploit these types of interactions as sources of comparative advantage. Similar approaches have been adopted by Levchenko (2007), Nunn (2007), and Costinot (2009), who investigate the impact of institutions and the contracting environment on the flows and composition of international trade. They have introduced and tested new sources of comparative advantage through the complementary connections between relationship-specific investments at the industry level and the rule of law at the country level, or the complementary relation between the complexity of industries and the quality of a country's institutions or its endowment of human capital.

Our study differs from previous work in two respects. First, we focus on the extensive margin as we want to know to what extent the traditional sources of comparative advantage explain the variation in the range of goods that countries export within a sector. Second, and more importantly, we want to determine which types of sector characteristics, tend to be more prone to respond, along the extensive margin to international trade frictions related to distance and higher tariff rates. It is here that the tenuous but interesting link to international fragmentation of production becomes most pronounced. We find that sectors with a higher intermediate-input intensity and thus with higher potential for international fragmentation of production are more sensitive to trade frictions. In particular, countries that are closer to the U.S. and that benefit from lower trade barriers export a larger share of the goods in industries that are more intermediate intensive.

In what follows, Section II discusses our baseline econometric specification and its extensions. In Section III, we describe the data measures and sources as well as some of the stylized facts related to the data. Section IV proceeds with a discussion of the estimation results before we conclude in Section V.

II. EMPIRICAL MODEL

We first investigate the importance of the traditional sources of comparative advantage on the extensive margin of trade before we extend the model to allow for industries that may be internationally fragmented. We modify the empirical model employed by Rajan and Zingales (1998), Romalis (2004), and others to add a role for intermediate intensity and to apply the model to the extensive margin. As indicated, we are primarily interested in the pattern of trade along the extensive margin, rather than in the actual volume of trade flows. The following regression describes our fairly intuitive starting estimation equation.[7] We relate a measure of country's pattern of extensive margin exports to the U.S. to a set of variables that captures factor intensity and factor costs; variables that measure trade costs with the U.S., such as tariffs; and a full set of country and industry dummies. We also allow for a complementary effect of intermediate intensity and intermediate prices to play a role. Our primary specification is

$$\begin{aligned}\pi_{ic} = \mu_i + \mu_c + \beta_1[\alpha_{i,U}A_{c,U}] + \beta_2[\alpha_{i,S}A_{c,S}] + \beta_3[\alpha_{i,K}A_{c,K}] \\ + \beta_4[\alpha_{i,int}P_c] + \beta_5 \ln(1+\tau_{ic}) + \varepsilon_{ic} \qquad (1)\end{aligned}$$

[7]As a matter of fact, one can directly relate specification (1) to an extended version of the Eaton and Kortum (2003) model with multiple sectors and factors of production. Furthermore, the Pareto distribution that characterizes the productivity draws for all goods *within* a sector would be defined at the sector-country level. Our earlier version of the paper contained such an extension, a variation of which can also be found in Cho (2007) and Mostashari (2007).

where π_{ic} denotes the share of total goods (measured as the number of goods) within an industry i that are exported by country c to the U.S.; μ_i and μ_c denote industry- and country-fixed effects. The term $\alpha_{i,f}$ is a measure of the factor intensity of factor f in industry I, which are assumed to be the same across countries; $A_{c,f}$ is a measure of the factor abundance of factor f in country c. We consider three factors of production in our analysis: unskilled labor (U), skilled labor (S), and capital (K). It is well understood that the interactions between the factor-abundance measures and the intermediate-good-intensity variables, $\alpha_{i,f}A_{c,f}$, proxy for a country's comparative advantage in producing particular types of goods. For example, we expect that a more capital-abundant country, with higher $A_{c,K}$, exports relatively more in capital-intensive sectors, with higher $\alpha_{i,K}$. We therefore expect positive signs for the coefficients β_1, β_2 and β_3 in regression (1). Countries export greater shares of goods in the industries that make intense use of their abundant factors. $\alpha_{i,\text{int}}$ is a measure of intermediate-good intensity, and P_c is a price index of country c that is meant to capture the overall level of prices of intermediate goods.[8] We expect a negative sign on coefficient β_4, such that countries with high intermediate costs will export relatively less in industries that make intensive use of intermediates; τ_{ic} is the U.S. tariff that is imposed on country c for industry i goods. We expect a negative sign for β_5, such that countries export less in industries that are subject to higher tariffs.

Our primary focus is to investigate whether trade frictions pose a greater deterrent to trade along the extensive margin in industries that are more prone to fragmentation than in other industries. To answer this question, we test the significance of the cross-partial effects of trade friction variables interacted with measures of industry fragmentation. Therefore, we extend our baseline regression (1) in the following way:

$$\pi_{ic} = \mu_i + \mu_c + \beta'\tilde{A} + \eta(\mathit{frag}_i\,\mathit{friction}_c) + \varepsilon_{ic} \tag{2}$$

where $\tilde{A}$ includes all previous variables from regression equation (1), frag_i is a measure of the degree of fragmentation in industry i, and $\mathit{friction}_c$ is a measure of the degree of trade frictions between country c and the U.S. If there is a magnified effect of trade frictions in industries characterized

[8]We think of the intermediate commodity as being a composite good assembled from all consumption goods.

by a larger degree of fragmentation, we expect the coefficient η to have a negative sign. As measures of trade friction, we consider a country's distance from the U.S. as well as the U.S. tariff imposed on imports from country c in industry i. We consider two measures of fragmentation. The first is the share of total expenditures on labor and intermediates that go to intermediate goods, thereby indicating the importance of intermediate costs relative to labor. A drawback of this measure is that it does not give a sense of the different stages of production or the number of intermediates that are involved in the production process. We therefore introduce a second measure of intermediate intensity that is derived from the Herfindahl index of the input concentration, denoted H_i where $H_i = \sum_{j=1}^{n} S_{ji}^2$ and S_{ji} stands for the value of input j used in sector i as a fraction of the total value of inputs used in sector i. Since H_i is larger for industries that employ few intermediates, we use the measure $(1 - H_i)$, which lies between zero and one and increases with the number of intermediates used.[9] Another appealing aspect of this measure is that it does not give excessive weight to relatively small components that are used in the production process. We also note that use of a broad range of inputs does not necessarily imply a large intermediate share. Therefore, this measure could be high even for an industry where intermediates make up a relatively small portion of overall costs relative to labor. Moreover, these measures address different aspects of more fragmented industries.

III. DATA

To estimate Equations (1) and (2), we draw from a range of data sources. For U.S. import data we use the U.S. International Trade Commission's *U.S. Imports/Exports (Dataweb)* which records bilateral trade flows for the U.S. at the 10-digit Harmonized Tariff Schedule (HTS10) level. For the trade data, we use the bilateral U.S. imports for 1999. As Pierce and Schott (2009) have documented, there was significant instability in both the U.S. import

[9]The Herfindahl index of input concentration has been used by Clague (1991a,b) as an indicator of how "self-contained" an industry is, which might indicate a reliance on a developed transportation, communication, and distribution infrastructure. Blanchard and Kamer (1997) and Levchenko (2004) use it to measure a good's "complexity" to capture reliance on superior institutions. Nunn (2007) uses it as a measure of the degree of the fragmentation of production.

and export code classifications, which poses a particular challenge when attempting to define a distinct set of goods and to concord these with other more aggregate industry variables coming from different time periods. We therefore focus on manufacturing categories that were consistently defined over the time period from 1989 to 2007, thus omitting goods that have been redefined or reclassified. Our analysis uses 7,324 HTS10 level goods. Using this disaggregate trade data for our sampled countries, we first consider the importance of (net) extensive-margin real trade growth to overall real trade growth.[10] Among all non-restructured countries for which the U.S. did not have any formal trade sanctions, we find that net extensive margin growth accounted for approximately 14% of real growth in exports to the U.S. between 1989 and 1999.[11]

Our tariff data are taken from the U.S. International Trade Commission's *Tariff Database* defined at the eight-digit Harmonized Tariff Schedule (HTS8) level. The database includes the *ad valorem*, specific, and estimated *ad valorem* equivalent tariffs based on the Most Favored Nation (MFN) status. In addition, the file indicates commodities that are eligible for tariff preference programs and the applicable tariffs under these programs. As a measure for tariffs, we use the estimated *ad valorem* equivalent tariff for a particular country applicable under the relevant preference program. If a country/good qualifies for more than one preference program, we use the minimum tariff of all qualifying programs.

We concord the trade and tariff data with the production data of the *Bureau of Economic Analysis* (BEA)'s Input–Output industry classification, so for our analysis a sector i will correspond to one of the BEA's output industries. We measure the total number of goods in a sector i as the total number of HTS10-digit goods categories in that sector. Our left-hand-side

---

[10]We use the Bureau of Labor Statistics import price indices to calculate real trade volumes in 1989 and 1999.

[11]We calculate this measure by the following method. We let z index goods and c index countries exporting to the U.S. d_{11} is an indicator for a good traded in both 1989 and 1999, d_{10} is an indicator for a good traded in 1989 but not 1999, d_{01} is an indicator for a good traded in 1999 but not 1989. $E^c_{z,t}$ are real exports to the U.S. by country c, in industry z, in year t. Then net extensive margin growth's share of real growth in exports to the U.S. between 1989 and 1999 is given by. $\frac{\Delta EM}{\Delta EXPORTS} = \frac{\sum_z \sum_c (d_{01}{}^* E^c_{z,1999}) - \sum_z \sum_i (d_{10}{}^* E^c_{z,1989})}{\sum_z \sum_c [(d_{01}+d_{11})^* E^c_{z,1999} - (d_{10}+d_{11})^* E^c_{z,1989})]}$. This measure tells how much of real trade growth is accounted for by goods not previously traded less trade of those goods that were no longer traded in 1999.

variable, the share of goods coming from a country in a sector, is then the number of HTS10-digit goods exported to the U.S. by that country within the industry over the total number of goods belonging to that industry. In our dataset, we observe all relevant data for 66 countries and 180 industries, which yields a balanced panel of 11,880 observations at the country/industry level for 1999. Table 1 lists the countries that are included in the analysis.

Table 1. Countries included in the analysis

Argentina	Madagascar
Australia	Malawi
Austria	Malaysia
Bangladesh	Malta
Belgium	Mauritius
Bolivia	Mexico
Brazil	Morocco
Cameroon	Netherlands
Canada	New Zealand
Chile	Nigeria
Colombia	Norway
Costa Rica	Pakistan
Denmark	Panama
Ecuador	Papua New Guinea
Egypt	Peru
El Salvador	Philippines
Fiji	Portugal
Finland	Singapore
France	South Africa
Germany	Spain
Ghana	Sri Lanka
Greece	Suriname
Guatemala	Sweden
Honduras	Syrian Arab Republic
Hong Kong	United Republic of Tanzania
Iceland	Thailand
India	Tunisia
Indonesia	Turkey
Ireland	United Kingdom
Italy	Uruguay
Jamaica	Venezuela
Japan	Zambia
South Korea	Zimbabwe

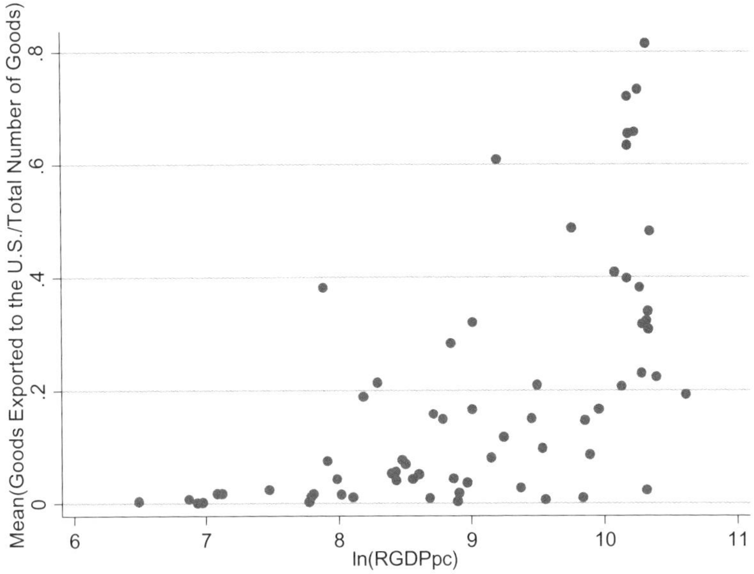

Fig. 1. Average share of # of exported goods versus per capita GDP.

In Figure 1, we plot per exporting country the average (across industries) of the left-hand-side variable against per capita GDP and in Figure 2 against GDP. GDP and per capita GDP are both taken from *Penn World Tables 6.3*. While these relationships will all be subsumed in the country effects in the empirical analysis, the plots do illustrate the consistency of our data with earlier findings reported by Hummels and Klenow (2005). Indeed, more goods are being exported, the higher the exporters' per capita GDP and GDP. In Figure 3, we also plot the average left-hand-side variable for exporting countries against the import tariff that they face in the U.S. Contrary to what one might expect, except for Canada and Mexico, we do not find a strong negative relationship between the extent of the extensive margin of exports and the level of the tariff. Figure 3 suggests that tariffs by themselves cannot play a very strong role in explaining the extensive margin of trade.[12]

To focus our analysis on the sector characteristics and how they interact with country characteristics, we draw on much of the data from Nunn

[12]See Debaere and Mostashari (2009).

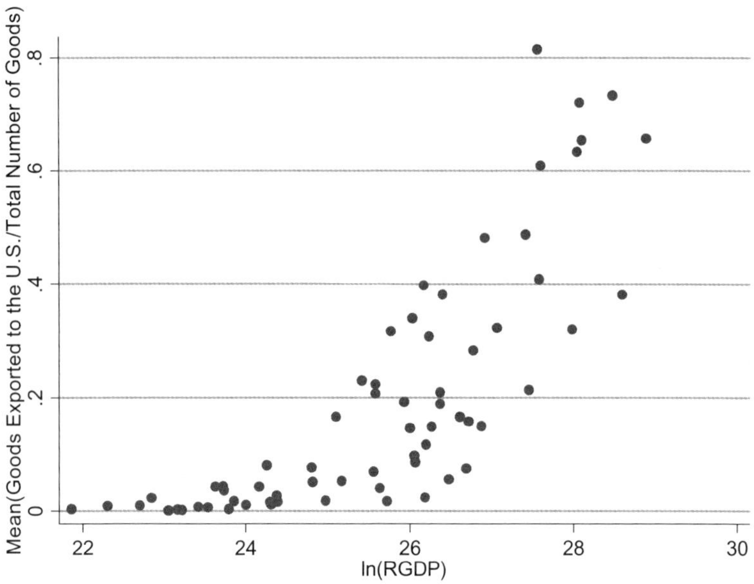

Fig. 2. Average share of # of exported goods versus GDP.

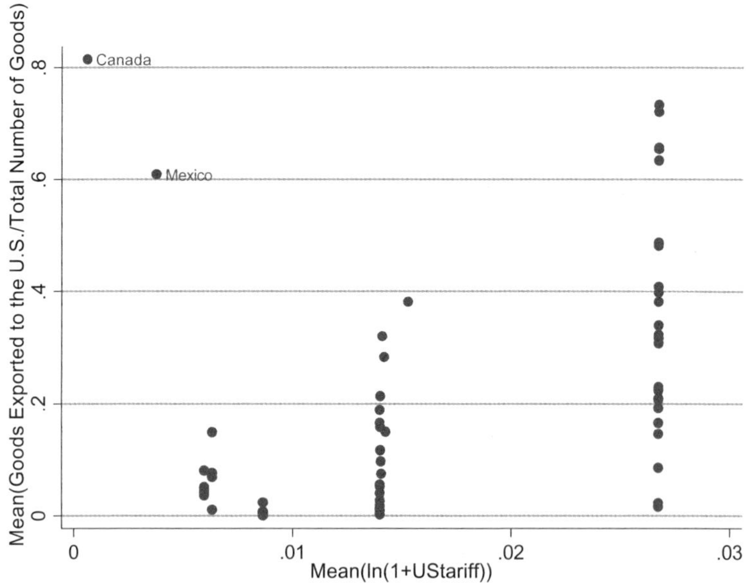

Fig. 3. Average share of # of exported goods versus import tariff.

(2007). In our empirical analysis, we have three main production factors besides intermediates: unskilled labor, skilled labor, and capital. As proxies for a country's factor costs of unskilled labor, skilled labor, and capital, similar to Nunn (2007) and Romalis (2004), we use measures of factor abundance. Making use of Nunn's (2007) data, both human capital stock and the capital stock measures are drawn from Antweiler and Trefler (2002). The human capital stock is the natural log of the ratio of workers completing high school to those not completing high school for 1992. The unskilled labor stock is then the negative of the human capital stock measure, the natural log of the ratio of workers not completing high school to those that did. The capital stock is the natural log of the average capital stock per worker, also for 1992. Because recent papers, including Levchenko (2007), have found institutional quality to be an important source of comparative advantage for industries that are more institutionally dependent, we also take from Nunn's data the measure of the rule of law originally sourced from Kaufmanm, Kraay, and Mastruzzi (2003). For intermediate costs, $P_{\text{int},c}$, we use the natural log of the exporting country's Price Level of GDP also taken from *Penn World Tables 6.3*.

We have two main sources for factor intensity measures: the BEA's 1997 Input–Output Use Tables and the NBER-CES Manufacturing Industry Database by Bartelsman and Gray (1996). We first calculate the share of expenditures on labor and intermediates attributed to intermediate goods from the BEA 1997 Benchmark Input–Output Use Tables. We henceforth refer to this measure as the intermediate cost share in sector i, $\alpha_{i,\text{int}}$. To get measures of skilled and unskilled labor intensity, we first calculate the labor-cost share from the BEA's 1997 Input–Output Use Tables as $1 - \alpha_{i,\text{int}}$. The unskilled labor share is then the share of production wages in total wages, taken from Bartelsman and Gray (1996), also used by Nunn (2007), multiplied by labor's cost share. Similarly, skill intensity is the share of non-production wages in total wages times labor's share. Capital intensity is measured as total real capital stock divided by total value added, also taken from Bartelsman and Gray (1996).

Our measures of fragmentation also come from the BEA 1997 Benchmark Input–Output Use Tables. The first measure is the intermediate cost share described above, $\alpha_{i,\text{int}}$. As one can infer from Figure 4, there is quite a bit of dispersion in intermediate shares around an average of 0.76. Our

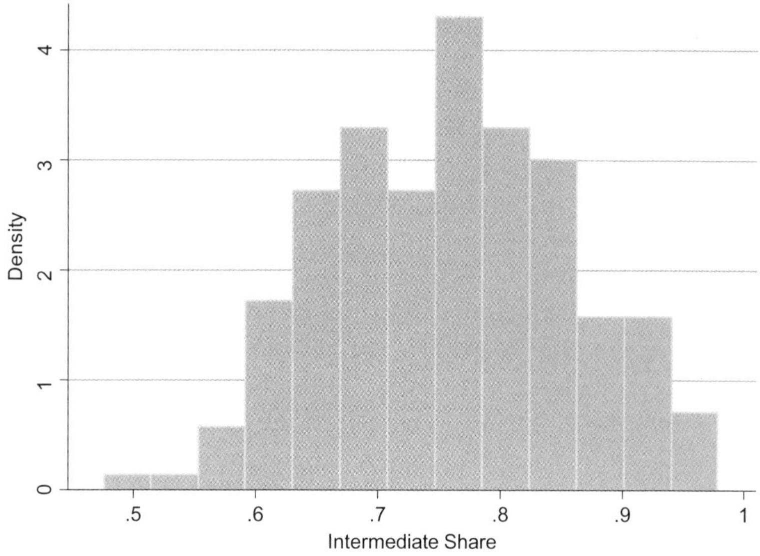

Fig. 4. Distribution of intermediate cost share.

second measure of fragmentation $(1 - H_i)$ has a distribution that is skewed toward higher values as one can see from Figure 5. In our dataset, the average value of $(1 - H_i)$ is 0.89. Since Nunn (2007) considers the well-known Grubel–Lloyd (GL) index of intra-industry trade an indicator of fragmentation, we will also include this measure in our study. We include the histogram of the distribution of the GL index in the lower half of Figure 6.[13] The average value of the GL index in our dataset is 0.67. To give a sense of how the various indices relate to the specific sectors, we list in Table 2 the 20 sectors with, respectively, the lowest and the highest intermediate-cost shares and the corresponding measures of $(1-H_i)$ and the GL index. As one can see, sectors with low intermediate-cost shares tend to have high $(1-H_i)$ measures, and sectors with high intermediate-cost shares tend to have low $(1 - H_i)$ measures. Table 3 shows the correlations of the different measures of intermediate intensity. As one can see, the intermediate-cost share and

[13]The Grubel–Lloyd index for industry i is calculated from U.S. international trade data. The formula for the index is $GL_i = 1 - [|EX_i - IMP_i|| / (EXP_i + IMP_i)]$. The Grubel–Lloyd index increases with the degree of international intra-industry trade. For example, if the sector exports and imports are of equal value, then the GL index is 1.

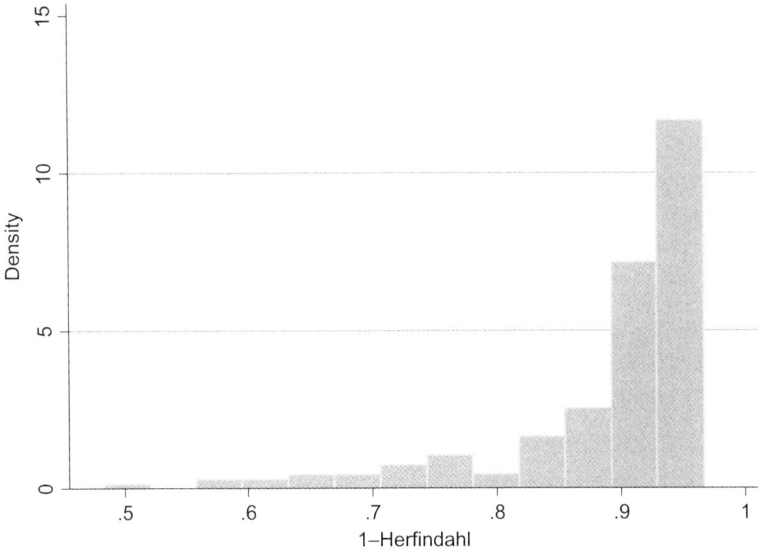

Fig. 5. Distribution of $1-H_i$.

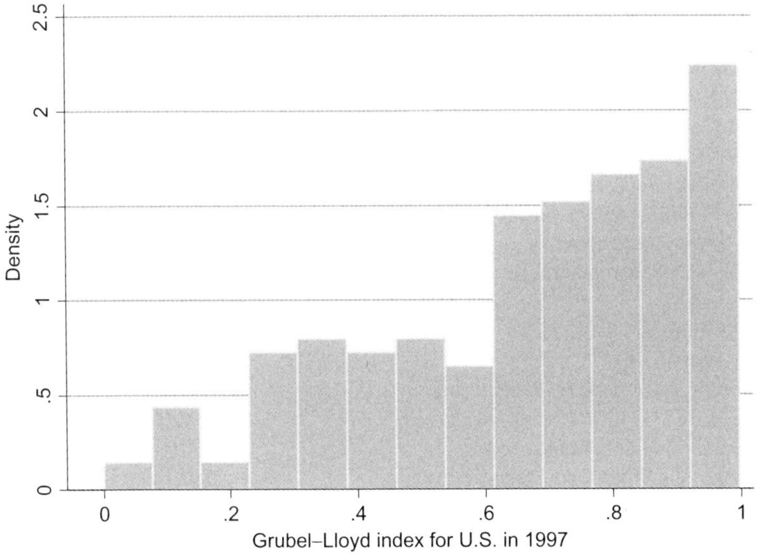

Fig. 6. Distribution of GL.

Table 2. **Industries with the lowest and highest intermediate cost shares**

Industry Description	Intshare	Invherf	GL
Twenty Lowest Intermediate Shares			
Industrial mold manufacturers	0.48	0.94	0.75
Newpaper publishers	0.52	0.92	0.42
Search, detection, & navigation instruments	0.55	0.93	0.75
Vitreous china & earthenware articles manufacturers	0.56	0.93	0.61
Cutting tool & machine tool accessory manufacturers	0.57	0.94	0.98
Turned product & screw, nut, & bolt manufacturers	0.58	0.95	0.87
Small arms manufacturers	0.60	0.95	0.28
Porcelain electrical supply manufacturers	0.60	0.95	0.65
Bread & bakery product, except frozen, manufacturers	0.60	0.95	0.80
Fluid power cylinder & actuator manufacturers	0.60	0.94	0.92
Cut stone & stone product manufacturers	0.61	0.92	0.08
Hand & edge tool manufacturers	0.61	0.94	0.78
Ophthalmic goods manufacturers	0.61	0.94	0.39
Packaging machine manufacturers	0.61	0.95	0.86
Power boiler & heat exchanger manufacturers	0.62	0.94	0.30
Ferrous metal foundaries	0.62	0.96	0.93
Speed changers & mechanical power transmission	0.62	0.94	0.76
Optical instrument & lens manufacturers	0.63	0.95	0.97
Musical instrument manufacturers	0.63	0.90	0.67
Narrow fabric mills & schiffli embroidery	0.63	0.89	0.98
Twenty Highest Intermediate Shares			
Soybean processing	0.98	0.48	0.07
Petroleum refineries	0.97	0.57	0.69
Fats & oils refining & blending	0.94	0.85	0.79
Other oilseed processing	0.94	0.76	0.72
Prim. smelting & refining of copper	0.94	0.59	0.26
Other animal food manufacturers	0.94	0.89	0.30
Cheese manufacturers	0.93	0.73	0.40
Coffee & tea manufacturers	0.93	0.76	0.22
Rice milling	0.93	0.67	0.38
Flour milling	0.92	0.65	0.50
Wet corn milling	0.92	0.73	0.94
Animal, except poultry, slaughtering	0.92	0.65	0.67
Distilleries	0.92	0.86	0.33
Breakfast cereal manufacturers	0.91	0.86	0.77
Automobile & light truck manufacturers	0.91	0.68	0.38
Phosphatic fertilizer manufacturers	0.91	0.91	0.37
Plastics material & resin manufacturers	0.90	0.87	0.64
Nitrogenous fertilizer manufacturers	0.89	0.87	0.00
Soft drink & ice manufacturers	0.89	0.89	0.73
Cigarette manufacturers	0.89	0.88	0.05

Table 3. Correlations among measures of fragmentation

	Intshare	Invherf	GL
Intshare	1		
Invherf	−0.56*	1	
GL	−0.22*	0.20*	1

Correlation coefficients are reported. *Indicates significance at the 1% level

Table 4. Correlations among factor intensity and fragmentation

	Intshare	Invherf	GL
Unskilled intensity	−0.85*	0.43*	0.16*
Skilled intensity	−0.78*	0.50*	0.19*
Capital intensity	0.30*	−0.26*	0.03*
Value added/shipments	−0.67*	0.56*	0.07*

Correlation coefficients are reported. *Indicates significance at the 1% level.

the $(1 - H_i)$ term are indeed negatively correlated, so that a larger share of intermediates in a sector does not necessarily imply that there are more stages or components to the sector. Also, the data show that the $(1 - H_i)$ term tends to be positively correlated with the GL index, which is in line with Nunn (2007).

In Table 4, we produce another set of correlations that help describe the relationships among the input-intensity measures. We show the correlations with the intermediate intensity measures with the other factor-intensity measures and the share of value added in shipments, taken from Bartelsman and Gray (1996). Probably most telling is the very different correlation between our fragmentation measures and the value-added measure. The $(1-H_i)$ term, and to some extent the GL index, correlate positively with value added, which is the exact opposite of our intermediate-cost-share measure. Also the intermediate-cost share correlates positively with the capital intensity, whereas the $(1 - H_i)$ term and GL index correlate negatively with that measure. By construction, the intermediate-cost share is negatively correlated with labor's share and consequently, with unskilled and skilled intensity. The opposite is true for the $(1 - H_i)$ term, which is positively correlated with the labor-share terms. In sum, the intermediate share and the $(1 - H_i)$ appear to identify different characteristics of fragmented goods. While the intermediate share gets at the overall importance of intermediates relative to labor costs, the $(1 - H_i)$ term is an indicator of the complexity of an industry and the degree to which many intermediates must be assembled and coordinated in a good's production.

In our empirical analysis, we interact sector characteristics of intermediate intensity with measures of trade friction such as the U.S. tariffs and the distance from the U.S. Specifically, we interact the intermediate-intensity measures with the natural log of the gross U.S. tariff and the natural log of the distance from the U.S., as measured as the great circle distance between countries' capital cities. As indicated, in a world in which fragmentation of production is increasingly pervasive, we expect these friction variables to have a greater negative impact for those industries that are more prone to international fragmentation of production.

IV. RESULTS

In this section, we discuss the regression results of Tables 5–8. We report standardized beta coefficients in all tables, so that one can directly compare the relative magnitudes of the interaction terms across specifications. Furthermore, all significance levels are reported using robust standard errors.

The results for the baseline regression that are given by Equation (1) are included in the first column of Table 5. As can be seen, all coefficient estimates, except for the interaction between capital intensity and capital abundance, have the expected sign and are significantly different from zero. In other words, we find evidence that supports the traditional patterns of comparative advantage based on factor abundance and factor intensity as relevant determinants of the extensive margin of U.S. imports. We also find that the U.S. tariff term negatively affects the range of goods that are exported in a sector, which is also in line with our expectations. However, the coefficient on tariffs is not significant in all specifications, which in light of our previous work that undermines the quantitative importance of the role played by tariffs in determining the extensive margin of exports is no surprise. Consistent with our expectations, we also find a negative

Table 5. Regression results

	(1)	(2)	(3)	(4)
lnustar	−0.088***	−0.081***	−0.080***	−0.080***
Unskill interaction	0.080***	0.113***	0.110***	0.109***
Skill interaction	0.107***	0.083***	0.081***	0.076***
Capital interaction	−0.098***	−0.092***	−0.085***	−0.113***
Intshare interaction	−0.976***	−0.557***	−0.558***	−0.551***
Intshare_Judicial Quality		−0.539***	−0.440***	−0.431***
(1−Herfindahl)_Judicial Quality			0.231***	
GL_Judicial Quality				0.204***
Country-fixed effects	yes	yes	yes	yes
Industry-fixed effects	yes	yes	yes	yes
R2	0.71	0.71	0.71	0.71
Number of observations	11,880	11,880	11,880	11,880

Standardized beta coefficients are reported.
All regressions conducted with robust standard errors.
***Indicates significance at the 10% level.
**Indicates significance at the 5% level.
*Indicates significance at the 1% level.

coefficient on the interaction of the intermediate share and the price index in the exporting country: Higher price levels make intermediate intensive industries less competitive.

In the next few columns of Table 5, we introduce our measures of intermediate input intensity interacted with a country measure of judicial quality. Introducing these interactions follows Levchenko (2007) and Nunn (2007), who take the quality of a country's institution as a source of comparative advantage. Looking at Columns 2 and 3 in Table 5, it is clear that the $(1 - H_i)$ term and the intermediate cost share are getting at very different characteristics of sectors. Countries with strong institutional quality export relatively more goods in industries that require the coordination of a large number of intermediate industries, which is consistent with the existing literature. However, we find that countries with strong institutional quality export relatively less in the industries that have large intermediate shares, or put another way, they export relatively more in high value added industries. In Column 4, we employ the GL index as a proxy for the $(1 - H_i)$ measure and find a consistent positive and significant sign. The results for the extensive margin of trade in Table 5 are thus to a large extent

Table 6. **Regression results with distance interactions**

	(1)	(2)	(3)	(4)
lnustar	−0.080***	−0.075***	−0.075***	−0.076***
Unskill interaction	0.110***	0.094***	0.094***	0.094***
Skill interaction	0.081***	0.094***	0.094***	0.093***
Capital interaction	−0.085***	−0.084***	−0.085***	−0.085***
Intshare interaction	−0.558***	−0.688***	−0.688***	−0.688***
Intshare_Judicial Quality	−0.440***	−0.328***	−0.327***	−0.328***
(1−Herfindahl)_Judicial Quality	0.231***	0.232***	0.234***	0.232***
Intshare × ln(distance)		−0.449***	−0.394***	−0.465***
(1−Herfindahl) × ln(distance)			0.103	
GL × ln(distance)				−0.071
Country-fixed effects	yes	yes	yes	yes
Industry-fixed effects	yes	yes	yes	yes
R2	0.71	0.71	0.71	0.71
Observations	11,880	11,880	11,880	11,880

Standardized beta coefficients are reported.
All regressions conducted with robust standard errors.
***Indicates significance at the 10% level.
**Indicates significance at the 5% level.
*Indicates significance at the 1% level.

in line with what the existing empirical literature finds on international trade along the intensive margin of trade.

In Table 6, we turn to what is the primary focus of our analysis. We introduce the interactions between the measures of fragmentation and the distance between the exporting country and the U.S. A few striking results stand out. In Column 1, we take our baseline regression with the basic determinants of comparative advantage, including those relating intermediate intensity to the rule of law that we introduced in Column 3 of Table 5. In Column 2, we add the interaction of bilateral distance to the U.S. and our intermediate-cost-share measure. As one can see, we obtain a negative and significant coefficient for this variable. We interpret this negative coefficient as an indication that closer countries export larger shares of goods that are more intermediate intensive, which suggests an additional sensitivity to trade frictions particular to these types of goods. Note that when we include the interactions between the $(1 - H_i)$ term and the GL index with distance in Columns 3 and 4, we do not observe significant coefficients.

Table 7. **Regression results with distance and tariff interactions**

	(1)	(2)	(3)	(4)
lnustar	−0.075***	0.080	0.455*	0.034
Unskill interaction	0.094***	0.096***	0.096***	0.097***
Skill interaction	0.094***	0.094***	0.095***	0.094***
Capital interaction	−0.085***	−0.085***	−0.085***	−0.086***
Intshare interaction	−0.688***	−0.650***	−0.644***	−0.645***
Intshare_Judicial Quality	−0.327***	−0.318***	−0.296***	−0.322***
(1−Herfindahl)_Judicial Quality	0.234***	0.233***	0.287***	0.220***
Intshare × ln(distance)	−0.394***	−0.347***	−0.322***	−0.347***
(1−Herfindahl) × ln(distance)	0.103	0.096	0.146	0.082
Intshare × lnustariff		−0.156	−0.281**	−0.169
(1−Herfindahl) × lnustariff			−0.254*	
GL × lnustariff				0.059**
Country-fixed effects	yes	yes	yes	yes
Industry-fixed effects	yes	yes	yes	yes
R2	0.71	0.71	0.71	0.71
Observations	11,880	11,880	11,880	11,880

Standardized beta coefficients are reported.
All regressions conducted with robust standard errors.
***Indicates significance at the 10% level.
**Indicates significance at the 5% level.
*Indicates significance at the 1% level.

In Table 7, we introduce the interaction of the intermediate-intensity measures with the U.S. import tariff as another trade friction. We only find the interaction between U.S. tariffs and intermediate-cost shares significant when we also control for the $(1 - H_i)$ term. Both interactions imply that countries with higher tariffs tend to export a greater share of goods in less fragmented industries. However, when we include the GL measure as a proxy for the $(1 - H_i)$ term, we get an unexpected positive coefficient, suggesting that countries with higher trade barriers tend to export a larger share of goods in industries characterized by greater intra-industry trade.

To extend the analysis of the intermediate intensity and to see how robust our results are, we also use Nunn's (2007) interaction of rule of law with his index that increases with the investment specificity of intermediate inputs and indicates a greater dependence on institutional quality. Nunn's measure combines U.S. Input–Output tables with Rauch's classification of goods into three different types: those that are traded on exchanges, those that are referenced priced and, finally, those that are neither. This is a valuable measure for us, to the extent that it characterizes in greater detail the intensity of the relationship specific investments needed to acquire intermediate goods. In particular, Nunn specifies the fraction of the inputs in a sector that are not traded on exchanges or that are not referenced priced, as a measure for the investment intensity of an industry. In particular, for sector i, $Z_i = \sum_j \theta_{ji} R_{ji}$, with θ_{ij} indicates the value of input j used industry i, and R_{ji} is the proportion of input j that is neither sold on an organized exchange nor referenced priced. Z_i then increases with the investment specificity of intermediate inputs and indicates a greater dependence on institutional quality. We follow Nunn and include this measure interacted with institutional quality since this may be an important source of comparative advantage for industries that are intermediate intensive. In Table 8 we include

Table 8. Regression results with distance, tariff, and judicial quality interactions

	(1)
lnustar	0.410*
Unskill interaction	0.060***
Skill interaction	0.070***
Capital interaction	−0.009
Intshare interaction	−0.637***
Intshare_Judicial Quality	−0.183***
(1−Herfindahl)_Judicial Quality	0.158**
Intshare × ln(distance)	−0.336***
(1−Herfindahl) × ln(distance)	0.129
Intshare × lnustariff	−0.254*
(1−Herfindahl) × lnustariff	−0.21
Judicial Quality Interaction	0.250***
Country-fixed effects	yes
Industry-fixed effects	yes
R2	0.71
Observations	11,880

Standardized beta coefficients are reported.
All regressions conducted with robust standard errors.
***Indicates significance at the 10% level.
**Indicates significance at the 5% level.
*Indicates significance at the 1% level.

this measure of relation-specific investments interacted with rule of law. In line with studies of international trade patterns along the intensive margin, countries with stronger institutions tend to export more in the sectors requiring more specific investment relationships to acquire intermediate goods. In addition, we still find a negative and significant coefficient of the intermediate-cost share interacted with the trade friction variables and no significance of the interaction of the trade friction variables with the $(1-H_i)$ term. One possible interpretation of this result is that production of goods that are more complex and more reliant on a secure contracting environment is less likely to be fragmented internationally, such that distance does not have a magnified effect for these industries. Also, the interactions of the cost-share terms and trade frictions are quantitatively larger than the labor and capital interactions combined. Consistent across all specifications in Tables 5 through 8, we find that the interaction that is most quantitatively important is that of the price index and the intermediate-share variable. In particular, going by the final specification, a one standard deviation increase in this term decreases the share of the number of goods that a country exports in an industry by 0.637 standard deviations.

V. CONCLUSION

"International fragmentation of production," "slicing the value chain," and "off-shoring" are all terms that refer to an increasingly internationalized production process that has received growing attention in the academic literature as well as in the press. However, to evaluate international fragmentation empirically is a challenge when one is not able to observe which traded goods are actually intermediates and which are finals. In this chapter, we therefore have taken an indirect approach. We relate industry characteristics of the intermediate intensity of a sector to the range of 10-digit goods that are traded within that sector. On the one hand, we find that the interactions between a sector's factor intensities and the factor abundances of the exporting countries reveal that the regular comparative advantage factors also determine the extensive margin within a sector. More importantly, we find that countries that are closer to the U.S. as well as countries that are benefiting from lower U.S. tariffs tend to export greater shares of goods in sectors with larger intermediate shares. This finding is consistent with the interpretation that, because of international fragmentation of production in these sectors, international trade in these sectors is more sensitive to trade frictions. Note that we do not find a significant complementary effect of trade frictions for sectors with more intermediate components, as measured by one minus the Herfindahl index of input concentration, which corresponds to sectors that tend to rely more on better institutional quality.

REFERENCES

Anderson, M. A., Balistreri, E. J., Fox, A. K. and R. H. Hillberry (2005). "Taste Parameters as Model Residuals: Assessing the 'Fit' of an Armington Trade Model." *Review of International Economics*, 13(5): pp. 973–984.

Antweiler, W. and D. Trefler (2002). "Increasing Returns to Scale and All That: A View From Trade." *American Economic Review*, 92: pp. 93–119.

Bernard, A., J. Eaton, J. B. Jensen and S. Kortum (2003). "Plants and Productivity in International Trade." *American Economic Review*, 93: pp. 1268–1290.

Bernard, A., S. Redding and P. Schott (2010). "Multiple-Product Firms and Product Switching." *American Economic Review*, 100(1): pp. 70–97.

Bernard, A., S. Redding and P. Schott (2007). "Comparative Advantage and Heterogeneous Firms." *Review of Economic Studies*, 74: pp. 31–66.

Besedes, T. and T. Prusa (2003). On the Duration of Trade. NBER Working Paper 9936.

Blanchard, Olivier and Michael Kremer (1997). "Disorganization." *Quarterly Journal of Economics*, 112: pp. 1091–1126.

Broda, C. and D. Weinstein (2006). "Globalization and the Gains from Variety." *Quarterly Journal of Economics*, 121: pp. 541–585.

Cho, D. (2007). "Unpacking the Sources of Comparative Advantage," Working Paper. Hong Kong Management University.

Clague, C. (1991a). "Factor Proportions, Relative Efficiency and Developing Countries' Trade." *Journal of Development Economics*, 35: pp. 357–380.

Clague, C. (1991b). "Relative Efficiency, Self-Containment, and Comparative Costs of Less Developed Countries." *Economic Development and Cultural Change*, 39: pp. 507–530.

Costinot, A. (2009). "On the Origins of Comparative Advantage." *Journal of International Economics*, 77: pp. 255–264.

Debaere, P. and S. Mostashari (2010). "Do Tariffs Matter for the Extensive Margin of Trade? An Empirical Analysis." *Journal of International Economics*, 81: pp. 163–169.

Dornbusch, R., S. Fischer and P. Samuelson (1977). "Comparative Advantage, Trade, and Payments in a Ricardian Model with a Continuum of Goods." *Quarterly Journal of Economics*, 95: pp. 203–224.

Eaton, J. and S. Kortum, (2003). "Technology, Geography and Trade." *Econometrica*, 70: pp. 1741–1780.

Evenett, S. and A. J. Venables, (2002). "Export Growth in Developing Countries: Market Entry and Bilateral Trade." Working Paper, London School of Economics.

Feenstra, R. (1994). "New Product Varieties and the Measurement of International Prices." *American Economic Review*, 84: pp. 157–177.

Feenstra, R. C. and H. Kee (2004). "Export Variety and Country Productivity," NBER Working Paper 10830.

Feenstra, R. C., J. Romalis and P. Schott (2002). "U.S. Imports, Exports and Tariff Data, 1989–2001," NBER Working Paper 9387.

Feinberg, S. E. and M. P. Keane (2009). "Tariff effects on MNC decisions to engage in intra-firm and arm' s-length trade." *Canadian Journal of Economics*, 42(3): pp. 900–929.

Felbemayr, G. and W. Kohler (2006). "Exploring the Intensive and Extensive Margins of World Trade." *Review of World Economics*, 127(4): pp. 642–674.

Helpman, E., M. Melitz and Y. Rubinstein (2004). "Trading Partners and Trading Volumes," Working Paper Harvard–Tel Aviv.

Heston A., R. Summers and B. Aten, Penn World Table Version 6.3, Center for International Comparisons of Production, Income and Prices at the University of Pennsylvania, August 2009.

Hilberry, R. and C. McDaniel (2002). "A Decomposition of North American Trade Growth since NAFTA," ITC Working Paper.

Hummels, D. and P. Klenow (2005). "The Variety and Quality of a Nation's Exports." *American Economic Review*, 95: pp. 704–723.

Levchenko, Andrei (2007). "Institutional Quality and International Trade." *Review of Economic Studies*, 74(3): pp. 791–819.

Kang, K. (2004). "The Path of the Extensive Margin (Export Variety), Theory and Evidence," Working Paper, University of California, Davis.

Kaufmann, A. Kraay and M. Mastruzzi (2003). "Governance Matters III: Governance Indicators for 1996–2002," World Bank Research Paper 3106.

Kehoe, T. and K. Ruhl (2002). "How Important is the New Goods Margin in International Trade? University of Minnesota and the Federal Reserve Bank of Minnesota Staff Report No. 324.

Klenow, P. and A. Rodriquez-Clare (1997). "Quantifying Variety Gains from Trade Liberalization," Working Paper.

Krugman, P. (1980). "Scale Economies, Product Differentiation and the Pattern of Trade." *American Economic Review*, 70: pp. 950–959.

Melitz, M. (2003). "The Impact of Trade on Intra-Industry Reallocations and Aggregate Industry Productivity." *Econometrica*, 71: pp. 1695–1725.

Mostashari, S. (2007). "The Contribution of Tariff Policy under Vertical Specialization to U.S. Import Growth between 1989 and 1999," Working Paper, University of Texas, Austin.

Nunn, Nathan (2007). "Relationship-Specificity, Incomplete Contracts and the Pattern of Trade." *Quarterly Journal of Economics*, 122(2): pp. 569–600.

Pierce, J. and P. Schott (2009). "Concording U.S. Harmonized System Categories over Time. 1989 to 2006," Yale School of Management (mimeo).

Rajan, Raghuram and Luigi Zingales (1998). "Financial Dependence and Growth." *American Economic Review*, 88(3): pp. 559–586.

Romalis, J. (2004). "Factor Proportions and the Structure of Commodity Trade." *American Economic Review*, 94(1): pp. 67–97.

Romalis, J. (2007). "NAFTA's and CUSFTA's Impact on International Trade." *Review of Economics and Statistics*, 89(3): pp. 416–435.

Ruhl, K. (2005). "The Elasticity Puzzle in International Economics," Working Paper University of Texas, Austin.

Xiang, Chong, (2008). "How long are Product Cycles?" Working paper, Purdue University.

Yi, K. (2003). "Can Vertical Specialization Explain the Growth of World Trade?" *Journal of Political Economy*, 111: pp. 52–102.

Comment

Andrei A. Levchenko

I. INTRODUCTION

The so-called "extensive margin" has received a great deal of attention in the international trade literature. The remarkably fruitful interaction of groundbreaking theory (exemplified by Melitz, 2003), and equally important empirical work (surveyed by Bernard *et al.*, 2007) has transformed our understanding of the role of firms in international trade. Naturally, when the unit of analysis is the firm, a great deal of attention in both theory and empirics has been devoted to the firm's decision to enter the export market — the extensive margin.

Having developed a comprehensive set of stylized facts on the extensive margin, a natural next question is, what are its determinants? This is a potentially important direction of research for two related reasons. First, we know almost nothing about the determinants of the extensive margin beyond the role of country size and distance (see, e.g., Eaton, Kortum, and Kramarz, 2008). And second, the extensive margin — for instance, the number of product varieties that a country imports — may have an important impact on welfare. Thus, examining the determinants of the extensive margin in a cross-section of countries can — down the road — lead us to a better understanding of some very important issues, such as the role of trade in economic development, as well as the three-way interactions among trade, institutions, and growth.

The chapter by Peter Debaere and Shalah Mostashari is a welcome step in that direction. Using an estimating equation derived from a multi-sector version of the Eaton–Kortum model, they demonstrate that countries with better institutions tend to export more product categories in sectors that have (i) lower intermediate use intensity and (ii) higher product complexity.

I will concentrate my comments in two areas. The first will focus on disentangling the role of institutions for the extensive margin vs. the overall trade volumes. The second will argue that in spite of the large amount of empirical and theoretical work in this area, we do not yet have a good grasp of whether, and how, the extensive margin of trade has an appreciable impact on welfare.

II. EXTENSIVE MARGIN VERSUS TRADE VOLUMES

The paper's main estimating equation has the form:

$$\pi^{i}_{US,c} = \alpha + \beta INST_c \times HERF_i + \gamma X_{ic} + \delta_i + \delta_c + \varepsilon_{ic} \qquad (1)$$

where i indexes industries, c countries, and $\pi^{i}_{US,c}$ is the share of finely disaggregated product categories in industry i that are imported from country c in the total number of products that the U.S. imports in industry i — country c's extensive margin in industry i. One of the main coefficients of interest is the interaction of the country's institutional quality, $INST_c$, with industry i's complexity, measured by the Herfindahl index of intermediate input shares, $HERF_i$.

In some of my own earlier work (Levchenko, 2007), I estimated a specification with nearly identical right-hand-side variables, but with the overall trade shares as the dependent variable:

$$\frac{M^{i}_{US,c}}{M^{i}_{US}} = \alpha + \beta INST_c \times HERF_i + \gamma X_{ic} + \delta_i + \delta_c + \varepsilon_{ic} \qquad (2)$$

where now $\frac{M^{i}_{US,c}}{M^{i}_{US}}$ is the import volume in sector i coming from country c as a share of total U.S. imports in sector i. This type of empirical specification, with import volume shares on the left-hand-side and explanatory variables that are interactions of country characteristics and sector characteristics is in fact quite common in the recent trade literature (see, among many others, Romalis, 2004; Nunn, 2007; Costinot, 2009; and Chor, 2009) for the variety of explanatory variables that have been used in this context). I am singling out my own work simply because one of the main right-hand-side variables of interest is identical to my paper, which helps make my point more precise.

I see two potential issues that Equation (2) raises for interpreting Equation (1). Econometrically, my earlier result that institutions affect trade volumes implies that there is an omitted variables problem. The paper's estimates could simply be driven by a mechanical correlation between the overall trade volumes and the number of product categories as recorded in the trade data. We must therefore sort out the impact of institutions on the extensive margin as distinct from its impact on the total trade volumes. One way to proceed would be to control for $\frac{M^i_{US,c}}{M^i_{US}}$ directly in estimation, although I suspect that the trade share is extremely highly correlated with $\pi^i_{US,c}$, making inference about the other coefficients unreliable.

Conceptually, it is important to sort out what is different about the extensive margin, holding the amount of trade constant. Indeed, the Eaton–Kortum framework adopted by this paper implies that trade shares and the extensive margin are exactly equal: $\pi^i_{US,c} = \frac{M^i_{US,c}}{M^i_{US}}$. This is the famous Eaton–Kortum result that the share of product categories and the share of trade volumes are not identified separately. As we can see, the theory adopted by the authors is not helpful for sorting out this issue. Looking beyond their theoretical framework, we must come to grips with the question of why it matters whether the country exports, say, \$100 in one product category, rather than \$1 in 100 different product categories.

III. EXTENSIVE MARGIN AND WELFARE IN HETEROGENEOUS FIRMS MODELS

Why do we care about the extensive margin? There are two important potential reasons. The first is consumers' gain from "love for variety" (Broda and Weinstein, 2006). The other source of gain receiving more attention recently is that a greater range of (imported) intermediate inputs increases productivity (see, among others, Amiti and Koenings, 2007; Kahasara and Rodrigue, 2008).

Indeed, there appears to be a strong positive correlation between the number of goods a country imports and per capita income. The solid dots in Figure C1 display the scatterplot of the (log) total number of 4-digit SITC product categories that a country imports (left scale), against the log PPP-adjusted per capita income on the x-axis. There is substantial variation in

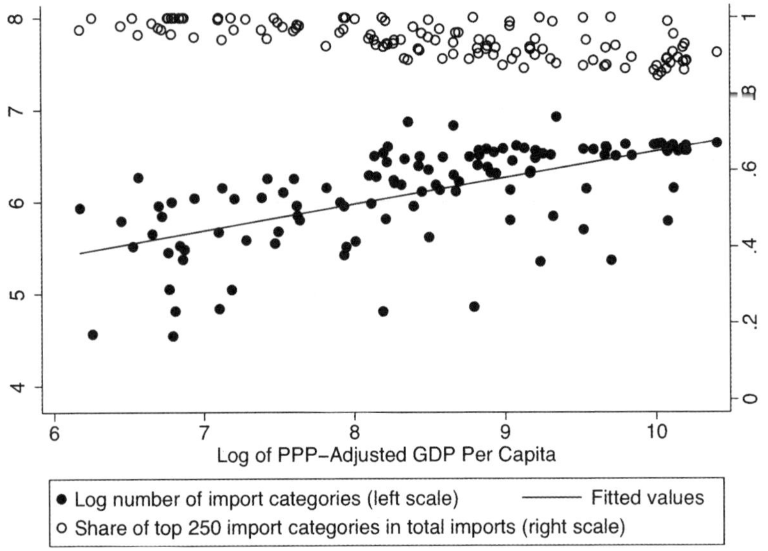

Note: The solid dots (left scale) display the log number of four-digit SITC product categories imported by an individual country over the period 1991–2000 against log PPP-adjusted per capita income, along with an OLS fit. The hollow dots (right scale) display the percentage of total import volume accounted for by the top 250 four-digit STIC categories.

Fig. C1. Imported varieties and per capita income.

the extensive margin of imports: the country in the 90th percentile imports about 750 product categories, compared to about 250 for a country in the 10th percentile. The positive relationship between the number of product categories and per capita income, depicted by the least-squares fit through the data, is indeed highly statistically significant.

However, in order to evaluate the welfare impact of the extensive margin of trade, we need a model. di Giovanni and Levchenko (2009) build and calibrate a multi-country model of international trade with heterogeneous firms in the spirit of Melitz (2003) and Eaton, Kortum, and Kramarz (2008), and compute the impact of increasing import varieties on welfare. The results are striking. The extensive margin of imports is responsible for only 3.5% of the total welfare gains from a 10% reduction in trade barriers. The overwhelming majority of the gains from a fall in trade costs is due to the intensive margin: existing firms selling more at lower prices. This is in spite of the fact that the extensive margin itself, as it would be measured in the data, is very large: there is an average 28% increase in the number of imported varieties.

What is the intuition for this result? The model is calibrated to the observed distribution of firm size, the so-called Zipf's Law (Axtell, 2001). It turns out that in the data, the distribution of firm size is extremely fat-tailed: the economy is dominated by a few very large firms. The distribution of firm size in turn contains information about the relative importance of the inframarginal firms relative to the marginal ones. In particular, Zipf's Law implies that the inframarginal, large firms are vastly more important for welfare than the much smaller firms that will drive the changes on the extensive margin of trade. The calibrated model makes this idea more precise, by using the observed distribution of firm size to discipline the quantitative exercise.

These results suggest that the marginal varieties are small, and therefore unimportant for welfare. As an illustration of this idea, the hollow dots in Figure C1 depict the share of the top 250 four-digit SITC categories in total imports for each country (right scale). As mentioned above, the country in the 10th percentile of the distribution of import categories imports in about 250 SITC sectors. Thus, we take the 250 largest sectors in each country, and compute the share of total imports captured by those sectors. On average in this sample of countries, the top 250 categories are responsible for more than 90% of the total exports. The minimum value in this sample of more than 100 countries is 84%. This indeed suggests that beyond some relatively low number of import categories, additional import sectors contribute very little to the overall imports, and presumably to the overall welfare as well.

IV. CONCLUSION

Though the extensive margin has been the focus of large amount of research in recent years, a great deal about it remains unknown, both empirically and theoretically. As I argued in this comment, on the theory side we have not yet come to grips with whether, and how much, the extensive margin really matters for welfare. Empirically, very little is known about the determinants of the extensive margin, beyond country size and distance. The authors demonstrate that institutions matter for the extensive margin as well, providing a welcome addition to the literature.

REFERENCES

Amiti, Mary and Jozef Konings (2007). "Trade Liberalization, Intermediate Inputs, and Productivity." *American Economic Review*, 97(5): pp. 1611–1638.

Axtell, Robert L. (2001). "Zipf Distribution of U.S. Firm Sizes." *Science*, 293(5536): pp. 1818–1820.

Bernard, Andrew, J. Bradford Jensen, Stephen Redding, and Peter Schott (2007). "Firms in International Trade." *Journal of Economic Perspectives*, 21: pp. 105–130.

Broda, Christian and David Weinstein (2006). "Globalization and the Gains from Variety." *Quarterly Journal of Economics*, 121(2): pp. 541–85.

Chor, Davin (2009). "Unpacking Sources of Comparative Advantage: A Quantitative Approach," Singapore Management University (mimeo).

Costinot, Arnaud (2009). "On the Origins of Comparative Advantage." *Journal of International Economics*, 77(2): pp. 255–264.

di Giovanni, Julian, and Andrei A. Levchenko (2009). "Firm Entry, Trade, and Welfare in Zipf's World," RSIE Discussion Paper 591.

Eaton, Jonathan, Samuel Kortum, and Francis Kramarz (2008). "An Anatomy of International Trade: Evidence from French Firms," NBER Working Paper No. 14610.

Kasahara, Hiroyuki and Joel Rodrigue (2008). "Does the Use of Imported Intermediates Increase Productivity? Plant-level Evidence." *Journal of Development Economics*, 87: pp. 106–118.

Levchenko, Andrei A. (2007). "Institutional Quality and International Trade." *Review of Economic Studies*, 74(3): pp. 791–819.

Melitz, Marc J. (2003). "The Impact of Trade on Intra-Industry Reallocations and Aggregate Industry Productivity." *Econometrica*, 71(6): pp. 1695–1725.

Nunn, Nathan (2007). "Relationship-Specificity, Incomplete Contracts and the Pattern of Trade." *Quarterly Journal of Economics*, 122: pp. 569–600.

Romalis, John (2004). "Factor Proportions and the Structure of Commodity Trade." *American Economic Review*, 94: pp. 67–97.

CHAPTER 9

Modes of East Asian Trade and Foreign Direct Investment: U.S. and Japan

K. C. Fung*, Hitomi Iizaka†, and Alan Siu‡

*University of California, Santa Cruz, CA 95064, USA
†Aoyama Gakuin University, Tokyo, Japan
‡APEC Study Centre, University of Hong Kong, Hong Kong

I. INTRODUCTION

East Asia[1] has experienced a substantial increase in the extent of intra-regional trade during the past 20 years. An important development that has added to the expansion of East Asian trade has been identified as international production fragmentation, where the production process of a final product is split into several steps and each production stage is undertaken in different countries or locations. Many alternative names have been given for such a phenomenon, including "slicing the value chain" (Krugman, 1995), "vertical specialization" (Hummels, Ishii, and Yi, 2001; Dean, Fung, and Wang, 2008), "international production sharing" (Ng and Yeats, 2001), production fragmentation (Athukorala, 2006) and "outsourcing" (Hanson *et al.*, 2001). There is increasing evidence of the large increase in international fragmentation of production around the world in a variety of sectors, including textiles and apparel, automobiles, consumer electronics, toys, and furniture. The extent of international production fragmentation and the depth of the production networks, however, vary according to industries and geographic regions (Fung, Garcia-Herrero, and Siu, 2009; Aminian, Fung, and Ng, 2009). As pointed out by Hiratsuka (2008), international production fragmentation in industries such as clothing involves

[1] In this study, East Asia covers the following countries/regions: China, Taiwan, Hong Kong, Japan, Republic of Korea, Indonesia, the Philippines, Malaysia, Singapore, and Thailand.

a relatively simple disintegration of procurement and production. In contrast, a much more sophisticated and well-developed production network exists in electronics and computer-related industries.

It has often been suggested that multinational enterprises (MNEs) or foreign direct investment (FDI) play a very important role in creating and coordinating the activities of production networks. MNEs can combine many resources available at different locations across national borders while they establish their production networks. In East Asia, the rapid growth of intra-regional trade has also been associated with a rising amount of FDI. Partly because of this, East Asia (excluding Japan) has gained in importance as recipients of FDI over time. Recent improvements in service links which lead to lower transportation and communication costs as well as progressive liberalizations and deregulations of international trade and FDI in the region also contribute to this trend. In addition, production networks created by such fragmentation appear to be significantly more extensive in East Asia than in other regions such as Latin America (Fung, Garcia-Herrero, and Siu, 2009; Athukorala, 2006, 2008; Ng and Yeats, 2001, 2003).

The formation of regional production networks can have various important implications for international trade. When MNEs engage in production fragmentation, initially, production may be geographically fragmented across national boundaries but organizationally confined within the boundaries of the firm. Affiliates of MNEs may rely heavily on imported intermediate products from their home countries if they are faced with limited choice of local suppliers. This will be the case if intermediate inputs require specialized production techniques that are not yet available in the host countries. It is often pointed out that a significant amount of trade in the global economy is indeed carried out in the form of intra-firm trade, which can explain the prevalence of FDI-based production fragmentation. Moreover, as production is fragmented across locations, exports of capital goods required to produce parts and components from an FDI source country may also expand. It may also increase imports by an FDI source country as the host country increases exports of finished goods back to the source country.

Over time, these networks disseminate knowledge and skills to local suppliers in the host countries (Ernst, 2000). Advanced knowledge possessed by the MNEs may be spilled over through contractual relationship with local firms. Production linkages as well as procurement relationships between the foreign affiliates and the domestic firms can also lead to improved technological capabilities of the local suppliers. Furthermore, as global competition intensifies, MNEs are under increasing pressure to reduce their costs of sourcing intermediate products, regardless of their origins. Regional production networks then cover both intra-firm and inter-firm transactions, joint ventures with its subcontractors, suppliers as well as service providers. When foreign affiliates start sourcing intermediate goods locally, it will partially offset the trade-creating effect of FDI.

At the same time, with economies of scale, industrial clusters may form covering affiliates and non-affiliates. Countries then tend to specialize more narrowly within industries to define their own niche markets to achieve scale economies. As an example, take the hard disk drive industry in Thailand. Parts and components are procured locally as well as from other countries in Asia. Indeed, several suppliers located in different countries supply the same parts and components to several assemblers on behalf of Seagate, Western Digital, Hitachi, Fujitsu, etc. (Hiratsuka, 2008). Evidence of industrial clusters can be found in various parts of East Asia; examples include the Shanghai–Jiangsu corridor and Guangzhou in China, the Eastern Seaboard in Thailand, Penang in Malaysia, and parts of Hsingchu and Taoyuang in Taiwan. The establishment of a number of industrial clusters subsequently leads to the expansion of international trade of parts and components within East Asia.

We have increasing evidence of the strong effects of international production networks on the volume and the direction of regional trade flows. But, is it really true that FDI systematically facilitates trade in parts and components, particularly in East Asia? This paper is an attempt to examine the question for two of the most important foreign direct investors in the developing economies of Asia: the U.S. and Japan. More specifically, we attempt to analyze the FDI-trade linkages in intra-regional exports and imports in East Asia focusing on aggregate, Japanese, and U.S. investment in East Asia in order to examine whether various production networks have different implications on intra-regional trade. Our analysis will be conducted on intra-regional exports and imports of parts and components, capital goods, consumption goods, and semi-finished goods.

The remainder of the paper is organized as follows: Section II describes some characteristics of international trade in East Asia, particularly the extent of intra-regional trade and the characteristics of trade by stages of production for each country. Section III presents an empirical analysis investigating the effects of FDI from these three countries on the volume of trade in various East Asian countries. It begins with a description of the variables used in the regression analysis, followed by the estimation methodology. The results for all regressions are reported and analyzed in Section III.II. Concluding remarks are given in Section IV.

II. PATTERNS OF TRADE IN EAST ASIA[2]

Intra-regional Trade

Tables 1a and 1b examine the changes in the share of geographic direction of individual East Asian imports and exports, respectively for 1985, 1995, 2003, and 2006. These tables also include figures for North America and EU15 for comparisons. East Asia in general appears to have gone through significant changes in the direction of their imports. The share of East Asia's imports from other East Asian countries increased from 23.0% in 1985 to 40.9% in 2003 and to 45.2% in 2006, indicating heightened dependence on regional trade. The increase is largely attributed to the newly industrializing economies (NIEs) and China. China's share more than doubled from 5.9% to 12.5% in 2003 and further increased to 16.3% in 2006, whereas the share of the NIEs rose from 10.7% to 18.4% in 2003 and appears to have leveled off since. Table 1 reports a relatively small gain in ASEAN's share — by 3.6% between 1985 and 2006. In contrast, a sizeable decline occurred in Japan's share — by almost 11.3% during the same period. Despite the setback, however, Japan still remains the single largest import-sourcing country for East Asia. The shares of U.S. and Canada as well as EU15 in East Asian imports also declined.

Increased reliance on regional trade can be seen for all East Asian countries, although sizeable differences regarding the extent of the dependence exist among various countries. For example, the share of East Asia in Philippines' imports increased by 12.8%, whereas the corresponding figures for Indonesia and China were both 29.9%. At the same time, the dependence on North America and EU15 as an import source declined for all East Asian countries.

[2]In this chapter East Asia includes China, Hong Kong, China, Indonesia, Japan, Republic of Korea, Malaysia, Philippines, Singapore, Taiwan Province of China, and Thailand.

Table 1a. The geographic destinations of East Asian imports: 1985, 1995, 2003, 2006

		East Asia	Japan	China	NIEs	ASEAN4	North America	EU15
East Asia	1985	23.0%	25.7%	5.9%	10.7%	6.4%	17.1%	13.6%
	1995	33.6%	22.8%	10.0%	16.0%	7.5%	15.8%	13.9%
	2003	43.3%	17.5%	14.3%	18.4%	10.7%	11.3%	11.0%
	2006	45.2%	14.4%	16.3%	18.4%	10.4%	9.6%	9.8%
Japan	1985	25.9%		5.1%	7.7%	13.1%	24.0%	7.6%
	1995	34.7%		10.8%	12.3%	11.5%	25.9%	14.5%
	2003	42.4%		19.7%	10.2%	12.5%	17.6%	12.8%
	2006	41.4%		20.5%	9.8%	11.1%	13.7%	10.0%
Korea	1985	10.6%	24.2%	0.0%	3.5%	7.1%	22.8%	11.0%
	1995	15.4%	24.6%	5.6%	4.2%	5.6%	24.7%	13.4%
	2003	26.8%	20.3%	12.3%	7.1%	7.5%	15.0%	10.8%
	2006	28.3%	16.8%	15.7%	5.6%	7.0%	11.9%	9.4%
Taiwan	1985	9.6%	27.6%	0.0%	3.8%	5.7%	25.5%	11.1%
	1995	18.8%	29.2%	3.0%	8.8%	7.0%	21.6%	14.4%
	2003	30.4%	25.7%	8.7%	11.4%	10.3%	14.2%	10.4%
	2006	31.8%	23.0%	12.3%	10.9%	8.6%	11.9%	8.6%
Hong Kong	1985	45.8%	23.1%	25.5%	17.5%	2.8%	9.8%	12.3%
	1995	59.6%	14.8%	36.2%	18.8%	4.6%	8.4%	10.8%
	2003	67.0%	11.8%	43.3%	17.1%	6.6%	5.9%	8.3%
	2006	70.7%	10.3%	45.8%	18.4%	6.6%	5.2%	7.1%
Singapore	1985	32.6%	17.0%	8.6%	6.8%	17.2%	15.5%	12.2%
	1995	36.5%	21.1%	3.3%	11.8%	21.5%	15.5%	13.4%
	2003	46.8%	11.3%	8.1%	10.7%	28.0%	13.6%	11.7%
	2006	49.2%	8.3%	11.4%	12.5%	25.3%	13.1%	10.9%
China	1985	14.0%	35.8%		11.9%	2.1%	14.6%	16.5%
	1995	32.6%	22.0%		28.1%	4.5%	14.2%	16.1%
	2003	42.2%	18.0%		27.6%	8.4%	9.3%	12.8%
	2006	43.9%	14.6%		25.9%	8.7%	8.5%	11.0%
Thailand	1985	23.4%	26.5%	2.4%	13.7%	7.2%	12.6%	16.1%
	1995	24.7%	30.7%	3.0%	15.3%	6.4%	12.7%	15.9%
	2003	33.4%	24.1%	8.0%	13.8%	11.6%	10.0%	10.0%
	2006	36.3%	20.1%	10.6%	13.6%	12.1%	7.1%	8.4%
Malaysia	1985	31.0%	23.2%	2.1%	22.4%	6.6%	16.4%	16.1%
	1995	31.0%	28.1%	2.3%	23.7%	5.0%	17.1%	15.6%
	2003	45.9%	17.2%	8.8%	25.1%	12.0%	16.0%	11.8%
	2006	49.7%	13.2%	12.1%	25.2%	12.5%	13.0%	11.1%

(*Continued*)

Table 1a. (*Continued*)

		East Asia	Japan	China	NIEs	ASEAN4	North America	EU15
Philippines	1985	30.6%	14.4%	5.4%	13.7%	11.5%	25.9%	9.3%
	1995	29.2%	22.1%	2.3%	21.0%	5.9%	19.9%	10.7%
	2003	35.5%	13.0%	9.1%	20.8%	10.2%	9.3%	10.9%
	2006	43.4%	9.0%	10.9%	23.9%	11.3%	7.8%	9.7%
Indonesia	1985	17.2%	25.8%	2.4%	13.5%	1.2%	18.7%	19.0%
	1995	24.6%	22.7%	3.7%	17.0%	3.9%	13.7%	20.1%
	2003	40.1%	19.5%	4.6%	21.5%	9.4%	22.4%	8.1%
	2006	46.0%	14.2%	7.2%	26.2%	10.0%	16.6%	8.3%
North America	1985	13.9%	17.7%	1.0%	10.2%	2.7%	27.9%	19.9%
	1995	20.4%	14.6%	5.6%	9.8%	5.1%	27.5%	16.4%
	2003	22.6%	8.5%	11.4%	6.8%	4.4%	24.3%	18.1%
	2006	24.4%	7.3%	14.8%	5.5%	4.1%	22.2%	16.3%
EU15	1985	3.0%	3.5%	0.4%	1.7%	0.9%	8.4%	56.2%
	1995	6.4%	4.1%	1.7%	3.0%	1.6%	8.1%	61.5%
	2003	8.4%	3.1%	4.1%	2.5%	1.8%	7.2%	58.5%
	2006	9.8%	2.4%	5.7%	2.5%	1.5%	6.4%	53.9%

Source: Compiled from UN Comtrade database and author's calculation.

The rising importance of China as an import source country can be seen in all East Asian countries, particularly for more advanced economies such as Japan, Korea, Taiwan, and Hong Kong. China has also become an increasingly important partner for non-regional markets. The increase in the share of China in the imports of North America between 1985 and 2006 was 13.8%. Intra-regional trade dominated in imports by EU15 which accounted for 53.9% in 2006, China managed to gain its share by 5.3% since 1985. Table 1a also shows that there have been significant changes in the pattern of China's imports as well. In 1985, more than one-third of its imports originated from Japan. Two decades later, its reliance on Japan declined to 14.6%. On the other hand, the share of intra-regional imports increased from 14% in 1985 to 43.9% in 2006. The rise is largely due to the increase in the share of the NIEs in China's imports.

On the export side, on average, the share of intra-regional exports increased from 25.5% to 40.7% (see Table 2). Of all the countries examined, significant increases in the shares of intra-regional exports are reported for Taiwan (42.2%) and Korea (28.9%), followed by Singapore, Japan, and

Table 1b. The geographic destinations of East Asian exports: 1985, 1995, 2003, 2006

		East Asia	Japan	China	NIEs	ASEAN4	North America	EU15
East Asia	1985	25.5%	16.9%	4.7%	15.1%	5.7%	29.4%	11.4%
	1995	38.0%	12.9%	8.7%	20.9%	8.4%	21.1%	13.9%
	2003	41.0%	10.6%	12.6%	20.1%	8.3%	19.4%	14.2%
	2006	40.7%	8.9%	13.1%	19.7%	7.9%	17.9%	14.2%
Japan	1985	24.1%		7.1%	12.8%	4.2%	40.2%	13.2%
	1995	42.0%		5.0%	25.0%	12.1%	28.9%	15.9%
	2003	44.9%		12.2%	23.5%	9.2%	26.5%	15.3%
	2006	45.7%		14.3%	23.2%	8.1%	24.3%	13.6%
Korea	1985	10.8%	15.0%	0.0%	7.4%	3.4%	39.7%	11.7%
	1995	31.1%	13.7%	7.5%	15.9%	7.7%	21.3%	13.3%
	2003	38.3%	8.9%	18.1%	13.6%	6.6%	19.2%	12.9%
	2006	39.7%	8.2%	21.3%	12.7%	5.6%	14.8%	12.5%
Taiwan	1985	15.1%	11.3%	0.0%	12.0%	3.1%	51.4%	9.4%
	1995	38.5%	11.8%	0.3%	29.6%	8.5%	25.0%	13.1%
	2003	51.0%	8.6%	15.9%	28.3%	6.8%	19.4%	13.1%
	2006	57.3%	7.6%	24.3%	25.2%	7.7%	16.0%	10.4%
Hong Kong	1985	36.6%	4.2%	26.0%	7.0%	3.6%	33.2%	13.6%
	1995	44.0%	6.1%	33.3%	7.1%	3.6%	23.3%	15.0%
	2003	52.1%	5.3%	41.7%	7.0%	3.4%	19.5%	13.7%
	2006	55.8%	4.8%	46.3%	6.2%	3.2%	15.9%	13.7%
Singapore	1985	31.4%	9.4%	1.5%	9.3%	20.6%	21.9%	11.0%
	1995	44.2%	7.8%	2.3%	15.4%	26.5%	18.8%	13.4%
	2003	53.4%	6.1%	6.3%	17.1%	30.0%	13.1%	12.1%
	2006	54.7%	5.5%	9.7%	16.7%	28.2%	10.5%	10.6%
China	1985	36.4%	22.2%		33.7%	2.7%	9.4%	9.2%
	1995	36.8%	19.1%		33.1%	3.7%	17.7%	12.9%
	2003	30.1%	13.6%		26.1%	4.0%	22.4%	16.5%
	2006	29.1%	9.5%		25.2%	4.0%	22.7%	17.5%
Thailand	1985	25.6%	13.4%	3.8%	15.4%	6.3%	20.9%	19.8%
	1995	30.9%	16.8%	2.9%	23.0%	4.9%	18.9%	15.1%
	2003	34.7%	14.2%	7.1%	17.9%	9.7%	18.2%	14.7%
	2006	35.3%	12.7%	9.0%	16.6%	9.6%	16.0%	13.0%
Malaysia	1985	36.4%	23.8%	1.1%	29.1%	6.3%	13.7%	14.9%
	1995	40.4%	12.7%	2.7%	31.6%	6.2%	21.5%	14.2%
	2003	43.0%	10.7%	6.5%	28.7%	7.8%	20.2%	12.1%
	2006	43.1%	8.9%	7.2%	26.7%	9.2%	19.4%	12.1%

(*Continued*)

Table 1b. (*Continued*)

		East Asia	Japan	China	NIEs	ASEAN4	North America	EU15
Philippines	1985	20.6%	18.9%	1.6%	12.9%	6.1%	37.5%	16.2%
	1995	24.6%	15.9%	1.2%	16.2%	7.2%	37.4%	16.9%
	2003	42.4%	22.3%	6.2%	21.5%	7.7%	12.7%	13.1%
	2006	41.3%	21.6%	8.3%	20.9%	8.2%	11.7%	11.5%
Indonesia	1985	18.4%	46.2%	0.5%	16.1%	1.9%	22.0%	6.4%
	1995	31.0%	27.1%	3.8%	22.2%	5.0%	14.7%	14.9%
	2003	35.4%	15.9%	5.9%	25.5%	11.0%	21.0%	16.3%
	2006	37.3%	16.7%	9.8%	22.4%	9.1%	18.9%	18.0%
North America	1985	9.1%	8.8%	1.6%	5.9%	1.6%	37.9%	18.9%
	1995	15.3%	9.5%	1.9%	10.2%	3.3%	35.9%	17.5%
	2003	13.6%	5.8%	3.2%	7.6%	2.9%	40.5%	16.6%
	2006	14.0%	4.8%	4.3%	7.3%	2.3%	38.4%	16.3%
EU15	1985	3.0%	1.2%	0.8%	1.5%	0.7%	10.8%	57.8%
	1995	5.7%	2.1%	1.0%	3.2%	1.6%	7.3%	61.8%
	2003	4.7%	1.6%	1.6%	2.2%	0.9%	9.7%	60.9%
	2006	4.9%	1.3%	1.9%	2.1%	0.8%	9.0%	59.1%

Source: Compiled from UN Comtrade database and author's calculation.

Hong Kong by 23.4%, 21.6%, and 19.2%, respectively. The increases in the shares of intra-regional exports in all countries are largely attributed to China. Increased dependence on regional exports is seen for all Asian countries except China. China's share shrank from 36.4% to 29.1%.

While over 36% of Chinese goods were destined for other East Asian countries in 1985, the figure declined to 29.1% in 2006. In contrast, a much higher portion of Chinese goods is absorbed by both North America and to lesser extent by EU15 in 2006. As we have shown in the import side, the reliance on North America declined for all other East Asian countries except China and Malaysia. The decline in the dependence appears to be even larger on the export side. For Taiwan in particular, the share of Taiwanese exports going to North America declined from 51.4% in 1985 to 16.0% in 2006.

Composition of Trade by Stage of Production in East Asia

The earlier section leads to the conclusion that East Asian countries have generally become increasingly interdependent. This section considers

Table 2. Average growth rate of total manufactured goods, intermediate goods, and final goods, 1998–2007

	Imports			Exports		
	Total	Intermediate goods	Final goods	Total	Intermediate goods	Final goods
Asian Nations	12.4%	13.6%	10.2%	12.7%	13.3%	12.0%
Japan	8.0%	10.2%	5.8%	7.1%	7.9%	6.1%
East Asia	13.7%	14.4%	12.1%	14.8%	15.5%	14.2%
China	22.1%	21.6%	23.5%	24.1%	26.8%	22.6%
Hong Kong	8.1%	10.6%	5.1%	8.3%	11.9%	4.8%
Indonesia	10.7%	10.3%	11.6%	11.9%	13.3%	9.2%
Malaysia	10.5%	10.8%	10.0%	9.8%	10.3%	9.2%
Philippines	2.4%	2.1%	4.7%	1.8%	1.6%	2.8%
Republic of Korea	16.2%	14.6%	21.1%	12.4%	12.0%	13.1%
Singapore	9.8%	11.2%	7.2%	10.8%	14.1%	4.9%
Thailand	13.5%	14.2%	12.1%	12.2%	13.7%	11.0%
EU15	8.9%	9.0%	8.8%	8.7%	8.8%	8.5%
North America	7.4%	6.8%	7.9%	6.0%	6.0%	5.9%
Others	11.5%	11.3%	11.8%	12.2%	13.2%	11.1%
World	9.8%	10.1%	9.4%	9.9%	10.3%	9.5%

Source: Compiled from UN Comtrade database and author's calculation.

composition of trade by stage of production in East Asia. Table 2 examines the annual growth rate of trade in total manufactured goods and compares them with the rate of growth of trade in finished and intermediate goods. The table provides strong evidence that trade in intermediate goods which can be used as a measure of international production sharing has been the engine driving intra-Asian trade during recent years. Between 1998 and 2007, exports of intermediate goods grew at a rate of 13.3% among Asian economies on average, which is faster than the growth rate of 12.0% for exports of final goods. On the import side, trade in intermediate goods grew over 3% faster than trade in final goods. Compared with other parts of the world, the growth rate in intermediate goods is much faster among Asian economies, both for exports and imports. The growth rate of exports of intermediate goods for the world, EU15, and North America were 10.3%, 8.8%, and 6.0%, respectively, while those of imports were 10.1%, 9.0%, and 6.8%, respectively.

Table 3 further distinguishes different types of intermediate goods, i.e., parts and components (IMPC) and semi-finished goods (IMSF). Finished goods are also further classified into consumption goods (FC) and capital goods (FCA). Primary goods (P) form the last category. This classification by different stages of production is useful in showing how each East Asian economy is involved in production fragmentation and to what extent they differ from other regions of the world. The classification is explained in Appendix 1.

The most notable difference between the world and the East Asian economies can be found in the trade pattern of parts and components. At the global level, approximately one-fifth of both imports and exports consist of the exchange of parts and components. That share remained relatively stable between 1998 and 2006 although both import and export share show a slight decline during recent years. Table 3 shows very different trends for different regions. For example, North America experienced declines of 6.0% and 4.2%, respectively, in its import and export shares of parts and components from 1998 to 2006. EU15 also experienced a similar declining trend in its parts and components trade, although more moderately relative to North America. The trend in East Asia contrasts markedly with the other regions, with the share of the parts and components trade increasing during the same period. It accounted for 27.0% of imports in 2006, which was 3.7% higher than the share in 1998. The upward trend can also be found, although to a lesser extent, on the export side, the share of which increased from 24.6% in 1998 to 26.4% in 2006.

For finished products, the most distinguishing difference between the world and the Asian economies can be found in the trade pattern of consumption goods, particularly on the import side. Approximately 22% of world imports take the form of consumption goods. In the case of North America, the share is almost 28%. Among East Asian countries, the corresponding share only amounts to 11.4% in 2006, which was a decline of more than 6.9% from 1998.

Another interesting point to note is the gradual decline in the import share of capital goods, which can be seen in all Asian economies examined, except Hong Kong and Korea. However, one must use caution about BEC classification for capital goods. Capital goods (41) include producers' goods that are defined in the System of National Accounts (SNA) as part of fixed

Table 3. **Trade pattern by stage of production 1998–2006**

Imports		China	China, Hong Kong SAR	Indonesia	Japan	Malaysia	Philippines	Republic of Korea	Singapore	Thailand	Asia	North America	European Union 15	World
1998	FC	4.4%	32.9%	6.1%	28.3%	6.2%	8.6%	5.0%	12.7%	8.3%	18.3%	29.5%	27.4%	24.8%
	FCA	19.4%	15.6%	21.5%	12.7%	18.2%	10.4%	12.0%	21.0%	17.3%	15.8%	18.1%	16.1%	17.0%
	IMPC	21.8%	19.2%	16.3%	13.2%	46.1%	46.7%	24.3%	39.7%	26.7%	23.3%	21.1%	17.6%	18.9%
	IMSF	44.5%	28.6%	37.5%	23.6%	21.7%	24.7%	33.0%	16.4%	34.6%	28.6%	20.1%	27.7%	27.1%
	P	8.2%	2.1%	12.6%	19.1%	3.7%	9.5%	22.7%	6.0%	11.2%	11.4%	6.4%	7.7%	8.3%
1999	FC	4.6%	33.0%	8.5%	28.8%	7.3%	8.7%	6.1%	12.5%	7.7%	18.1%	29.5%	27.7%	24.9%
	FCA	19.2%	14.7%	12.9%	13.1%	14.7%	9.3%	13.7%	19.3%	15.3%	15.1%	18.2%	16.7%	17.0%
	IMPC	23.5%	21.0%	12.1%	13.5%	47.3%	45.3%	25.6%	41.6%	27.9%	24.3%	21.1%	17.8%	19.4%
	IMSF	41.6%	27.5%	39.7%	22.9%	23.2%	25.0%	30.9%	15.3%	34.0%	27.7%	19.2%	26.1%	25.8%
	P	8.7%	2.1%	18.0%	18.3%	3.8%	11.7%	20.9%	5.7%	12.1%	11.6%	6.8%	7.7%	8.6%
2000	FC	4.2%	30.2%	6.0%	26.3%	6.6%	7.4%	6.5%	11.2%	6.8%	16.1%	28.1%	24.9%	22.8%
	FCA	17.5%	15.4%	14.1%	12.6%	14.9%	9.6%	15.7%	18.4%	14.2%	15.0%	18.1%	16.2%	16.6%
	IMPC	24.2%	24.5%	13.7%	14.5%	48.6%	46.1%	23.9%	42.8%	31.1%	25.5%	20.1%	17.4%	19.5%
	IMSF	38.1%	26.3%	39.1%	22.9%	21.2%	22.6%	27.8%	14.0%	31.1%	26.4%	18.9%	25.2%	25.1%
	P	13.5%	1.9%	16.7%	19.9%	4.4%	13.0%	22.9%	7.3%	14.3%	13.5%	9.1%	9.7%	10.7%

(Continued)

Table 3. (*Continued*)

Imports		China	China, Hong Kong SAR	Indonesia	Japan	Malaysia	Philippines	Republic of Korea	Singapore	Thailand	Asia	North America	European Union 15	World
2001	FC	4.4%	30.4%	5.6%	27.6%	7.3%	7.5%	8.3%	11.8%	7.1%	16.6%	30.2%	26.8%	24.3%
	FCA	20.1%	16.8%	15.3%	12.3%	16.3%	8.6%	14.2%	19.1%	17.2%	15.8%	17.6%	15.9%	16.5%
	IMPC	25.1%	24.5%	14.1%	13.9%	44.8%	47.6%	22.1%	40.3%	28.4%	24.6%	18.2%	17.2%	18.7%
	IMSF	35.8%	24.8%	37.6%	22.9%	21.8%	22.5%	28.9%	14.5%	30.6%	26.3%	19.1%	25.6%	25.4%
	P	12.2%	2.0%	19.2%	19.5%	5.4%	12.6%	23.1%	7.2%	14.6%	13.3%	8.9%	9.2%	10.2%
2002	FC	4.5%	29.6%	6.6%	27.7%	7.6%	6.9%	9.8%	11.9%	7.6%	16.1%	32.1%	28.8%	25.3%
	FCA	21.0%	16.0%	14.0%	12.3%	15.0%	7.0%	14.5%	17.2%	17.5%	15.8%	17.4%	14.9%	16.1%
	IMPC	27.4%	26.9%	13.8%	14.4%	47.0%	55.5%	22.7%	41.4%	27.1%	26.4%	17.4%	16.5%	18.5%
	IMSF	34.7%	24.2%	35.6%	22.5%	20.8%	19.4%	29.5%	14.7%	31.6%	26.2%	19.0%	25.7%	25.3%
	P	10.6%	2.0%	19.5%	19.3%	4.7%	9.5%	20.2%	7.0%	14.3%	12.3%	8.7%	9.1%	10.0%
2003	FC	4.5%	27.3%	7.4%	26.4%	7.7%	7.1%	9.2%	11.7%	7.7%	14.8%	31.7%	29.1%	24.9%
	FCA	21.6%	15.2%	12.5%	12.1%	13.3%	7.1%	15.0%	16.8%	17.3%	16.0%	17.1%	14.4%	15.9%
	IMPC	28.4%	29.9%	13.4%	14.3%	48.3%	52.9%	22.4%	41.9%	26.7%	27.0%	16.4%	16.1%	18.2%
	IMSF	32.0%	24.1%	34.6%	23.2%	20.4%	20.9%	29.9%	14.2%	31.4%	26.0%	19.0%	25.4%	25.4%
	P	11.8%	2.0%	21.1%	20.2%	5.3%	9.8%	20.0%	7.0%	14.7%	12.8%	10.3%	9.2%	10.5%

(*Continued*)

Table 3. (*Continued*)

Imports		China	China, Hong Kong SAR	Indonesia	Japan	Malaysia	Philippines	Republic of Korea	Singapore	Thailand	Asia	North America	European Union 15	World
2004	FC	4.0%	25.0%	7.3%	25.0%	7.6%	7.1%	8.0%	10.5%	7.3%	13.3%	29.8%	28.3%	23.6%
	FCA	21.1%	15.2%	14.5%	11.8%	14.7%	6.2%	15.6%	17.0%	15.6%	16.1%	17.0%	14.7%	16.1%
	IMPC	28.6%	32.4%	13.0%	14.5%	44.0%	52.4%	20.6%	42.0%	25.5%	27.1%	16.3%	15.6%	18.1%
	IMSF	29.3%	23.7%	37.5%	23.5%	22.7%	20.8%	31.2%	13.9%	33.0%	25.9%	20.1%	25.6%	25.7%
	P	15.0%	1.9%	17.0%	21.3%	5.6%	9.5%	21.3%	8.0%	16.4%	14.2%	11.3%	9.9%	11.4%
2005	FC	4.0%	23.6%	6.1%	23.1%	7.5%	7.6%	8.1%	10.1%	7.4%	12.4%	28.1%	27.4%	22.6%
	FCA	19.4%	15.7%	13.8%	11.5%	14.6%	6.4%	15.1%	13.9%	15.8%	15.3%	16.7%	14.6%	15.8%
	IMPC	29.5%	34.2%	12.2%	13.7%	43.1%	50.3%	19.2%	42.2%	22.9%	26.8%	15.6%	15.0%	17.6%
	IMSF	28.2%	22.4%	31.9%	22.9%	22.5%	20.1%	30.3%	14.4%	32.1%	25.1%	20.0%	25.5%	25.4%
	P	17.0%	1.9%	17.7%	24.7%	6.5%	11.5%	24.2%	10.1%	19.0%	16.4%	13.2%	11.5%	12.9%
2006	FC	4.2%	21.6%	6.5%	20.8%	7.5%	7.7%	8.3%	9.0%	7.7%	11.4%	27.9%	25.8%	21.5%
	FCA	19.2%	16.1%	14.6%	11.0%	14.4%	6.6%	14.6%	14.6%	14.3%	15.2%	16.4%	14.2%	15.5%
	IMPC	30.5%	36.2%	10.5%	13.7%	41.4%	48.4%	17.6%	40.7%	22.9%	27.0%	15.1%	14.5%	17.3%
	IMSF	26.0%	21.5%	31.3%	23.5%	22.9%	19.6%	30.3%	14.3%	32.0%	24.4%	20.3%	26.1%	25.2%
	P	17.9%	2.1%	19.2%	26.8%	7.6%	13.2%	26.1%	9.3%	20.3%	17.6%	14.0%	12.1%	13.5%

(*Continued*)

Table 3. (*Continued*)

Exports		China	China, Hong Kong SAR	Indonesia	Japan	Malaysia	Philippines	Republic of Korea	Singapore	Thailand	Asia	North America	European Union 15	World
1998	FC	47.9%	42.6%	20.5%	20.0%	14.0%	17.7%	19.2%	10.9%	37.4%	27.0%	16.6%	27.2%	24.9%
	FCA	15.0%	12.3%	4.1%	27.4%	18.5%	12.2%	20.2%	28.4%	13.0%	20.1%	21.3%	19.2%	17.9%
	IMPC	9.8%	17.6%	4.7%	29.6%	36.5%	59.6%	22.0%	37.4%	24.8%	24.6%	26.3%	17.9%	19.4%
	IMSF	22.9%	24.9%	36.3%	19.4%	23.9%	9.0%	34.5%	13.9%	18.8%	22.6%	24.1%	28.3%	26.5%
	P	3.8%	1.5%	17.5%	0.4%	5.3%	1.5%	0.8%	0.8%	4.0%	2.3%	6.8%	3.1%	7.0%
1999	FC	46.8%	42.1%	24.3%	20.5%	12.5%	14.0%	19.7%	9.4%	35.5%	26.5%	17.0%	27.6%	24.6%
	FCA	15.9%	12.8%	4.3%	26.4%	17.9%	13.4%	22.0%	26.6%	13.3%	20.1%	21.0%	19.1%	17.7%
	IMPC	11.6%	19.0%	6.4%	30.2%	41.0%	64.3%	24.9%	40.1%	25.4%	26.6%	27.0%	18.1%	20.0%
	IMSF	21.8%	24.0%	42.2%	19.3%	21.2%	6.8%	29.1%	14.4%	18.3%	21.6%	23.8%	27.3%	25.3%
	P	3.3%	1.5%	18.8%	0.3%	5.4%	1.4%	0.4%	0.7%	3.5%	2.2%	6.3%	3.3%	7.8%
2000	FC	43.8%	39.3%	22.4%	18.7%	12.4%	14.4%	18.2%	8.2%	32.0%	24.8%	16.0%	25.8%	22.6%
	FCA	17.3%	13.5%	8.1%	26.5%	18.9%	15.7%	21.6%	24.1%	13.2%	20.3%	20.3%	19.0%	17.2%
	IMPC	12.8%	22.2%	8.7%	31.7%	40.0%	60.3%	27.7%	44.2%	27.0%	28.1%	27.4%	17.9%	20.2%
	IMSF	21.4%	23.2%	40.5%	19.1%	20.0%	7.1%	26.9%	12.7%	19.2%	21.0%	24.0%	27.0%	24.5%
	P	3.7%	1.5%	17.7%	0.3%	6.0%	1.3%	0.3%	0.6%	3.9%	2.3%	7.1%	3.7%	9.7%

(*Continued*)

Table 3. (*Continued*)

Exports		China	China, Hong Kong SAR	Indonesia	Japan	Malaysia	Philippines	Republic of Korea	Singapore	Thailand	Asia	North America	European Union 15	World
2001	FC	42.3%	38.4%	23.1%	20.2%	13.4%	16.2%	19.8%	8.6%	34.1%	26.2%	16.9%	27.6%	24.2%
	FCA	18.4%	14.0%	6.8%	24.8%	21.2%	16.6%	24.8%	23.2%	12.8%	20.2%	19.8%	19.1%	17.2%
	IMPC	14.0%	23.4%	8.8%	30.2%	35.6%	57.7%	22.3%	42.4%	25.1%	26.2%	26.1%	17.6%	19.2%
	IMSF	20.9%	22.4%	39.6%	20.0%	21.4%	7.4%	27.4%	14.2%	19.2%	21.4%	24.0%	27.0%	24.7%
	P	3.4%	1.5%	19.5%	0.6%	5.1%	1.3%	0.3%	0.6%	3.7%	2.5%	7.6%	3.2%	9.3%
2002	FC	40.2%	35.9%	20.8%	22.4%	12.7%	14.8%	19.4%	8.5%	33.1%	26.3%	17.6%	29.2%	25.1%
	FCA	20.0%	14.7%	8.2%	23.0%	18.8%	17.0%	26.2%	22.0%	14.9%	20.1%	18.9%	18.3%	16.7%
	IMPC	15.6%	25.5%	8.7%	29.6%	38.2%	59.3%	24.3%	42.8%	23.3%	26.7%	25.7%	17.1%	19.0%
	IMSF	20.3%	22.2%	40.4%	20.2%	22.2%	6.5%	25.9%	15.1%	19.9%	21.3%	24.4%	27.0%	24.8%
	P	2.9%	1.4%	19.5%	0.4%	5.1%	1.4%	0.3%	0.7%	4.5%	2.4%	7.5%	3.4%	8.9%
2003	FC	37.4%	33.0%	20.1%	21.6%	11.9%	15.0%	19.2%	8.1%	31.0%	25.2%	17.7%	29.4%	24.9%
	FCA	23.3%	14.3%	6.5%	22.9%	17.8%	14.4%	26.1%	20.2%	15.7%	20.6%	18.1%	17.4%	16.3%
	IMPC	16.0%	28.4%	9.1%	30.2%	36.8%	60.0%	25.2%	42.3%	23.5%	27.0%	24.7%	16.8%	18.6%
	IMSF	19.6%	22.4%	41.8%	20.5%	24.3%	7.6%	25.6%	17.4%	20.8%	21.5%	24.9%	27.1%	25.1%
	P	2.6%	1.7%	19.9%	0.5%	6.0%	1.4%	0.4%	0.7%	5.5%	2.4%	8.9%	3.4%	9.4%

(*Continued*)

Table 3. (*Continued*)

Exports		China	China, Hong Kong SAR	Indonesia	Japan	Malaysia	Philippines	Republic of Korea	Singapore	Thailand	Asia	North America	European Union 15	World
2004	FC	34.2%	30.3%	21.8%	20.0%	11.5%	13.4%	18.0%	7.5%	29.8%	23.6%	17.2%	28.5%	23.9%
	FCA	25.2%	13.9%	7.1%	23.9%	19.2%	18.8%	26.2%	18.7%	16.0%	21.6%	18.3%	17.4%	16.5%
	IMPC	16.7%	31.6%	9.5%	30.0%	33.4%	56.8%	26.3%	43.2%	23.1%	27.1%	23.7%	16.6%	18.4%
	IMSF	21.2%	22.4%	39.2%	21.0%	25.2%	8.2%	25.2%	17.4%	21.8%	22.0%	25.9%	27.4%	25.6%
	P	1.9%	1.6%	19.8%	0.7%	6.9%	1.8%	0.4%	0.7%	5.8%	2.2%	9.3%	3.8%	9.7%
2005	FC	32.6%	28.8%	18.2%	19.9%	11.3%	13.4%	16.2%	7.4%	28.7%	22.9%	17.1%	28.0%	22.9%
	FCA	26.4%	14.6%	6.4%	22.6%	19.8%	18.1%	26.3%	16.9%	17.8%	21.7%	18.2%	17.7%	16.3%
	IMPC	16.9%	34.8%	8.4%	29.6%	32.3%	56.1%	26.9%	42.9%	21.3%	26.8%	22.8%	16.6%	17.8%
	IMSF	21.1%	20.1%	41.2%	22.1%	24.5%	8.8%	24.9%	16.8%	22.5%	22.0%	25.9%	27.7%	25.3%
	P	1.9%	1.4%	23.6%	0.8%	7.9%	2.2%	0.4%	0.6%	5.8%	2.5%	10.0%	4.0%	11.3%
2006	FC	31.1%	26.5%	17.1%	20.6%	10.6%	13.2%	14.8%	7.7%	27.2%	22.4%	16.6%	26.8%	22.1%
	FCA	26.8%	14.9%	5.8%	22.1%	20.4%	15.6%	27.6%	14.4%	17.9%	21.8%	18.9%	18.2%	16.6%
	IMPC	17.4%	36.4%	7.1%	28.5%	30.9%	53.7%	25.9%	44.4%	21.3%	26.4%	22.1%	16.3%	17.6%
	IMSF	22.2%	20.3%	41.8%	22.5%	25.3%	12.6%	25.1%	16.1%	22.6%	22.5%	26.1%	28.1%	25.7%
	P	1.4%	1.6%	25.5%	0.9%	8.4%	2.5%	0.5%	0.7%	6.6%	2.6%	10.2%	4.2%	11.3%

Source: Compiled from UN Comtrade database and author's calculation.

capital formation. However, there are items in capital goods (41 and 51) that can be used as intermediate products in the related industry. Examples include motors, diesel and semi-diesel engines, generators, transformers, radiators, rectifiers, and so on.

Furthermore, there is considerable variation in the trade patterns across East Asian countries. A general picture of the division of production processes in East Asia can be drawn from Table 3 as follows: China's trade structure can be characterized by a larger import share of parts and components and semi-finished products, and by a large export share of consumption goods as well as capital goods. This reflects China's role in production fragmentation as a processing and assembly base for finished products destined for the world market.

The general feature of three ASEAN countries, Malaysia, the Philippines, and Indonesia, is a large share of intermediate goods among both imports and exports. The decomposition of intermediate goods shows that while parts and components account for a large share of imports and exports in Malaysia and the Philippines, semi-finished goods account for a large share in Indonesia. The import structure of Thailand is similar to the above-mentioned three ASEAN countries; however, the distinctive difference can be found in its export structure, i.e., a much larger share of exports of consumption goods. In this comparison, Singapore is treated separately from the four other ASEAN countries due to its relatively high wages, and is discussed in later paragraphs.

Japan's trade structure is quite different compared to those of developing Asia. Japan is a large supplier of parts and components, reflecting Japanese industries turning to other countries of the region for the assembly of Japanese products (Jones *et al.*, 2004). The trend is also marked by a small export share of consumption goods. Table 3 also indicates that capital goods hold a large share of Japan's exports. Production fragmentation has been facilitated greatly by multinational corporations and consequent FDI, which has had a significant impact on exports from investing countries to host countries. This may be due to the fact that new production facilities need to be equipped using capital goods from the investing country or because new capital goods are required for expanding existing production capacities.

A large share of parts and components trade can also be found in economies such as Singapore and Hong Kong where wage costs are much higher relative to other developing countries of East Asia. In Singapore, parts and components make up a substantial share of its imports and exports. Over 40% of both imports and exports are induced by the need for parts and components. This represents Singapore's pivotal role as an outsourcing centre in East Asia, particularly high-tech manufacturing, and as a hub for many leading international firms. Both Hong Kong and Singapore have efficient logistics sector as well as finance industries, which facilitate the formation of world-class supply chain hubs in the region.

Hong Kong is a trading hub for electronic parts and components in Asia. It hosts a number of multinational manufacturers that source parts of key components and takes advantage of its free port status. At the same time, the electronics industry in Hong Kong is characterized by its heavy dependence on imported parts of components. Local firms source worldwide as well as from Chinese companies. Hong Kong's import share of parts and components increased dramatically from 19.2% in 1998 to 36.2% in 2006. On the export side, electronics is the largest export industry, accounting for nearly 50% of Hong Kong's total exports in 2006.

III. FOREIGN DIRECT INVESTMENT IN EAST ASIA

General Trend in FDI Inflow in East Asia

Table 4 shows that although global FDI inflow continued to be dominated by the EU15 since 1980, East Asia (without Japan) has gained in importance as recipients of FDI over time until mid-1990s in terms of both the volume of inward flows and their world shares. Total value of inflows of FDI into eight East Asian economies that amounted to US$ 4.5 billion in 1985 increased to US$ 71.8 billion in 1995. Their shares in total world inflows rose from 7.7% in 1985 to 22.9% in 1995. The surge of FDI came to a halt, however, in 1997 with the Asian financial crisis. The swift recovery from the crisis in terms of FDI volume in 1998 was only followed by another sharp downturn in 2001. Since 2003, FDI inflows to the region rose again. It reached US$ 127.49 billion in 2004, a 50% increase over 2003 with a backdrop of improved economic performance, a more favorable FDI policy environment and a rise in merger and acquisition activities in the

Table 4. Inward FDI and the share in world inward FDI, 1985–2005

US$ million	1985	1990	1995	2000	2001	2002	2003	2004	2005
Japan	642.0	1,753.0	41.5	8,322.7	6,241.3	9,239.3	6,324.3	7,815.7	2,775.0
Republic of Korea	218.0	759.0	1,250.0	8,591.0	3,692.0	2,975.0	3,785.0	7,687.0	7,198.0
Taiwan Province of China	342.0	1,330.0	1,559.0	4,928.0	4,109.0	1,445.0	453.0	1,898.0	1,625.0
Hong Kong, China	−267.2	3,275.1	6,213.4	61,924.1	23,776.5	9,681.9	13,623.6	34,034.7	35,897.0
China	1,956.0	3,487.1	37,520.5	40,714.8	46,877.6	52,742.9	53,505.0	60,630.0	72,406.0
Singapore	1,046.8	5,574.7	11,591.3	16,484.5	14,121.6	5,821.5	9,330.8	16,059.8	20,083.0
Thailand	160.0	2,575.0	2,070.0	3,350.0	3,886.0	947.0	1,952.0	1,064.0	3,687.0
Malaysia	694.7	2,611.0	5,815.0	3,787.6	553.9	3,203.4	2,473.2	4,624.2	3,967.0
Phillipines	12.0	550.0	1,459.0	1,345.0	899.0	1,792.0	347.0	469.0	1,132.0
Indonesia	310.0	1,092.0	4,346.0	−4,550.0	−2,978.4	145.0	−596.9	1,023.0	5,260.0
E. Asia	4,472.2	21,253.9	71,824.2	136,575.0	94,937.2	78,753.7	84,872.6	127,489.7	151,255.0
ASEAN 5	2,223.5	12,402.7	25,281.3	20,417.1	16,482.1	11,908.9	13,506.0	23,240.0	34,129.0
N. America	21,862.0	56,004.0	68,027.0	380,788.0	187,144.0	96,608.0	60,761.0	123,910.0	133,265.0
EU15	15,965.0	89,459.0	116,324.0	674,278.0	362,418.0	283,863.0	240,572.0	185,227.0	387,858.0
World	57,959.0	201,614.0	340,336.0	1,409,568.0	832,248.0	617,732.0	557,869.0	710,755.0	916,277.0

(*Continued*)

Table 4. (*Continued*)

%	1985	1990	1995	2000	2001	2002	2003	2004	2005
Japan	1.1%	0.9%	0.0%	0.6%	0.7%	1.5%	1.1%	1.1%	0.3%
Republic of Korea	0.4%	0.4%	0.4%	0.6%	0.4%	0.5%	0.7%	1.1%	0.8%
Taiwan Province of China	0.6%	0.7%	0.5%	0.3%	0.5%	0.2%	0.1%	0.3%	0.2%
Hong Kong, China	−0.5%	1.6%	1.8%	4.4%	2.9%	1.6%	2.4%	4.8%	3.9%
China	3.4%	1.7%	11.0%	2.9%	5.6%	8.5%	9.6%	8.5%	7.9%
Singapore	1.8%	2.8%	3.4%	1.2%	1.7%	0.9%	1.7%	2.3%	2.2%
Thailand	0.3%	1.3%	0.6%	0.2%	0.5%	0.2%	0.3%	0.1%	0.4%
Malaysia	1.2%	1.3%	1.7%	0.3%	0.1%	0.5%	0.4%	0.7%	0.4%
Phillipines	0.0%	0.3%	0.4%	0.1%	0.1%	0.3%	0.1%	0.1%	0.1%
Indonesia	0.5%	0.5%	1.3%	−0.3%	−0.4%	0.0%	−0.1%	0.1%	0.6%
East Asia	7.7%	10.5%	21.1%	9.7%	11.4%	12.7%	15.2%	17.9%	16.5%
ASEAN 5	3.8%	6.2%	7.4%	1.4%	2.0%	1.9%	2.4%	3.3%	3.7%
North America	37.7%	27.8%	20.0%	27.0%	22.5%	15.6%	10.9%	17.4%	14.5%
EU15	27.5%	44.4%	34.2%	47.8%	43.5%	46.0%	43.1%	26.1%	42.3%

Note: East Asia excludes Japan.
Source: World Investment Report, various years.

region. Considering 27% increase in global FDI inflow in 2004, a gain in the region's FDI inflow is spectacular. It continued to grow in 2005 reaching US$151.26 billion, which was up almost 34-fold from 1985. The region accounted for over one-fifth of global FDI inflow in 2005.

The largest contributor to the region's rising share in global FDI inflow has been China. FDI inflows to China have grown dramatically over the past two decades since China initiated its "open-door" policy in 1978. It was in the mid-1980s when FDI inflows surged and marked the beginning of China's globalization process. After it achieved unprecedented growth during the early 1990s, however, FDI inflows started to decline. This downturn continued until the next wave of FDI inflows hit China in 2000. Despite the widespread decline in global FDI inflows between 2000 and 2002, China was able to increase FDI inflow with expectations of further deregulations and opening up following that country's accession to WTO in 2001. In 2005, FDI in China was 37 times higher than in 1985, accounting for 7.9% of global FDI inflow and almost 48% of aggregate FDI inflows to East Asia.

ASEAN 5 (Singapore, Thailand, Malaysia, Philippines, and Indonesia) experienced a significant increase in FDI inflows during the early 1990s, accounting for 7.4% of global FDI inflow in 1995. The Asian financial crisis in 1997 triggered a sharp overall decline in the region's FDI inflow of 40% during 1998, although individual national performances varied greatly. In order to enhance the attractiveness of the region for FDI inflows, the ASEAN Investment Area was established in 1998 and required the member countries to reduce or eliminate investment regulations and conditions that might impede investment flows. This provided a new impetus for economic integration among ASEAN member countries. The ASEAN Free Trade Area (AFTA) became fully operational on 1 January 2003 and this added momentum to economic integration in the region. FDI inflows to the ASEAN 5 continued to increase for two consecutive years, reaching US$34 billion in 2005.

Among the ASEAN 5, Singapore has been a leader in attracting FDI, which has played a pivotal role in that country's economy. A liberal open-door policy and extensive FDI promotion policies toward foreign investors attracted a massive amount of FDI. In 2005, Singapore retained its position as third-largest recipient in East Asia, attracting US$20 billion, which accounted for approximately 59% of total FDI inflow to the ASEAN 5.

FDI inflows to the East Asian "Tigers" (Hong Kong, China, Korea, and Taiwan) began to increase rapidly in the early 1990s against the backdrop of strong economic growth and the liberalization of investment regimes. The slowdown of the domestic economy and the regional economic situation as a result of the Asian financial crisis prompted the sharp decline of FDI inflows to Taiwan in 1998. As a result, the share of the East Asian "Tigers" in global FDI declined to 2.8% during the year. Since then, the share of these economies has quickly picked up and reached 5.4% in 2000. Their combined share in global FDI inflow peaked at 6.1% in 2004 before declining slightly to 4.9% in 2005.

Hong Kong experienced an unprecedented FDI boom in 1999 after it recovered from the turmoil of the Asian financial crisis. The surge reflected Hong Kong's role as a financial hub for business in the region, particularly in China. Hong Kong is by far the largest foreign investor in China, and its investment increased dramatically since the early 1980s. A significant portion of the investment originates from China itself. Much of China's capital outflows take place either through legal or illegal channels to Chinese firms located in Hong Kong, and such funds find its way back to China as FDI. This type of "round tripping" of funds is mostly used to escape regulations such as barriers to trade or to gain eligibility for incentives available only to foreign investors (e.g., tax concessions). Hong Kong is also used as a stepping stone for investment to China. A large number of foreign firms use affiliates in Hong Kong to invest in China on their behalf. In addition, many overseas companies have regional offices as well as regional headquarters in Hong Kong.

Hong Kong has been experiencing another surge in FDI inflows during recent years. This partly reflects the Closer Economic Partnership Arrangement (CEPA) signed between Hong Kong and China, which opened up new opportunities not only for firms in Hong Kong but also for other foreign investors. In 2005, Hong Kong attracted almost 25% of the FDI inflows into the region, which accounted for 3.9% of global FDI inflows.

Since the 1997 Asian financial crisis, Korea has adopted extensive policy reforms in favor of FDI such as simplifying the approval procedure, the removal of various restrictions on foreign ownership, strengthening tax incentive systems and financial support for foreign investors, among others. As a result, FDI inflows began to surge in 1997 and maintained strong growth until 2000. In 2004, the inflows picked up once again and Korea absorbed more than 1% of global FDI inflow.

The inflows of FDI to Taiwan grew rapidly, particularly toward the end of the 1990s, due to a large-scale reform of various laws and regulations on FDI inflows as well as further opening up of the financial sector. However, after 2001, the absolute magnitude of FDI in Taiwan has been small, which is a clear contrast to the recent surge in FDI inflows in Korea.

Inward FDI in East Asia from Japan and the U.S.

Figure 1 shows the stock of Japanese and U.S. direct investments in the individual countries within East Asia between 1985 and 2006. A relatively stable increase in the FDI stock from both countries can be seen in all countries until 1997, when the Asian economic crisis hit. In contrast to the relatively similar FDI developments displayed by Japan and the U.S. until the crisis, the FDI stock of those two countries appears to have begun to follow the different path immediately after the crisis. Japanese direct investment outflows to the crisis-stricken economies declined sharply after the crisis. The pace of Japanese FDI outflows moderated due to the severe economic slowdown in Japan as well. The total dollar amount of Japanese direct investment in all nine countries combined continued to stay below 1997 level until 2005, although the size and the duration of the decline varies among those countries. The sharpest and lasting drop hit Indonesia and to a lesser extent Thailand. Consequently, as of 2006, the stock of Japanese investment has not recovered to the pre-crisis level in those two countries. In contrast, in China, although Japanese investment position plummeted in 1997 and 1998, it made a swift recovery relative to other East Asian economies.

Although Japan was more dominant in its direct investment position in East Asia in 1997, the stock of U.S. investment as of 2006 became larger than that of Japan's in all countries examined here except China and Thailand. Singapore and Hong Kong are the most important U.S. investment markets in the region. U.S. international investment position as of 2006 stood at over US$60 billion and US$38 billion in Singapore and Hong Kong, respectively. In contrast, although the amount of U.S. direct investment to many of these economies shrank during the next couple of years after the crisis, the overall upward trend of investment position was recovered shortly.

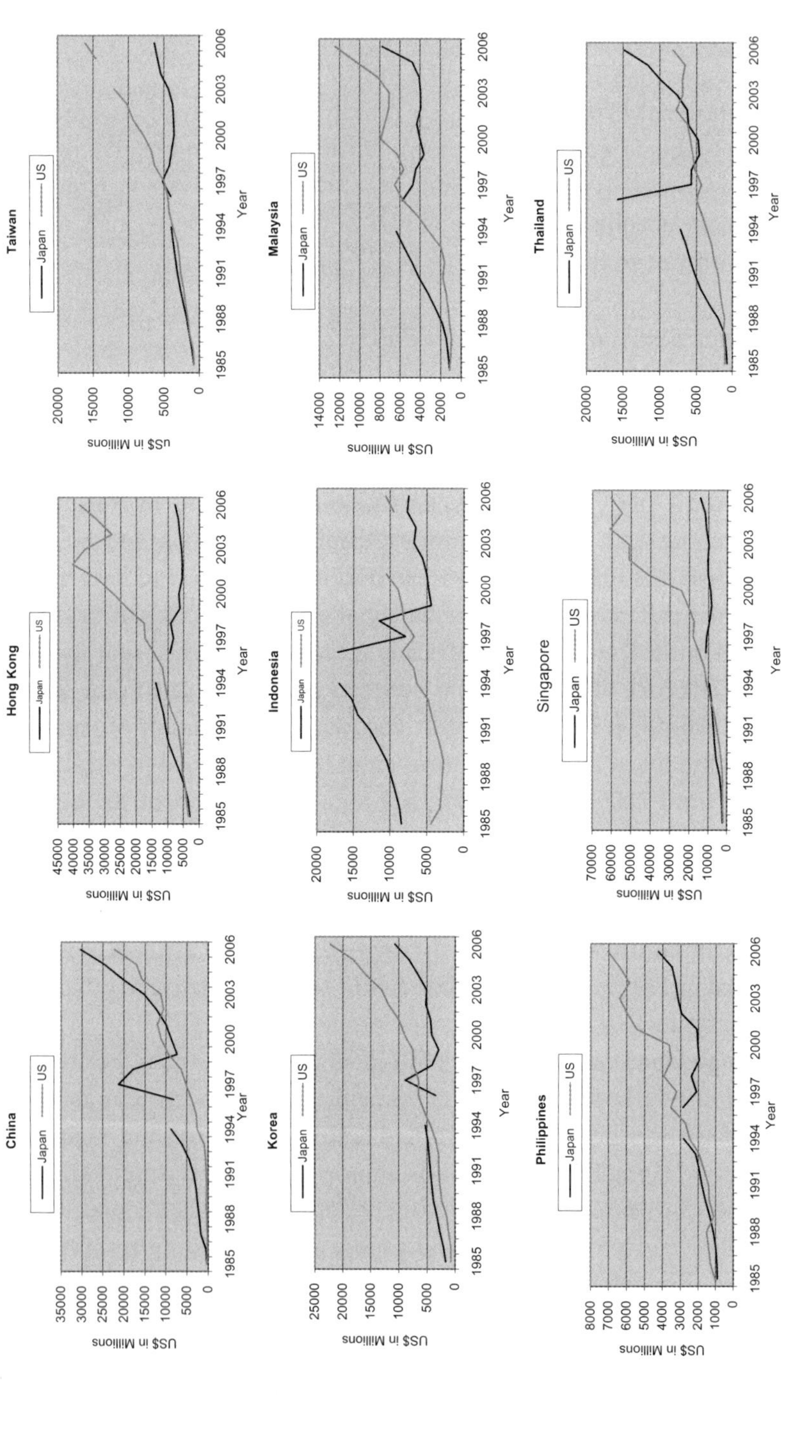

Fig. 1. U.S. and Japanese FDI stock in Asia.

IV. GRAVITY EQUATION

Model Specification and Estimation Method

The gravity model has been widely applied in various studies of international trade and FDI (Feenstra *et al.*, 2001). The gravity equation in international trade using cross-country data is commonly written as:

$$X_{ij} = f(GDP_i, GDP_j, F_{ij}) \tag{1}$$

where X_{ij} is the value of the trade flow of goods from country i to country j, GDP_i and j are the GDP in country i and j, respectively, and F_{ij} is a vector of factors that influence the trade flow. The factors commonly used include the physical distance between the two countries i and j, which is used as a proxy for transportation or trade costs and a dummy variable assuming the value 1 if i and j share a common land border and 0 otherwise.

The model specification is augmented in order to examine the economic impact of FDI inflows on the host country's trade. China, Hong Kong, Singapore, South Korea, Thailand, Malaysia, the Philippines, Indonesia, and Japan are included in the estimation here for 1998–2006. Of particular interest is the impact of U.S. and Japanese FDI on the various forms of intra-regional trade in East Asia. One possible specification issue for including FDI in the gravity analysis is the endogeneity problem. More specifically, the causal relationship between FDI and trade may be driven by unobserved common factors such as variation in government policy, technology, tastes, etc. The strategy adopted here to deal with this issue is to estimate FDI at the first stage using various instrumental variables while in the second stage, bilateral trade is estimated with the predicted value of FDI as the additional independent variable. The error term in the FDI equation then is uncorrelated with the error term in the trade equation.

The model predicts that FDI flow and bilateral trade flows between any two countries as:

$$\begin{aligned} FDI_i = {} & \alpha_0 + \beta_1 DIFPGDP_{ij} + \beta_2 DIFWAGE_{ij} + \beta_3 DUTY_i + \beta_4 CTAX_i \\ & + \beta_5 CORRUPT_i + \beta_6 GSTAB_i + \beta_7 LAW_i + \beta_8 TEL_i + \varepsilon_{ij} \end{aligned} \tag{2}$$

$$\begin{aligned} T_{ij} = {} & \gamma_0 + \rho_1 GDP_i + \rho_2 GDP_j + \rho_3 DIST_{ij} \\ & + \rho_4 DMB_i + \rho_5 FDI_i + \delta_{ij} \end{aligned} \tag{3}$$

where subscripts i and j refer to the reporting country (e.g., the country that is reporting the imports and the exports) and the partner country. The definition of the variables in the above equation is listed below. Annual data for nine economies from 1998 to 2006 are used in the estimation. Equation (3) is run for trade in parts and components, capital goods, consumption goods, and semi-finished goods separately. In addition, the impact of each explanatory variable on bilateral import flows and export flows are examined separately.

- FDI_i — the level of U.S. or Japanese FDI stock in the reporting (host) country.
- $DIFPGDP_{ij}$ — the absolute value of the difference in per capita GDP between i and j.
- $DIFWAGE_{ij}$ — the absolute value of the difference in wages between i and j.
- $DUTY_i$ — import tariff of the host country.
- $CTAX_I$ — corporate tax rate of the host country.
- $CORRUPT_i$ — an index of corruption in the host country.
- $GSTAB_i$ — an index of government stability in the host country.
- LAW_i — an index of rule of law in the host country.
- TEL_i — the number of telephone main lines per 1,000 people in the host country.
- $DIST_{ij}$ — the geographical distance between the most important cities in i and j.
- T_{ij} — the volume of exports or imports by country i to or from j in trade in parts and components and trade in capital goods.
- GDP — gross domestic product.
- DMB_{ij} — a dummy variable that is 1 if i and j share a common border and 0 otherwise.

The independent variables included in Equation (2) are believed to exert an influence on inward FDI in each East Asian economy by changing the investment environment through institutional and policy changes as well as economic conditions.

Two variables have been incorporated in this analysis that may influence the level of foreign production — the absolute difference of per capita GDP (DIFPGDP) and wages (DIFWAGE). The gap in per capita GDP and wages between a reporting country and a partner country should have a positive influence on FDI of the vertical type.[3] Trade in intermediate goods can be very sensitive to cost differences between two countries. Factor price differentials between countries allow fragments to be produced more cheaply in another country (Deadorff, 2001).

Policy-related variables, tariff barriers proxied by import duty, and corporate tax rates have also been included. MNEs, which set up vertical production networks, may be encouraged to invest in a country with relatively low tariff barriers due to lower costs of their imported intermediate products. Under such an arrangement, goods-in-process may cross multiple borders while they are being produced. Since a tariff may be imposed each time these goods-in-process cross a border, the effect of the lower tariff rate on the reduction in the cost of production of these goods can be magnified.

Another policy-related variable that can influence a host country's location advantage is the host country's corporate or other tax rates. As global profit maximizers, MNEs should be sensitive to tax factors, since such factors have a direct effect on their profits. Evidence of significant negative influence from corporate tax rates on FDI have been reported in previous studies by Wei (1997); Gastanaga, Nugent, and Pashamova (1998); and Hsiao (2001).

Also included in Equation (2) are institutional factors, the level of corruption, the stability of each government, and the rule of law. Corruption can discourage FDI by inducing a higher cost of doing business. Hines (1995) showed that FDI from the U.S. grew more rapidly in less corrupt countries than in more corrupt countries after 1977. Wei (1997) presented an alternative explanation of the negative and significant effect of corruption on FDI. Unlike taxes, corruption is not transparent and involves many factors that are more arbitrary in nature. Wei demonstrated the fact that this type of uncertainty induced by corruption leads to a reduction in FDI. Political stability of a government and a sound system of the rule of law can also be important factors in the inflow of FDI. Uncertain political environments and their related risks can impede FDI inflows despite favorable economic conditions.

---

[3] For a very interesting study on how vertical intra-industry trade helps integrate East Asia, see Wakasugi (2007).

The last variable, TEL, included in Equation (2) is a proxy for the quality of infrastructure. On the other hand, as theorized by Jones and Kierzkowski (1990), production fragmentation is not costless. A high quality of infrastructure can induce investors to invest in particular locations to facilitate production sharing.

We now turn to Equation (3). The volume of trade in both intermediate and final products is expected to be positively related the market sizes of the two countries concerned. The variable GDP captures the idea that larger countries trade more than small countries as they can offer more differentiated products to satisfy a wide variety of consumers. At the same time, for producers of both intermediate products as well as capital goods, the larger the market size of both exporting and importing countries due to the presence of economies of scale, the larger the volume of trade. According to the theory of fragmentation outlined by Jones *et al.* (2004), scale of production would determine the lengths to which the division of labor can proceed since the level of the workers' specialization increases as the scale of production rises. As Grossman and Helpman (2005) proposed, the variable can also be treated as a proxy for the "thickness" of the markets; this has a positive impact on the location of outsourcing, as the likelihood of the firms finding an appropriate partner in their search increases as the size of a country increases.

The distance variable is considered to be a crucial factor in explaining international trade since distance increases trade costs, which negatively influences the bilateral trade volume. In particular, transport or trade costs can have a larger impact on decisions concerning production fragmentation, as each intermediate product that belongs to the same value-added chain often crosses borders multiple times. Geographical proximity, on the other hand, promotes bilateral trade flows as it reduces transportation needs, information costs, cultural unfamiliarity, etc. Therefore, the expected sign of the variable is negative.

The final variable is a dummy variable with regard to whether the importing country and exporting country are adjacent. The dummy variables may capture various factors that lead to reduced business transaction costs. For example, firms in adjacent countries are likely to have a better understanding of business practices than firms from a different business environment. Such familiarity also helps reduce the difficulty of finding an appropriate outsourcing partner in production networks. As the variable is assumed to capture additional proximity between trading partners that facilitate trade, it is expected to have a positive sign.

Except for the dummies, all variables are log-linearized. Sources for the variables are listed in Appendix 2.

V. ESTIMATION RESULTS

Tables 5 and 6 represent the results of the estimations by random effect model. Our results show a positive and statistically significant influence of all Japanese, and U.S. direct investment on trade in parts and components, semi-finished goods, consumption goods as well as capital goods, indicating a complementary relationship between such modes of trade and U.S. and Japanese FDI in East Asia. However, a large variation exists in the magnitude of the impact of the variable between the U.S. and Japan, and across the two types of disaggregated data.

With regard to trade in parts and components, Japanese direct investment appears to have a much larger effect relative to the U.S. direct investment. On the export side, it shows that 1% increase in Japanese direct investment inflow leads to 0.61% increase in intra-Asian bilateral exports, whereas for U.S. direct investment inflows, they only lead to 0.37% increase. The impact of Japanese direct investment exerted on regional bilateral exports of parts and components is approximately 1.7 times as large as that of the U.S. direct investment. On the import side, similar difference exists between FDI from these countries. The coefficient for Japan is approximately 1.8 times as large as that for the U.S. case.

Electrical industries as well as automobile industries consist of layers of subcontractors in Japan. Small and Medium Enterprises (SMEs) as subcontractors to larger multinationals function as suppliers of intermediate goods. After large Japanese manufacturers shifted their production from Japan to various Asian countries in 1970s and 1980s, SMEs also established their overseas production to extend the long-term close business ties they have created with the MNEs back in Japan. A large part of FDI by Japanese MNEs is thus also conducted by SMEs, which is a distinctive characteristic of Japanese FDI. These SMEs produce parts and machinery for the large manufacturers and they establish support industries in the East Asian

Table 5. Regression results for Japanese FDI stock: 1998–2006

Explanatory variables	Exports					Imports				
	TotalEX coefficient	SF coefficient	PC coefficient	CA coefficient	Con coefficient	TotalIM coefficient	SF coefficient	PC coefficient	CA coefficient	Con coefficient
Random Effects Model										
GDP, reporter	0.715***	0.691***	0.715***	0.791***	0.402***	0.681***	0.688***	0.879***	0.833***	0.494***
	(0.129)	(0.042)	(0.059)	(0.059)	(0.052)	(0.038)	(0.425)	(0.059)	(0.058)	(0.048)
GDP, partner	0.770***	0.703***	0.747***	0.703***	0.784***	0.657***	0.612***	0.641**	0.707***	0.802***
	(0.125)	(0.040)	(0.056)	(0.056)	(0.050)	(0.041)	(0.045)	(0.063)	(0.061)	(0.051)
DIST	−0.235***	−0.604***	−1.194***	−0.949***	−0.907***	−0.663***	−0.493***	−1.080***	−0.811***	−0.815***
	(0.323)	(0.143)	(0.201)	(0.178)	(0.186)	(0.143)	(0.158)	(0.228)	(0.185)	(0.183)
DB	1.674**	1.169***	−0.225	0.394	0.585*	0.541*	0.906**	−0.301	0.272	0.621*
	(0.834)	(0.376)	(0.526)	(0.464)	(0.488)	(0.377)	(0.414)	(0.599)	(0.483)	(0.479)
FDIHAT	0.488***	0.263***	0.613***	1.094***	0.308***	0.493***	0.174***	0.619***	0.858***	0.420***
	(0.325)	(0.069)	(0.098)	(0.109)	(0.083)	(0.066)	(0.072)	(0.098)	(0.110)	(0.081)
LM	1%	1%	1%	1%	1%	1%	1%	1%	1%	1%
No. of observations	648	643	643	643	643	643	643	643	643	643

Table 6. Regression results using U.S. FDI stock: 1998–2006

	Exports					Imports				
Explanatory variables	TotalEX coefficient	SF coefficient	PC coefficient	CA coefficient	Con coefficient	TotalIM coefficient	SF coefficient	PC coefficient	CA coefficient	Con coefficient
Random Effects Model										
GDP, reporter	0.726***	0.697***	0.758***	0.912***	0.404***	0.662***	0.659***	0.875***	0.820***	0.486***
	(0.123)	(0.041)	(0.061)	(0.061)	(0.051)	(0.041)	(0.044)	(0.063)	(0.061)	(0.051)
GDP, partner	0.707***	0.687***	0.751***	0.734***	0.753***	0.695***	0.597***	0.701***	0.787***	0.865***
	(0.126)	(0.041)	(0.061)	(0.062)	(0.051)	(0.041)	(0.044)	(0.064)	(0.061)	(0.052)
DIST	−0.135	−0.582***	−1.183***	−0.987***	−0.870***	−0.646***	−0.453***	−1.080***	−0.805***	−0.828***
	(0.326)	0.146	(0.224)	(0.198)	(0.184)	(0.153)	(0.159)	(0.244)	(0.196)	0.194
DB	1.827**	1.185***	−0.219	0.329	0.614	0.547*	0.943**	−0.314	0.261	0.598
	(0.839)	(0.382)	(0.585)	(0.516)	(0.482)	(0.399)	(0.415)	(0.638)	(0.511)	0.508
FDIHAT	0.657***	0.194***	0.371***	0.485***	0.253***	0.304***	0.193***	0.332***	0.475***	0.190***
	(0.183)	(0.048)	(0.070)	(0.076)	(0.058)	(0.047)	(0.050)	(0.071)	(0.075)	(0.058)
LM	1%	1%	1%	1%	1%	1%	1%	1%	1%	1%
# of obs.	648	643	643	643	643	643	643	643	643	643

countries. Japanese manufacturing industries over time concentrated production of components and part through their *keiretsu* business networks in East Asia (METI, 2008). The large impact of Japanese direct investment on the intra-regional trade of parts and components may be attributed to this distinctive characteristic of Japanese business organization.

The results also indicate that FDI by both Japan and the U.S. cause intra-Asian bilateral exports and imports of parts and components to increase. Thus inward FDI of different sources and trade are complementary. Furthermore, the predicted impact on exports is insignificantly different from the predicted impact on imports of parts and components for the Japanese and the U.S. cases. This indicates that increased levels of Japanese and U.S. FDI have insignificant impact on the trade balance of parts and components of these Asian countries.

A significantly positive impact of FDI inflow is also found on trade in capital goods for the two FDI source countries. On the import side, the result may be attributed to various trade liberalization policies and institutional changes that many East Asian economies pursued during the 1990s. For example, many East Asian economies unilaterally eliminated their tariffs on capital and intermediate goods. In addition, duties on trade in information technology products were completely eliminated due to the adoption of the Information Technology Agreement (ITA). This is important because among the products actively traded in the East Asian region (excluding Japan) the leading category is information technology products. With respect to institutional changes, the establishment of Export Processing Zones (EPZ), where manufacturers enjoy import duty exemption on imported inputs as well as duty drawbacks on imported parts and components used for the production of exports, effectively reduces the impact of tariff barriers on trade.

More interestingly, however, the size of the impact of Japanese direct investment is 2.3 times as large as that of the U.S. direct investment on the export side. An equally large difference in the sizes of the coefficients can also be found on the import side. The coefficient for Japan is 1.8 times as large as those for the U.S. The difference can partly be due to an importance of Japanese machinery production in Asia and to the fact that a wide range of goods that can be used as intermediate inputs in related industries is being classified as "Capital Goods" in the BEC.

The overseas structure of Japanese general machinery industry is characterized by the continual expansion in the number of production bases around the world. The geographical spread of general machinery affiliates is diverse, but they tend to follow firms in the electrical, electronics, and automotive industries (Farrell, 2008). In 2003, 18% of general machinery industry affiliates were located in China, 16% in North America, 15% in ASEAN, and 8% in the NIEs3 economies (JBIC, 2004). Furthermore, with the *keiretsu* system and the assistance of local Japanese government in deploying overseas operation for SMEs (at the prefecture and the ward level), intra- and inter-industry relationships originating from Japan remain strong even when the firms are going abroad.

Another key feature of the Japanese machinery industries is that they have been strong and highly competitive industries since WWII. Japan was the early adaptor and developer of the new Numeric Control technology (NC), which was then prominently applied to Japanese products with continual improvements. Indeed by 1982, Japan has become the largest machine tool producer of the world. At its peak production in 1990, Japan produced US$13 billion worth of machine tools.

With the aid of the NC technology, Japan was able to remain competitive in a wide range of industries. A large impact of Japanese direct investment on the bilateral intra-regional trade in Asia can be best understood by the wide spectrum of manufacturing exports from Japan and from their affiliates in Asia, many of which fall under the "Capital Goods" classification.

On the impact of FDI on bilateral Asian trade of consumption good, Japanese FDI again have higher coefficients than those associated with U.S. FDI, with the Japanese impact being even higher on the import side. As for semi-finished goods, we have the usual pattern that Japanese FDI has a larger impact on such mode of exports. However, on the import side, the U.S. uncharacteristically has a larger coefficient. Thus U.S. FDI plays a larger role in facilitating imports of semi-finished goods in East Asian economies.

The coefficients for the two standard variables, the market sizes of the trading partners and the distance have the expected signs and are statistically significant at the 1% level. The overall results for GDP are consistent with the hypothesis that larger countries with a large production capacity are more likely to enjoy economies of scale and to export more, while at the same time importing more due to a higher capability of absorption.

Table 7. Regression results using the aggregated FDI stock: 1998–2006

Explanatory variables	Exports					Imports				
	TotalEX coefficient	SF coefficient	PC coefficient	CA coefficient	Con coefficient	TotalIM coefficient	SF coefficient	PC coefficient	CA coefficient	Con coefficient
Random Effects Model										
GDP, reporter	0.685***	0.739***	0.847***	1.023***	0.475***	0.745***	0.638***	0.767***	0.870***	0.879***
	(0.035)	(0.039)	(0.056)	(0.056)	(0.047)	(0.036)	(0.040)	(0.056)	(0.054)	(0.046)
GDP, partner	0.731***	0.683***	0.737***	0.726***	0.729***	0.648***	0.646***	0.855**	0.814***	0.492***
	(0.038)	(0.042)	(0.060)	(0.060)	(0.050)	(0.038)	(0.043)	(0.060)	(0.057)	(0.049)
DIST	−0.721***	−0.558***	−1.159***	−0.097***	−0.840***	−0.597	−0.420***	−1.040***	−0.756***	−0.791***
	(0.141)	(0.523)	(0.212)	(0.186)	(0.176)	(0.132)	(0.154)	(0.217)	(0.174)	(0.176)
DB	0.682**	1.175***	−0.260	0.267	0.598*	0.533*	0.938*	−0.342	0.217	0.594*
	(0.367)	(0.397)	(0.552)	(0.482)	(0.458)	(0.343)	(0.401)	(0.567)	(0.450)	(0.460)
FDIHAT	0.308***	0.227***	0.364***	0.453***	0.286***	0.362***	0.241***	0.359***	0.501***	0.243***
	(0.044)	(0.050)	(0.071)	(0.074)	(0.059)	(0.046)	(0.051)	(0.071)	(0.071)	(0.058)
LM	1%	1%	1%	1%	1%	1%	1%	1%	1%	1%
No. of observations	643	643	643	643	643	643	643	643	643	643

Distance is found to be an important deterrent for trade flows of both exports and imports of all types of trade. Distance is likely to represent not only transportation costs but also other trade costs such as communication costs and local distribution and regulatory costs. Lowering the costs of these service links that connect two production sites is crucial for countries to successfully integrate in production networks.

The adjacency dummy included to capture additional advantages arising from geographical proximity is found to have only some significant influence on regional bilateral trade.

As a further comparison, we introduce results for aggregate FDI (i.e., FDI from all sources) in Table 7. Looking at Tables 5–7, it is clear that results for the U.S. FDI resemble those for the aggregate FDI. However, Japanese FDI again has larger impact on all modes of trade except for imports of semi-finished goods. The difference is particularly produced for trade in parts and components and in capital goods. Thus compared with other sources of FDI, Japanese FDI seems to play a larger role in enhancing intra-Asian trade.

VI. CONCLUSION

In this paper we document the growing importance of intra-East Asian trade of parts and components as well as other forms of trade. Our empirical analysis shows that FDI does play an important and *independent* or *exogenous* role in facilitating the trade of parts and components in East Asia. This is true for aggregate FDI as well as FDI from the two important source countries: the U.S. and Japan. Furthermore, FDI is also complementary to trade in capital goods, consumption goods and semi-finished goods.

Furthermore, our empirical studies show that FDI from Japan has a particularly strong influence on both trade in parts and components as well as trade in capital goods. With respect to capital goods, it is fairly well known that the Japanese engineering and machinery sector has a long history of being competitive and the sector continues to be an important part of the economy. It seems likely that Japanese affiliates are set up abroad to import machinery from Japan or to manufacture and export some of such capital goods to other Asian economies. Thus for the case of Japan, trade in capital goods and trade in parts are both facilitated by Japanese direct investment.

In addition, FDI rather than local supply is needed both because of the high quality of the machinery as well as the importance of safeguarding the intellectual content of such capital goods. Other complementary explanations of the significant influence of Japanese FDI on the two modes of intra-East Asian trade include the activities of the small and medium enterprises as well as other *keiretsu* suppliers that follow the Japanese multinationals when they go abroad. In contrast, investments from the U.S. also facilitate trade in parts and components, capital goods, semi-finished goods and consumption goods but they lack the focused activities of their machinery sectors. They may also have stronger tendencies to use local suppliers as well as supplies from other non-U.S. foreign affiliates. In addition, Japanese FDI also plays a stronger role than U.S. FDI in facilitating trade in consumption goods as well as exports of semi-finished goods. Aggregate FDI is also found to be complementary to trade in Asia. The impacts of aggregate FDI on trade are similar to those associated with U.S. FDI. Thus Japanese FDI has some unusually high effects on Asian trade. One can argue that Japanese multinationals play a particularly strong role in trade integration among East Asian economies.

Some policy implications emerge from our studies. For example, there are other Asian economies which so far have been outside of the Asian production network, including much of South Asia. It is clear that to promote trade in parts and components, these economies will need to adopt policies that are friendly not only to trade but also to FDI. A set of policies that are of importance to both trade and FDI will be the improvement of infrastructure, including ports, highways, and airports. In addition, existing studies show that the quality of institutions (rule of law, corruption, intellectual property rights protection, etc.) is also likely to be an important factor in attracting FDI, which in turn facilitates the formation of the production network.

ACKNOWLEDGMENTS

We would like to thank the discussant and the participants at the conference for excellent and very useful comments. We are grateful to the APEC Study Centre at the University of Hong Kong for providing us with research support. All errors are ours.

APPENDIX 1

Commodity Code	
1	Food and beverages
11	Food and beverages, primary
111	Food and beverages, primary, mainly for industry (P)
112	Food and beverages, primary, mainly for household consumption (F-C)
12	Food and beverages, processed
121	Food and beverages, processed, mainly for industry (IM-SF)
122	Food and beverages, processed, mainly for household consumption (F-C)
2	Industrial supplies nes
21	Industrial supplies nes, primary (P)
22	Industrial supplies new, processed (IM-SF)
3	Fuels and lubricants
31	Fuels and lubricants, primary (P)
32	Fuels and lubricants, processed
321	Fuels and lubricants, processed, motor spirit
322	Fuels and lubricants, processed (other than motor spirit) (IM-SF)
4	Capital goods (except transport equipment), and parts and accessories thereof
41	Capital goods (except transport equipment) (F-CA)
42	Parts and accessories of capital goods (except transport equipment) (IM-PC)
5	Transport equipment, and parts and accessories thereof
51	Transport equipment, passenger motor cars (F-C)
52	Transport equipment, other
521	Transport equipment, other, industrial (F-CA)
522	Transport equipment, other, non-industrial (F-C)
53	Parts and accessories of transport equipment (IM-PC)
6	Consumption gods nes
61	Consumption goods nes, durable (F-C)
62	Consumption goods nes, semi-durable (F-C)
63	Consumption goods nes, non-durable (F-C)
7	Goods nes

Note: P: Primary goods; IM-SF: Semi-finished goods under Intermediate goods; IM-PC: Parts & components under Intermediate goods; F-CA: Capital goods under Final goods; F-C: Consumption goods under Final goods; 321 and 7 are treated as "others."

APPENDIX 2

Source of Variables

FDI: Aggregate FDI inflows of each country, aggregate FDI inflows to East Asia, and aggregate FDI to the world are from UNCTAD.

CORRUPT: An index of corruption from the International Country Risk Guide by the PRS Group. It ranges from 0 to 6, with a higher number indicating a lower level of corruption.

GSTAB: An index of government stability from the International Country Risk Guide by the PRS Group. The range is from 0 to 12. A higher score means higher stability of a government.

Law: An index of Law and Order from the International Country Risk Guide by the PRS Group. It ranges from 0 to 6, where a higher number indicates a better system of law and order.

DUTY: Import duties are from the International Monetary Fund's *Government Finance Statistic Yearbook.*

WAGE: Average wages in manufacturing from the United Nations Common Database, LABORSTA and official country websites.

CPTAX: Corporate income tax rate, measured in percentage points, from *Worldwide Summary* by PricewaterhouseCoopers website.

TEL: Telephone mainlines (per 1,000 people) from World Development Indicators.

GDP: GDP in U.S. dollars are from EconStats.

PGDP: Per capita GDP are from EconStats.

REFERENCES

Aminian, N., K. C. Fung and F. Ng (2009). "A Comparative Analysis of Trade and Economic Integration in East Asia and Latin America." *Economic Change and Restructuring*, 42: pp. 105–137.

Athukorala, P. C. (2008). "China's Integration into Global Production Networks and its Implications for Export-Led Growth Strategy in Other Countries in the Region," Economics RSPAS Working Paper, Australian National University.

Athukorala, P. C. (2006). "Product Fragmentation and Trade Patterns in East Asia." *Asian Economic Papers*, 4(3): pp. 1–27.

Dean, J., K. C. Fung and Z. Wang (2008). "How Vertically Specialized is Chinese Trade?" USITC Working Paper, The Government of the U.S.: Washington, D.C.

Deardorff, A. V. (2001). "Fragmentation across Cones," in S. W. Arndt and H. Kierzkowski (Eds.), *Fragmentation: New Production Patterns in the World Economy*, pp. 35–51, Oxford: Oxford University Press.

Ernst, D. (2000). "Evolutionary Aspects: The Asian Production Networks of Japanese Electronics Firms," in M. Borrus, D. Ernst and S. Haggard (Eds.), *International Production Networks in Asia: Rivalry or Riches?* pp. 79–107. London, New York: Routledge.

Farrell, R. S. (2008). *Japanese Investment in the World Economy: A Study of Strategic Themes in the Internationalization of Japanese Industry*, Northampton, MA: Edward Elgar Publishing.

Feenstra, R. C., J. R. Markusen and A. K. Rose (2001). "Using the Gravity Equation to Differentiate Among Alternative Theories of Trade." *Canadian Journal of Economics*, 34(2): 430–437.

Fung, K. C., A. Garcia-Herrero and A. Siu (2009). "Production Sharing in Latin America and East Asia," BBVA Working Paper 09-01.

Gastanaga, V. M., J. B. Nugent and B. Pashamova (1998). "Host Country Reforms and FDI Inflows: How Much Difference Do They Make?" *World Development*, 26(7): pp. 1299–1314.

Grossman, G. M. and E. Helpman (2005). "Outsourcing in a Global Economy." *Review of Economic Studies*, 72(1): pp. 135–159.

Hanson, G. H., R. J. Mataloni, Jr. and M. J. Slaughter (2001). "Expansion Strategies of U.S. Multinational firms," in S. M. Collins and D. Rodrik (Eds.), *Brookings Trade Forum 2001*, pp. 245–282. Washington, D.C.: Brookings Institution Press.

Hines, J. R., Jr (1995). "Forbidden Payment: Foreign Bribery and American Business After 1977," National Bureau of Economic Research Working Paper, No. 5266, Cambridge, MA, U.S.

Hiratsuka, D. (2008). "Japan's Outward FDI in the Era of Globalization", in R. S. Rajan, R. Kumar and N. Virgill (Eds.), *New Dimensions of Economic Globalization: Surge of Outward Foreign Direct Investment from Asia*, pp. 87–114, Singapore: World Scientific Publishing.

Hsiao, C. (2001). "Efficient Estimation of Dynamic Panel Data Models — with an Application to the Analysis of Foreign Direct Investment to Developing Countries," Paper prepared for the 2001 Econometric Society Far Eastern Meeting in Kobe, Japan.

Hummels, D., J. Ishii and K.-M. Yi (2001). "The Nature and Growth of Vertical Specialization in World Trade." *Journal of International Economics*, 54(1): pp. 75–96.

Japanese Bank of International Cooperation (2004). *JBIC Review*, Tokyo: Government of Japan.

Jones, R. W., and H. Kierzkowski (1990). "The Role of Services in Production and International Trade: A Theoretical Framework," in R. Jones and A. Krueger (Eds.), *The Political Economy of International Trade: Festschrift in Honor of Robert Baldwin*, pp. 31–48, Oxford: Basil Blackwell.

Jones, R. W., H. Kierzkowski and C. Lurong (2004). "What does the Evidence Tell Us About Fragmentation and Outsourcing." *International Review of Economics and Finance*, 14(3): pp. 305–316.

Krugman, P. (1995). "Growing World Trade: Causes and Consequences." *Brooking Papers on Economic Activity*, 1: pp. 327–377.

White Paper on International Economy and Trade 2008, Ministry of Economy, Trade and Industry, Japan.

Ng, F. and A. Yeats (2001). "Production Sharing in East Asia: Who does What for Whom, and Why?" in L. K. Cheng and H. Kierzkowski (Eds.), *Global Production and Trade in East Asia*, pp. 63–109, Boston: Kluwer Academic.

Ng, F. and A. Yeats (2003). "Major Trade Trends in East Asia: What are their Implications for Regional Cooperation and Growth?" Policy Research Working Paper No. 3084, World Bank, Washington, D.C.

Wakasugi, R. (2007), "Vertical Intra-Industry Trade and Economic Integration in East Asia." *Asian Economic Papers*, 6(1): pp. 26–39.

Wei, S.-J. (1997). "Why is Corruption So Much More Taxing Than Tax? Arbitrariness kills," National Bureau of Economic Research Working Paper, No. 6255, Cambridge, MA, U.S.

Comment

Theresa Greaney

This is a well-informed and well-documented account of recent trends in East Asian trade, with particular emphasis on measuring and explaining increases in intra-regional trade. The growth in intra-regional trade has coincided with increases in both foreign direct investment (FDI) and production fragmentation in the region. The authors present detailed descriptive statistics to document the simultaneous growth in intra-regional trade, intermediates trade, and FDI in East Asia, and they reference some of the related literature on multinational enterprises (MNEs) and international trade to back up their hypothesis that these three growth trends are tightly connected. The authors also identify the U.S., Japan, and South Korea as major sources of FDI for East Asia, and multinational firms from these countries play a major role in generating these trends.

The descriptive analysis is extremely detailed and informative, but the use of a gravity model to analyze the authors' research questions needs further development, so my comments focus on this later section of the chapter. The gravity model traditionally is used to predict bilateral trade based on GDPs of trade partners, distance between trade partners, and other factors (e.g., common language, common border, etc.). To give the gravity model a more solid theoretical foundation, Anderson and van Wincoop (2003) added a multilateral resistance term to the gravity model using price indices. Feenstra (2002) provided a simpler way of accounting for multilateral resistance by showing that country fixed effects could be used in place of difficult-to-measure price indices. This chapter makes quite a few changes from the traditional usage of a gravity model by: (1) omitting the multilateral resistance term; (2) restricting the sample of trading countries to only nine East Asian countries; and (3) changing the dependent variable to parts of bilateral trade (i.e., parts and components, and capital goods) rather than total bilateral trade.

To address these issues, I would suggest that the authors include benchmark results for total bilateral trade involving many countries in addition to East Asian countries, and include a dummy variable when both trade partners are located in East Asia. If the East Asia dummy variable is significant and presumably positive, then that provides evidence that something is different about trade in this region — these countries are trading within East Asia more than we would expect based on their GDPs and trading distances, which justifies further inquiry. I would also recommend including more trade partners throughout the authors' use of the gravity model. To measure the impact of FDI on intra-regional trade, we need to include inter-regional trade along with intra-regional trade in the estimations. The authors might consider using an interaction term to see to what extent FDI from each of their three target investors — the U.S., Japan, and South Korea — impacts all trade involving East Asian countries and, in particular, how it affects intra-regional trade.

I would also suggest including benchmark results for total bilateral trade versus results for just parts and components trade or just capital goods trade to see if the results differ when trade is broken down into sub-groupings. When trade is broken up, should we expect that a country's GDP is a good predictor of how much a country exports or imports of a particular category of intermediate goods? Maybe the authors could consider using gross industrial output or gross output of final goods, rather than GDP, as predictors of trade in intermediates.

To assess the impact of FDI on trade but avoid the inherent endogeneity problem, the authors use instrumental variables to estimate FDI and then use these estimated values as independent variables in the gravity model. While the approach seems reasonable, the authors' description of their methodology could be improved. It was confusing to see only one subscript on the variable FDI_i which I thought represented a bilateral flow or stock involving two countries. Regarding the independent variable $DUTY_i$, the text should clarify how the "import tariff of the host country" is measured. Is this a trade-weighted average tariff for manufactured goods? Since so many exceptions are made for export-processing firms that are hypothesized to be key players in intra-regional intermediates trade in East Asia, should tariffs really be an important predictor of FDI? Regarding the independent variables $DIFPGDP_{ij}$ and $DIFWAGE_{ij}$ which are defined as the absolute value of differences in per capita GDP and wages, respectively, I believe that the signs of these differences matter in predicting FDI. Do we expect the same coefficient on $DIFWAGE_{ij}$ in predicting FDI from South Korea into a country with 10% lower wages and into one with 10% higher wages? The authors also could strengthen this section by showing their results from Equation (2) so that the readers can assess the accuracy of their predicted value of FDI.

Once these issues have been clarified, the authors' results will add to the growing literature that seeks to explain recent changes in East Asian trade. I suspect they will provide robust evidence that FDI plays a key, independent role in facilitating trade in intermediate products in East Asia.

REFERENCES

Anderson, J. A. and van Wincoop, E. (2003). "Gravity with Gravitas: A Solution to the Border Puzzle." *American Economic Review*, 93: pp. 170–192.

Feenstra, R. C. (2002). "Border Effects and the Gravity Equation: Consistent Methods for Estimation." *Scottish Journal of Political Economy*, 49: pp. 491–506.

CHAPTER 10

The Influence of Multinational Exposure on Private Chinese Trade

Deborah L. Swenson

Department of Economics, University of California, Davis, USA
NBER, Cambridge, Massachusetts, USA

I. INTRODUCTION

The sustained growth of Chinese exports has been notable on many dimensions. In addition to its unusually high rate of growth, Chinese trade is also distinguished by the large degree of foreign firm involvement and for the importance of outsourcing trade. The rapid growth of Chinese trade has been accompanied by an emerging debate on whether Chinese exporters have moved into export industries that are more sophisticated than are typically observed for countries otherwise similar to China.[1] Taken together, the confluence of these developments raises the question of how the multinational company (MNC) presence in China is altering the trade environment and the capability of local firms.[2]

There are many reasons to expect that multinationals will have a positive effect on local firms. For example, exposure to multinationals may provide informational spillovers about production techniques or technologies, new

[1] Rodrik (2006); Schott (2008); and Kiyota (2008).

[2] The question of multinational spillovers is not new. In the trade context, Aitken, Hanson, and Harrison (1997); Greenaway, Sousa, and Wakelin (2004); and Ma (2006), uncover a positive association between MNC presence and export probabilities or export volumes, while Swenson (2008) notes an association between multinational presence and the creation of new trade at the extensive margin. Similarly, Head, Jing, and Swenson (2009) find that the expansion of large retailers in China is associated with the increases in export capabilities. However, exporting spillovers are not observed in all contexts. Summaries of the large literature on multinational spillovers is provided by Blomstrom and Kokko (1998); Navaretti and Venables (2004); and Gorg and Greenaway (2004).

products, or destination market opportunities, which in turn, elevates the export capabilities of local firms.[3] Nonetheless, MNC presence has other effects that may exert a negative influence on local firm export outcomes. In particular, if MNCs cause congestion in local factor markets, or if MNCs directly compete with local firms in product markets, the net effect of multinational presence may instead be negative.[4] Because multinationals are likely to simultaneously render both positive and negative effects in local production markets, the net effect of multinational exposure deserves empirical exploration since it cannot be determined by theory alone.

Due to the characteristics of Chinese trade development, China's trade provides an ideal setting in which to examine the relationship between MNC activities and private local-firm export capabilities. First, thanks to the tremendous influx of foreign investment in the 1990s and early 2000s, there was sizable variation in the evolution of multinational activity at the city-sector level which can be used to identify multinational spillovers to local private export outcomes. In addition, as Figure 1 illustrates, MNCs

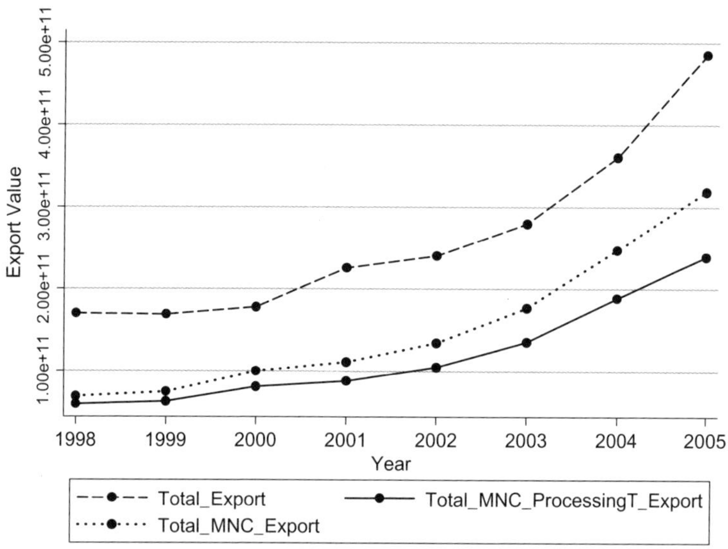

Source: Customs General Administration of the People's Republic of China.

Fig. 1. Multinational firm contribution to Chinese trade.

[3]See Rauch (1999) and Rauch and Trindade (2003) for background on information and trade.

[4]For discussion and evidence on negative multinational spillovers, see Aitken and Harrison (1999).

were responsible for more than half of China's exports between 1998 and 2005, and therefore, the scale of multinational exposure was sufficient to generate effects, if MNCs are an important conduit.

A further benefit of turning to the Chinese experience is that one can examine different factors in MNC engagement in trade, thus searching for evidence that provides information on the types of multinational contact that help or hinder the expansion of private local export. Of particular interest is the relative influence of processing trade. As Figure 1 shows, the majority of MNC exports involved processing trade activity, where foreign firms produced products in China for export. Therefore, it is also possible to test whether contact with firms engaged in processing trade rendered different effects than contact with firms involved in ordinary trade.

Empirical examination of China's trade between 1998 and 2005 shows that private Chinese firms achieved superior export outcomes when local firms were surrounded by a growing presence of MNCs. This result is apparent even after one controls for city-sector fixed effects, as well as contemporaneous measures of economic activity at the sector and city level that provide controls for the rapid rate of growth in trade. Evaluated with the most conservative parameter estimates, which are based on regressions that include contemporaneous demand and supply variables, the estimated coefficients indicate that the increases in multinational exposure experienced by the average city-SITC3 sector between 1998 and 2005 would have generated a 7.2% increase in private export transactions.

Following the general analysis, this chapter asks whether a particular channel — the import of intermediate inputs — contributed to the improved export outcomes for local private firms exposed to MNCs. The answer appears to be in affirmative, as about half of the original effect appears to be driven by multinational import of inputs, and the effect is observed only in manufacturing, but not in non-manufacturing industries. This is consistent with recent work which suggests that local firm productivity may be improved when firms gain better access to a greater variety of imported inputs.

As a final check on this result, the chapter also tests whether the effect of MNCs on local firm export outcomes can be explained by MNCs' capital equipment imports. The results indicate that MNC capital equipment imports were associated with improved local private firm export volumes, although the effect is again restricted to private export in manufacturing sectors. Further, if capital equipment imports are disaggregated between those imported by foreign-invested enterprises (FIEs) versus those imported by multinationals for use in processing trade, it appears that the strongest spillover benefits were driven by the former category of capital equipment imports, those of (FIEs).

II. DATA AND TRENDS IN CHINESE EXPORT

To measure private trade outcomes and multinational involvement in China, I use Chinese trade data as reported in the Customs General Administration of the People's Republic of China for 1997–2005.[5] The unusual and useful aspect of these data is their highly disaggregated reporting of firm ownership type and Chinese city-district of origin, in addition to the typical information on trade volume, destination or origin country partner, and HS8 product classification. The data on ownership type are especially useful, since it means that one can separately identify and distinguish between the trade transactions of foreign firms and of Chinese-owned entities.

The primary measure of interest in this chapter is the level of export by private Chinese firms. To display the role of various actors in the data set, the original HS8 transactions for 1998 to 2005 for each firm type are aggregated to the national level. These trade numbers are then used to calculate the trade shares for each Chinese exporter group, and displayed in Figure 2. The notable development that emerges is that the relative private share of Chinese export trade grew more than four-fold during the period of analysis. Over the same interval, the share of China's exports attributable to MNCs remained fairly stable, while the share of trade that was related to state-owned enterprises and other residual groups shrank. Exposure to the influx of MNCs may have helped private Chinese firms to learn about new products and processes, especially if the MNCs were more advanced than their Chinese counterparts.[6]

---

[5]These data were used under license to the CID at the University of California, Davis.

[6]Brambilla (2006) finds that the rate of new product introduction was twice as rapid by multinational firms in China than it was for private Chinese firms.

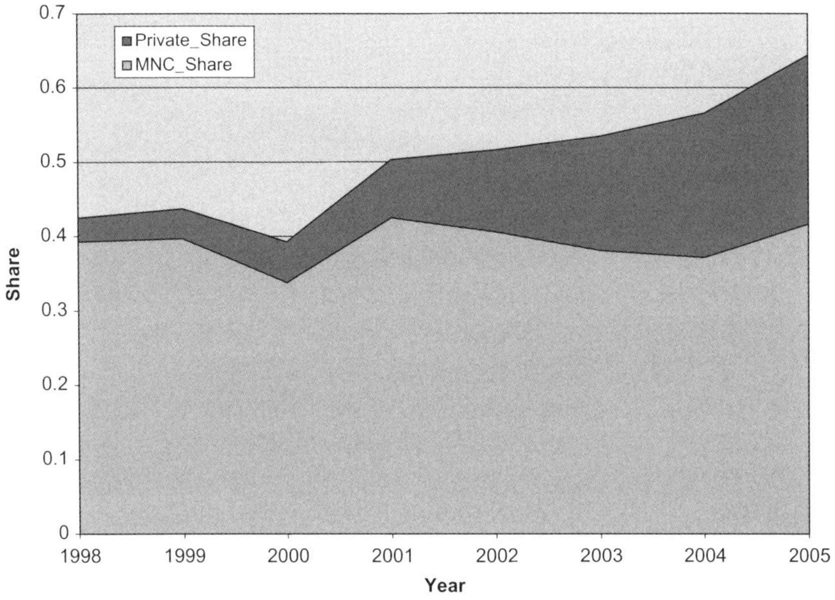

Source: Customs General Administration of the People's Republic of China.

Fig. 2. The composition of Chinese exports, 1998–2005.

For a second view on developments in Chinese exports, Figure 3 depicts Chinese processing exports by agent. Chinese processing trade developments are a bit different than those for all trade flows. In this trade segment, private Chinese firms exhibited only small increases in export share, while the share attributable to MNCs grew from 65% to 87% of all Chinese processing exports.

While the original data set records transactions at the fine HS8 digit level of detail, the empirical analysis examines the data at the city-sector level, where alternative measures of sector (three-digit and four-digit SITC) are used. At this level, it is possible to measure local private export performance at the city-sector level either by export volumes, or by the count of unique export transactions.[7]

[7]Uniqueness of transactions stems from differences in city-district origin, firm type, destination country, and HS8 product.

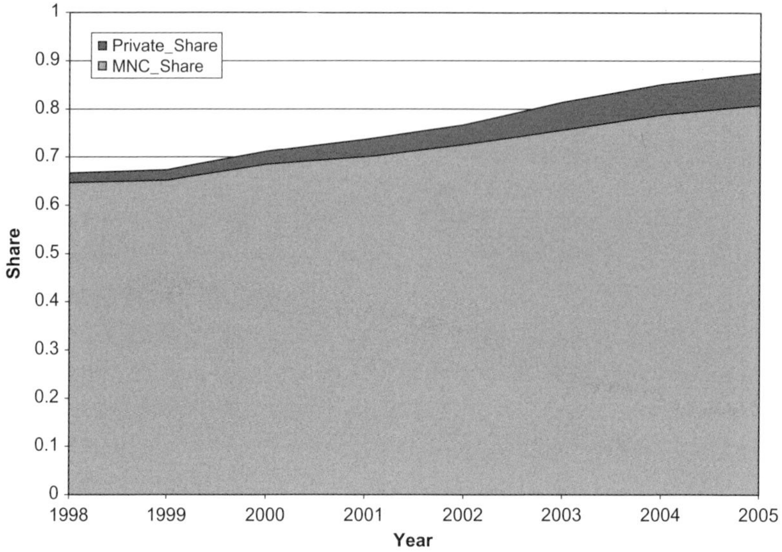

Source: Customs General Administration of the People's Republic of China.

Fig. 3. The composition of Chinese processing exports, 1998–2005.

To capture the economic influence of MNCs, I also turn to the data on Chinese HS8 trade transactions. Using the information on the organization conducting each trade transactions, all transactions that involved at least some multinational influence were coded as multinationals. This includes transactions that are listed under the categories "foreign-invested enterprises," "joint ventures," and "equity joint ventures." First, to measure multinational presence, I created a multinational variable that is a synthetic count of "firms," where firms were defined by each unique combination of the city-origin, country-destination, regime-type, and firm-type identifiers in the data set.[8]

To illustrate the degree of change in MNC presence variable, Table 1 reports the average level of MNC contact for two-digit SITC manufacturing industries. These observations for the years 1997 and 2004 represent the average MNC presence of active three-digit SITC-city observations within

[8]This concept of "firms" originates in Feenstra and Hanson (2005). While the data record HS8 export transactions, the fine disaggregation of transaction identifier (HS8 product, city of production, city-zone ownership type, and processing regime) generates information that is close in nature to that available in firm-level data sets.

Table 1. Multinational involvement at the city-SITC3 level, count measures

Two-digit SITC	Industry description	No. of MNCs in 1997	No. of MNCs in 2004
61	Leather, leather manufactures, N.E.S., and dressed furskins	2.22	4.35
62	Rubber manufactures, N.E.S.	3.8	9.99
63	Cork and wood manufactures other than furniture	7.72	13.93
64	Paper, paperboard, and articles of paper pulp, paper or paper board	5.27	17.41
65	Textile yarn, fabrics, made-up articles, N.E.S., and related products	4.89	15.83
66	Nonmetallic mineral manufactures, N.E.S.	5.03	10.59
67	Iron and steel	0.93	2.17
68	Nonferrous metals	0.92	2.92
69	Manufactures of metals, N.E.S.	6.72	20.43
71	Power generating machinery and equipment	1.57	5.57
72	Machinery specialized for particular industries	1.35	4.68
73	Metalworking machinery	0.8	2.75
74	General industrial machinery and equipment, N.E.S., and machine parts, N.E.S.	2.72	12.75
75	Office machines and automatic data processing machines	5.12	16.57
76	Telecommunications and sound recording and reproducing apparatus and equipment	14.87	46.33
77	Electrical machinery, apparatus and appliances, N.E.S., and electrical parts thereof	11	30.47
78	Road vehicles (including air-cushion vehicles)	2.52	10.69
79	Transport equipment, N.E.S.	0.67	1.47
81	Prefabricated buildings; sanitary, plumbing, heating and lighting fixtures and fittings, N.E.S.	5.98	14.66
82	Furniture and parts thereof; bedding, mattresses, mattress supports, cushions and similar stuffed furnishings	22.81	71.29
83	Travel goods, handbags and similar containers	28.89	50.54
84	Articles of apparel and clothing accessories	26.21	53.11
85	Footwear	36.35	57.5
87	Professional, scientific and controlling instruments and apparatus, N.E.S.	3.88	12.89
88	Photographic apparatus, equipment and supplies and optical goods, N.E.S.; watches and clocks	8.07	13.95
89	Miscellaneous manufactured articles, N.E.S.	19.79	42.04

Note: # of MNCs reports the average number of distinct MNC transactions at the city level, for three-digit industries within each of the two-digit SITC manufacturing industries.

the two-digit industries.[9] The striking detail in this table is the growth in average level of multinational contact. For 22 of the 26 two-digit manufacturing industries, the *frequency* measure of multinational contact in 2004 was at least twice as large as it was in 1997, and in some industries, the growth was much more rapid yet. The base numbers on growth, as well as the standard deviation, suggest that wide differences across time and location should provide sufficient variation in the multinational measures to help identify spillover effects in the regression analysis.

The second measure of multinational contact is based on the volume of multinational export transactions, again at the city-sector level of aggregation. This variable was formed by aggregating all HS8 product trade transactions at the city-year level to the sector level. Here too, the underlying variables doubled over the estimation period, and exhibited significant variation across time and location that is exploited for identification in the regression analysis.

III. ESTIMATION FRAMEWORK AND RESULTS

The empirical goal of this chapter is to examine how the export capability of private Chinese firms is influenced by the evolution of their exposure to MNCs at the city level. For this purpose, the primary dependent variable is the level of year t exports by private Chinese firms at the city (c) and sector (s) level, $\text{Private\_EXP}_{\text{cst}}$. The first regression, specification (1) relates the current value of private exports to the level of multinational activity in the previous year.

$$\begin{aligned}\ln(\mathit{Private\_EXP}_{\text{cst}}) = \alpha &+ \beta_1 \times \ln(\mathit{Sector\_MNC}_{\text{cs},t-1}) \\ &+ \beta_2 \times \ln(\mathit{Ind\_MNC}_{\text{cs},t-1}) \\ &+ \beta_3 \times \ln(\mathit{OtherInd\_MNC}_{\text{cs},t-1}) + \Sigma Y_t + \varepsilon_{\text{cst}}. \quad (1)\end{aligned}$$

In this regression, *sector* refers to private or multinational economic activity at the three-digit or four-digit SITC level.

[9]Since the analysis tests how previous multinational presence affected current private exports, the multinational data for 1997–2004 are used to explain private trade outcomes between 1998 and 2005.

In the three-digit (four-digit) regressions, *OwnSec_MNC* refers to multinational exports in $t - 1$ for the same city three-digit (four-digit) sector level as the private firm. Similarly, *OwnInd_MNC* is the measure of multinational exports in $t - 1$ for the city in the one-digit sector that contains the private firm observation. To avoid double counting, time $t - 1$ multinational exports reported for the same city three-digit (four-digit) sector level which were already included in *OwnSec_MNC* are excluded from the measure *OwnInd_MNC*. The final measure of multinational exposure *OtherInd_MNC* includes all multinational exports from the city in year $t - 1$, excluding the multinational exports that are included in the previous two variables.

The variables referencing multinational spillovers are all lagged one period relative to the private outcome variables, under the assumption that multinational spillovers act with a lag due to learning and/or implementation lags. In the case of learning lags, it may take some time before private Chinese firms observe the nature of MNC activities and opportunities. Alternatively, lags will occur if local private firms learn only after they hire workers who choose to move from MNCs to local employers. When local private firms decide to implement the production techniques they have observed, or to form new export contracts with partners they learned of through multinational contact, they face a second lag.

While the multinational exposure variables are lagged one period to reflect the nature of firm decisions, the use of lags also has econometric benefits. In particular, the use of lagged regressors alleviates simultaneity issues by ensuring that the multinational variables are predetermined relative to the dependent variable.

The original specification is estimated using fixed-effect panel regression techniques, which assume that the error term includes a fixed component at the city-sector level. City-sector fixed effects are particularly important for this estimating framework, since there are many unobserved factors that are likely to make cities suited for export in some sectors and not others. No doubt, the set of relevant determinants include specific factors, such as natural resource availability or particular worker skills, and available infrastructure. City-sector effects, also reflect the local policy environment, and whether the policy setting is beneficial to particular industries. Any of these elements have the potential to foster both private export and multinational export. Since it is not feasible to collect all relevant variables for the full set of cities in this project, all regressions are estimated using panel specifications which include city-sector fixed effects.[10] The choice of this framework implies that the effects of multinational contact are identified by within variation since the use of fixed effects removes time-invariant factors that help to stimulate both MNC and private firm exports. Such an assumption is appropriate as long as the comparative advantage factors that stimulated exports by private or MNCs remained static at the city-sector level during the period of estimation.

Finally, each regression estimated also includes fixed-year effects. These are useful for capturing changes over time due to macroeconomic developments such as changes in prices or the business cycle, or due to China's entry into the WTO, which made exporting more or less favorable for all exporters, are swept out. While the coefficients for the fixed year effects are not reported in the regression tables, they grow in magnitude over the panel, and are always statistically significant. Thus, the time effects confirm that changes in China's environment were indeed important to both multinational and private firm exports.

Initial Estimates of the Basic Regression Framework

The estimation results for the basic specification are displayed in Table 2. Whether private export volumes are measured at the three-digit or four-digit level, the regression uncovers a positive association between changes in own-sector multinational exposure, and the subsequent level of private exports by local firms in the same city-sector. For the manufacturing sector, the coefficient estimates imply that a one-standard deviation increase in the level of own-sector multinational exposure at the four-digit (three-digit) SITC level was associated with a 11.5% (15.5%) increase in private firm exports. These regressions also show a positive association for non-manufacturing sectors, although the implied increase in private exports in non-manufacturing sectors is associated with much smaller changes — a 6.7% (4.2%) increase if multinational exposure in non-manufacturing

[10]The coefficients on the multinational exposure terms are dramatically larger in magnitude if the regressions are estimated using OLS, even when the regressions are augmented to include dummy variables for city and SITC sector.

Table 2. General multinational exposure and the value of exports by private exporters, 1998–2005

	Four-digit SITC		Three-digit SITC	
	Mfg	Non-Mfg	Mfg	Non-Mfg
Multinational Export Volume,	0.014[a]	0.009[a]	0.019[a]	0.014[a]
City-Sector	(0.001)	(0.002)	(0.001)	(0.000)
Multinational Export Volume,	0.014[a]	−0.004	0.006[b]	0.001
City-Industry	(0.003)	(0.003)	(0.003)	(0.003)
Multinational Export Volume,	0.039[a]	0.033[a]	0.014[a]	0.020[a]
City-Other Industries	(0.004)	(0.006)	(0.004)	(0.005)
Year Dummies	Yes	Yes	Yes	Yes
City-Sector Fixed Effects	Yes	Yes	Yes	Yes
Within R^2	0.313	0.239	0.355	0.263
Between R^2	0.021	0.004	0.003	0.007
Overall R^2	0.027	0.018	0.003	0.022
Observations	225,411	71,152	114,718	51,889
Groups	68,929	24,855	32,919	17,350

Note: All variables measured in logs. Dependent variable, private export volume at the city sector level. Standard errors in paranthesis.
[a]Significance at the 1% level.
[b]Significance at the 5% level.
[c]Significance at the 10% level.

sectors measured by four-digit (three-digit) SITC industry increased by one standard deviation.

Multinational contact as measured by the evolution at the other industry level has an even stronger association in the estimates. This suggests that multinational presence brings general benefits to the local market area. In addition, since this coefficient is larger than the own-sector effect, it suggests that competition in product markets, or congestion of sector-specific factor markets attenuate the benefits from multinational contact.

Input Imports and the Effects of Multinational Contacts

While the basic regression provides evidence of a positive relationship between growth in MNC exposure at the city level, and the subsequent growth of private exporter activity, the regression does not provide any indication of the reasons for the association. First, the association could be driven by information. Here, private firms could learn of their export opportunities, by observing the opportunities available to their MNC neighbors, or by learning from workers who leave MNC employers to work in private firms. Alternatively, the growth of MNC activity in a city could foster the influx of trade intermediaries to the city, such as buyers, distributers and shippers. Subsequently, the presence of new local buyers and trade intermediaries may enable the local private firms to make their own connections in international markets, even if they are not directly interacting with the MNCs themselves. Finally, MNCs, due to their import of inputs, may increase the availability of inputs at the local level. Since the availability of new inputs has the potential to increase firm productivity, the local firms may experience improvements in their ability to export.[11]

To test how proximity to MNCs and their imports affected local private Chinese firms, the basic regression specification is augmented with three new regressors that measure the dollar value of MNC imports at the city-year level. As before, the MNC variables are lagged one year relative to the dependent variable, which is the value of private exports at the city-sector-year level.

$$\begin{aligned}
&\ln(\mathit{Private_EXP}_{\mathrm{cst}}) \\
&\quad = \alpha + \beta_1 \times \ln(\mathit{Sector_MNC}_{\mathrm{cs},t-1}) + \beta_2 \times \ln(\mathit{Ind_MNC}_{\mathrm{cs},t-1}) \\
&\qquad + \beta_3 \times \ln(\mathit{OtherInd_MNC}_{\mathrm{cs},t-1}) + \gamma_1 \times \ln(\mathit{Sector_MNC_IMP}_{\mathrm{cs},t-1}) \\
&\qquad + \gamma_2 \times \ln(\mathit{Ind_MNC_IMP}_{\mathrm{cs},t-1}) \\
&\qquad + \gamma_3 \times \ln(\mathit{OtherInd_MNC_IMP}_{\mathrm{cs},t-1}) + \Sigma Y_t + \varepsilon_{\mathrm{cst}}. \qquad (2)
\end{aligned}$$

[11] Using firm-level data from India, Goldberg *et al.* (2008) are able to show that firms that were able to import larger varieties of inputs due to India's trade liberalization in the 1990s introduced more new products. In related work, Kasahara and Rodrigue (2008) find that when Chilean firms become importers of intermediate inputs, they experienced an increase in productivity. However, while Amiti and Konings (2007) find that cuts in Indonesian tariffs had effects that were especially large when the tariffs cut were on intermediate inputs, and with the productivity effects concentrated in importing firms, Arkolakis *et al.* (2008) do not find similar benefits from increased import varieties in Costa Rica. In the U.S., Ellison, Glaeser, and Kerr (2007) attribute the largest benefit of agglomeration as arising from the collocation of firms in related industries, which increases the output of inputs.

In contrast with the original "MNC" variables that are based on the export presence of values of MNCs, the new variables *MNC_IMP*, are constructed based on the import transactions data for Chinese imports that were purchased by MNCs. The first variable *Sector_MNC_IMP* is formed by aggregating all MNC imports that match the four-digit or three-digit SITC aggregation of the dependent variable. Moving to the coarser levels, *Ind_MNC_IMP* includes all multinational import activity in the one-digit SITC, aside from the multinational imports already reflected in *Sector_MNC_IMP*. Finally, the variable *OtherIND_MNC_IMP*, contains all multinational imports at the city level that were not contained in the previous two variables. Two maintained assumptions are implicit in the method that is used to represent the exposure to imported intermediate inputs brought in by MNCs. First, it is assumed that private firms produce their preferred product variety and do not benefit from collocation and use of multinational inputs that are in their three- or four-digit sector. Second, since I do not have a detailed input–output matrix for Chinese production which maps the use of inputs at the fine product level, I assume that firms (on average) use a greater share of inputs from their own industry, than from other outside industries.

Table 3 reports the results from running regression specification (2). Beginning with the results based on private firm exports at the SITC4 level, three results emerge. First, once variables capturing the effects of exposure to MNC import are added to the regression specification, the estimated coefficient for the impact of own-sector exposure to multinational export activity falls by half. This suggests that one conduit for the positive influence of MNC exposure operates through channels affecting the availability, and possibly the price, of imported intermediate inputs. Second, the benefits of multinational import are observed primarily due to multinational imports outside of the private firm's sector. Finally, the distinction between manufacturing and non-manufacturing private Chinese firms is especially stark. The data indicate that the positive associations related to MNC presence are almost entirely observed in the manufacturing sector.

When the analysis of regression specification (2) is repeated at the three-digit SITC level, the contrast between private firms in manufacturing versus non-manufacturing sectors is less dramatic. However, the three-digit regression results also support the notion that local private firms benefit

Table 3. General and import multinational exposure and the value of exports by private exporters, 1998–2005

	Four-digit SITC		Three-digit SITC	
	Mfg	Non-Mfg	Mfg	Non-Mfg
Multinational Export Volume, City-Sector	0.007[a] (0.001)	0.006[a] (0.002)	0.018[a] (0.001)	0.014[a] (0.000)
Multinational Export Volume, City-Industry	0.012 (0.009)	−0.017[b] (0.008)	0.002 (.003)	−0.000 (0.003)
Multinational Export Volume, City-Other Industries	0.060[a] (0.016)	0.025 (0.025)	0.004 (0.004)	0.017[a] (0.005)
Multinational Import Volume, City-Sector	0.002[a] (0.001)	−0.001 (0.000)	0.007[a] (0.002)	0.004[a] (0.002)
Multinational Import Volume, City-Industry	0.038[a] (0.007)	0.021 (0.009)	0.008[a] (0.003)	0.008[a] (0.003)
Multinational Import Volume, City-Other Industries	0.070[a] (0.010)	0.005 (0.017)	0.018[a] (0.003)	0.005 (0.004)
Year Dummies	Yes	Yes	Yes	Yes
City-Sector Fixed Effects	Yes	Yes	Yes	Yes
Within R^2	0.363	0.289	0.356	0.263
Between R^2	0.010	0.001	0.019	0.006
Overall R^2	0.039	0.023	0.039	0.021
Observations	225,411	71,152	114,718	51,889
Groups	68,929	24,855	32,919	17,350

Note: All variables measured in logs. Dependent variable, private export volume at the city sector level. Standard errors in paranthesis.
[a]Significance at the 1% level.
[b]Significance at the 5% level.
[c]Significance at the 10% level.

when multinational contact exposes local firms to greater imports of inputs, and that the effect is strongest for manufacturing sectors.

To better understand why exposure to multinational imports is associated with improved export ability for local private firms, I turn to a specific category of import — capital equipment. Since work by Lee (1995) and Eaton and Kortum (2001) suggests that capital goods imports are associated with increased higher levels of economic growth at a country level, multinationals may be particularly beneficial when they introduce private firms to new capital, or when MNCs begin to produce parts in China, that they make available locally. To test this idea, the basic regression specification is now supplemented with measures of capital goods import by MNCs.

$$\begin{aligned}\ln(Private\_EXP_{cst}) &= \alpha + \beta_1 \times \ln(Sector\_MNC_{cs,t-1}) + \beta_2 \times \ln(Ind\_MNC_{cs,t-1}) \\ &\quad + \beta_3 \times \ln(OtherInd\_MNC_{cs,t-1}) \\ &\quad + \gamma_1 \times \ln(OtherSector\_MNC\_CAPGood_{cs,t-1}) + \Sigma Y_t + \varepsilon_{cst}. \quad (3)\end{aligned}$$

The new measure *OtherSector_MNC_CAPGood* comprises total capital goods imports by MNCs, whether for use by FIEs, or by multinational outsourcing firms. In each regression, the measure includes all capital goods imports outside of the three- or four-digit sector, at which the private firm export is measured. This is because own-sector exposure may bring direct competition with the private firms, while other-sector capital goods imports may convey information spillovers, or may increase the inputs that are available to local firms.

The effects of adding multinational capital goods imports to the regression are displayed in Table 4. In manufacturing sectors, the results show that MNC capital goods imports had a strong positive association with subsequent private firm export ability in manufacturing sectors. At the same time, no association is found for private firm export ability outside of the manufacturing sectors. The coefficient estimates for the manufacturing sectors are economically meaningful. For example, in the case of three-digit sector private manufacturing export, the estimated coefficient implies that a one standard deviation increase in the level of multinational capital goods imports would boost private exports by 9.9%.

In investigating the effects of capital equipment imports by MNCs, it is possible to make a distinction between capital equipment that was imported by multinational outsourcing firms, versus capital equipment imports made by foreign invested firms. To this end, Equation (3) is modified to include two separate coefficients to reflect these two types of capital equipment imports. As before, the results in Table 5 show that there is no positive effect of these imports on the export abilities of private firm exporters in non-manufacturing industries. By contrast, all of the effects are noted in the manufacturing sectors, and the effects are found to be most pronounced for capital equipment imports by FIEs rather than for capital goods imports by outsourcing firms.

Table 4. **General and total capital equipment multinational exposure and the value of exports by private exporters, 1998–2005**

	Four-digit SITC		Three-digit SITC	
	Mfg	Non-Mfg	Mfg	Non-Mfg
Multinational Export Volume,	0.007[a]	0.009[a]	0.018[a]	0.014[a]
City-Sector	(0.001)	(0.002)	(0.001)	(0.002)
Multinational Export Volume,	0.013[a]	−0.004	0.004	0.001
City-Industry	(0.003)	(0.003)	(0.003)	(0.003)
Multinational Export Volume,	0.038[a]	0.033[a]	0.011[a]	0.020[a]
City-Other Industries	(0.004)	(0.006)	(0.004)	(0.005)
Total City Other Sector Capital	0.012[a]	0.003	0.014[a]	0.000
Equipment Imports	(0.002)	(0.003)	(0.002)	(0.003)
Year Dummies	Yes	Yes	Yes	Yes
City-Sector Fixed Effects	Yes	Yes	Yes	Yes
Within R^2	0.314	239	0.355	0.263
Between R^2	0.019	0.004	0.025	0.007
Overall R^2	0.028	0.018	0.035	0.002
Observations	225,411	71,152	114,718	51,889
Groups	68,929	24,855	32,919	17,350

Note: All variables measured in logs. Dependent variable, private export volume at the city sector level. Standard errors in paranthesis.
[a]Significance at the 1% level.
[b]Significance at the 5% level.
[c]Significance at the 10% level.

IV. ROBUSTNESS CHECKS AND DISCUSSION

Outsourcing

The regression analysis focuses on total trade, which comprises both ordinary trade and outsourcing trade. However, the magnitude of private outsourcing trade responses may be stronger or weaker. In addition, private outsourcing trade may be shaped by a different set of factors than those that move other forms of commerce. Finally, multinational activity that is oriented toward outsourcing activities may have differential spillovers effects when compared with multinational activity directed to the conduct of ordinary trade. To ask whether outsourcing trade should be treated separately, Table 6 considers some alternate specifications. To begin, in the first two columns I use the original dependent variable, total private export

Table 5. General and capital equipment multinational exposure and the value of exports by private exporters, 1998–2005

	Four-digit SITC		Three-digit SITC	
	Mfg	Non-Mfg	Mfg	Non-Mfg
Multinational Export Volume,	0.007[a]	0.006[a]	0.018[a]	0.014[a]
City-Sector	(0.001)	(0.002)	(0.001)	(0.000)
Multinational Export Volume,	0.021[b]	−0.017[b]	0.004	−0.000
City-Industry	(0.009)	(0.008)	(0.003)	(0.003)
Multinational Export Volume,	0.092[a]	0.025	0.011[a]	0.020[a]
City-Other Industries	(0.015)	(0.025)	(0.004)	(0.005)
City Capital Equipment Imports	−0.002[b]	−0.004[c]	0.003[b]	−0.001
By Outsourcing firms	(0.001)	(0.003)	(0.001)	(0.002)
City Capital Equipment	0.043[a]	0.002	0.014[a]	0.000
Imports by FIEs	(0.005)	(0.009)	(0.002)	(0.002)
Year Dummies	Yes	Yes	Yes	Yes
City-Sector Fixed Effects	Yes	Yes	Yes	Yes
Within R^2	0.363	0.289	0.355	0.263
Between R^2	0.012	0.005	0.023	0.007
Overall R^2	0.038	0.023	0.037	0.022
Observations	225,411	71,152	114,718	51,889
Groups	68,929	24,855	32,919	17,350

Note: All variables measured in logs. Dependent variable, private export volume at the city sector level. Standard errors in paranthesis.
[a]Significance at the 1% level.
[b]Significance at the 5% level.
[c]Significance at the 10% level.

at the city-sector level, but separate the multinational variable into two components that distinguish the multinational outsourcing activity from multinational engagement in ordinary trade. Controlling for capital equipment imports, it appears that the general export presence of MNC firms involved in ordinary trade has a larger positive effect on private firm exports than does the presence of MNC firms involved in outsourcing.[12]

One reason for this differential may be that multinational outsourcing stimulates private outsourcing, while it is not similarly helpful to local firms

[12]If the regressors for capital goods import are removed from the specifications in columns 1 and 2 in Table 6, the coefficients on the multinational export variables do not change appreciably.

Table 6. Multinational outsourcing exposure and private exporter outcomes in manufacturing, 1998–2005

	Private export value city-four-digit SITC total		Private outsourcing export value, city-four-digit SITC total		Private export transactions city-four-digit SITC number	
MNC Outsourcing Exports City-Sector Value	0.006[a] (0.001)	0.006[a] (0.011)	0.031[a] (0.002)	0.030[a] (0.002)	0.004[a] (0.000)	0.004[a] (0.000)
MNC Outsourcing Exports City-Other Sector Value	0.011[b] (0.002)	0.012[b] (0.002)	0.015[b] (0.005)	0.017[b] (0.005)	0.009[b] (0.001)	0.011[a] (0.001)
MNC Ordinary Exports City-Sector Value	0.015[a] (0.011)	0.015[a] (0.011)	0.007[a] (0.002)	0.007[a] (0.002)	0.009[a] (0.001)	0.010[a] (0.000)
MNC Ordinary Exports City-Other Sector Value	0.050[a] (0.004)	0.049[a] (0.004)	0.072[a] (0.010)	0.070[a] (0.010)	0.045[a] (0.002)	0.044[a] (0.002)
Total City Other Sector Capital Equipment Imports	0.011[a] (0.002)		0.013[a] (0.002)		0.008[a] (0.001)	
City Capital Equipment Imports by Outsourcing firms		0.005[a] (0.001)		0.004[a] (0.002)		0.001[a] (0.000)
City Capital Equipment Imports by FIEs		0.002[b] (0.001)		0.012[a] (0.002)		0.003[a] (0.000)
Year Dummies	Yes	Yes	Yes	Yes	Yes	Yes
City-Sector Fixed Effects	Yes	Yes	Yes	Yes	Yes	Yes
Within R^2	0.520	0.315	0.041	0.041	0.524	0.524
Between R^2	0.026	0.014	0.002	0.002	0.001	0.001
Overall R^2	0.062	0.034	0.019	0.019	0.088	0.088

Note: All variables measured in logs. Dependent variable, private export volume at the city four-digit SITC sector level. Each four-digit regression has 225,411 (68,929) observations (groups). Standard errors in paranthesis.

[a] Significance at the 1% level.
[b] Significance at the 5% level.
[c] Significance at the 10% level.

that are engaged in private ordinary export. To test this idea, the dependent variable in the third and fourth columns is replaced with private outsourcing export value rather than the total value of private exports. As predicted, the coefficients on the multinational export terms increase in magnitude.

What is surprising, however, is that the effect of capital goods imports by FIEs on private outsourcing exports is especially large in comparison with the effects related to the import of equipment by multinational outsourcing firms.

As a final check for distinctions that are relevant to outsourcing trade, the final two columns in Table 6 test how the number of distinct private export transactions is influenced by the multinational environment at the city-sector level. These results show that ordinary multinational trade has a stronger effect on the number of private city-sector trade transactions than does multinational outsourcing trade. Furthermore, while all multinational capital equipment imports have a positive association with private export transactions, the effect is again stronger for capital goods imports by FIEs.

Contemporaneous Changes in Export Demand or City Capability

The key maintained assumption of the panel regressions is that fixed effects for city-sector (SITC3 or SITC4), fully capture characteristics that make some city locations in China better for private exports or multinational trade activity than others, and that the fixed effects are time invariant. In the context of an eight-year panel, the assumption of time invariance may be reasonable. However, given the rapid changes in China over the last decades, this assumption is not guaranteed to hold. For this reason, the basic regression specification (1) is augmented with additional time-varying regressors to deal with concerns about changes in city and market conditions. The results for these new regressions are displayed in Tables 7 and 8. First, the regressions include the current (year t) level of total Chinese export in a sector. This is done to account for export-market demand shocks manifested in time t, which is contemporaneous to the dependent variable private exports. If some portion of these shocks is anticipated by MNC firms, and private firms are slower to become aware of the true level of export demand, then the earlier coefficients on the MNC variables could simply reflect differential timing responses to developments in the foreign demand for Chinese products. The first and fourth columns of Table 7 show that there is indeed a large correlation between overall Chinese exports in a sector and the level of sector export by a city. Nonetheless, the coefficients

Table 7. **Multinational exposure and the value of exports by private exporters in manufacturing, 1998–2005**

	Observations and variables measured at three-digit SITC level			Observations and variables measured at four-digit SITC level		
Value of Multinational Exports in City-Sector	0.012[a] (0.011)		−0.017[a] (0.002)	0.008[a] (0.000)		−0.021[a] (0.001)
Value of Multinational Export in City-Other Sectors	−0.002[a] (0.004)		−0.016[a] (0.004)	−0.003 (0.004)		−0.030[a] (0.005)
Number of Multinational Exports in City-Sector		0.210[a] (0.011)	0.296[a] (0.015)		0.196[a] (0.008)	0.319[a] (0.011)
Number of Multinational Exports in City-Other Sectors		0.101[a] (0.018)	0.140[a] (0.020)		0.146[a] (0.016)	0.205[a] (0.019)
Total Chinese Export in Sector	0.600[a] (0.026)	0.570[a] (0.026)	0.572[a] (0.026)	0.687[a] (0.016)	0.661[a] (0.016)	0.659[a] (0.016)
Total City Export in other industries	0.512[a] (0.019)	0.430[a] (0.018)	0.430[a] (0.018)	0.446[a] (0.019)	0.322[a] (0.016)	0.325[a] (0.016)
Provincial GVIO	−0.029[b] (0.013)	−0.031[b] (0.013)	−0.033[b] (0.013)	−0.011 (0.011)	−0.014 (0.011)	−0.016 (0.011)
Year Dummies	Yes	Yes	Yes	Yes	Yes	Yes
City-Sector Fixed Effects	Yes	Yes	Yes	Yes	Yes	Yes
Within R^2	0.369	0.372	0.373	0.326	0.329	0.330
Between R^2	0.070	0.108	0.140	0.042	0.060	0.064
Overall R^2	0.180	0.220	0.224	0.136	0.161	0.166

Note: All variables measured in logs. Dependent variable private export volume at the city sector level. Four-digit regressions have 225,411 (68,929) observations (groups), three-digit regressions have 114,718 observations (72,089 groups). Standard errors in paranthesis.
[a]Significance at the 1% level.
[b]Significance at the 5% level.
[c]Significance at the 10% level.

on multinational activity remain almost identical to those shown in the earlier regression specifications that do not include total Chinese exports in the sector.[13]

[13]While city-sector-time shocks could explain the remaining positive effect of local multinational presence, the idea that multinationals may have a positive influence on local firms despite the fact that they are likely to intensify product market competition, is not entirely without precedent. Greenstone, Hornbeck, and Moretti (2008) show that local incumbent firms experience TFP increases in the period after a large plant enters their local market.

Table 8. Multinational exposure and the number of private exporters in manufacturing, 1998–2005

	Observations and variables measured at four-digit SITC level				Observations and variables measured at three-digit SITC level			
Value of Multinational	0.009[a]		0.006[a]		0.010[a]		0.007[a]	
Exports in City-Sector	(0.000)		(0.000)		(0.000)		(0.001)	
Value of Multinational Export	0.041[a]		0.013[a]		0.013[a]		0.004[b]	
in City-Other Sectors	(0.002)		(0.002)		(0.002)		(0.002)	
Number of Multinational Exports		0.161[a]		0.150[a]		0.187[a]		0.176[a]
in City-Sector		(0.002)		(0.003)		(0.006)		(0.005)
Number of Multinational Exports		0.274[a]		0.190[a]		0.229[a]		0.158[a]
in City-Other Sectors		(0.005)		(0.006)		(0.009)		(0.010)
Total Chinese Export			0.247[a]	0.226[a]			0.211[a]	0.185[a]
in Sector			(0.006)	(0.006)			(0.014)	(0.014)
Total City Export			0.274[a]	0.146[a]			0.279[a]	0.182[a]
in other industries			(0.005)	(0.006)			(0.009)	(0.010)
Provincial GVIO			0.001	−0.002			−0.004	−0.005
			(0.004)	(0.004)			(0.008)	(0.008)
Year Dummies	Yes	Yes	Yes	Yes	Yes	Yes	Yes	Yes
City-Sector Fixed Effects	Yes	Yes	Yes	Yes	Yes	Yes	Yes	Yes
Within R^2	0.521	0.540	0.534	0.546	0.562	0.581	0.576	0.589
Between R^2	0.023	0.049	0.057	0.118	0.010	0.225	0.186	0.310
Overall R^2	0.070	0.208	0.218	0.281	0.058	0.286	0.247	0.256

Note: All variables measured in logs. Dependent variable, private export volume at the city sector level. Four-digit regressions have 225,411 (68,929) observations (groups), three-digit regressions have 114,718 observations (72,089 groups). Standard errors in paranthesis.

[a]Significance at the 1% level.

[b]Significance at the 5% level.

[c]Significance at the 10% level.

Changes over time may also be relevant and systematic if cities differentially changed in their infrastructure, amenities, or policy environment, as these environmental factors should simultaneously boost both private trade and multinational activity in the city. If so, a correlation of MNC and private trade could reflect the rise or fall in the city's export capability, instead of spillover benefits moving from multinational to private firms. To control for this possibility, the regressions in Tables 7 and 8 also include a regressor for total city exports in other industries. This variable is also measured in year t, to make it contemporaneous with the dependent variable, private exports at the city-sector level. This control is appropriate if unmeasured shocks at the city-year level made some cities more attractive for all types of export activities. The large and statistically significant coefficient on this variable suggests that ongoing developments at the city level enabled all sectors, whether served by MNC or private firms, to grow faster or slower in some cities than in others. However, while this variable helps to explain private export outcomes, it does not cause the positive coefficients on multinational exposure to disappear. Finally, to control for economic spillovers at the provincial level, the regressions also include provincial gross value of industrial output in year t.[14] However, the coefficients on this variable are either negative or statistically indistinguishable from zero.

Count Measures of Multinational Presence

Another question that arises is whether the benefits of multinational proximity are related to the size of multinational operations, or whether the benefits stem from the diversity of multinational activities. To test this, the number of multinational contacts is added to a number of regressions in Table 7. The results show that there is a strong positive association between increases in the number of multinational contacts and the growth of private exports at the city-sector level. In addition, if the regressions include measures of the *volume* of multinational contacts and the *frequency* of multinational contacts, the results show that the positive effects of multinational contact are related to contact frequency, while there are negative effects that are due to the volume of multinational contact. Such an outcome supports

[14] I use provincial gross value of industrial output, rather than city-level, since the majority of cities would be dropped from the sample if the city measure were used instead.

the idea that the negative spillovers may reflect increases in competition, or congestion effects driven by increases in local wages and other factor costs.

The results displayed in Table 7 represent a lower bound on the effects of multinational exposure, as these conservative parameter estimates are based on regressions including contemporaneous demand and supply variables. Nonetheless, the estimated parameters imply that the growth in MNC contact had economically meaningful effects on private exporters in China. For example, the coefficients for the three-digit SITC regressions indicate that private exports at the city sector level would increase 1.2% when exposed to a 10% increase in the volume of multinational export transactions, or by 21% if exposed to a 10% increase in the number of distinct multinational export transactions at the city-sector level. Alternatively, if the increases in multinational exposure in terms of volume and presence experienced by the average city-SITC3 industry between 1998 and 2005 are used (and combined with the coefficient estimates from the 3rd column in Table 7), the implied effect of multinationals is a 7.2% increase in private export transactions.

Count Measures of Private Exporter Outcomes

To provide an alternative view on the results, Table 8 repeats the regressions contained in Table 7 with a new dependent variable that measures the *count* of active private export transactions at the city-sector level. Such a specification asks whether a growing exposure to MNCs enables local private firms to increase their number of products exported, or the number of locations to which they export. The results show that there is indeed a positive effect, which suggests that the benefits of multinational exposure are not solely on the intensive margin, but also on the extensive margin.

V. CONCLUSIONS

Examination of China's trade between 1998 and 2005 shows that private Chinese export outcomes were superior when local firms were surrounded by a growing presence of MNCs. This result is apparent even after one controls for city-sector fixed effects, and for city and sector measures that control for the rapid rate of growth in trade. Evaluated with the most conservative parameter estimates, which are based on regressions including contemporaneous demand and supply variables, the coefficients indicate that the increases in multinational exposure experienced by the average city-SITC3 industry between 1998 and 2005 would have generated a 7.2% increase in private export transactions.

Following the general analysis, this chapter asks whether a particular channel — the import of intermediate inputs — contributed to the improved export outcomes for local private firms exposed to MNCs. The answer appears to be in affirmative, as about half of the original multinational exposure effect appears to be driven by multinational import of inputs, and the effect is observed only in manufacturing, but not non-manufacturing industries. This is consistent with recent work that suggests that local firm productivity may be improved when firms gain better access to a greater variety of imported inputs.

As a final check on this result, the chapter also tests whether the effect of MNCs on local firm export outcomes can be explained by the MNC's import of capital equipment. Again, it is found that multinational import of capital equipment imports is associated with improved local private firm export volumes, although the effect is again restricted to manufacturing sectors. Further, if capital equipment imports are disaggregated between those imported by FIEs, versus those imported by MNCs for use in processing trade, it appears that the positive effects are driven by the former category of capital equipment imports by multinationals.

In the future, it would be interesting to use more tailored measures of multinational contact. One way of pushing this issue further would be to use detailed input–output matrices, to verify that the import of intermediate inputs by multinationals is indeed beneficial to local private firms that are situated in sectors that could use those same categories of inputs. In this fashion, it would be possible to better identify how imported input quality and imported input diversity affect subsequent export growth by local Chinese firms.

REFERENCES

Aitken, B. J. and A. E. Harrison (1999). "Do Domestic Firms Benefit from Direct Foreign Investment? Evidence from Venezuela," *American Economic Review*, 89(3): pp. 605–618.

Aitken, B., G. H. Hanson, and A. E. Harrison (1997). " Spillovers, foreign investment, and export behavior," *Journal of International Economics*, V43(N1–2): pp. 103–132.

Amiti, M. and J. Konings (2007). "Trade Liberalization, Intermediate Inputs and Productivity," *American Economic Review*, 97: pp. 1611–1638.

Arkolakis, C., S. Demidova, P. Klenow, and A. Rodriguez-Clare (2008). "Endogenous Variety and the Gains from Trade," *American Economic Review Papers and Proceedings*, 98: pp. 444–450.

Blomstrom, M. and A. Kokko (1998). "Multinational Corporations and Spillovers," *Journal of Economic Surveys*, 12: pp. 247–277.

Brambilla, I. (2009). "Multinationals, Technology, and the Introduction of Varieties of Goods," *Journal of International Economics*, 79(1): pp. 89–101.

Eaton, Jonathan and Samuel Kortum. (2001). "Trade in Capital Goods," *European Economic Review*, 45(7): pp. 1195–1235.

Ellison, G., E. L. Glaeser and W. Kerr (2007). "What Causes Industry Agglomeration? Evidence from Coagglomeration Patterns," NBER 13068.

Feenstra, R. C. and G. H. Hanson (2005). "Ownership and Control in Outsourcing to China: Estimating the Property-Rights Theory of the Firm," *Quarterly Journal of Economics*, 120: pp. 729–761.

Goldberg, P. K., A. Khandelwal, N. Pavcnik and P. Topalova (2008). "Imported Intermediate Inputs and Domestic Product Growth: Evidence from India," NBER Working Paper, 14, 416.

Gorg, H. and D. Greenaway (2004). "Much Ado about Nothing? Do Domestic Firms Really Benefit from Foreign Direct Investment?" *World Bank Research Observer*, 19(2): pp. 171–197.

Greenstone, M., R. Hornbeck, and E. Moretti (2008). "Identifying Agglomeration Spillovers: Evidence from Million Dollar Plant," NBER 13, 833.

Head, K., R. Jing, and D. Swenson (2009). "From Beijing to Bentonville: Do Multinational Retailers Link Markets?"

Kasahara, H. and J. Rodrigue (2008). "Does the Use of Imported Intermediates Increase Productivity? Plant-level Evidence," *Journal of Development Economics*, 87(1): pp. 106–118.

Kiyota, K. (2008). "Are U.S. Exports Different from China's Exports? Evidence from Japan's Imports," Yokohama National University and University of Michigan manuscript.

Lee, J.-W. (1995). "Capital Goods Imports and Long-Run Growth," *Journal of Development Economics*, 48(1): pp. 91–110.

Ma, A. (2006). "Export Spillover to Chinese Firms: Evidence from Provincial Data," *Journal of Chinese Economics and Business Studies*, 4(2): pp. 127–149.

Navaretti, G. B. and A. J. Venables (2004). *Multinational Firms in the World Economy*, Princeton and Oxford: Princeton University Press.

Rauch, James E. (1999). "Networks versus Markets in International Trade," *Journal of International Economics*, 48: pp. 7–35.

Rauch, J. E. and V. Trindade (2003). "Information, International Substitutability, and Globalization," *American Economic Review*, 93(3): pp. 775–791.

Rodrik, D. (2006). "What's So Special About China's Exports?" *China & World Economy*, 14(5): pp. 1–19.

Schott, P. K. (2007). "The Relative Sophistication of Chinese Exports," *Economic Policy*, 53: pp. 5–49.

Swenson, D. L. (2008). "Multinational Firms and New Chinese Export Transactions," *Canadian Journal of Economics*, 41(2): pp. 596–618.

Comment

Lucia Tajoli

The paper by Deborah Swenson looks at a strongly debated issue: the impact of multinational firms on the host economy. As acknowledged by the author, there is a large theoretical and especially empirical literature dealing with this issue, highlighting a number of different possible effects created by the presence of multinational corporations (MNC). Given the lack of a clear-cut general prediction on the results of hosting foreign firms, the matter becomes an empirical one. From a policy perspective, a proper understanding of the circumstances that give rise to a specific outcome is crucial to put in place suitable measures to attract or deter foreign investors, and possibly to select them.

Even if theoretical models allow both for positive and negative effects of the presence of multinational corporations, most empirical studies have shown that the hosting countries benefit from receiving foreign direct investments in many ways: technological spillovers and access to superior organization forms, more information on foreign markets and competitors, wage increases, decrease in the unemployment rate, increased tax revenue for the government are often associated with MNCs' presence. The existing empirical evidence confirms a positive outcome also for China (see for example Zhang, 2001 or Liu *et al.*, 2009). What is most interesting here is that a specific effect, possibly more controversial, is examined: is the export capacity of Chinese domestic firms enhanced or reduced by the presence of MNCs? The answer is *a priori* uncertain because there exists the possibility that foreign firms displace domestic firms through some form of crowding out, by increasing the competitive pressure or rising the price of factors of production (see Barrios *et al.*, 2005). This concern is especially relevant for smaller economies (the Irish case is a relevant example), but it seems less pertinent for very large and fast growing economies such as China. However, the uncertainty of the final outcome makes an empirical analysis of the issue very appropriate.

The evidence provided in the paper suggests that there are indeed positive spillover effects from foreign MNCs to domestic private firms: foreign MNCs' presence in a Chinese city (measured in terms of exports generated by those MNCs) is positively associated with exports of domestic private firms located in the same city, rejecting the existence of relevant crowding out effects.

One of the main contributions of this work is that it not only looks at the impact of MNCs but also aims at identifying the channels creating this effect. In particular, it considers the role of inputs imported by MNCs: the availability of a larger set of inputs could increase the productivity of the domestic firms, enhancing their exports. The empirical results show that MNCs' imports are also positively associated with domestic firms' export, as expected.

These very interesting results could be made more convincing by tackling some issues that are not yet fully addressed in the paper. The first is a peculiarity of Chinese exporting firms, which for a large fraction are state-owned. State-owned firms are responsible for a relevant share of overall exports (more than 20% of total exports, according to data of the Chinese Department of General Economic Affairs), but state-owned enterprises (SOEs) are not considered in the analysis. Are they affected in a similar manner by MNCs, or not affected at all?[15] The answer to this question could shed some light on the channels through which MNCs exert their influence. Furthermore, data reported in the paper show a decline in the export share of SOEs together with an increase in exports from private firms. The question arises on whether the increase of private exports is due to "new" exports or instead to a privatization process, which has turned SOEs' exports into private exports. Some mention about the privatization of SOEs in China would be useful, possibly also introducing control variables for this process and for the presence of SOEs in the regressions.

Another specificity of the Chinese case is the very rapid increase of overall Chinese exports to the world, accompanied by many important changes in the Chinese economy, in its endowment of infrastructures, and so on. One might suspect that the transformation of the Chinese economy

[15]For example, one might expect that Chinese private firms are more willing to adopt foreign organization forms than the SOEs, or that they benefit more from a larger set of inputs being available because they are subject to tighter constraints in importing them.

is the key factor pushing the export propensity of Chinese private firms, and therefore it should be taken in due account. This is done toward the end of the paper, as a robustness check on the results. The results of the regressions that include the trend of Chinese exports and some transformations at the provincial level are much more convincing, even if inevitably the use of these control variables in the regressions lowers to some extent the coefficients of the variables of interest. In addition to the changes mentioned above, related to the Chinese economy, a number of other important changes occurred in the world economy, affecting the possibility to access to foreign markets for Chinese firms, probably with different sectoral effects. Examples are the WTO membership, the elimination of the Multifiber Agreement, etc. It would be useful to introduce in the regressions a variable controlling for changes in market access at the sector level, because the sector fixed effects that are used cannot do it.

Examining the mechanism that is driving the results, there can be some problem in introducing MNCs' imports into the regression. In fact, at the aggregate level, there is a very high correlation between Chinese export flows and import flows, both growing at a very fast pace.[16] This correlation can be lower at a disaggregated and local level, but still an issue of multicollinearity between MNCs' export and import values in the regressions could arise. Some check on this should be provided. Other variables could be used to capture the effect that seems to be at work. For example, an indicator of the number of intermediate inputs used by MNCs, or an index of input prices could be used as proxies of the spillovers generated by MNCs (assuming that such data are available).

The author also considers the role played by a specific type of imports of the MNCs, imports of capital equipment. While the use of technologically advanced capital equipment could increase the productivity of the MNCs, it is not clear which kind of spillovers they could generate that could affect the exports of the private Chinese firms. Therefore, the results on the positive role of imports of capital goods are difficult to interpret.

A very large share (over 50%) of Chinese exports is given by processing trade, which is connected to the operations of foreign firms. The chapter

[16]The correlation between aggregate Chinese export and import flows between 1997 and 2007 as recorded in the WTO database is equal to 0.99.

therefore considers also the influence of MNCs on this specific type of exports. Here again the mechanism through which spillovers might occur is not completely spelled out, and therefore it is not evident which results should be expected. To the extent that exports classified as processing trade imply a production process not entirely internalized by a foreign firm, but some form of "production sharing" between foreign and domestic firms, productivity spillovers and learning effects should be larger than for "ordinary trade." Some results go against this intuition, as the general exports of MNC firms involved in ordinary trade have a stronger effect on private firms exports than the presence of MNCs involved in outsourcing trade, and the same is true for the effect of capital goods imports. It is possible that capital goods imported for outsourcing are more obsolete than capital goods imported for in-house production done by MNCs, and therefore they generate weaker technological spillovers. There is some anecdotal evidence on very mature capital goods being exported to some less-developed countries, and this could be the case also for China. These unexpected results could be analyzed more deeply, as they might hint at some non-obvious transmission mechanism.

Finally, some robustness check could be done on the estimation techniques. The use of lagged variables in panel estimates can make the OLS estimates inconsistent, therefore some other estimation methods could be tested. Also, given the suspicion that the result is given by a general strong upward trend in most variables, it would be a useful robustness check to run a regression using differentiated variables rather than levels.

In conclusion, in spite of some caveats mostly related to the specificity of the Chinese case, this paper provides a number of interesting insights on the channels through which MNCs can affect a country's export potential. The issue of what is driving exports and what makes some firms trade abroad while others do not is becoming more and more central in the debates around international trade, for the positive and normative implications that this can have. Therefore, a paper like this one by Deborah Swenson that takes a closer look into the mechanisms fostering exports is certainly a welcome step forward in the understanding of these processes.

REFERENCES

Barrios, Salvador, Holger Görg, and Eric Strob (2005). "Foreign direct investment, competition and industrial development in the host country," *European Economic Review*, 49(7): pp. 1761–1784.

Liu, Xiaming, Chengang Wang, and Yingqi Wei (2009). "Do local manufacturing firms benefit from transactional linkages with multinational enterprises in China?" *Journal of International Business Studies*, 40(7): pp. 1113–1130.

Zhang, Kevin H. (2001). "How Does FDI Affect Economic Growth in China?" *Economics of Transition*, 9(3): pp. 679–693.

CHAPTER 11

The Effects of Foreign Direct Investment on China's Labor Market

Theresa M. Greaney[*,‡] and Yao Li[†,§]

[*] Department of Economics, University of Hawai'i, Hawai'i, USA
[†] School of Management and Economics
University of Electronic Science and Technology of China
Chengdu, Sichuan, China
[‡] greaney@hawaii.edu
[§] liyao@vestc.edu.cn

I. INTRODUCTION

Although much of the attention regarding offshoring effects has focused on the impacts on labor markets in source countries, such as the U.S., the impacts are likely to be more extensive on labor markets in host countries. This hypothesis is based on the simple observation that the foreign direct investment (FDI) flows usually represent a larger share of host country, rather than home country, national income. This chapter seeks to examine how FDI has affected the labor market in China. In particular, we analyze industrial and regional data from the National Bureau of Statistics of China to assess how FDI has impacted wages and employment. Since most of the data from China distinguishes between FDI from overseas Chinese investors (i.e., those located in Hong Kong, Macao, and Taiwan) and FDI from foreign investors, we examine possible differences in investment patterns and effects across these different FDI sources.

China is a particularly interesting case study because it has become the world's largest developing country recipient of FDI, boasts the world's fastest economic growth, and has the world's largest labor force. In addition, as a transition economy, China's industrial sector involves mixtures of state ownership, state control, collective ownership, domestic private ownership, and foreign ownership. The gradual movement away from state ownership in many industries coincides with large inflows of FDI, making it difficult to separate privatization influences from FDI influences. This added feature of China's market has not deterred some recent efforts at examining these relationships. Gong, Gorg, and Maioli (2006) find that foreign acquisition increases employment in China while domestic privatization slows employment growth compared with firms that remain state-owned. Karlsson *et al.* (2009) find positive employment effects of FDI on both foreign- and domestic-owned private firms in China using a large firm-level dataset for 1998–2004. These positive effects are found even after controlling for other firm characteristics that may lead to faster employment growth. Wang (2005) also finds a positive relationship between FDI growth and employment growth. On the other hand, Yang, Yu, and Wang (2009) find that FDI has a significant negative effect on employment and no significant effect on wages. They incorporate a Cobb–Douglas production function into Agosin and Mayer's (2000) FDI Crowd-in-Crowd-out model to derive employment and wage functions and then use firm-level data from Chinese manufacturers from 1987–2004.

While most of the aforementioned studies focus on finding employment effects, there are even more investigations into the effect of FDI on China's wages. Some researchers have found a significant positive relationship between FDI and China's average wage level (e.g., Ge, 2006; Wang and Lan, 2008). Zhao (2001) and Wu (2001a) take a different approach by investigating FDI's effect on China's wage composition. They find that FDI increased the relative wages of skilled labor in China due to existing market distortions. Wu (2001b) reports the same relationship, but attributes it to better intellectual property rights protection of foreign-invested enterprises rather than to market distortions.

There are many studies that have looked for a "foreign ownership wage premium" for countries other than China. Lipsey and Sjoholm (2001) find a foreign ownership premium of 12% for blue-collar workers and 22% for white-collar workers in Indonesian factories after controlling for region, industry, plant size, and worker characteristics. In fact, the opening sentence of their paper reads "It seems to be a universal rule that in every country, foreign-owned firms and plants pay higher wages, on average, than domestically owned ones." They point out that this holds true for developed countries as well as for developing countries. Heyman, Sjoholm, and Tingvall (2007) examine this proposition using detailed matched employer–employee data from Sweden and find a smaller wage premium associated with foreign ownership than previous studies found. They find that foreign-owned firms do pay more than domestic-owned firms but the former do not pay more for identical workers. The higher wages paid in foreign firms can be explained by firm and worker characteristics.

In this chapter, we investigate the impact of FDI on China's labor market first by using our data to present a descriptive analysis of China's industrial sector in 2004. We focus on industry-level and regional differences in the shares of capital coming from the state; from Hong Kong, Macao, and Taiwan; from foreigners; and from others. We use our descriptive analysis to guide our regression analysis in looking for the effects of FDI on earnings and employment in China's manufacturing industries, while controlling for other determinants of earnings and employment. Our regression analysis seeks to explain variations in earnings and employment across industries using capital ownership as an explanatory variable. We attempt to identify FDI effects separately from privatization effects by considering the effects of capital contributions sourced from the state, from collectives, and from private domestic investors, as opposed to those sourced from FDI. We also conduct separate analyses of two particularly large employment industries — textiles and communication equipment, computers, and electronics — where we seek to explain earnings and employment variations across regions. The advantages of our study are the use of an extensive and relatively new data source, *China's Economic Census Yearbook 2004*, our method of allowing ownership to be defined as a continuous variable based on capital contributions from different sources, our ability to examine the effects of investment from overseas Chinese separately from investment from foreigners, and our in-depth inquiries into two specific industries as case studies of a labor-intensive sector and a capital-intensive sector. In the following section, we describe our data sources, followed by our data analysis.

II. DATA

China's Economic Census Yearbook 2004, produced by the National Bureau of Statistics of China (NBSC), presents detailed industry-level data for industrial enterprises. Considering manufacturing, mining, and utilities to be one-digit industry aggregates, the Economic Census includes 30 manufacturing industries, 6 mining industries, and 3 utilities industries at the two-digit level of aggregation. Due to space constraints in presenting some tables, these industries are aggregated to show 23 manufacturing industries, plus mining and utilities as aggregated industries, in some tables. The manufacturing industries that combine two sub-industries are textiles, apparel, and footwear; wood products and furniture; chemicals and chemical products; smelting and processing of metals; and general- and special-purpose machinery. The food and beverages industry combines three sub-industries.

The Economic Census also presents some data only for "enterprises above designated size," which is defined as enterprises with annual sales of at least 5 million yuan. This minimum size cut-off would include all large- and medium-sized firms, along with some small firms as designated by the NBSC. For ease of reference, we refer to this subset of industrial enterprises as "large enterprises." This allows us to separate state-controlled enterprises, FDI enterprises, and private-owned enterprises in a later section of the chapter. We also use these data at the three-digit industry level with 521 industries for our regression analysis.

Although the Economic Census provides us with one year's (2004) data for cross-industry and cross-region analysis, to pursue time-series and panel-data analysis for the years 2001–2007, we utilized other data sources. *China's Labor Statistical Yearbook* (2002–2008), produced by the NBSC, provided data on average annual earnings of urban workers. Since we focus on industrial sectors and most industrial enterprises are located in cities, the lack of data for rural workers should not be a major concern. Our employment and other operational data for industrial enterprises are from the NBSC's *China Industrial Economic Statistical Yearbook* (2002–2004, 2006–2008) and the *China Economic Census Yearbook 2004.*[1]

III. DESCRIPTIVE ANALYSIS

Sectoral Analysis of all Enterprises

Tables 1 and 2 show main indicators of all industrial enterprises by industry in 2004. The tables cover 1.38 million enterprises in mining, utilities,

[1] The statistical yearbooks published by NBSC annually report the previous year's statistical data. NBSC did not publish the *China Industrial Economic Statistical Yearbook* in 2005, and the related 2004 data are included in the *China Economic Census Yearbook 2004.*

Table 1. **Main indicators of all industrial enterprises by industry, 2004**

Sector	Number of enterprises (thousands)	Gross Industrial Output (GIO) (billion yuan)	Annual average number employed (thousands)	Money-losing enterprises (share)	Average number of employees per enterprise
Total	1375.3	22231.6	93039.4	17.9	67.7
Mining	78.9	1242.2	8684.6	8.0	110.0
Utilities	37.8	1593.3	3548.6	22.1	94.0
Manufacturing	1258.6	19396.1	80806.2	18.4	64.2
Food & Beverages	125.1	1556.9	5781.7	14.2	46.2
Tobacco	0.3	259.7	202.1	16.7	704.3
Textiles, Apparel, & Footwear	131.4	1632.4	12451.7	21.2	94.8
Leather, Fur, Feather & Related Products	22.7	313.3	2759.7	16.3	121.6
Wood Products & Furniture	63.9	349.8	2655.0	13.2	41.6
Paper & Paper Products	39.7	397.1	2009.0	18.4	50.6
Printing & Recorded Media Reproduction	41.2	174.4	1270.1	21.2	30.8
Articles For Culture, Education & Sport Activities	14.6	142.8	1485.6	21.6	101.6
Coking & Processing of Petroleum & Nuclear Fuel	7.2	908.9	779.9	19.7	108.9
Chemicals & Chemical Products	78.6	1602.2	4880.2	20.8	62.1
Pharmaceuticals	11.3	336.6	1324.8	31.0	117.3

(*Continued*)

Table 1. (*Continued*)

Sector	Number of enterprises (thousands)	Gross Industrial Output (GIO) (billion yuan)	Annual average number employed (thousands)	Money-losing enterprises (share)	Average number of employees per enterprise
Rubber	15.2	204.8	1091.4	18.9	71.8
Plastics	69.8	525.3	2915.9	19.4	41.8
Non-metallic Mineral Products	157.9	995.1	8397.5	10.6	53.2
Smelting & Pressing of Metals	35.7	2355.4	4565.3	18.9	127.8
Metal Products	81.0	636.0	3502.5	18.9	43.2
General & Special Purpose Machinery	168.9	1609.6	8377.8	19.7	49.6
Transportation Equipment	53.9	1453.8	4327.7	21.0	80.4
Electrical Machinery & Equipment	60.1	1203.7	4453.8	23.3	74.1
Communication Equip., Computers & Other Electronics	27.3	2259.4	4354.8	32.6	159.3
Measuring Instruments & Office Machinery	16.7	240.9	1139.5	28.6	68.2
Artwork & Other Manufacturing	32.6	212.0	1993.5	16.7	61.2
Recycling & Disposal of Waste	3.6	26.1	86.6	12.0	24.4

Source: Authors' analysis of data from *China's Yearbook of* 2004 Economic Census.

Table 2. More main indicators of all industrial enterprises by industry, 2004

Sector	Share in Total Paid-in Capital				Export share of GIO (share)	Average annual pay per employee (Y1000)	Average GIO per employee (Y1000)	Average assets per employee (Y1000)
	State-owned	From HK, Macao & Taiwan	From foreigners	Others				
Total	24.8	8.9	13.8	52.5	18.7	12.9	238.9	258.7
Mining	45.7	1.1	0.5	52.6	3.2	14.8	143.0	195.5
Utilities	56.1	2.3	3.1	38.4	0.6	23.6	449.0	1190.1
Manufacturing	15.1	11.3	17.8	55.8	21.2	12.2	240.0	224.6
Food & Beverages	9.9	8.5	19.9	61.7	9.5	10.2	269.3	231.2
Tobacco	89.3	0.3	0.3	10.0	1.0	47.5	1285.0	1494.5
Textiles, Apparel, & Footwear	6.6	21.0	13.9	58.6	33.1	10.1	131.1	115.1
Leather, Fur, Feather & Related Products	1.9	28.1	21.8	48.2	52.1	10.4	113.5	73.0
Wood Products & Furniture	6.3	15.3	14.8	63.6	29.1	9.2	131.7	111.7
Paper & Paper Products	10.9	11.9	23.4	53.8	6.9	10.4	197.7	244.1
Printing & Recorded Media Reproduction	14.8	13.3	7.0	64.9	7.1	11.7	137.3	173.7
Articles For Culture, Education & Sport Activities	2.1	39.1	20.4	38.5	61.8	10.6	96.2	76.7
Coking & Processing of Petroleum & Nuclear Fuel	33.6	3.9	3.6	59.0	2.5	18.8	1165.4	683.0
Chemicals & Chemical Products	18.3	7.3	15.5	58.9	8.5	13.0	328.3	335.7
Pharmaceuticals	12.5	5.2	13.7	68.6	10.3	14.9	254.1	398.7

(*Continued*)

Table 2. (*Continued*)

Sector	Share in Total Paid-in Capital: State-owned	Share in Total Paid-in Capital: From HK, Macao & Taiwan	Share in Total Paid-in Capital: From foreigners	Share in Total Paid-in Capital: Others	Export share of GIO (share)	Average annual pay per employee (Y1000)	Average GIO per employee (Y1000)	Average assets per employee (Y1000)
Rubber	9.4	14.4	29.8	46.4	23.3	11.1	187.6	191.3
Plastics	4.4	22.1	19.2	54.3	22.3	10.9	180.2	174.3
Non-metallic Mineral Products	11.4	7.5	10.9	70.1	8.1	8.9	118.5	138.5
Smelting & Pressing of Metals	34.2	5.2	6.3	54.3	6.7	17.6	515.9	478.2
Metal Products	5.9	15.0	16.3	62.8	25.6	11.3	181.6	158.0
General & Special Purpose Machinery	14.0	7.0	16.7	62.3	12.8	12.8	192.1	209.1
Transportation Equipment	27.5	5.0	19.9	47.6	9.4	15.9	335.9	357.1
Electrical Machinery & Equipment	7.9	13.3	22.7	56.2	26.7	13.3	270.3	238.6
Communication Equip., Computers & Other Electronics	6.7	18.6	42.1	32.7	61.1	18.2	518.8	382.5
Measuring Instruments & Office Machinery	10.3	17.4	25.7	46.6	50.1	14.5	211.4	196.9
Artwork & Other Manufacturing	8.4	23.0	16.4	52.2	45.0	10.3	106.3	86.7
Recycling & Disposal of Waste	2.4	8.5	14.1	75.1	0.5	10.8	300.8	186.0

Source: Authors' analysis of data from *China's Yearbook of* 2004 Economic Census.

and manufacturing industries. As shown in Table 1, manufacturing industries account for the largest number of industrial enterprises, with 1.26 million enterprises compared to mining's 78,900 or utilities' 37,800. Within manufacturing, the industries with the largest numbers of enterprises are general- and special-purpose machinery with 168,900; non-metallic mineral products, with 157,900; and textiles, apparel, and footwear, with 131,400. In terms of Gross Industrial Output (GIO), the largest manufacturing industries are smelting and pressing of metals (2355.4 billion yuan), communication equipment, computers, and other electronics (2259.4 billion yuan), and textiles, apparel, and footwear (1632.4 billion yuan). Other large GIO producers are general- and special-purpose machinery (1609.6 billion yuan), chemicals and chemical products (1602.2 billion yuan), and food and beverages (1593.3 billion yuan).

Table 1 also presents the annual average number of people employed by each industry as an indicator of the size of the industry in labor-market terms. Mining industries combined employed the largest number, with 8.7 million, followed by non-metallic mineral products and general- and special-purpose machinery with just under 8.4 million each. Food and beverages employed about 5.8 million, while chemicals and chemical products employed 4.9 million and smelting and processing of metals employed 4.6 million. With the exception of non-metallic mineral products, these top six employers are combined two-digit industries, but the next three industries are single industries. Electrical machinery and equipment; communication equipment, computers, and other electronics; and transportation equipment each employed between 4.3 and 4.5 million workers.

The Census asks managers to indicate whether their enterprise has lost money over the past year. The shares of enterprises that report having lost money range from a low of 8.0% for mining to highs of 28.6%–32.6% for measuring instruments and office machinery; pharmaceuticals; and communication equipment, computers, and other electronics. Overall, 18.4% of the enterprises in manufacturing industries reported losses.

The next column in Table 1 calculates the average number of employees per enterprise in each industry. The outlier here is the tobacco industry, with 704.3 employees per enterprise, while the average across all industrial enterprises is only 67.7. The next highest number of employees per enterprise is 159.3, reported by communication equipment, computers, and other electronics. Smelting and pressing of metals also reported large average enterprise sizes, with 127.8 employees per firm. The industries that reported the smallest average enterprise sizes are recycling and disposal of waste (24.4 employees per enterprise) and printing and recorded media reproduction (30.8 employees per enterprise). Both are small industries in terms of GIO.

Table 2 continues to present main indicators for all industrial enterprises by industry. The first four columns show the ownership shares for total paid-in capital for each industrial sector. The breakdown provided in the data is state-owned capital; capital from Hong Kong, Macao, and Taiwan; capital from foreigners; and capital from others. The "Others" column includes collective capital, private capital, and corporate capital, where the last is defined as capital from other enterprises.[2] The tobacco industry again is an outlier in having such a high share of its capital coming from the state, at 89.3%, compared with the average across all industries of only 24.8%. Utilities (56.1%) and mining (45.7%) are the only other industries with state-owned capital shares that are quite high. The tobacco, utilities, and mining enterprises are predominantly state-owned, and these industries are highly regulated by the government so that existing firms have a large degree of monopoly power. The heavy government role in these industries and the corresponding monopoly power lead to less FDI, larger-sized enterprises in terms of number of employees per firm, higher capital-intensity in terms of assets per employee, and higher paid workers.

Industries with high shares of capital coming from Hong Kong, Macao, and Taiwan include articles for culture, education, and sports activities[3] (39.1%); leather, fur, feather, and related products (28.1%); artwork and other manufacturing (23.0%); and plastics (22.1%). Capital from foreigners has flowed into some of the same industries, but the largest shares are in communication equipment, computers, and other electronics (42.1%); rubber (29.8%); measuring instruments and office machinery (25.7%);

[2]These other enterprises may involve mixtures of state-owned capital, collective capital, foreign capital, and private capital, but the data are not broken down by ultimate beneficial owner.

[3]This industry includes stationary, pens, pencils, sporting goods, toys, games, and musical instruments.

paper and paper products (23.4%); and electrical machinery and equipment (22.7%). Overall, the contribution of "Others" provides the majority of capital in China, at 52.5%, including 55.8% for all manufacturing industries combined. The industries with the highest shares of capital coming from "Other" sources are recycling and disposal of waste (75.1%), nonmetallic mineral products (70.1%), and pharmaceuticals (68.6%).

The next column of Table 2 presents the export share of GIO.[4] The industries with the highest exports shares are articles for culture, education, and sports activities (61.8%), communication equipment, computers, and other electronics (61.1%), leather, fur, feather, and related products (52.1%), measuring instruments and office machinery (50.1%), and artwork and other manufacturing (45.0%). All of these industries were mentioned earlier as having high shares of capital from overseas Chinese investors or foreign investors. The correlations between foreign capital shares and export shares will be presented after discussing the final columns of Table 2.

The last three columns of Table 2 show per employee averages for annual earnings,[5] GIO and enterprise assets. The tobacco industry has the highest values for all three measures with annual earnings per employee of 47,500 yuan, GIO per employee of 1.3 million yuan, and assets per employee of 1.5 million yuan. The industries ranked second (23,600 yuan) through fifth (17,600 yuan) in terms of employee earnings were utilities; coking and processing of petroleum and nuclear fuel; communication equipment, computers, and other electronics; and smelting and pressing of metals. These same industries appear in the top five for average GIO per employee, with slightly different ordering, and all but one appear in the top five for average assets per employee.[6] As these rankings suggest, the values in these three columns are highly correlated.

---

[4]This is derived by dividing the delivery value of exports by the gross industrial output for each industry.

[5]We calculate average annual earnings per employee using data on total salaries paid and average annual number employed. Throughout the chapter we use the terms earnings and pay interchangeably in referring to average annual earnings per worker, but these terms should not be confused with hourly wages which we cannot determine.

[6]That industry, communication equipment, computers and other electronics, takes sixth place behind pharmaceuticals which is ranked fifth.

Table 3 presents the various correlations of interest across the variables shown in Table 2. The first four columns examine how the different ownership shares are related to export shares, annual employee pay, GIO per employee, and assets per employee. The table is divided into three sections depending on whether we include all industries, or whether we exclude industries with the heaviest concentrations of state-owned capital, which involve highly regulated, monopolistic industries. The heavy state involvement and monopoly power of these enterprises are likely to distort some of the relationships when these industries are included. For example, when we include all industries, state-ownership appears to be very positively correlated with annual pay, GIO per employee, and assets per employee, with correlation coefficients of 0.89, 0.73, and 0.89, respectively. However, these relationships appear much less strong if we exclude the industries with the heaviest state-ownership of capital, which are also industries involving state-owned monopolies or heavily regulated industries (i.e., tobacco, utilities, mining, smelting and pressing of metals, and coking and processing of petroleum and nuclear fuel). The coefficients drop to 0.43 for employee pay, 0.31 for GIO per employee, and 0.59 for assets per employee, and they drop even further if we also exclude transportation equipment (i.e., use a cut-off of 1/4 state-ownership of capital rather than 1/3).

The impact of the industries with heavy state-ownership also is seen in the relationships between annual pay and capital coming from overseas Chinese versus foreign sources. Enterprises with higher shares of overseas Chinese investment seem to pay less (−0.46 correlation coefficient) when all industries are included, but the strength of this relationship is much lower when the state-dominated industries are excluded (−0.16 correlation coefficient using the 1/4 state-ownership cut-off). The impact of the state-dominated industries on the correlation between foreign ownership and pay is even stronger. With all industries included, it appears that foreign ownership is negatively related to employee pay (−0.40 correlation coefficient), but the relationship is positive and fairly large when we exclude state-dominated industries (0.53 or 0.57 correlation coefficients, depending on the state-ownership cut-off). In fact, the correlation coefficients for all of the variables with foreign capital ownership change dramatically from fairly large negative values to fairly large positive values when the state-dominated industries are excluded. Overall, the examination of correlation

Table 3. **Correlation coefficients between ownership shares and other main indicators by industry**

	Share in Total Paid-In Capital						
Variables	State-owned	From HK, Macao & Taiwan	From foreigners	Others	Annual pay per employee	GIO per employee	Assets per employee
All Industries							
Export share of GIO	−0.53	0.87	0.67	−0.27	−0.29	−0.35	−0.44
Annual Pay per Employee	0.89	−0.46	−0.40	−0.75		0.83	0.92
GIO per Employee	0.73	−0.49	−0.36	−0.50			0.83
Assets per Employee	0.89	−0.56	−0.47	−0.63			
*Industries with less than 1/3 State-Ownership**							
Export share of GIO	−0.50	0.83	0.55	−0.76	0.17	−0.08	−0.32
Annual Pay per Employee	0.43	−0.25	0.53	−0.42		0.79	0.81
GIO per Employee	0.31	−0.42	0.56	−0.23			0.84
Assets per Employee	0.59	−0.62	0.32	−0.07			
*Industries with less than 1/4 State-Ownership***							
Export share of GIO	−0.51	0.82	0.57	−0.83	0.27	−0.03	−0.28
Annual Pay per Employee	0.25	−0.16	0.57	−0.39		0.78	0.77
GIO per Employee	0.17	−0.38	0.58	−0.19			0.83
Assets per Employee	0.51	−0.59	0.34	0.00			

*Excludes tobacco, utilities, mining, smelting and pressing of metals, and coking and processing of petroleum and nuclear fuel.

**Excludes all of the above plus transportation equipment.

coefficient between ownership shares and per employee averages for pay, GIO, and assets confirms that state-dominated sectors tend to have higher pay and higher per employee GIO and assets.[7] Setting these industries aside, however, foreign capital has the strongest positive relationship with pay and GIO per employee, while state-ownership still has the strongest positive relationship with assets per employee. Investment from overseas Chinese tends to be negatively related to pay, GIO per employee, and assets per employee, and investment from other sources is negatively related to the first two variables. We cannot conclude causal relationships from these correlations, but this evidence is suggestive that ownership matters in determining employee compensation.

Table 3 also shows correlation coefficients between ownership sources and the export share of GIO. As we might expect, capital inflows into China appear to be positively related to trade outflows. The correlation coefficient between the export share of GIO and the capital share from overseas Chinese is 0.87, and the corresponding coefficient between the export share and the capital share from foreign is 0.67.[8,9] The influence of state-dominated industries is weaker on these coefficients, since the values decrease only slightly when these industries are excluded.

Finally, Table 3 shows correlations between the variables that are not related to ownership. As one might expect, there are strong positive relationships between annual pay, GIO per employee, and assets per employee. Firms that are more productive and have higher capital-to-labor ratios

[7]At the aggregate level for industrial enterprises, Aizenman and Geng (2009) find similar results that state-owned enterprises have higher markups over marginal cost than do foreign-funded enterprises, but the difference shrinks over time as SOE's markups have fallen dramatically compared to smaller declines for FFE markups.

[8]These results correspond with Chen and Song (2003). They find that the overseas Chinese invested firms in China are more likely to be exported-oriented small- and medium-size firms attracted by cheap labor costs while the foreigners-invested firms are more likely to be large enterprises with higher requirements for human capital and attracted by China's huge market potential.

[9]It will be interesting to see whether this strong correlation weakens over time since China had to revise its law on foreign capital enterprises as part its successful bid for entry into the World Trade Organization (WTO). The relevant 1986 law required foreign-invested enterprises to use advanced technology and to export most of their products. The revised law in 2000 softened the language to merely encouraging these activities. See Wang, Johnson, and Yang (2003).

tend to pay more, and firms with higher-paid labor and higher capital–labor ratios tend to more productive, etc. Interestingly, the relationship between pay and export share is slightly negative when all industries are included, but it becomes slightly positive when state-dominated industries are excluded. The state-dominated industries tend to have very low export shares of GIO. Excluding these industries with their low participation in exporting, we find that industries with higher export shares tend to pay slightly more and have slightly lower assets per employee (i.e., be more labor-intensive rather than capital-intensive).

Regional Analysis of all Enterprises

Tables 4 and 5 present the Census data organized by regions rather than by industry. The regions are grouped as coastal, inland, and minority regions because China has set different FDI policies for these regions over time. The coastal regions were the first to allow FDI and then actively encourage FDI, followed by the inland regions.[10] The minority regions have been the slowest to open to FDI. The coastal regions combined host the largest numbers of enterprises, produce the most GIO, and employ the most workers, followed on each measure by the inland regions and then the minority regions. The inland regions on average have lower shares of money-losing enterprises (15.6%) relative to the coastal regions (18.9%) and the minority regions (25.8%), but there are significant variations within these regions. Inland regions of Henan (7.4%) and Hunan (9.0%) reported the lowest shares of money-losing enterprises, while the top three provinces for shares of money-losing enterprises fall in all three regions. The minority region of Xinjiang tops with 42.4%, followed by the inland region of Beijing at 40.0%, and then by the coastal region of Hainan at 35.6%.

The last column in Table 4 shows the average number of employees per enterprise, with the largest numbers reported in minority regions (83.9) and the smallest in the coastal regions (65.5). Large state-owned enterprises continue to play major roles in the economies of the minority regions in particular. Among large enterprises in Tibet, state-owned enterprises produced 75% of the total GIO. For Qinghai (also a Tibetan region) and

[10]See Fung, Iizaka, and Tong (2004) for a detailed description of the policies involved in the progressive opening of China's market to FDI.

Table 4. **Main indicators of all industrial enterprises by region, 2004**

Region	Number of enterprises (thousands)	Gross Industrial Output (GIO) (billion yuan)	Annual average number employed (thousands)	Money-losing enterprises (share)	Average number of employees per enterprise
Total	1375.3	22231.6	93039.4	17.9	67.7
Coastal Regions	**843.1**	**14694.4**	**55245.9**	**18.9**	**65.5**
Liaoning	54.6	914.1	3542.0	31.8	64.9
Shandong	120.7	2467.8	9359.3	11.0	77.6
Tianjin	25.7	611.9	1689.3	31.7	65.9
Jiangsu	188.8	2947.7	10189.1	18.2	54.0
Shanghai	55.8	1459.4	3409.3	21.3	61.1
Zhejiang	188.9	2122.7	8615.9	13.6	45.6
Fujian	49.8	751.6	3645.3	16.1	73.1
Hainan	2.1	42.9	147.7	35.6	71.5
Guangdong	137.7	3152.0	13381.3	26.1	97.2
Guangxi	19.1	224.2	1266.7	20.6	66.4
Inland Regions	**493.5**	**6802.7**	**34553.5**	**15.6**	**70.0**
Jilin	16.4	355.2	1382.9	22.0	84.5
Heilongjiang	20.3	395.6	1874.8	24.0	92.3
Anhui	39.3	423.6	2358.1	17.6	60.1
Beijing	31.7	597.5	1580.3	40.6	49.9
Hebei	64.6	1019.4	4409.9	10.0	68.2
Shannxi	28.9	417.4	2781.3	12.7	96.3
Jiangxi	29.5	273.7	1791.7	10.4	60.8
Henan	76.9	923.7	5302.5	7.4	69.0
Hubei	29.3	532.9	2354.8	22.6	80.5
Hunan	43.9	434.2	2624.0	9.0	59.7
Chongqin	20.5	259.9	1446.2	15.8	70.5
Sichuan	43.8	530.4	2973.1	17.2	67.9
Guizhou	11.1	154.6	938.9	26.5	84.4
Shanxi	25.8	315.1	1754.3	13.1	68.0
Gansu	11.7	169.6	980.9	18.8	84.1
Minority Regions	**38.6**	**734.6**	**3240.0**	**25.8**	**83.9**
Inner Mongolia	11.8	232.7	1101.4	16.0	93.0
Ningxia	4.0	60.5	331.1	25.0	82.4
Xinjiang	5.8	165.6	568.1	42.4	97.8
Yunnan	14.4	234.4	1035.3	26.9	71.9
Qinhai	2.2	38.8	181.0	31.3	82.3
Tibet	0.4	2.5	23.1	15.2	64.9

Source: Authors' analysis of data from *China's Yearbook of 2004 Economic Census*.

Table 5. More main indicators of all industrial enterprises by region, 2004

Region	Share in Total Paid-in Capital				Export share of GIO (share)	Average annual pay per employee (Y1000)	Average GIO per employee (Y1000)	Average assets per employee (Y1000)
	State-owned	From HK, Macao & Taiwan	From foreigners	Others				
Total	24.8	8.9	13.8	52.5	18.7	12.9	238.9	258.7
Coastal Regions	**14.2**	**14.1**	**20.4**	**51.3**	**25.6**	**13.4**	**266.0**	**248.6**
Liaoning	38.6	3.4	12.6	45.5	14.3	13.5	258.1	345.8
Shandong	26.6	3.3	12.8	57.3	12.2	11.1	263.7	219.6
Tianjin	17.4	3.6	25.0	54.0	24.1	15.0	362.2	363.7
Jiangsu	8.0	12.5	28.5	51.0	23.7	13.1	289.3	248.1
Shanghai	9.4	9.0	33.4	48.1	28.0	20.9	428.1	456.8
Zhejiang	6.3	10.5	12.5	70.7	23.1	13.1	246.4	236.5
Fujian	12.2	24.8	20.1	42.8	32.3	12.6	206.2	190.3
Hainan	28.0	3.8	23.0	45.2	6.9	13.8	290.7	498.1
Guangdong	6.4	32.7	19.0	41.9	42.3	13.7	235.5	198.1
Guangxi	34.9	4.5	8.5	52.2	6.0	11.7	177.0	236.5
Inland Regions	**38.5**	**2.2**	**5.7**	**53.6**	**5.2**	**12.0**	**196.9**	**263.0**
Jilin	44.8	1.5	7.5	46.2	3.1	12.5	256.8	333.5
Heilongjiang	25.6	0.6	3.2	70.6	2.0	12.1	211.0	300.7
Anhui	36.2	3.8	9.7	50.3	6.3	11.2	179.6	210.5
Beijing	50.0	2.0	9.1	39.0	11.7	21.7	378.1	851.2

(Continued)

Table 5. (*Continued*)

Region	Share in Total Paid-in Capital				Export share of GIO (share)	Average annual pay per employee (Y1000)	Average GIO per employee (Y1000)	Average assets per employee (Y1000)
	State-owned	From HK, Macao & Taiwan	From foreigners	Others				
Hebei	33.4	3.1	6.2	57.3	4.9	11.2	231.2	216.8
Shannxi	39.5	1.1	2.0	57.5	5.7	12.1	150.1	240.6
Jiangxi	29.9	6.2	3.3	60.7	6.4	10.2	152.7	173.7
Henan	27.8	1.9	2.5	67.8	3.8	9.6	174.2	172.2
Hubei	44.7	2.0	9.0	44.3	4.5	12.6	226.3	339.0
Hunan	28.4	2.9	4.2	64.5	5.6	11.6	165.5	180.9
Chongqin	24.6	3.1	7.3	65.0	5.4	12.0	179.7	215.0
Sichuan	34.3	1.7	4.5	59.6	5.0	11.8	178.4	253.9
Guizhou	44.6	2.1	1.7	51.6	4.3	13.1	164.7	284.9
Shanxi	43.1	1.9	2.6	52.3	3.4	12.7	179.6	283.2
Gansu	51.6	0.6	0.9	46.9	3.7	13.7	172.9	272.6
Minority Regions	**38.2**	**1.3**	**2.1**	**58.4**	**4.2**	**14.5**	**226.7**	**385.2**
Inner Mongolia	27.3	1.1	2.0	69.6	4.7	13.4	211.3	331.2
Ningxia	42.4	0.3	4.7	52.6	7.0	13.9	182.8	287.6
Xinjiang	54.2	2.2	0.8	42.8	1.9	18.1	291.5	478.1
Yunnan	33.3	1.4	3.0	62.3	4.2	13.7	226.4	387.2
Qinhai	34.5	0.7	0.9	63.9	6.7	15.6	214.4	574.8
Tibet	81.5	0.0	0.2	18.2	0.4	15.6	107.6	500.4

Source: Authors' analysis of data from *China's Yearbook of 2004 Economic Census*.

Xinjiang (a Muslim region), large state-owned enterprises contributed 81% and 80% of total GIO, respectively.

Table 5 shows regional variations in capital ownership in the first four columns. State-ownership is much stronger in the inland and minority regions, at about 38% each, than it is in the coastal regions, where the state-owned share is only 14%. The state-ownership shares vary widely across individual regions, from lows of only 6% in Zhejiang and Guangdong to Tibet, which appears to be an outlier at 81.5% state-ownership of capital, and Xinjiang at 54.2%. The pattern of ownership by overseas Chinese and foreigners is the opposite of that observed in state-ownership, with much larger shares on average in the coastal regions than in the inland and minority regions. The individual regions with the highest shares of capital from overseas Chinese are Guangdong (34.7%) and Fujian (24.8%), while Shanghai and Jiangsu received the largest shares of capital from foreigners (33.4% and 28.5%, respectively). Unsurprisingly, these same four coastal regions reported the highest export shares of GIO, between 24% and 42%.

The regions with the highest average annual pay per employee are Beijing (21,700 yuan), Shanghai (20,900 yuan) and Xinjiang (18,100 yuan), one region from each grouping of regions. Beijing also has the second largest GIO per employee and the largest assets per employee. This is likely due to Beijing's unique status as the capital of China and the center of education in China, which has led to Beijing hosting many large state-holding companies and many large high-technology enterprises. Shanghai has been China's economic center with rigorous market competition for many years. Only enterprises with high productivity and high pay to attract quality employees can survive the competitive conditions in Shanghai. Therefore, we find that Shanghai has the largest GIO per employee and the second highest average annual pay per employee. Minority regions such as Qinhai, Tibet, and Xinjiang have relatively high levels of assets per employee and average annual pay. This is because most of their enterprises are state-holding enterprises in capital-intensive monopoly industries such as mining and related manufacturing or energy-related industries. The influence of these industries pushes up the average earnings for workers across all minority regions (14,500 yuan) to exceed that of workers in coastal regions (13,400 yuan) and those in inland regions (12,000 yuan).

Sectoral Analysis of Large Enterprises by Ownership Type

Table 6 shows main indicators for large enterprises by industry and ownership type. Due to space constraints, the table presents only industries with above average GIO, which are 11 out of 30 two-digit industries. As noted previously, enterprises must have annual income from principal business above 5 million yuan in 2004 to be included as a "large enterprise." Comparing Table 6 to Table 1, we can see that 20.4% of manufacturing enterprises qualify as large enterprises, but these enterprises account for 90.4% of total GIO and 70.1% of total employment among manufacturing enterprises. The advantage of the data on large enterprises is that reporting divides the enterprises in each industry into state-controlled, foreign-invested, and domestic privately owned enterprises (POEs). The state-controlled grouping, which we called state-owned enterprises (SOEs) for convenience, includes entirely SOEs and state-holding enterprises, where the latter involve mixed ownership but the state represents the largest single share-holder in the enterprise. The foreign-direct-invested enterprises (FDIE) group includes all industrial enterprises registered as joint-ventures, cooperatives, or sole (exclusive) investment enterprises, and limited liability corporations with foreign funds, inclusive of overseas Chinese funds.[11] The domestic POEs include enterprises registered as domestically privately owned.[12]

Of the 11 industries shown in the table, 6 report higher average annual earnings per employee at FDI enterprises than at SOEs, and the lowest earnings at POEs. Five industries shown have the highest earnings reported at SOEs, followed by FDIEs and then POEs. Among the full industry breakdown of 30 industries, 17 have the following ranking of earnings: FDIE > SOE > POE; 3 have FDIE > POE > SOE; and 10 have SOE > FDIE > POE. This means that FDIEs report higher average earnings per worker than POEs in all industries, and FDIEs report higher earnings than SOEs in 20 out of 30 industries.

[11]We note that some enterprises may be included as both state-controlled and foreign-invested, so there may be some overlap between the SOE and FDI rows within each industry.

[12]Domestic private capital and corporate capital would be the funding sources for these enterprises, but not collective capital. All three of these sources are combined in the "Other" category of paid-in capital in Tables 1–5.

Table 6. Main indicators of large manufacturing enterprises, industries with above average GIO, 2004

Sector	Ownership	Number of enterprises	GIO (Bn yuan)	Annual average number employed (thousands)	Average number of employees per enterprise	Share in Total Paid-in Capital: State-owned	From HK, Macao & Taiwan	From foreigners	Others	Average annual pay per employee (Y1000)	Average GIO per employee (Y1000)	Average assets per employee (Y1000)
Manufacturing	All	256,999	17528.3	56673.4	220.5	18.4	11.7	20.0	50.0	14.0	309.3	281.6
	SOE	27,071	4849.5	12275.4	453.5	48.5	2.1	5.3	44.1	18.4	395.1	494.2
	FDI	56,412	6366.7	17354.8	307.6	4.3	27.8	47.9	20.0	16.3	366.9	294.6
	POE	114,838	3407.7	14503.6	126.3	0.3	0.3	0.3	99.1	10.5	235.0	157.2
Agricultural and Sideline Foods Processing	All	14,097	834.5	1965.1	139.4	11.3	8.5	18.2	61.9	10.1	424.7	259.9
	SOE	2,057	97.1	296.9	144.3	57.3	2.7	4.2	35.8	10.5	326.9	316.8
	FDI	2,133	250.0	461.6	216.4	4.2	22.8	50.6	22.4	12.3	541.6	319.2
	POE	6,742	251.1	637.0	94.5	0.5	0.4	0.2	99.0	8.7	394.2	189.0
Textile Industry	All	24,192	1035.6	5879.2	243.0	9.5	20.5	13.8	56.2	10.2	176.1	159.1
	SOE	1,253	93.2	897.2	716.0	54.7	3.0	2.6	39.8	9.0	103.9	176.9
	FDI	5,236	280.9	1471.5	281.0	2.1	45.7	30.6	21.6	12.4	190.9	186.7
	POE	13,783	392.4	2075.3	150.6	0.0	0.4	0.6	99.0	10.0	189.1	131.5
Petroleum Processing, Coking and Nuclear Fuel Processing	All	2,019	892.7	679.7	336.7	36.2	4.0	3.6	56.2	20.3	1313.3	753.0
	SOE	278	695.9	351.8	1265.5	46.5	3.7	0.4	49.4	28.3	1978.1	999.0
	FDI	164	90.7	50.0	304.9	2.2	26.4	27.6	43.8	26.9	1813.7	1345.0
	POE	967	67.0	143.0	147.9	0.3	0.0	0.0	99.7	9.6	468.7	423.9
Raw Chemical Material & Chemical Products	All	18,759	1295.3	3263.5	174.0	21.4	6.6	16.9	55.1	14.8	396.9	390.5
	SOE	2,251	429.1	1163.3	516.8	41.2	1.1	2.4	55.4	17.3	368.8	507.0
	FDI	3,011	338.9	397.7	132.1	4.0	22.1	56.7	17.2	25.2	852.1	752.7
	POE	7,930	235.1	750.2	94.6	0.2	0.2	0.1	99.5	10.6	313.4	206.5

(*Continued*)

Table 6. (*Continued*)

Sector	Ownership	Number of enterprises	GIO (Bn yuan)	Annual average number employed (thousands)	Average number of employees per enterprise	Share in Total Paid-in Capital: State-owned	From HK, Macao & Taiwan	From foreigners	Others	Average annual pay per employee (Y1000)	Average GIO per employee (Y1000)	Average assets per employee (Y1000)
Non-metal Mineral Products	All	19,960	746.0	4153.2	208.1	15.4	9.0	13.9	61.7	10.9	179.6	225.7
	SOE	2,450	115.6	788.0	321.6	49.9	1.9	3.6	44.6	11.9	146.7	337.2
	FDI	2,423	145.5	546.0	225.3	4.2	28.4	43.9	23.4	15.6	266.5	383.5
	POE	8,932	241.2	1386.8	155.3	0.8	0.1	0.1	99.0	9.7	173.9	151.0
Smelting & Pressing of Ferrous Metals	All	7,141	1694.9	2772.7	388.3	40.2	4.2	5.9	49.6	20.4	611.3	562.4
	SOE	553	858.6	1436.7	2598.0	61.2	1.9	1.2	35.7	27.5	597.6	705.7
	FDI	512	214.3	191.1	373.2	7.0	24.7	39.6	28.7	19.1	1121.3	896.6
	POE	4,028	300.6	582.9	144.7	0.7	0.2	0.1	99.0	10.7	515.6	282.9
Smelting & Pressing of Non-ferrous Metals	All	5,300	598.7	1273.3	240.2	28.3	7.4	6.9	57.4	15.2	470.2	425.1
	SOE	534	213.3	586.3	1097.9	53.6	2.5	1.6	42.3	18.7	363.9	485.2
	FDI	651	102.0	141.5	217.4	6.5	31.8	31.7	30.0	17.0	720.6	637.4
	POE	2,568	133.4	256.7	100.0	0.2	0.4	0.1	99.3	11.2	519.6	263.9
Ordinary Machinery	All	20,568	852.4	3437.4	167.1	16.2	6.6	22.1	55.0	14.4	248.0	258.6
	SOE	2,305	211.4	885.6	384.2	45.9	1.0	8.9	44.2	17.0	238.7	401.4
	FDI	3,081	246.5	584.0	189.5	3.9	16.8	57.3	22.0	21.5	422.2	418.1
	POE	9,863	234.4	1057.5	107.2	0.3	0.2	0.5	99.1	11.6	221.6	153.0
Transport Equipment	All	11,824	1379.6	3413.1	288.7	30.8	4.3	20.8	44.2	17.7	404.2	422.8
	SOE	2,403	767.7	1565.9	651.6	44.8	1.4	13.3	40.5	21.5	490.2	589.5
	FDI	2,008	590.1	685.7	341.5	14.6	9.4	48.6	27.4	25.6	860.6	700.7
	POE	4,494	149.4	628.8	139.9	0.3	0.2	0.3	99.1	11.1	237.6	169.7

(*Continued*)

Table 6. (*Continued*)

Sector	Ownership	Number of enterprises	GIO (Bn yuan)	Annual average number employed (thousands)	Average number of employees per enterprise	Share in Total Paid-in Capital: State-owned	From HK, Macao & Taiwan	From foreigners	Others	Average annual pay per employee (Y1000)	Average GIO per employee (Y1000)	Average assets per employee (Y1000)
Electric Machines	All	16,145	1123.3	3486.8	216.0	9.0	13.5	25.3	52.1	14.6	322.2	272.0
and Apparatuses	SOE	1,273	126.1	411.0	322.9	43.6	2.0	7.5	46.9	17.4	306.8	470.5
	FDI	3,926	434.9	1398.1	356.1	2.7	27.6	52.0	17.7	16.3	311.1	235.9
	POE	6,652	207.7	776.7	116.8	0.1	0.1	0.3	99.6	11.9	267.4	182.5
Communications	All	9,161	2226.0	3787.9	413.5	7.3	18.1	44.1	30.5	19.4	587.7	416.0
Equipment,	SOE	1,038	338.3	500.1	481.8	27.6	2.4	11.0	59.0	23.7	676.4	756.6
Computer and	FDI	4,677	1852.6	2690.1	575.2	1.9	23.9	58.7	15.5	19.9	688.7	406.5
Other Electronic Equipment	POE	2,370	75.4	342.4	144.5	0.1	0.1	0.1	99.7	12.7	220.2	159.8

Note: Industries shown have above average GIO, which means industry GIO greater than 1/30th of the total GIO for all 30 industries, (17528.3/30 = 584.3); SOE includes state-sole-owned enterprises and state-holding companies; FDI includes all enterprieses classified as freign-invested enterprieses; POE includes domestic privately owned enterprises.

source: Authors' analysis of data from *China's Yearbook of 2004 Economic Census.*

In summary, we observe suggestive evidence that FDIE are associated with higher pay within industries, but they are also associated with higher productivity (GIO per employee) and higher capital–labor ratios (assets per employee). We cannot identify a possible relationship between ownership and earnings until we can control for these other variables, which we will attempt to do in our regression analysis.

Regional Analysis of Large Enterprises in Two Selected Industries

We have selected two different industries to focus on with industry-level analysis. For our analysis of a labor-intensive industry, we focus on the textiles industry. For a relatively capital-intensive industry, we chose the communication equipment, computers, and other electronics industry. Another reason for choosing these industries is that the former has a relatively high share of capital sourced from overseas Chinese investors while the latter has a large share coming from foreign investors. Table 7 shows the main indicators for large enterprises in the textiles industry, with regional observations for 2004. For this industry, the "large enterprises" represented in Table 7 account for 29.1% of the total number of enterprises, 88.9% of the gross industrial output, and 77.0% of the annual average number employed in the industry. These large firms are funded primarily by "others" (which includes collective, corporate and personal sources for capital) with 56.2% of the paid-in-capital, followed by overseas Chinese investors (20.5%), foreign investors (13.8%), and lastly by state capital (9.5%), although these ownership shares vary widely by region.

Table 8 shows main indicators for large enterprises in communication equipment, computers, and other electronics industries in 2004. For this industry, Table 8 covers 33.6% of the enterprises in the industry, but these large enterprises account for 98.5% of GIO and 87.0% of the employment for this industry. The large firms in this industry receive 44.1% of the capital from foreigners, 30.5% from others, 18.1% from overseas Chinese, and 7.3% from the state.

Comparing across Tables 7 and 8, large firms in communication equipment, computers and other electronics rely more on export sales (61.8% versus 29.4% export share of GIO), pay more on average per worker (19,400 yuan versus 10,200 yuan annual pay), have higher output

Table 7. Main indicators of large enterprises in texiles industries by region, 2004

Region	Number of enterprises (units)	Money-losing firms (share)	GIO (Y bn)	Annual average # employed (1000)	Share in Total Paid-in Capital				Export share of GIO (share)	Average annual pay per employee (Y1000)	Average GIO per employee (Y1000)	Average assets per employee (Y1000)
					State-owned	From HK, Macao & Taiwan	From foreigners	Others				
Total	24,192	22.2	1035.6	5879.2	9.5	20.5	13.8	56.2	29.4	10.2	176.1	159.1
Coastal Regions	20,227	20.7	853.2	4249.3	5.4	24.2	15.8	54.6	32.1	11.2	200.8	175.3
Liaoning	374	47.3	12.3	96.6	25.0	8.2	18.6	48.3	34.3	8.2	127.8	171.2
Shandong	2,326	15.5	156.8	856.0	8.2	7.9	16.5	67.4	23.4	8.5	183.2	150.2
Tianjin	329	50.5	7.3	72.1	38.0	3.0	14.1	44.8	40.8	9.8	101.5	286.7
Jiangsu	6,498	23.2	257.6	1203.3	6.4	14.1	21.6	57.9	24.1	11.4	214.1	164.6
Shanghai	1,109	22.0	34.9	186.0	2.4	19.6	25.4	52.7	37.9	15.3	187.8	196.7
Zhejiang	6,647	16.2	247.0	1042.9	1.2	17.0	10.0	71.9	36.9	12.3	236.9	214.0
Fujian	796	15.7	37.7	195.1	2.2	46.8	14.8	36.2	25.9	11.4	193.1	172.5
Hainan	10	50.0	1.1	7.0	2.2	14.1	15.7	68.0	48.3	16.6	150.6	307.3
Guangdong	2,040	23.0	95.3	550.9	2.9	59.2	13.7	24.2	55.2	12.3	173.0	149.2
Guangxi	98	48.0	3.1	39.4	24.8	5.2	3.0	67.0	10.3	8.1	79.6	81.4
Inland Regions	3,706	29.4	162.0	1483.8	25.8	5.5	6.0	62.8	15.6	7.5	109.2	105.6
Jilin	73	41.1	3.1	29.1	50.4	0.2	28.5	21.0	24.2	6.5	106.3	152.3
Heilongjiang	92	40.2	3.5	50.8	20.7	5.8	1.6	72.1	21.5	6.8	69.4	111.0
Anhui	344	41.3	15.1	134.7	16.5	4.6	13.0	65.9	20.4	8.0	112.3	121.4
Beijing	181	28.7	5.9	39.4	14.8	5.2	20.6	59.4	27.3	15.0	150.8	228.1
Hebei	600	15.2	34.8	216.9	23.7	8.5	6.3	61.5	14.3	7.4	160.4	124.1
Shannxi	73	38.4	2.8	45.2	59.7	1.0	3.6	35.7	8.6	5.7	61.6	88.4

(Continued)

Table 7. (*Continued*)

Region	Number of enterprises (units)	Money-losing firms (share)	GIO (Y bn)	Annual average # employed (1000)	Share in Total Paid-in Capital				Export share of GIO (share)	Average annual pay per employee (Y1000)	Average GIO per employee (Y1000)	Average assets per employee (Y1000)
					State-owned	From HK, Macao & Taiwan	From foreigners	Others				
Jiangxi	261	29.1	7.7	81.2	26.9	16.3	4.1	52.8	27.5	8.1	94.5	75.7
Henan	662	18.9	30.3	283.4	28.9	2.3	0.7	68.1	9.7	6.5	106.8	93.7
Hubei	559	38.5	25.0	224.1	11.6	7.3	3.2	77.9	14.8	7.5	111.5	98.2
Hunan	265	33.6	9.9	96.2	11.8	9.6	3.7	75.0	12.1	8.6	103.3	77.1
Chongqin	111	35.1	3.9	50.3	45.5	0.2	0.1	54.1	23.5	7.5	77.9	84.5
Sichuan	304	23.7	12.6	115.3	17.9	3.4	1.5	77.1	15.6	7.0	109.1	95.5
Guizhou	32	43.8	0.4	8.1	78.0	2.8	0.0	19.2	3.1	7.0	44.2	122.2
Shanxi	98	62.2	5.9	90.3	55.6	3.4	0.7	40.3	16.8	7.3	65.6	107.3
Gansu	51	39.2	1.1	18.8	36.2	0.0	0.0	63.7	5.1	6.5	59.3	126.2
Minority Regions	259	39.0	20.3	146	24.2	7.0	6.7	62.1	25.8	8.8	139.3	230.6
Inner Mongolia	125	27.2	10.9	57.9	8.8	4.5	15.9	70.7	37.7	10.4	187.7	289.9
Ningxia	26	26.9	2.5	6.1	1.3	0.0	4.0	94.7	20.5	5.4	410.2	418.2
Xinjiang	73	60.3	6.0	60.3	42.7	12.4	0.0	44.9	6.2	8.2	98.8	173.0
Yunnan	24	45.8	0.6	17.3	34.2	0.0	1.4	64.4	23.3	6.6	36.2	118.8
Qinhai	9	33.3	0.4	4.2	24.1	0.3	0.0	75.2	32.4	11.2	89.8	412.4
Tibet	2	100.0	0.0	0.2	100.0	0.0	0.0	0.0	77.8	10.0	45.0	535.0

Source: Authors' analysis of data from *China's Yearbook of 2004 Economic Census.*

Table 8. Main indicators of large enterprises in communication equipment, computers and other electronics industries by region, 2004

Region	Number of enterprises (units)	Money-losing firms (share)	GIO (Y bn)	Annual average # employed (1000)	Share in Total Paid-in Capital				Export share of GIO (share)	Average annual pay per employee (Y1000)	Average GIO per employee (Y1000)	Average assets per employee (Y1000)
					State-owned	From HK, Macao & Taiwan	From foreigners	Others				
Total	9,161	26.4	2226.0	3787.9	7.3	18.1	44.1	30.5	61.8	19.4	587.7	416
Coastal Regions	7,795	26.3	1997.8	3339.4	4.5	20.9	49.3	25.4	65.8	19.2	598.2	390.8
Liaoning	217	35.9	39.6	68.1	17.9	3.2	41.9	37.0	62.8	17.7	581.7	581.2
Shandong	461	18.9	80.0	148.3	10.5	6.7	41.8	41.0	30.7	14.3	539.6	338.5
Tianjin	333	34.8	136.8	124.0	5.5	2.2	69.0	23.3	61.1	26.8	1103.3	623.4
Jiangsu	1,639	27.2	435.9	653.6	4.3	22.2	60.7	12.8	72.8	18.5	666.9	432.8
Shanghai	695	22.7	284.4	236.6	3.1	7.4	63.7	25.9	70.7	31.0	1202.1	953.2
Zhejiang	1,015	13.6	90.9	214.5	3.6	17.8	26.8	51.9	36.7	17.2	423.9	392.1
Fujian	352	19.0	117.9	158.1	3.3	25.9	40.7	30.1	58.2	19.2	745.4	429.0
Hainan	6	33.3	0.3	0.8	1.4	78.3	0.0	21.0	45.9	22.5	383.8	506.3
Guangdong	3,027	31.1	810.0	1726.5	2.9	37.8	33.8	25.5	69.3	18.1	469.1	274.3
Guangxi	50	32.0	1.9	8.9	22.0	11.7	12.1	54.0	5.6	14.0	218.3	398.8
Inland Regions	1,336	27.5	221.8	439.3	21.0	4.3	19.5	55.2	26.9	20.8	504.8	602.0
Jilin	33	48.5	2.2	11.7	77.5	0.6	3.2	18.7	36.5	14.3	186.5	580.3
Heilongjiang	30	33.3	1.6	4.5	7.2	2.8	37.4	52.6	7.2	10.9	356.7	1389.8
Anhui	87	28.7	7.8	22.4	23.5	7.2	4.4	64.8	6.7	14.1	349.2	291.5
Beijing	498	25.1	123.6	100.2	5.2	4.9	32.0	57.9	34.5	39.9	1233.1	1085.4
Hebei	73	21.9	5.7	21.6	30.1	0.8	3.1	66.0	10.1	13.6	264.5	346.5
Shannxi	29	24.1	1.1	9.2	29.7	26.4	0.0	43.9	2.3	10.2	115.8	275.5

(*Continued*)

Table 8. (*Continued*)

Region	Number of enterprises (units)	Money-losing firms (share)	GIO (Y bn)	Annual average # employed (1000)	Share in Total Paid-in Capital				Export share of GIO (share)	Average annual pay per employee (Y1000)	Average GIO per employee (Y1000)	Average assets per employee (Y1000)
					State-owned	From HK, Macao & Taiwan	From foreigners	Others				
Jiangxi	49	28.6	3.2	22.0	47.8	5.8	7.5	38.8	18.5	9.8	146.3	190.4
Henan	45	24.4	8.2	17.5	29.1	11.2	7.6	52.2	16.5	23.4	469.5	871.4
Hubei	92	31.5	14.2	27.7	25.3	11.3	7.0	56.4	13.1	18.3	513.9	504.5
Hunan	84	31.0	8.4	23.6	9.1	2.6	35.6	52.6	28.8	13.7	357.0	545.3
Chongqin	24	20.8	3.8	7.0	28.3	1.9	12.4	57.3	2.4	16.7	536.9	555.9
Sichuan	183	21.9	24.2	89.9	36.6	1.0	9.7	52.8	22.3	16.9	269.4	471.0
Guizhou	30	63.3	2.8	11.4	19.4	2.2	7.6	70.8	33.6	17.1	249.9	463.5
Shanxi	66	28.8	13.9	58.4	31.5	0.8	1.9	65.7	15.4	14.1	238.0	398.5
Gansu	13	38.5	1.0	12.2	54.5	0.0	0.0	45.5	15.6	9.1	80.8	412.0
Minority Regions	30	23.3	6.5	9.3	18.5	17.1	2.0	62.4	2.4	19.9	702.2	698.6
Inner Mongolia	16	31.3	5.0	4.3	6.6	37.7	4.2	51.5	0.4	13.3	1154.2	760.2
Ningxia	2	50.0	0.1	0.8	71.4	0.0	0.0	28.6	49.0	20.0	120.0	393.8
Xinjiang	1	0.0	0.6	2.3	0.0	0.0	0.0	100.0	8.2	24.3	269.1	615.7
Yunnan	11	9.1	0.9	1.9	24.3	6.7	1.1	68.3	4.0	29.5	448.4	787.9
Qinhai	na	na	na	na	na	na	na	na	na	na	na	na
Tibet	na	na	na	na	na	na	na	na	na	na	na	na

Source: Authors' analysis of data from *China's Yearbook of 2004 Economic Census*. na = not available.

per worker (587,700 yuan versus 176,100 yuan), and are more capital-intensive (416,000 yuan versus 159,100 yuan in assets per worker). These two industries will be used for industry-specific regression analysis in a later section of the paper.

IV. REGRESSION ANALYSIS

Cross-Industry Regression Analysis of Large Enterprises

We use the Economic Census 2004 data at the three-digit industry level to estimate the effect of different sources of capital on average annual earnings and on employment. We start this inquiry with standard OLS regressions on the following equation:

$$\ln Y_i = \alpha + \beta_1 \ln X_i + \beta_2 Z_i + \beta_3 \delta_i + \varepsilon_i \qquad (1)$$

where Y_i represents either earnings or employment in three-digit industry i, X_i represents control variables for industry i, Z_i represents our ownership variables of interest for industry i, and δ_i represents two-digit level industry dummy variables. We use capital–labor ratios to control for differing levels of K-intensity across industries and total paid-in-capital to control for industry size when we measure ownership variables in shares.[13] The ownership variables for capital supplied by the State, Collective, Personal,[14] Overseas Chinese (OC), or Foreign Direct Investment (FDI) are expressed as either log values of the investment or as shares of the total paid-in-capital for an industry.

Tables 9 and 10 show our regression results for Equation (1), using all of the industrial sector observations in the columns on the left and using only the manufacturing industries in the columns on the right.[15] Table 9

[13]Total paid-in-capital is highly positively correlated with its various components, so it is dropped in regressions that measure ownership variables in log capital amounts.

[14]"Personal capital" represents capital sourced from domestic private investors. In the earlier tables, personal, collective and corporate capital are grouped together as "other" capital, but we separate these sources for the regression analysis. Corporate capital is dropped from the regressions to avoid multi-collinearity in the independent variables and because this capital source involves mixtures of the other capital sources, so that interpreting resulting coefficients would be difficult.

[15]Heavy state control and regulation in mining and utilities sectors lead us to investigate the results while excluding these industries.

Table 9. Cross-industry regression results for earnings, 2004

Independent variables	All Industrial			Manufacturing only		
	Benchmark	log K	K share	Benchmark	log K	K share
ln(K/L)	0.308**	0.268**	0.260**	0.304**	0.268**	0.261**
	(0.031)	(0.028)	(0.028)	(0.030)	(0.029)	(0.029)
ln(TotalK)	0.008		0.000	0.012		−0.001
	(0.008)		(0.007)	(0.008)		(0.007)
StateK		0.005	−0.003**		0.002	−0.003**
		(0.009)	(0.001)		(0.009)	(0.001)
CollectiveK		−0.009	−0.007**		−0.006	−0.006**
		(0.010)	(0.002)		(0.010)	(0.002)
PersonalK		−0.072**	−0.006**		−0.073**	−0.006**
		(0.019)	(0.001)		(0.020)	(0.002)
OCK		0.020^	−0.001		0.019^	−0.001
		(0.010)	(0.001)		(0.011)	(0.001)
FDIK		0.050**	0.001		0.051**	0.001
		(0.009)	(0.001)		(0.009)	(0.001)
_cons	0.832**	1.837**	2.373**	1.105**	1.845**	2.354**
	(0.191)	(0.173)	(0.249)	(0.122)	(0.178)	(0.259)
Observations	521	470	470	479	445	445
R^2	0.657	0.732	0.741	0.618	0.714	0.723

Note: ** = significant at the 1% level; * = significant at the 5% level; ^ = significant at the 10% level. Robust standard errors in parentheses; all regressions include industry dummy variables.

uses the log of earnings as the dependent variable. For all industrial sectors, the benchmark case shows that almost 66% of the variation in earnings at the three-digit industry level can be explained by variations in capital intensity and total capital across industries, along with industry dummies. More capital-intensive industries pay more and labor-intensive industries pay less, with a 10% increase in an industry's capital–labor ratio estimated to increase annual earnings by 3.08% in the benchmark case. The coefficient on the capital–labor ratio becomes slightly smaller when we added our variables of interest in the next two columns, but is still highly significant. Across the two different specifications for ownership variables, only personal ownership had a significant estimated impact in both specifications. Personal ownership negatively impacts earnings. A 10% increase in an industry's financing from personal capital is associated with 0.72% lower

Table 10. **Cross-industry regression results for employment, 2004**

Independent variables	All industrial			Manufacturing only		
	Benchmark	log K	K share	Benchmark	log K	K share
ln(K/L)	−0.883**	−0.858**	−0.913**	−0.907**	−0.854**	−0.905**
	(0.034)	(0.056)	(0.030)	(0.035)	(0.058)	(0.031)
ln(Total K)	0.982**		0.995**	0.992**		0.996**
	(0.010)		(0.011)	(0.011)		(0.011)
StateK		0.272**	0.001		0.255**	0.001
		(0.023)	(0.001)		(0.021)	(0.002)
CollectiveK		0.107**	0.006^		0.089**	0.006^
		(0.028)	(0.003)		(0.026)	(0.003)
PersonalK		0.295**	0.000		0.313**	0.000
		(0.040)	(0.002)		(0.039)	(0.002)
OCK		0.124**	−0.004**		0.136**	−0.003*
		(0.018)	(0.001)		(0.019)	(0.001)
FDIK		0.013**	−0.005**		0.138**	−0.006**
		(0.018)	(0.001)		(0.018)	(0.001)
_cons	7.633**	12.636**	8.221**	7.677**	12.731**	8.173**
	(0.211)	(0.408)	(0.256)	(0.147)	(0.416)	(0.265)
Observations	521	470	470	479	445	445
R^2	0.974	0.937	0.977	0.972	0.940	0.977

Note: ** = significant at the 1% level; * = significant at the 5% level; ^ = significant at the 10% level. Robust standard errors in parentheses; all regressions include industry dummy variables.

earnings. A one percentage point increase in the share of capital financed by personal capital is associated with 0.6% lower earnings. State capital and collective capital also show significant and negative coefficients, but only for the specification using capital shares. A positive and marginally significant (at the 10%) coefficient is found for OCK when ownership is measured in log capital amounts rather than in shares, where the coefficient is insignificant. A 10% increase in an industry's financing from overseas Chinese corresponds with 0.2% higher earnings. For FDIK, a positive and highly significant coefficient is found when using log capital amounts. A 10% increase in an industry's FDI corresponds with 0.5% increase in earnings. When we limit our observations to just manufacturing industries, as shown in the right-side panel of Table 9, our results change only marginally.

Table 10 shows the regression results using the log of employment as the dependent variable. As seen in the benchmark case for all industrial sectors, the vast majority (i.e., 97%) of the variation in employment across three-digit industries can be explained by our capital intensity and size variables, along with industry dummies. As one would expect, more capital-intensive industries tend to employ fewer workers, while larger industries as measured by their total paid-in-capital tend to employ more workers. Adding our variables of interest slightly increases the fit of our estimating equation when we use capital shares in addition to total capital. When we break up total capital into its various sources, we are able to explain a little less of the variation in employment across industries, but each of the capital sources reports a highly significant, positive coefficient, as one would expect. The more capital invested in an industry from any source, the more employment in that industry. The largest estimated effect is for personal capital, where a 10% increase in personal capital corresponds with 2.95% more employment in an industry. The smallest effect is estimated for FDIK, where a 10% increase in investment corresponds with only 0.13% more employment.

Measuring capital contributions as shares, we find positive and barely significant coefficients on collective capital, but negative and significant coefficients for OCK and FDIK coefficients. Over all industrial sectors, a one percentage point increase in collective capital's share of total capital is associated with 0.6% more employment in an industry. A similar one percentage point increase in OCK's or FDIK's share of total capital is associated with 0.4% or 0.5% less employment in an industry, respectively. Similar results are found when we limit our observations to just manufacturing industries.

Summing up what we learn from this regression analysis, industries that receive higher shares of their funding from state, collective, and personal capital sources tend to pay less, and a higher share of collective capital also is associated with higher employment, after controlling for different capital-intensities and size across industries. Among the two capital inflows into China, OCK and FDIK are associated with higher pay when measured in log capital amounts. They are associated with fewer workers at the industry level when they are measured in capital shares. Comparing these results with what we found using simple correlation coefficients in Table 3 highlights the importance of controlling for other industry characteristics in looking at pay and ownership shares across industries. While we found a positive correlation between the state's share of total capital and pay in Table 3 this contrary result can be explained by noting the following: (1) many of the industries that are dominated by state monopolies, such as coking and processing of petroleum and nuclear fuel, and smelting and pressing of metals, are also very capital-intensive which leads to higher wages; and (2) the simple correlation coefficients in Table 3 assign equal weights to each industry and some industries that are dominated by state monopolies, such as tobacco, are actually quite small in terms of output and employment. By controlling for capital intensity and size differences across industries, we have greater confidence in the estimated coefficients found in Tables 9 and 10, so we conclude that state ownership is associated with lower pay. Collective capital and personal capital are part of the "Others" category in Table 3 (along with corporate capital), and both simple correlations and regression results indicate lower earnings associated with these capital sources. Both the simple correlations (excluding state-dominated industries) and the regression results suggest that FDI may be associated with higher pay across industries. We discuss the robustness of these results in the appendix.

Fixed Effect Panel Regression Analysis of Large Enterprises in Two Selected Industries

Our next attempt to examine the relationship between ownership types and labor-market variables is by using data for our two specific industries. For both industries, we have annual regional observations of main indicators for years 2001–2007. With 31 regions and 7 years of data, we have 217 potential observations for each industry, but there are a few missing observations, particularly for the different sources of capital. Our estimating equation is as follows:

$$\ln Y_{ij}^{t} = \alpha + \beta_1 \ln X_{ij}^{t} + \beta_2 Z_{ij}^{t} + \varepsilon_{ij}^{t} \qquad (2)$$

where $i =$ textiles or communication equipment, computers and other electronics industries in separate regressions; $j =$ region is the group index; $t =$ year is the time index. The control variables in X are the same as in the last section, and the variables of interest are limited to state capital, OC capital and FDI capital due to data availability.

The regression results for the textiles industry are shown in Table 11. Adding our ownership variables significantly improves our ability to explain the within group and overall variation in earnings across regions. Regions that have more capital-intensive textile enterprises and/or more total capital in this industry tend to have higher pay for textiles workers. Regions that have higher state capital investments or higher shares of state capital in total paid-in capital are associated with lower earnings for textile workers. The negative and significant coefficient on state capital means that a 10% increase in capital contributions from the state corresponds with 0.82% lower earnings in a region. Alternatively, a one percentage point increase in the share of capital coming from the state corresponds with 0.7% lower earnings for textile workers in a region. OCK and FDIK produce positive and significant (at the 5% level) coefficients when measured in log amounts, not shares. A 10% increase in OC capital contributions corresponds with 0.52% higher earnings in textiles and a similar increase in FDI corresponds with 0.34% higher textiles earnings in a region.

In the employment results shown in the right-side panel of Table 11, regions with more labor-intensive enterprises (i.e., lower capital–labor ratios) and/or more total capital tend to employ more textile workers, as one would expect. Among the variables of interest, all of the types of capital have positive and significant effects on textiles employment when measured in log capital amounts. The coefficient on FDIK is the largest, at 0.107, followed by OCK (0.074) and then state capital (0.048), but the state capital coefficient remains highly significant in the capital shares specification, while the coefficient on FDIK is significant only at the 10% level and the OCK coefficient becomes insignificant.

Table 12 shows similar fixed effect panel regression results for the communication equipment, computers, and other electronics industry. Focusing on the earnings results on the left-hand side of the table, we find that state capital produces a negative coefficient regardless of the specification, although the significance level varies. A 10% increase in state capital corresponds with 0.48% lower earnings in the communications equipment, etc. industry, while a one percentage point increase in the share of capital sourced from the state corresponds with 0.5% lower earnings. The

Table 11. Fixed effect panel regression results for textiles industry, 2001–2007

Independent variables	Earnings by Region				Employment by Region			
	Benchmark 1	Benchmark 2	log K	K share	Benchmark 1	Benchmark 2	log K	K share
ln(K/L)	0.155*	0.070	0.313**	0.079	−0.058	−0.696**	−0.617**	−0.737**
	(0.076)	(0.094)	(0.095)	(0.071)	(0.231)	(0.070)	(0.155)	(0.081)
ln(TotalK)		0.096*		0.159**		0.728**		0.738**
		(0.044)		(0.058)		(0.054)		(0.080)
StateK			−0.082**	−0.007**			0.048**	0.003**
			(0.015)	(0.001)			(0.017)	(0.001)
OCK			0.052*	0.001			0.074*	0.001
			(0.021)	(0.003)			(0.030)	(0.003)
FDIK			0.034*	0.003			0.107**	0.009^
			(0.015)	(0.003)			(0.033)	(0.005)
_cons	8.175**	7.853**	7.510**	7.450**	4.393**	1.960**	6.514**	2.006**
	(0.369)	(0.313)	(0.455)	(0.384)	(1.139)	(0.436)	(0.804)	(0.577)
Observations	216	216	165	191	216	216	165	191
Within R^2	0.036	0.077	0.486	0.475	0.002	0.794	0.309	0.770
Overall R^2	0.177	0.331	0.583	0.477	0.070	0.976	0.760	0.963
log likelihood	83.6	88.3	135.1	145.3	−37.3	133.2	67.5	155.9
df	31	32	28	35	31	32	28	35
AIC	−163	−171	−260	−279	79	−260	−125	−300

Note: ** = significant at the 1% level; * = significant at the 5% level; ^ = significant at the 10% level. Robust standard errors in parentheses.

Table 12. Fixed effect panel regression results for communication equipment, computers and other electronics industry, 2001–2007

Independent variables	Earnings by region				Employment by region			
	Benchmark 1	Benchmark 2	log K	K share	Benchmark 1	Benchmark 2	log K	K share
ln(K/L)	0.023	0.001	0.030	0.032	0.012	−0.100**	−0.018	−0.042^
	(0.034)	(0.025)	(0.026)	(0.027)	(0.099)	(0.028)	(0.031)	(0.025)
ln(TotalK)		0.137**		0.122^		0.742**		0.546**
		(0.037)		(0.067)		(0.067)		(0.075)
StateK			−0.048^	−0.005**			−0.012	−0.002
			(0.028)	(0.002)			(0.039)	(0.001)
OCK			0.067**	−0.003			0.194**	0.006
			(0.024)	(0.004)			(0.044)	(0.004)
FDIK			0.004	−0.005			0.150**	0.006*
			(0.028)	(0.003)			(0.045)	(0.003)
_cons	9.357**	8.427**	9.240**	8.558**	3.109**	−1.948**	1.884**	−0.759
	(0.196)	(0.232)	(0.278)	(0.449)	(0.573)	(0.570)	(0.530)	(0.564)
Observations	204	203	168	174	204	203	168	174
within R^2	0.009	0.120	0.165	0.170	0.001	0.696	0.529	0.668
Overall R^2	0.025	0.227	0.226	0.501	0.010	0.940	0.826	0.896
log likelihood	46.6	58.0	70.8	72.6	−112.1	8.9	21.5	55.2
df	30	31	30	31	30	31	30	31
AIC	−89	−110	−132	−133	228	−12	−33	−98

Note: ** = significant at the 1% level; * = significant at the 5% level; ^ = significant at the 10% level. Robust standard errors in parentheses.

coefficient on OCK is positive and highly significant when measured in log capital amounts, but it becomes negative and insignificant when measured in capital shares. For employment in this industry, both OCK and FDIK produce significant and positive coefficients when measured in log capital amounts, and the result for FDIK is robust to changing the specification to capital shares. Similar to the textiles industry, we find that FDIK has a positive impact on employment in the communication equipment, computers and other electronics industry across regions using both specifications. A 10% increase in FDIK corresponds with a 1.5% increase in employment, and a one percentage point increase in the share of capital coming from FDI is associated with a 0.6% employment increase.

Overall, our results from fixed-effect panel regressions on two specific industries show a negative relationship between state capital and earnings in both industries, a possible positive relationship between OCK and earnings in both industries, and a possible positive relationship between FDIK and earnings only in the textiles industry.[16] For employment, we find a positive relationship between FDIK and employment in both industries, a positive relationship between state capital and employment only in the textiles industry, and a possible positive relationship between OCK and employment in both industries.

V. CONCLUSIONS

We use relatively new Chinese data to investigate the impact of FDI on China's labor market. We find that two-digit industries with high shares of capital coming from Hong Kong, Macao, and Taiwan include articles for culture, education and sports activities; leather, fur, feather, and related products; artwork and other manufacturing; and plastics. Capital from foreigners has flowed into some of the same industries, but the largest shares are in communication equipment, computers, and other electronics; rubber; measuring instruments and office machinery; paper and paper products; and electrical machinery and equipment. Many of these industries

[16]We use the terminology "possible relationship" to indicate a significant coefficient was found using only one of our two methods of measuring capital contributions from different sources.

also report high capital–labor ratios, high output per worker, and high earnings, so isolating the impact of ownership shares on earnings requires us to control for some of these other industry characteristics.

Results from our regression analysis indicate that industries that receive higher shares of their funding from state, collective and domestic private capital sources tend to have lower annual pay, and a higher share of collective capital also is weakly associated with higher employment, after controlling for differing capital intensities and size across industries. We find that higher shares of capital sourced from overseas Chinese and foreign investors are associated with less employment at the industry level, but that industries that receive higher amounts of capital from these sources tend to have higher annual pay. In addition to cross-industry analysis, we conduct detailed analysis across regions and time for two specific industries — textiles and communication equipment, computers and other electronics. We find that regions that receive higher shares or amounts of capital from the state report lower earnings in both industries and higher employment only in the textiles industry. FDI has a positive effect on regional employment in both industries, regardless of how we measure FDI, but a positive relationship with earnings is found only for FDI measured in log amounts and only for the textiles sector. Larger amounts of capital sourced from overseas Chinese investors also are associated with higher earnings and higher employment in both industries. Overall, our evidence is suggestive that capital inflows have had some positive effects on both earnings and employment in China.

ACKNOWLEDGMENTS

The authors would like to thank discussant Francesc Ortega and other conference participants for helpful comments.

APPENDIX
ROBUSTNESS ISSUES

By controlling for differing capital–labor intensities and/or differing industry size (i.e., total capital) across industries in identifying wage and employment effects of FDI and other sources of capital, we may be understating the potential impact of these capital flows. The FDI may work through higher capital intensities or more total capital to increase wages, for example.[17] Tables A1 and A2 are comparable to Tables 9 and 10 in the main text, but we have dropped our control variables from the regressions. We see that collective capital and personal capital still display negative and significant relationships with earnings, while FDIK shows a positive and significant relationship with earnings.

The results for state capital and OCK differ somewhat from previous results found with control variables included. In Table A1, stateK has a significant positive relationship with earnings when measured in log capital amounts, but a significant negative relationship with earnings when measured in capital shares. Only the latter relationship was significant in Table 9, although the sign reversal on coefficients was the same. The positive relationship between stateK amounts and earnings may reflect the capital-intensive nature of some of the state-dominated sectors, which results in

Table A1. Cross-industry regression results for earnings, 2004, dropping control variables independent variables

Independent variables	All industries		Manufacturing only	
	log K	K share	log K	K share
StateK	0.038**	−0.005**	0.035**	−0.005**
	(0.008)	(0.001)	(0.009)	(0.001)
CollectiveK	−0.018	−0.011**	−0.013	−0.010**
	(0.012)	(0.003)	(0.012)	(0.003)
PersonalK	−0.092**	−0.011**	−0.094**	−0.011**
	(0.022)	(0.001)	(0.023)	(0.002)
OCK	0.005	−0.006**	0.003	−0.006**
	(0.013)	(0.001)	(0.014)	(0.001)
FDIK	0.077**	0.000	0.080**	0.000
	(0.012)	(0.001)	(0.012)	(0.001)
_cons	3.628**	4.472**	3.640**	4.466**
	(0.090)	(0.130)	(0.094)	(0.141)
Observations	470	470	445	445
R^2	0.584	0.604	0.556	0.576

Note: ** = significant at the 1% level; * = significant at the 5% level. Robust standard errors in parentheses; all regressions include industry dummy variables.

[17] The authors thank discussant Francesc Ortega for this suggestion.

Table A2. Cross-industry regression results for employment, 2004, dropping control variables

Independent variables	All industrial		Manufacturing Only	
	log K	K share	log K	K share
StateK	0.164**	0.003	0.148**	0.000
	(0.030)	(0.009)	(0.030)	(0.010)
CollectiveK	0.137**	−0.030	0.111**	−0.035
	(0.038)	(0.021)	(0.035)	(0.021)
PersonalK	0.359**	−0.023*	0.381**	−0.023*
	(0.064)	(0.009)	(0.063)	(0.009)
OCK	0.172**	0.014^	0.187**	0.013
	(0.032)	(0.009)	(0.035)	(0.009)
FDIK	0.047^	−0.009	0.046^	−0.010
	(0.026)	(0.007)	(0.027)	(0.007)
_cons	6.892**	4.774**	7.015**	5.118**
	(0.295)	(0.883)	(0.292)	(0.914)
Observations	470	470	445	445
R^2	0.863	0.265	0.863	0.243

Note: ** = significant at the 1% level; * = significant at the 5% level; ^ = significant at the 10% level. Robust standard errors in parentheses; all regressions include industry dummy variables.

higher wages in these sectors and a significant coefficient when we do not control for K/L ratios. The finding of a significant negative relationship between shares of OCK and earnings in an industry also differs from previous results where a negative, but insignificant, coefficient was reported. This likely reflects higher shares of OCK in industries such as textiles and apparel which tend to be labor-intensive with lower wages.

In comparing Table A2 to Table 10, we find robust results that capital contributions from any source tend to increase employment in an industry, when the contributions are measured in log capital amounts. When the contributions are measured in shares, our results change when we exclude the control variables. Collective capital shares were found to have a weakly positive relationship with employment, while OCK and FDIK shares were found to have significant negative relationships with employment with control variables included. As shown in Table A2, excluding these controls results in a negative relationship between personal capital and employment and a weakly positive relationship between OCK and employment. Since industry employment is so strongly correlated with industry size, we have more confidence in the results in Table 10, where industry size is controlled and ownership is measured by capital shares.

Another potential problem with our regressions in the main text is the issue of multicollinearity between our control variables and our ownership variables of interest. For example, FDIK is highly correlated with TotalK. From the descriptive analysis in Section III, we know that FDIEs tend to export more and have high K/L, GIO/K and GIO/L ratios. We tried to use Export/GIO, GIO/K and GIO/L ratios as instrumental variables for FDIK. But these variables are also correlated with TotalK. We also considered using each industry's share of export in total export as an instrumental variable since resource-oriented FDI tends to flow into a host country's comparative advantage industries where exports are high. Unfortunately, this variable is also highly correlated with TotalK. We did not succeed in identifying a good instrumental variable for FDI.

REFERENCES

Agosin, M. R. and R. Mayer (2000). "Foreign Investment In Developing Countries, Does It Crowd In Domestic Investment?" UNCTAD Discussion Papers 146, United Nations Conference on Trade and Development.

Aizenman, J. and N. Geng (2009). "Adjustment of State Owned and Foreign-Funded Enterprises in China to Economic Reforms, 1980s–2007: A Logistic Smooth Transition Regression (LSTR) Approach," NBER Working Paper No. 15274.

Chen, J. and Y. Song (2003). "FDI in China: Institutional Evolution and its Impact on Different Sources," *Proceedings of the 15th Annual Conference of the Association for Chinese Economics Studies Australia* (ACESA).

Fung, K. C., H. Iizaka, and S. Tong (2004). "Foreign Direct Investment in China: Policy, Recent Trend and Impact," *Global Economic Review*, 33(2): pp. 99–130.

Ge, Y. (2006). "The Effect of Foreign Direct Investment on Urban Wage, an Empirical Examination," *Urban Studies*, 43(9): pp. 1439–1450.

Gong, Y. D., H. Görg, and S. Maioli (2006). "Employment Effects of Privatization and Foreign Acquisition of Chinese State-owned Enterprises," Research Paper No. 2006/32. Leverhulme Centre for Research and Economic Policy (University of Nottingham).

Heyman, F., F. Sjoholm, and P. G. Tingvall (2007). "Is There Really a Foreign Ownership Wage Premium? Evidence from Matched Employer-Employee Data," *Journal of International Economics*, 73: pp. 355–376.

Karlsson, S., N. Lundin, F. Sjoholm, and P. He (2009). "Foreign Firms and Chinese Economy," *The World Economy*, 32(1): pp. 178–201.

Lipsey, R. and F. Sjoholm (2001). "Foreign Direct Investment, Education and Wages in Indonesian Manufacturing," *Journal of Development Economics*, 73: pp. 415–422.

Wang, G., M. Johnson, and X. Yang (2003). "China's Revised FDI Laws and WTO Entry Create Changing Patterns of FDI in China: Implications for Investors and Policy Makers," *Journal of Emerging Markets*, 8(3): pp. 5–13.

Wang, J. (2005). "Measuring the Effects of Employment Creation of FDI in China," *Statistical Research*, 25(3): pp. 29–32 (in Chinese).

Wang, T. and Y. Lan (2008). "The Effects of FDI on Wages of China's Domestic Firms—An Empirical Study Based on Different Regions and Different Types of Labor," *Modern Economic Science*, 30(5): pp. 21–25 (in Chinese).

Wu, X. (2001a). "The Impact Of Foreign Direct Investment on the Relative Return to Skill," *The Economics of Transition*, 9(3): pp. 695–715.

Wu, X. (2001b). "FDI, Intellectual Property Rights and China's Wage Inequality," *China Economic Review*, 11(2): 361–384.

Yang, Y., Z. Yu, and M. Wang (2009). "Test of FDI Effect on China's Employment," *Economist*, 2009(5): pp. 5–14 (in Chinese).

Zhao, Y. (2001). "Foreign Direct Investment and Relative Wages: The Case of China, *China Economic Review*, 12(1): pp. 40–57.

Comment

Francesc Ortega

I. INTRODUCTION

This paper addresses an important question: what are the labor-market effects of FDI (capital flows) in the destination economies? Conceptually, this is very similar to the question: what are the labor-market effects of Immigration (labor flows) in the destination economies? Both questions need to address a common empirical challenge: coming up with a convincing empirical strategy to uncover causal effects.

The immigration literature has made a lot of progress thanks to creative instrumental-variable strategies. The key has been access to within-country regional variation in labor inflows by country of origin. The best example on how to use these data effectively is the ethnic networks instrument (Card, 2001).

In my view, the most important feature of the data used by Greaney and Yi is precisely the availability of disaggregation of FDI flows by destination region and (partially) by origin.

II. BRIEF SUMMARY OF THE PAPER

New Data

The authors mainly rely on aggregate region-industry for year 2004, complemented with some annual data for period 2004–2008, although limited to urban areas. The main variables of interest in the dataset are: number of firms, output, exports, employment, assets, wage bill, ownership shares. In addition there are a number of variables on ownership structure: State-owned, Overseas Chinese, Foreigners, and Others (Personal, Collective, and Corporate).

Descriptive Analysis

The authors concentrate on a description of the data by industry, region, and region-industry for selected industries and, in particular, on within-industry differences in wages, worker productivity and export share by ownership. Their findings suggest that firms with high FDI pay higher wages and have high worker productivity. Another interesting finding of the data arises from the comparison between FDI flows from Overseas Chinese versus FDI from the rest of the world. In my view, the most interesting fact is the existence of differences in specialization: while the former specialize in "Culture, Sports, and Education," the latter specialize in "Communication equipment, computers, and electronics."

Regression Analysis

The regression analysis is mostly cross-sectional, aggregated by industry, using data for year 2004. The dependent variables are earnings and employment. The authors also report region-fixed-effects regressions for two selected industries. The main finding is that foreign ownership is associated with higher earnings and higher employment. However, the results do not appear to be very robust to changes in specification.

III. COMMENTS ON DESCRIPTIVE ANALYSIS

My first suggestion is to provide more background information on the goals of FDI in China. In particular, it would be interesting to know whether FDI is mainly aimed at serving the Chinese domestic market or to re-export. Does the answer vary by industry?

Second, it would be interesting to use regression analysis to produce sets of stylized facts on the average firm characteristics by ownership structure. I would find it particularly interesting to focus on the following set of outcomes: wages, output per worker, relative size (in employment or output), export share of output, capital intensity. The regression should include industry fixed effects.

IV. COMMENTS ON REGRESSION ANALYSIS

Cross-sectional Regression

The authors consider three regressions models which, in essence, correspond to the following three equations:

$$\text{Model 0:}\quad \ln y_i = \alpha_I + \beta \ln K_i + \gamma \ln(K/N)_i + \varepsilon_i$$

$$\text{Model 1:}\quad \ln y_i = \alpha_I + \beta_1 \ln K_{1i} + \beta_1 \ln K_{2i} + \gamma \ln(K/N)_i + \varepsilon_i$$

$$\text{Model 2:}\quad \ln y_i = \alpha_I + \beta_1 \ln \theta_{1i} + \beta_1 \ln \theta_{2i} + \gamma \ln(K/N)_i + \delta \ln K_i + \varepsilon_i.$$

There are some concerns about these specifications. First, I would suggest to drop $\ln K$ from Model 0. It is not entirely clear why this variable should appear in the model, and it is likely to be highly correlated with K/N. Second, a bit of algebra shows that Model 1 is nested in Model 2. Since the current estimates differ widely between the two models, the data appear to reject Model 1 (the most restricted).

It is also worth noting that including both K/N and K in Models 1 and 2 is likely to reduce the effect of FDI. By including them, we are ruling out the effect of FDI on wages operating through higher capital intensity.

In my view, a more suitable specification for the cross-sectional models is:

$$\text{Model 3:}\quad \ln w_i = \alpha_I + \beta_1 \ln \theta_{1i} + \beta_1 \ln \theta_{2i} + \varepsilon_i$$

where identification is based on cross-industry differences.

One could take this specification further and estimate

$$\text{Model 4:}\quad \ln w_{ir} = \alpha_I + \beta_1 \ln \theta_{1ir} + \beta_1 \ln \theta_{2ir} + \varepsilon_{ir}$$

where identification is based on cross-region, within-industry differences. The main advantage here is that we can account for time-invariant differences across industries.

Within-country, Over-time Relationship

The authors also present some analysis based on variation over time. My main concern here is that I suspect the data contain too little time-variation in just four years in ownership. This analysis shares some of the concerns discussed in the previous section as well.

V. SUGGESTION NEW INSTRUMENTAL-VARIABLES APPROACH

Let us now come back to the key empirical challenge, that is, the following endogeneity problem: Does foreign ownership in an industry lead to higher productivity? Or is FDI attracted by high productivity in an industry?

My suggestion is to attempt the construction and implementation of the following instrumental-variables strategy. Let the main explanatory variable in the analysis be the industry share of foreign-ownership from Overseas Chinese (θ_{1i}). It is plausible to expect that origin countries will do FDI in industries in which they have technological superiority. To implement this idea, we can build the following instrument: the industry share in exports from Overseas Chinese (Hong Kong, Macao, and Taiwan) to the rest of the world, that is, $Z_i = X_{i,HMT}/X_{HMT}$.

We can take this idea further. Suppose our main explanatory variable varies by industry and region (θ_{1ir}). Then it is feasible to add interactions with distance between each region and Hong Kong, Macao, and Taiwan, that is,

$$Z_{i,r} = (X_{i,\mathrm{HMT}}/X_{\mathrm{HMT}}) \times \mathrm{dist}(r, \mathrm{HMT})$$

VI. CONCLUSIONS

I conclude my discussion with three final sets of remarks. The first is about the data used. The main limitation of the data is that, unfortunately, there are no firm-level observations. If it were possible to obtain such data, it would greatly increase the possibilities. The main strength of the data is that China is a great case study.

The second set of remarks concerns the descriptive analysis. Currently, it contains perhaps an excessive amount of information and should be more focused. It would be interesting to focus on presenting a set of stylized facts on average firm characteristics by ownership, controlling for industry. This could become an important benchmark for future studies on FDI in China.

Finally, the last set of concerns is about the regression analysis in the paper. It seems to me that there is room to exploit the existing data further. In particular, I think it is worth pursuing the instrumental-variables approach sketched earlier.

CHAPTER 12

Clusters, Productivity, and Exports in Taiwanese Manufacturing Industries

Eric Y. Cho* and Hideki Yamawaki†

*Foxconn Technology Group
†Peter F. Drucker Graduate School of Management
Claremont Graduate University, USA

I. INTRODUCTION

The emergence of China as a world's major exporting country was one of the most important phenomena in the world economy in the past decades. As well documented elsewhere, the most obvious and significant consequence of the rise of China has been its bilateral trade surpluses with the U.S. and the European Union. While it is more subtle, another important consequence of China's economic emergence is its impact on neighboring economies. For example, Japan's economic relationships with China had grown significantly since the mid-1990s. China (including Hong Kong) became Japan's largest trading partner by the mid-2000s. And China had become one of the most important production locations for Japanese manufacturing firms through their intensive foreign direct investments.

Taiwan's economic links with the Chinese Mainland also grew substantially in the past decade. Taiwan's trade with China had been closely linked with Hong Kong until 2001. In fact, Taiwan's exports to Hong Kong reached U.S.$18 billion in 1993, while its exports to the Chinese Mainland were minuscule at U.S.$16 million in the same year. The role of Hong Kong as the key entry point to the Chinese Mainland, however, changed in the early 2000s when Taiwan's exports to the Chinese Mainland exceeded its exports to Hong Kong in 2004. In 2007, Taiwan's exports to the Chinese Mainland reached U.S.$62 billion, while its exports to Hong Kong were U.S.$38 billion (Figure 1). The relative importance of the U.S. as the most important destination of Taiwan's exports also changed in 2004, when the

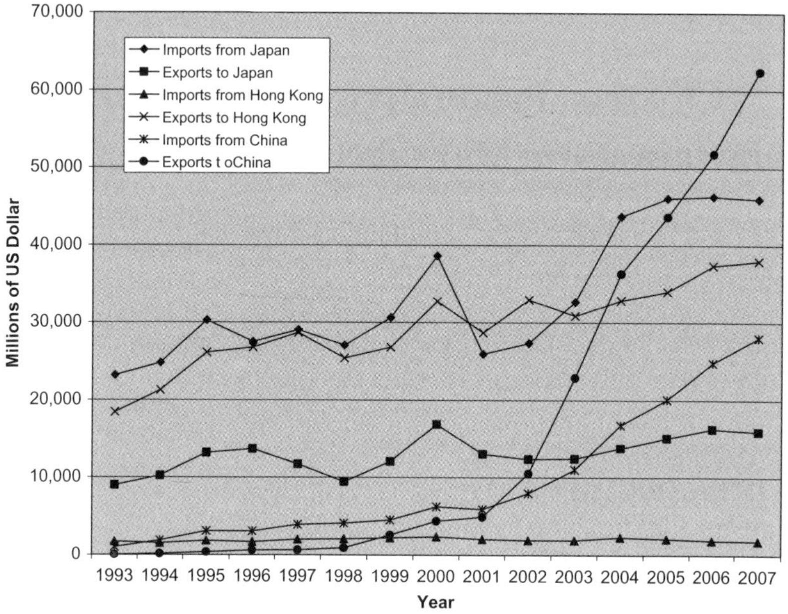

Source: Directorate General of Customs, Ministry of Finance, ROC.

Fig. 1. Taiwan's trade with China/Hong Kong and Japan, 1993–2007.

Chinese Mainland took over the position. The U.S. accounted for 15.8% of total Taiwanese exports while the Chinese Mainland accounted for 19.9% in 2004. By 2007, the relative importance of the Chinese Mainland grew further for Taiwan, accounting for 25.3% of its total exports.

From the 1960s through the 1980s, Taiwan's industries focused on manufacturing, notably for the emerging markets, and attained international recognition for their competitive advantages in efficiency. They competed predominantly on price and efficiency and set priority for developing and obtaining access to cost-reducing and process-improving technologies (Jenkins, Kuo, and Sun, 2003). By the late 1990s, however, Taiwanese firms started to face many internal and external challenges as their once-successful manufacturing industries were exposed to strong competitive pressure from China. At this juncture, the critical policy question addressed by Taiwanese companies and the government facing the emerging economic importance of China was how to build on its distinctive competitive advantages and create a new economic relationship with China.

As China established itself as a low-cost manufacturing center in the world and started to offer access to a potentially vast domestic market, the economic relationship to China became inevitably important for the future growth of Taiwanese industries. One of the policy initiatives that the Taiwanese government adopted was the cluster-centered industrial development initiative to promote industrial clusters and the transition to an innovation-driven economy (e.g., MOEA, 2004, 2006). With an overarching goal of creating a mutually beneficial relationship with China, the idea that formed the foundation of this policy was to make Taiwan specialize in the area where its industries could offer a range of economic activities that lack or are comparatively weak in China. Emulating the successful model of Taiwan's first government-led industrial cluster, Hsinchu Science Park, the government spearheaded a series of cluster-building initiatives. These include the projects for expanding the existing HSP created in 1980 and building several new clusters such as the Central Taiwan Science Park, Southern Taiwan Science Park, and the Taipei Technology Corridor. These clusters are normally comprised several Parks specialized in specific products and technologies. For example, the world's leading semiconductor manufacturers such as Taiwan Semiconductor and United Microelectronics reside in Hsinchu Science Park. Southern Taiwan Science Park was built to target precision machinery, optoelectronics, integrated circuit, telecommunication, and biotechnology. On the other hand, Taipei Technology Corridor focuses on Taiwan's software industry.

Did these clusters help Taiwanese industries improve their market performance and enhance their international competitiveness? This chapter addresses this question and examines empirically the effect of industrial clusters on industrial performance in Taiwan. Our study is the first attempt in the literature to quantify Taiwan's industrial clusters and test the hypothesis that clusters play a significant role in determining industrial performance. For this purpose, we constructed locational GINI coefficients for the four-digit SIC industries in Taiwan. A GINI coefficient measures the degree to which industry employment is concentrated in a particular region. The statistical analysis finds some evidence that supports the hypothesis that highly clustered industries are more likely to show higher productivity growth and higher export intensity than less clustered industries.

The remainder of this chapter is organized as follows: Section II provides a brief overview of the Taiwanese industries and the development of industry clusters. Section III develops the hypotheses for empirical analysis. The statistical model and data are presented in Section IV. Empirical tests in the form of regression analysis of labor productivity growth and export intensity are provided in Section V. The final section summarizes the main findings and concludes.

II. TAIWANESE MANUFACTURING INDUSTRIES AND INDUSTRY CLUSTERS

From the 1950s through the present day, the main focus of policy adopted by the government in Taiwan has been to promote and sustain export activities of small-and medium-sized firms (Jenkins, Kuo, and Sun, 2003; Murray and Efendioglu, 2003; and Aw, 2002). An important factor widely known to have contributed to the success of Taiwanese industries is the development of industry clustering. The most prominent cluster is the Hsinchu Science Park, which was established in 1980 in Hsinchu County and part of Taoyuan County, and is the home of Taiwan's world-known semiconductor and computer firms including Taiwan Semiconductor (TSMC) and United Microelectronics (UMC). The cluster's DRAM production capacity ranked number one in the world and accounted for 23% of the world's total capacity in the early 2000s. Moreover, it is the home of Taiwan's IC design, manufacturing, and packaging industries. The IC design industry was ranked number two, and the IC manufacturing and packaging industries were both ranked number one in the world with over 70% of the world market share in the early 2000s. The Hsinchu Science Park is also the home base of Taiwan's highly successful export products, including large-screen LCD monitors, laptop and desktop computers, motherboards, servers, CRT monitors, and optical storage devices, which account for 90% of Taiwan's total production in the information hardware industry.

Emulating the successful model of clustering achieved by Hsinchu Science Park, the Taiwanese government has spearheaded a series of cluster-building initiatives. The existing Hsinchu Science Park was expanded to include new fields such as biomedical (Hsinchu Biomedical Park). The Central Taiwan Science Park (CTSP) was established in the early 2000s and hosts Central Taiwan Precision Machinery Industrial Cluster, which focuses on precision machinery. Southern Taiwan Science Park (STSP),[1] which consists of Tainan Science Park, Kaohsiung Science Park, and Kaohsiung Biotechnology Park, is targeted to promote precision machinery, optoelectronics, integrated circuit, telecommunication, biotechnology, as well as computer and peripheral industries.

The Taipei Technology Corridor was conceptualized with an emphasis on the software industry. It comprised the Neihu Technology Park, the Nangang Software Park, and the Beitou-Shilin Technology Park. The Neihu Technology Park focuses on computer, communications, and consumer electronics, while the Nangang Software Park is dedicated to the development of IC design, biotechnology, and digital content. The Beitou-Shilin Technology Park, which is close to the financial center of Taiwan, is designed to become the center of biotechnology, media communication, and information technology.

There are other industrial park projects that focus on different areas including biotechnology and pharmaceutical technology (Kaohsiung Science Park, Agricultural Biotechnology Park, Nangang Biotechnology Plaza, and Yilan Marine Life Science & Technology Park), and environmental sciences (Environmental Science & Technology Parks (ESTP) in Tainan, Kaohsiung, Taoyuan, and Pingtung).

Finally, the textile cluster in Chunghua County has been growing since the 1960s and is generating more than 50% of the total revenue for this industry. Kinmen County hosts production of ceramic ornaments and utensils, while Taichung County is the home for musical instruments and the bicycle industries. Furthermore, Chiayi County produces the award-wining high-quality green tea. Figure 2 shows a map of selected industrial science parks in Taiwan in the early 2000s.[2]

[1]"Southern Taiwan Science Park," published by Southern Taiwan Science Park Administration, Taiwan, R.O.C., May 2006.

[2]Based on information provided in the following government publications: "The Core of the Cluster: Taiwan InnoValue, " Ministry of Economic Affairs (MOEA), Department of Investment Services and Taiwan External Trade Development Council, 2006; "The Investment Environment of the R.O.C. on Taiwan," Industrial Development & Investment Center, MOEA, 2005; "Why Taiwan: Reasons to Invest in Taiwan, R.O.C.," Industrial Development & Investment Center, MOEA, 2005; "Development of Key Industries in Taiwan," Industrial Development & Investment Center, MOEA, 2004; and "Hsinchu Science Park Annual Report 2005," Science Park Administration, April 2006.

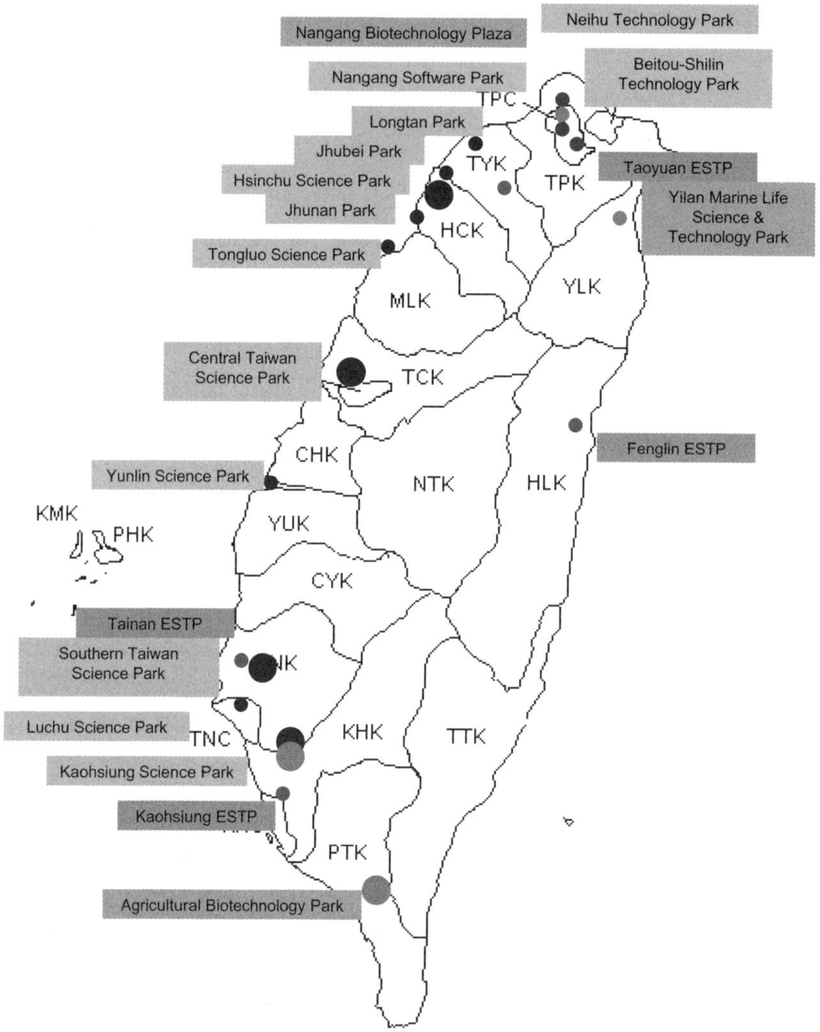

Fig. 2. Industrial/science parks in Taiwan.

III. HYPOTHESES ON CLUSTERING AND INDUSTRY PERFORMANCE

Interpreting the seminal work of Marshall (1920), Krugman (1991) pointed out that the advantage of concentrated production is generated by three distinctive sources: labor-market pooling, specialized inputs, and technological spillovers. In essence, the existence of external economies, which are obtainable from the environment in which the firms reside, is the key to the advantage of clustering (Fujita and Thisse, 2002). By concentrating a number of firms in an industry in the same location, a localized industry gains an advantage from offering a pooled market for workers with specialized skills. Both workers with specialized skills who seek employment and firms that seek such workers are better off if they get access to the pooled labor market in the same location (Marshall, 1920; Krugman, 1991).

Agglomeration is created in a localized industry because it can support suppliers with specialized skills and capabilities. Capacity utilization of specialized machinery can be increased and maintained at a high level in a localized industry that produces the same kind of products. This in turn makes the localized industry more efficient (Marshall, 1920; Krugman, 1991). If the minimum efficient scale of production varies across a range of products and through different stages of production process, manufacturers can choose an optimal combination of operations by working closely with many specialized suppliers. The availability of firms with complementary skills also allows manufacturers to produce a large variety of products. If variety is produced through a wide range of materials and components that are handled efficiently by specialists as well as through stages of specialized operations, manufacturers then will benefit from working with localized suppliers with such capabilities. As Porter (1990, 1998) notes, the key factor for clusters to generate economic advantages is that interconnected companies, specialized suppliers and service providers, firms in related industries, and associated institutions in particular fields compete but also cooperate within a cluster.[3]

Because firms in a localized industry are proximate, information flows easily among them. Localization, therefore, generates knowledge spillovers between nearby firms (Marshall, 1920). Previous empirical research that examines the extent of knowledge spillovers shows that knowledge spillovers tend to be bounded geographically within a geographic area where new knowledge is created (Jaffe, Trajtenberg, and Henderson, 1993;

[3]For evidence on the importance of diversities of business activities that are complementary to each other in clusters, see Klimenko (2004), and Audretsch and Feldman (1996).

Audretsch and Feldman, 1996; and Ellison and Glaeser, 1999). Knowledge spillovers within clusters are likely to be generated by informal exchange of information, labor turnover, industry events, and often from working relationships with suppliers and buyers (Yamawaki, 2002; Forni and Paba, 2002; Malmberg and Power, 2005).

In addition to these traditional sources of cluster advantage, some researchers argue that a major advantage realized from clustering is innovation (Porter, 2000; Porter and Stern, 2001). The external environment in a cluster where firms reside, they argue, plays an important role for promoting innovation. Highly clustered localities where the intensive competition in obtaining new ideas is the norm that could be more conducive for innovative activities than the ones that are characterized by monopoly (Audretsch and Feldman 1996; Feldman and Audretsch, 1999).[4]

These arguments, in general, imply that clustering of firms in a region creates knowledge, skills, and new technologies, which promote productivity growth and enhance industrial competitiveness. The primary question we address is therefore: Does agglomeration of economic activities in a region enhance productivity and competitiveness? Despite the importance of this question, past empirical research that addresses this question is quite scarce, at least for Taiwan.[5]

IV. PRODUCTIVITY AND CLUSTERING

The Statistical Model

We test the hypothesis that clustering contributes to the growth rate of productivity due to creation and accumulation of knowledge and skills. We propose a simple production function model where output (Q) of the ith industry at time t is assumed to be a function of the stock of capital (K), the number of employees (L), the degree of geographic concentration of economic activities (C), and a factor accounting for disembodied technical change ($Ae^{\lambda t}$), as in

$$Q_{it} = Ae^{\lambda t} Q(K_{it}, L_{it}, C_{it}) \qquad (1)$$

[4]Enright (2003) provides an extensive survey of the existing literature on clusters.

[5]See Otsuka (2006) for the development pattern of cluster developments in East Asia. Sonobe and Otsuka (2006) examine the formation of clusters in Taiwan.

Assuming the production function is Cobb–Douglas and separable in C and totally differentiating (1), we can derive an expression in terms of rates of growth:

$$q_i = \lambda + \beta c_i + \alpha k_i + (1 - \alpha) l_i \tag{2}$$

where β and α are output elasticities with respect to geographic concentration of economic activities, C, and capital, K, and lower case letters are used to indicate rates of growth of Q, K, L, and C.[6] Rearranging terms to derive a labor productivity equation:

$$(q - l)_i = \lambda + \beta c_i + \alpha (k - l)_i \tag{3}$$

where $(q - l)_i$ is the growth rate of labor productivity in industry i, c_i is the growth rate of concentrated activities, and $(k - l)_i$ is the growth rate of the capital–labor ratio.

Equation (3) will be estimated for a cross-section of 214 four-digit industries matched between 1996 and 2001. The degree of concentrated economic activities (the intensity of clustering) in a specific industry is measured by two variables in our analysis: the GINI coefficient (GINI) and Location Quotients (LQ). The definitions of GINI coefficient and LQ are given in the appendix. Both GINI coefficients and LQ were calculated for the four-digit industries in our sample for 1996 and 2001. While the GINI coefficient is constructed for a specific industry, Location Quotients vary across industry and region. We therefore propose to estimate a model for a cross-section of industry and a model for cross-sections of industry and municipals:

$$QLGR_i = a_0 + a_1 GINIGR_i + a_2 KLGR_i + e_i \tag{4}$$

$$QLGR_{ij} = b_0 + b_1 LQGR_{ij} + b_2 KLGR_{ij} + \Sigma_{i=1} b_{i+2} D_i + u_{ij} \tag{5}$$

Subscript j indicates region (municipality) j, subscript i indicates industry i, *QLGR* is the growth rate of labor productivity, *KLGR* is the growth rate of the capital–labor ratio, *GINIGR* is the growth rate of the GINI coefficient, *LQGR* is the growth rate of Locational Quotients, *D* is the industry dummy at the two-digit level, and *e* and *u* are the disturbance terms.

[6] We assume constant returns to scale with respect to capital and labor.

In addition to the relationship between the growth rate of labor productivity and clustering, we examine the relationship between the level of labor productivity and clustering. From (1), we can derive the following equations for estimation:

$$\ln QL_i = c_0 + c_1 \ln GINI_i + c_2 \ln KL_i + c_3 \ln L_i + e_i \quad (6)$$

$$\ln QL_{ij} = d_0 + d_1 \ln LQ_{ij} + d_2 \ln KL_{ij} + d_3 \ln L_{ij} + \Sigma_{i=1} d_{i+3} D_i + u_{ij} \quad (7)$$

where *QL* is labor productivity, *GINI* is the GINI coefficient, *KL* is the capital–labor ratio, *L* is the number of employees, *LQ* is Locational Quotients, *D* is the industry dummy, and *e* and *u* are the disturbance terms.

Data and Variables

The data we use were collected from the Taiwanese Census for Manufacturing & Services compiled by the Directorate of General Budgetary, Accounting and Statistics (DGBAS) for the years, 1996 and 2001. The Census for service and manufacturing sectors at the national level are conducted every five years. In our dataset, the number of business establishments surveyed in the censuses was 894,629 for 1996 (the ninth national census) and 971,500 for 2001 (the tenth census). Since the Taiwanese SIC system was modified in 1996 and 2001, we were forced to drop a number of observations from our sample to keep the industry classification at the SIC four-digit level compatible between the two sample years.

In Taiwan, there are 25 municipalities, which comprise either cities or counties. Since these municipalities are comparable to each other in terms of geographic scope and geopolitical significance, we use municipality as a unit of observation for clustering in our analysis of clusters in Taiwan.[7] The Census data that we collected from the Directorate of General Budgeting, Accounting, and Statistics contain aggregate and disaggregate data at the level of the entire nation, municipalities (i.e., cities or counties) or districts

[7]There are some different views regarding what level of aggregation is relevant to study industry clusters. While Krugman (1991) argues that states are not the right geographic units, Feldman and Audretsch (1999) claim that the relevant geographic unit of observation is at the city level. After summarizing the existing literature, Enright (2003) reported that around 50% of previous studies using city or smaller were close to the size of city as measurement of clusters.

that comprise individual municipalities. While information such as firm establishments and labor forces is available at the district level, most industry data are available only at the municipal or more aggregated national level. Two levels of aggregation were therefore used in the present study: national level and municipal level. For the analysis at the national level, the number of observations is 462 for the pooled cross-section of 1996 and 2001 data. For the municipal-level sample, the number of observations is 7,831 for the pooled cross-section of 1996 and 2001 data.

There exist three standard indices for measuring the spatial concentration of industries: Spatial Concentration Ratio, spatial Hirschman–Herfindahl index (HHI), and Locational GINI coefficient. The spatial concentration ratio (SCR) is measured by employment shares of an industry in the most concentrated four or eight geographic areas. The major drawback of SCR is that it is sensitive to the number of geographical regions selected, and the information of employment distribution outside the selected regions is neglected. HHI is calculated by first taking the differences between the share of employment for a particular industry in a region and the share of total employment in that region, and taking the squared sum of the above differences across all regions. The limitation of this method is that if the number of establishments in an industry is less than the number of regions, it may falsely result in a high concentration. Finally, the Locational GINI Coefficient is derived from the GINI coefficient widely utilized in the fields of economics and ecology. This measurement also has a disadvantage due to its inability to distinguish between random and non-random causes of concentration. Since our objective is to examine the effects of clustering on industrial performance rather than the cause or origin of clustering formation, the disadvantage of the Locational GINI Coefficient is considered less significant than the other two measures. Therefore, we chose the Locational GINI Coefficients (denoted *GINI*) and Location Quotients (denoted *LQ*) as the measure of clustering in our statistical analyses.

The definitions of these variables are described in Appendix 2. The Locational GINI Coefficient has a minimum value of "0" when the distribution of employment shares for an industry is totally dispersed across regions and a maximum value of "0.5" if the industry employment is completely concentrated in one region. One disadvantage resulted from using

"Locational GINI coefficients" is the artifact that if an industry is composed of a small number of firms, the value could be biased and higher. For example, if there is one only firm in the industry, it frequently tends to result in a high coefficient. In an effort to minimize the bias caused by a small number of firms, we excluded industries comprising less than 100 establishments in our analysis.

Results

We first tested the hypothesis that the extent of industry clustering is positively associated with labor productivity by using the four-digit industry data. In Equation (4), the inter-industry variation of the growth rate of labor productivity is explained by the cluster variable, *GINIGR*. The definitions of the variables used in the statistical analysis are provided in Appendix 1. The second column of Table 1 shows the estimation results of Equation (4), where the dependent variable is the growth rate of labor productivity between 1996 and 2001. The coefficient of *GINIGR* is statistically significant at the 1% level of significance and has a positive sign, suggesting that clustering building contributed to labor productivity growth in Taiwanese manufacturing industries between 1996 and 2001.

The estimation result of Equation (5) that uses *LQGR* as the independent variable is shown in the third column of Table 1. In the estimation, industry dummies are included in the specification to control for the industry-specific variance in the growth rate of labor productivity. The coefficient of *LQGR* is statistically significant and has a positive sign as we expected, suggesting that fast growth of clustering is likely to increase the growth rate of labor productivity in a region.

Finally, Table 2 presents the regression results for Equations (6) and (7) where labor productivity is in level form. After controlling for the capital–labor ratio and employment size, the coefficient for *GINI* is statistically significant and has a positive coefficient.[8] In the regression using the

[8]We performed a Hausman test for the hypothesis that the individual effects are random. The null hypothesis was rejected at the 99% confidence level for the equation using *GINI*, while the null was not rejected for the equation using *LQ*. Hence, the estimation result of the random-effect model is presented for the equation using *LQ*, while the estimation result of fixed-effect model is presented for the equation using *GINI*.

Table 1. Regression equations explaining labor productivity growth (*QLGR*) in Taiwanese manufacturing industries, 1996–2001

	$QLGR_i$		$QLGR_{ij}$	
GINIGR	0.3587	(2.49)***		
LQGR			0.0222	(7.09)***
KLGR	0.6697	(10.47)***	0.1681	(18.27)***
D13			−0.1105	(−1.14)
D14			−0.2486	(−2.34)***
D15			−0.2895	(−1.87)**
D16			−0.2196	(−1.91)**
D17			−0.2660	(−1.93)**
D18			−0.0827	(−0.68)
D19			0.3218	(2.45)***
D21			−0.2157	(−1.82)**
D22			−0.0804	(−0.76)
D23			0.3200	(1.50)
D24			−0.0582	(−0.39)
D25			−0.1234	(−1.20)
D26			−0.2734	(−3.17)***
D27			−0.1575	(−1.50)
D28			−0.1511	(−1.56)
D29			−0.2070	(−2.80)***
D31			−0.0444	(−0.57)
D32			−0.2273	(−2.11)**
D33			−0.0260	(−0.21)
D39			−0.0440	(−0.38)
Constant	0.4294	(9.07)***	0.2534	(4.67)***
N	214		2848	
Adj. R-squared	0.346		0.129	

Note: Subscript *i* indicates industry *i* and *j* indicates municipal *j*. Numbers attached to the dummy variables correspond to Taiwanese SIC 2-digit code: 13 (food and beverages); 14 (apparel); 15 (leather and fur products); 16 (wood products); 17 (furniture and fixtures); 18 (pulp, paper, and paper products); 19 (printing); 21 (chemicals); 22 (chemical products); 23 (petroleum and coal products); 24 (rubber products); 25 (plastic products); 26 (non-metal mineral products); 27 (basic metals); 28 (fabricated metal products); 29 (machinery and equipments); 31 (electrical and electronic machinery); 32 (transportation equipments); 33 (precision instruments); and 39 (other industrial products).

t-values are in parentheses.

**Denotes 95% significance level.

***Denotes 99% significance level.

Table 2. Regression equations explaining labor productivity (QL) in Taiwanese manufacturing industries, 1996 and 2001

	$\ln QL_i$		$\ln QL_{ij}$	
ln*GINI*	0.1158	(2.17)***		
LQ			0.0160	(4.00)***
ln*KL*	0.2633	(8.54)***	0.2669	(42.48)***
ln*L*	0.1635	(5.77)***	0.0723	(23.19)***
DYear	0.0516	(9.61)***	0.0163	(9.19)***
D12			1.7477	(5.93)***
D13			0.0115	(0.27)
D14			−0.1165	(−2.49)***
D15			−0.0409	(−0.51)
D16			−0.0860	(−1.51)*
D17			−0.1036	(−1.66)**
D18			0.0080	(0.14)
D19			0.0214	(0.31)
D21			0.2061	(3.65)***
D22			0.0605	(1.20)
D23			0.2355	(2.39)***
D24			0.0152	(0.21)
D25			−0.0253	(−0.47)
D26			−0.0167	(−0.41)
D27			0.1038	(2.33)***
D28			0.0060	(0.13)
D29			0.0463	(1.26)
D31			0.1288	(3.49)***
D32			0.1195	(2.55)***
D33			0.0634	(1.15)
D39			0.0274	(0.49)
Constant	−99.7361	(9.21)***	−28.4826	(−8.06)***
N	462		7831	
Adj. R-squared	0.513		0.356	

Note: Subscript i indicates industry i and j indicates municipal j. Numbers attached to the dummy variables correspond to Taiwanese SIC two-digit code: 13 (food and beverages); 14 (apparel); 15 (leather and fur products); 16 (wood products); 17 (furniture and fixtures); 18 (pulp, paper, and paper products); 19 (printing); 21 (chemicals); 22 (chemical products); 23 (petroleum and coal products); 24 (rubber products); 25 (plastic products); 26 (non-metal mineral products); 27 (basic metals); 28 (fabricated metal products); 29 (machinery and equipments); 31 (electrical and electronic machinery); 32 (transportation equipments); 33 (precision instruments); and 39 (other industrial products).
t-values are in parentheses.
**Denotes 95% significance level.
***Denotes 99% significance level.

municipal data, the coefficient for *LQ* is significant and has a positive sign, suggesting that highly concentrated municipals are more likely to show high labor productivity.

V. EXPORTS AND CLUSTERING

The Model

To the extent that clustering creates knowledge, skills, new technology, and thereby externalities, we expect that firms that operate in industrial clusters have advantages to compete in international markets and hence are more likely to engage in export activities than those firms that operate in isolated areas. We therefore test the hypothesis that the intensity of clustering is positively associated with the propensity to export in the Taiwanese industry. We have the following relation:

$$EXP_i = f(GINI_i, QL_i, KL_i, PROF_i) \tag{8}$$

where EXP_i is export intensity in industry i, $GINI_i$ is the level of industrial clustering, QL_i is labor productivity, KL_i is the capital–labor ratio, and $PROF_i$, is industry profitability. The recent literature on the relationship between productivity and the export propensity of plants and firms (Bernard *et al.* 2003; Bernard and Jensen, 2004) suggests that high productivity leads a firm to export, and exporters are normally larger and more productive in the years before they begin to export. We, therefore, expect that labor productivity, *QL*, is positively related to export intensity, *EXP*.

In addition to the export enhancing effect of clustering that arises from externalities, firm clustering may promote exports through enhancing the extent of local competition. Porter (1990) points out that vigorous local competition not only sharpens advantages at home but also pressures domestic firms to sell abroad in order to grow. Sakakibara and Porter (2001) provide empirical evidence that supports this hypothesis for Japanese manufacturing industries.

Two other variables are added to the model to control for the variance in export intensity between industries. Capital intensity in the Taiwanese industry (*KL*) is included in the specification as traditionally used in the previous literature on the determinants of trade flows (e.g., Stern and Maskus, 1981; Deardorff, 1984). Although it is a crude measure, industry profitability is added to the model specification to control for the depth of financial resources that firms can dip into when they need to invest in distribution in the local market. Bergsten, Horst, and Moran (1978) have pointed out that a manufacturer's success in a market abroad hinges critically on its sales efforts and non-manufacturing activities organized in the local market. In particular, they argued that direct investments in ancillary activities tend to promote exports since they enable the manufacturer to develop a goodwill asset in the local market and to circumvent the inefficiency associated with arm's-length transactions. Yamawaki (1991) provides some evidence that supports the hypothesis that successful exporters tend to commit their resources heavily in the local market and control their local distribution systems. Since these expenditures are usually irreversible "sunk" costs that have to be incurred before firms enter the export market, firms may need to generate profit to fund these investments before they start exporting. We use the net earning–sales ratio (*PROF*) as a proxy to measure the industry's financial capacity to fund ancillary investment in the export market.[9]

Results

The OLS result of Equation (6) that uses the sample for 2001 is:

$$\underset{}{EXP} = \underset{(0.24)}{-0.014} + \underset{(2.17)^{**}}{0.449 GINI} + \underset{(0.11)}{3.37E-06 QL} - \underset{(1.23)}{0.002 KL} + \underset{(0.82)}{0.251 PROF(-1)}{}^{10}$$

$N = 208$, Adj. R-squared $= 0.416$,
**denoted 95% significance level

where t-values are in parentheses. In estimation, 21 two-digit SIC industry dummies are included to control for sector-specific factors that are

[9]On the contrary, Chou (1986) argues that profitability creates resistance for firms to export because profitable firms tend to protect their markets and avoid entries of foreign firms in Taiwan.

[10]Because industry profits may have a simultaneous relationship with exports, *PROF* is constructed as a lagged variable by using the value for 1996. In addition to the OLS estimate for 2001, we re-ran the regression by using pooled cross-section for 1996 and 2001 data. The coefficient for *GINI* was statistically significant and had a positive sign.

not captured by the variables included in the specification. In particular, we consider Taiwan's past industrial policy that selected strategic industries and promoted their export activities as potentially important factors to determine the inter-industry variation of exports. Industry policy and cluster-based policy are essentially different in the ways in which competition among firms is promoted and cross-industry linkages and complementarities are emphasized.

The coefficient for *GINI* is statistically significant at the 5% level of significance and has a positive sign. This result suggests that an increase in cluster intensity is likely to promote exports in a four-digit industry within a two-digit sector. In other words, highly clustered industries tended to export more in Taiwan in 2001. Neither the productivity nor factor intensity showed a significant contribution to export performance after *GINI* was included in the regression.

VI. CONCLUSIONS

In this study, we constructed the Locational GINI Coefficients at the aggregate (industry) level as well as Location Quotients at the disaggregated (municipal) level for the manufacturing sector in Taiwan. We found some evidence that provides support for the hypotheses that industrial clustering promotes labor productivity at both the industry and regional (municipal) levels.

A general concern for the Taiwanese economy in recent years has been the decentralization of its manufacturing industries to low-cost locations such as the Chinese Mainland or other Asian countries. If the creation of new ideas based on tacit knowledge cannot easily be transferred across distance, one would argue that it is quite important for Taiwan to transform the foundation of its industrial advantages from cost-driven to knowledge-driven. Indeed, the Taiwanese government has vigorously implemented a policy to promote geographic concentration of economic activities with a goal of improving international competitiveness of her industries. Our empirical results seem to provide some evidence that highly clustered industries and municipalities in Taiwan are more productive. They are likely to export more at least in the early 2000s.

Although our empirical analysis is not designed to capture the mechanism through which a cluster enhances labor productivity and exports, it is important to note that the key success factor for clustering is not the mere presence of firms in a certain geographic area. There must be creation of new ideas, innovation, and skill formation through interconnected relationships of firms and their activities in the region. And, the existence of infrastructure to support such innovative activities should be considered an integral part of success factors.

Does the presence of cluster in a region improve productivity in other countries such as Japan? Despite the importance of this question, empirical research that addresses this question is rather scarce. A study by Morikawa (1997) examined the relationships between various measures of regional economic performance and agglomeration during the period of 1975–1991 in Japan. By using data sample at the level of prefectures, his study found that real labor productivity growth in the region was not statistically related to the level of agglomeration measured by population density and regional GDP per geographic area. While we find a positive relation between clustering and labor productivity growth for Taiwan, Morikawa's study for Japan finds no statistical evidence for a linkage between labor productivity growth and agglomeration at a regional level. Because the definitions of variables used to measure cluster intensity are different in the two studies, we are unable to draw any implications unequivocally from these findings. Further research that uses a comparable research method is needed for making any meaningful comparison of cluster effects between countries.

Our statistical results find a general link between clustering and economic performance of industry. However, it is important to note that not every industry is suitable for clustering, nor do all locations possess the necessary conditions to support cluster building. Industries that operate with complicated supply chains use diverse competencies, rely heavily on "tacit" knowledge rather than codified information, and require product transportability, could potentially benefit more from forming or residing in clusters.

ACKNOWLEDGMENTS

We are grateful to Kozo Kiyota, Alan Deardorff, Kyoji Fukao, Wilhelm Kohler, Vitor Trindade, and other conference participants at the University of Michigan for helpful comments and suggestions.

APPENDIX 1

Variable Definitions

Productivity Equation

Labor Productivity (*QL*):	Gross value added divided by total employment.
Location Quotient (*LQ*):	See Appendix 2 for the definition of this variable. This variable measures the level of clustering in an industry within a specific geographic region (municipal).
GINI Coefficient (*GINI*):	See Appendix 2 for the definition of this variable. This variable measures the level of clustering in an industry.
Capital–Labor Ratio (*KL*):	Gross fixed assets divided by total employment.

The growth rate of labor productivity (*QLGR*), the growth rate of the capital–labor ratio (*KLGR*), the growth rates of GINI (*GINIGR*) and Location Quotient (*LQGR*) are constructed using the Census data for 1996 and 2001. *QL*, *QLGR*, *KL*, *KLGR*, *LQ*, and *LQGR* are constructed both for a four-digit SIC industry and for a four-digit SIC industry in a specific municipal whenever data are available.

Export Equation

Export (*EXP*):	Total industry exports divided by total industry shipments.
Profitability (*PROF*):	Price-cost margin. Value added minus payroll divided by shipments.

EXP and *PROF* are constructed for a four-digit SIC industry.

All these variables are constructed from the data obtained in *Taiwanese Census of Manufacturing and Services*, the Directorate of General Budgetary, Accounting and Statistics (DGBAS) for the years of 1996 and 2001.

APPENDIX 2

Location Quotient and Locational GINI Coefficient

Location Quotient

Location quotients are widely used in measuring regional development of certain industries, employment condition of certain types of activities, representation and resource allocations of certain businesses, import/export conditions. (Isard *et al.*, 1998; Yamawaki, 2006). Although there are number of variations, we use the following definition:

$$(EMP_i^j/EMP_i)/(EMP^j/EMP)$$

EMP_i^j = The number of people employed in industry i and in region j.
EMP^j = The total number of people employed in manufacturing sector in region j.
EMP_i = The total number of people in the nation employed in industry i.
EMP = The total number of people in the nation employed in manufacturing sector.

For a specific region (municipal in this paper), it is the share of employed activities for a certain industry normalized by the national share of employed activities in the region. For a specific industry, it is the employed activities of a region normalized by the share of industrial activities among the whole manufacturing sector of a nation.

GINI Coefficient

First, we listed all the regions (municipal) in a particular industry. For each of the locational units in our sample, we calculate both the share of total national manufacturing employment and the share of national employment in the industry. We indicate this ratio by L_x and denote the industrial employment share of whole manufacturing sector as x. Second, we rank L_x from the highest to the lowest. Thirdly, we plot (L_i, i), where L_i is the cumulative L_x and i, the cumulative x corresponding to each L_x. Lastly, we calculate the size of the area (gray area in the figure below) enclosed by the Lorenz curve and the line of inequality to obtain the Locational Gini Coefficients (Krugman, 1991; Isard *et al.* 1998).

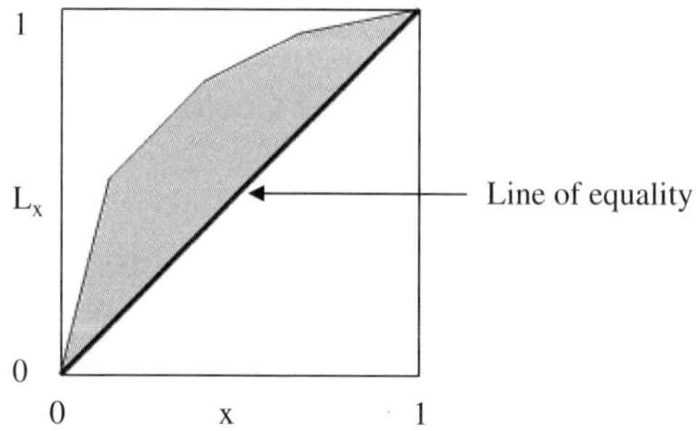

APPENDIX 3

Locational GINI coefficients in Taiwanese manufacturing, 2001

SIC2	SIC3	SIC4	GINI	SIC2	SIC3	SIC4	GINI
08			0.15			1021	0.27
	081	0810	0.11			1022	0.23
	082	0820	0.32			1023	0.26
	083		0.15			1024	0.29
		0831	0.21			1029	0.26
		0832	0.18		103	1030	0.23
		0833	0.31		104		0.19
		0834	0.09			1041	0.25
	084		0.23			1042	0.35
		0841	0.29			1043	0.34
		0842	0.22		105	1050	0.28
	085		0.12		109	1090	0.25
		0851	0.23	11			0.16
		0852	0.22		111		0.18
		0853	0.09			1111	0.20
	086		0.38			1112	0.32
		0861	0.41		112		0.26
		0869	0.24			1121	0.26
	087		0.19			1122	0.27
		0871	0.41		113	1130	0.34
		0872	0.41		114		0.29
		0873	0.22			1141	0.39
		0874	0.21			1142	0.23
		0875	0.34			1149	0.27
		0879	0.26		119		0.17
	088		0.25			1191	0.35
		0881	0.40			1199	0.19
		0882	NA	12	120		0.17
		0883	0.27			1201	0.20
	089		0.15			1202	0.23
		0891	0.21			1203	0.22
		0892	0.23			1209	0.18
		0893	0.26	13	130		0.08
		0894	0.15			1301	0.09
		0895	0.25			1302	0.17
		0899	0.16			1303	0.15
09	090	0900	0.41			1304	0.22
10			0.22			1305	0.20
	101		0.28			1309	0.10

(*Continued*)

(*Continued*)

SIC2	SIC3	SIC4	GINI	SIC2	SIC3	SIC4	GINI
		1011	0.27	14			0.14
		1012	0.35		141		0.11
		1013	0.28			1411	0.12
		1014	0.33			1412	0.27
		1019	0.3			1419	0.16
	102		0.22		142	1420	0.18
	143	1430	0.34	21	210		0.16
15			0.12			2101	0.25
	151	1510	0.38			2102	0.16
	152		0.18			2103	0.18
		1521	0.28			2104	0.20
		1522	0.16			2105	0.26
	153	1530	0.23			2106	0.20
	154	1540	0.11			2109	0.18
	159		0.26	22			0.12
		1591	0.31		221		0.28
		1599	0.21			2211	0.34
16			0.25			2212	0.35
	161	1610	0.29			2213	0.31
	162	1620	0.24			2214	0.33
	163	1630	0.32			2215	0.33
	169	1690	0.27			2219	0.23
17			0.20		222		0.17
	171		0.27			2221	0.17
		1711	0.24			2222	0.32
		1712	0.34			2223	0.31
		1713	0.24			2229	0.24
	172	1720	0.30		223		0.11
	173		0.24			2231	0.40
		1731	0.24			2232	0.05
		1732	0.33			2233	0.09
	179	1790	0.27		224	2240	0.23
18			0.16		225	2250	0.23
	181	1810	0.22		229		0.16
	182		0.16			2291	0.14
		1821	0.25			2292	0.26
		1822	0.18			2293	0.31
		1823	0.23			2294	0.24
		1824	0.13			2299	0.23
		1825	0.39	23			0.13
		1826	0.29		231		0.13

(*Continued*)

(*Continued*)

SIC2	SIC3	SIC4	GINI	SIC2	SIC3	SIC4	GINI
	183	1830	0.29			2311	0.23
	184	1840	0.15			2312	0.16
	189	1890	0.20			2313	0.21
19			0.35			2314	0.17
	191	1910	0.41			2315	0.22
	199	1990	0.07			2319	0.10
20	200		0.22		232		0.17
		2001	0.34			2321	0.23
		2002	0.20			2322	0.25
		2009	0.20			2323	0.19
	233		0.18			2545	0.29
		2331	0.41			2546	0.19
		2332	0.23			2547	0.19
		2333	0.19			2548	0.29
	234		0.40			2549	0.15
		2341	NA		255		0.13
		2342	0.40			2551	0.12
		2343	NA			2552	0.31
	239	2390	0.17		256	2560	0.28
24			0.16		257	2570	0.18
	241		0.17		258		0.20
		2411	0.17			2581	0.17
		2412	0.39			2582	0.24
	242	2420	0.27			2583	0.20
	243		0.08			2584	0.22
		2431	0.09			2585	0.25
		2432	0.06		259		0.21
	244		0.13			2591	0.18
		2441	0.22			2592	0.24
		2442	0.15			2593	0.19
	245		0.17	26			0.28
		2451	0.17		261		0.30
		2452	0.18			2611	0.37
	249		0.18			2612	0.28
		2491	0.24			2613	0.28
		2492	0.22			2614	0.30
		2493	0.25			2619	0.30
		2494	0.17		262		0.29
		2499	0.19			2621	0.34
25			0.18			2622	0.27
	251		0.11		263		0.29

(*Continued*)

(*Continued*)

SIC2	SIC3	SIC4	GINI	SIC2	SIC3	SIC4	GINI
		2511	0.15			2631	0.34
		2512	0.16			2632	0.28
	252	2520	0.11			2639	0.31
	253		0.22		264	2640	0.31
		2531	0.26	27			0.20
		2532	0.18		271	2710	0.27
		2533	0.24		272	2720	0.24
		2534	0.28		273	2730	0.35
		2539	0.21		279		0.21
	254		0.18			2791	0.34
		2541	0.18			2792	0.21
		2542	0.23			2799	0.28
		2543	0.36	28			0.20
		2544	0.27		281		0.23
		2811	0.21		311		0.16
		2812	0.27			3111	0.16
	282		0.22			3112	0.14
		2821	0.29			3113	0.29
		2822	0.38			3114	0.28
		2823	0.22		319		0.20
		2824	0.28			3191	0.27
		2829	0.23			3192	0.27
	283		0.20			3199	0.20
		2831	0.27				
		2832	0.22				
	284	2840	0.23				
	289	2890	0.23				
29			0.12				
	291		0.33				
		2911	0.34				
		2912	0.28				
		2913	NA				
	292		0.40				
		2921	0.41				
		2922	0.36				
	293		0.16				
		2931	0.29				
		2932	0.17				
	294		0.19				
		2941	0.32				
		2942	0.18				
	295		0.28				

(*Continued*)

(*Continued*)

SIC2	SIC3	SIC4	GINI	SIC2	SIC3	SIC4	GINI
		2951	0.25				
		2952	0.31				
	296		0.36				
		2961	0.37				
		2962	0.32				
	299	2990	0.14				
30			0.19				
	301		0.25				
		3011	0.26				
		3019	0.25				
	302		0.19				
		3021	0.28				
		3022	0.25				
		3029	0.37				
	303	3030	0.25				
	304	3040	0.22				
31			0.17				

APPENDIX 4

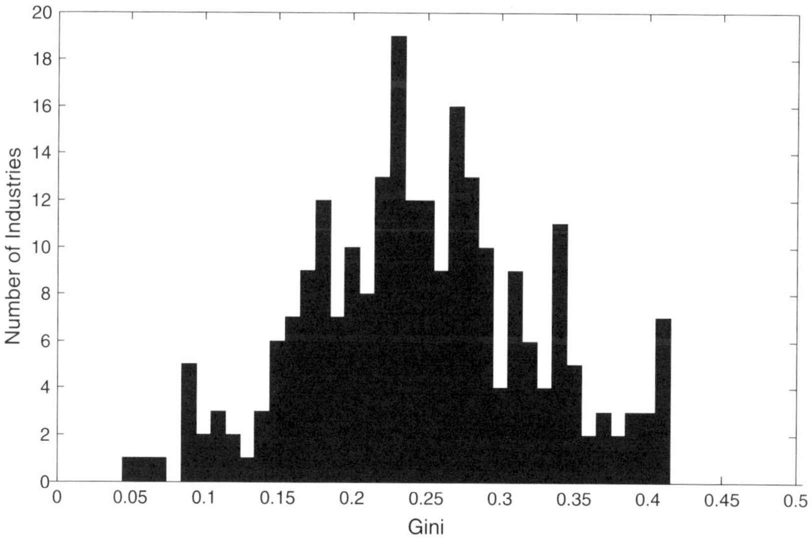

Histogram — Locational GINI coefficients of Taiwanese manufacturing industries in 2001 (Four-digit SIC industries)

REFERENCES

Audretsch, D. and M. Feldman (1996). "R&D Spillover and the Geography of Innovation and Production," *The American Economic Review*, 86: pp. 630–640.

Aw, B. Y. (2002). "Productivity Dynamics of Small and Medium Enterprises in Taiwan," *Small Business Economics*, 18: pp. 69–84.

Bergsten F. C., T. Horst, and T. H. Moran (1978). *American Multinationals and American Interests*, Washington, D.C.: Brookings Institution.

Bernard, J. R., J. Eaton, J. B. Jensen, and S. Kortum (2003). "Plants and Productivity in International Trade," *American Economic Review*, 93: pp. 1268–1290.

Bernard, J. R. and J. B. Jensen (2004). "Why Some Firms Export?" *Review of Economics and Statistics*, 86: pp. 561–569.

Chou, T. C. (1986). "Concentration, Profitability and Trade in a Simultaneous Equation Analysis: The Case of Taiwan," *Journal of Industrial Economics*, 34: pp. 429–443.

Deardorff, A. V. (1984). "Testing Trade Theories and Predicting Trade Flows," in R. W. Jones and P. B. Kenen (Eds.), *Handbook of International Economics*, Vol. 1. pp. 467–517, Amsterdam: North-Holland.

Ellison, G. and E. Glaeser (1999). "The Geographic Concentration of Industry: Does Natural Advantage Explain Agglomeration?" *American Economic Review*, 89: pp. 311–316.

Enright, M. J. (2003). "Regional Clusters: What We Know and What We Should Know," in J. Brocker, D. Dohse, R. Soltwedel (Eds.), *Innovation Clusters and Interregional Competition*, Berlin: Springer.

Feldman, M. P. and D. B. Audretsch (1999). "Innovation in Cities: Science-based Diversity, Specialization, and Localized Competition," *European Economic Review*, 43: pp. 409–429.

Forni, M. and S. Paba (2002). "Spillover and the Growth of Local Industries," *Journal of Industrial Economics*, 51: pp. 151–171.

Fujita, M. and J. Thisse (2002). *Economics of Agglomeration — Cities, Industrial Location, and Regional Growth*, Cambridge: Cambridge University Press.

Isard, W., I. Azis, M. Drennan, R. Miller, S. Saltzman, and E. Thorbecke (1998). *Methods of Interregional and Regional Analysis*, Burlington: Ashgate Publishing Company.

Jaffe, A. M., M. Trajtenberg, and R. Henderson (1993). "Geographic Localization on Knowledge Spillovers as Evidence by Patent Citations," *Quarterly Journal of Economics*, 63: pp. 577–598.

Jenkins G., C. Kuo, and K. Sun (2003). *Taxation and Economic Development in Taiwan*, Cambridge, MA: Harvard University Press.

Klimenko, M. (2004). "Competition, Matching, and Geographical Clustering at Early Stages of the Industry Life Cycle," *Journal of Economics and Business*, 56: pp. 177–195.
Krugman, P. (1991). *Geography and Trade*, Cambridge, MA: MIT press.
Malmberg, A. and D. Power (2005). "(How) Do (Firms in) Clusters Create Knowledge?" *Industry and Innovation*, 12: pp. 409–431.
Marshall, A. (1920) *The Principles of Economics*, New York: Macmillan.
Ministry of Economic Affairs (MOEA), Taiwan (2004). "Development of Key Industries in Taiwan," Industrial Development & Investment Center.
Ministry of Economic Affairs (MOEA), Taiwan (2006). "The Core of the Cluster: Taiwan InnoValue," Department of Investment Services and Taiwan External Trade Development Council.
Morikawa, M. (1997). "Machinery Industry and Regional Economic Growth: Factors in the Economic Development of Japan's Prefectures," *Tsusankenkyu Review*, 10: pp. 64–90 (In Japanese).
Otsuka, K. (2006). "Cluster-Based Industrial Development: A View from East Asia," *Japanese Economic Review*, 57: pp. 361–376.
Porter, M. (1990). *The Competitiveness of Nations*, London: Macmillan Press.
Porter, M. (1998). "Clusters and the New Economics of Competition," *Harvard Business Review*, 76: pp. 77–90.
Porter, M. (2000). "Location, Competition, and Economic Development: Local Clusters in a Global Economy," *Economic Development Quarterly*, 14: pp. 15–34.
Porter, M. and S. Stern (2001). "Innovation: Location Matters," *MIT Sloan Management Review*, 42: pp. 28–36.
Sakakibara, M. and M. Porter (2001). "Competing at Home to Win Abroad: Evidence from Japanese Industry," *Review of Economics and Statistics*, 83: pp. 310–322.
Sonobe, T. and K. Otsuka (2006). "The Division of Labor and the Formation of Industrial Clusters in Taiwan," *Review of Development Economics*, 10: pp. 71–86.
Stern, R. M. and K. E. Maskus (1981). "Determinants of the Structure of U.S. Foreign Trade, 1958–76," *Journal of International Economics*, 11: pp. 207–224.
Yamawaki, H. (1991). "Exports and Foreign Distributional Activities: Evidence on Japanese Firms in the U.S.," *Review of Economics and Statistics*, 73: pp. 294–300.
Yamawaki, H. (2002). "The Evolution and Structure of Industrial Clusters in Japan," *Small Business Economics*, 18: pp. 121–140.
Yamawaki, H. (2006). "The Location of American and Japanese Multinationals in Europe," *International Economics and Economic Policy*, 3: pp. 157–173.

Comment

Kozo Kiyota

I. SUMMARY

This chapter examines empirically whether clusters have positive effects on labor productivity and exports in Taiwan. It uses industry-level data that are from the Taiwanese Census for Manufacturing & Services for the years 1996 and 2001. To measure the clusters, it utilizes two variables: the Locational GINI coefficient and Location Quotients. The regression results indicate that "clustering enhances the growth rate of labor productivity and promotes exports in Taiwanese manufacturing industries."

II. GENERAL REMARKS

Several studies have examined the effects of clusters on productivity and exports (e.g., Porter, 2000). However, none of the previous studies examined Taiwanese manufacturing industries explicitly. One of the contributions of this chapter is its focus on Taiwanese manufacturing industries to examine the effects of industry clusters, which adds another national perspective to the literature. The empirical analyses are clear and concise. My comments and suggestions for clarifications are as follows .

Motivation and Analysis

The motivation of the chapter comes from the increases in the construction and development of industrial and science parks by the Taiwanese government. The chapter then asks whether the clusters promote the growth of labor productivity and exports. However, there is no discussion about the effects of Taiwanese industrial policy on the clusters. If the clusters are formed by factors other than industrial policy, it is difficult to justify the Taiwanese industrial policy. It may thus be important to examine the effects of the Taiwanese industrial policy on the clusters to obtain some policy implications from the analysis.

Productivity

Are there any specific reasons why this chapter focuses on labor productivity rather than total factor productivity (TFP)? Krugman (1994) pointed out that the growth of East-Asian countries was largely attributable to factor accumulation. Kiyota and Okazaki (2005, 2010) have examined the effects of Japanese industrial policies on the productivity of firms. Kiyota and Okazaki (2005, 2010) have found that the Japanese industrial policies had positive effects on labor productivity but not on TFP, implying that the effects of the industrial policies on TFP could be different from the effects on labor productivity. It is thus interesting to focus on TFP rather than labor productivity.

Productivity and Clustering #1

Regression equation (6) in Section IV is:

$$\ln \frac{Q_i}{L_i} = c_0 + c_1 \ln \mathrm{GINI}_i + c_2 \ln \frac{K_i}{L_i} + c_3 \ln L_i + e_i$$

which is derived from the production function. Note that this chapter assumes the following Cobb–Douglas production function:

$$\frac{Q_{it}}{L_{it}} = ae^{\lambda t} C_{it}^{\beta} \left(\frac{K_{it}}{L_{it}} \right)^{\alpha}$$

Dropping t to simplify the notations and using the Locational GINI coefficient as a proxy for the degree of geographic concentration of economic activities C, we have:

$$\ln \frac{Q_i}{L_i} - \ln Ae^{\lambda} + \beta \ln GINI_i + \alpha \ln \frac{K_i}{L_i}$$

It is thus not clear why the regression equation needs the number of employees (L_i) in addition to the capital–labor ratio (K_i/L_i). Similar arguments can be applied to equation (7).

Productivity and Clustering #2

Regression equations (6) and (7) are estimated by OLS, pooling years 1996 and 2001. However, the results in Table 2 show that the number of observations is large enough to control for industry-specific fixed/random effects. To check the robustness of the results, it might be useful to control for unobservable industry heterogeneity (i.e., fixed/random effects), employing panel data estimation methods. In this connection, the analysis would be improved if the analysis could add the data for 2006.

Exports and Clustering

To examine the effects of clustering on exports, OLS is used to estimate the following equation:

$$\mathrm{EXP}_i = a_1 + a_2 GINI_i + a_2 \frac{Q_i}{L_i} + a_3 \frac{K_i}{L_i} + a_4 \mathrm{PROF}_i + e_i$$

However, the regression equation (6) suggests that labor productivity should be treated as an endogenous variable because it also depends upon the clusters:

$$\ln \frac{Q_i}{L_i} = c_0 + c_1 \ln GINI_i + c_2 \ln \frac{K_i}{L_i} + c_3 \ln L_i + e_i$$

Therefore, more explanation about this possible endogeneity problem would be helpful.

Implications

It might be helpful if there were discussion of some possible implications for Japanese and/or U.S. international trade.

REFERENCES

Kiyota, K. and T. Okazaki (2005). "Foreign Technology Acquisition Policy and Firm Performance in Japan, 1957–1970," *International Journal of Industrial Organization*, 23: pp. 563–586.

Kiyota, K. and T. Okazaki (2010). "Industrial Policy Cuts Two Ways: Evidence from Cotton Spinning Firms in Japan, 1956–1964," *Journal of Law and Economics*, 53(3): pp. 587–609.

Krugman, P. (1994). "The Myth of Asia's Miracle," *Foreign Affairs*, 73: pp. 62–78.

Porter, M. (2000). "Location, Competition, and Economic Development: Local Clusters in a Global Economy," *Economic Development Quarterly*, 14: pp. 15–34.